P9-DJK-753

NORTON ANTHOLOGY OF

WESTERN MUSIC

VOLUME 3: TWENTIETH CENTURY

SIXTH EDITION

NORTON ANTHOLOGY OF WESTERN MUSIC

VOLUME 3: TWENTIETH CENTURY

SIXTH EDITION

Edited by

J. Peter Burkholder

and

Claude V. Palisca

W. W. NORTON & COMPANY
NEW YORK LONDON

Printed in the United States of America

ISBN 978-0-393-93240-9 (pbk.)

W. W. Norton & Company, Inc., 500 Fifth Avenue, New York, N.Y. 10110
www.wwnorton.com

W. W. Norton & Company Ltd., Castle House, 75/76 Wells Street, London W1T 3QT

1 2 3 4 5 6 7 8 9 0

CONTENTS

MAKING CONNECTIONS: HOW TO USE THIS ANTHOLOGY

The *Norton Anthology of Western Music* (NAWM) is a companion to *A History of Western Music*, Eighth Edition (HWM), and *Concise History of Western Music*, Fourth Edition. It is also designed to stand by itself as a collection representing the most significant traditions, trends, genres, national schools, innovations, and historical developments in the history of music in Europe and the Americas.

The editions of the scores are the best available for which permission could be secured, including several editions especially prepared for NAWM. Where no publication or editor is cited, Claude V. Palisca or I have edited the music from the original source. All foreign-language texts are accompanied by English translations by one or both coeditors, except where another translator is credited. These are literal to a fault, corresponding to the original line by line, often word for word, to facilitate understanding of the ways the composer has set the text.

Each selection is followed by a detailed commentary, separate from the discussion of the piece in HWM, that describes the piece's origins, points out its important features and stylistic traits, and addresses issues of performance practice, including any unusual aspects of notation.

Recordings

An anthology of musical scores is greatly enhanced by recordings. Excellent, authoritative recorded performances of all the items in NAWM are included on the *Norton Recorded Anthology of Western Music*. Many are new to this edition. The recordings feature some of the best performers and ensembles working today, alongside classic recordings from earlier generations. For music composed prior to 1780, the performers on the recordings use period instruments and seek to reflect the performance practice of the time, to the extent that we understand it today. The recordings also include performances with period instruments for several works composed during the late eighteenth and nineteenth centuries, including symphonies by Haydn, Mozart, Beethoven, Berlioz, and Schumann and vocal works by Mendelssohn and Stephen Foster. The ragtime and jazz recordings all feature the original artists, and several of the twentieth-century pieces appear in performances by the composer or by the performers for whom they were written. In many periods and genres, musicians were expected to improvise, embellish, or otherwise alter the written music, as evident in many of the performances on the accompanying recordings. When these or other discrepancies occur between score and recording, we have provided an explanation in the commentary.

To make listening easier, compact disc numbers and track numbers have been added to the scores—in grayed rectangles for the complete 14-CD set and in plain rectangles for the 6-CD Concise set. The CD number is located in the running header at the top of the page, and the track numbers placed in the score itself. Tracks are positioned not only at the beginning of each selection or movement but also at major sections, themes, and other events in the music, especially those pointed out in the commentaries.

Why These Pieces?
We have aimed to include outstanding works that represent their makers, genres, and times. Only a small fraction of the music worthy of attention could be included, making it important for us to choose pieces that could accomplish several purposes at once. Knowing the thinking behind our choices will help students and teachers make the best use of this collection. The rest of this preface explains several of the themes that determined our selections.

Placing Music in Historical Context
The title *Norton Anthology of Western Music* needs one important qualifier: this is a *historical* anthology of the Western musical tradition. Rather than serve up great works to be studied in splendid isolation, this anthology seeks to place each piece in a historical context, relating it to the society from which it came and to other music that the composer used as model or inspiration. Studying music in its contexts can illuminate the choices composers made, the values of the society they lived in, and the meanings of the pieces themselves. Just as composers did not create in a musical void, standing aloof from their predecessors and contemporaries, so the historically oriented listener must have access to the primary material in order to establish connections. This anthology invites students and teachers to make such connections.

Breadth and Depth of Repertoire
Making connections depends on having a wide range of examples. The repertoire in this edition of NAWM is broader than ever before. The twentieth century is now represented by over fifty selections, including new works by Satie, Milhaud, Bartók, Hindemith, Prokofiev, Varèse, Cowell, Cage, Feldman, Stockhausen, Boulez, Berio, Reich, Adams, Ligeti, Schnittke, and Daugherty. Coverage of major genres is fuller, adding symphonies by Mozart (NAWM 116), Schumann (132), Tchaikovsky (151), and Hindemith (174); chamber music by Schubert (133) and Brahms (148); choral works by Lassus (49), Gabrieli (74), Lully (83), Haydn (113), and Prokofiev (175); and operas by Scarlatti (90), Bellini (138), Meyerbeer (139), and Puccini (143), plus the Prelude to Wagner's *Tristan und Isolde* (141a). Women composers are represented across the centuries—in the twelfth century by Hildegard of Bingen (7) and Beatriz de Dia (9); in the seventeenth by Barbara Strozzi (72) and Elisabeth-Claude Jacquet de la Guerre (85); in the nineteenth by Clara Schumann (134), Fanny Hensel (136), and Amy Cheney Beach (153); and in the twentieth by Bessie Smith (170), Ruth Crawford Seeger (180), Ellen Taaffe Zwilich (200), and Sofia Gubaidulina (202). Music of Spain and Latin America is well represented, with a medieval cantiga (12), a Renaissance motet and mass (48),

a secular villancico (50), works for vihuela (63), a South American Christmas villancico (88), the first opera composed and staged in the New World (87), and a symphonic picture of an Afro-Cuban ritual by Mexico's Silvestre Revueltas (177). Coverage of French music from the Middle Ages through the Baroque has been expanded, adding new chansons by Machaut (26), Caserta (28), Busnoys (38), and Lassus (57), Ockeghem's *Missa prolationum* (39), an air de cour (73), a Gaultier lute dance (84), and a grand motet by Lully (83). The African-American traditions of ragtime, blues, and jazz are included, with a Joplin rag (155), Bessie Smith's *Back Water Blues* (170), Louis Armstrong's rendition of *West End Blues* (171), Duke Ellington's *Cotton Tail* (172), and Charlie Parker and Dizzy Gillespie's *Anthropology* (183). Also here are classics of band literature, from Sousa (154) to Husa (196). The coverage of American and East European music is the best ever, including works by seventeen composers from Eastern Europe and twenty-nine working in the United States.

Breadth of repertoire is matched by depth. Several composers are represented by more than one work to permit comparison of early and later styles (for example, Josquin, Monteverdi, Beethoven, Schubert, Schoenberg, Stravinsky, and Cage) and to show distinct approaches by a single composer to diverse genres (for example, Adam de la Halle, Machaut, Du Fay, Josquin, Byrd, Bach, Haydn, Mozart, Schumann, Mendelssohn, and Brahms). Instead of relying solely on excerpts to give a taste of multimovement genres, NAWM includes complete examples of a Gregorian chant Mass, Baroque keyboard suite, Corelli trio sonata, Vivaldi concerto, Bach cantata, and Haydn symphony, to show how such works are constructed and what types of movements they contain. In the same spirit, complete scenes from operas by Monteverdi, Rameau, Handel, Mozart, Rossini, Meyerbeer, Weber, Verdi, and Berg demonstrate how differently these composers construct a scene.

Styles and Genres

Perhaps the primary role of a historical anthology is to present examples of the most important styles and genres in music history and to trace their development through time. The generally chronological organization of NAWM follows the order in which these selections are discussed in HWM. Volume 1 highlights changes in both style and genre from ancient Greece (1–2), medieval monophony (3–13), and early polyphony (14–23) through the fourteenth century (24–31); the first, middle, and later generations of Renaissance composers (32–37, 38–43, and 44–65); and the early, middle, and late Baroque period (66–81, 82–92, and 93–100). Volume 2 includes the Classic era (101–117) and the first and second halves of the nineteenth century (118–140 and 141–154). Volume 3 focuses on the twentieth century, divided by World War II (155–182 and 183–205).

Genres, styles, conventions, and forms develop only because composers pick up ideas from each other and replicate or build on them in their own music, a process that can be observed again and again through the pieces in this anthology. The monophonic songs of the troubadours in southern France (8–9) inspired those of the trouvères in the north (10), Minnesinger in Germany (11), and cantiga composers in Spain (12). Later generations of poet-musicians, active in the fourteenth century, wrote polyphonic secular songs and codified standard forms for them, notably the French virelai (26 and 38), rondeau (27 and 34), and ballade

(28 and 35) and the Italian madrigal, caccia, and ballata (29–31). In the Renaissance, new forms and styles of secular song emerged with the Spanish villancico (50), German Lied (40), Italian frottola and madrigal (51–55 and 66–67), and new types of song in French (43, 56–58, and 73) and in English (59–61). In the nineteenth century, the song for voice and piano became the mainstay of home music-making, exemplified by the Lieder of Schubert and Schumann (121–123) and the parlor songs of Stephen Foster (124), but then splintered into two different traditions: art songs, like those of Ives (168) and Barber (186), and popular songs, like those by Oliver (171a) and Gershwin (169). Outgrowths of the art song include the orchestral song, such as Mahler's *Kindertotenlieder* (150), and the song for voice and chamber ensemble, as in Boulez's *Le marteau sans maître* (191).

Similar paths can be traced in religious music from Gregorian chant (3–5) to the modern style of Pärt (201), and in opera from its creation in Italy (68–70) through its diffusion to other lands (71, 82, 86, and 87) and the many changes in style throughout the eighteenth (90, 99, 101–4, and 117), nineteenth (137–146), and twentieth centuries (162 and 185). Exploring and explaining changes in these and other genres is a central theme of this anthology and of HWM.

Musicians frequently use an old word to mean new things, so that the very nature of a genre may change. Through this anthology, the listener can follow the motet as it changes from a work that adds text to existing music (21a) to a new work based on chant (21c–d); acquires rich rhythmic patterning in the lowest voice, as in Adam de la Halle's motets (22) and the isorhythmic motets of Vitry (24); is redefined as a newly composed Latin sacred work with equal voices in motets by Dunstable (33), Josquin (41), Victoria (48a), and Lassus (49); and is broadened in meaning in the seventeenth century to embrace sacred works with instrumental accompaniment for any number of voices from one (75) to many (74 and 83). Even more surprising is the change in meaning of *concerto*, which in the early seventeenth century designated a work for voices and instruments, such as Schütz's sacred concertos (77–78), but came to mean a piece for one or more solo instruments with orchestra. The latter type is represented here by a Vivaldi violin concerto (93), illustrating the genre's first maturity in the late Baroque; piano concerto movements from the Classic era by J. C. Bach (110) and Mozart (115), showing the latter's debt to the former; the finale of Mendelssohn's Violin Concerto (131), representing the Romantic concerto; and Schnittke's Concerto Grosso No. 1 (203), a postmodern reinterpretation of a Baroque genre.

Similar chains of development can be seen in instrumental music. Dance music in the Middle Ages (13) and Renaissance (62) led to stylized dances of many types: songs in the form of dances, such as Dowland's *Flow, my tears* (61); independent pieces for keyboard or lute, including those by Byrd (64), Gaultier (84), Chopin (126), and Dvořák (152); keyboard dance suites in the Baroque period, such as those by Jacquet de la Guerre (85) and François Couperin (94), a genre revived in the modern era by Schoenberg (161) and others; and dance movements in other works, including Corelli's trio sonatas (81d) and symphonies from Haydn (112c) to Shostakovich (176). Ballets or dance episodes appear in operas, as in the scenes included here from Gluck's *Orfeo ed Euridice* (104) and Berg's *Wozzeck* (162). Stravinsky's *Rite of Spring* (164) and Copland's *Appalachian Spring* (181), known today primarily as orchestral works, were originally composed as dance music for ballets, as was Milhaud's *La création du monde* (173). More generally, dance rhythms infect many vocal and instrumental works, including the air in minuet rhythm from Lully's opera *Armide* (82b); Araujo's *Los coflades de la estleya* (88) and Torrejón y Velasco's *La púrpura de la rosa*, both full of Spanish dance rhythms; the aria in gigue rhythm in Scarlatti's cantata *Clori vezzosa, e bella* (89b); the sarabande-influenced aria from Handel's opera *Giulio Cesare* (99b); the waltzes in Schumann's *Carnaval* (125); Gottschalk's *Souvenir de Porto Rico* (129), suffused with rhythms from Latin American dances; and the seguidilla from Bizet's *Carmen* (144).

The canzonas of Gabrieli (65) and others established a tradition of extended instrumental works in several sections with contrasting meters, tempos, and moods, leading to the sonatas of Marini (81) and the multimovement sonatas of Corelli (91) and later composers. Out of this tradition grew the string quartet, represented here by movements from quartets by Haydn (111), Beethoven (120), Ruth Crawford Seeger (180), and George Crumb (193); string quintets, including Schubert's (133); and chamber works with piano, such as Clara Schumann's Piano Trio (134) and piano quintets by Brahms (148) and Amy Beach (153). The symphony grew from its Italian beginnings, represented by Sammartini (108), to become the major instrumental genre of the late eighteenth and nineteenth centuries, dominated by Austrian and German composers such as Stamitz (109), Haydn (112), Mozart (116), and Beethoven (119). Symphonists after Beethoven reinterpreted the tradition in varying ways, including Berlioz's programmatic *Symphonie fantastique* (130), reconceptions of form in Schumann's Fourth Symphony (132) and Tchaikovsky's *Pathétique* Symphony (151), and Brahms's embrace of the past in his Fourth Symphony (147). The symphony was a continuing presence in the twentieth century, represented here by Webern (163), Stravinsky (165), Hindemith (174), Shostakovich (176), Still (182), and Zwilich (200).

Descriptive instrumental passages in opera, like Rameau's picture of a stormy sea in *Hippolyte et Aricie* (95), inspired composers to write instrumental music intended to convey a mood, character, scene, or story, as in the character pieces of Schumann (125), Liszt (128), Gottschalk (129), Scriabin (158), Satie (159), and Cowell (179) and the orchestral tone poems and descriptive pieces by Strauss (149), Debussy (156), Revueltas (177), Penderecki (195), and Adams (198).

As suggested by these descriptions, almost every genre has roots in an earlier one. Here is where the evolutionary metaphor so often applied to music history seems most applicable, tracing lines of development both within and among genres. This anthology provides ample material for making these connections.

Techniques

In addition to genres, composers often learn techniques from their contemporaries or predecessors and extend them in new ways. Compositional practices that start in one genre or tradition often cross boundaries over time. To give just one example, imitative counterpoint, developed in the medieval canon (23) and caccia (30), became a structural principle in Renaissance vocal music from the late fifteenth century, illustrated by Busnoys's chanson *Je ne puis vivre* (38) and Josquin's motet *Ave maria . . . virgo serena* (41), through the early seventeenth century, as in Weelkes's madrigal *As Vesta was* (60). The technique was taken over into instrumental music through the canzona (65) and ricercare (80), and the latter developed into the fugue (see the fugues in 92 and 96). Fugal passages occur in many types of work, from oratorios (100c and 135) to symphonies (112a, 116, 119, and 130), and imitation remains a device learned by every student of Western music.

Forms morph into new forms or combine with others. Binary form, invented for dance music (62a, 84, and 85), was used for abstract sonata movements by Corelli (91d), Domenico Scarlatti (98), and others and developed into sonata form as used in piano sonatas (107, 114, and 118), chamber works (113, 148, and 153), and symphonies (108, 109, 112a and d, 116, 119, and 132). A small binary form could also be expanded into a longer movement by serving as the theme for a movement in rondo form, as in the finale of Haydn's *Joke* String Quartet (111). The elements of sonata form could in turn be combined with ritornello form in a concerto first movement (110 and 115) or with rondo form in a sonata-rondo, used often for finales (120b and 131).

Styles also cross genres and traditions. Vocal music served as the basis for early instrumental works, like the intabulations and variations of Narváez (63). Moreover, the styles and gestures of vocal music have been imitated by instrumental composers again and again, including recitative and vocal monody in Marini's violin sonata (81), singing styles in piano sonatas by C. P. E. Bach (107) and Mozart (114), and bel canto operatic style in Chopin's nocturnes (127). Musicians cannot afford to know only the literature for their own instrument, because composers are constantly borrowing ideas from other repertoires, and performers need to know how to reflect these allusions to other styles in their performances.

Several selections document the influence of vernacular and traditional music on art music. Medieval English singers improvised polyphony with parallel thirds and sixths, which entered notated music in the thirteenth-century *Sumer is icumen in* (23), fifteenth-century carols (32), and the works of English composer John Dunstable (33) and exercised a profound influence on Continental composers such as Binchois (34) and Du Fay (36). Debussy adapted the texture and melodic idiom of Asian music to his own orchestral conception in *Nuages* (156). Satie borrowed from Parisian café music in *Embryons desséchés* (159). Stravinsky simulated Russian folk polyphony in *The Rite of Spring* (164). Bartók borrowed elements of Hungarian peasant song in *Staccato and Legato* (166) and Serbo-Croatian song and Bulgarian dance styles in his *Music for Strings, Percussion and Celesta* (167). Milhaud's *La création du monde* (173) draws on jazz and blues, and Still's *Afro-American Symphony* (182) incorporates the twelve-bar blues (170–171), African-American spiritual, and instrumental sounds from jazz. Daugherty evokes popular styles from boogie-woogie to Las Vegas lounge music in *Dead Elvis* (204). Sheng makes the cellist imitate the sounds and playing styles of Chinese instruments in his *Seven Tunes Heard in China* (205).

Twentieth-century composers have introduced a constant stream of innovations, and this anthology includes a number of pioneering works. Notable are Schoenberg's *Pierrot lunaire* (160), his most famous atonal piece and the first to use Sprechstimme; his Piano Suite (161), the first complete twelve-tone work; Webern's Symphony (163), a model of *Klangfarbenmelodie* and pointillism; Stravinsky's *Rite of Spring* (164), whose block construction influenced so many later composers; Varèse's *Hyperprism* (178), which reconceives music as sound masses moving through space; Cowell's *The Banshee* (179), based on new sounds produced by playing directly on the strings of a piano; Ruth Crawford Seeger's *String Quartet 1931* (180), whose novel approach to counterpoint made it a classic of the American experimentalist tradition; Cage's *Sonatas and Interludes* (187) for prepared piano and *Music of Changes* (188), one of the first pieces composed using chance operations; Feldman's *Projection I* (189), a pioneer of indeterminacy; Stockhausen's *Kreuzspiel* (190) and Boulez's *Le marteau sans maître* (191), which extend serialism to duration and dynamics; Crumb's *Black Angels* (193), full of new sounds from an electrified string quartet; Babbitt's *Philomel* (194), an early example of combining a live singer with electronic music on tape; Penderecki's *Threnody* (195), which produces novel clusters of sound from a string orchestra; Adams's *Short Ride in a Fast Machine* (198), which applies minimalist techniques to create a gradually changing canvas of sound; and Ligeti's *Vertige* (199), an exercise in micropolyphony.

Learning from History

Besides learning from their contemporaries and immediate predecessors, many composers have reached back across the centuries to revive old methods or genres, often producing something remarkably new in the process. Inspired by the ancient Greek idea of suiting music to the rhythm and mood of the words, illustrated here by the *Epitaph of Seikilos* (1), Renaissance composers sought to capture the accents and feelings of the text, evident in motets by Josquin (41) and Lassus (49), in the new genre of the madrigal (52–55), and in the *musique mesurée* of le Jeune (58). Among the tools Renaissance composers borrowed from ancient Greek music and music theory was chromaticism, found in Euripides' *Orestes* (2); after madrigal composers like Rore (53), Marenzio (54), and Gesualdo (55) used it as an expressive device, it became a common feature in instrumental music as well, such as in Frescobaldi's chromatic ricercare (80), and later composers from Bach (96–97) to Wagner (141) made it an increasingly central part of the musical language. In a classic example of creating something really new by reaching into the distant past, the attempt to revive the principles of ancient Greek tragedy led to the invention of opera and recitative in Peri's *Euridice* (68).

Romantic and modern composers have often sought to revive the spirit of earlier music. Recollections of Baroque music include Beethoven's fugue in his String Quartet in C# Minor (120a), Brahms's chaconne in the finale of his Fourth Symphony (147), and Schoenberg's passacaglia in *Nacht* from *Pierrot lunaire* (160a). Webern's Symphony (163) contains elaborate canons modeled on those of the Renaissance, and Reich's *Tehillim* (197) reconciles canons with minimalist procedures. Messiaen borrowed the isorhythmic techniques of Vitry (24) and Machaut (25) in his *Quartet for the End of Time* (184), and Barber echoed medieval chant, heterophony, and open-fifth harmonies in his picture of a medieval monk (186).

Reworkings

In addition to drawing on general styles, genres, and techniques, composers have often reworked particular compositions, a process that can be traced through numerous examples in this anthology. In one notable case a single chant gave rise to a chain of polyphonic accretions. *Viderunt omnes* (3d) was elaborated by Leoninus and colleagues in an organum for two voices (17), which in turn was refreshed by his successors with new clausulae (18) that substituted for certain passages in the original setting. His younger colleague Perotinus wrote a four-voice organum on the same chant (19). Meanwhile, anonymous musicians fitted words to the upper parts of some of the clausulae, creating the new genre of the motet (21a). Later composers borrowed the tenor line of a clausula (21b) or a passage from the original *Viderunt omnes* chant (21c, 21d, and 22) and added one, two, or three new voices to create ever more elaborate motets.

NAWM contains many other instances in which composers reworked existing music into new pieces, a recurring thread in music history. Anonymous medieval church musicians added monophonic tropes (6) to the chant *Puer natus* (3a) and developed early types of polyphony that add other voices to a chant (14–15). Machaut based the Kyrie of his *La Messe de Nostre Dame* (25) on the chant *Kyrie Cunctipotens Genitor* (3b). Many Renaissance composers wrote masses that rework existing models using a fascinating variety of methods, including Du Fay's cantus-firmus mass based on his own polyphonic ballade *Se la face ay pale* (37), Josquin's paraphrase mass on the chant hymn *Pange lingua* (42), and Victoria's imitation mass on his own motet *O magnum mysterium* (48). Du Fay elaborated a Gregorian hymn in fauxbourdon style (36), and Luther recast another chant hymn (44a) as a Reformation chorale (44b), later used by J. S. Bach as the basis for a cantata (98). Luther's chorale *Ein feste Burg* (44c) was set in four parts by Johann Walter (44d), one of over a hundred reworkings of that famous tune. J. S. Bach's setting of *Durch Adams Fall* (97) exemplifies an entire genre of chorale preludes for organ.

Such elaborations of existing material are not confined to religious music. Narváez's *Cancion Milles regres* (63a) is a reworking for vihuela of Josquin's chanson *Mille regretz* (43), and Byrd's *Pavana Lachrymae* (64) recasts Dowland's lute song *Flow, my tears* (61) into an idiomatic keyboard piece. Gottschalk's *Souvenir de Porto Rico* (129) uses a melody of Puerto Rican street musicians. Berlioz's *Symphonie fantastique* (130), Crumb's *Black Angels* (193), and Daugherty's *Dead Elvis* (204) all borrow phrases from the Gregorian chant *Dies irae*. Luther's *Ein feste Burg* makes a dramatic appearance in Meyerbeer's opera *Les Huguenots* (139) as a symbol of the Reformation. Puccini borrowed two Japanese songs to depict his title character in *Madama Butterfly* (143), and identified her American husband with *The Star-Spangled Banner*. The Coronation scene from Musorgsky's *Boris Godunov* (145) incorporates a Russian folk song, and Stravinsky's *Rite of Spring* (164) uses several. The repeating bass figure in the chaconne finale of Brahms's Fourth Symphony (147) is adapted from a chaconne movement of a Bach cantata. The theme of the finale of Beach's Piano Quintet (153) is modeled on a theme from Brahms's Piano Quintet (148). Ives's *General William Booth Enters into Heaven* (168) is based on a hymn tune and quotes a drum pattern and a minstrel show song. Both Ellington's *Cotton Tail* (172) and Parker and Gillespie's *Anthropology* (183) borrow the harmonic progression from the chorus of Gershwin's song *I Got Rhythm* (169). Copland's *Appalachian Spring* (181) includes variations on a Shaker hymn, Husa's *Music for Prague* (196) derives much of its material from a Czech hymn, and the first movement of Sheng's *Seven Tunes Heard in China* (205) varies the melody of a Chinese song.

Improvisation

Improvisation has been part of the Western tradition since ancient times. Every type of medieval organum (14–19) was an improvisatory practice before it was a written one. Singers and instrumentalists from the Renaissance to the early nineteenth century often improvised ornaments and embellishments to decorate the written music, as represented on many of the recordings that accompany this anthology. Lutenists and keyboard players demonstrated their skill through elaborate improvisations, exploring a mode or introducing another work; from these developed the written tradition of the toccata and prelude, represented by examples from Frescobaldi (79), Jacquet de la Guerre (85a), Buxtehude (92), and J. S. Bach (96). Part of the individuality of the keyboard music of C. P. E. Bach (107), Schumann (125), Chopin (127), Liszt (128), Rachmaninov (157), and Scriabin (158) derives from textures or passages that sound improvisatory, however carefully calculated they may be. The invention of sound recording has made possible the preservation of improvisations themselves, which are a fundamental part of the blues and jazz tradition, represented here in the recordings of Jelly Roll Morton playing Joplin's *Maple Leaf Rag* (155b), Bessie Smith's blues (170), Louis Armstrong's performance on King Oliver's *West End Blues* (171b), Ben Webster's solo in Ellington's *Cotton Tail* (172), and Charlie Parker's solo in *Anthropology* (183).

Reception

Certain pieces won a place in this anthology because contemporary critics or the composers themselves singled them out. A legend developed that when some Catholic leaders sought to ban polyphonic music from church services, Palestrina saved it by composing his *Pope Marcellus Mass* (47). Giovanni Maria Artusi attacked Monteverdi's *Cruda Amarilli* (66) in his 1600 treatise. Caccini wrote that *Vedrò 'l mio sol* (67) was one of his pioneering attempts to write a new type of solo song. Cesti's *Intorno all'idol mio* (71b) was one of the most frequently cited arias of the mid-seventeenth century. Athanasius Kircher praised the final scene of Carissimi's *Jephthe* (76) as a triumph of the powers of musical expression. Jean-Jacques Rousseau roundly criticized and Jean le Rond d'Alembert carefully analyzed Lully's monologue in *Armide, Enfin il est en ma puissance* (82b). Pergolesi's *La serva padrona* (101) was a hit with the public in Italy and provoked a battle between critics in France. The opening chorus of Haydn's *The Creation* (113) was hailed as the height of the sublime in music. The first movement of Beethoven's *Eroica* Symphony (119) and Stravinsky's *The Rite of Spring* (164) were both objects of critical uproars after their premieres. Britten's *Peter Grimes* (185) was the first English opera to win international acclaim in over two centuries, and Zwilich's Symphony No. 1 (200) earned her the first Pulitzer Prize in music awarded to a woman. The reactions to these compositions are exemplars of "reception history," a field that has attracted considerable attention among teachers and historians.

Relation to Politics

Finally, musical influences are not the only connections that can be made among these pieces. For example, many grew out of a specific political context, and studying the ways those links are reflected in the music can be illuminating. Walther von der Vogelweide's *Palästinalied* (11) is a crusade song, celebrating the

Christian warriors from Western Europe who sought to wrest the Holy Land from the Muslims. *Fole acostumance/Dominus* (21b) attacks hypocrisy and deception in the church and in French politics. Du Fay's *Resvellies vous* (35) and Peri's *Euridice* (68) were both written for aristocratic weddings, and many other works in NAWM were composed for royal or aristocratic patrons. Indeed, Lully's operas and church music (82–83) were part of a political program to glorify King Louis XIV of France and centralize his power through the arts. Schütz's *Kleine geistliche Konzerte* (77) were written for reduced forces in response to the Thirty Years' War. Gay's *The Beggar's Opera* (103) spoofed social norms by taking a criminal as its hero. Beethoven originally dedicated his *Eroica* Symphony (119) to Napoleon, whom he saw as the embodiment of republican ideals, then tore up the dedication when Napoleon named himself emperor. Political commentary is a recurrent theme in twentieth-century music, including Berg's appeal for better treatment of the poor in *Wozzeck* (162), Britten's condemnation of social ostracism in *Peter Grimes* (185), Crumb's reflections on the Vietnam War in *Black Angels* (193), Penderecki's memorial for the first victims of nuclear war (195), and Husa's protest against the Soviet invasion of Czechoslovakia in *Music for Prague 1968* (196). Sometimes the role of politics is unclear, even if inescapable; musicians and critics are still trying to puzzle out the intended meanings of Hindemith's *Symphony Mathis der Maler* (174), written in Germany during the Nazi era, and Shostakovich's Fifth Symphony (176), composed in the Soviet Union during the height of Stalin's repression.

Your Turn

All of these and many other potential connections can be made through the works in this anthology. But they remain unrealized until you, the reader, make them real for yourself. We invite you to study each piece for what it shares with others as well as for its own distinctive qualities. You will encounter much that is unfamiliar, perhaps including pieces you will grow to love and others that may never suit your tastes. At the end, the goal is to understand as much as possible about why those who created this music made the choices they did, and how each piece represents a trend, genre, style, and time that played an important role in our long and ever-changing tradition of Western music.

—J. Peter Burkholder
October 2008

ACKNOWLEDGMENTS

The creative efforts of many people are represented in these pages. W. W. Norton and I appreciate the individuals and publishers cited in the source notes who granted permission to reprint or adapt material under copyright. I am especially grateful to John Hajdu Heyer for his edition of Lully's *Te Deum*, to Edward H. Roesner for his edition of *Viderunt omnes* by Leoninus and colleagues, and to Rebecca A. Baltzer for her editions of *Factum est salutare/Dominus and Fole acostumance/Dominus* and her editorial revisions of Adam de la Halle's *De ma dame vient/Dieus, comment porroie/Omnes*, which were prepared specifically for NAWM. Thomas J. Mathiesen kindly provided phonetic transliterations of the Greek poetry and new engravings of the music for NAWM 1 and 2. David Budmen contributed the beautiful layout and elegantly typeset several items that were not reproduced from existing editions. Samuel Rosenberg and Robert A. Green helped with French translations. Derek Stauff researched the backgrounds of dozens of pieces, helped with bibliography, and scanned several new items. I had assistance in writing several of the commentaries, from Roger Hickman (NAWM 175, 176, 193, 195, 201, and 205), Felicia Miyakawa (169–172 and 183), Drew Edward Davies (88), Kunio Hara (143), and Patrick Warfield (154). I am deeply indebted to all of them for their assistance.

Members of the Editorial Advisory Board for HWM—Nicole Baker, Ira L. Braus, Anna Maria Busse Berger, Catherine J. Cole, Vincent Corrigan, Andrew Dell'Antonio, Charles Dill, Cathy Ann Elias, Margot Fassler, Jonathan Gibson, James Grier, Stephen E. Hefling, Robert Hopkins, Steven Huebner, Steven Johnson, Dennis Leclaire, Melanie Lowe, Kathryn Lowerre, David Metzer, Heather Platt, Jeremy L. Smith, Pamela F. Starr, R. Larry Todd, and Stephen A. Willier—made very helpful suggestions, from choice of repertoire to details in the commentaries. Rika Asai, Katherine Baber, Jonathan Gibson, Robert A. Green, Barbara Russano Hanning, Kunio Hara, David R. Hurley, Gesa Kordes, Luiz Fernando Lopes, Thomas J. Mathiesen, Brent C. Reidy, Alexander Silbiger, Kristen Strandberg, Travis Yeager, and Christopher Young suggested pieces to include, asked clarifying questions, and offered ideas. Over four hundred instructors provided extensive feedback about the previous edition and suggestions for changes. Alan Matheson identified the quotation in Parker's *Anthropology* solo (NAWM 183). Their help has made this a much better anthology, and I am very grateful.

Assembling the recordings was an especially complex task. I began with an initial list, matching editions to recordings wherever possible. Roger Hickman found other high-quality recordings. He also worked with Ronnie Thomas from Naxos to ensure that the mastering of each CD was precise. Roger meticulously checked and rechecked each of the disks, and Ronnie carefully mastered the CDs. Amy Miles, licensing and production manager for Naxos, oversaw the production of the CD sets, and along with Diamond Time, Ltd., negotiated the licensing for each track—a laborious and complicated effort. Their enthusiastic work brought the recording set to fruition, and I greatly appreciate their contributions.

For some works, no satisfactory recordings were available. Paul Elliott once again organized, directed, and sang in new performances along with Wolodymyr Smishkewych, William Hudson, and Dominic Lim. Konrad Strauss and his staff produced the recordings, and Indiana University's Jacobs School of Music generously offered the performing space. New recordings were also contributed by the medieval performing group Altramar, featuring singers Angela Mariani and David Stattelman and instrumentalists Jann Cosart and Christopher Smith. Their wonderful performances have made the recording set better and more complete, and I warmly thank them.

In addition, I remain indebted to the many people who assisted in preparing the previous edition, especially John Anderies, David N. Baker, Jonathan Bellman, Jane A. Bernstein, Geoffrey Block, Michael Broyles, Felix O. Cox, Richard Crawford, Stephen A. Crist, Luis Dávila, Andrew Dell'Antonio, Matthew Dirst, Kristine Forney, James Franklin, Jonathan Glixon, Halina Goldberg, Bruce Gustafson, Jan Herlinger, Steven Huebner, Steven Johnson, Jeffrey Kallberg, William Kinderman, Melanie Lowe, Claudia Macdonald, Jeffrey Magee, Roberta Montemorra Marvin, Daniel Melamed, Alison Mero, Felicia Miyakawa, Kevin N. Moll, Margaret Murata, Russell E. Murray, Jessie Ann Owens, William F. Prizer, Ann Shaffer, Rex Sprouse, Larry Starr, Pamela F. Starr, Scott Stewart, Patrick Warfield, and Neal Zaslow. Their contributions continue to enhance this new edition.

It has been a pleasure to work with the staff at W. W. Norton. Allison Courtney Fitch oversaw and coordinated the entire NAWM project, secured permissions, facilitated communication between all of the project's contributors, and offered encouragement. Kathy Talalay copyedited the entire manuscript and suggested numerous improvements. Maribeth Anderson Payne, music editor, has been a constant source of ideas and enthusiasm for NAWM as well as HWM, and her careful scrutiny of the commentaries helped make them clearer and more accurate. Jane Searle oversaw production and made the schedule work when I fell behind. I cannot thank them all enough for their skill, dedication, care, and counsel.

Thanks finally but most of all to my family, especially Donald and Jean Burkholder, who introduced me to the love of music; Bill, Joanne, and Sylvie Burkholder, whose enthusiasm renewed my own; and P. Douglas McKinney, whose patient support made this whole project possible. I look forward to sharing the music in this anthology with them, and with all who use and enjoy it.

—J. Peter Burkholder
October 2008

RECORDINGS

Recordings accompanying this anthology are available under the titles *Norton Recorded Anthology of Western Music* (14 CDs containing all of the pieces in the three volumes) and *Concise Norton Recorded Anthology of Western Music* (6 CDs containing 97 of the pieces in the three volumes). The corresponding CD numbers are indicated in the scores. Track numbers for both sets of CDs are indicated in the scores as follows:

14-CD set (tracks indicated in shaded boxes):

CD 1: NAWM 1–20
CD 2: NAWM 21–41
CD 3: NAWM 42–62
CD 4: NAWM 63–75 and 77
CD 5: NAWM 76 and 78–90
CD 6: NAWM 91–100
CD 7: NAWM 101–113
CD 8: NAWM 114–124
CD 9: NAWM 125–135 and 137
CD 10: NAWM 136 and 138–143
CD 11: NAWM 144–154
CD 12: NAWM 155–171
CD 13: NAWM 172–190
CD 14: NAWM 191–205

6-CD set (tracks indicated in plain boxes):

CD 1: NAWM 1–48
CD 2: NAWM 49–78 and 82
CD 3: NAWM 79 and 85–111
CD 4: NAWM 112–128
CD 5: NAWM 130–156
CD 6: NAWM 160–205

PITCH DESIGNATIONS

In this book, a note referred to without regard to its octave register is designated by a capital letter (A). A note in a particular octave is designated in italics, using the following system:

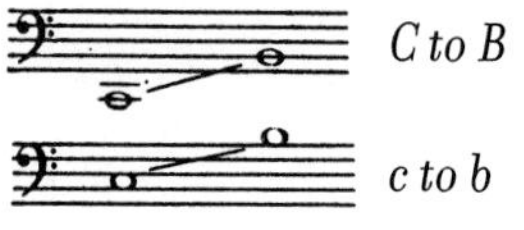

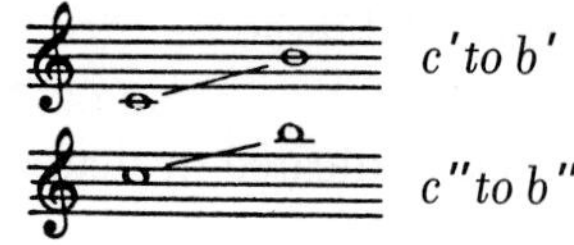

Scott Joplin (1867/8–1917)

Maple Leaf Rag

Piano rag

1899

[Joplin recording]	CD 12|1	CD 5|69
(Morton recording)	CD 12|5	CD 5|73

Tempo di marcia.

2	70
6	74

From Scott Joplin, *Maple Leaf Rag* (Sedalia, Mo: John Stark & Son, 1899). Reprinted in Scott Joplin, *Complete Piano Works*, ed. Vera Brodsky Lawrence (New York: The New York Public Library, 1971), 26–28.

3 71
7 75

TRIO.
49
54
4 72
8 76
60
1.
2.
65
70
76
1.
2.

Scott Joplin named his *Maple Leaf Rag* after the Maple Leaf Club in Sedalia, Missouri, where he performed regularly as a pianist in the late 1890s. Instead of selling the piece outright to a publisher, as was a frequent practice of composers at the time, he negotiated with his publisher, John Stark, for a royalty of one cent per copy. The first year only about four hundred copies were sold, but eventually buyers took home more than a million copies, making it the most famous piano rag in history and the first piece by an African American to sell so well. Although ragtime was a type of popular music, Joplin intended his rags as classical works, equivalent to other stylized dances, such as Chopin's mazurkas and waltzes (compare NAWM 126).

The form of a rag is like that of a march, with two repeated sixteen-measure strains followed by a trio, usually in a key a fourth higher, that features two more strains. *Maple Leaf Rag* is unusual in that it lacks the typical four-measure introduction, repeats the first strain once again after the second strain and before the trio, and returns to the original key in the last strain. Thus its form is AABBACCDD, in which the C strain is in the subdominant D♭ major and the others in the tonic A♭ major. The contrasts of melody and figuration between and within strains are strong, as in Sousa's march (NAWM 154), but the logical form and several recurring rhythmic figures lend the piece a satisfying unity.

In a rag, the left-hand accompaniment keeps a steady beat in eighth notes while the right hand plays syncopated figures above it. The most common accompanimental pattern for rags is the alternation of a bass octave on the beat with chords on the offbeats, as at measures 17 and 49, but *Maple Leaf Rag* also includes other patterns, like those at measures 1 and 9. Throughout the rag, the syncopations in the right hand vary tremendously, with well over a dozen different possible combinations of rhythms within a measure. Longer or accented notes often fall on the sixteenth note just before or just after the beat. These constantly changing rhythms give the music much of its energy. But the harmony is also colorful, with chromatic passing tones, lowered sixth chords (measure 5), changes of mode (to minor in measure 7), diminished seventh chords (measure 9), ninth chords (measures 31 and 49), and other effects. All strains but the first begin away from the tonic chord, and all cadences involve some chromaticism, providing momentum toward resolution.

The accompanying recording includes two performances. The first is by Scott Joplin himself, recorded on a player piano roll in April 1916. Player pianos literally play themselves, with an internal mechanism that depresses the keys. As a paper roll passes over a metal cylinder that has a small hole for each key on the piano keyboard, a suction pump draws in air wherever a hole is cut in the paper, and a mechanical mechanism presses the corresponding key, sounding that note. Many famous pianists—including several composers, such as Joplin—recorded music this way. Piano rolls were one form in which music was sold in the late nineteenth and early twentieth centuries, and they helped to popularize Joplin's music. His roll gives us a good sense of his playing: steady, clear, and not too fast (he often admonished players not to play ragtime fast). He adds notes and flourishes here and there, especially to the bass line.

The second performance is by Jelly Roll Morton (1890–1941), recorded in June 1938 for the Library of Congress as part of a project by Alan Lomax to record, document, and preserve the work of artists who had contributed to the jazz and blues traditions. Morton was one of the pioneers of jazz, and his playing shows the characteristics of the early New Orleans style. While Joplin played the piece more or less as notated (as a classical piece would be played), Morton renders the sixteenth notes in the swinging style associated with jazz, in which the notes on the beat (here, on each eighth note) are elongated and those on the offbeats shortened, creating a rhythm like triplets alternating eighth and sixteenth notes. Moreover, he freely changes the material, adding an introduction (based on the second half of the first strain), adding new syncopations, changing the accompanimental patterns in the left hand, introducing a fair amount of chromaticism, and altering some passages almost beyond recognition. His performance imitates the sound of a New Orleans jazz band, the right hand suggesting the style of the trumpet and clarinet melody instruments, and the left the trombone and piano (see NAWM 170). He also omits the repetitions of the first two strains, to keep the piece under the three- to four-minute limit for 78-rpm records, resulting in the form Intro ABACCDD.

Claude Debussy (1862–1918)

Nocturnes: No. 1, *Nuages* (Clouds)

Symphonic poem

1897–99

CD 12|9 CD 5|77

Modéré

2 FLUTES

2 HAUTBOIS

1 COR ANGLAIS

2 CLARINETTES SI ♭

1er et 2e BASSONS

3e BASSON

1er et 2e CORS A PISTONS EN FA

3e et 4e CORS A PISTONS EN FA

TIMBALES

HARPE

Modéré

VIOLONS

ALTOS

VIOLONCELLES

CONTREBASSES

1o pp

pp très expressif

pp très expressif

più pp

pp

pp

più pp

Div. Sourdines

Div. Sourdines

Div. Sourdines

Sourdines

From Claude Debussy, *Nocturnes*, ed. Clinton F. Nieweg (New York: E. F. Kalmus, 1990, 2004), 2–18. Used by permission.

5
10
78
1
Fl.
pp
COR ANG.
expressif
3
p
Cl.
pp
1er et 2e Bons
pp
pp
CORS
pp
TIMB.
tr
ppp
pppp
1
8
pp
Div. en 6
pp
pp

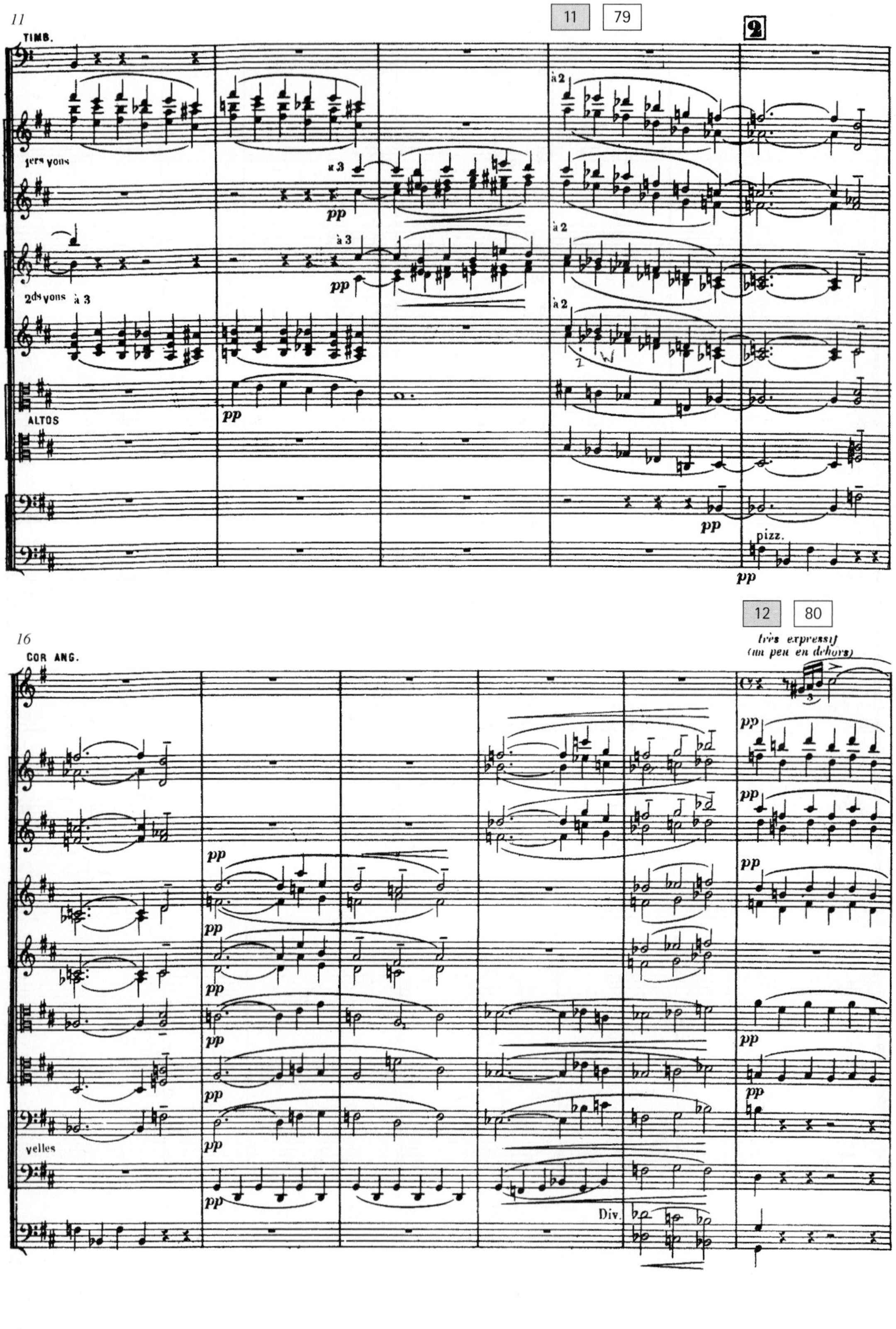

11

11 79

2

TIMB.

à 2

1ers vons

à 3

pp

à 3

pp

à 2

2ds vons à 3

à 2

pp

ALTOS

pp

pizz.

pp

22
COR ANG.
3
p
1o
p
CORS
3o
p
2ds vons
ALTOS
pp
velles
pp
pp

13 81

32
HAUTB.
1o
CL.
Bons
CORS
p
pp

37
HAUTB.
à 2
p
cre - scen - do
CL.
Bons
p cre - scen - do
a 4

42 **4** 14 82

HAUTB
COR ANG
CL
BONS
CORS
1º
3º
4
pizz.
pizz.
pizz.
pizz.
Div.
f *pp*

46
COR ANG.
5
1er COR
sourdines
p
5
pizz.
pizz.
arco
pizz.
arco
pp

50

COR ANG.

1er et 2e BONS

pp

1er COR

p

p

più p

p

più p

pp

pp

pp

pp

54

HAUTB.

6

p expressif

COR ANG.

pp

pp

ALTO SOLO

sans sourdines

p expressif

ppp

ppp

ppp

59
HAUTB.
pp
CL.
pp
pp
BONS
pp
pp
pp
pp
pp
ALTO SOLO
più p
pp
pp
pp
pp
pp
pp
pp
pp

15 83

64
7 Un peu animé
1re Fl.
1"
très expressif
Cl.
pp
1er et 2e Bons
pp
HARPE
pp
(Sol ♭, Réb, La ♭, Mi ♭, Si ♭)
7 Un peu animé
pp

69
1re FL
CL.
1o sourdines
pp
CORS
3o sourdines
HARPE
1 Von SOLO (sans sourdines)
p très expressif et très soutenu
p
ALTO SOLO
très expressif et très soutenu
velle SOLO
sans sourdines
très expressif et très soutenu
pizz.
arco

74
1re Fl.
Cl.
1er et 2e Bons
1o
Cors
3o
Harpe
8
Von solo
Alto solo
Velle solo
p
pp
ppp

79
16
84
1er FL.
1° tempo
più p molto dim.
pp
COR ANG.
sf > p
p
p
CL.
sf > p
pp
p
1er et 2e Bons
1°
sf > p
pp
CORS
3°
> p
più p > pp
HARPE
1° tempo
sur la touche
pp

85
HAUTB.
1°
9
p
più p pp
COR ANG.
p molto dim.
CL.
CORS
3°
p
più p pp
TIMB.
tr
ppp
9
pp
pp
pp
pp
pp
pp
à 4
sur la touche
pp

91
COR ANG
Plus lent
10
1er et 2e Bons
pp
1o
TIMB.
tr
ppp
à 8
à 4
ppp
97
1re FL.
Encore plus lent
Soto
Sourdines
CORS
ppp
pizz.
pp
3

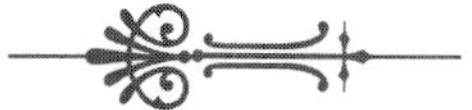

Claude Debussy began his three *Nocturnes* as a set of pieces for solo violin and orchestra for violinist Eugène Ysaÿe, but soon recast them as symphonic poems for orchestra alone. They took him almost three years to complete (1897–99), between work on other projects. The name *Nocturnes* was not meant to evoke the genre Chopin had helped to popularize (see NAWM 127) but was borrowed from a series of impressionist paintings that James McNeill Whistler (1834–1903) titled *Nocturne*. Like Whistler's paintings, Debussy's orchestral pictures evoke scenes that are at the same time ordinary and a bit mysterious: *Nuages* (Clouds), evoking shifting clouds; *Fêtes* (Festivals), depicting evening festivities; and *Sirènes* (Sirens), bringing to life the Sirens of ancient Greece with a wordless women's chorus behind the orchestra. The first two movements were performed in 1900, and the complete piece was published later that year.

Like all of Debussy's orchestral music, *Nuages* is a play of musical images, each characterized by instrumental color, motive, pitch collection, rhythm, and register. In the course of the movement, images are juxtaposed, superimposed, repeated, and altered, creating a kind of musical experience that seems almost visual, rather than following the older literary or rhetorical model of music that presents, develops, and recapitulates themes. *Nuages* consists of three sections in a modified ABA' form, with the A section (measures 1–63) far longer than the others (measures 64–79 and 80–102 respectively).

The opening image, a pattern of alternating fifths and thirds adapted from a song by Musorgsky, suggests movement without a strong sense of direction, an apt musical representation of slowly moving clouds. It changes almost every time it recurs: the winds are replaced by strings (measure 11), the oscillations by parallel ninth chords (measure 14) or triads (measure 29), the open fifths and thirds by full triads (measure 21) or seventh chords (measure 43, joined by pizzicato offbeats), and so on. In the brief A' section the pattern is heard only in fragments (measures 94–97), as if the clouds were scattering.

Juxtaposed with or superimposed upon the opening image is a motive in the English horn, set off in a meter of its own (4/4 against 6/4 in the other instruments), that quickly rises and slowly descends through a portion of the octatonic scale, spanning a tritone (measures 5–8). Unlike the constantly changing clouds, this figure changes little. The final notes are sometimes omitted or repeated, but the motive is otherwise the same at each appearance, never developed, transposed, or played by another instrument, and the English horn never plays anything else. After most statements, the horns answer with a tritone (as at measure 23) or another brief gesture, drawing their notes from the same octatonic scale as the English horn (or, in the A' section, from a whole-tone scale). At the end, the final notes of the English horn motive echo a couple of times, and then it disappears.

The shifting cloud and steady English horn ideas are interspersed with contrasting episodes: a chordal idea in the strings (measures 15–20) and a unison melody, perhaps derived from the cloud figure, that gradually rises in sequence and crescendos (measures 33–42). The profoundly calm middle section features sustained strings and a pentatonic tune in flute and harp that evokes the sound world of Asia—perhaps a Japanese flute or *koto* melody, or a Javanese *gamelan* (gong and percussion orchestra).

As in works by Musorgsky (see NAWM 145) and Fauré, chords in *Nuages* are not used to shape a phrase by tension and release. Instead, each chord is conceived as a sonorous unit in a phrase whose structure is determined more by melodic shape or color than by harmonic movement. Oscillating chords, parallel triads and ninth chords, and sustained chords all serve to create distinctive musical images. However, such a procedure does not necessarily negate tonality, which Debussy maintains in *Nuages* through pedal points and frequent returns to the primary chords of B minor, the key of the A sections.

Often, Debussy uses different pitch collections to distinguish blocks of sound from one another as they are juxtaposed. The opening cloud figure features a B-minor scale tinged with chromaticism, which contrasts with the octatonic scale in the English horn motive and its accompanying chords. The B section inhabits a contrasting tonal world centered on the D♯ Dorian scale (measures 64–68).

Debussy's writing for orchestra is full of striking touches, including the identification of the English horn with a single motive, the use of the horns for only brief gestures, and the bell-like combination of flute in unison with harp. The strings are muted and divided (the violins in as many as twelve parts, the violas and cellos in two), giving a rich but distant sound, and independent lines for solo violin and viola add contrasting colors. Very soft timpani rolls, barely heard near the beginning and end of the piece, underscore the stillness.

Sergei Rachmaninov (1873–1943)

Prelude in G Minor, Op. 23, No. 5

Piano prelude

1901

157

CD 12|17

From Sergei Rachmaninoff, *Prelude, Opus 3, No. 2 in C-sharp Minor; Ten Preludes, Opus 23,* ed. Ruth Laredo (New York: C. F. Peters, 1985), 24–29.

13
f
18
17
f
20
f
23
ff
sost.
ff
26

29
dim.
32
p
dim.
19
Un poco meno mosso
35
pp
37
39
cresc.
mf

41
p
p
43
r.h.
45
r.h.
cresc.
47
mf
p
49
rit.
20
pp poco a poco accelerando e cresc.

51
54
57
Tempo I
f
cresc.
60
ff
63
f

66
69
f
cresc.
ff
Sost.
72
21
ff
75
78
dim.
mp

Sergei Rachmaninov composed his Prelude in G Minor in 1901 as a freestanding work, then in 1903 added nine more and published them as his Ten Preludes, Op. 23. Later, he wrote thirteen more preludes for his Op. 32 (1910). These two collections, together with the C♯-minor prelude of 1892, constituted a complete set of twenty-four preludes in every major and minor key, following the model of Chopin's Preludes, Op. 28, and of Bach's *Well-Tempered Clavier.* Yet because they were initially conceived individually, Rachmaninov's preludes are longer than those of Chopin and Bach and are rarely played as a group.

The form of the Prelude in G Minor is relatively simple: ABA Coda, with the A section itself in aaba song form. Yet almost every time an idea repeats, Rachmaninov introduces new variants, maintaining interest through constant if subtle changes:

Section:	A				B			A				Coda
Figure:	a	a'	b	a''	c	c'	trans (a)	a'''	a''''	b	a'''''	(from a)
Harmony:	i		mod	i	V			i	iv	mod	i	
Measure:	1	10	17	25	35	42	50	54	58	64	72	82

The two main sections differ greatly in character. The A theme is marchlike, with repeated sixteenth notes on the offbeats suggesting drumrolls, and builds to a powerful climax. The B theme is lyrical and passionate, over rolling arpeggiations in the accompaniment. Such stark contrasts of material and such strongly etched emotions are quintessential Rachmaninov.

Rachmaninov was not the innovator in harmony that his contemporaries Strauss, Debussy, Scriabin, and Schoenberg were. But he developed a highly individual and recognizable style within the musical language of Romanticism, which is perhaps an even more difficult feat. One element that set him apart was his gift for creating melodies that sounded familiar yet fresh, moving in unexpected ways yet always sounding right in retrospect. The opening melody, in the bass, is little more than an arpeggiated G-minor triad followed by an embellished stepwise descent from G to D, but its striking rhythm and the sixteenth-note figures that decorate its main notes make it unique and memorable. The middle-section theme hovers around A, straining to rise and sinking back twice, then climbs almost an octave before falling back into place again. Subtle connections link this theme to that of the first section, including a prominent diminished fourth between F♯ and B♭ (compare measures 36 and 5) and another bass stepwise descent from G to D (measures 39–40). The second time through (measure 42), a countermelody appears in the tenor, pressing upward and heightening the sense of yearning.

Another factor in Rachmaninov's individual style was his use of innovative textures on the piano, such as the figuration in the A section, where both hands move constantly back and forth between melody and accompaniment and between higher and lower registers. Even the treatment of harmony is unusual. The music never leaves the key of G minor; instead, Rachmaninov introduces motion up the circle of fifths (measures 17–21) to suggest a modulation within the A section, then focuses on the dominant seventh chord in the B section, in both cases relying on the major thirds in the chords to create a sense of contrast with the prevailing minor of the opening theme.

The performance on the accompanying recording is by Rachmaninov himself, recorded in April 1920 on a piano roll that, when replayed on an Ampico reproducing piano, reproduces not only the notes themselves (like the recording of Scott Joplin in NAWM 155) but also the pedaling, the dynamic level, and the emphasis the pianist gave to each note. Recordings of this sort had advantages over audio records of the time because they could go beyond the three- to four-minute limit for 78-rpm records, could be corrected by the artist, and could sound truer than any record because they were played on actual pianos. Rachmaninov's piano roll shows his dynamic playing, his variety of touch, his use of the pedal, and the fluctuating tempo that was part of the Romantic performing aesthetic. Arpeggiated chords in the middle section and an added note at the end suggest the freedom Romantic pianists took with music, especially their own.

Alexander Scriabin (1872–1915)

Vers la flamme, Op. 72

Tone poem for piano

1914

CD 12|22

Allegro moderato

pp sombre *pochiss.* *con sord.* *pp* *p* *mp* *p* *pp* *poco* *sf poco*

From Alexander Skriabin, *Ausgewählte Klavierwerke*, ed. Günter Philipp, vol. 2, *Préludes, Poèmes, und andere Stücke* (Leipzig: Edition Peters, 1967), 64–72.

34
sf poco
24
40
avec une émotion naissante
pp
p
pochiss.
5
45
avec une joie voilée
pp
49
53
57

25
61
de plus en plus animé
p
cresc. poco a poco
65
avec une joie de plus en plus tumultueuse
p
cresc. poco a poco
68
71
m.s.
74
m.s.

26
77
m.s.
m.d.
78
79
80
27
81
Éclatant, lumineux
comme une fanfare
ff
ma dolce
82

83
84
85
m.s.
m.d.
86
m.s.
87
f cresc.
88

89
90
91
92
93
m. s.
m.d.
94
m.s.

28
95
f cresc.
96
m.d.
m.s.
98
f cresc.
100
102
p cresc.
104

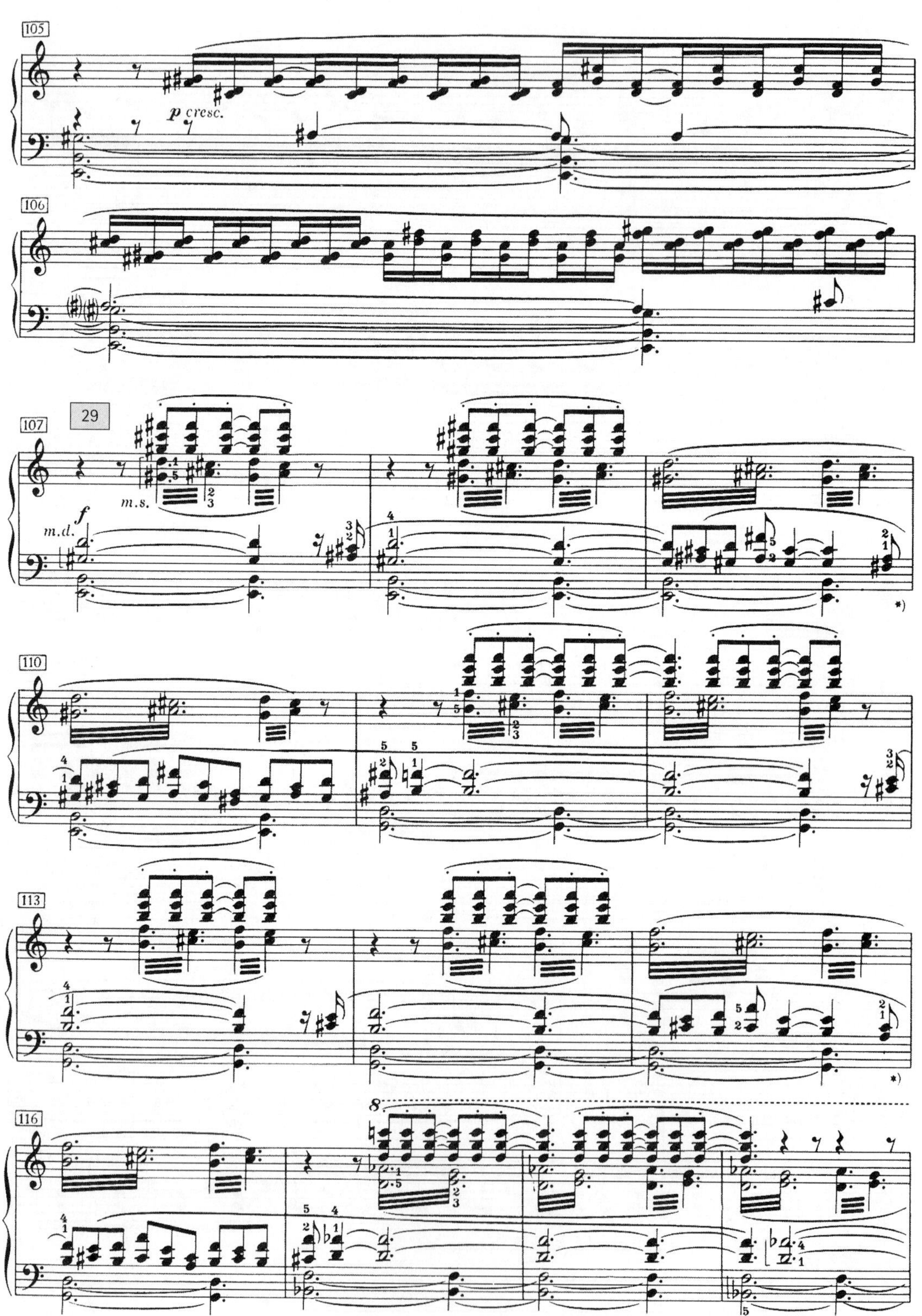
105
p cresc.
106
29
107
f
m.d.
m.s.
*)
110
113
*)
116
8

120
125
30
m.d.
m.s.
ff
129
m.d.
ff
133

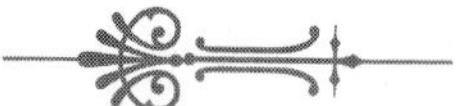

Alexander Scriabin composed *Vers la flamme* (Toward the Flame) in early 1914, conceiving it first as an orchestral work, and then as a sonata, before settling on the novel genre of a tone poem for piano, in emulation of the symphonic poem. The title suggests a journey toward enlightenment or even immolation, without specifying the course of events. Accordingly, the piece presents a series of abstract ideas, gradually increasing in activity and dynamic level and expanding upward in register until it reaches a transcendent climax at the end.

There are two main thematic ideas that define the form, which may be called theme A (measures 1–6) and theme B (measures 27–34). Theme A always involves two voices moving together in counterpoint, and theme B is a single melody. Both begin with repeated neighbor-note motion, then reach upward, fall back, and rise again, an apt image for the sense of striving implied by the piece's title and overall shape. The piece unfolds as a series of textures, delineating four large sections that place the two thematic elements in new contexts:

Section	Measure	Texture	Theme
1	1 27	Block chords under melodies	A B
2	41 65	Stratified layers, oscillating bass and middle voice in 5 against 9 Stratified layers, oscillating middle voice, arpeggios in bass	half-step motive from B half-step motive from B, later part of A (measures 70, 74)
3	77 81 95	Rapid triplets over chords Rapid triplets over leaping bass Rapid triplets alternating with tremolos/high pulsed chords	A' B (repeats at measure 89) transition
4	107 125	Tremolos and high pulsed chords	A B (beginning only)

The work is not tonal in a conventional sense. Rather, a referential sonority of two interlocked tritones announced at the beginning, E–A♯–G♯–D, often embellished with C♯ or F♯, serves as a kind of tonic chord, transposed and varied over the course of the movement. Variants appear at measures 28, 41, 65, 77, 95, 107, and 125. Several of these substitute B for A♯ or include both, thereby creating a sonority that resembles a dominant seventh chord with added notes. At the end the D is raised to D♯ (measure 125), resolving any remaining tension in a climactic apotheosis marked by the widest range and highest pitches of the whole movement. Although theme B appears in a new transposition each time, theme A returns in sections 3 and 4 at its original pitch, creating a sense of stability in the second half of the piece akin to a return to the tonic in a piece of tonal music.

Scriabin's use of harmonic relationships by thirds in this piece is characteristic of his work in general. Theme A is almost entirely octatonic (excepting only the F♯), and Scriabin treats it in sequence by minor third (measures 1–12). Theme B highlights a chord of stacked thirds (B–D–F♯–A♯–C♯) that moves by minor third as well (measures 29–32). Other passages also feature movement by major third (see the bass line in measures 41–64) or minor third (measures 68–77). Most chords have four or more notes, and the final sonority has six, combining traditional tertian structure in the lower notes with stacks of fourths in the upper register. The many dissonances do not require resolution; instead, as in the music of Musorgsky (NAWM 145) or Debussy (NAWM 156), they provide harmonic color that serves to distinguish one block of ideas from another, while the movement from one complex chord to the next conveys a sense of harmonic progression.

A virtuoso showpiece, *Vers la flamme* poses numerous difficulties for the performer, including rhythms of five against nine (see the passages beginning at measures 41 and 81) and rapid leaps around the keyboard. At the end, Scriabin requires three staves to notate his massive sonorities (measure 125).

159

Erik Satie (1866–1925)

Embryons desséchés (Dried Embryos): No. 3, *de Podophthalma*

Character piece

1913

CD 12|31

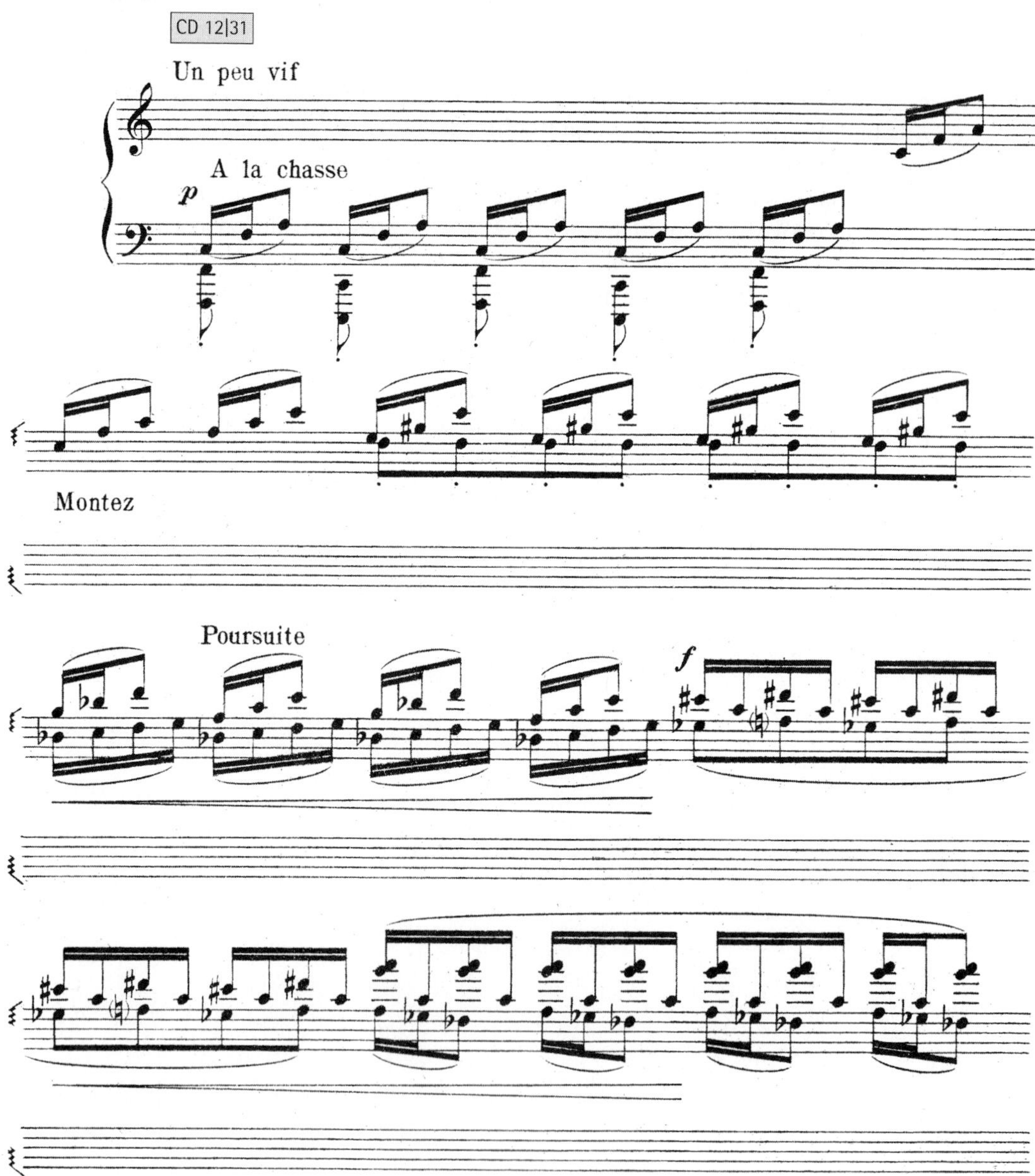

III: Of a Podophthalma. Fairly brisk. Out hunting. Mount. Pursuit.

From Erik Satie, *Gymnopédies, Gnossiennes and Other Works for Piano* (New York: Dover Publications, Inc., 1989), 140–43. In the commentary below, the discussion of Satie's uses of borrowed material in the piece draws on Steven Moore Whiting, *Satie the Bohemian: From Cabaret to Concert Hall* (Oxford: Oxford University Press, 1999).

An adviser. He's right! Pause. Slower. In order to cast a spell over the game. Rallentando.

Resume, getting gradually faster. What is it? The adviser.

Cadence obligée *(de l'Auteur)*

ff

4 Juillet 1913

Obligatory cadenza (by the composer). July 4, 1913.

Erik Satie composed his *Embryons desséchés* (Dried Embryos) between June 30 and July 4, 1913, and it was published later that year. The third of the three pieces, *de Podophthalma* (Of the Podophthalma), was dedicated to Jane Mortier, who apparently gave the premiere. In an introduction to the set that Satie drafted but did not include in the publication, he wrote:

> This work is absolutely incomprehensible, even for me. With a singular profundity, it always astonishes me. I wrote it in spite of myself, impelled by Destiny.
>
> Perhaps I wanted to make jokes? That will not surprise me and would be quite my style. However, I will not have any indulgence for those who treat it with disdain. Let them be aware.

Here Satie parodies the Romantic idea that music comes from a divine source, and the composer is merely the unwitting conduit through which it passes. He also spoofs the serious tone of most Romantic music, while insisting that his joke—if it is a joke—be taken seriously. Nothing ruins a joke like explaining it, but by teasing out the strands of his humor, we can see Satie's purpose: to question some of our basic assumptions about music, and particularly to critique musical Romanticism.

The subject of these character pieces—dried embryos of sea creatures—is absurd, and therefore mocks the very notion of program music, character pieces, and representation in music. The absurdity is heightened by the academic airs Satie puts on by using scientific rather than common names for his creatures: in the first piece, Holothuria, a genus of sea cucumber, and in the other two, Edriophthalma and Podophthalma, two classes of crustaceans (no longer used in taxonomy), the former with fixed eyes (such as small shrimp) and the latter with eyes on stalks (like crabs and lobsters). Satie may have been inspired by *Für Darwin* (1864; published in English as *Facts and Arguments for Darwin*, 1869), a book by Swiss-born biologist Fritz Müller that includes chapters on the developmental history of Podophthalma and Edriophthalma, with pictures of their embryos. Satie includes with each piece a short note that combines correct scientific description with a bit of fantasy. Since it is impossible to portray dried embryos in music—which is part of Satie's point—he focuses his note on the living creatures. The note for the third piece reads as follows:

> Crustaceans with eyes placed on movable stalks. They are skillful, tireless hunters. They are found in all the oceans. The meat of the Podophthalma constitutes a tasty food.

The one part of this note that can be suggested in music is the idea of the hunt, and that is what Satie does. He hints at the plot of his tale with marginal annotations in the music, which are translated at the bottom of the page in this edition. He starts with an active rising figure to suggest the chase, creating a sense of growing excitement by moving from low to high on the keyboard and from F major to whole-tone chords and melodies. Then "an adviser" appears, with his own leitmotive that is labeled at each appearance—a satirical jab at analyses of Wagner operas that carefully point out every appearance of a leitmotive. The leitmotive is harmonized with chromatic chords, perhaps another Wagner reference. A hunting call in C major tries to cast a spell on the game being hunted, but it does not seem to work. The adviser leitmotive alternates with the opening music, culminating with a statement of the leitmotive in canon, and then the piece ends with a long triumphant cadence, even though there is no sign that the hunt was successful. Throughout, the sea creatures are anthropomorphized by the stirring music, dialogue with the counselor, and hunting call (imagine the sound of horns underwater), which makes the entire program ridiculous.

Of course, all these programmatic indications are visible only to the player, not to the audience. It would take longer to explain the program to an audience than it does to play the piece. By designing the work to be fully comprehensible (to the extent that it is comprehensible—see his note above) only to the performer, Satie takes it out of the realm of concert music and places it squarely in the tradition of keyboard music to be played for one's own pleasure. This upends the hierarchy that had developed, in which concert music had become far more prestigious and ambitious than music for amateur performance at home. Also visible only to the performer is the unusual notation: even though the piece is in F major and $\frac{2}{4}$ meter (changing to $\frac{6}{8}$ for the hunting call), Satie notates the music without key signature or barlines, a pointed rejection of convention.

Satie is critiquing the concert tradition in another way as well. Steven Whiting has shown that Satie was drawing elements of the Parisian popular tradition, especially the music sung at the cabaret and café-concert, into the tradition of art music. He does so here in part through musical borrowing. The advisor's melody is taken from the refrain of "The Song of the Orangutan" in Edmond Audran's operetta *La Mascotte* (1880):

En n'trem-blez donc pas comm' ça On le rat-tra - pe - ra.

Don't tremble like that, we'll catch it.

Whiting notes that any Frenchman would have recognized the tune and its text, which suggests what the adviser is saying. The hunting call that follows is adapted from one called "La Royale," which was normally played after the hunters had slain the prey; in this context, it suggests a bit of premature celebration or wishful thinking. This hunting call was featured in a musical scene performed in 1900 at the Concert des Ambassadeurs (depicted in the painting on the cover of this book), placing it in the context of the café-concert. Moreover, the very ideas of musical humor and parodistic borrowing were common in music of the cabaret and café-concert. By pulling all of these elements into a suite of three piano pieces published in the format of art music, Satie was blurring the categories and thus questioning the hierarchy of prestige that placed art music at the top and dismissed popular music as beneath notice.

Finally, these critiques—which have required some explanation—seem subtle in comparison to the satire of Romantic art music in the piece's ending, which anyone can catch on first hearing. In an "obligatory cadenza (by the composer)," Satie parodies the long cadences at the end of Beethoven's symphonies. The key of F major suggests he is thinking of Beethoven's Symphony No. 8, whose finale needs a long assertion of the tonic after its complex harmonic adventures. But at the end of Satie's brief and light piece, it sounds like a bombastic cliché and thus implies that all of Beethoven is a bombastic cliché.

Satie's piece is irreverent and iconoclastic in mocking the sacred cows of Romanticism, antagonistic in reacting against convention, and nihilistic in negating the traditions of concert music, including the classics of the past. These characteristics place it in the avant-garde, a movement Satie helped to inspire that has had an enduring effect on music ever since.

Arnold Schoenberg (1874–1951)

Pierrot lunaire, Op. 21: Excerpts

Melodrama (song cycle) for speaker and chamber ensemble

1912

(a) No. 8: *Nacht* (Night)

33
2
Etwas rascher.
B-Kl. (B)
Vel.
am Steg
Flag.
(pp aber deutlich hörbar)
gesungen (womöglich die tieferen Noten)
Etwas rascher.
gesprochen
ruht der Ho - ri-zont,
verschwie - gen.
Aus dem Qualm ver - lor - ner
Etwas rascher.
Flatterzunge
am Steg
cresc.
pp dim.
ppp
Tie - fen steigt ein Duft,
Erinnrung mordend!
Fin - stre, schwar - ze
stacc.
ohne Ped.
cresc.
34
3
I. Tempo
am Griffbrett
dim.
I. Tempo
Rie - senfal - ter tö - te - ten der Sonne Glanz.
dim.

B-Kl. (B)
Vcl.
espress.
Flag.
p
f
pp
molto legato
Und vom Him - mel er - denwärts sen-ken sich mit schwe - ren Schwin - gen

B-Kl. (B)
Vcl.
20
p dim.
dim.
un - - sichtbar die Un - - ge - tü - me auf die Men - schen-

B-Kl. (B)
Vcl.
mf
dim.
her - - zen nie - der... fin - stre, schwar - ze
8

(b) No. 13: *Enthauptung* (Beheading)

35 4

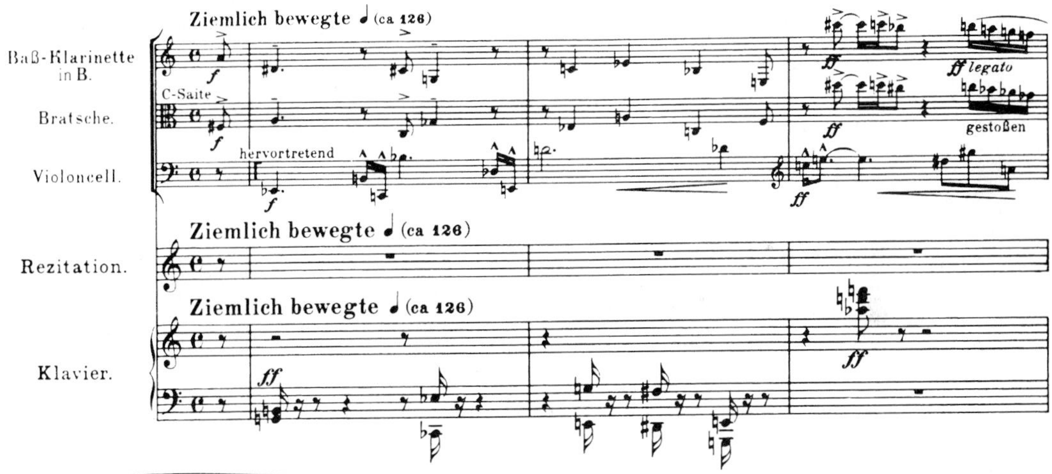

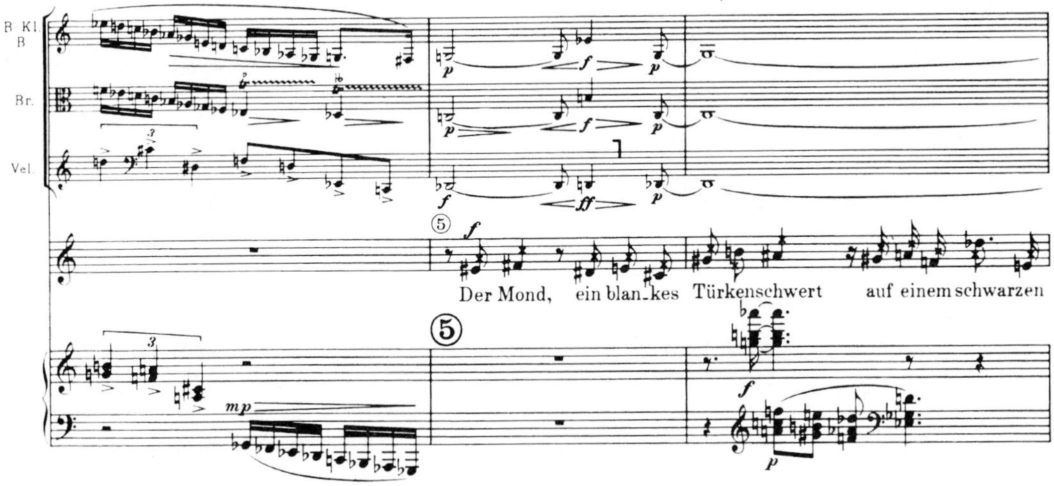

Ziemlich bewegte ♩ (ca 126)

Baß-Klarinette in B.
C-Saite
Bratsche.
hervortretend
Violoncell.
f ff legato gestoßen

Ziemlich bewegte ♩ (ca 126)

Rezitation.

Ziemlich bewegte ♩ (ca 126)

Klavier.
ff

B-Kl. B
Br.
Vel.
p f p ff mp

5

Der Mond, ein blan-kes Türkenschwert auf einem schwarzen

B-Kl. B
Br.
Vel.
fff
p
sf
p espress.
Sei-denkis-sen, ge-spen-stisch groß-dräut er hin-ab durch schmer-
pp
Ped.
bedeutet Hauptstimme.
36
5
sehr ruhig und gleichmäßig
pp sehr ruhig und gleichmäßig
10
-zens-dunk-le Nacht.
psf
sff
Pier-rot irrt oh-ne Rast um-her und starrt empor in To-
pizz.
arco
pp sehr ruhig und gleichmäßig

B-Kl. (B)
Br.
Vel.
arco
pizz.
(15)
- des - ängsten zum Mond dem blan - ken Tür - kenschwert auf einem schwar - zen
37
6
rit.
Tempo
Sei - denkis - sen.
Es schlottern un - ter ihm die Knie,
hervor
accel.
ohn - mächtig bricht er jäh zusammen. Er wähnt: es sause strafend schon auf sei - nen Sündenhals her -

B-Kl. (B)
Br.
Vel.
gliss.
G-Saite
ff
20
nie-der der Mond_____, das blan-ke Tür-kenschwert.
fff
martellato
38 7
langsam (♩ ca 96-100)
Gr. Flöte.
25
espress.
pp begleitend
nimmt Klarinette in A
ppp
Fl.
Kl. (A)
fpp
30
fp
poco espress.
pizz.
arco
trem. am Steg

folgt: **Die Kreuze**
unmittelbar anschließend.
Klavier (anfangs allein) später dazu Flöte, Klar. (A), Geige, Vcll.

⌐ ¬ bedeutet Hauptstimme.

NACHT

Finstre, schwarze Riesenfalter
Töteten der Sonne Glanz.
Ein geschloßnes Zauberbuch,
Ruht der Horizont—verschwiegen.

Aus dem Qualm verlorner Tiefen
Steigt ein Duft, Erinnrung mordend!
Finstre, schwarze Riesenfalter
Töteten der Sonne Glanz.

Und vom Himmel erdenwärts
Senken sich mit schweren Schwingen
Unsichtbar die Ungetüme
Auf die Menschenherzen nieder . . .
Finstre, schwarze Riesenfalter.

NIGHT

Dark black giant moths
killed the radiance of the sun.
A sealed book of magic,
the horizon rests, keeping silence.

From the vapor of forgotten depths
rises a fragrance, killing memory!
Dark black giant moths
killed the radiance of the sun.

And from heaven earthwards
they sink with ponderous oscillations,
invisible monsters,
down to the hearts of men . . .
Dark black giant moths.

ENTHAUPTUNG

Der Mond, ein blankes Türkenschwert,
Auf einen schwarzen Seidenkissen,
Gespenstisch groß—dräut er hinab
Durch schmerzensdunkle Nacht.

Pierrot irrt ohne Rast umher
Und starrt empor in Todesängsten
Zum Mond, dem blanken Türkenschwert
Auf einem schwarzen Seidenkissen.

Es schlottern unter ihm die Knie,
Ohnmächtig bricht er jäh zusammen.
Er wähnt: es sause strafend schon
Auf seinen Sündenhals hernieder
Der Mond, das blanke Türkenschwert.

—ALBERT GIRAUD, TRANSLATED FROM THE FRENCH BY O. ERICH HARTLEBEN

BEHEADING

The moon, a polished scimitar
on a black silken cushion,
ghostly vast, menaces downwards
through pain-dark night.

Pierrot wanders about, restless,
and stares on high in mortal terror
at the moon, the polished scimitar
on a black silken cushion.

His knees knock together under him;
swooning, he suddenly collapses.
He imagines: in punishment, it is already
rushing down on his guilty neck,
the moon, the polished scimitar.

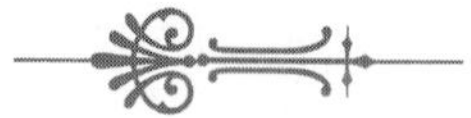

Arnold Schoenberg wrote *Pierrot lunaire* in the spring of 1912, after moving from Vienna to Berlin with his family the previous fall. The full title of this cycle of songs translates as "Three times seven poems from Albert Giraud's *Pierrot lunaire*." He composed it at the request of Albertine Zehme, an actress who asked for a piano accompaniment over which she could recite the poetry. As Schoenberg worked on it, he added other instruments, and the result was a piece scored for a speaker and five musicians, some of whom double on a second instrument: flute (piccolo), clarinet (bass clarinet), violin (viola), cello, and piano. By using a different combination of instruments for every song in the cycle, Schoenberg achieves a maximum variety of color. Throughout the cycle, the voice declaims the text in what Schoenberg called *Sprechstimme* (speaking voice), following the notated rhythm exactly but only approximating the written pitches in gliding tones of speech. He indicated this effect—an innovative synthesis of melodrama and song—with an x through the stem of each note. Schoenberg conducted the premiere with Zehme in October 1912, and then they took the work on tour through Germany and Austria. It was well received and helped to establish his reputation as a leading modernist composer of his generation. When *Pierrot lunaire* was published in 1914, Schoenberg designated it Opus 21, the same number as there are songs in the cycle.

For his text, Schoenberg selected poems from a collection by Albert Giraud, a Belgian symbolist poet, translated into German by O. Erich Hartleben. Giraud imagined Pierrot, the stock comic character from the improvised theatrical tradition of *commedia dell'arte*, pursued by fantastic, threatening visions of the moon. The extreme situations and vivid images prompted Schoenberg to use an intense and dissonant musical language in the instruments, heightened by the eerie effect of the gliding, inexact pitches in the voice. Just as certain expressionist painters, such as Oskar Kokoschka and Egon Schiele, distorted representations of real objects to reflect their feelings about their surroundings and themselves, so Schoenberg used exaggerated graphic images and speech inflections in this work to express the feelings conveyed in the poetry.

The poems in the cycle are unrhymed but follow a strict form: each is thirteen lines long, divided in two quatrains and a quintain, and uses the first two lines as a refrain, repeating them as lines 7–8 and stating line 1 again as line 13. In most of the songs, Schoenberg reflected this form by including instrumental interludes after each quatrain and by highlighting repeated lines of text with an allusion to their original music at the same pitch level. As we will see, the two songs included here reflect the poetic form in very different ways.

Pierrot lunaire is *atonal*, meaning that no pitch serves as a tonal center. Instead, Schoenberg relies on motivic development to give his music coherence and shape, using the method he called *developing variation*, presenting a basic idea at the outset and then continuously drawing out new variants of that idea. Many of the songs evoke old forms or genres or rely on traditional techniques—such as canons—to ensure unity and give the listener something familiar to grasp.

In No. 8, *Nacht* (Night), Pierrot sees giant black moths casting gloom over the world, shutting out the sun. The basic motive, a rising minor third followed by a descending major third, reappears constantly in various note values throughout the parts, often overlapping itself. At the beginning, for example, the first three notes, *E'–G'–E♭'*, form a statement of the motive, but the second note initiates another statement (*G'–B♭'–G♭'*), whose second note in turn initiates another (*B♭'–D♭–A'*), and so on, until six intertwined statements appear in the first three measures. (These overlapping statements can be hard to see in the score, since Schoenberg divides each three-note figure between the hands or between instruments. Note that the bass clarinet in B♭ sounds a major ninth lower than written, so that the cello and bass clarinet share a statement of the motive, *E–G–E♭*.) This three-note motive suffuses the entire piece, in various transformations including inversion and retrograde, and its omnipresence creates a fitting musical image of Pierrot's obsession with the giant moths. The transformations can be subtle and more all-pervading than might be suspected at first; for instance, in measure 8, the bass clarinet has three statements of the motive, whose first notes themselves form another statement of the motive. At one point (measure 10), the voice stops speaking and sings the motive. Even the motive's shape, in original form or inverted, suggests the wings of the moths.

Schoenberg calls this song a *passacaglia*, a set of variations over a repeated bass, but it is an unusual one. The bass ostinato consists of the basic motive on E (E–G–E♭) followed by a chromatic descent. The ostinato is first stated in measures 4–6 by the bass clarinet and imitated at one-measure intervals by the cello and the two hands on the piano. It reappears varied over ten more times, usually in the piano left hand, returning with particular prominence at measures 11, 16, 23 (in the voice), and 24 to mark the refrains and musical interludes, thus reflecting the poetic structure in a readily audible way. At the end (measures 24–25), the original complex of overlapping statements of the basic motive (from measures 1–3) repeats at pitch, modified to include the chromatic descent that characterizes the bass ostinato. Despite the atonal harmonies, this frequent repetition of the passacaglia ostinato and its opening notes E–G–E♭ creates a sense of tonal location, allowing Schoenberg to establish a home region, depart from it, and return at significant points and at the end, just as in tonal music.

In No. 13, *Enthauptung* (Beheading), Pierrot imagines that he is beheaded by the moonbeam for his crimes. The first five measures encapsulate the poem and include a cascade of notes in the bass clarinet and viola—using both whole-tone scales one after the other—that illustrates the sweep of the scimitar. The next ten measures depict the atmosphere of the moonlit night and Pierrot scurrying to avoid the moonbeam. Even though it may appear to the listener that thematic development has been abandoned for free improvisation shaped by the text, the ideas presented at the outset return frequently in new guises. The poetic structure is reflected by repetitions in the music, though much more subtly than in *Nacht*. When the opening lines of the poem return, they are declaimed using variations of the original rhythm (compare measures 5–7 in the voice to measures 14–16 and 20–21). At the first return, the instruments echo the frenetic texture if not the notes of measures 3–4, and a more explicit though still varied repetition follows immediately: augmented chords in the piano move in parallel in a rhythm and melodic contour taken from the cello and piano parts in the opening measures to evoke the image of Pierrot's knees knocking together (measure 17). As the voice declaims the final refrain, the piano performs the downward runs played by viola and bass clarinet in measures 3–4, at the same pitch level as before, while the other instruments play glissandos. An Epilogue recalls the music of No. 7, *Der kranke Mond* (The Sick Moon).

On the accompanying recording, the vocalist renders the Sprechstimme by touching or approximating each pitch, then slowly gliding to the next one, varying the timbre of her voice in an exaggerated manner to convey the changing moods and images of the text. Schoenberg calls for some special playing techniques; for example, in *Nacht*, the cello bows over the bridge (*am Steg*, measure 10), producing a thin metallic sound, or plays harmonics (*Flag.* for *Flageolet*, measure 11), and the bass clarinet uses flutter-tonguing (measure 13). In some passages, such as the opening of *Enthauptung*, Schoenberg uses brackets to indicate the leading voice, or *Hauptstimme* (here, the cello).

Arnold Schoenberg (1874–1951)

Piano Suite, Op. 25: Excerpts

Suite

1921–23

161

(a) Prelude

CD 12|39 CD 6|8

From Arnold Schoenberg, *Complete Works*, part 2, *Klavier- und Orgelmusik*, ser. A, vol. 4, *Werke für Klavier zu zwei Händen*, ed. Eduard Steuermann and Reinhold Brinkmann (Mainz: B. Schott's Söhne, and Vienna: Universal Edition, 1968), 44–45 and 54–56.

poco rit.
sf
dim.
p
f
accel.
f
cresc.
ff
sfp
sf
etwas langsamer
rit.
tempo
ff
sf
accel.
pp
cresc.
sf
f cresc.

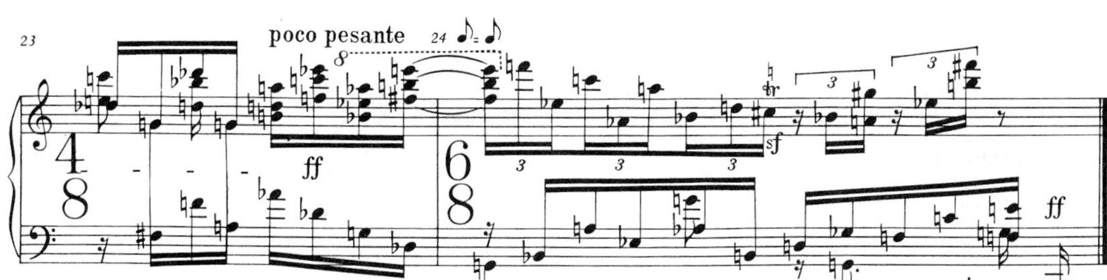

(b) Minuet and Trio

40 9

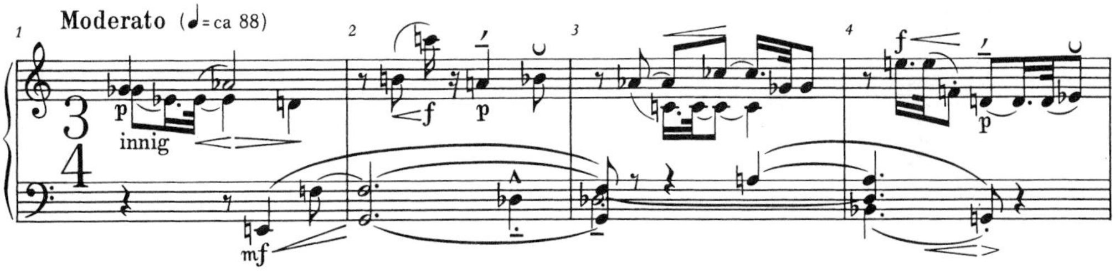

Moderato (♩= ca 88)

innig

rit. - - - tempo

41 10

tempo
rit.
f
p
f
rit.
tempo
ff
poco rit.
tempo
p
f
p

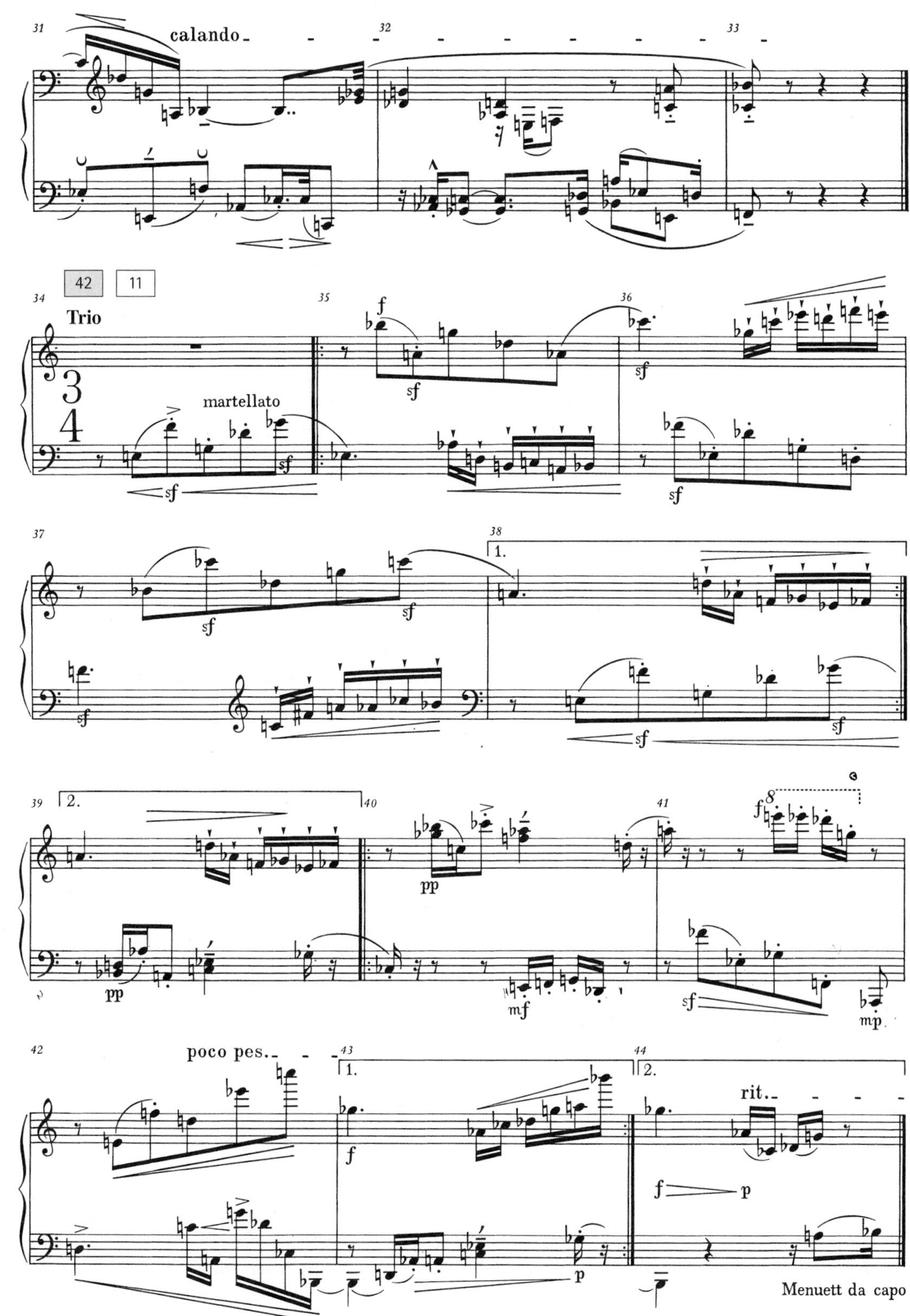
31
calando
32
33
42 11
34
Trio
martellato
sf
35
f
sf
36
sf
sf
37
sf
sf
sf
38
1.
sf
sf
39
2.
pp
40
pp
mf
41
f
8
sf
mp
42
poco pes.
43
1.
f
p
44
2.
rit.
f
p
Menuett da capo

In the late 1910s, Schoenberg became preoccupied with how to recreate what he called "the structural functions of tonality" in his atonal music. In *Pierrot lunaire* (NAWM 160), he created a sense of tonal location by presenting an idea at a certain pitch level and restating it later at the same pitch level (or octave equivalent), paralleling a fundamental procedure of tonal music: the establishment of a tonic, departure from it, and return to it. But he had no analogue to the function of a dominant chord as the opposite pole of the tonic nor an analogue to harmonic progression and resolution, and so could not create extended forms without relying on a text to give a work coherence.

He found the solution in the *twelve-tone method*, which he codified in his Piano Suite. The Prelude was the first twelve-tone piece he composed, in July 1921, and he began the Intermezzo the same month. In February and March 1923, he added the other movements—Gavotte, Musette, Minuet and Trio, and Gigue—to create a suite of dances on the Baroque model. By this time, always obsessed with numbers, Schoenberg was publishing one opus a year, whose number usually matched the year of publication; the Piano Suite, Op. 25, was issued in June 1925.

A twelve-tone *row*, or *series*, consists of all twelve notes of the chromatic scale arranged in an order that provides the sequence of intervals and motives the composer wishes to use. By including all twelve notes, the row avoids emphasizing any one as the tonal center. Instead, the row itself functions as a kind of tonal region, and its transformations (described below) serve as contrasting regions. Typically, a piece uses the same row throughout, creating both motivic and tonal consistency. The row for the Piano Suite is shown in the example below.

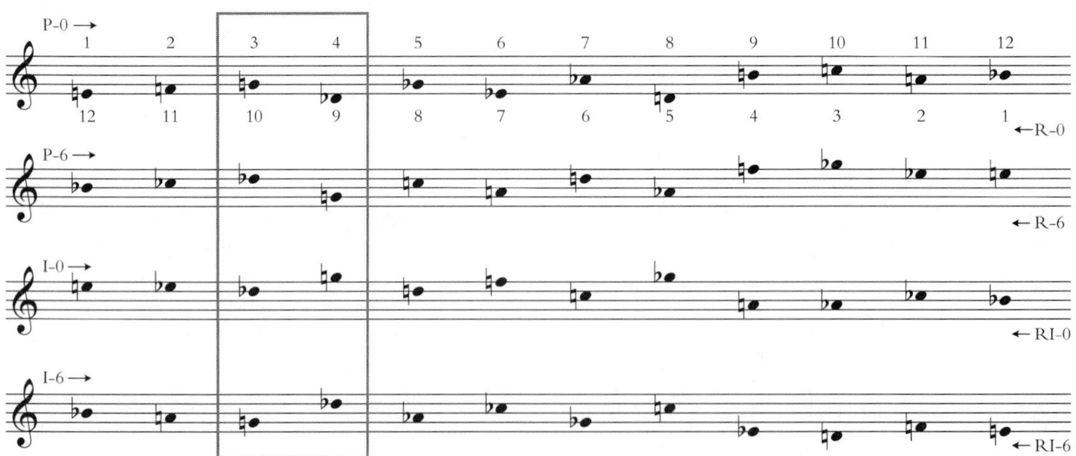

A row can be presented in its original, or *prime*, form but also in *inversion* (upside down), *retrograde* (backward), or *retrograde inversion* (upside down and backward), and each of these forms may appear in any of twelve possible transpositions. In the Piano Suite, Schoenberg used only two transpositions of each form, as shown in the example: P-0, the untransposed prime form beginning on E; P-6, the prime form transposed up six semitones; I-0, the inversion beginning on E; I-6, the inversion transposed up six semitones; and their retrogrades, R-0, R-6, RI-0, and RI-6 respectively. He had designed the row so that each of these transpositions begins on E and ends on B♭ or the reverse, and that each prime or inverted form has the tritone G–D♭ in notes 3 and 4 (shown by the box in the example). These shared characteristics relate these row forms to each other and distinguish them from all other possible transpositions of the row. In Schoenberg's mind, the use of these eight row forms exclusively was analogous to establishing a key in tonal music, and by using the same eight in each movement he preserved that consistency throughout the suite, just as all the dances in a Baroque suite are usually in the same key. Indeed, in a sketch, he designated P-0 "tonic" and P-6 "dominant," showing that he was thinking of analogies to functional tonality.

Schoenberg often broke the series into smaller units that he used to form motives and chords. Here the most frequent division is into three segments of four notes, called *tetrachords*. The first four notes of R-0, B♭–A–C–B♮, form the letters B–A–C–H in German nomenclature, a salute to the composer whose suites Schoenberg meant to emulate. Variants of this distinctive motive pervade the entire suite, linking Schoenberg's music intimately to Bach's.

The opening passages of the movements included here illustrate Schoenberg's procedures. At the start of the Prelude, P-0 is in the right hand as a melody (measures 1–3) and P-6 accompanies in the left hand, with the second tetrachord (C–A–D–G♯), stated simultaneously with the third (F–F♯–E♭–E). (Enharmonic notes are considered the same, so G♯ and A♭ are used interchangeably, as are G♭ and F♯.) The pickup to measure 4 begins a statement of I-6, with the first tetrachord in the lowest contrapuntal voice (B♭–A–G–D♭, completed on the second beat of measure 5), the second tetrachord in the top voice (A♭–C♭–G♭–C♮), and the third tetrachord in the middle. R-6 follows in measure 5, with the three tetrachords similarly layered in counterpoint (the G and D♭ overlap with the previous row), and then a brief rest marks a cadence. In Schoenberg's analogy, the first phrase moved from "tonic" (P-0) to "dominant" (R-6, the retrograde of P-6).

As the work proceeds, it can be a challenge to locate and identify the rows. Since Schoenberg consistently divides the row into tetrachords, the best strategy is to find one of the tetrachords, figure out what row form it is from, and then search for the other tetrachords from that row form nearby. For instance, the D♭–G–F–E from the end of measure 5 to the downbeat of measure 6 is from R-0, and the other tetrachords of that row appear in the next eight notes. It can be ambiguous whether a retrograde form is being used, because sometimes the order of notes within a tetrachord is reversed or otherwise changed.

The Prelude is somewhat free-form, in the tradition of the Baroque prelude (see NAWM 85a for an example). But the Minuet and Trio follows a strict dance form, and it is intriguing to see the ways that Schoenberg has reflected the traditional genre in his new language. It is typical of a trio to be lighter in texture than the minuet that frames it, and that is true here. Schoenberg uses two-part counterpoint in the Trio: P-0 in the left hand (measure 34) is imitated in inversion by I-6 in the right hand, followed by I-0 in the left hand (measure 36) and P-6 in the right. These four measures repeat, and a similar canon constitutes the second half of the Trio. The result cunningly evokes both the spirit of a Bach invention, through a little canon in inversion, and the two-measure phrasing and binary form of a minuet.

At the beginning of the Minuet, the periodic phrasing and the lilting, dance-like rhythms are apparent even without looking for the rows. Each measure-long unit in the right hand is set off from the next by a brief rest. The second two-measure phrase echoes the rhythmic and melodic motives of the first, forming an antecedent-consequent pair. Both of these two-measure phrases end with an allusion to leading-tone motion at a cadence; the fact that the second ends a fifth lower than the first is a reference to the dominant-tonic relationships of traditional tonality. When we do look for the rows, we find that the first two measures present P-0, using the first tetrachord (E–F–G–D♭) in the left hand as an accompaniment to the other two, which occupy one measure each; measures 3–4 present I-6 in a similar arrangement, with some internal reordering of notes within the tetrachords.

The presentation of one complete row statement every two measures creates a kind of harmonic rhythm. Schoenberg then picks up the pace, completing the next three row statements in four beats (P-6), three beats (I-0), and two beats (P-0) respectively, before settling down to one row statement per measure until the repeat mark at the end of the first section. Once again, rhythmic and motivic repetition on the surface, such as the sequences in measures 5–6 and measures 9–10, articulate the changes of row form. This twelve-tone rhythm is quite a close analogy to the use of chord progressions in tonal music to establish the meter and phrasing through harmonic motion. Thus in many ways, Schoenberg's complex twelve-tone method provided the tools he needed for recreating the functions of tonality in a musical language that did not define a central pitch.

The Minuet follows the standard rounded binary form, except that the second section is not repeated. The first five measures of the second section offer contrasting material derived from the first measure of the movement, then a varied restatement of the first section begins at measure 17. At first it is quite distant, but by measure 21 the motives from measures 5–8 are readily apparent, and measures 29–31 repeat the end of the first section almost exactly. Throughout, Schoenberg marks the ends of important subsections with ritardandos, making it easy to see how he himself envisioned the formal divisions. A brief coda in measures 32–33 ends the Minuet with the same two row forms with which it began, P-0 in the right hand and I-6 in the left, providing an analogy in twelve-tone terms to the closure granted by a V-I cadence at the end of a tonal work.

The question almost everyone asks about twelve-tone music is "Can you really hear the rows?" One response is to note that the piece can be perfectly coherent even without recognizing a single row form. The inverted canon of the Trio and the antecedent-consequent phrasing and sequences in the Minuet are evident in the musical contours, without tracing the exact intervals or pitches. In Schoenberg's music, it is less important to hear and identify entire rows than to recognize the motives he draws from the row, like the tetrachords in the Piano Suite, and perhaps to be aware of the harmonic rhythm marked off by successive segments of music containing all twelve tones. These are things listeners can train themselves to hear and performers can quickly locate in the score and represent in performance, without doing a complete analysis of the rows.

Schoenberg meticulously marked the dynamics, articulation, phrasing, and tempo fluctuations, knowing that in such an unfamiliar idiom the performer would have difficulty making choices in such matters without guidance. In some places, such as measure 22 of the Prelude and measures 2 and 4 of the Minuet, he used marks derived from poetry to indicate notes that should be stressed (ʹ) or left unstressed (˘) in cases where his intended accentuation contradicts the regular meter.

Alban Berg (1885–1935)

Wozzeck, Op. 7: Act III, Scene 3

Opera

1917–22

CD 12|43 CD 6|12

Vorhang rasch auf 3. Szene Eine Schenke (Nacht, schwaches Licht)
Curtain rises quickly 3rd Scene *A low tavern (badly lit, Night)*

Schnellpolka von einem Burschen ungemein roh und *sempreff* gespielt
Fast Polka played very coarsely and sempreff by one of the young men

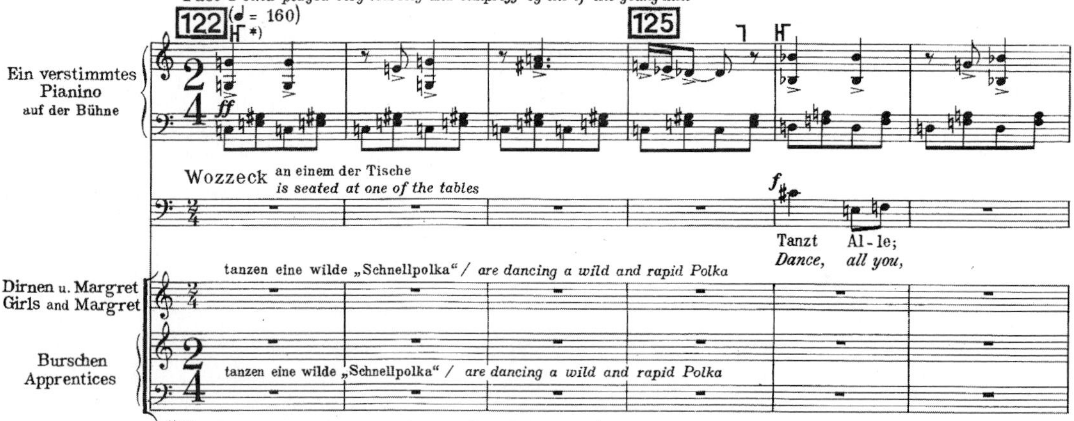

122 (♩ = 160) H *) 125

Ein verstimmtes Pianino auf der Bühne

ff

Wozzeck an einem der Tische
is seated at one of the tables

f

Tanzt Al - le;
Dance, all you,

Dirnen u. Margret
Girls and Margret

tanzen eine wilde „Schnellpolka" / *are dancing a wild and rapid Polka*

Burschen
Apprentices

tanzen eine wilde „Schnellpolka" / *are dancing a wild and rapid Polka*

*) H bedeutet in dieser Szene Hauptrhythmus (siehe Takt 114-115)

130

Pianino

sempre ff

Wozz.

tanzt nur zu, springt, schwitzt ______ und
dance a - way! Leap, sweat ______ and

135

Pianino

Wozz.

stinkt, es ______ holt Euch doch
reek! For ______ some day soon

From Alban Berg, *Wozzeck*, ed. H. E. Apostel (Vienna: Universal Edition, 1955), 419–36. English singing translation by Eric Blackall and Vida Harford.

140
Pk.
p
poco cresc.
Pianino
sempre ff
stürzt ein Glas Wein hinunter
dashes down a glass of wine
Wozz.
noch ein-mal der Teu-fel!
he'll fetch you, the Dev-il!
♩ = ♩ (𝅗𝅥 = daher 80)
145
1. 2. Kl. in B 3. 4.
1. 2. Hr. in F o. D. 3. 4.
mf
Pk.
kl. Tr.
f mf pp
Pianino
den Klavierspieler überschreiend
then, shouting down the pianist
Wozz.
Es rit-ten drei Rei-ter wohl an den Rhein, Bei ei-ner Frau Wir-tin da
Three horse-men came rid-ing up to the Rhine, And went to my host-ess to
♩ = ♩ (𝅗𝅥 = daher 80)
145
1. Vl.
2. Vl.
Vla
Vlc.
pizz.
f

etwas ruhiger (𝅗𝅥 = 70)
150
1. 2.
Kl. in B
3. 4.
1. 2.
Hr. in F
o. D.
3. 4.
Trgl
Hfe
p immer gebrochen
gleichsam versuchend, eine Begleitung für das Lied Wozzecks zu finden
149
150
Das Pianino a. d. Bühne
ff
p dolce
Wozz.
kehr-ten sie ein. Mein Wein- ist gut, mein Bier- ist klar, Mein Töch - ter - lein
taste of her wine. My wine- is good, my ale- is clear, my daugh - ter dear
etwas ruhiger (𝅗𝅥 = 70)
150
arco
1. 2. Solo
1. Vl.
3. 4. Solo
1. Vl.
d. Übrig.
2. Vl.
Vla
Vlc.

subito meno allegro (𝅗𝅥 = 60)
a tempo (𝅘𝅥 = 𝅘𝅥 = 160)
155
1. Hr. in F o. D.
2. Hr. in F o. D.
3.
3. Pos. o. D.
Btb. o. D.
gestopft
ff
fp
(o. Dpf.)
Pk.
f
Trgl
Hfe
nicht gebrochen
Pianino
subito meno allegro
a tempo 155
Schnellpolka
verklingen lassen
quasi in den Tanz Wozzecks einfallend
Margret
mit Wozzeck tanzend
dancing with Wozzeck
Wozz.
sich unterbrechend
interrupts himself
springt auf
jumps up
tanzt mit Margret ein Paar Sprünge
dances a few steps with her
liegt auf der... Ver-dammt! Komm, Mar-gret!
lies on her... Be damned! Come, Mar-gret!
1. 2. Solo
1. Vl.
3. 4. Solo

rit. - - Wieder meno allegro
(ritardierte 𝅗𝅥 = neue 𝅗𝅥 = 60)
poco rit.
160
Englh.
die Singstimme fortsetzend
dimin.
nimmt 4. Ob.
gestopft
1.2. nehmen Dpf.
1. 2. 3.
Hr. in F o. D.
4.
3. o. D.
Pos.
4. m. D.
m. Dpf.
nimmt Dpf.
Dpf. ab
Btb. o. D.
(ohne rit.) Plötzliche Unterbrechung
Pianino
Marg.
bleibt plötzlich stehen
then suddenly stops
führt sie an seinen Tisch und zieht sie auf seinen Schoß nieder
leads her to his table, and pulls her on his lap
Wozz.
Komm setz Dich her, Mar - gret!
Come, let's sit down, Mar - gret!
rit. - - Wieder meno allegro
poco rit.
160
get. Griffbrett arco
2. Vl.
Vla get.
Vlc.
(die Pos. nicht übertönend)
Kb.
(die Btb. nicht übertönend)
molto p

*) Triller ohne Nachschlag

165
44
13
168
1.2. Fl.
nehmen 1.u.2.Picc.
1.2. Fg.
3.
Kfg.
1.2.Hr.in F m.D.
Dpf.ab
1. m.D.
Pos.
2. o.D.
(o.Dpf.)
(m.Dpf.)
quasi Echo
mf
p
Hfe
nicht gebrochen
Die Margret begleitend
(𝅗𝅥=𝅘𝅥=120)
Das Pianino a.d.Bühne
ff
m. d. Pianino
Marg.
In's
To
Wozz.
dolce
kalt
cold
wer - den!
al - so!
Kannst nicht sin - gen?
Can't you sing, girl?
1. Vl.
2. Vl.
Vla
Vlc.
Kb.
gewöhnlich

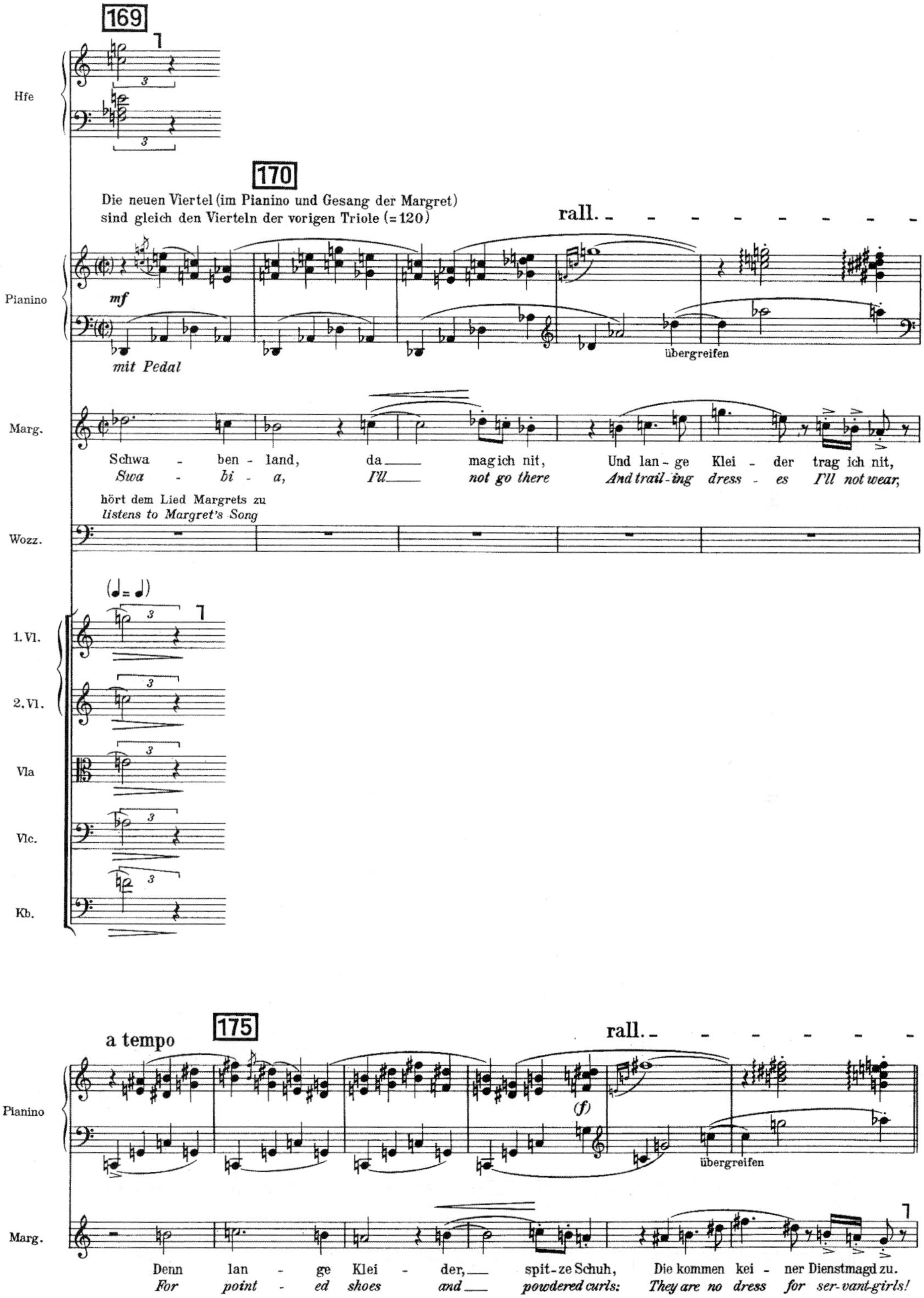

169

Hfe

170

Die neuen Viertel (im Pianino und Gesang der Margret) sind gleich den Vierteln der vorigen Triole (=120)

rall.

Pianino

mf

mit Pedal

übergreifen

Marg.

Schwa - ben - land, da___ mag ich nit, Und lan - ge Klei - der trag ich nit,
Swa - bi - a, I'll___ not go there And trail - ing dress - es I'll not wear,

hört dem Lied Margrets zu
listens to Margret's Song

Wozz.

(♩= ♩)

1. Vl.

2. Vl.

Vla

Vlc.

Kb.

plötzlich noch langsamer (♩ = 80)
180
1.2. Picc. 3.4.
1.2. Ob. 3.4.
1.2. Hr. in F o.D. 3.
1.3. Trp. in F m.D. 2.4.
m. Dpf.
a 2
o.Dpf.
4. Pos. o.D.
Btb. o.D.
gr. Tr.
Xyl.
Hfe
auffahrend
flaming up
Wozz.
Nein! kei-ne Schuh, man kann auch bloß - fü-ßig in die Höll' geh'n! Ich möcht heut
No! wear no shoes, one can go bare - foot-ed down to hell fire! I feel like
plötzlich noch langsamer (♩ = 80)
180
Doppelgriff
1.Vl.
2.Vl.

45
14
185
1.u.2. Picc. nehmen 1.u.2. Fl.
1.2.
Picc.
3.4.
1.2.
Ob.
3.4.
1.2.
Kl. in B
3.4.
Echoton
pp
Echoton
a 2
1.
Fg.
2.3.
Kfg.
1.2.3.Hr. in F o.D.
1.2.3.4.Trp. in F m.D.
1.3. a 2
2.4. a 2
4.Pos. o.D.
subito p (Echo)
Btb. o.D.
subito p (Echo)
Pk.
Xyl.
Cel.
f
Hfe
Marg.
mf
A - ber was hast Du
But what is that, there
Wozz.
rau - fen, rau - fen
fight - ing, fight-ing!
185
m. Dpf.
Solo m.D.
1.Vl.
d.Übrig.
2.Vl.

kurzer Halt
poco Allegro (¢)
voriges ♩ = neue 𝅗𝅥 (= 80)
1. 2.
Kl. in B
3. 4.
1.
Fg.
2. 3.
Kfg.
4. Pos. o. D.
Btb. o. D.
Pk.
Cel.
Hfe
Marg.
an der Hand?
on your hand?
Rot!
Red
Blut!
blood!
Wozz.
Ich?
Mine?
ich?
Mine?
poco Allegro (¢)
voriges ♩ = neue 𝅗𝅥 (= 80)
kurzer Halt
Dpf. ab
Solo m.D. 1. Vl.
1. Solo Vlc. o.D.
o. Dpf.
col legno gestr.
Solo Kb. o.D.
o. Dpf.
col legno gestr.

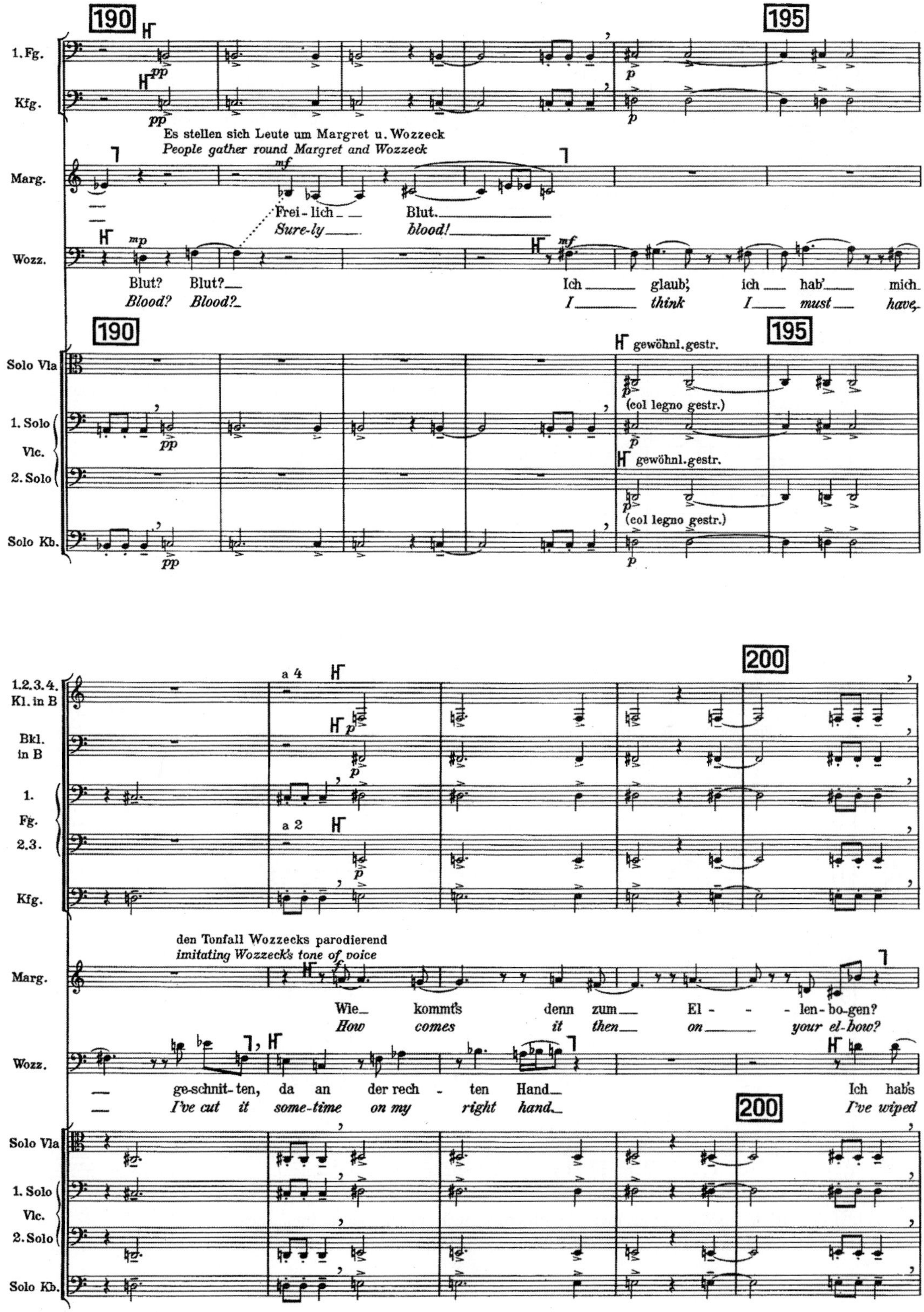

200
1.2.3.4. Kl. in B
a 4
Bkl. in B
1. Fg. 2.3.
a 2
Kfg.
den Tonfall Wozzecks parodierend
imitating Wozzeck's tone of voice
Marg.
Wie kommt's denn zum El- - len-bo-gen?
How comes it then on your el-bow?
Wozz.
ge-schnit-ten, da an der rech - ten Hand
I've cut it some-time on my right hand
Ich hab's
I've wiped
200
Solo Vla
1. Solo Vlc. 2. Solo
Solo Kb.

*If the Chorus encounters insuperable difficulties with pitch, their entrances can be sounded by the onstage piano (audible only to the singers).

1,2,3,4.Kl. in B
Bkl. in B
1,2,3.Fg.
Kfg.
Hfe
Soprane
Frei - lich da stinkt's nach
Sure - ly it smells of
ev. das Pianino a.d.Bühne
1. Bässe Blut Blood
2. Ten. Blut Blood
2. Bässe Blut Blood
Marg.
stinkt's nach Men - schen - blut!
smells of hu - man blood!
Wozz.
Bin ich ein Mör - der? Platz! o - der es geht
Am I a murd' rer? Off! or else some - one
(alle Soprane)
Dirnen Sopr.
Frei - lich da stinkt's nach
Sure - ly it smells of
Alt
Burschen Ten.
Baß
(col legno gestr.)
Vla
(gew.)
2 Soli Vlc. die Übrig.
(gew.)
get.
Kb.

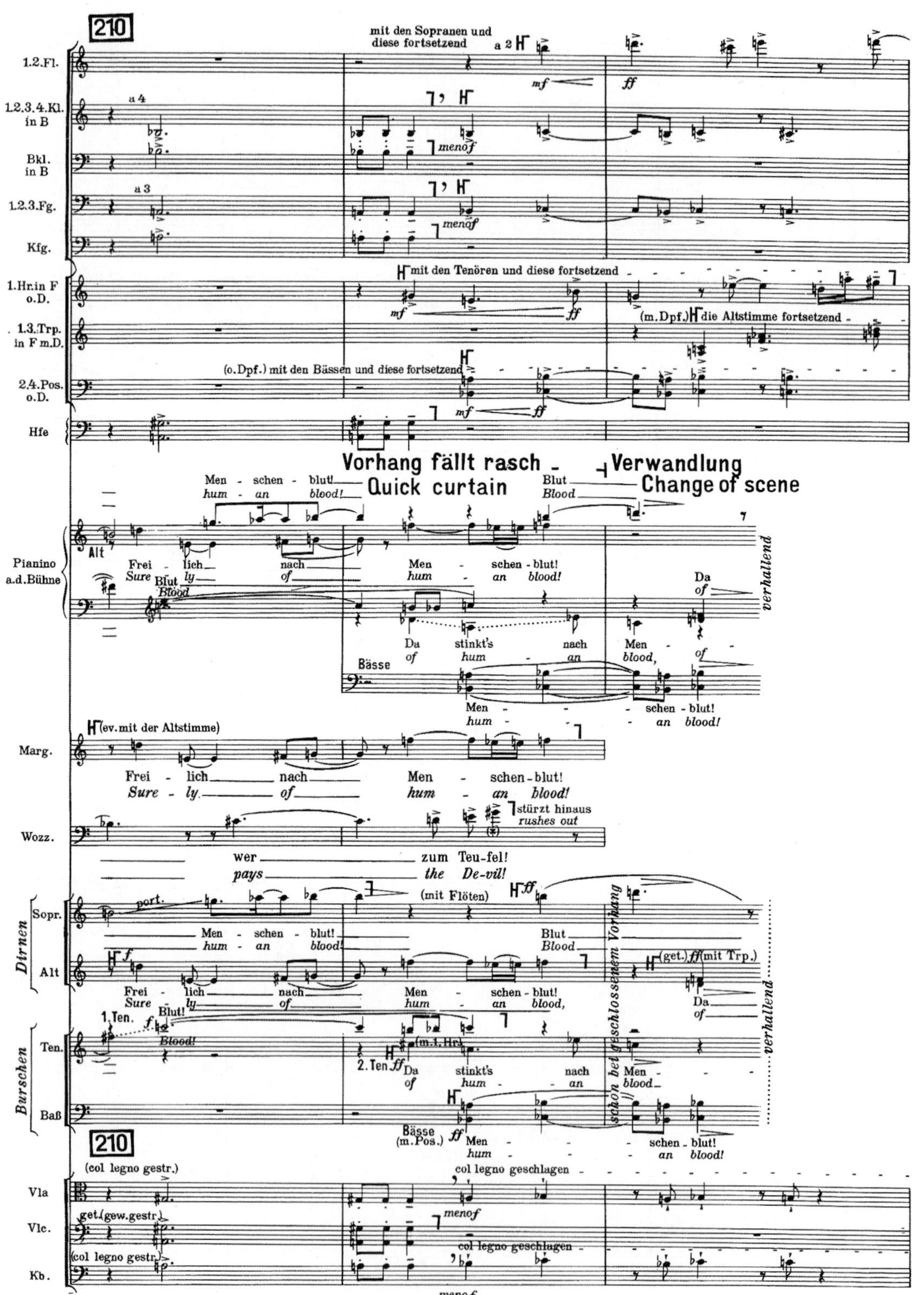
210
Vorhang fällt rasch
Quick curtain
Verwandlung
Change of scene
Men - schen - blut!
hum - an blood!
Frei - lich nach
Sure - ly of
wer zum Teu-fel!
pays the De-vil!
stürzt hinaus
rushes out
Da stinkt's nach
of hum - an
Blut
Blood
Men - schen - blut!
hum - an blood!
schon bei geschlossenem Vorhang
verhallend
col legno geschlagen

215
3.4.Picc.
a 2
ff
1.2.Fl.
1.2.
Ob.
3.4.
a 2
ff
1.2.
Kl.in B
3.4.
a 3
1.2.3.Fg.
1.3. Trp. inF m.D.
2.4.Pos. o.D.
1.Vl.
fff
fp
2.Vl.
gew. gestr.
Vla
Vlc. get.
gew. gestr.
Kb.

etwas schwerer
(𝅗𝅥 = 50-60)
1.2.Fl.
1.2.3.4.Ob.
1.2.3.4.Kl. in B
Bkl. in B
1.2.3.Fg.
1.2.3.4.Hr. in F o.D.
2.4.Pos. o.D.
Btb. o.D.
kl.Tr. womöglich mehrere
a 2
a 4
a 3
fff
fp
nehmen Dpf.
fp cresc.
sempre marc.
etwas schwerer
(𝅗𝅥 = 50-60)
1.Vl. get.
2.Vl.
Vla
Vlc. get.
col legno geschl.
nehmen Dpf.
Vorhang auf
(𝅗𝅥=𝅗𝅥)
1.2.3.4.Tp. in F m.D.
m.D. kurz gestoßen
pp(quasi Echo)
3.4.Dpf.ab
1.3.Pos. m.D.
Dpf.ab
kl.Tam-Tam
pp ohne cresc.
abdämpfen

In 1824, Johann Christian Woyzeck was executed for killing the woman he lived with, although many believed he was innocent by reason of insanity. A young doctor and writer, Georg Büchner (1813–1837) wrote a play based on the incident, casting the central figure as a poor soldier who is a powerless victim of circumstances, but Büchner died before finishing it. Decades later, Büchner's play was assembled by a literary scholar (who misread the y as a z and transcribed the name as *Wozzeck*). This version was published in 1879 and, finally, staged in 1913. Alban Berg saw the Vienna production the next year and immediately decided to set the play as an opera, adapting his libretto from the original text and reordering some of the scenes. His own service in the Austrian military during World War I gave him a sense of Wozzeck's life as a soldier and provided details for the opera. He completed the music in 1922 and had the vocal score printed in order to stimulate interest. The work was finally premiered in 1925 at the Berlin State Opera, to excellent reviews. Within a few years it became established as one of the most successful modern operas and by far the most popular atonal opera.

The story centers on Franz Wozzeck, a poor soldier, who is mocked by his Captain, has apocalyptic visions, and submits to a Doctor's experiments in order to earn extra money. (The poor characters all have names, but the well-to-do ones have only titles, a symbol of the power they wield in Wozzeck's world.) Wozzeck has a child with his common-law wife Marie, but with his many part-time jobs he has little time for them. When the Drum Major woos Marie, she gives in to his attentions. Wozzeck learns of their affair, and, driven mad by despair, he kills her and then accidentally drowns while seeking to hide the bloody knife. In the heartbreaking final scene, their orphaned child rides his hobby horse, not comprehending what has happened, while other children run to look at Marie's body.

Berg laid out the libretto in three acts with five scenes each. In addition to using leitmotives throughout the opera, he composed each scene as a traditional musical form. These forms help to describe the characters and convey the dramatic situation, but they also show Berg's interest in reflecting on the music of the past, a common theme of modernist composers. The first act introduces the characters, with a Baroque suite to suggest the Captain's devotion to convention; a rhapsody for Wozzeck's visions; a march and lullaby as Marie glimpses the Drum Major and sings to her child; a passacaglia for the Doctor's fixation on his experiments; and a rondo as the Drum Major repeatedly tries to seduce Marie and finally succeeds. The second act is a symphony in five movements, portraying the dramatic developments through a sonata-form movement, a fantasia and fugue, a ternary slow movement, a scherzo, and a rondo, as Wozzeck learns of the affair, ineffectually fights for Marie, and sinks into despair. The third act is a series of six inventions, each on a single element—a theme, a single note, a rhythmic pattern, a chord, a key, and a duration—suggesting Wozzeck's obsessions. The music in each act is continuous, with linking orchestral interludes between scenes. The longest interlude, before the last scene, is like a symphonic Adagio that sums up the tragedy.

The scene included here is the invention on a rhythm. Wozzeck sits in a tavern, having just murdered Marie in the previous scene. An onstage piano, mistuned to suggest the sound of a cheap barroom piano, introduces the rhythmic pattern—a series of eight durations—in the form of a fast polka. Throughout the scene, the rhythmic pattern repeats incessantly, in its original values, in augmentation, and in diminution, and in both instruments and voices, often in more than one form at a time. Berg indicates every instance with the sign of an H attached to a bracket, a symbol Schoenberg had invented to designate the main melodic line (H standing for *Hauptstimme*, main voice) but used here to indicate the main rhythm (*Hauptrhythmus*). These constant repetitions envelop Wozzeck, symbolizing his obsession with his guilt.

Wozzeck picks up the rhythm as he watches the dancers (measures 130–41), then briefly frees himself from it by singing a folk song, using a tune from Marie's Act I lullaby (at measure 145). He asks Marie's friend Margret to dance with him, then sits down with her on his lap and asks her to sing a song. But there is no respite for him—even her song is in the obsessive rhythm of the scene (measures 168–79). She notices blood on his hand, singing again in that rhythm (measures 185–93). As others gather around them, Wozzeck says he must have cut himself, but she points out the blood on his elbow and says it smells of human blood, and the others agree. By this point all of them are singing only in the scene's main rhythm, and Wozzeck sings it at twice the speed of the others in a sign of his growing panic (measures 197–207). Throughout this passage (measures 187–211), the orchestra plays its own statements of the rhythm, each on repeated pitches a major seventh apart, rising by whole steps and then half steps as the scene builds to a climax. Surrounded by the emblem of his guilt, Wozzeck flees in a frenzy while overlapping statements of the rhythm sound in the orchestra.

Berg's music is atonal (not twelve-tone), but he frequently imitates the styles and textures of tonal music, as in the triadic accompaniment to the piano polka; the prominent fourths, triadic shapes, and melodic sequences of Wozzeck's imitation folk song; and the rocking accompaniment, balanced phrases, and arching lines of the popular-style song Margret sings. By constantly using familiar elements like these, Berg makes his music both dramatically effective and accessible to a wide range of listeners.

It can be difficult for singers to find their pitches in atonal music. Sometimes the pitches of the vocal lines are contained in the harmonies that accompany them, as in Wozzeck's folksong at measure 145, but that is not always the case. Berg recognized the difficulty, and in measures 202–12 he provided an optional part for the onstage piano that includes a transcription of the parts for the Chorus. This part may be played—audible only to the singers—if they need assistance in finding their pitches.

ANTON WEBERN (1883–1945)

Symphony, Op. 21: First movement, Ruhig schreitend

Symphony

1927–28

CD 12|46

*Sounds as notated (i.e., not transposed)

From *Symphonie*, Op. 21 (Vienna: Universal Edition, 1929), 2–8.

calando
tempo
calando
tempo
Kl.
Bkl.
offen
1.
Hrn.
2.
Hrf.
1. Gg.
2. Gg.
Br.
Vlc.
pizz.
arco
Dämpfer auf
m Dpf
dim.

rit.
tempo
rit.
Kl.
Bkl.
1.
Hrn.
2.
Hrf.
1. Gg.
2. Gg.
Br.
Vlc.
Dämpfer auf
Solo
Alle
arco
Solo
pizz.
arco am Steg
Dämpfer ab
dim.

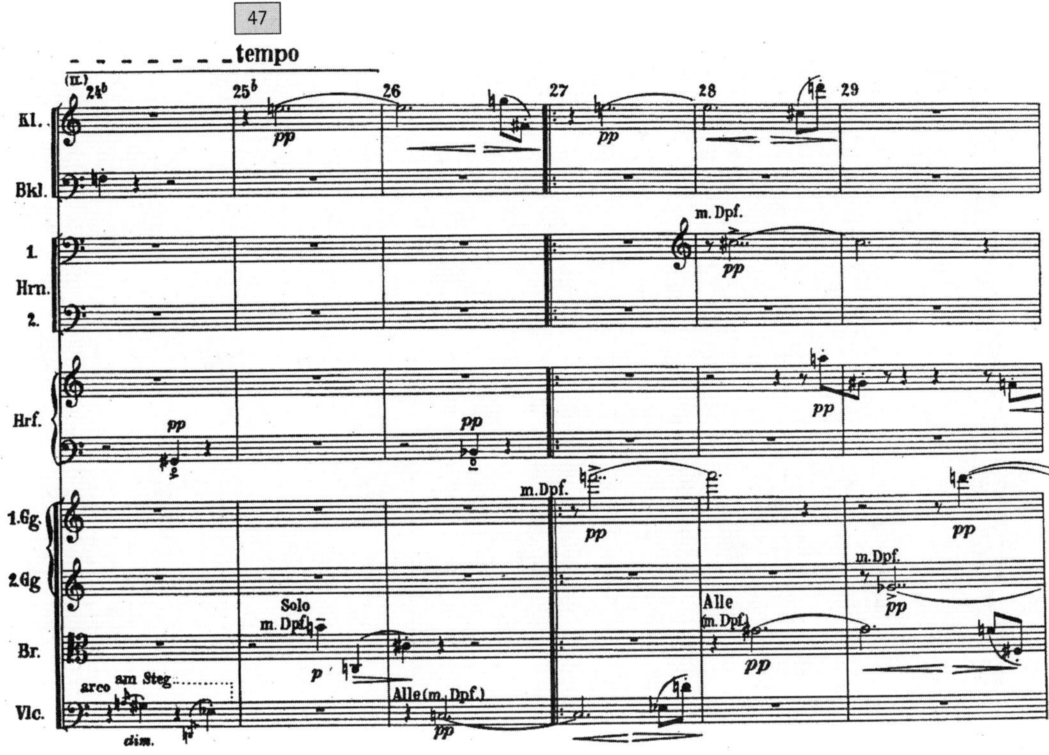
47
tempo
Kl.
Bkl.
1.
Hrn.
2.
m. Dpf.
Hrf.
1.Gg.
2.Gg
Br.
Vlc.
Solo
m. Dpf.
Alle
(m. Dpf.)
arco
am Steg
Alle (m. Dpf.)
dim.

Kl.
Bkl.
1.
Hrn.
2.
Hrf.
1.Gg.
2.Gg.
Br.
Vlc.
dim.
am Steg

Kl.
Bkl.
1.
Hrn.
2.
Hrf.
1. Gg.
2. Gg.
Br.
Solo
Vlc.
pp

48

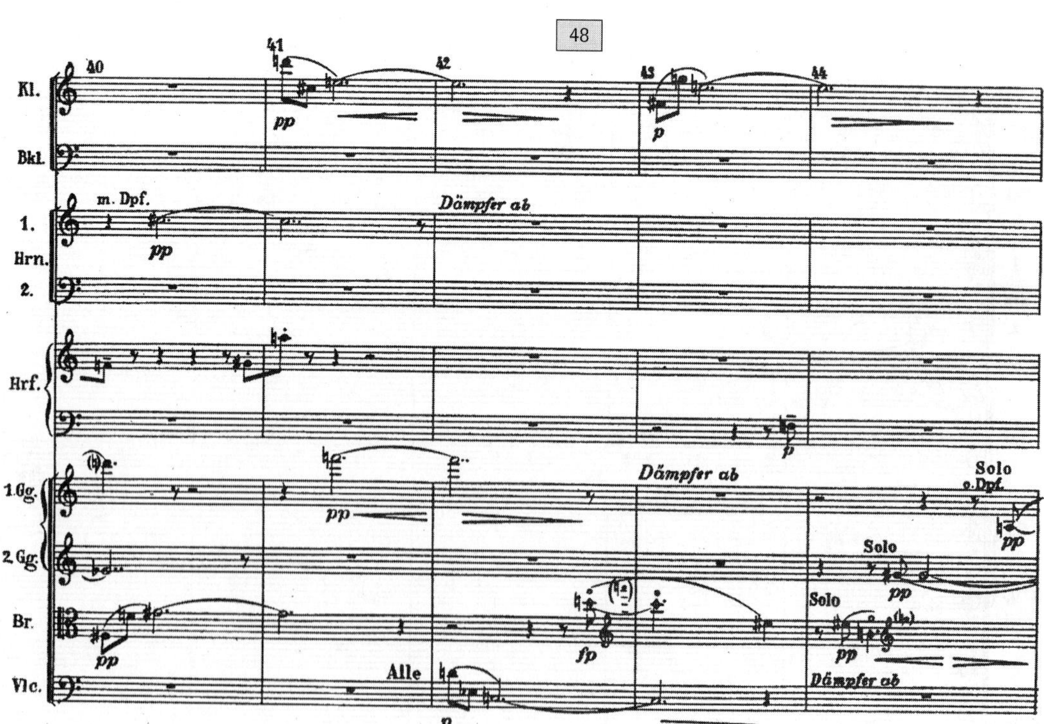

Kl.
Bkl.
m. Dpf.
Dämpfer ab
1.
Hrn.
2.
Hrf.
Dämpfer ab
Solo
o. Dpf.
1. Gg.
Solo
2. Gg.
Solo
Br.
Alle
Dämpfer ab
Vlc.
pp
fp
p

rit.
tempo
rit.
tempo
Kl.
Bkl.
1.
Hrn.
2.
gedämpft
Hrf.
Alle (o. Dpf.)
Solo
Alle
1.Gg.
2.Gg.
Alle
o. Dpf.
Dämpfer ab
Alle o. Dpf.
Dämpfer ab
Br.
o. Dpf.
Vlc.

Kl.
Bkl.
(o. Dpf.)
Dämpfer auf
1.
Hrn.
2.
Hrf.
Solo
Alle
1.Gg.
Solo
Alle
2.Gg.
Br.
Alle
Solo
Vlc.

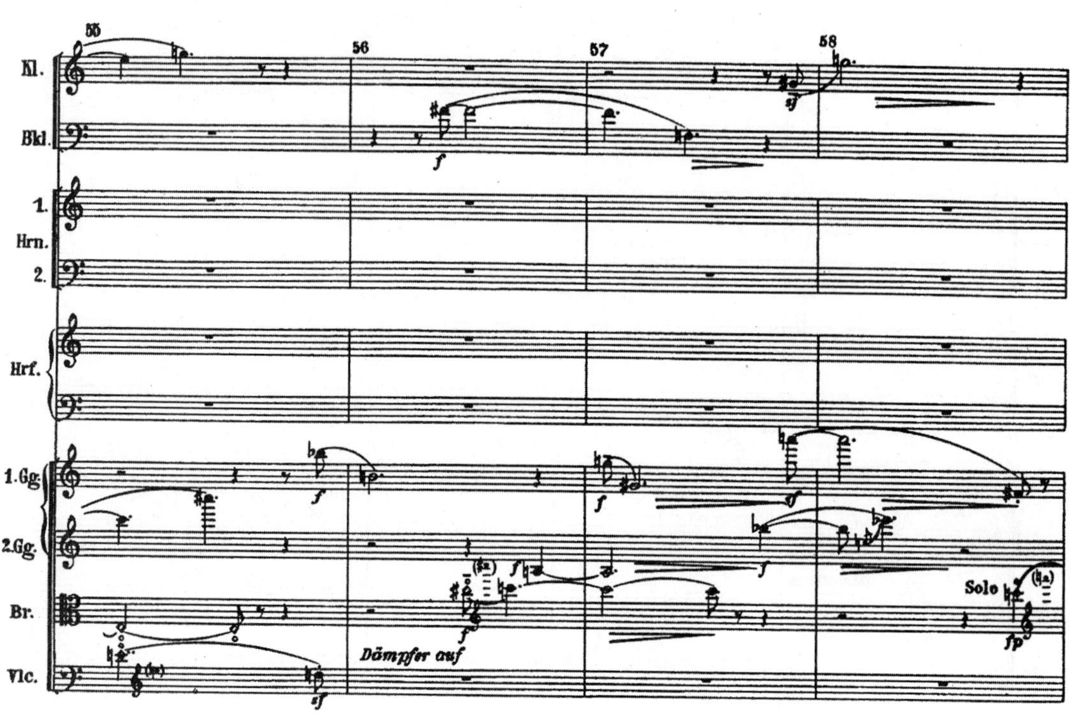
Kl.
Bkl.
Hrn.
Hrf.
1. Gg.
2. Gg.
Br.
Vlc.
Dämpfer auf
Solo

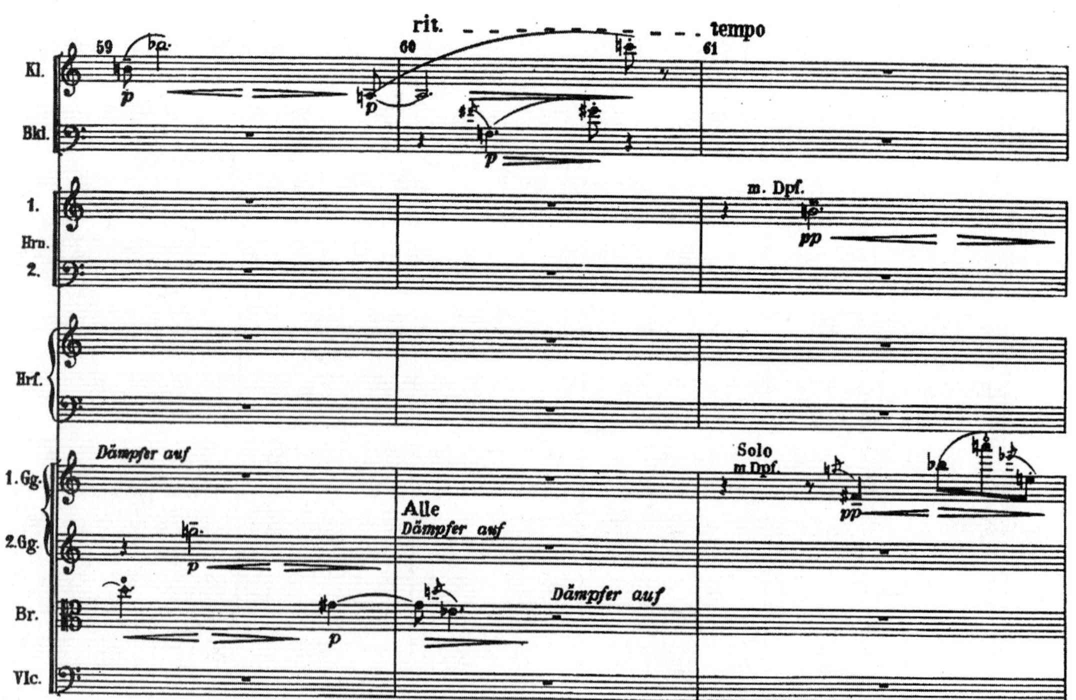
rit.
tempo
Kl.
Bkl.
Hrn.
m. Dpf.
Hrf.
Dämpfer auf
1. Gg.
2. Gg.
Br.
Vlc.
Alle
Dämpfer auf
Dämpfer auf
Solo
m. Dpf.

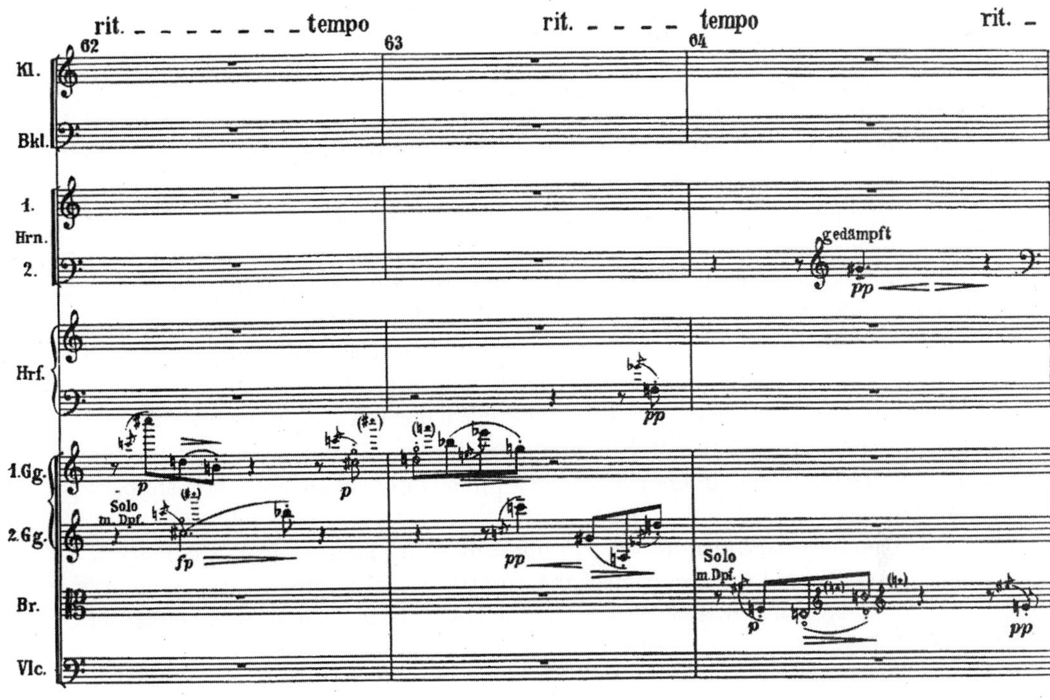
rit.
tempo
rit.
tempo
rit.
62
63
64
Kl.
Bkl.
1.
Hrn.
2.
gedämpft
pp
Hrf.
pp
1.Gg.
p
p
Solo
m. Dpf.
2.Gg.
fp
pp
Solo
m.Dpf.
Br.
p
pp
Vlc.

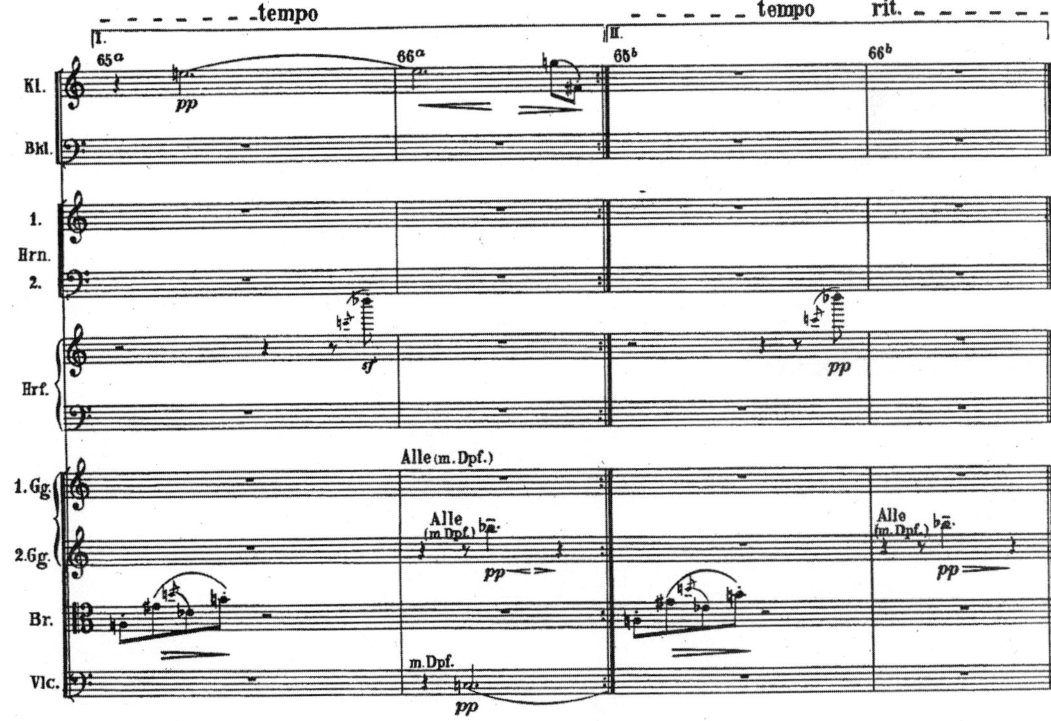
tempo
tempo
rit.
I.
II.
65a
66a
65b
66b
Kl.
pp
Bkl.
1.
Hrn.
2.
Hrf.
sf
pp
Alle (m. Dpf.)
1.Gg.
Alle
(m. Dpf.)
2.Gg.
pp
Alle
(m. Dpf.)
pp
Br.
m.Dpf.
Vlc.
pp

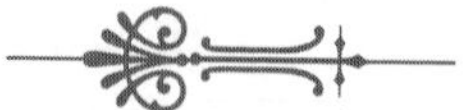

After a decade in which he composed only songs, Anton Webern adopted Schoenberg's twelve-tone method in the mid-1920s, finding in it the solution to writing extended instrumental works in an atonal language. The second such work was his Symphony, Op. 21, scored for a small chamber orchestra in emulation of eighteenth-century symphonies. It has only two movements, the first based on sonata form and the second a theme with seven variations. By invoking these forms and the genre of the symphony, Webern sought to link his modernist twelve-tone language to the conventional forms and tonality of the classical tradition.

To gain an understanding of how he remade past elements in twelve-tone terms requires a detailed look at how he used the rows. Fortunately, Webern made it easier to trace the twelve-tone rows through the music by notating the clarinet, bass clarinet, and horns at actual pitch (rather than in their customary transpositions).

The overall binary form of the first movement is apparent from the marked repetitions, but Webern reconceives the exposition, development, and recapitulation of sonata form in a new way. In the exposition, instead of two contrasting themes, he presents two simultaneous canons in inversion, using statements of his twelve-tone row in the canonic voices (see HWM, p. 828, for a simplified score that shows the beginnings of the canons). Thus he substitutes the Renaissance texture of imitative polyphony for the melody-and-accompaniment texture typical of classical symphonies. However, rather than present any of the canonic voices in a single instrument, he makes the change of instrumental timbre itself part of the melody, an effect Schoenberg called *Klangfarbenmelodie* (tone-color-melody).

The leading voice of the first canon begins in horn 2, continues in the clarinet, and concludes the first row statement in the cello, with each instrument stating one tetrachord (four-note segment) from the row (P–0), as shown here:

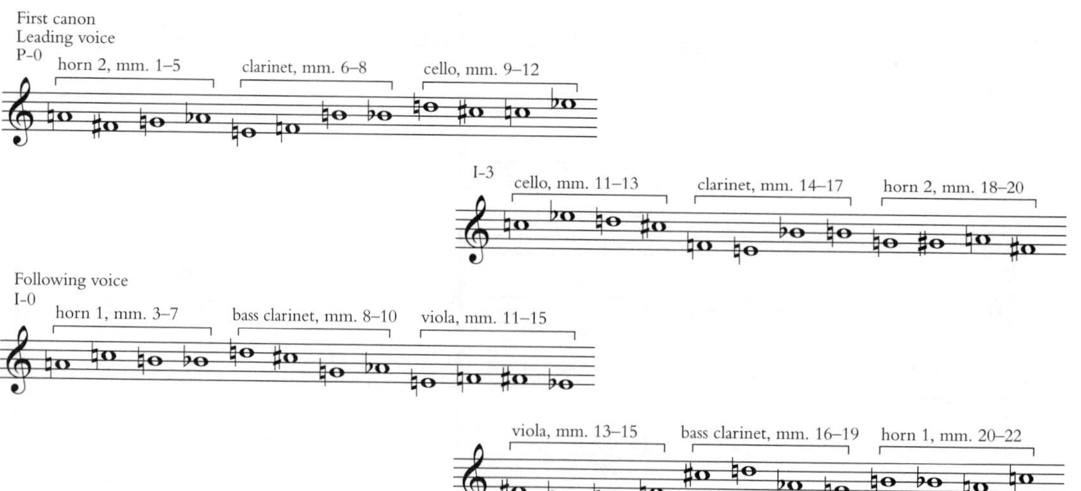

The last two notes of the row overlap with I-3, an inverted statement of the row, which moves from cello back to clarinet and horn 2, as shown in the example, again highlighting the division of the row into tetrachords. Webern has so designed the row that this inversion results in the same sequence of tetrachords (allowing for internal reordering of notes) but in reverse order, a symmetry highlighted by the symmetry of timbres.

The following voice of the canon, an inversion of the first voice that starts on the same note (I-0) exactly two measures later, traces a similar path from horn 1 to bass clarinet to viola, then back again, using the same kinds of timbres as the leading voice and in the same order (brass, single-reed wind, and string instrument), as shown in the example. The symmetries of timbre and tetrachord echo a symmetry in the row itself: its transposed retrograde R-6 is the same as P-0, making the row a virtual palindrome (something that is the same backward as it is forward, like "Able was I ere I saw Elba").

The first canon exhibits the short phrases and frequent rests typical of Webern's music. The second canon is even more short-breathed, with sometimes just one note in an instrument. The result is a succession of tiny points, or wisps, of sound, a texture described as *pointillism* that is often the most immediately recognizable aspect of a Webern score. The leading voice in the second canon begins in the harp (measure 2), then moves through plucked and bowed cello (measures 3–5), violin 2 (measure 6), harp (measures 7–8), horn 2 (measures 9–10), harp (measures 11–12, overlapping with a new row statement), horn 2 (measures 12–13), violin 1 (14–15), harp (measure 16), viola (measures 16–17, overlapping with another row statement), and so on. Meanwhile, the following voice, in inversion, begins two measures later and traces a similar path through harp, viola, violin 1, and so on. The use of so many timbres in each canonic voice and the appearance of notes from more than one canonic line in each instrument combine to make the canons very difficult to hear.

In the exposition, the somewhat more lyrical first canon serves as "first theme," and the more rapidly changing and pointillistic second canon serves as "second theme." The sense of a "home key" is created by registration, another source of symmetry. Except for E♭/D♯, which can appear in the octave either just above or just below middle C, every other note of the chromatic scale appears in one, and only one, octave during the entire exposition, sounding the pitches shown here:

All these pitches taken together form a symmetrical arrangement around the opening *a*, ranging in fourths down from the *e♭'* above it or up from the *d♯* below it. This symmetrical array is possible because of the strict canon in inversion, equally spaced around the central pitch *a*. The recurrence of these specific pitches throughout the exposition provides a very strong sense of location, although A does not function as a traditional tonic.

The recapitulation reprises the same row forms in the same order as the exposition, but the surface looks and sounds very different, making it hard to hear the return. The recapitulation begins on the last eighth note of measure 42 (highlighted with a *forte-piano* marking), with a statement of the pitches from the first canon's leading voice in viola (through measure 45), cello (measures 46–47), violin 1 (last eighth of measure 47 through measure 53), and again viola (measures 54–55) and violin 1 (measures 55–58). (Some notes in the strings are written as harmonics, and Webern indicates the sounding pitch in small notes.) The following voice of the canon appears exactly two measures later, as it did in the exposition, moving from violin 1 to viola, clarinet, cello, viola, and back to clarinet. The second canon can be traced in similar fashion, beginning with the harp notes in measures 43 and 45.

In the recapitulation, the pitches are again symmetrical, in an arrangement shown here:

Some pitches are in the same octave as in the exposition, others one to three octaves higher, and the axis of symmetry is now *e♭''*. This recapitulation resembles traditional ones by restating the material from the exposition, but it does so in a novel way.

The relatively brief development is a palindrome, providing another kind of symmetry. It begins with the clarinet in measure 25b and concludes with the clarinet in measures 43–44, overlapping the beginning of the recapitulation, and measures 34–35 form its center point. The development and recapitulation repeat as a unit, as in many early symphonies (see NAWM 108).

All these canons, symmetries, and palindromes may be difficult or even impossible to hear, reflecting Webern's interest in structural devices that are not necessarily audible. He absorbed this interest, along with his fondness for canons, from his studies of medieval and Renaissance music as a doctoral student of musicology at the University of Vienna. More audible is the subtle progress of the composite rhythm (the rhythm of all parts taken together), which begins by repeating a gentle syncopated figure (quarter note, half note, quarter note) in almost every measure, then gradually introduces an articulation on every quarter note (measure 13), then increases the pace to use eighth notes in the development, and uses more continuous eighth notes in the recapitulation. Webern did not want his performers to analyze the row structure. Instead, he insisted that performers should focus on the musical surface—making each note as expressive as an entire phrase of a Romantic symphony—and he believed that the music's coherence would be clear.

Igor Stravinsky (1882–1971)

The Rite of Spring: Excerpts

Ballet

1911–13

(a) *Danse des adolescentes* (Dance of the Adolescent Girls)

CD 12|49 CD 6|15

From Igor Stravinsky, *The Rite of Spring*, reengraved edition (London: Boosey & Hawkes, 1967), 10–28 and 121–53.

14
15
Fl. picc. 1 2
sf
Ob. 1 2
f
C. ing.
come sopra
Cl. picc. in Re
Cl. in Sib 2 3
Cor. in Fa 1.2 3.4 5.6 7.8
come sopra
Tr. in Do 1
Solo con sord.
mf
pizz.
Vl. I
Vl. II
Vle.
Vc.
Cb.
20
16
Ob. 1.2 3
1.2 a2
C. ing.
Fag. 1 2
mf
Tr. in Do 1
(pizz.)
poco meno f
pizz.

26

17

Fl. picc. 1 2

Fl. gr. 1 2

Fl. alto

Ob. 1.2 3

C. ing.

Cl. picc. in Re

Cl. in La 1

Cl. in Sib 2 3

Fag. 1 2

Cor. in Fa 4

Tr. picc. in Re

Tr. in Do 1.2 3.4

Vl. I

Vl. II

Vle.

Vc.

Cb.

Flttzg.

1.2 a2

sempre simile

sim.

con sord.

pizz.

sf meno f

ff mf f sf

32
18
Fl. picc.
Fl. gr.
Fl. alto
sim.
Ob.
1,2 a2
C. ing.
Cl. picc. in Re
sim.
muta in Mi♭
Cl. in La
muta in Si♭
Cl. in Si♭
Fag.
Cor. in Fa
4 senza sord.
sf sempre
Tr. picc. in Re
Tr. in Do
senza sord.
Vl. I
arco
f (non div.)
sempre sim.
Vl. II
div.
unis.
Vle.
come sopra
Vc.
Cb.

39
19
1.2 a2
Fag. 1.2 3
C. Fag. 1
Cor. in Fa 1.2 3.4 5.6 7.8
Vl. I
Vle.
Vc.
Cb.
p sub.
f
47
20
piùf
Trbn. 1
mf

55
21
Ob. 1 2
1.2 a2
Fag. 1.2 3
C. Fag. 1
Vl. I
Vle.
Vc.
Cb.
f
p sub.
63
Fl. gr. 1
più f
1.5 2.6 Cor. in Fa 3.7 4.8
1.5 a2
2.6 a2
3.7 a2
4.8 a2
Trbn. 1 2
Tbe. 1 2
sff
Timp.
G.C.
Vl. II
pizz.
arco
ff

50 16

72
22
23
Fl. picc.
Fl. gr. 1
Ob.
C. ing.
Cl. in Sib
Fag. 2
Tr. picc. in Re
Tr. in Do 1
Trbn.
Vl. Solo
Vl. I
Vl. II
Vle.
pizz.
arco
Solo
stucc.
marc.
79
24
Solo
marc.
C. ing.
Cl. in Sib
Fag.
Tr. in Do 1
2 Vl. Soli
sul Sol
Vl. I
Vl. II
Vle.
Vc.
col legno sino al segno
col legno sino al segno

51
17
86
25
C. ing.
p sub.
Fag.
p
tr
Cor. in Fa
mp (mais en dehors)
Solo
2 Vl. Soli
p sub.
Vl. I
Vl. II
col legno al.
mf
Vle.
Vc.
93
Solo
Fl. gr.

99
26
Soli
Ob.
Cl. in Si♭
Fag.
Solo
Tr. in Do
Solo
con sord.
senza sord.
2 Vl. Soli
Vl. I
Vl. II
div.
Vle.
Vc.
106
27
Fl. gr.
Fl. alto
Cor. in Fa

52
18
113
28
Fl. gr.
Fl. alto
Cl. picc. in Mib
Cl. in Sib
Cl. bas. in Sib
Fag.
C. Fag.
Cor. in Fa 5
Trbn.
Timp.
2 Vl. Soli
Vl. I
Vl. II div.
Vle.
Vc.
Cb.
pizz.
pizz.

119
29
Fl. picc.
Fl. gr.
Fl. alto
Ob.
Cl. picc. in Mib
Cl. in Sib
Cl. bas. in Sib
Fag.
C. Fag.
Tr. in Do
mp cantab.
Trbn.
Timp.
Triang.
bacch. di legno
Cym. ant.
Vl. I
legg. 5.6
legg. 7.8
Tutti div.
Vl. II div.
Vle. div. a3
3 Soli Vc.
arco
marcatiss. e molto cantabile
gli altri
Cb.
stacc.

127
Fl. picc. 1 2
Fl. gr. 1 2
Fl. alto
Ob. 1 2 3
C. ing. 1 2
mp
ff
C.ing. 2 muta in Ob. 4
Cl. picc. in Mib
Cl. in Sib 1 2 3
p
Cl. bas. in Sib
p
Fag. 1 2 3 4
Fag. 4 muta in C. Fag. 2
Cor. in Fa 1 2 3 4 5 6 7 8
f
sim.
p
Tr. in Do 1 2 3 4
Trbn. 1 2
Timp.
Triang.
Cym. ant.
Vl. I div.
Vl. II div.
Vle. div. a3
f
3 Soli Vc. gli altri
Cb.

133 30
Cl. picc. in Mi♭
Cl. in Si♭
Cl. bas. in Si♭
sempre sf
30
Vl. I div.
p sub. e stacc.
Vl. II div.
pizz.
p sub.
meno f
4 Sole
Vle.
le altre
sul Sol
3 Soli
Vc.
gli altri
p sub.
Cb.
139
31
Solo
mf grazioso
Fl. picc. 1
Ob.
C. ing.
muta in Re
C. Fag.
a2
Cor. in Fa 4
cresc.
(pizz.)
sim.
(sempre sim.)
Tutte
Tutti div.
sff

145
32
Fl. picc. 1
Fl. gr.
Fl. alto
Ob.
C. ing.
Cl. picc. in Re
Cl. in Si♭
Fag. 3
C. Fag.
a2
(a2)
sf
Cor. in Fa
Tr. in Do
Vl. I div.
arco
sff
mf
Vl. II div.
Vle. div.
mf cresc.
Vc. div.
unis. arco
Cb.

151

Fl. picc. 1 2
Fl. gr. 1 2
Fl. alto
Ob. 1 2 3 4
C. ing.
Cl. picc. in Re
Cl. in Si♭ 1 2 3
Fag. 1 2 3
C. Fag. 1
Cor. in Fa 1.2 3.4 5.6 7.8
Tr. picc. in Re
Tr. in Do 1 2 3 4
Tbe. 1 2
Vl. I div.
Vl. II div.
Vle. div.
Vc.
Cb.

f sempre *sim.* *f* *mf* Flttzg. *mf* *2mf* *4mf* arco *mf cresc.* *f* arco

156
33
Fl. picc. 1 2
Fl. gr. 1 2
Fl. alto
Ob. 1 2 3 4
C. ing.
Cl. picc. in Re
Cl. in Si♭ 1 2 3
Fag. 1 2 3
C. Fag. 1 2
Cor. in Fa 1.2 3.4 5.6 7.8
Tr. picc. in Re
Tr. in Do 1 2 3 4
Tbe. 1 2
Vl. I div.
Vl. II div.
Vle. div.
Vc. div.
Cb.
Flttzg.
sempre sim.
stacc.
a 2
sim. sempre
pizz.

160
34
Fl. picc. 1 2
Fl. gr. 1 2
Fl. alto
Ob. 1 2 3 4
C. ing.
Cl. picc. in Re
Cl. in Sib 1 2 3
Cl. bas. in Sib
Fag. 1 2 3
C. Fag. 1 2
Cor. in Fa 1.2 3.4 5.6 7.8
Tr. picc. in Re
Tr. in Do 1.2 3.4
Trbn. 1 2 3
Tbe. 1 2
Vl. I div.
Vl. II div.
Vle. div.
Vc. div.
Cb. div.
Flttzg.
stacc.
poco più
f assai
arco
sim.

164
35
Fl. picc. 1 2
Fl. gr.
Fl. alto
Ob.
C. ing.
Cl. picc. in Re
Cl. in Si♭
Cl. bas. in Si♭
Fag.
C. Fag.
Cor. in Fa
Tr. picc. in Re
Tr. in Do
Trbn.
Tbe.
Timp.
secco
come sopra
Vl. I div.
Vl. II div.
Vle.
unis.
div.
Vc. div.
Cb. div.

169
36
a 2
Fl. picc. 1 2
Fl. gr. 1 2
Fl. alto
Ob. 1 2 3 4
C. ing.
Cl. picc. in Re
Cl. in Sib 1 2 3
Cl. bas. in Sib
a 3
Fag. 1 2 3
a 2
C. Fag. 1 2
C. Fag. 2 muta in Fag. 4
gliss.
Cor. in Fa 1 2 3 4 5.6 7.8
Tr. picc. in Re
Tr. in Do 1.2 3.4
Trbn. 1 2 3
Tbe. 1 2
Timp.
36
Vl. I div.
Vl. II div.
div.
unis.
Vle.
Vc. div.
Cb. div.
sff

(b) *Danse sacrale* (Sacrificial Dance)

11
144
145
Fl. picc. 1 2
Fl. gr. 1 2
Fl. alto
Ob. 1 2 3 4
C. ing.
Cl. picc. in Mib
Cl. in Sib 1 2 3
Cl. bas. in Sib
Cor. in Fa 1 2 3 4 5 6 7 8
Tr. picc. in Re
Tr. in Do 1 2 3
Tr. bas. in Mib
Trbn. 1 2 3
Tba. 1
Timp.
Vl. I
Vl. II
Vle.
Vc.
Cb.
ff marc.
sim.
f marc.
sff
a 3
sf e stacc. sempre
sempre
div.
unis.
div. a 2
div. a 3
a 2
ff subito
sempre
ff

19
146
147
Ob.
C. ing.
1. et 3. ordinérement
Cor. in Fa
Tr. picc. in Re
sff
Tr. in Do
sff
Tr. bas. in Mi♭
sff
a 3
Trbn.
sf
Tba.
Timp.
div.
unis.
div.
unis.
div.
unis.
Vl. I
div. a 3
unis.
div. a 3
unis.
div. a 3
unis.
Vl. II
div. a 3
unis.
div. a 3
unis.
Vle.
Vc.
Cb.

54
28
148
149
Fl. picc. 1 2
Fl. gr. 1 2
Fl. alto
Ob. 1 2 3 4
C. ing.
Cl. picc. in Mi♭
Cl. in Si♭ 1 2 3
Cl. bas. in Si♭
Fag. 1 2
C. Fag.
Cor. in Fa 1 2 3 4 5 6 7 8
Tr. picc. in Re
Tr. in Do 1 2 3
Tr. bas. in Mi♭
Trbn. 1 2 3
Tba. 1
Timp.
Vl. I
Vl. II
Vle.
Vc.
Cb.
sff
pp sempre
senza sord.
muta in Tr. 4 in Do
div.
div. a 3
unis.
p sempre

36
150
Fag. 1 2
C. Fag.
Cor. in Fa 1 2 4
Vl. II
Vle.
Vc.
Cb.
45
151
152
Ob. 1
C. ing.
p
con sord.
sf
senza sord.
Solo con sord.
f marc.
Soli con sord.
a 3
f marc.
sim.
Tr. picc. in Re
Tr. in Do 1
Trbn. 1 2 3
Vl. I
div.
p cresc.

53
153
Fl. gr. 1
Fl. alto
Ob. 1
C. ing.
Fag. 1 2
C. Fag.
Cor. in Fa 1 2 4
Tr. picc. in Re
Tr. in Do 1
Timp.
Soli f
Tam-t.
colla bacch. di Triang.
gliss.
pp
sf
Vl. I div.
Vl. II
Vle.
Vc.
Cb.

62
154
155
Soli a 2
Solo
f marc.
Fl. picc. 1 2
Cl. picc. in Mi♭
Fag. 1 2
C. Fag.
Cor. in Fa 1 2 4
Tr. picc. in Re
senza sord.
non div.
sempre sf
Vl. I
Vl. II div.
div. a 3
Vle. div.
Vc.
Cb.
70
156
157
sim.
Fl. picc. 2 muta in Fl. gr. 3
Tr. in Do 1
Solo marc.
Vl. II div. a 2
Vle. div. a 2
div. a 2
a 3
ff

77
158
159
Fl. picc.
Fl. gr.
Fl. alto
Ob.
C. ing.
Cl. picc. in Mib
Cl. in Sib
Cl. bas. in Sib
Fag.
C. Fag.
Cor. in Fa
Tr. picc. in Re
Tr. in Do 1
Vl. I div. a 3
Vl. II div. a 3
Vle. div. a 3
Vc. div. a 3
Cb.
a 2
non div.
unis.

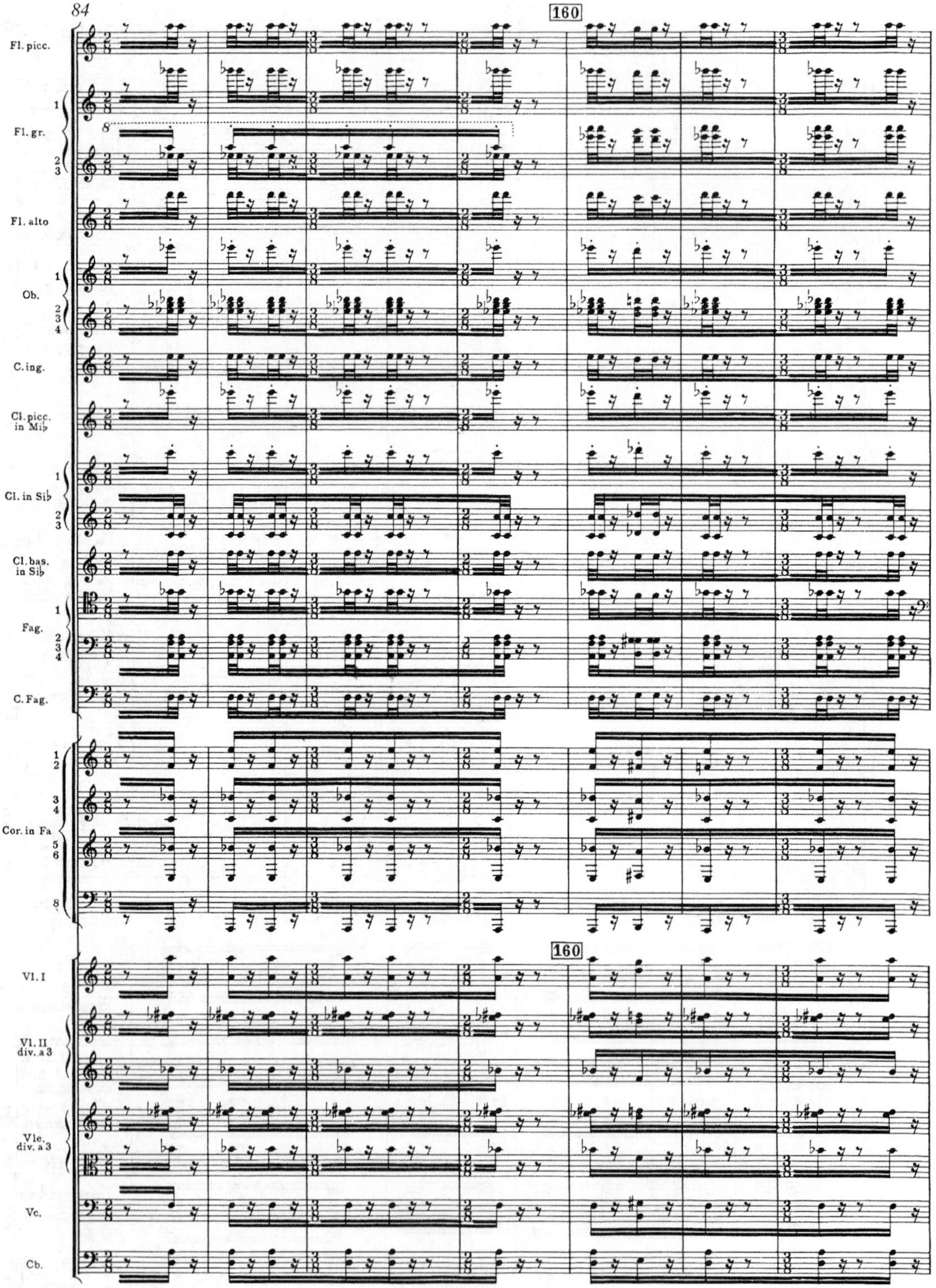

84

160

Fl. picc.
Fl. gr. 1, 2 3
Fl. alto
Ob. 1, 2 3 4
C. ing.
Cl. picc. in Mi♭
Cl. in Si♭ 1, 2 3
Cl. bas. in Si♭
Fag. 1, 2 3 4
C. Fag.
Cor. in Fa 1 2, 3 4, 5 6, 8
Vl. I
Vl. II div. a 3
Vle. div. a 3
Vc.
Cb.

91
161
162
Solo
Fl. picc.
Flttzg.
fff
Fl. gr.
a 2
Fl. alto
Ob.
C. ing.
Cl. picc. in Mi♭
Cl. in Si♭
Fag.
Fag. 4 muta in C. Fag. 2
pp sempre
C. Fag.
Cor. in Fa
ff
Tr. picc. in Re
fff marcatissimo
Tr. in Do
Tr. 4 muta in Tr. bas. in Mi♭
senza sord.
Soli a 3
Trbn.
fff marcatiss.
Tbe.
Vl. I
div.
Tutti
div. a 3
Vl. II div. a 3
unis.
p sempre
Vle. div. a 3
Vc.
Cb.

95
163
Fag. 1 2
C.Fag. 1
Cor. in Fa 1 2 3 4
con sord.
Trbn. 1 2 3
Soli con sord. a 3
f marc.
Vl.II
Vle.
Vc.
Cb.
102
164
Fl. gr. 1
Ob. 2
p cresc.
Tr. picc. in Re
Solo con sord.
f marc.
Tr. in Do 1
senza sord.
sim.
Vl.I
div. sul pont. sino al segno ⊕

107
165
166
Fl. picc.
Fl. gr.
Ob.
C. ing.
Cl. picc. in Mi♭
Cl. in Si♭
Cor. in Fa
Tr. picc. in Re
(con sord.)
cresc.
Vl. I
Vl. II
Vle.
Vc.
Cb.
unis.
div.

112
accelerando e cresc.
Fl. picc.
Fl. gr. 1
Ob.
C. ing.
Cl. picc. in Mi♭
Cl. in Si♭
Cor. in Fa
Tr. picc. in Re
Tr. in Do
Trbn.
Tba.
(senza sord.)
(senza sord.)
senza sord.
cresc.
accelerando e cresc.
Vl. I
Vl. II div.
Vle. div.
Vc. div.
Cb.
pizz.

116
167
55
168
Ob.
ff sempre
C. ing.
ff sempre
Fag.
a2
sempre sf
sempre sim.
C. Fag.
a2
sempre sf
sempre sim.
1.3 sempre cuivré e f
Cor. in Fa
sempre sf
semprc sf
sempre sf
Tr. picc. in Re
(con sord.)
sf
Tr. in Do
con sord.
Tr. bas. in Mi♭
con sord.
Trbn.
con sord.
f
sf
Timp.
sempre f e secco
167
168
Vl. I
f sempre
sempre
div.
unis.
Vl. II
unis. arco
f sempre
div. a 3
Vle.
unis. arco
f sempre
div. a 3
sempre
Vc.
unis. arco
f sempre
div.
unis.
Cb.
arco
sempre sf

125
169
170
Fl. picc. 1 2
Fl. gr. 1 2
Fl. alto
Ob. 1 2 3 4
C. ing.
Cl. picc. in Mi♭
Cl. in Si♭ 1 2 3
Cl. bas. in Si♭
Fag. 1 2
C. Fag. 1 2
Cor. in Fa 1 2 3 4 5 6 7 8
Tr. picc. in Re
Tr. in Do 1 2 3
Tr. bas. in Mi♭
Trbn. 1 2 3
Tba. 1
Timp.
Vl. I
Vl. II
Vle.
Vc.
Cb.
ff marc.
f marc.
stacc. e f sempre
unis.
div.
div. a 3
a2
a3

134
171
172
Ob.
C. ing.
Fag.
a2
C. Fag.
Cor. in Fa
1. et 3. ordinérement
Tr. picc. in Re
sff
Tr. in Do
Tr. bas. in Mib
Trbn.
a3
sf
Tba.
Timp.
Vl. I
div.
unis.
Vl. II
div. a3
Vle.
Vc. div.
Cb.

142
173
174
56
♪ = ♩ = 126
Fl. picc. 1 2
Fl. gr. 1 2
Fl. alto
Ob. 1 2 3 4
C. ing.
Cl. picc. in Mi♭
Cl. in Si♭ 1 2 3
Cl. bas. in Si♭
Fag. 1 2
C. Fag. 1 2
a2
sff
ff
Cor. in Fa 1 2 3 4 5 6 7 8
Tr. picc. in Re
Tr. in Do 1 2 3
Tr. bas. in Mi♭
Trbn. 1 2 3
Tbe. 1 2
senza sord.
a3 gliss.
Timp. picc.
Timp. gr.
muta in Mi♭
Do♯ muta in Si♭
Tam-t.
G.C.
f secco
Vl. I
Vl. II
Vle.
Vc. div.
Cb.
div.
div. a3
unis.
sim.
sempre molto pesante e f

150
175
a2
C. Fag. 1 2
sempre sim.
Cor. in Fa 1 2 3 4 5 6 7 8
f
a3
Trbn. 1 2 3
sempre sim.
Tbe. 1 2
Timp. picc.
Timp. gr.
Tam-t.
G.C.
sempre sim.
175
Vl. I
Vl. II
Vle.
Vc.
Cb.

154
176
Fl. picc. 1 2
a2
Fl. gr. 1 2
Ob. 1 2 3 4
Cl. picc. in Mib
Cl. in Sib 1 2 3
C. Fag. 1 2
Cor. in Fa 1 2 3 4 5 6 7 8
Soli marc.
marc.
1 pavillon en l'air
5 pavillon en l'air
Tr. picc. in Re
f(cuivrez)
Tr. in Do 1 2 3
Tr. bas. in Mib
a3
Trbn. 1 2 3
Tbe. 1 2
Timp. picc.
Timp. gr.
Tam-t.
G. C.
Vl. I
Vl. II
Vle.
Vc.
Cb.
pizz.
div.
div. pizz.
unis.
arco
ben marcato
sim.

158
177
Fl. picc. 1 2
a2
sf
Fl. gr. 1 2
Ob. 1 2 3 4
sff
Cl. picc. in Mib
Cl. in Sib 1 2 3
C. Fag. 1 2
Cor. in Fa 1 2 3 4 5 6 7 8
sim.
ff
gliss.
Tr. picc. in Re
Tr. in Do 1 2 3
Tr. bas. in Mib
poco sf
Trbn. 1 2 3
a3
Tbe. 1 2
Timp. picc.
Timp. gr.
Tam-t.
G.C.
Vl. I
Vl. II
Vle.
Vc.
Cb.
unis.
arco
div. pizz.
div.
sffz

164
178
179
Cl. picc. in Mib
Cl. in Sib 1 2
C. Fag. 1 2
a2
f
a2
Cor. in Fa
Tr. picc. in Re
Tr. in Do
Tr. bas. in Mib
Trbn. 1 2 3
a3
Tbe. 1 2
Timp. picc.
Timp. gr.
Tam-t.
G.C.
Vl. I
Vl. II div.
unis.
div.
Vle.
Vc.
Cb.

172
180
57
♩=♪=126
Fl. picc. 1 2
Fl. gr. 1 2
Ob. 1 2 3 4
C. ing.
Cl. picc. in Mib
Cl. in Sib 1 2 3
C. Fag. 1 2
Cor. in Fa 1 2 3 4 5 6 7 8
Tr. picc. in Re
Tr. in Do 1 2 3
Tr. bas. in Mib
Trbn. 1 2 3
Tbe. 1 2
Timp. picc.
Timp. gr.
Tam-t.
G. C.
Vl. I
Vl. II
Vle.
Vc.
Cb.
a2
ff
sff
sfff
energico
più sf
più f
cuivrez
secco e f
div.
unis.

181
Fl. picc.
Fl. gr.
Fl. alto
Ob.
Cl. picc. in Mi♭
Cl. in Si♭
Fag.
C. Fag.
Cor. in Fa
Tr. in Do
Tr. bas. in Mi♭
Trbn.
Tbe.
Timp. picc.
Timp. gr.
Tam-t.
G. C.
Vl. I
Vl. II
Vle.
Vc.
Cb.
182
ouvert
come sopra
Soli a 2
Solo
maestoso
unis.
con tutta forza

188
183
184
Fl. picc.
Fl. gr.
Fl. alto
Ob.
C. ing.
Cl picc. in Mib
Cl. in Sib
Fag.
C. Fag.
Cor. in Fa
Tr. picc. in Re
Tr. in Do
Tr. bas. in Mib
Trbn.
Tbe.
Timp. picc.
Timp. gr.
Tam-t.
G.C.
Vl. I
Vl. II
Vle.
Vc.
Cb.
a 2
a 3
ff
fff
cresc.
ouvert
1 pav. en l'air e fff
3 pav. en l'air e fff
5 et 7 pav. en l'air e fff
Solo
a 2 Soli
gliss.
poco meno
en dehors
fff marcatiss.
mf

196
185
Soli
a 2
fff
Fl. picc.
Fl. gr.
Fl. alto
Ob.
C. ing.
Cl. picc. in Mi♭
Cl. in Si♭
Fag.
C. Fag.
sim.
Cor. in Fa
Tr. picc. in Re
Tr. in Do
cresc.
Tr. bas. in Mi♭
Trbn.
Tbe.
Timp. picc.
Timp. gr.
Tam-t.
G. C.
Vl. I
Vl. II
Vle.
Vc.
Cb.

203
186
58
187
Fl. picc.
Fl. gr.
Fl. alto
Ob.
C. ing.
Cl. picc. in Mib
Cl. in Sib
Fag.
C. Fag.
Cor. in Fa
Tr. picc. in Re
Tr. in Do
Tr. bas. in Mib
Trbn.
Tbe.
G. C.
Vl. I
Vl. II
Vle.
Vc.
Cb.
sempre stacc. e secco
f marc.
sempre sf
sempre ben marcato
div.
sempre marc.

211
188
189
Fl. gr.
Fl. alto
Ob.
C. ing.
Cl. picc. in Mi♭
Cl. in Si♭
Fag.
C. Fag.
a 2
fff
f marc.
Cor. in Fa
poco sf
Tr. picc. in Re
Tr. in Do
Tr. bas. in Mi♭
Trbn.
Tbe.
Timp.
mf
G. C.
Vl. I
Vl. II
Vle.
Vc.
Cb.
div.
div. a 3
unis.

219
190
191
Fl. gr.
Fl. alto
Ob.
C. ing.
Cl. picc. in Mib
Cl. in Sib
Cl. bas. in Sib
Fag.
C. Fag.
a 2
Cor. in Fa
Timp.
G. C.
Vl. I
Vl. II
Vle.
Vc. div.
Cb.
cresc.
sim.
mf cresc.
poco a poco cresc.
div. a 2
marc.
sempre sim.
f marc.

227
192
193
Fl. gr.
Fl. alto
Ob.
C. ing.
Cl. picc. in Mi♭
Cl. in Si♭
Cl. bas. in Si♭
Fag.
C. Fag.
Cor. in Fa
Tr. picc. in Re
Tr. in Do
Tr. bas. in Mi♭
Trbn.
Tbe.
Timp.
G. C.
Vl. I
Vl. II
Vle.
Vc.
Cb.
div. a 3
unis.
meno f
a 2
(a 2)

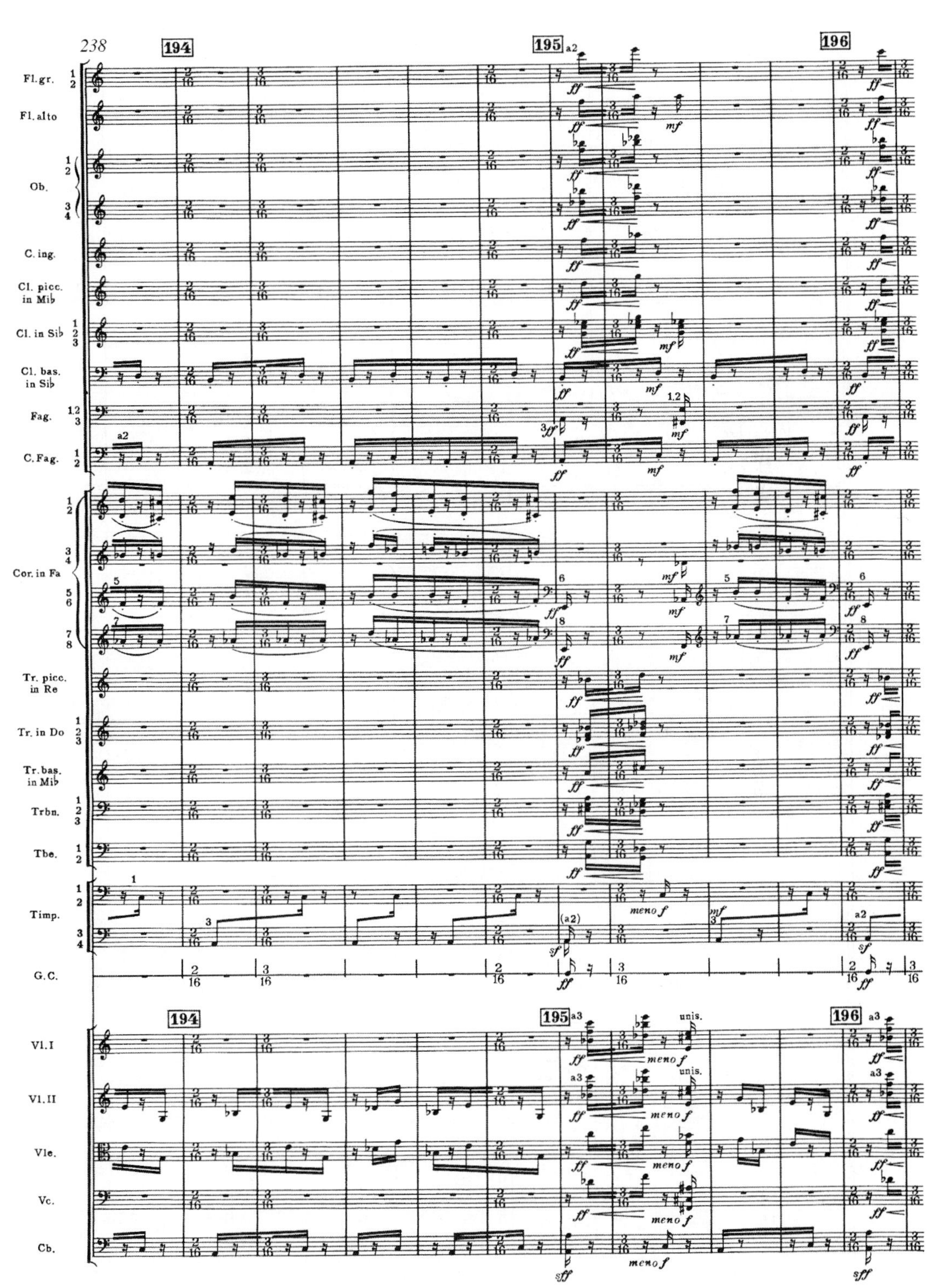

238
194
195
196
Fl. gr.
Fl. alto
Ob.
C. ing.
Cl. picc. in Mib
Cl. in Sib
Cl. bas. in Sib
Fag.
C. Fag.
Cor. in Fa
Tr. picc. in Re
Tr. in Do
Tr. bas. in Mib
Trbn.
Tbe.
Timp.
G.C.
Vl. I
Vl. II
Vle.
Vc.
Cb.
a2
a3
unis.
meno f

249
197
198
Fl. picc. 1 2
Fl. gr. 1 2
Fl. alto
Ob. 1 2 3 4
C. ing.
Cl. picc. in Mib
Cl. in Sib 1 2 3
Cl. bas. in Sib
Fag. 1.2 3
C. Fag. 1 2
Cor. in Fa 1 2 3 4 5 6 7 8
Tr. picc. in Re
Tr. in Do 1 2 3
Tr. bas. in Mib
Trbn. 1 2 3
Tbe. 1 2
Timp. 1 2 3 4
G.C.
Vl. I
Vl. II
Vle.
Vc.
Cb.
sim.
sempre sim.
meno f
più sf
a2
a3
unis.

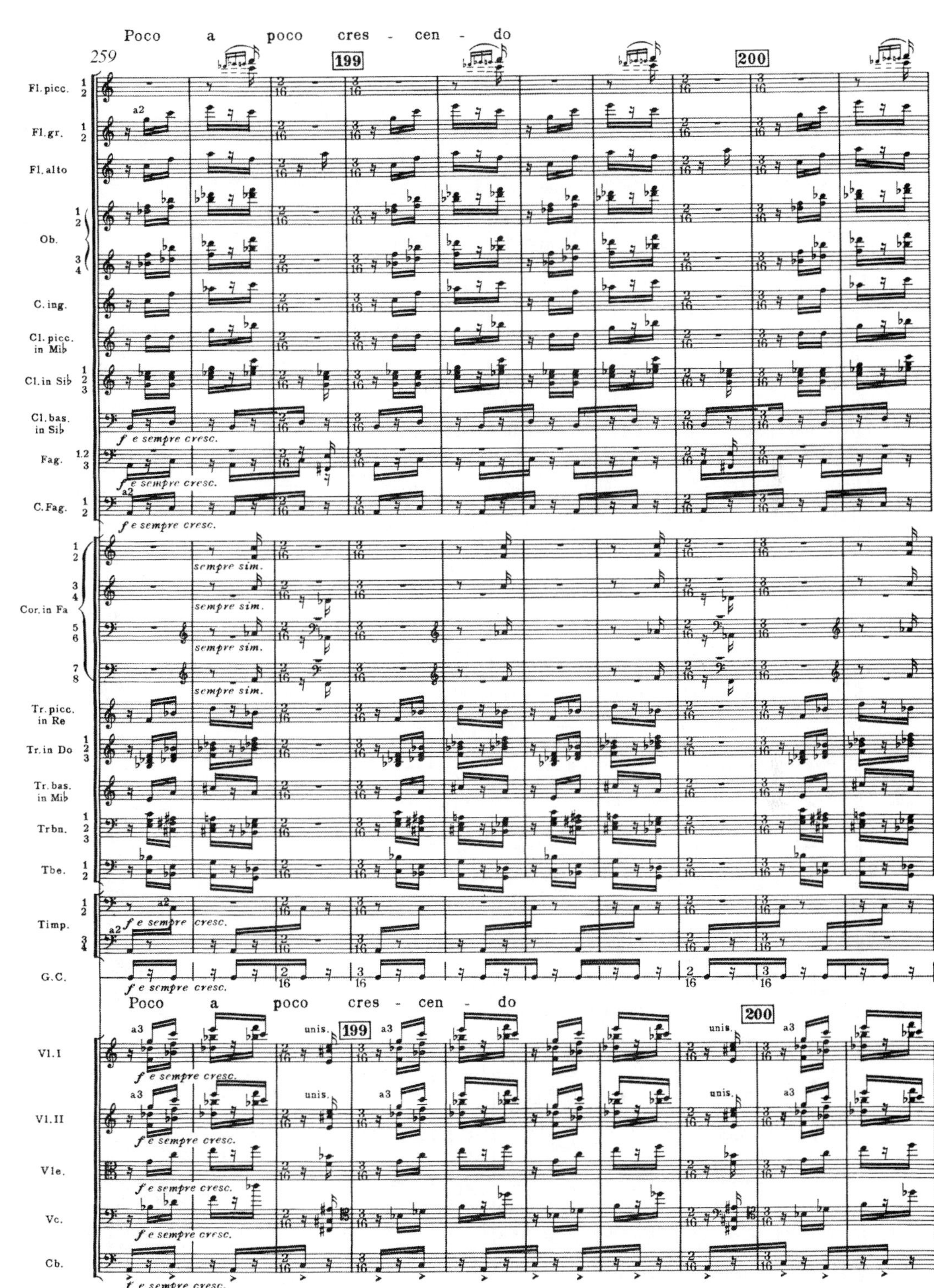
Poco a poco cres - cen - do
259
199
200
Fl. picc.
Fl. gr.
Fl. alto
Ob.
C. ing.
Cl. picc. in Mib
Cl. in Sib
Cl. bas. in Sib
Fag.
C. Fag.
Cor. in Fa
Tr. picc. in Re
Tr. in Do
Tr. bas. in Mib
Trbn.
Tbe.
Timp.
G.C.
Vl. I
Vl. II
Vle.
Vc.
Cb.
f e sempre cresc.
sempre sim.
unis.
a2
a3

269
201
Fl.picc.
Fl.gr.
Fl.alto
Ob.
C.ing.
Cl.picc. in Mi♭
Cl.in Si♭
Cl.bas. in Si♭
Fag.
C.Fag.
Cor.in Fa
Tr.picc. in Re
Tr.in Do
Tr.bas. in Mi♭
Trbn.
Tbe.
Timp.picc.
Timp.gr.
G.C.
Vl. I
Vl. II
Vle.
Vc.
Cb.
non cresc.
colla parte
p non cresc.
sul ponticello
unis.
rapido
div.
non arpeggiato
Descendez le „la" un demi-ton plus bas

The Rite of Spring was the third ballet Igor Stravinsky wrote for the Ballets Russes (Russian Ballet) in Paris, following his phenomenally successful *Firebird* (1910) and *Petrushka* (1911). The company's impresario, Serge Diaghilev, sought in his productions to fuse the arts in collaborative works drawing on Russian culture. Stravinsky first conceived of *The Rite of Spring* in 1910, imagining a pagan ritual in prehistoric Russia in which a young girl is chosen to dance herself to death as a sacrifice to the god of Spring. He worked out the scenario for the ballet with Nikolai Roerich, an artist and expert on the ancient Slavs.

The goal of the collaborators was not to tell a story, as in previous ballets, but to show a ritual on stage, invoking the spirit of primitive life as a balm for the ills of modern urban society. Roerich designed the sets and costumes, working from Russian peasant designs. Choreographer Vaclav Nijinsky invented deliberately awkward movements for the dancers, the opposite of the refined, graceful motions of traditional ballet. For the music, Stravinsky drew from folk songs, as was his practice, but invented an anti-Romantic, dissonant, and sometimes shocking musical language to suggest primitivism.

At the premiere in May 1913, the audience protested in one of the most notorious scandals in music history (see HWM, p. 834, for Stravinsky's account). Their outrage was aimed more at the choreography than at the music, which was a great success when performed as a concert work in Moscow and Paris in 1914. Ironically, this composition that Stravinsky intended as part of a collective artwork has rarely been performed as a ballet since, and instead it became one of the most popular and frequently played orchestral works of the twentieth century.

After an Introduction, the curtain rises on the *Danse des adolescentes* (Dance of the Adolescent Girls). The strings, using double stops and downbows on every chord, reiterate a sonority that includes all seven notes of an A♭ harmonic minor scale. The dissonance is intense, but there is no expectation of resolution; the chord is simply a musical object, one of many that Stravinsky juxtaposes throughout the piece, and the striking dissonance evokes a primal feeling. The barring is regular, but because each chord in the first two measures is played in exactly the same manner there is no clear indication of the meter. An unusual pattern of accents, reinforced by eight horns, destroys any feeling of metrical regularity. The effect of the unpredictable accents is to reduce meter to mere pulsation on every eighth note, strongly conveying the idea of primitivism by emphasizing pulse, the most elemental aspect of rhythm.

This texture suddenly breaks off, and we hear another: an ostinato in the English horn, a four-note figure common in Slavic folk music, over arpeggiated triads in bassoons and cellos. Although this sounds quite different from what precedes it, there is more continuity between these blocks than may be apparent, since all the pitches of the preceding chord appear here as well, with only two new ones (one new note, *c*, and one octave doubling, low *G*). Such combinations of contrast with continuity are typical of Stravinsky's music and occur throughout *The Rite of Spring*.

The pounding chords resume, with an abbreviated form of the accent pattern (measures 13–16 repeat measures 2–5). At measure 17, the English horn ostinato appears over the chords, and other ideas are added, creating a texture of superimposed layers that is characteristic of the entire ballet. Typically, each idea is given its own timbre or group of timbres as well as a unique figuration. The chords break off but the ostinato continues as new ideas are superimposed. Often, blocks of sound are juxtaposed in close succession: for instance, a fanfare figure of stacked fifths in the brass and clarinets at measure 26, repeated in measures 28 and 29, alternates with an embellished running idea in flutes and violin I in measures 27 and 30–33, while the other parts play ostinatos. In the original choreography, many of these alternating ideas accompanied motions by different groups of dancers on stage, and the effect is strongly visual, like cross-cutting between shots in a film or music video. The music moves forward by layering, juxtaposing, and alternating ideas in this fashion rather than through motivic development or any of the other sophisticated means of traditional classical music; this is another emblem of the primitive.

The pounding chords return (measure 35), then grow suddenly quieter. Here Stravinsky at last introduces a melody based on a Russian folk tune (bassoons, measure 43), repeating and varying it several times. After a sudden pause (measures 70–71), the English horn ostinato returns, now passed back and forth among other instruments, and it remains a constant presence through the end of the dance. Material heard earlier sometimes returns in new guises (compare measures 78–81 to measures 9–12; measures 99–106 to measures 18–22; and the rhythm in the clarinets at measures 133–40 to the opening rhythm in the horns). But from measure 83 to the end, Stravinsky gradually increases the intensity by building up layers of activity. The leading melody in this section is a folklike tune introduced by solo horn and immediately varied by the flute (measures 89–96). Another folklike melody briefly joins it, presented in cellos and in parallel thirds by the trumpets (measure 119). Then the texture thins suddenly and gradually builds again, adding layer on layer and crescendoing until the next dance suddenly begins. This pattern of building intensity by repeating and overlaying ideas is characteristic of *The Rite of Spring* and appears in almost every dance.

Stravinsky was a master of orchestration, often using special instrumental effects. In *The Rite of Spring*, he includes the unusual timbres of instruments like the low alto flute, the high clarinet, and the trumpet in D, and devices such as mutes and flutter-tonguing. Frequent staccatos and detached playing produce a dry sound, quite far from the lush orchestral sounds of most Romantic composers. Additionally, Stravinsky often divided complex figures between instruments to make them easier to execute, like the piccolo figuration in measures 27–33. At measures 78–81, the violas play a harmonic glissando, moving the finger up and down the C string (without pressing it against the fingerboard) to obtain different notes from the harmonic series, a technique Stravinsky learned from his teacher, Rimsky-Korsakov.

The last dance in *The Rite of Spring* is *Danse sacrale*, the sacrificial dance of the chosen one. Here Stravinsky uses two techniques to undermine meter and reduce rhythm to pulsation: constant changes of meter, as at the beginning, and repeating chords interspersed with rests in unpredictable ways (beginning at measure 34).

The dissonant chords, unexpected accents, and loud dynamics convey an atmosphere of violence appropriate to the disturbing events on stage.

The opening section, A, repeats its main idea (measures 2–5) many times, sometimes alternated with other figures of a similar character (as at measures 11–12 and 16). A new section, B (measure 34), begins softly with pulsing chords interrupted by frequent rests; adds a chromatic idea above the chords (measures 47–48); builds to a frightening climax (measures 91–92); then suddenly returns to its opening dynamic level and gradually builds again. The A section returns, transposed down a semitone (measure 116). Then a new section, C, begins (measure 149), signaled by heavy percussion and a whole-tone tune introduced by the horns (measure 154), soon transformed into a folklike melody (measures 160–71). The opening of section A briefly interrupts (measures 174–80). Finally, ideas from A return over an A–C–A–C ostinato in the bass (at measure 203), the music builds to a final climax, and the chosen one collapses to rising chromatic scales in the flutes.

Throughout the ballet, Stravinsky elevates rhythm and tone color to a position equal to pitch and motive as determinants of the form, shape, and progress of the music. His prominent use of ostinatos, changing meters, unpredictable rests and attacks, rhythm and melody reduced to their elements, juxtaposed blocks of sound, layering, discontinuity, and motives identified with specific timbres all had a significant impact on later composers, making *The Rite of Spring* one of the most influential pieces of music ever written.

165

Igor Stravinsky (1882–1971)

Symphony of Psalms: First movement

Choral symphony

1930

CD 12|59

6
1
Fl. gr.
Oboi
C. I.
Fag.
C-Fag.
Tr-ni
Tr-ne (basso)
Timp.
Gr.C.
1
Arpa
P.-f. 1 2
V-C.
C-B.

12
2
Fl. gr.
Oboi
C.I.
Fag.
C-Fag.
Cor.
Tr-ni
Tr-ne (basso)
Timp.
Gr.C.
Arpa
Piano 1
Piano 2
V-C.
C-B.
1º
mf
p
8va bassa
Arco unis.

17
cant. espressivo
mf
3
Cor. 1 2
Piano 1
8a bassa
Piano 2
Una corda (secco)
mf
Arco
V-Cello Solo
V-C. Solo
Gli altri V-Celli
mf cant.
Gli altri V-C.
C-B.
22
4
60
Oboi 1 2
3 4
mf
p
C.I.
Fag. 1
2 3
Cor. 1 2
A.
mf cant.
E - - xau - -
Piano 1
8a bassa
Piano 2
V-C. Solo
Gli altri V-C.
C-B.

27
Oboi
C.I.
Fag.
A.
-di o - ra - ti - o - nem me - am, Do - mi - - - ne
32
5
mf
Oboi
C.I.
Fag.
S.
A.
T.
B.
f cant.
Et de - pre - ca - ti - o - nem me - - - am.
Tutti V-C. div. a 2
mf cant.

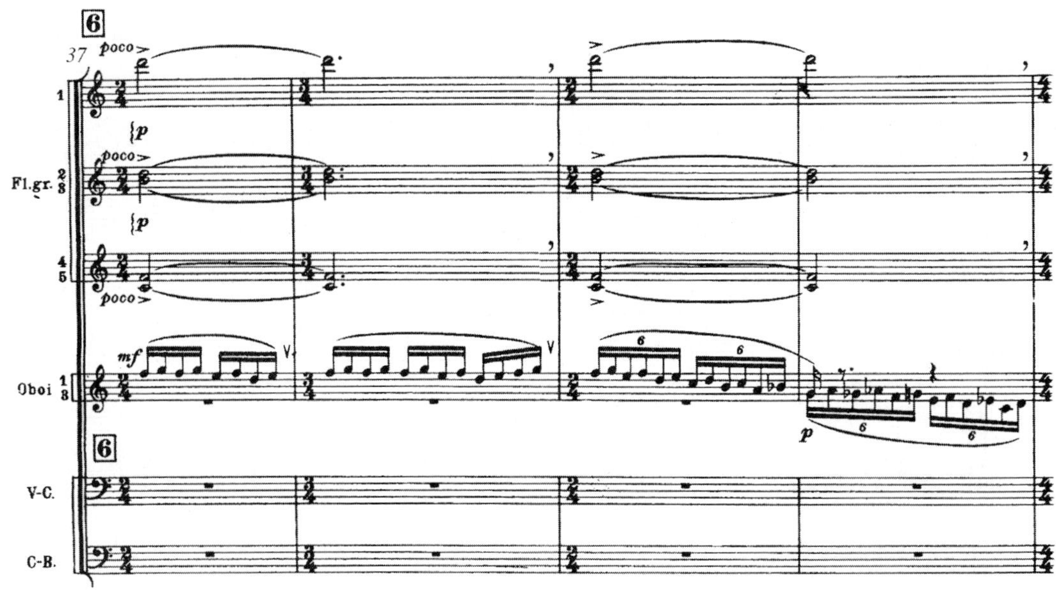
6
37
poco
p
Fl.gr.
Oboi
V-C.
C-B.

7
8
41
espressivo
mf
p
Oboi
C.I.
Fag.
mf cant.
A.
Au - ri - bus per - ci - pe lac - ri-mas me -
Unis.
V-C.
C-B.

61
46
9
Fl.gr.
ben marc.
a 2
f sempre ben marc.
Fl.gr.5 = Fl.piccolo
Oboi
C.I.
Fag.
f sempre ben marc.
C-Fag.
Tr-ne
Tr-ne 3 (basso)
Timp.
Gr.C.
A.
as.
T.
Ne si -
Arpa
Piano 1
Piano 2
V-C.
Div. Pizz.
Unis. Arco
C-B.
Div. Pizz.
Unis. Arco

50
Fl. gr.
Oboi
C.I.
Fag.
simili
C-Fag.
Tr-ni
Tr-ne (basso)
Timp.
Gr. C.
S.
Ne si - le - as.
T.
- le - as, ne si - le - as.
Arpa
Piano 1
Piano 2
etc. simile
V-C.
Div. Pizz.
C-B.
Div. Pizz.

62
53
10
mf stacc. e ben marc.
C.I.
Fag.
mf stacc. e ben marc.
Tr-ni
leggiero ma marcato
Tr-ne (basso)
10
ben cant.
A.
Quo - ni - am ad - ve - na
ben cant.
B.
Quo - ni - am ad - ve - na
56
C.I.
Fag.
très court
très court
C-Fag.
très court
Cor.
Solo staccatissimo
Tr-ni
Tr-ne (basso)
Tuba
ben cant.
S.
e - go sum a - pud
A.
e - go sum a - pud
T.
ben cant.
a - pud
B.
e - go sum a - pud

59
11
a 2
f ben cant.
Oboi
f ben cant.
Fag.
C-Fag.
1º
Cor.
Tr-ba picc. Re
mf ben cant.
Tr-be Do
mf ben cant.
Tr-ni
etc. simile
Tr-ne (basso)
Tuba
11
S.
A.
T.
B.
te et pe - - - re - gri - - - nus,

62
Fl. picc.
Fl. gr.
a 2
Oboi
C. I.
détaché et bien marqué
Fag.
C-Fag.
Cor.
Tr-ba picc. Re
Tr-be Do
Tr-ni
Tr-ne (basso)
Tuba
S.
A.
T.
B.
cres - cen - do
si - - cut om - - nes pa - - tres

63
65 12
etc. sim.
Fl. picc.
Fl. gr.
a 2
ff
etc. sim.
Fag.
ff sempre marcatissimo
C-Fag.
Cor. 1.3. 2.4.
sim.
Tr-ba picc. Re
Tr-be Do
sf
Tr-ne (basso) e Tuba
8a bassa
S.
A.
T.
B.
me - i Re - - mit - - te mi - hi,
Piano 1
ff marcatissimo
Piano 2
ff marcatissimo
V-C. unis.
Arco
C-B. unis.
sff

68
Fl. picc.
sempre sfp
Fl. gr.
sempre sfp
sempre sfp
Oboi
sempre stacc.
sempre stacc.
C.I.
Fag.
sub. p
sempre stacc.
sempre stacc.
S.
mf
re - - mit - te
A.
sub. meno f
re - mit - te mi - hi, ut re - fri -
T.
sub. meno f
re - mit - te, re - mit - te mi - hi, ut re - fri -
B.
mf
re - mit - te
Arpa
mf staccatissimo sempre simile
muta LA♯ in LA♭
V-C.
sub. p
C-B.

71
13
Fl. picc.
Fl. gr. 1
Oboi
a 2
C.I.
Fag.
C-Fag.
mf pesante
mf pesante
13
S.
mi - - - hi, pri - us quam a - be - - -
A.
- - ge - rer pri - us quam a - be - -
T.
- - ge - rer pri - us quam a - be - - -
B.
mi - - - hi, pri - us quam a be - - -
Arpa
Piano 1
mf
Piano 2
f
V-C.
mf e ben pesante
C-B.

74
senza dim.
Fl. picc.
Fl. gr.
Oboi
C.I.
Fag.
C-Fag.
Cor.
Tr-ba picc. Re
Tr-be Do
Tr-ni
Tr-ne (basso)
Tuba
senza dim.
S.
A.
T.
B.
-am et ampli - us non e - - ro.
Piano 1
Piano 2
8a bassa
Div. a 2
V-C.
C-B.
Enchainez

Exaudi orationem meam, Domine, et deprecationem meam:	Hear my prayer, Lord, and my supplication:
auribus percipe lacrimas meas.	give ear to my tears.
Ne sileas.	Do not keep silence.
Quoniam advena ego sum apud te et peregrinus, sicut omnes patres mei.	For I am a stranger to you and a wanderer, like all my fathers.
Remitte mihi, ut refrigerer prius quam abeam et amplius non ero.	Pardon me, that I may be refreshed before I depart and am no more.

—Psalm 38:13–14 (39:12–13)

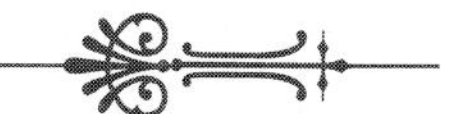

In late 1929, Serge Koussevitzky, conductor of the Boston Symphony Orchestra, commissioned Stravinsky to compose a symphonic piece for the fiftieth anniversary of the Orchestra, occurring the following year. Stravinsky's response was *Symphony of Psalms*, a three-movement work that set three Latin psalms, combining orchestra with chorus. The first movement uses the last two verses of Psalm 38 in the Latin Vulgate Bible (Psalm 39 in the Protestant numbering).

In this work and others during his neoclassical period (1920–51), Stravinsky applied the trademarks of his mature style, developed in *The Rite of Spring* (NAWM 164), to pieces that echoed the styles, genres, and forms of music from the eighteenth century or earlier. Such works were no longer nationalist, like the early ballets, but were intended as universal statements. Stravinskian traits abound. Just in the opening measures, we hear sudden discontinuities and juxtapositions of material; rapid changes of meter; and unpredictable rhythms and rests that tend to emphasize elemental pulsation rather than meter. Later passages use ostinatos and superimpose multiple layers (as in measures 26–36). Yet the music is less dissonant than the *Rite*, and there are frequent references to the language and styles of the past, including many triads and diatonic scales, an imitation of liturgical chant in the vocal lines, and the fugue in the second movement.

After an introduction, there are two main musical ideas that alternate, A and B, and a contrasting middle section, C:

Music:	Intro	A	trans	B1	B2	trans	B1'	A'	C	A"	B1"	B2'	Cadence
Measure:	1	15	18	26	33	37	41	49	53	65	68	72	75

Considering only the portion with text (measures 26–78), the form might be described as an arch, with C at the center. Theme A is associated with the most direct appeals to God, at "Ne sileas" (Do not keep silence) and "Remitte mihi" (Pardon me), and section C with the psalmist's description of himself as a wanderer. The juxtaposition of contrasting blocks of material, common in Musorgsky (see NAWM 145) and other Russian composers as well as in Stravinsky's early ballets, is here used no longer as a national characteristic but as a device to articulate an abstract form.

One of the most important aspects of neoclassical music is that it is *neotonal*, establishing a tonal center not through traditional harmony but through repetition and assertion. At the beginning of the first movement, an E-minor chord, repeated irregularly over the next several measures, creates a center on E, but the prominence of G in the chord (G occurs in four octaves, and E in only the lower and uppermost octaves) suggests that the G will be important as well. The A sections are primarily diatonic, using the notes of the E Phrygian scale and sustaining a drone E in the bass. The B sections are largely octatonic, offering a tonal contrast while (at least in the B1 sections) featuring G–B–E sonorities on the downbeats. The transitions and the first B2 section hint strongly at G as an alternate center, and in the closing cadence (measures 74–78) the bass marches down stepwise from E to G while the voices rise from E through F to G. The way Stravinsky juxtaposes E and G as two rival centers, then leads the music from the former rival to the latter, is a novel reinterpretation of traditional tonality, the sort of reinvention of past conventions that is at the heart of neoclassicism.

Another aspect of neoclassicism, particularly in Stravinsky's hands, was an attempt to avoid the emotionalism associated with Romantic music. Among the ways the composer avoided Romanticism in this piece were his exclusion of violins and violas from the orchestra, shunning the instruments that most often carry emotional melodies in nineteenth-century symphonies while favoring what Stravinsky regarded as the more objective sounds of wind instruments, and his choice to avoid tempo markings that suggested moods (such as Allegro or Vivace) and to use simple metronome markings instead. Beginning in the 1920s, he often conducted his own works, both as a way to make money and as a model for others of how to conduct his music without indulging in interpretive excess. The performance on the accompanying recording was conducted by Stravinsky himself in 1963, when he was eighty-one, and it exemplifies his preference that the music should speak for itself.

Béla Bartók (1881–1945)

Mikrokosmos: No. 123, *Staccato and Legato*

Étude

1926, 1932–39

CD 12|64

a Allegro, ♩ = 126

f

From Béla Bartók, *Mikrokosmos*, vol. 5 (London: Boosey & Hawkes, 1940), 6–7.

b
65
p
mf
f

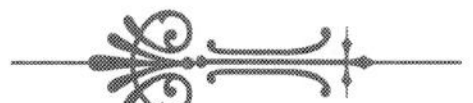

A piano teacher as well as a composer, Béla Bartók wrote *Mikrokosmos* to introduce piano students to the techniques and sounds of modern music. The 153 pieces are in six volumes arranged from simplest to most challenging. The collection began to take shape in 1936, when his son Péter began to study piano and Bartók wrote pieces for him to learn. Bartók completed the project during the next three years, incorporating some pieces written a decade earlier. He played excerpts from *Mikrokosmos* in recitals beginning in 1937, performing this piece, *Staccato and Legato*, for the first time in January 1938. The whole collection was published in 1940 by the British publisher Boosey & Hawkes, to whom Bartók had switched from his Viennese publisher Universal Edition after Nazi Germany annexed Austria in 1938.

As the title suggests, the entire set represents a microcosm of Bartók's style. *Staccato and Legato* offers both a practical étude for the student—an exercise in playing legato and staccato in alternation within each hand and simultaneously between both hands—and an illustration of Bartók's synthesis of elements derived from peasant music with characteristics of classical music. The synthesis works by emphasizing not only the elements that most distinguish these two traditions but also those elements they have in common.

From the classical tradition, this piece is modeled on Bach, resembling a two-part invention. The two hands are in exact canon, first at an octave and fourth below with entrances a measure apart (measures 1–11) and then, after a sly transition, at an octave and fifth below with entrances half a measure apart (measures 13–22). The subject and answer are both inverted at measure 13. After the cadence in measure 24, Bartók presents a second version of the piece (marked **b**), which repeats the original version but with the counterpoint inverted—that is, with the second voice transposed to be above rather than below the first. Canon, inversion, and invertible counterpoint are all typical of Bach.

The contrast of legato and staccato is also a trait from the classical tradition, and it is used here to point out the canon, as was typical performance practice for playing Bach at the piano; each entrance begins legato, then turns to staccato to make it easier to hear the answer in the other voice.

The tonal structure has a classical shape. The piece starts in a tonal region centered on C, with a subject that spans from C to F and an answer that spans from G to C. The music then repeats, varied, a fifth higher on G (measures 7–12), mimicking a move in tonal music from tonic to dominant. The third phrase is in a region on F, with an inverted subject spanning F to C and an answer that moves from B♭ to F, and the piece closes on C. The overall structure, moving from C to G to F and back to C, is like that of many eighteenth-century pieces that go from tonic to dominant and then somewhere else before returning to the tonic.

But there are folk elements here too. The shape of the opening phrase, rising and falling in the span of a fourth, is common in Hungarian peasant songs. So are several other features in the right-hand melody of the section marked as **a**: the melodic structure of a series of short phrases, each marked off with a rest; the transposition of the first phrase up a fifth (as happens here at measure 6), thereby filling in the rest of the octave; the immediate variation of a phrase rather than repeating it exactly, as we see here with each successive pair of phrases; and the overall contour of the melody, rising from the opening note to the upper octave and then returning. These traits are evident in many of the Hungarian peasant melodies Bartók collected, including this one that he recorded in the Pest region near Budapest in 1907:

In addition to sharing these general characteristics, this Hungarian peasant tune closely resembles Bartók's melody in certain respects: its first measure shares the short-short-long rhythm of measures 2–3 in Bartók's melody, and the melodic contour of those measures of the Bartók is like an inverted chromatic variant of the first measure of the peasant melody. Whether Bartók had this particular tune in mind or not, its similarities to the melody of *Staccato and Legato* show how closely he modeled the latter on Hungarian melodies.

Another feature of *Staccato and Legato*, its chromaticism, may also have a Hungarian source. Several Hungarian peasant melodies mix modes, for instance by shifting between the Dorian and Mixolydian modes (which changes the third of the scale from minor to major). Here the rising gestures suggest the major scale (like the C-major scale spelled out by the first four notes of the subject and answer respectively), and the falling gestures suggest the chromatic scale or Phrygian scale. In the diatonic context established by the opening figure, the chromatic notes sound like ornamental tones, and indeed Bartók observed in his studies of Hungarian folk music that some tunes featured chromatic ornaments within mostly diatonic melodies.

Of course, the contrast of diatonicism and chromaticism is also common in the classical tradition, as are melodies that rise and fall and are formed from phrases that are repeated or varied. We have also seen that both traditions provide a source for the overall motion in *Staccato and Legato* from C to G and back to C. Bartók's synthesis of the two traditions depends upon such common features, even while highlighting what makes each tradition distinctive.

Béla Bartók (1881–1945)

Music for Strings, Percussion and Celesta: Third movement, Adagio

Symphonic suite

1936

CD 12|66 CD 6|19

Adagio, ♩ ca 66 — allarg. — — — al — Adagio molto, ♩ ca 40

Timpani

Xylophon

rubato

mf p

5

Timp.

Xyl.

1.Vle.

1.Vlc.

1.Cb.

tr dim. pp p

10

Timp.

Xyl.

2.Vl.

1.Vle.

1.Vlc.

1.Cb.

tr mf p pp

Timp.
Xyl.
2.Vl.
1.Vle.
1.Vlc.
1.Cb.
15
poco ral
1.Vl.
3.Vl.
4.Vl.
2.Vle.
2.Vlc.
p,espr.
mf

lentando
a tempo
Timp.
Xyl.
1. Vl.
2. Vl.
1. Vle.
1. Vlc.
1. Cb.
3. Vl.
4. Vl.
2. Vle.
2. Vlc.
2. Cb.
dim.
sul pont.
pp
mf
p

67
20
A
20 Più andante, ♩ ca 56
Gr. cassa
Tam-tam
Timp.
Xyl.
Cel.
Pfte.
1. Vl.
2. Vl. div.
1. Vle.
1. Vlc.
1. Cb.
3. Vl.
4. Vl.
2. Vlc.
2. Cb.
pp
tr
p
mf
mf, espr.
2 Soli
p, espr.
con sord.
ord.
div.

25
Cel.
Pfte.
2 soli
1.Vl.
2.Vl.
div.
con sord.
pp
1.Vle.
pp
II
1.Vlc.
pp
div.
tr
3.Vl.
tr
div.
tr
4.Vl.
tr

30
rallent. _ _ al Più lento, ♩ ca 46
Timp.
Xyl.
Cel.
Pfte.
1.Vl.
tutti
2.Vl. div.
1.Vle.
1.Vlc.
1.Cb.
3.Vl.
4.Vl.
2.Vlc.
2. Cb.

68
21
35
B Più andante, ♩ ca 66
Timp.
Cel.
pp
20
Arpa
p
ppp
gliss.
Pfte.
ppp
gliss.
10
1. Vl.
1. Vle.
1. Vlc.
1. Cb.
2. Vlc.
2. Cb.
p

Timp.
p
Cel.
20
20
20
Arpa
Pfte.
gliss.
gliss.
gliss.
unis.
senza sord. flaut.
2.Vl.
pp
flaut.
1.Vle.
pp
flaut.
1.Vlc.
pp
senza sord.
flaut.
4.Vl.
pp
flaut.
2.Vle.
pp
flaut.
2.Vlc.
pp
2.Cb.

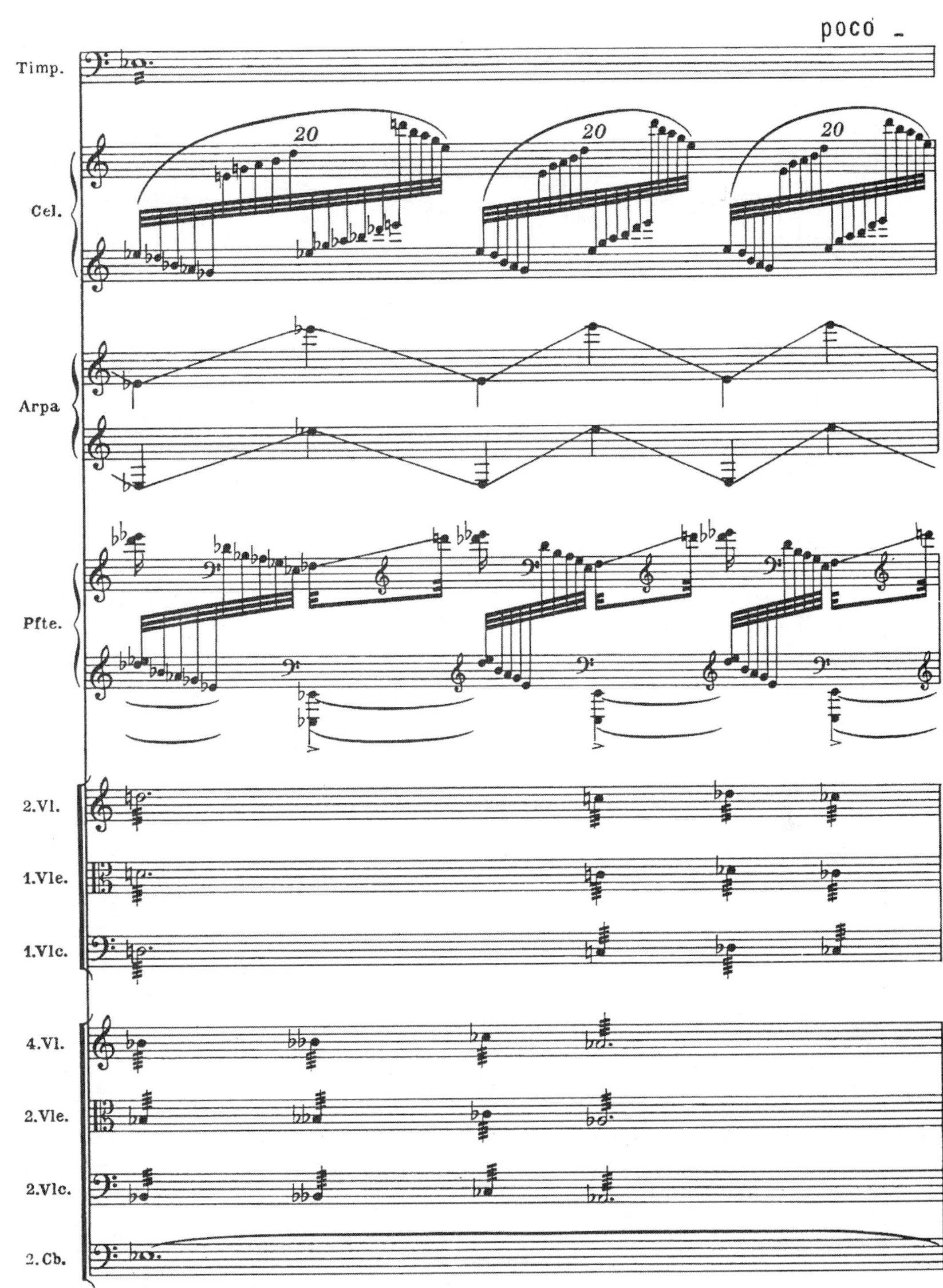
poco
Timp.
20
20
20
Cel.
Arpa
Pfte.
2.Vl.
1.Vle.
1.Vlc.
4.Vl.
2.Vle.
2.Vlc.
2. Cb.

a
poco
Timp.
cresc.
Cel.
20
20
20
cresc.
Arpa
cresc.
Pfte.
cresc.
2. Vl.
cresc.
1. Vle.
cresc.
1. Vlc.
cresc.
4. Vl.
cresc.
2. Vle.
cresc.
2. Vlc.
cresc.
2. Cb.
cresc.

stringendo
Timp.
Cel.
20
20
20
Arpa
Pfte.
10
10
10
2. Vl.
1. Vle.
1. Vlc.
4. Vl.
2. Vle.
2. Vlc.
2. Cb.

40
Timp.
20
20
20
Cel.
Arpa
10
10
10
Pfte.
2.Vl.
1.Vle.
1.Vlc.
4.Vl.
2.Vle.
2.Vlc.
2. Cb.

Timp.
Cel.
f
5
Arpa
Pfte.
gliss.
10
(ord.)
1. Vl.
mp
2. Vl.
1. Vle.
1. Vlc.
1. Cb.
4. Vl.
2. Vle.
2. Vlc.
2. Cb.

Timp.
mf
Arpa
mf
Pfte.
10
10
10
f
1. Vl.
cresc.
2. Vl.
ord.
cresc.
1. Vle.
ord.
mf cresc.
1. Vlc.
ord.
mf cresc.
1. Cb.
mf
3. Vl.
senza sord.
(ord.)
mp cresc.
4. Vl.
ord.
mf cresc.
2. Vle.
ord.
mf cresc.
2. Vlc.
2. Cb.
mf

*) kleineres Instrument mit höherem Ton / *instrument plus petit au son plus clair*
smaller cymbal with higher tone

*) kleineres Instrument / *instrument plus petit*
smaller cymbals

quasi a tempo, ♩ ca 80
Piatti
Timp.
Xyl.
Arpa
Pfte.
1. Vl.
2. Vl.
1. Vle.
1. Vlc.
1. Cb.
3. Vl.
4. Vl.
2. Vle.
2. Vlc.
2. Cb.
pizz.
arco

55
Allegretto, ♩ ca 104
Cel.
mf
Arpa
p
Pfte.
sempre stacc.
p
8
pizz.
div.
1. Vl.
2. Vl.
1. Vle.
1. Vlc.
1. Cb.
3. Vl.
4. Vl.
2. Vle.
2. Vlc.
2. Cb.
(non div.)

70
23
60
poco a poco rallent - - - (D) Meno mosso, ♩ ca 76
Pfte
p
arco
pp,dolce
pizz.
1.Vl.
2.Vl.
1. Vle.
1. Vlc.
1.Cb.
arco
pp
3.Vl.
4.Vl.
2.Vle.
2.Vlc.
2.Cb.

65 Adagio, ♩ ca 56
Cel.
p
14
14
11
11
Arpa
p
Pfte.
1. Vl.
2. Vl.
1. Vle.
2 Soli
div.
3. Vl.
p
2. Vle.
p dolce
arco
2. Vlc.
p dolce

Cel.
14
14
14
14
Arpa
sf
Pfte.
1. Vl.
2. Vl.
1. Vle.
3. Vl.
2. Vle.
2. Vlc.

Cel.
14
14
14
14
Arpa
Pfte.
1. Vl.
2. Vl.
1. Vle.
3. Vl.
2. Vle.
2. Vlc.

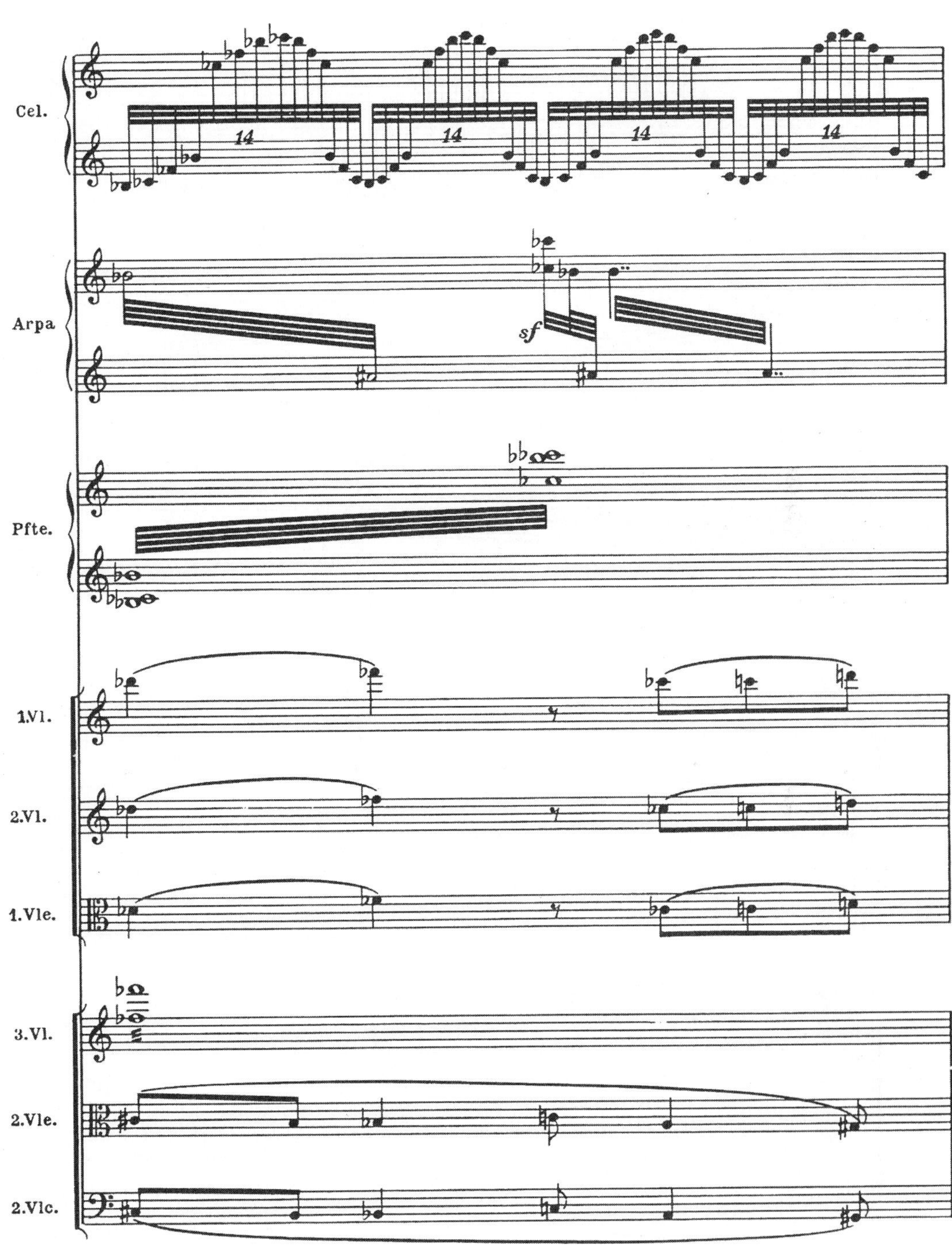
Cel.
14
14
14
14
Arpa
sf
Pfte.
1.Vl.
2.Vl.
1.Vle.
3.Vl.
2.Vle.
2.Vlc.

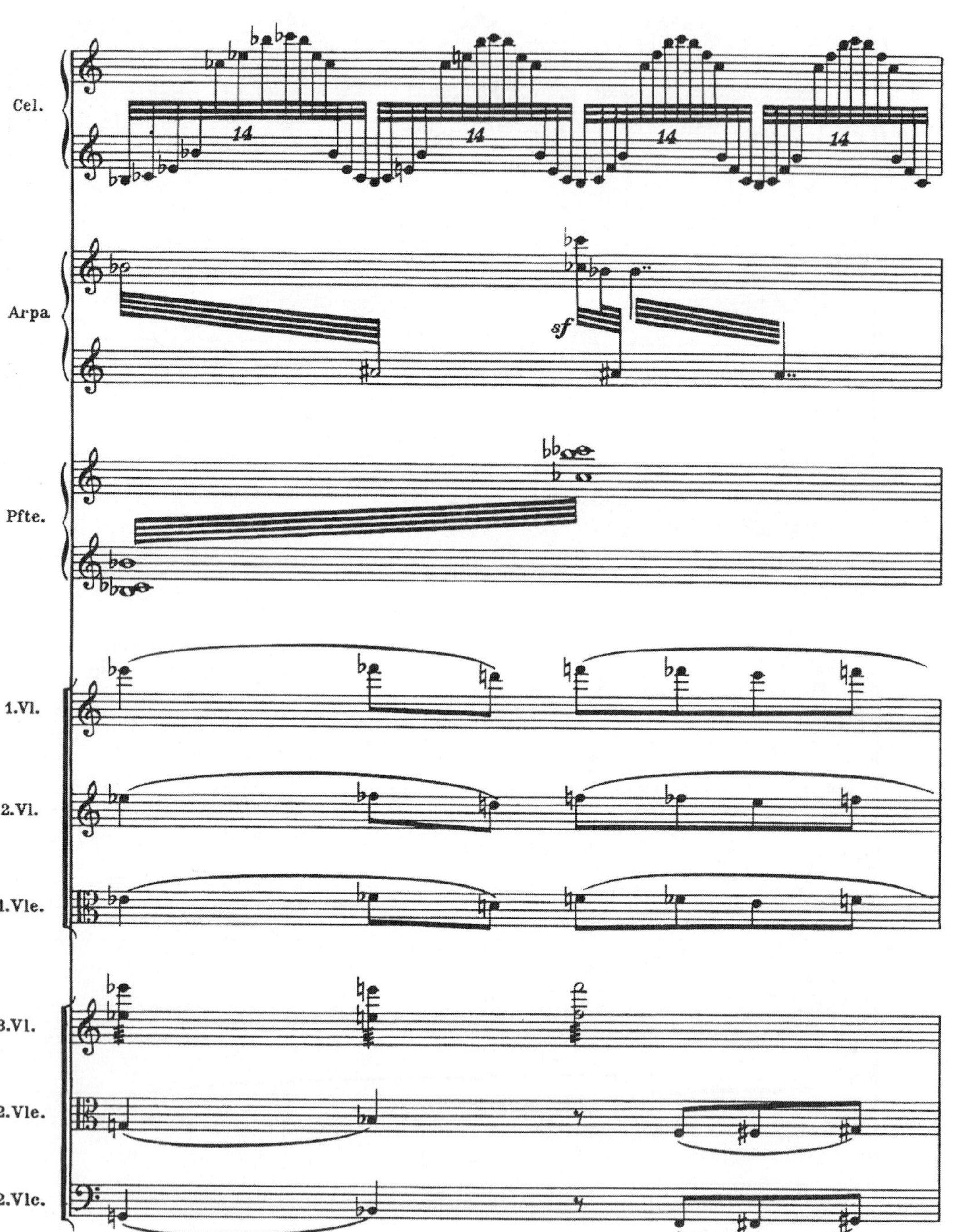
Cel.
14
14
14
14
Arpa
sf
Pfte.
1.Vl.
2.Vl.
1.Vle.
3.Vl.
2.Vle.
2.Vlc.

rallen
70
Cel.
14
14
14
14
Arpa
sf
Pfte.
1. Vl.
2. Vl.
1. Vle.
3. Vl.
2. Vle.
2. Vlc.

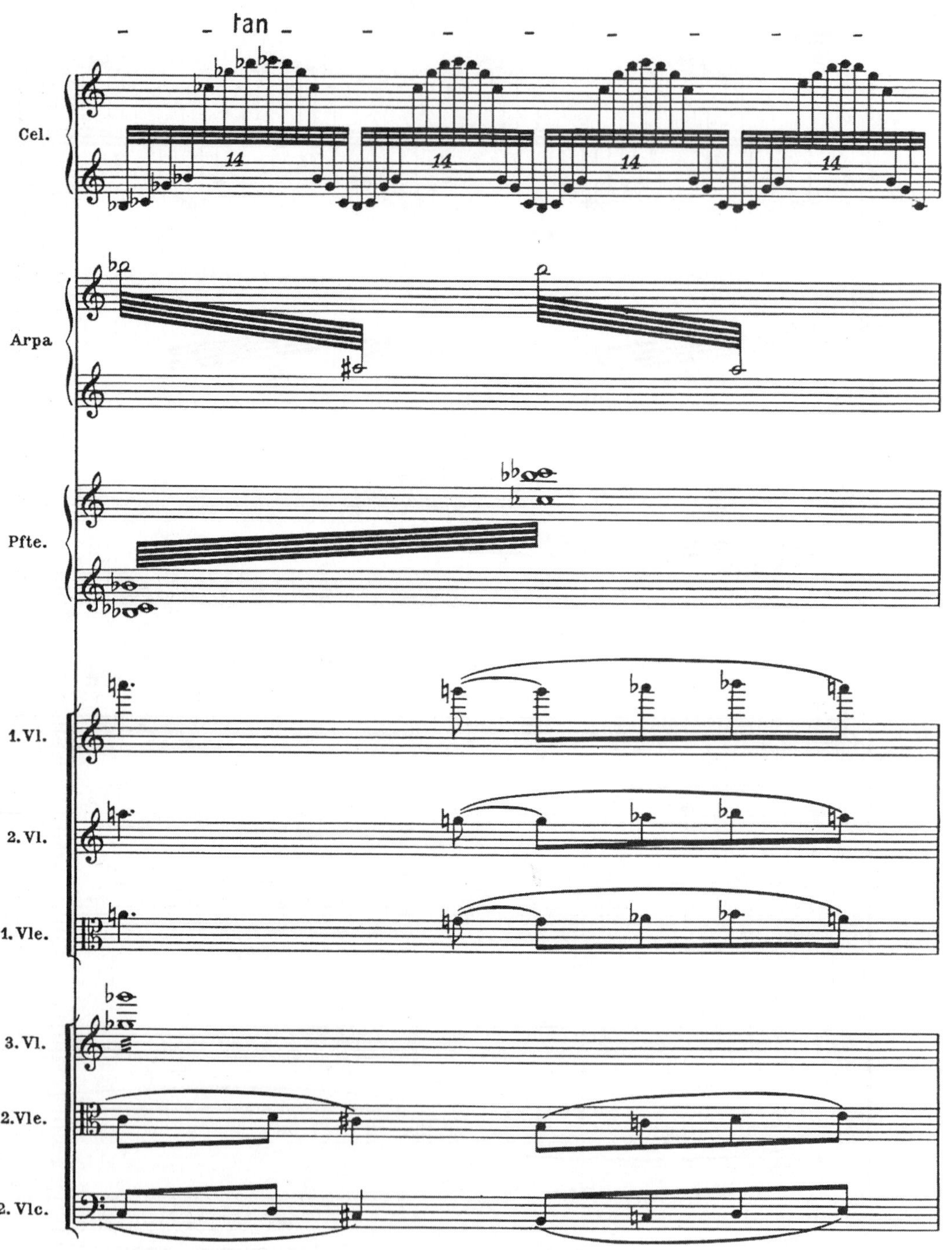
tan
Cel.
14
14
14
14
Arpa
Pfte.
1. Vl.
2. Vl.
1. Vle.
3. Vl.
2.Vle.
2. Vlc.

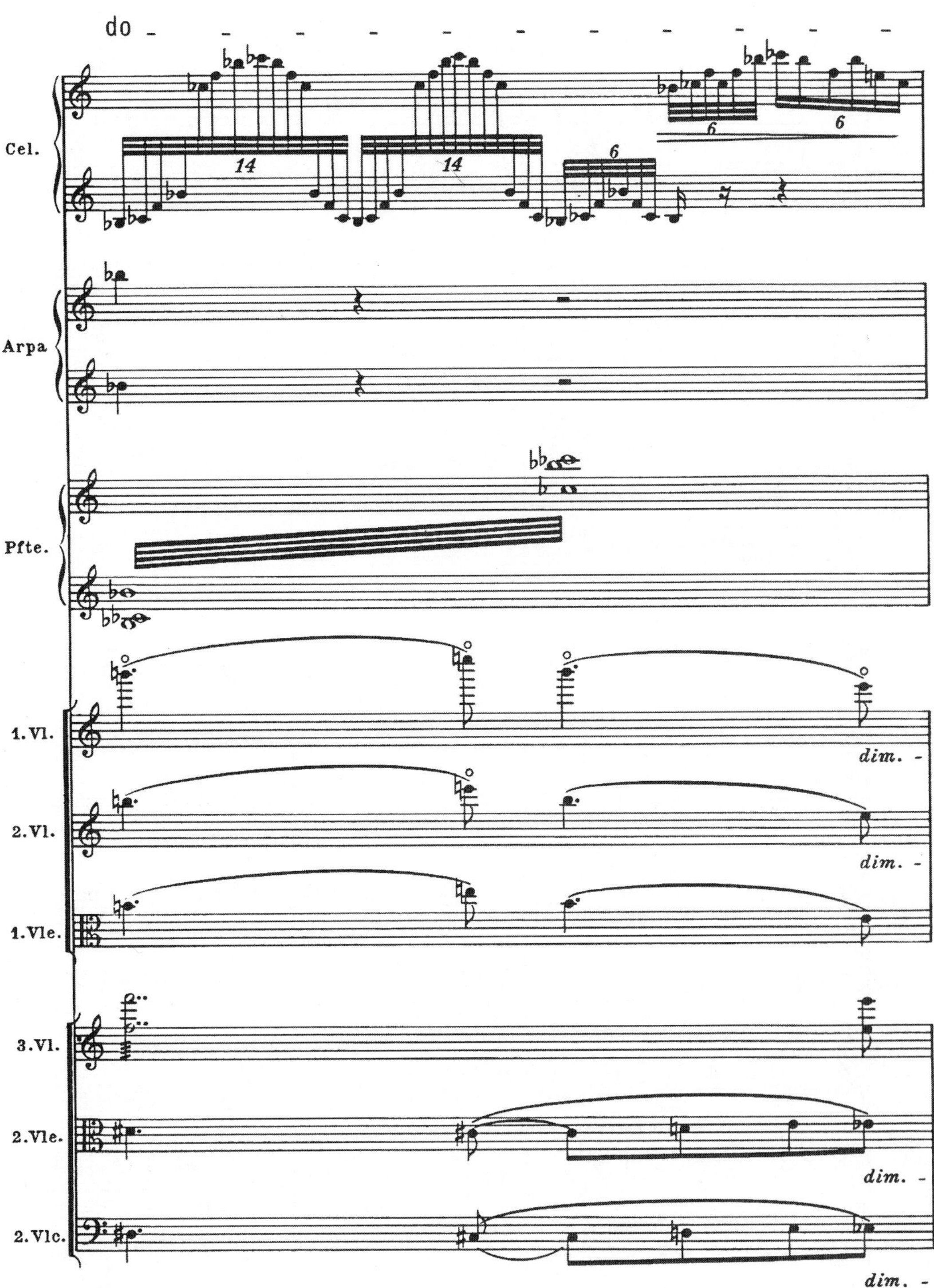
do
Cel.
14
14
6
6
6
Arpa
Pfte.
1. Vl.
dim.
2. Vl.
dim.
1. Vle.
3. Vl.
2. Vle.
dim.
2. Vlc.
dim.

71
24
al ♪ ca 70
E
Quasi a tempo
75
♩ ca 50, rallent.
Cel.
5
pp
Arpa
ff près de la table
Pfte.
pp
pizz.
1. Vl.
ff
2. Vl.
pizz.
1. Vle.
f
pizz.
1. Vlc.
f
pizz.
1. Cb.
f
sul pont.
2. Vle.
pp
p
2. Vlc.
pp
f
arco
2. Cb.
f

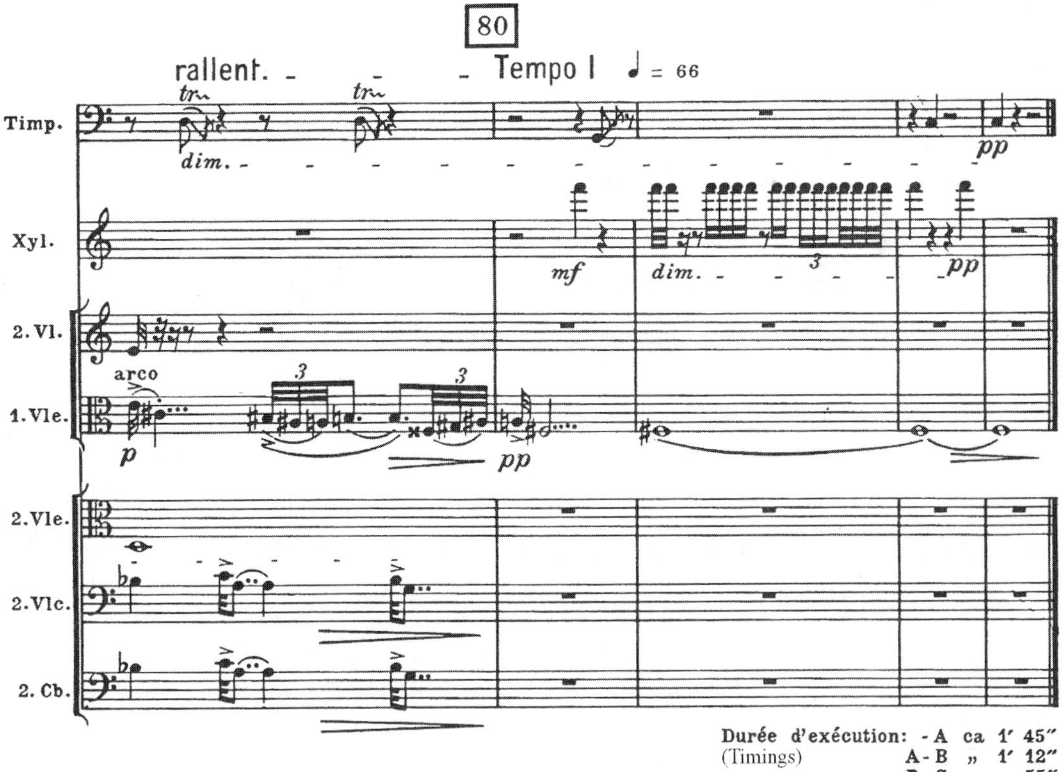

Durée d'exécution: (Timings)

-A	ca	1′ 45″
A-B	„	1′ 12″
B-C	„	55″
C-D	„	57″
D-E	„	58″
E-	„	48″
	ca	6′ 35″

Béla Bartók wrote *Music for Strings, Percussion and Celesta* in the summer of 1936 for the Basel Chamber Orchestra and its conductor, Paul Sacher. Bartók's concept for the piece was so clear in his mind that he wrote it out from the start in full score, rather than beginning with a reduced score as composers usually do for orchestral works. It was premiered the next January in Basel, Switzerland, to such great applause that the orchestra played the fourth movement again as an encore.

The work has four movements: a slow fugue, a fast sonata form, a slow arch form, and a rondo finale. The fugue theme is recalled in each later movement. The movements are also linked by a symmetrical scheme of tonal centers—A for the outer movements, with the notes a minor third above (C) and below (F♯) serving as centers for the second and third movements respectively. Like *Symphony of Psalms* (NAWM 165), the piece is neotonal, rather than based on traditional harmony. In each movement, the note a tritone away from the tonal center serves as an opposite pole. Another symmetrical aspect of the music is the layout of the orchestra itself: the strings are divided into two halves (violins 1 and 2, viola 1, cello 1, and bass 1 on the left, curving from front to back, with the others on the right in a mirror arrangement), and the piano, harp, celesta, and percussion are in the middle.

The slow movement, included here, exhibits symmetries on both a minute and a large scale. The opening xylophone solo is a palindrome centered on the first beat of measure 3—that is, the rhythm from that beat is the same going in either direction. The form is also palindromic (though not exactly so), punctuated by the four phrases of the fugue theme (FT) from the first movement:

Section:	A	FT1	B	FT2	C	FT3	B'	FT4	A'
Measure:	1	19	20	34	35	60	63	74	75

The A section is marked by four striking sounds: the xylophone, which repeats a single pitch (*f'''*); glissandos on the timpani between F♯ and C, the two tonal poles of the movement; low string tremolos on C and F♯; and figures in violas and violins that snake through chromatic space. After the first phrase of the fugue appears (in viola 1 and cello 1 at measure 19), two solo violins and celesta share the B theme, accompanied by an eerie background of trills in the strings and parallel major sevenths articulated by the piano, violin glissandos, and string tremolos.

After another fugue segment, the C section begins with glissandos and two mutually exclusive pentatonic scales played rapidly in the harp, piano, and celesta, over which a twisting theme in parallel octave tremolos gradually rises. This texture has become known as Bartók's "night music," named for the movement *Musiques nocturnes* in his piano suite *Out of Doors* (1926). The twisting theme builds to a climax as celesta, harp, and piano drop out. At the peak, the last segment of the twisting theme is transformed into a transposed, modified retrograde: omitting the bracketed notes, A–A♯–[D♯]–E♯–[F♯]–E–G (violin 1, measures 44–45) becomes C–A–B♭–E♭–D (measure 46). This new motive is itself heard in retrograde in alternation with its original form (measures 48 and 50) or in counterpoint with it (measures 51–53), as if to emphasize the symmetries. The new motive suffuses the texture, imitated in every instrument. Then, as the third phrase of the fugue theme enters (violin 3 and viola 2, measures 60–63), we may hear a hidden connection: the new motive turns out to derive from the last five notes of this phrase of the fugue theme, changing the whole steps into larger intervals (compare D–C–D♭–C♭–B♭ in measures 61–63, from the fugue theme, with the new motive C–A–B♭–E♭–D in measure 46).

A modified reprise of the B theme follows, treated in canon at the tritone and accompanied by a texture reminiscent of the first half of the C section, with tremolos and arpeggios in piano, harp, and celesta and violin tremolos in a high register. The last phrase of the fugue theme appears in piano and celesta, and an abbreviated recollection of the A section closes the movement.

Bartók drew on folk music, not just as a way to evoke a national or folklike style, but as a source of ideas for renewing modern music. That is evident in this movement, which does not sound folklike in the least but draws many elements from folk styles. The string melodies in the A sections borrow their short on-beat accents (as in measure 6) from a rhythm common in Hungarian folk tunes, and take their rapid, snaking figuration (as in measures 7–8) from the ornate, partly chromatic vocal ornaments of Serbo-Croatian folk songs. The B section and the climax of the C section (measures 45–59) both—in different ways—echo a technique of Bulgarian dance orchestras, in which instruments play in octaves against drones and a chordal tapestry of sound is produced by plucked instruments. In the latter passage, the $\frac{5}{4}$ meter suggests the Bulgarian dance rhythm of 2 + 3 (the *paidushko*). Thus, in this movement, and throughout *Music for Strings, Percussion and Celesta*, Bartók has fully assimilated elements of folk music into one of his most original works of art music.

This piece is highly individual in style, form, and even genre. It is clearly related to the four-movement symphony but differentiated from the symphony by its movement structure and prominent percussion and keyboard parts. Paradoxically, such a high degree of individuality is typical of the twentieth century, when composers sought both to follow in the footsteps of the classical masters of the past and to stake out new territory, forging distinctive identities for themselves and for each new piece.

Charles Ives (1874–1954)

General William Booth Enters into Heaven

Song

1914

CD 12|72 CD 6|25

Allegro moderato *(March time)*

(marcato)

Booth led bold - ly with his big bass drum (Are you washed in the blood of the Lamb? Are you washed in the blood of the Lamb, of the Lamb?)

Hal - - le - lu - yah

Saints smiled grave - - ly and they said, "He's come" {(Washed / are you washed} in the blood of the

*Both small and large notes in voice part are sung if there is a chorus.

From Charles Ives, *Nineteen Songs* (Bryn Mawr, Pa.: Theodore Presser, 1935), 2–7. Reprinted by permission of Carl Fischer on behalf of Theodore Presser.

17
73
26
Lamb? The blood of the Lamb?)
p f
Oct's 8va basso ad lib.
21
f
Walk - ing lep - ers fol - lowed rank on rank,
Lurch-ing brav - oes from the ditch - es dank
mf
cresc.
25
f
Drabs from the al - ley - ways and drug fiends
f
28
pale Minds still pas-sion rid-den, soul powers frail: Ver-min-eat-en saints with moul-dy
32
(ad lib.)
breath, Un - washed legions with the ways of Death (Are you washed in the blood of the
ff mf
l.h. sfz
ff mf
3

36
74 27
Lamb? Are you washed in the blood of the Lamb?)
dim. e poco rit.
p
40
f marcato
Ev - 'ry slum had sent its half -
leggiero
44
a - score The round world o - ver. (Booth had groaned for more). Ev - 'ry ban - ner
f
48
animato poco a poco
75 28
that the wide world flies, Bloomed with glo - ry and trans - cen - dent dyes.
52
molto animato
ff
Big - voiced lass - ies made their ban - jos bang, bang, bang, made
(sempre marcato)

55
— their ban - jos, — Tranced, fan - a - tical they shrieked and sang — They shrieked and — sang: 'Are you? Are you washed in the blood?
fff
fff
59
(shouted)
In the blood of the Lamb — of the Lamb? Hal-le-lu-jah! Hal - le-lu - jah
sf
ff
63
ff
Hal - le - lu-jah, Lord, Hal - - le - lu-jah, Lord,
76 29
65
Hal - le - lu - jah! It was queer to see Bull-necked con-victs,
l.h.
r.h.
r.h.
l.h.
ff
68
Bull - necked con - victs with that land — make free. Loons — with trum - pets blowed —

72
mf
— a blare On, on, up - ward thro' the
poco meno
mf
75
f
gold - en air! (Are you washed in the blood in the blood of the Lamb, in the
ff
ff
ff
6
78
mf
blood of the Lamb, the Lamb of the Lamb, the Lamb?
meno mosso
l.h.
mf
dim. e rit. poco a poco
77
30
Adagio
81
p
pp
p
Je - sus came from the court house door, Streched his hands a - bove the pass - ing
p
pp
Adagio and with dignity
p
p
pp
85
poor. Booth saw not, but led his queer ones, Round and round round and round and round
the mighty court - house square,
l.h.

89
and round_ and_ round and round_ and round and round Yet! in an instant all that
poco e poco rit. e decresc.
Allegro
93
blear re-view Marched_ on, marched_ on marched on marched on_ marched
cresc. e accel. molto animato
Allegro risoluto
78 31
97
on marched_ on marched on_ spot-less, clad in rai - ment_ new. The lame_ were_
Broadly - but very slightly slower
101
(upper voices as a shout)
Hal-le-lu-yah
straight - ened, with-ered limbs un-curled And blind_ eyes opened on a new sweet
ritard
poco rit. e decresc.
105
Adagio
world Are you washed in the blood of the Lamb?_ Are you washed in the blood of the
poco rit.
(A little faster recalling the march)

Charles Ives found the poem *General William Booth Enters into Heaven* by American poet Vachel Lindsay (1879–1931) in a 1914 review of Lindsay's first book of poetry. There was probably no poet better suited for Ives's musical idiom than Lindsay, who infused his poems (and his onstage readings of them) with the rhythms and performing styles of hymns, vaudeville, and ragtime. Ives based his song on only the extracts printed in the review: the first, second, and fourth stanzas of the seven-stanza poem. The song remained unpublished until 1935, when Henry Cowell produced nineteen of Ives's songs as an issue of *New Music*, a quarterly journal of works by modern composers.

Lindsay wrote the poem on the death of William Booth, evangelist and founder of the Salvation Army, whom Lindsay pictures entering Heaven beating a bass drum at the head of an army of the souls he had saved. Appropriately, Lindsay drew inspiration from a gospel hymn, indicating that the poem was "to be sung to the tune of 'The Blood of the Lamb.'" He quoted the hymn's refrain line frequently ("Are you washed in the blood of the Lamb?"), and for the other lines he used the hymn's accent pattern of three stressed, three unstressed, and three stressed syllables.

Ives's setting is an art song in the classical tradition, but he incorporates elements from the band music and popular songs of the American vernacular tradition, from Protestant hymnody, and from the experimental music in which he was a pioneer. At the opening, he evokes Booth's bass drum through his technique of imitating drumbeats as dissonant chords on the piano, an experiment from his teen years; the bass notes arrive after the rest of the chord, just as on a bass drum the resonance of the drum head is heard just after the sound of the initial impact. The rhythm here is the "street beat" (measures 1–2), the pattern drummers use to keep marchers moving in step and one of the first things Ives would have learned as a drummer in his father's band. Ives based the vocal melody on motives paraphrased from the hymn "There Is a Fountain Filled with Blood," whose imagery closely matches that of the hymn Lindsay used.

In the second section of the song (measures 19–39), Lindsay describes Booth's followers, and Ives gives each group a different musical characterization, using ostinatos, parallel dissonant chords, and other modernist sounds. At each appearance of the refrain line "(Are you washed in the blood of the Lamb?)," Ives presents a new paraphrase of "There Is a Fountain."

When the marchers arrive at the center of Heaven—depicted as a "mighty courthouse square" like those in county seats across America—Ives suggests the milling crowd through a rising and falling whole-tone scale in the voice and repeating ostinatos in the piano (measures 40–51). At the line "Big-voiced lassies made their banjos bang" (measures 52–55), the piano paraphrases *Oh, Dem Golden Slippers* by James A. Bland, a minstrel song about going to Heaven whose second verse begins "Oh my ole banjo." Later Ives adds a bugle call for the line "Loons with trumpets blowed a blare," and a hint of the hymn "Onward, Upward" where the words of Lindsay's poem almost quote it (measures 70–74). All these elements show Ives's affectionate, good-humored approach to depicting the motley crowd, although both Lindsay's poem and Ives's song are entirely serious.

When Jesus appears at the court house door and blesses the marchers, Ives states most of "There Is a Fountain," slightly reworked, in the piano (measures 82–88), accompanying a repeating motive in the voice that depicts the crowd still circling around the square. This is the first mostly diatonic passage in the song, and its slow, soft, dignified character reflects Jesus' serenity. Booth does not see Jesus at first (he was blind when he died), and continues to lead the march even as he and all the marchers are cleansed and healed by Jesus' blessing. At the climactic moment of transformations, over the drum pattern in the piano, the singer presents the complete verse of "There Is a Fountain," set awkwardly to Lindsay's words as if to express the force of will it took Booth to motivate his followers. This moment is the culmination of the drama in Lindsay's poem and also of the thematic process of the whole song, a gradual emergence of the hymn tune as the principal theme. The song is thus an example of *cumulative form*, the form Ives used most often, in which the main theme is heard first in fragments and paraphrases and appears complete only at the end.

In the final measures, the action stops, and the closing refrain is set twice, over soft arpeggiated chords and then in the four-part harmony of Protestant hymns. The stark contrasts of style seen here and throughout the song are typical of Ives, who used them to articulate his cumulative form and for expressive purposes, just as Mozart used contrasting styles in his music (see the commentaries for NAWM 114 and 117). In this context, the use of a familiar style amid so many novel sounds suggests the humble devotion of a hymn, and thus brings the message of the song home. The moment quickly passes, and the parade fades away in the distance.

After writing this song, Ives sketched an arrangement for unison choir and chamber orchestra. When he published the song more than twenty years after writing it, he included a number of passages in small notes, indicating that they should be sung if the piece was performed by a choir, and these are sometimes included even when it is sung by a soloist.

George Gershwin (1898–1937)

I Got Rhythm, from *Girl Crazy*

Broadway show song

1930

CD 12|79 CD 6|32

[Instrumental Introduction]

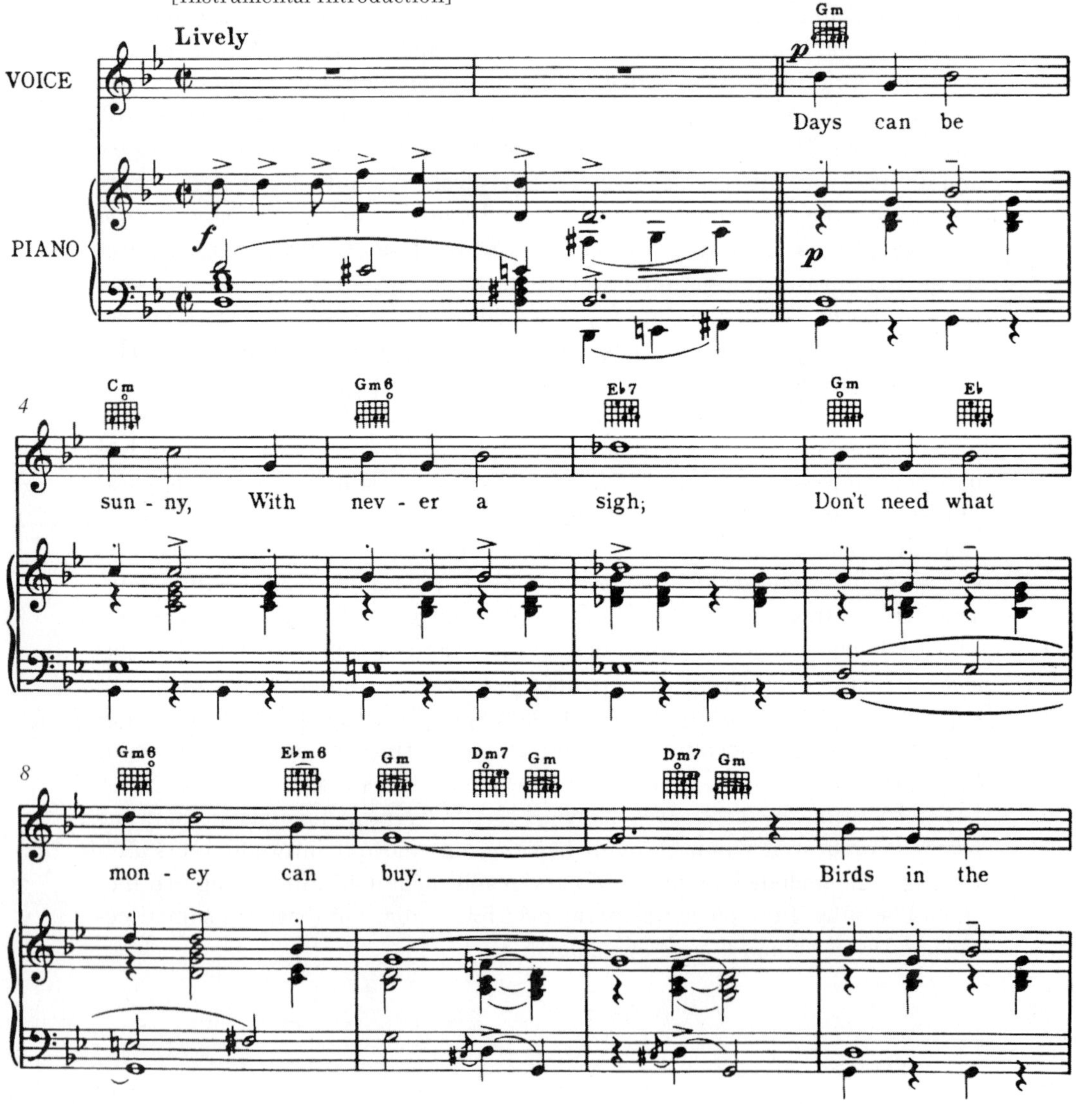

80 33

Lively

VOICE

PIANO

Days can be sun - ny, With nev - er a sigh; Don't need what mon - ey can buy. Birds in the

12
Cm
Gm6
E♭7
Gm
Gm7
tree sing Their day - ful of song, Why should - n't
16
Cm7
F7
B♭
Fm7
B♭
Fm7
B♭
D
D7
we sing a - long?
I'm chip - per
sf
20
Faug5
D7
Cm7
E♭7
D
D7
all the day, Hap - py with my lot. How do I
sf
24
Faug5
D7
Cm7
F7
Edim
G♭7
F7
B♭m6
Ddim
F7
get that way? Look at what I've got:
f

81 34

REFRAIN (with abandon)
29
p-mf
B♭ B♭6 Cm7 F7 B♭6 Edim Cm7 F7
I — got rhy - thm, I — got mu - sic, —
33
B♭ B♭6 Cm7 F7 E♭m6 B♭ F7 B♭ C♯dim F7
I — got my man — Who could ask for an - y - thing more?
37
B♭ B♭6 Cm7 F7 B♭6 Edim Cm7 F7 B♭ B♭6
I — got dais - ies — In — green pas - tures, — I — got
42
Cm7 F7 E♭m6 B♭ F7 B♭ D7 Am7
my man Who could ask for an - y - thing more? Old — Man

46
Fm6 D7 G Daug 5 Dm G7 C7 Gm7 Ebm6 C9
Troub - le, I don't mind him, You won't find him
51
C7-5 F7 C7 F7 Bb Bb6 Cm7 F7 Bb6 Edim
'Round my door. I got star - light, I got
56
Cm7 F7 Bb Bb6 Cm7 F7 Ebm Bb Fm
sweet dreams, I got my man Who could ask for an - y-thing
60
G7 C7 F7 1. Bb Ab Gb Db 2. Bb
more, Who could ask for an - y-thing more? more?
sfz
8

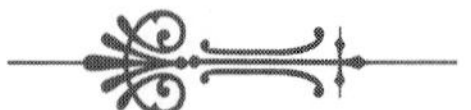

George Gershwin composed *I Got Rhythm*, with lyrics by his brother Ira, for the Broadway musical *Girl Crazy*, which premiered on October 14, 1930, at the Alvin Theater. George typically composed the melody first, and Ira then fitted it with lyrics, the practice also of several other Tin Pan Alley and Broadway songwriting teams. The show introduced Ginger Rogers and Ethel Merman, who became stars on Broadway and in the movies. Merman debuted *I Got Rhythm* in the role of Frisco Kate and later recorded the song in the version heard on the accompanying recordings. The song was published in 1930 in the version reproduced here, arranged with piano accompaniment and with guitar chords and fingerings.

Gershwin laid out *I Got Rhythm* in standard Tin Pan Alley form: verse plus thirty-two-bar chorus with phrases in an AABA' pattern (plus a two-bar tag). Following the trend at the time, the work has only one verse, and the main emphasis in the song is on the chorus, which is immediately repeated. To provide a clear contrast of mood and style, Gershwin set the verse and chorus in different keys. The verse begins in G minor, but modulates to the relative major, B♭, which remains the key area of the A sections of the chorus. The B section of the chorus, called the "bridge," shifts to the mediant, D major, and then travels down the circle of fifths to get back to B♭ in the final A section of the chorus. Ira's lyrics are fresh, modern, optimistic, and slangy, as they are in most of his songs; the opening phrase, for example, is not "I've got" or "I have," but the grammatically incorrect yet catchy "I got." Ira matches George's heavily syncopated rhythm with a punchy text that allows every syllable to be stressed (as in the first four measures of the chorus).

I Got Rhythm was an immediate popular hit, and not only in its original form. Instrumental versions based on the song's chorus began to appear, and soon this song became a jazz standard. However, in jazz performances of the song, it is not the melody that is the focus; rather, jazz performers have valued the harmony, which provided the framework for their improvisations. The "changes" (the jazz term for a specific harmonic progression) of this song became the basis for so many new jazz tunes in the following decades that this particular chord progression came to be known simply as "rhythm changes" (short for "the *I Got Rhythm* changes"). NAWM 172, Duke Ellington's *Cotton Tail*, is one example of a new jazz tune built over this harmonic progression.

Typically, the scores of Tin Pan Alley songs and indeed of most popular songs are merely guidelines for performance. The two-measure introduction can be repeated indefinitely as a vamp to set the stage for the singer. In Merman's recording, the band plays the entire melody of the chorus before returning to the two opening measures as written. Merman then enters with the verse, and follows with the chorus. The recording captures Merman's trademark nasal, chest-voiced performing style, nearly spoken delivery, and textual additions, such as interpolating the words "hanging 'round my front or back door" in the final statement of the chorus. The performance concludes with Merman's signature flourish: punching the final note of the chorus up a fifth and holding it for several measures as the orchestra finishes the melody.

Bessie Smith (1894–1937)

Back Water Blues

Blues

1927

CD 12|82 CD 6|35

1. When it rains five days and the skies turn dark at night,
When it rains five days and the skies turn dark at night,
Then trouble's takin' place in the lowlands at night.

2. I woke up this mornin', can't even get out of my door.
I woke up this mornin', can't even get out of my door.
That's enough trouble to make a poor girl wonder where she want to go.

3. Then they rowed a little boat about five miles 'cross the farm.
Then they rowed a little boat about five miles 'cross the farm.
I packed all my clothes, throwed them in and they rowed me along.

4. When it thunders and lightnin', and the wind begins to blow,
When it thunders and lightnin', and the wind begins to blow,
There's thousands of people ain't got no place to go.

5. Then I went and stood upon some high old lonesome hill.
Then I went and stood upon some high old lonesome hill.
Then looked down on the house where I used to live.

6. Back-water blues done caused me to pack my things and go.
   Back-water blues done caused me to pack my things and go.
   'Cause my house fell down and I can't live there no more.

7. (Moan . . .) I can't move no more,
   (Moan . . .) I can't move no more,
   There ain't no place for a poor old girl to go.

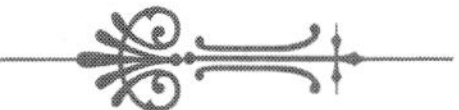

Bessie Smith, known as the "Empress of the Blues," wrote both lyrics and music for her hit song *Back Water Blues.* Columbia Records marketed Smith's recording, made on February 2, 1927, as a response to a flood in Mississippi in April of 1927, and it became one of her best-known records. She had composed the song several months earlier after a flood on Christmas Day, 1926, in Nashville, where she sang in a show a few days after the flood. As is true for much early blues, the text can be understood as a complaint against racial oppression and poverty.

Smith constructed the song in conventional blues form. Each of the seven stanzas shares the same AAB poetic form: the second line repeats the first, followed by a new line of poetry with the same end rhyme. The rhyme is often a near-rhyme, as in the pairing of "go" with "more" in the last two verses; the quality of the vowel is always more important than the ending consonants. The last line of each stanza either completes the thought begun by the first or packs a surprise by offering new information, as in the sixth verse.

Each stanza follows the form of a twelve-bar blues, with four measures for each line of poetry and a general harmonic pattern of tonic chords in the first phrase, subdominant to tonic in the second, and dominant to tonic in the third. After a brief piano introduction, the harmony settles into the tonic for four measures, with the piano moving to the subdominant in the second measure, as sometimes occurs in the form. The next four-measure phrase begins on the subdominant, moving back to the tonic after two measures. For the final line of the stanza, in measures 9–12 of the blues pattern, the harmony moves to the dominant for a measure, then to the subdominant (with added ninth and seventh) before moving back to the tonic for the final two measures. Each phrase of melody lingers around the fifth degree of the scale, decorating or repeating it, and then descends to the tonic. Here, as in many blues, the voice begins just before the first measure of each phrase and cadences on the third measure, allowing space in the third and fourth measures for the pianist to respond in an evocation of the call-and-response structure typical of African-American group singing.

The twelve-bar blues is a flexible harmonic pattern, used as a general framework. Exact adherence to the chords specified here is not crucial; rather, it is the combination of the harmonic framework, use of blue notes (flatted thirds and sevenths, sometimes also flatted fifths), poetic structure, and general mood that together give life to the blues.

The sheet music included here is merely an approximation for the performance, as Smith's recording reveals. Many blues were performed and recorded before they were written down in notation, and there are elements of the performance that the notation is not well equipped to capture. Smith sings a somewhat different melody for each verse, emphasizing the blue notes and altering the rhythm to fit the words of each stanza while following the same basic melodic shape. Pianist James P. Johnson, famed as an exponent of the stride piano style, responds to Smith's phrases with improvised additions of his own. Some of his figurations respond to the text, as when during the fourth stanza he produces a dramatic, downward skipping bass line to imitate the thunder, lightning, and blowing wind. His rocking accompaniment in the left hand throughout most of the song seems to suggest a reassurance that time and life go on and the flood will subside.

King Oliver [Joe Oliver] (1885–1938)

171

West End Blues, as performed by Louis Armstrong and His Hot Five

Blues

RECORDED 1928

(a) Original sheet music [not on recording]

15
3
way to the West End, And there's where troub - les will be - gin;
way to the West End, To lose those ug - ly West End blues,
3
Chorus
p-f
19
My man, my dan, low down, Mean houn' In
p-f
23
town with my best friend, run-nin' a - roun' Soon the
27
un - der-tak - er man, gon - na knock u - pon his door,

31
Folks in West End, Folks in West End,
35
Gon - na see some shoot-in' Like they nev - er have seen be - fore,
38
I mean my man and my best friend will nev - er cheat in West End an - y -
41
1.
more. My
2.
more.

(b) Transcription of recording by Louis Armstrong and His Hot Five

CD 12|83

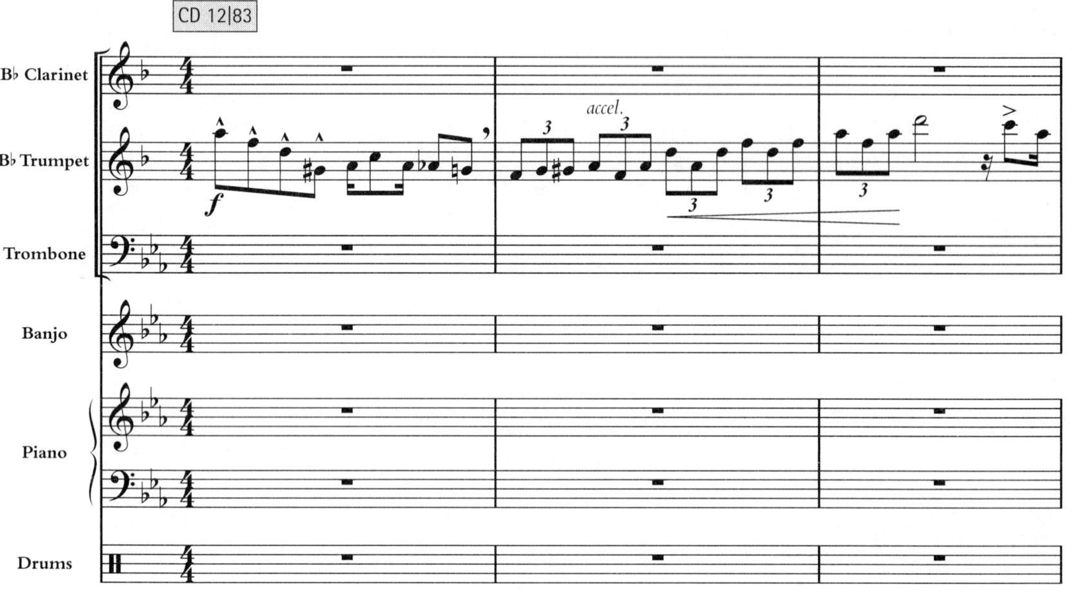

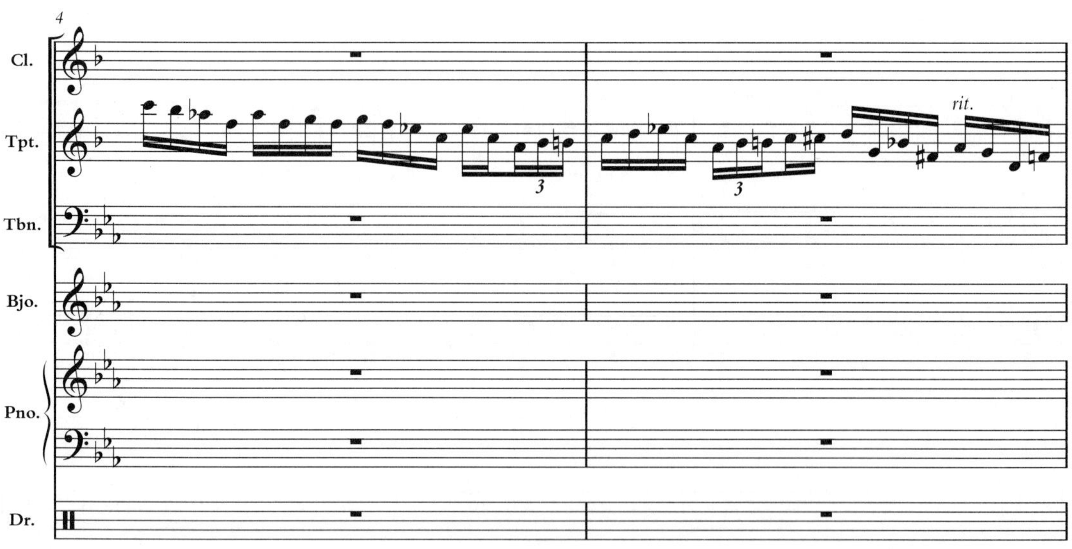

♩ = 84
Cl.
Tpt.
Tbn.
Bjo.
Pno.
Dr.
B♭+7
E♭
(play 1/4 notes throughout)
Brushes (snare)
simile
mf
lip
E♭7
A♭

13
Cl.
Tpt.
Tbn.
Bjo.
Pno.
Dr.
A♭m
E♭
G♭°7
16
84
B♭7
E♭
E♭7
A♭
B7
F7
B♭+7

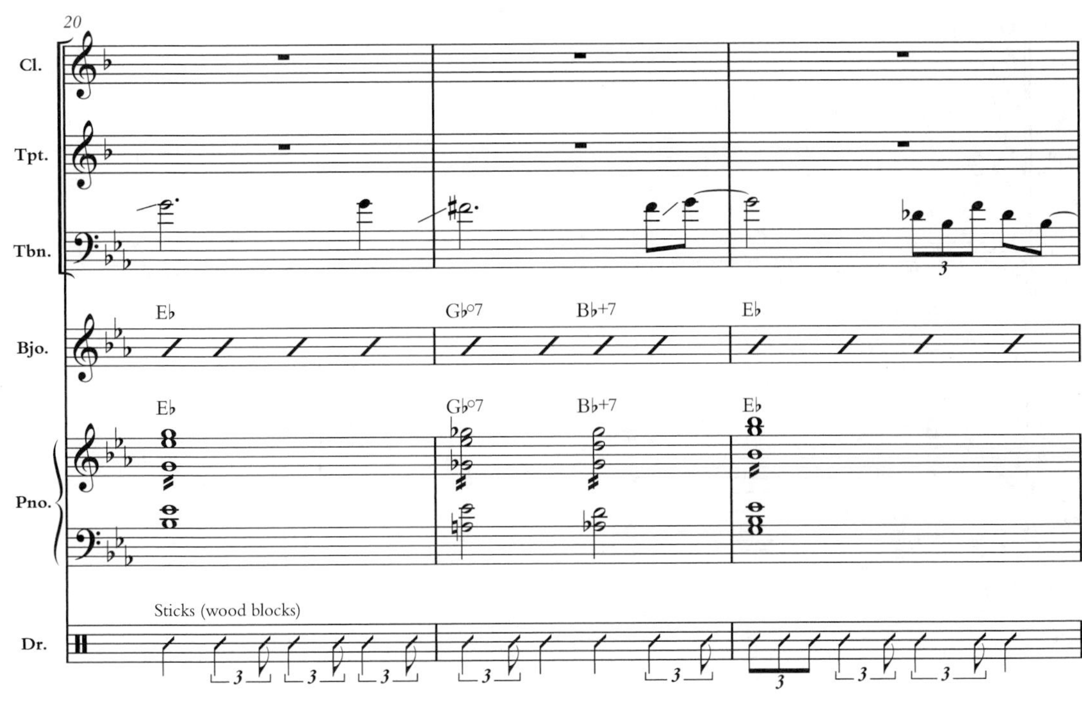
20
Cl.
Tpt.
Tbn.
Bjo.
Pno.
Dr.
Eb
Gb°7
Bb+7
Eb
Sticks (wood blocks)

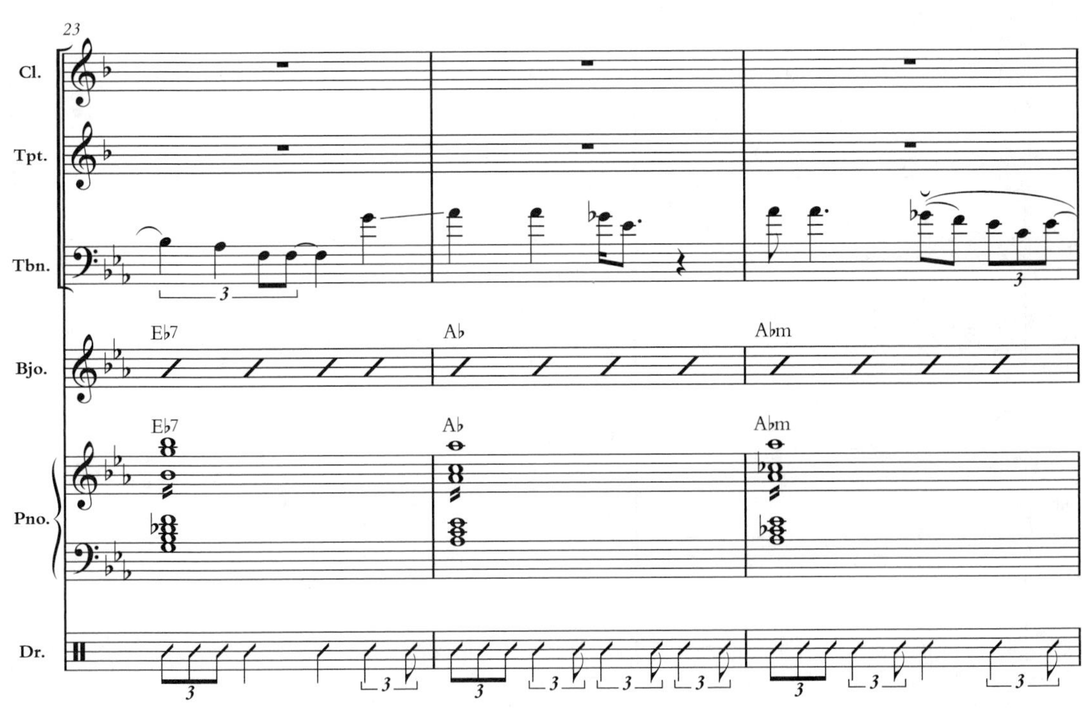
23
Cl.
Tpt.
Tbn.
Bjo.
Pno.
Dr.
Eb7
Ab
Abm

26
Cl.
Tpt.
Tbn.
Bjo.
Pno.
Dr.
E♭ G♭°7 B♭7
29
85
B♭7 E♭ E♭7 G♭°7 Fm7(♭5) E♭ F9 B♭7 B♭7+5

32
Cl.
Voice (actual pitch a 9th below)
Tpt.
Tbn.
E♭
Bjo.
E♭
simile
Pno.
Dr.

35
Cl.
Tpt.
Tbn.
E♭7
A♭
A♭m (major on recording)
Bjo.
E♭7
A♭
A♭m (major on recording)
Pno.
Dr.

38
Cl.
Tpt.
Tbn.
Bjo.
Pno.
Dr.
E♭
B♭7

41
86
Cl.
Tpt.
Tbn.
Bjo.
Pno.
Dr.
E♭ E♭7 G♭°7 Fm7(♭5) E♭ E°7 B♭7

44
Cl.
Tpt.
Tbn.
Bjo.
8va
3
Pno.
Ped.
Dr.

46
Cl.
Tpt.
Tbn.
Bjo.
8va
15ma
3
7
Pno.
Ped.
Dr.

48
Cl.
Tpt.
Tbn.
Bjo.
(8va)
8va
f
Pno.
Ped.
Ped.
Ped.
Ped.
Dr.

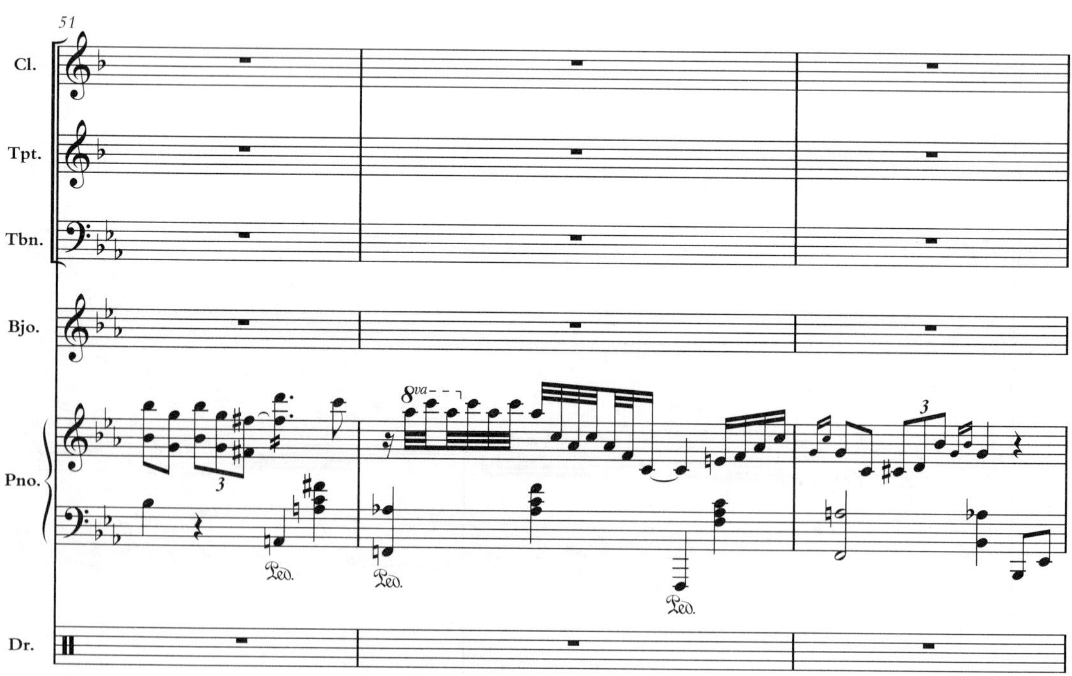
51
Cl.
Tpt.
Tbn.
Bjo.
3
8va
3
Pno.
Ped.
Ped.
Ped.
Dr.

87
54
Cl.
Tpt.
mf
Tbn.
Bjo.
Pno.
Dr.

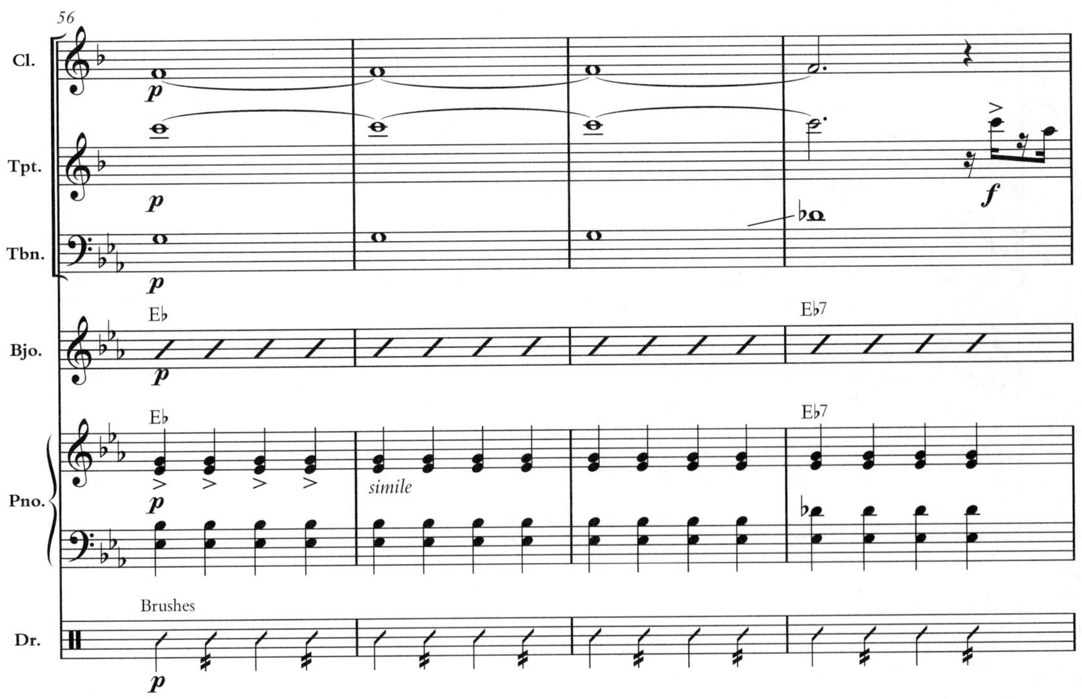
56
Cl.
p
Tpt.
p
f
Tbn.
p
E♭
E♭7
Bjo.
p
E♭
E♭7
Pno.
p
simile
Brushes
Dr.
p

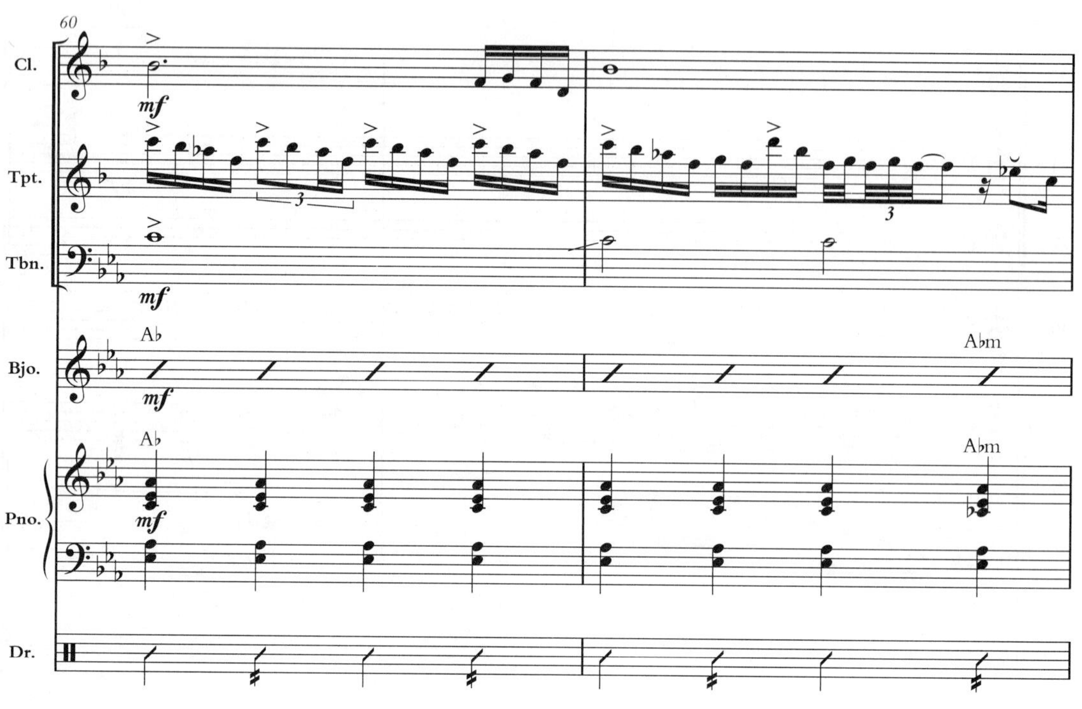
60
Cl.
Tpt.
Tbn.
Bjo.
Pno.
Dr.
mf
A♭
A♭m
3

62
Cl.
Tpt.
Tbn.
Bjo.
Pno.
Dr.
E♭
G♭°7
3

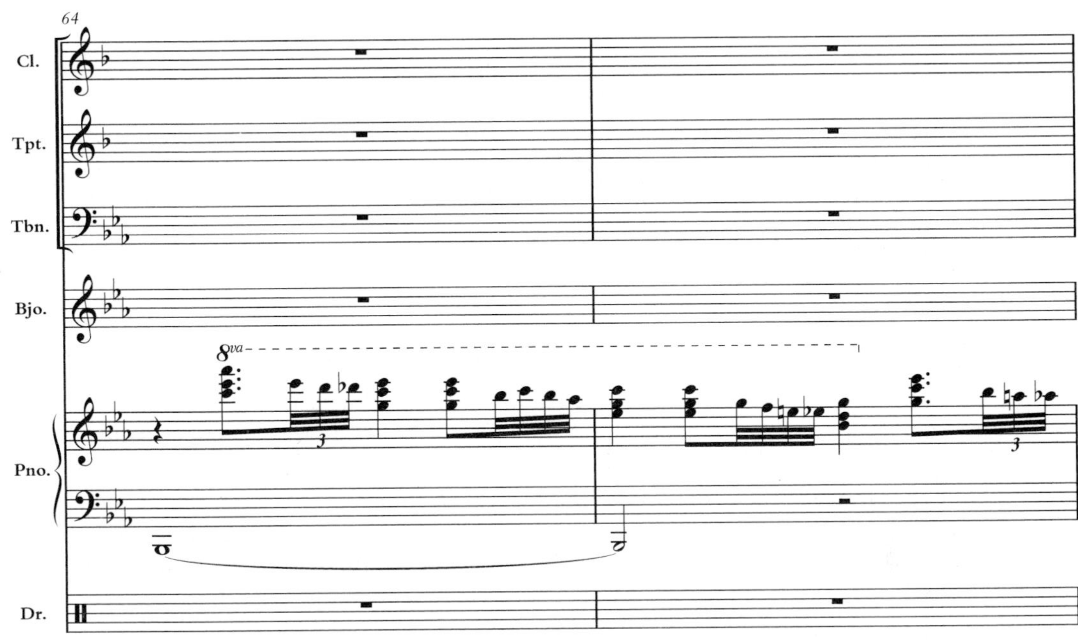
64
Cl.
Tpt.
Tbn.
Bjo.
8va
3
Pno.
Dr.

66
rit.
Cl.
Tpt.
Tbn.
p
A♭
B7
E♭
Bjo.
3
Pno.
8vb
Pop Cymbals
Dr.

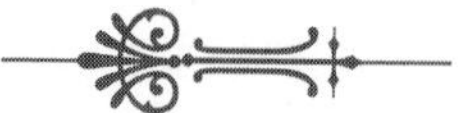

In the period between the two world wars, jazz and other types of popular music were sold both as recordings by star performers and as sheet music for amateurs to play at home or for other musicians to use in their own performances. These two versions of *West End Blues* illustrate the difference between the two formats, as well as the ways jazz performers used the songs they played as the basis for improvisation.

NAWM 171a shows the sheet music for *West End Blues* as composed and published in 1928 by Joe "King" Oliver (music) and Clarence Williams (lyrics). Typical of the popular songs in sheet music of the time, this song begins with a brief piano introduction and is laid out in verse-refrain form. The two bars leading into the first verse are labeled "Vamp," an instruction to the accompanist to keep repeating these measures until the singer joins in. The music for the verse is built over one complete statement of a twelve-bar blues progression (compare NAWM 170). The refrain, to be sung after each verse, presents two successive statements of the twelve-bar blues. Each time through the twelve-bar progression, Oliver writes a different melody and varies the harmony slightly, creating greater variety. The rhythm often features dotted eighths and sixteenths, a written approximation to the swinging rhythms typical of jazz, in which even eighth notes are played in a uneven pattern alternating long and short notes.

The same year Oliver and Williams wrote *West End Blues*, Louis Armstrong and His Hot Five—with Armstrong on trumpet backed by Jimmy Strong on clarinet, Fred Robinson on trombone, Earl Hines on piano, Mancy Cara on banjo, and Zutty Singleton on drums—recorded an instrumental version for OKeh Records in Chicago. This recording is on the accompanying CD set, and it is transcribed in NAWM 171b. The parts for the B♭ clarinet and B♭ trumpet both sound a whole step lower than written.

In place of the piano introduction, the recorded version begins with a virtuosic solo by Armstrong that spirals up to near the top of the trumpet's range and then cascades down to end near the bottom. The recorded version has no verse-refrain structure; it has, instead, five statements of the twelve-bar blues pattern, in which members of the group take turn playing solos that are either improvised or in the style of improvisation. In jazz parlance, each such statement is called a *chorus* (derived from, but different from, the alternate term for the refrain of a popular song). To mark the end of each chorus, the musicians substitute for the tonic chord that usually occupies the last two measures of a twelve-bar blues a quickly-moving chord progression known as a *turnaround*, which leads from the tonic to the dominant and prepares for the next chorus.

The entire ensemble plays the first chorus together, with Armstrong taking the melody—a flexible, freely decorated version of the vocal melody of the original song's verse that begins in utter simplicity, becomes more embellished with each phrase, and ends with the rising spirals from the introduction to close on a trilled high C (sounding B♭). The second chorus features Robinson on trombone, beginning with the opening notes of the chorus and then introducing new variations.

He is backed by the rhythm section of piano, banjo, and drum set, here played mostly on wood blocks. The third rendition of the blues progression features the clarinet alternating in call and response with Armstrong, who puts down his trumpet and sings in a novelty vocal style that he had made popular: he "scats," singing nonsense syllables to an improvised melody, making his voice sound like an instrument. Hines solos on the piano in the fourth chorus, alternating between two styles of playing in the right hand: rapid, elaborate figurations that resemble the passagework of classical pianists (compare NAWM 127 and 128) and syncopated melody in what has been called his "trumpet style." In the latter style, he often reinforces the melody in octaves (measures 48–51) or embellishes it with tremolos or quickly alternating notes (measures 51–53) that simulate the vibrato, trills, and grace notes of trumpet or clarinet players. The entire ensemble returns for the fifth and final chorus. Once again, Armstrong takes the lead, holding a single high pitch—the high C that concluded his first chorus—for four measures, then filling the next four bars with a virtuosic burst of inventive improvisation, repeating a descending figure five times and then extending and embellishing it. He cedes the stage to Hines for one last brief piano solo, and then the performance ends with a brief cadential tag.

This recording of *West End Blues* exemplifies two of Armstrong's innovative techniques that were seminal to the development of jazz. The first was scat singing, which allowed a voice to imitate an instrument. Scat remains an important technique for jazz singers. Armstrong also quickly became known as an outstanding soloist and paved the way for dynamic, improvised jazz solos, a crucial element of jazz's musical language.

172

Duke Ellington (1899–1974)

Cotton Tail

Jazz composition (contrafact)

1940

Duke Ellington, *Cotton Tail*, as recorded by Duke Ellington and His Orchestra on May 4, 1940. Transcribed by David Berger, edited by Brian Almeter.

5
A. Sax 1
A. Sax 2
T. Sax 1
T. Sax 2
B. Sax
Tpt. 1
mf
Tpt. 2
Tpt. 3
mf
Tbn. 1
Tbn. 2
mf
Tbn. 3
mf
Gtr.
B♭7(♭5) E♭ E♭m B♭/F F7(♭5) C7 F7(+5)
Pno.
B♭7(♭5) E♭ E♭m B♭/F F7(♭5) C7 F7(+5)
Bass
B♭7(♭5) E♭ E♭m B♭/F F7(♭5) C7 F7(+5)
Dr.

9
A. Sax 1
A. Sax 2
T. Sax 1
T. Sax 2
B. Sax
Tpt. 1
Tpt. 2
Tpt. 3
Tbn. 1
Tbn. 2
Tbn. 3
Gtr.
Pno.
Bass
Dr.
B♭ G-7 C-7 F7 B♭ G-7 C-7 F7

13
A. Sax 1
A. Sax 2
T. Sax 1
T. Sax 2
B. Sax
Tpt. 1
Tpt. 2
Tpt. 3
Tbn. 1
Tbn. 2
Tbn. 3
Gtr.
Pno.
Bass
Dr.
B♭7(♭5) E♭ E♭m B♭/F F7(♭5) C7 F7 B♭
f

17
A. Sax 1
A. Sax 2
T. Sax 1
T. Sax 2
B. Sax
Tpt. 1
Tpt. 2
Tpt. 3
Tbn. 1
Tbn. 2
Tbn. 3
Gtr.
Pno.
Bass
Dr.
D7♭9
G7(+5)
G7♯9
3
f

21
A. Sax 1
A. Sax 2
T. Sax 1
T. Sax 2
B. Sax
mf
Tpt. 1
Tpt. 2
Tpt. 3
Tbn. 1
Tbn. 2
Tbn. 3
C7(+5)
C7♭9
Fsus7
Gtr.
Pno.
Bass
To Sticks
Hi-Hat
Dr.

25
B
A. Sax 1
A. Sax 2
T. Sax 1
T. Sax 2
B. Sax
tr
Tpt. 1
Tpt. 2
Tpt. 3
f
mf
Tbn. 1
Tbn. 2
Tbn. 3
Gtr.
Pno.
Bass
Dr.
B♭7 A7 A♭7 G7 G♭7 F7 B♭ G♭7 F7

2 37

29

C

To Clarinet

T. Sax 1

T. Sax 2

mp

C

Gtr. B♭ G-7 C-7 F7 B♭ G-7 C-7 F7

Pno. B♭ G-7 C-7 F7 B♭ G-7 C-7 F7

Bass B♭ G-7 C-7 F7 B♭ G-7 C-7 F7

Dr.

37
T. Sax 2
vib.
3
Gtr.
Pno.
Bass
Dr.
Bb G-7 C-7 F7 Bb G-7 C-7 F7
41
T. Sax 1
T. Sax 2
Clarinet
mf
vib.
f
Tpt. 1
Tpt. 3
Tbn. 3
Bb7 Eb Ebm Bb Abmaj7

45
D
A. Sax 1
A. Sax 2
T. Sax 1
T. Sax 2
3
3
B. Sax
D
Tpt. 1
Tpt. 2
Tpt. 3
D
Tbn. 1
Tbn. 2
Tbn. 3
D
D7
G7
Gtr.
D7
G7
Pno.
D7
G7
Bass
Dr.

49
T. Sax 1
T. Sax 2
Tpt. 1
Tpt. 2
open
Tpt. 3
Tbn. 3
ff
C7
F7
B7
Gtr.
Pno.
Bass
Dr.
53
vib.
B♭
G-7
C-7
F7

57
A. Sax 1
A. Sax 2
T. Sax 1
T. Sax 2
B. Sax
Tpt. 1
Tpt. 2
Tpt. 3
Tbn. 1
Tbn. 2
Tbn. 3
Gtr.
Pno.
Bass
Dr.
ff
B♭7
E♭
E♭m
B♭
F7(+5)

3 38

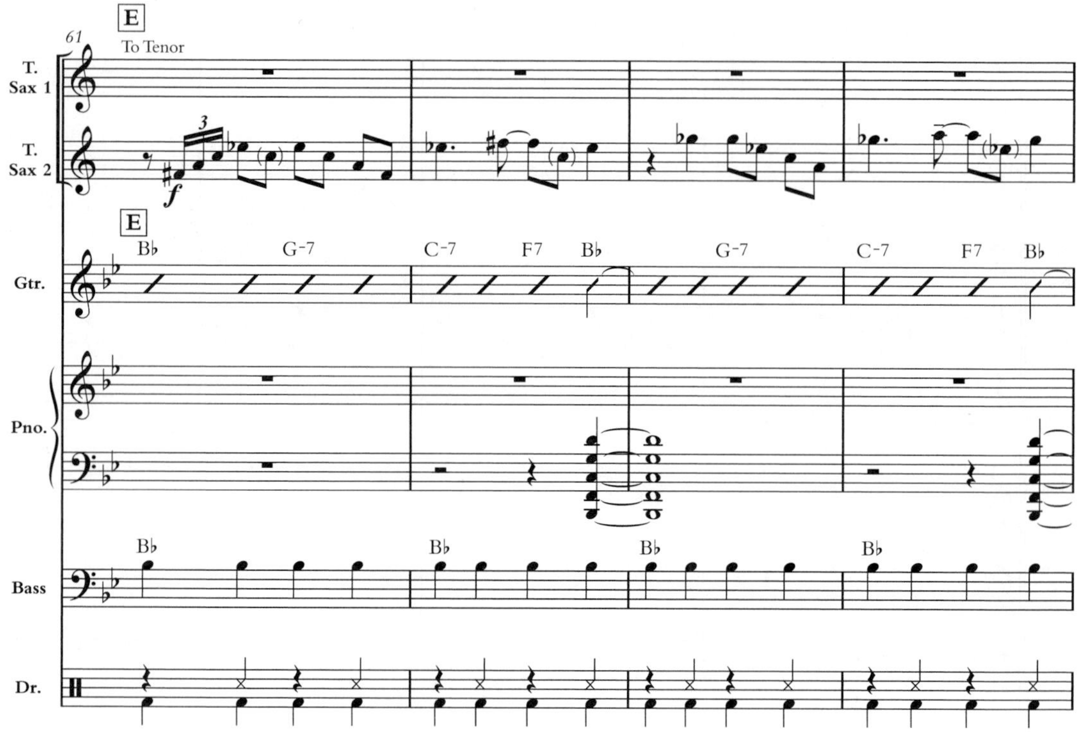

E
61
To Tenor
T. Sax 1
T. Sax 2
Gtr.
Pno.
Bass
Dr.
B♭ G-7 C-7 F7 B♭ G-7 C-7 F7 B♭
B♭ B♭ B♭ B♭

65
Growl
T. Sax 2
Gtr.
Pno.
Bass
Dr.
G-7 C-7 F7 B♭ G-7 B♭
B♭ B♭ B♭ B♭

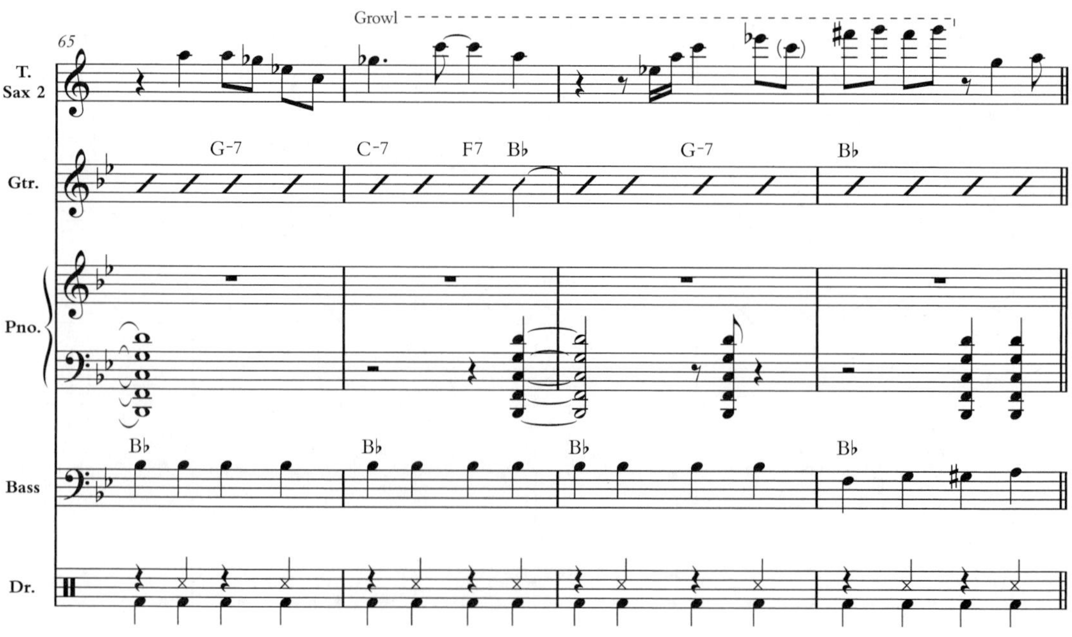

69
T. Sax 2
Wide Vib.
Gtr.
Pno.
Bass
Dr.
B♭
G-7
C-7
F7

73
T. Sax 2
Gtr.
Pno.
Bass
Dr.
B♭7
E♭
E♭m
B7(♭5)
B♭
F7
Hi-Hat
cont. Hi-Hat

77
A. Sax 1
A. Sax 2
T. Sax 1
T. Sax 2
B. Sax
Tpt. 1
Tpt. 2
Tpt. 3
Tbn. 1
Tbn. 2
Tbn. 3
Gtr.
Pno.
Bass
Dr.
f
D7
G7

81
A. Sax 1
A. Sax 2
T. Sax 1
T. Sax 2
B. Sax
Tpt. 1
Tpt. 2
Tpt. 3
Tbn. 1
Tbn. 2
Tbn. 3
C7
B7/F
F7
Gtr.
Pno.
Bass
Dr.

85
T. Sax 2
Gtr.
Pno.
Bass
Dr.
B♭ G-7 C-7 F7 B♭ G-7 C-7 F7

89
T. Sax 2
Gtr.
Pno.
Bass
Dr.
B♭7 E♭ E°7 B♭ G-7 C-7 F7(+5)
mp

4
39
93
F
A. Sax 1
A. Sax 2
T. Sax 1
T. Sax 2
B. Sax
Lead
Tpt. 1
Tpt. 2
Tpt. 3
Tbn. 1
Tbn. 2
Tbn. 3
Gtr.
Pno.
Bass
Dr.
f
B♭7 C-7 F7 B♭ A°7 Gm7 G♭7 Cm7(♭5) F7
cont. Hi-Hat, Hi-Hat backbeat

97
A. Sax 1
A. Sax 2
T. Sax 1
T. Sax 2
B. Sax
Tpt. 1
Tpt. 2
Tpt. 3
Tbn. 1
Tbn. 2
Tbn. 3
Gtr.
Pno.
Bass
Dr.
B♭7 B♭m E♭m6 B♭ A7 G-7 C7 F7 C7

101
A. Sax 1
A. Sax 2
T. Sax 1
T. Sax 2
B. Sax
Tpt. 1
Tpt. 2
Tpt. 3
Tbn. 1
Tbn. 2
Tbn. 3
Gtr.
Pno.
Bass
Dr.
B♭ D♭°7 C-7 F7(+5) B♭7 F6 G°7 G♭7 F7

105
A. Sax 1
A. Sax 2
T. Sax 1
T. Sax 2
B. Sax
Tpt. 1
Tpt. 2
Tpt. 3
Tbn. 1
Tbn. 2
Tbn. 3
Gtr.
Pno.
Bass
Dr.
B♭ Dm7(♭5) E♭ E°7 F7(+5) B♭ B°7 E♭7 C7(+5) F7 B♭

G
Solo
109
B. Sax
D7
G7
Gtr.
D7
G7
Bass
Hi-Hat
cont. Hi-Hat
Dr.
113
B. Sax
C7
F7
Gtr.
C7
F7
Bass
Dr.
117
H
B. Sax
B♭
G-7
C-7
F7
B♭
G-7
C-7
F7
Gtr.
Pno.
B♭
G-7
C-7
F7
B♭
G-7
C-7
F7
Bass
Dr.

5 40

121
A. Sax 1
A. Sax 2
Tenor
T. Sax 1
T. Sax 2
B. Sax
Tpt. 1
Tpt. 2
Tpt. 3
Tbn. 1
Tbn. 2
Tbn. 3
B♭7
E♭
F7
B♭
F7
Gtr.
Pno.
B♭7
E♭
F7
B♭
F7
Bass
Dr.

125
I
A. Sax 1
A. Sax 2
T. Sax 1
T. Sax 2
B. Sax
I
Tpt. 1
Tpt. 2
Tpt. 3
I
Tbn. 1
Tbn. 2
Tbn. 3
I
Bb C7 F7 C-7 A7 F7(+5) Bb Gm6 Gm7 B7 C7 F7(b9)
Gtr.
Pno.
Bass
ad lib., crosstick on snare
Dr.

129
A. Sax 1
A. Sax 2
T. Sax 1
T. Sax 2
B. Sax
Tpt. 1
Tpt. 2
Tpt. 3
Tbn. 1
Tbn. 2
Tbn. 3
Gtr.
Pno.
Bass
Dr.
B♭7 E♭7 E♭m B♭ F7 C7(♭9) F7(♭9) B♭6 F7

133
J
A. Sax 1
A. Sax 2
T. Sax 1
T. Sax 2
B. Sax
Tpt. 1
Tpt. 2
Tpt. 3
Tbn. 1
Tbn. 2
Tbn. 3
Gtr.
Pno.
Bass
Dr.
B♭ G-7 C-7 G♭7(♭5) F7 B♭ G-7 C7 F7

137
A. Sax 1
A. Sax 2
T. Sax 1
T. Sax 2
B. Sax
Tpt. 1
Tpt. 2
Tpt. 3
Tbn. 1
Tbn. 2
Tbn. 3
Gtr.
Pno.
Bass
Dr.
B♭7
E♭
E♭7(♭5)
B♭ F7(+5) B♭7 F7
E♭7 A7 B♭

141
K
A. Sax 1
A. Sax 2
T. Sax 1
T. Sax 2
B. Sax
K
Tpt. 1
Tpt. 2
Tpt. 3
K
Tbn. 1
Tbn. 2
Tbn. 3
K
D7 D7 D°7 D7 G7 F♯7 G7
Gtr.
D7 D7 D°7 D7 G7 F♯7 G7
Pno.
D7 D7 D°7 D7 G7 F♯7 G7
Bass
Dr.

145
A. Sax 1
A. Sax 2
T. Sax 1
T. Sax 2
B. Sax
Tpt. 1
Tpt. 2
Tpt. 3
Tbn. 1
Tbn. 2
Tbn. 3
Gtr.
Pno.
Bass
Dr.
C7
Gm7(♭5)
C7
F7
E7
F7
Hi-Hat

149
L
A. Sax 1
A. Sax 2
T. Sax 1
T. Sax 2
B. Sax
L
Tpt. 1
Tpt. 2
Tpt. 3
L
Tbn. 1
Tbn. 2
Tbn. 3
L
Gtr.
B♭ F-7 G-7 C-7 F7 E♭-7 B♭ F-7 G-7 G7 C7(♭9) F7
Pno.
B♭ F-7 G-7 C-7 F7 E♭-7 B♭ F-7 G-7 G7 C7(♭9) F7
Bass
B♭ F-7 G-7 C-7 F7 E♭-7 B♭ F-7 G-7 G7 C7(♭9) F7
Dr.
cont. Hi-Hat

6 41

153
A. Sax 1
A. Sax 2
T. Sax 1
T. Sax 2
B. Sax
Tpt. 1
Tpt. 2
Tpt. 3
Tbn. 1
Tbn. 2
Tbn. 3
Gtr.
Pno.
Bass
Dr.
ff
B♭ B♭7 E♭ E♭m B♭ G7 A°7 B♭ A7(♯9)

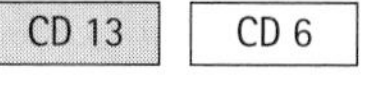

157 M

A. Sax 1 — *ff*

A. Sax 2 — *ff*

T. Sax 1 — *ff*

T. Sax 2 — *ff*

B. Sax — *ff*

M

Tpt. 1

Tpt. 2

Tpt. 3

M

Tbn. 1

Tbn. 2

Tbn. 3

M

Gtr. — B♭ G-7 | C-7 G♭7 F7 A7(♯9) | B♭ G-7 | C-7 F7(+5) A7(♯9)

Pno. — B♭ G-7 | C-7 G♭7 F7 A7(♯9) | B♭ G-7 | C-7 F7(+5) A7(♯9)

Bass — B♭ G-7 | C-7 G♭7 F7 A7(♯9) | B♭ G-7 | C-7 F7(+5) A7(♯9)

Dr.

161
A. Sax 1
A. Sax 2
T. Sax 1
T. Sax 2
B. Sax
Tpt. 1
Tpt. 2
Tpt. 3
Tbn. 1
Tbn. 2
Tbn. 3
Gtr.
Pno.
Bass
Dr.
f
ff
B♭7 B♭7(+5) E♭7 E♭m A7(♯9) B♭7 E♭ E♭m G-7 C7 F7 A7(♯9)

165
N
A. Sax 1
A. Sax 2
T. Sax 1
T. Sax 2
B. Sax
Tpt. 1
Tpt. 2
Tpt. 3
Tbn. 1
Tbn. 2
Tbn. 3
Gtr.
Pno.
Bass
Dr.
B♭ G-7 Gm6 E♭ F7 A7(♯9) B♭ G-7 Fsus7 F7(+5) A7(♯9)

169
A. Sax 1
A. Sax 2
T. Sax 1
T. Sax 2
B. Sax
Tpt. 1
Tpt. 2
Tpt. 3
Tbn. 1
Tbn. 2
Tbn. 3
B♭7
F7(+5) A7(+5)
B♭
Gtr.
Pno.
Bass
Dr.

173
O
A. Sax 1
A. Sax 2
T. Sax 1
T. Sax 2
B. Sax
O
Tpt. 1
Tpt. 2
Tpt. 3
O
Tbn. 1
Tbn. 2
Tbn. 3
O
D7 D7(♭9) E-9 G°7 A7(♯9) D7(♭9) G7 A♭7(♭9) B°7 D♭°7 E♭°7 F°7
Gtr.
D7 D7(♭9) E-9 G°7 A7(♯9) D7(♭9) G7 A♭7(♭9) B°7 D♭°7 E♭°7 F°7
Pno.
D7 D7(♭9) E-9 G°7 A7(♯9) D7(♭9) G7 A♭7(♭9) B°7 D♭°7 E♭°7 F°7
Bass
Dr.

177
A. Sax 1
A. Sax 2
T. Sax 1
T. Sax 2
B. Sax
Tpt. 1
Tpt. 2
Tpt. 3
Tbn. 1
Tbn. 2
Tbn. 3
Gtr.
Pno.
Bass
Dr.
C7 B7 C7 G7 D♭7 C7 F7 A7(+5) A♭7 G7(+5) G♭7(+5) F7(+5)

181
P
A. Sax 1
mf
A. Sax 2
T. Sax 1
T. Sax 2
B. Sax
mf
P
Tpt. 1
plunger/mute partly open (no inflections)
Tpt. 2
mf
Tpt. 3
P
Tbn. 1
mf
Tbn. 2
Tbn. 3
P
B♭ G-7 C-7 F7 B♭ G-7 C-7 F7
Gtr.
mf
B♭ G-7 C-7 F7 B♭ G-7 C-7 F7
Pno.
mf
B♭ G-7 C-7 F7 B♭ G-7 C-7 F7
Bass
mf
Dr.
mf

185
A. Sax 1
A. Sax 2
T. Sax 1
T. Sax 2
B. Sax
Tpt. 1
Tpt. 2
Tpt. 3
Tbn. 1
Tbn. 2
Tbn. 3
Gtr.
Pno.
Bass
Dr.
B♭7(♭5)
E♭
E♭m
B♭
F7(♭5)
C7
F7 B♭
Hi-Hat
rim click to end

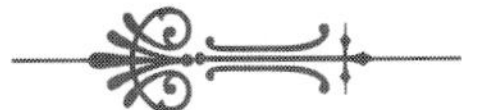

Throughout his career as a band leader and composer, Duke Ellington hired performers more for their individual sounds than for their ability to blend seamlessly into the ensemble, and he wrote music to showcase their particular abilities. In *Cotton Tail,* composed in 1940, Ellington took advantage of the talents of two new members of his band: virtuoso bassist Jimmy Blanton and tenor saxophonist Ben Webster. Both players brought new elements that Ellington incorporated into his own style. Blanton's bass playing is marked by fast-moving lines that reach high into the instrument's range and include many nonchord tones, helping to create contrapuntal textures, especially during the solos. His approach became the foundation for jazz bassists for over a generation and is still widely imitated. Webster began his career in Kansas City and played there with Bennie Moten's band, known for its fast, virtuosic playing and hot improvisation, a style that is evident in this solo.

Cotton Tail is a *contrafact,* a new tune composed over a harmonic progression borrowed from another song. Ellington composed a new melody (measures 1–28) to be played over the harmonic progression from the chorus of George Gershwin's *I Got Rhythm* (NAWM 169). Using a familiar harmonic progression was convenient, since players already knew the harmonies and could therefore extemporize with confidence, but adding a new tune and giving it a new name meant that no royalties had to be paid for recording or playing the original song. The harmonic progression from *I Got Rhythm* was used for more contrafacts than any other except the blues, in part because its structure provided interesting possibilities: the A phrases changed chords every half-measure, while the B section lingered on each chord for two measures, offering a strong contrast between rapid and slow harmonic rhythm (the pace of the harmonic progression). Ellington follows Gershwin's harmonies in general outline, but makes many small changes. For example, in measure 5, he underpins the unexpected E natural (equivalent to F♭, the flatted fifth) in the melody with a B♭^{7} chord with flatted fifth, enriched from a simple tonic B♭ major chord in the original. Later there are several passages in which the harmony is colored by substitute chords, though the overall structure of the progression is maintained.

After the opening statement of the new tune to Gershwin's progression (with its last eight-bar phrase shortened to four bars, measures 25–28), each subsequent statement, or chorus, of the AABA harmonic pattern is given different orchestration. The first two choruses (at measures 29 and 61) feature Ben Webster's blistering, agile solo on tenor sax, punctuated at times by chords from the band. Unlike most big-band solos of the time, which were composed or worked out in advance, Webster's is improvised, built at times from sequences (measures 29–32, 45–52, 61–66, and 77–84) or variation (measures 85–88) and at other times from seemingly free figuration, sometimes highlighted with the growls, rasps, or large vibrato that were among his signature sounds. His lines play off the four-measure phrasing and underlying harmonies but never obscure them, mixing syncopations and nonchord tones with enough notes that are on the beat and in the chord so that we never lose our orientation. Throughout, Blanton's bass line helps to drive the rhythm, adding contrapuntal interest and intensity as it climbs into a high range, even crossing above Webster in measures 31–33 (note that the bass sounds an octave lower than written, the tenor sax a major ninth lower than written).

The third chorus (measure 93) is divided into smaller units: the brass and rhythm sections play the first two A sections; Harry Carney on baritone sax takes the B section (measure 109); and Ellington himself rounds out the final A' with a brief piano solo. The fourth chorus (measure 125) features the reed section (saxophonists Webster, Carney, Barney Bigard, Otto Hardwick, and Johnny Hodges) in block chords (rhythmic unison). The fifth and final chorus (measure 157) is again divided. The first two A sections feature a trademark Ellington technique: brass and reed sections trading short, repeated melodic statements known as *riffs*, in call-and-response style. The entire band plays the B section, and the final A section returns to the tune from the beginning of the piece, with both reed and brass instruments playing the melody.

The accompanying CDs include the first recording of *Cotton Tail*, made on May 4, 1940, and featuring all the original musicians. The score shown here is a transcription from that recording. Thanks to rapid dissemination of the record, Webster's impressive solo became so associated with the tune that later musicians—and even Webster himself—refrained from improvising during the choruses and simply reproduced the solo note for note. In this way, recordings came to preserve performances, even improvised ones, in a form as permanent as notation.

Darius Milhaud (1892–1974)

La création du monde (The Creation of the World), Op. 81a: First tableau

173

Ballet

1923

CD 13|7

From Darius Milhaud, *La création du monde* (Paris: Max Eschig, 1969), 9–21.

16
Trp.
Trb.
1°
mp
Piano
C. cl.
T.in
G.C.
Sax.
C.B.
20
Trp.
Trb.
Piano
C.cl.
T.in
G.C.
Sax.
C.B.

8
24
Hb.
Bon
Cor
Trb.
Piano
B. de bois
Tambin
G.C.
Timb.
Vons
Sax.
Vlle
C.B.
f en dehors

28
Hb.
Cl.
à 2
f
Bon
f
Cor
f
Trb.
Piano
f
T. de basq.
Le trille indique le pouce, l'accent le coup frappé avec le poing
f
B. de bois
G.C.
Timb.
Vons
Sax.
f
Vlle
C.B.

32
Cl.
Bon
Cor
Piano
T. de B.
G C
Vons
Sax.
Vlle
C B.
36
Trp.
Trb.
à 2
gliss.

40
Cl.
Bon
Cor
Trp.
Trb.
gliss.
gliss.
Piano
T. de B.
G.C.
Vons
Sax.
Vlle
C.B.

9
44
Fl.
Cl.
Bon
Cor
Trp.
Trb.
Piano
T. de B.
Cymb.
C. cl.
G.C.
Timb.
Vons
Sax.
Vlle
C.B.
à 2
ff
gliss.
8a

48
Fl.
Cl.
Bon
Cor
Trp.
2o
Trb.
gliss.
Piano
Cymb.
C. cl.
G.C.
Timb.
Vons
Vlle
C.B.

52
Fl.
Cl.
Bon
Cor
Trp.
1o
2o
gliss.
Trb.
Piano
Cymb.
C.cl.
G C.
Timb.
Vons
fff
Vlle
C B.

56
Fl.
Cl.
Bon
Cor
Trp.
Trb.
gliss.
Piano
Cymb.
C.cl.
G.C.
Timb.
Vons
Vlle
C.B.
fff
pp
pp vibrez

During a concert tour to the United States in 1922–23, Darius Milhaud heard African-American jazz bands in Harlem and was profoundly affected by their music. Upon his return to Paris he proposed a ballet based on jazz style that would capitalize on the growing French interest in jazz and the continuing fashion for African art inspired by the French colonial presence in Africa. The result was *La création du monde,* written for the Ballets Suédois (Swedish Ballet), a company formed in Paris in 1920 that produced innovative collaborative projects along the lines of the Ballets Russes (see NAWM 164). Blaise Cendrars based the scenario on an African creation story, the cubist painter Fernand Léger designed the sets and costumes using African masks and figurines as models, and Jean Börlin created the choreography, drawing on African dance movements. The ballet premiered on October 25 to mixed reviews, but soon the piece was regarded as a pioneering blend of jazz and classical idioms. In 1926, Milhaud arranged the music as a concert suite for piano and string quartet, and it was published in both versions.

For Milhaud, jazz was an authentic expression of African-American experience, with roots in ancient African traditions. But it was also modern, up-to-date, and chic, in tune with the postwar French admiration for the brashness and vibrancy of American culture. By blending the raw energy of jazz with the classical European tradition, and particularly with the neoclassicism then current in France, Milhaud sought to meld the strengths of both in a fresh, modern idiom.

Milhaud scored the piece for an ensemble that reflects both traditions. It has the typical winds, brass, strings, and percussion of the European orchestra. But the strings are soloists, not orchestral sections, and he includes the sounds of a jazz band, with piano, lots of percussion, and a saxophone substituting for the viola.

The ballet begins with an overture, followed by five tableaux, of which the first is included here. Cendrars's scenario describes the scene:

> The curtain rises slowly on a dark stage. In the middle of the stage we see a confused mass of intertwined bodies: chaos prior to creation. Three giant dieties move slowly around the periphery. These are Nzame, Medere, and N'kva, the masters of creation. They hold counsel, circle around the formless mass, and utter magic incantations.

For this scene, Milhaud wrote a brief fugue in three sections, using a theme inspired by the blues scale and by the rhythms of jazz. The fugue was the quintessential contrapuntal form of the Baroque era, making the blend of jazz and classical traditions hard to miss. In addition, there are many of Milhaud's modernist traits, including *polytonality* (the superimposition of two or more keys at once) and *polyrhythm* (the superimposition of two or more metric or phrase groupings).

The first section (measures 1–23) is the fugal exposition:

- The piano and percussion establish a four-measure-long rhythmic ostinato, with a grouping of 3+3+3+3+4 beats marked by bass drum and piano that works against the notated meter. This evokes similar effects in ragtime (see the first four measures of Joplin's *Maple Leaf Rag,* NAWM 155).

- Over this, the contrabass enters in measure 3 with the fugue subject in D (sounding an octave lower than notated). The subject resembles a jazz riff, featuring short gestures that vary a basic idea. The rhythm includes the upbeats and syncopations typical of jazz, and the melody suggests blue notes on the third and seventh degrees of the scale by alternating minor and major forms and moving chromatically between them (see measures 4–6). The quick arpeggiation in the piano also has the blue third (F–F♯).
- After five measures, the trombone enters with the subject transposed to E (measures 8–13). The piano shifts to that chord, and the contrabass plays the countersubject, which also emphasizes blue thirds and sevenths.
- At measure 13, the E♭ alto saxophone presents the subject transposed to A (it sounds a major sixth lower than notated). The piano moves to A, as does the countersubject in the trombone. The contrabass introduces a second countersubject, which again plays on the blue third and seventh.
- At measure 18, the trumpet enters with the subject back on D, the piano shifts again, the saxophone takes up the countersubject and the trombone the second countersubject, and the contrabass harmonizes with the latter, adding to the mix yet another melody full of blue notes.

The process here is both a very proper fugue and a cunning imitation of the multiple layers of melody typical of group improvisation in New Orleans-style jazz of the early 1920s. The harmonic motion (I–II–V–I) evokes a standard progression in classical music but also hints at the I, IV–I, V–I progression of the twelve-bar blues. The rhythms are jazzy but also modern and polyrhythmic. The five-measure-long phrases established by the entrances of the fugue subject overlap the four-measure-long ostinato in piano and percussion, compounding the conflict of beat groupings mentioned above. As we will see, similar conflicts of phrase length appear throughout the tableau, suggesting that they are part of Milhaud's depiction of chaos.

The second section (measures 24–45) is not fugal, but superimposes material in layers:

- The section begins with a melody in D in cello and oboe (measures 24–28) that again features blue notes and derives from the tail end of the fugue subject (compare the contrabass in measures 6–8). It appears over three layers of ostinato with different cycles: (1) a pattern in parallel thirds in D major recurring every six beats (piano right hand, horn, and saxophone); (2) descending parallel triads in C major recurring every five beats (piano left hand, contrabass, trombone, and bassoon); and (3) D major/minor chords in violins and timpani with drum patterns, all recurring irregularly. The superimposition of two keys, C and D, is an instance of polytonality, which Milhaud uses frequently.
- In the rest of the section, the clarinet presents the fugue subject four times, shortened to four measures, in keys that travel up the circle of fifths: F (measure 29), C (measure 33), G (measure 37), and D (measure 41; note that the clarinet is in B♭ and sounds a whole step lower than written). The first and third of these statements reverse the major and minor thirds in

> the subject. The other instruments accompany with a repeating figuration that recurs in a 6+6+8 beat pattern, thus stretching over five measures, recreating the conflict of five- versus four-measure phrases from the first section. As part of this recurring idea, the bass line works its way down chromatically from F (measure 29) to C (measure 34) to G (measure 39), delaying the arrival on D until the first beat of the third section. Near the end of this progression, the trombone starts to add glissandi, a boisterous, jazzy touch (measures 39–45).

The third section (measures 46–59) returns to the tonic and combines elements from the other two sections. It begins with a varied restatement of the beginning of the second section, with elements rearranged; for example, the parallel triads are now in the D Dorian mode, the parallel third figure in the C Phrygian mode. In measure 50, these two parts of the texture return to their original relationship, and the fugue subject returns in the violins in its original key of D. At measure 54, the two violins are in stretto, with the fugue subject in the keys of A and D, while all the other parts reach a peak of intensity. Then, all of a sudden, the music quiets and moves on to the next tableau.

Throughout the ballet, Milhaud's synthesis of jazz and classical elements is masterful, showing that he understood jazz and blues well and saw how elements drawn from them could be used and reinterpreted in a neoclassical context. He was among the first classically trained composers to draw on jazz or blues, and he inspired many others to follow his example.

PAUL HINDEMITH (1895–1963)

Symphony Mathis der Maler: Second movement, *Grablegung* (Entombment)

Symphony

1933–34

CD 13|10

Sehr langsam (♩ etwa 54)

Große Flöten 1. 2.

Oboen 1. 2.

Klarinetten (B) 1. 2.

Fagotte 1. 2.

Hörner (F) 1. 2. 3. 4.

Trompeten (C) 1. 2.

Posaunen 1. 2. 3.

Baßtuba

Pauken

Schlagzeug

Sehr langsam (♩ etwa 54)

Violinen 1. 2.

Bratschen

Violoncelli

Kontrabässe

mit Dämpfer

p mp mf

From Paul Hindemith, *Sämtliche Werke*, vol. 2, fascicle 2, *Orchesterwerke 1932–34*, ed. Stephen Hinton (Mainz: B. Schott's Söhne, 1991), 114–19.

grFl
Klar (B)
Fg
Hr (F)
Vl
Br
Vc
Kb
zus.
nimmt kleine Flöte
mit Dämpfer
11
Ob
pizz.
dim.

18
grFl
Ob 1.
Vl 1. 2.
Br
pizz.
pp
mp
pp
cresc.
mp
23
grFl
Ob 1. 2.
Klar (B) 1. 2.
Hr (F) 1. 2. 3.
Trp 1. 2.
Pos 1. 2. 3.
Btb
Vl 1. 2.
Br
Vc
Kb
arco
mf
mp
cresc.
f

12
28
klFl
grFl
Ob
Klar (B)
Fg
Hr (F)
Trp
Pos
Bth
Pk
Vl
Br
Vc
Kb
f
mf
cresc.

32
13
klFl
grFl
Ob
Klar (B)
Fg
Hr (F)
Trp
Pos
Btb
Beck
Vl 1.
Vl 2.
Br
Vc
Kb
ff
mp
p
pp
f
mf

38
grFl
Ob
Klar (B)
Fg
zus.
Hr (F)
Btb
Vl 1.
Vl 2.
Br
Vc
Kb
f dim.
p
mf
dim.
pp
p dim.
cresc.
f
mf
pp

While Paul Hindemith was writing the libretto for his opera *Mathis der Maler* in 1933, he decided to compose some of the instrumental preludes and interludes for the opera and assemble them into an orchestral work that could be performed to promote the coming opera. This project had a political dimension. Many of his works had been banned from public performance by the new National Socialist (Nazi) government, because of their radical texts or modernist style, and as a result the opera was unlikely to be staged in Germany. But Hindemith planned to use a more widely accessible idiom in *Mathis der Maler* and saw the instrumental work as a way to attract support for producing the opera. The second movement, included here, was the first to be composed, in November 1933. The other movements—the overture as the first movement, and a finale consisting of the prelude and other passages destined for the opera's sixth tableau—were completed by February 1934, and the three-movement *Symphony Mathis der Maler* was premiered on March 12 by the Berlin Philharmonic Orchestra with Wilhelm Furtwängler conducting. It was a great success with the public and critics alike, and it remains one of the most popular and frequently performed symphonies composed between the wars. The critical reception was remarkable, because writers of differing ideological bents praised the piece for different reasons: to pro-Nazi reviewers, it showed Hindemith's turn away from his more dissonant earlier works, but to supporters of new music, it was a triumph of modernism. Ultimately, Hindemith was condemned by Nazi propaganda minister Joseph Goebbels as an "atonal noisemaker," and his music was banned. The opera was finally premiered in Switzerland in May 1938, and Hindemith moved there that September.

The opera is based on the life of Mathias Grünewald (Mathis Neithardt, ca. 1470–1528), painter of the Isenheim Altarpiece in Colmar, Alsace, and the symphony was linked directly with the altarpiece itself. In a program note for the symphony's premiere, Hindemith observed that "the three movements are related to the corresponding panels for the Isenheim Altarpiece. I tried through musical means to approach the same feeling that the pictures arouse in the viewer." Of the middle movement, based on the panel showing the entombment of Christ after the crucifixion (shown in HWM, Figure 34.3, page 886), he wrote: "In the 'Entombment,' the still, pale lifelessness of the first theme [measure 1] is contrasted with the warmth and gentleness of the second [measure 16]." This same music appears in the opera as an interlude in the seventh tableau, after the death of Mathis's beloved Regina, and its first and final sections are adapted as the last music in the opera, when Mathis places his few possessions in a trunk, including his paints and brushes, and prepares to die.

The movement flows like a single thought, aided by a pervasive rhythmic figure—quarter note, eighth rest, and eighth note (or its equivalent, dotted quarter and eighth)—that appears in almost every measure. This gently pulsing rhythm, like a very slow heartbeat, captures the cold stillness Hindemith meant to evoke at the beginning, reflecting the lifeless body being lowered into the tomb in Grünewald's painting, but also conveys the feelings of solace that emerge later in the movement. In a variant, heard throughout the opening theme, the eighth note is divided into two sixteenths. The tender theme of the middle section (measure 16) has more rhythmic variety, suggesting life and warmth: a diminution of the original rhythm (dotted eighth and sixteenth), triplets, and pulsing eighths in the accompaniment. The reprise of the opening theme (measure 28) adds regular sixteenth notes in an accompanying line, which combines with the full orchestration and *forte* dynamic level to suggest grandeur. The final section uses rhythmic figures from the first two sections, gradually diminishing in rhythmic variety until only the original rhythm remains, gently rocking between chords.

The form reflects this sense of continuous flow, offering open-endedness rather than closure:

Section:	A			B					A'	C	
Motive:	a	a'	b	c	c	a"	c'	a'''	a''''	d	e
Tone center:	C→G♯	C	C♯	C♯		mod			B♭→F♯	C♯	C♯
Measure:	1	6	10	16	20	23	24	26	28	34	39

The opening phrase (a) returns frequently, but it is varied and at a higher dynamic level each time it appears. The first two statements lead in different directions to music we never hear again, giving the first section no finality. The contrasting middle theme (c) is heard twice in oboe and flute over pizzicato strings, then the opening measures of the two themes alternate until the first theme returns for its final appearance. It sounds like a culmination, rounding off an ABA' form. But then the music continues, presenting new material that draws on the rhythmic and melodic figures already heard. Simultaneously new and yet familiar, this added section makes a fitting end to the contemplation of entombment: return is not possible, and one must move on.

The harmony is neotonal rather than tonal. It includes open fifths and octaves, triads, chords built on fourths, and dissonances of a second or seventh, all common devices for Hindemith. These are arranged in phrases according to his theory of "harmonic fluctuation," in which relatively consonant chords move toward greater dissonance and then gradually or suddenly move back to consonance. Most chords are pentatonic or diatonic, and most motion between chords is by step, making the flow from chord to chord sound logical and right, even if it could not be predicted in advance. The fifth- and fourth-chords of the first theme sound stark and hollow, evoking the emotional numbness that often follows the death of a beloved friend, while the third-based chords of measures 10–14 and of the final section (measures 34–45) sound warm and consoling in comparison, even when they are dissonant. Throughout, the orchestration heightens the contrasts between themes and reinforces the mood, from dry muted strings at the beginning to the full orchestra with brass at the grand final statement of the main theme.

Tone centers are suggested through arrival on chords that include a prominent octave and fifth above the lowest note, with or without the third. Thus the movement begins on C, cadences on G♯ in measure 4, returns to C in measure 6, and moves on to C♯ in measure 10. The tone center of the middle section is less clear, but the bass line and the mostly diatonic melody suggest the Dorian mode on C♯. The A′ section begins on B♭ and cadences emphatically on F♯. By this point, the harmony has traversed a tritone (C–F♯), echoing the overall progress of the symphony as a whole, which moves a tritone from G in the first movement to D♭ at the end of the third. But instead of ending on F♯ or returning to the opening tone center C, Hindemith begins and ends the final section on C♯, enharmonically the same as the last movement. Like the form, the harmony suggests moving forward, rather than closure, perhaps reflecting the knowledge of anyone viewing Grünewald's altarpiece that the entombment is not the end of the story.

Sergey Prokofiev (1891–1953)

175

Alexander Nevsky, Op. 78: Fourth movement, *Arise, ye Russian People*

Cantata (film score)

1938–39

CD 13|14 CD 6|42

From Sergei Prokofiev, *Alexander Nevsky,* Op. 78 (Moscow: Gosudarstvennoe Muzykal'noe Izdatsl'stvoe, 1959), 40–53.

7
2 Fl.
2 Cl.
Cl.b.
Sax.
C-fag.
ff
a 2
4 Cor.
a 2
ff
a 2
3 Tr-ni e Tuba
a 2
P-tti
ff
C-na
ff
T-tam
ff
S.
A.
рус-ски - е, на славный бой, на смертный бой, вста - вай-те, лю-ди воль-ны - е, за
Rus-sian folk, in bat-tle just, in fight to death. A - rise Ye Peo-ple, free, and brave, de -
T.
B.
V-ni I
V-ni II
V-le
V-c.
div.
arco
unis.
C-b.

12
2 Fl.
2 Cl.
Cl.b.
Sax.
C-fag.
4 Cor.
3 Tr-ni
e Tuba
P-tti
T-ro
C-na
T-tam
Arpa
Dob magg.
S.
A.
на - шу зем-лю, чест - ну - ю.
fend our fair, our na - tive land.
T.
Жи - вым бой-цам по чёт и честь, а мерт-вым сла-ва
To liv-ing war-riors high es - teem, im - mor-tal fame to
B.
V-ni I
V-ni II
V-le
V-c.
C-b.
div.
unis.
pizz.

17
a 2
2 Fl.
2 Cl.
Cl. b.
Sax.
C-fag.
f
4 Cor.
3 Tr-ni e Tuba
T-ro
Arpa
sol ♭
S.
A.
T.
веч-на - я. За от-чий дом, за рус-ский край, вста вай-те, лю-ди
war-riors slain. For na-tive home, for Rus-sian soil a - rise Ye Peo-ple,
B.
V-ni I
V-ni II
V-le
V-c.
C-b.
div.
unis.
div.

21
Picc.
2 Fl.
2 Cl.
Cl.b.
Sax.
C-fag.
4 Cor.
3 Tr-ni
e Tuba
P-tti
T-ro
C-na
T-tam
Arpa
S.
A.
Вста- вай - те, лю - ди
A - rise to arms, Ye
рус - ски - е, на
Rus - sian folk, in
слав - ный бой, на
bat - tle just. in
смертный бой, вста
fight to death. A
T.
рус - ски - е.
Rus - sian folk.
B.
V-ni I
V-ni II
V-le
V-c.
unis.
C-b.

26
poco rit.
Picc.
2 Fl.
2 Ob.
C. ingl.
2 Cl.
Cl. b.
Sax.
2 Fag.
C-fag.
Tr-be I.II
4 Cor.
3 Tr-ni e Tuba
P-tti
C-na
T-tam
Arpa
S.
A.
вай-те, лю-ди воль-ны-е, за на-шу зем-лю чест-ну-ю.
rise Ye Peo-ple, free and brave, defend our fair, our na-tive land.
T.
B.
poco rit.
V-ni I
V-ni II
V-le
V-c.
C-b.
div. arco
unis.
div.
arco
unis.

34
15
43
a tempo
2 Fl.
2 Cl.
Cl.b
2 Fag.
C-fag.
a 2
p cresc.
4 Cor.
Tuba
Alti
На Ру - си род - ной, на Ру-си боль-шой не бы-вать вра - гу. Под - ни-май-ся, встань,
In our Rus-sia great, in our na-tive Rus-sia no foe shall live. Rise to arms, a - rise,
a tempo
arco
V-ni I
V-ni II
V-le
V-c.
C-b.
div.
mp espress.
mf espress.
cresc.

45
Picc.
2 Fl.
Cl. I
Cl. b.
Fag. I
C-fag.
A.
B.
V-ni I
V-ni II
V-le
V-c.
C-b.
a 2
unis.
div.
non div.
мать род- на - я Русь!
na - tive moth - er Russ!
На Ру - си род - ной, на Ру - си боль - шой не бы-
In our Rus-sia great, in our na - tive Rus-sia no

16
44
55
Picc.
2 Fl.
2 Ob.
2 Cl.
Cl. b.
Sax.
2 Fag.
C-fag.
Tr-be I.II
4 Cor.
3 Tr-ni e Tuba
P-tti
C-na
T-tam
Arpa
S.
A.
T.
B.
вать вра - гу. Под - ни-май-ся, встань, мать род-на - я Русь!
foe shall live. Rise to arms, a - rise, na - tive moth - er Russ!
Вста-
A -
V-ni I
V-ni II
V-le
V-c.
C-b.
p cresc.
mf espress.
div.
unis.

66
Picc.
2 Fl.
2 Ob.
2 Cl.
C-fag.
Tr-be I.II
4 Cor.
3 Tr-ni e Tuba
P-tti
C-na
T-tam
Arpa
S.
вай - те, лю - ди
rise to arms, Ye
рус-ски - е.
Rus-sian folk.
Вста -
A -
вай-те, лю-ди
rise Ye Peo - ple,
A.
T.
На
In
славный бой, на
bat - tle just, in
смертный бой.
fight to death.
B.
V-ni I
V-ni II
V-le
V-c.
C-b.
pizz.
div.
arco
unis.
a 2
ff

71
2 Fl.
2 Cl.
Cl.b.
Sax.
2 Fag.
C-fag.
4 Cor.
3 Tr-ni e Tuba
P-tti
C-na
Cassa
T-tam
Sil.
solo
Arpa
S.
воль-ны - е.
free and brave.
Вра-гам на Русь не ха - жи - вать, пол -
No foe shall march' cross Rus - sian land, no
A.
T.
За на-шу зем-лю чест-ну - ю.
De - fend our fair, our na - tive land.
B.
V-ni I
V-ni II
V-le
V-c.
arco
C-b.
div.

76
2 Fl.
2 Cl.
Cl.b.
Sax.
2 Fag.
C-fag.
Cassa
Sil.
Arpa
S.
A.
T.
B.
V-ni I
V-ni II
V-le
V-c.
C-b.
a 2
mp
mf
ten.
ков на Русь не ва - жи - вать, пу - тей на Русь не ви - ды - вать, по -
for - eign troops shall Rus - sia raid. Un - seen the ways to Rus - sia are. No

80
Picc.
2 Fl.
2 Cl.
Cl.b.
Sax.
2 Fag.
C-fag.
4 Cor.
3 Tr-ni e Tuba
P-tti
C-na
Cassa
T-tam
Sil.
Arpa
S.
A.
T.
B.
V-ni I
V-ni II
V-le
V-c.
C-b.
-лей Ру - си не тап - ты-вать.
foe shall ra - vage Rus - sian fields.
Вста-вай-те, лю-ди рус-ски - е, на слав-ныи бой, на
A - rise to arms, Ye Rus-sian folk in bat - tle just, in

85
Picc.
2 Fl.
2 Ob.
C.-ingl.
2 Cl.
Cl.b.
Sax.
2 Fag.
C-fag.
I
Tr-be
II.III
4 Cor.
3 Tr-ni
e Tuba
P-tti
C-na
T-tam
Arpa
S.
A.
смерт - ный бой, вста - вай - те, лю - ди воль-ны - е, за на-шу зем - лю чест - ну - ю!
fight to death. A - rise Ye Peo-ple, free and brave, de - fend our fair, our na - tive land.
T.
B.
V-ni I
V-ni II
V-le
V-c.
C-b.

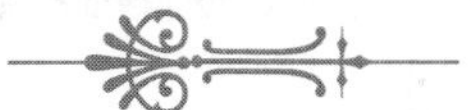

Two years after moving to the Soviet Union in 1936, Sergey Prokofiev was commissioned to compose the music for *Alexander Nevsky*, the first sound film by the renowned Soviet director Sergei Eisenstein (1898–1948). Alexander Nevsky was a thirteenth-century hero who as a young man led Russian armies to victories over invaders from Sweden in 1240 and from Germany in 1241–42. In the latter conflict Nevsky employed a brilliant strategy that enticed the Germans onto the slippery ice of the frozen Lake Pepius, where Nevsky's foot soldiers overwhelmed the German force and many of the heavily armored German knights drowned after cracking through the ice. Eisenstein's film focuses on this critical event in Russian history, and the epic battle serves as the spectacular climax. Made at a time of growing tensions in Europe just prior to World War II, this film showing Russians' valiant defense of their homeland was a powerful propaganda tool warning of potential invasion by Nazi Germany and of the sacrifices that would be needed to repel them. The film was completed in November 1938 and premiered in December.

As was his frequent practice, Prokofiev subsequently arranged excerpts from the film score as a concert work, which was premiered in May 1939 and published that year. He created a cantata, rather than an orchestral suite, from *Alexander Nevsky* because the film score contains a substantial amount of music for chorus, which takes part in the story and also comments on the events. The cantata contains seven excerpts from the film score. The order of the movements follows the chronology of the film and thus provides a miniature retelling of the story. The music is derived from two types of music in the film: *diegetic music* or *source music*, which is part of the story and is heard or performed by the characters in the film, and *nondiegetic music* or *underscoring*, which establishes a mood, character, or situation (like music in an opera) and is heard only by the audience. Much of the music in the cantata is lifted directly from the film score without extensive alteration other than some minor cuts, extensions through repetition, and rearrangements of material.

Prokofiev's music for the film and cantata reflects the doctrine of *socialist realism*, which called for the arts to help strengthen the Soviet state by celebrating socialism, progress, and the people, using techniques that were directly accessible to the masses. This required music that was relatively simple, immediately comprehensible, full of melody, and often folklike in style. It did not preclude dissonance or unusual effects if the meaning was clear and appropriate.

The fourth movement of the cantata, included here, is heard in the film when Nevsky gathers his army, underscoring scenes of peasants leaving their farms and their labors to take up whatever weapons they could find to use against the invaders. The text exhorts the people of Russia to fight to the death to defend their homeland. Both of the principal themes recur later in the film, where they accompany the rejoicing of the victorious Russian people. The movement is in ABA′ form. Both A sections are also small ABA′ forms, although each has different material in the middle section:

Section:	Introduction	A			B		A'		
Music:		a	b	a'	c	c'	a''	d	a'''
Key:	E♭	E♭	C♭ → b♭	E♭	D		E♭	C♭ → a♭	E♭
Measure:	1	6	14	22	34	50	66	74	82

The brief, clamorous orchestral introduction establishes a mood of fervency with conflicting rhythmic pulses, orchestration that suggests trumpet calls and pealing church bells, and a harmonic clash between a reiterated B♭ in the winds and brass and pizzicato second-inversion G-major chords in the strings. The latter imitates the seven-string Russian guitar, which has the same tuning (D–G–B–D–G–B–D), and the sound of plucked string chords continues throughout the A sections. The implied polytonality, double chromatic neighbors in the trumpets, and glissandos in the xylophone are modernist touches that recall Prokofiev's dissonant pre-Soviet style, but they work here as a noisy call to action within a socialist realist idiom.

Once the chorus enters, the music unfolds in regular four-measure phrases. The energetic A section has a folklike character, with its repetitive melody, limited range, and foot-stomping accents. The opening tune (measures 6–13) contains four two-measure units, each beginning with an upward gesture that mirrors the repetitions of the word "arise." The choral writing is homorhythmic, with just two independent lines: the sopranos and tenors present the melody, and the altos and basses provide a supportive counterpoint. The orchestra reinforces the accents in the chorus. Prokofiev's simplified musical language is evident in the diatonic melody and harmony, yet subtle features demonstrate his craft. The tune has modal characteristics, using the notes of the E♭-major scale and concluding on E♭ but emphasizing G and C to create a sense of ambiguity between E♭ major and C minor. This is reinforced by the harmony, which features traditional triads but unexpected progressions. The repeated B♭ in the introduction and the dominant seventh chord on B♭ on the last quarter note of measure 5 indicate the key of E♭, but the deceptive resolution in measure 6 suggests C minor, anticipated by the G-major triads in the introduction. Even after a solid V–I cadence on E♭ in measures 9–10, the music still sounds modal because it emphasizes the subdominant A♭. Simple it may look and sound, but Prokofiev makes sure that there are enough unexpected touches to keep the listener's interest.

The middle portion of the first section (measures 14–21) moves to C♭ major and then B♭ minor. The harmony includes occasional dissonances, while the melody, sung by the men of the choir, retains a modal character. The melodic accents are emphasized by drumrolls, harp chords, and rapid arpeggios in the winds. The opening melody returns with greater reinforcement from the orchestra, and the A section closes on a sustained E♭ major chord.

The B section (measures 34–65) is in a different tonal world, an untroubled D major. A mostly conjunct melody is sung by the altos over the warm accompaniment of bowed strings and pulsating horns, then repeated by the basses under ascending scales in the winds. Again, both melody and harmony are unpredictable enough to keep our interest and suggest the modal qualities of folk song. Although the section projects a calm, uplifting mood, the text is no less resolute and warlike.

When the A section returns, the women and men sing antiphonally at first. The middle portion, sung by the women, introduces a new melody and features the striking addition of a scalar figure in triplets played by the xylophone. By changing all these elements rather than simply repeating the first section, Prokofiev conveys a sense of forward progress that fits the film scene and creates a more convincing close.

The result is both effective film music and effective state propaganda, in a language fully adapted to the doctrine of socialist realism. It is also well suited for amateur choirs—it makes more demands on the orchestral players, who are likely to be professionals, than it does on the choir or on the listener—and thus serves another purpose as well. Prokofiev uses a traditional orchestra augmented by some unusual percussion (such as bells and tam-tam, a flat gong) and a saxophone, an instrument that he used often in his Soviet orchestral compositions. In this score, the transposing instruments (English horn, clarinets, saxophone, trumpets, and horns) are notated at sounding pitch.

Dmitri Shostakovich (1906–1975)

Symphony No. 5, Op. 47: Second movement, Allegretto

Symphony

1937

CD 13|17

48

Allegretto ♩ = 188

Violini I

Violini II

Viole

Violoncelli senza sord. *ff*

Contrabassi senza sord. *ff*

49

Fl. a2 *ff dim.* tr *p*

Ob. a2 *ff dim.* tr *p*

Cl. picc. solo *ff dim.* tr

Cl.(B) a2 *ff dim.* tr *pp*

Cor. a2 *f* a2 *f* *dim.* *p*

Archi

From Dmitri Shostakovich, *Sobranie Sochinenij* [Collected Works], vol. 3 (Moscow: Izdatelstvo Muzika, 1980), 52–82.

a 2
Fl.
Cl. picc.
p
Cor.
15
50
Ob.
Cl.
Fag.
p cresc.
f
marc.
f marc.
20
cresc.
ff
51
V-c.
C-b.
mf
dim.
25
senza sord.
Archi
31

52
tutti
senza sord.
f marc.
cresc.
ff
Archi
37
18
53
Picc.
Fl.
Ob.
Cl.
picc.
Cl.
Fag.
Tr-be
Tr-ni
e
Tuba
Timp.
P-tti
a2
mf
pizz.
fff
Archi
42

Picc.
a2
Fl.
a2
Ob.
Cl. picc.
a2
Cl.
Fag.
C-fag.
Cor.
I
Tr-be
Tr-ni e Tuba
Timp.
T-ro
P-tti
Arpe
[sempre a2]
Archi
47

Picc.
Fl.
a2
Ob.
a2
Cl. picc.
Cl.
a2
Fag.
marc.
C-fag.
Cor.
I
Tr-be
mf
mf
Tr-ni e Tuba
Timp.
mf
T-ro
P-tti
Archi
arco
f marc.
arco
f marc.
51

54
19
Picc.
a2
Fl.
a2
Ob.
Cl. picc.
a2
Cl.
Fag.
a2
ff
C fag.
soli
ff
Cor.
soli
ff
Tr-be
Tr-ni e Tuba
mf
mf
Timp
mf
f
T-ro
f
54
arco
ff marc.
arco
ff marc.
Archi
ff
ff
55

55
Picc.
Fl.
Ob.
Cl. picc.
Cl.
Fag.
C-fag.
Cor.
Tr-be
Tr-ni e Tuba
Timp.
T-ro
Archi
a 2
ff
II
p
sf
p subito
gliss.
arco
pizz.
60

Picc.
Fl.
II
Ob.
Cl. picc.
II
Cl.
Fag.
C-fag.
Cor.
Tr-be
Tr-ni e Tuba
Timp.
Archi
f
65

Picc.
Fl.
Ob.
Cl. picc.
Cl.
Fag.
C-fag.
Cor.
Tr-be
Tr-ni e Tuba
Timp.
Archi
f marc.
cresc.
mf cresc.
mf
p
69

56
Picc.
Fl.
Ob.
Cl. picc.
Cl.
Fag.
C-fag.
Cor.
Tr-be
Tr-ni e Tuba
Timp.
T-ro
Archi
a2
soli
ff
mf
f
arco
ff marc.
gliss.
74

Picc.
Fl.
Ob.
Cl. picc.
Cl.
Fag.
C-fag.
Cor.
Tr-be
Tr-ni e Tuba
Timp
T-ro
Archi
a2
ff
f
con sord.
gliss.
80

20
57
a2
Cor.
Arpe
p
V-no solo
gliss.
V-ni I
pizz.
V-c.
85
58
V-ni
91
rit.
a tempo
I solo
Fl.
V-le
97
59
Fag.
pp
V-ni II
103

60
Fl.
Fag.
gliss.
Arpe
p
arco sul C
pizz.
Archi
arco sul G
rit.
109
21
a tempo
61
tutti
arco
f marc.
114
senza sord.
Cor.
ff
div.
unis.
120

62
a 2
Fl.
Ob.
Cl.
mf
Cor.
sf
p subito
pp
Archi
dim.
pizz.
pp
p
127
Picc.
Fl.
Ob.
Cl. picc.
Cl.
Fag.
C fag.
ff
f
morendo
arco
div.
132

63
Picc.
a2
Fl.
a2
Ob.
Cl. picc.
a2
Cl.
a2
Fag.
C-fag.
a2
Cor.
a2
Tr-be
Tr-ni e Tuba
Timp.
63
unis.
Archi
137

Picc.
Fl.
Ob.
Cl. picc.
Cl.
Fag.
C-fag.
Cor.
Tr-be
Tr-ni e Tuba
Timp.
Arpe
Archi
a2
ff
sf
p sub.
p
141

64
a 2
Fl.
Ob.
Cl.
Cor.
Archi
mf
pp
dim.
pizz.
147
Picc.
Cl. picc.
ff
p
I
morendo
arco
div.
152

22
65
Picc.
pp
I
Fl.
pp
I.
Cl.
pp
I solo
Fag.
p
solo
C-fag.
p
a2
pp
Cor.
a2
pp
pp
unis.
pp
Archi
pp
pp
157
pp
I
Fag.
C-fag.
66
pizz.
p
pizz.
p
pizz.
p
Archi
163

Picc.
tr
p
Archi
170
67
I
Fag.
C-fag.
p
mf
pizz.
f
176
I
182

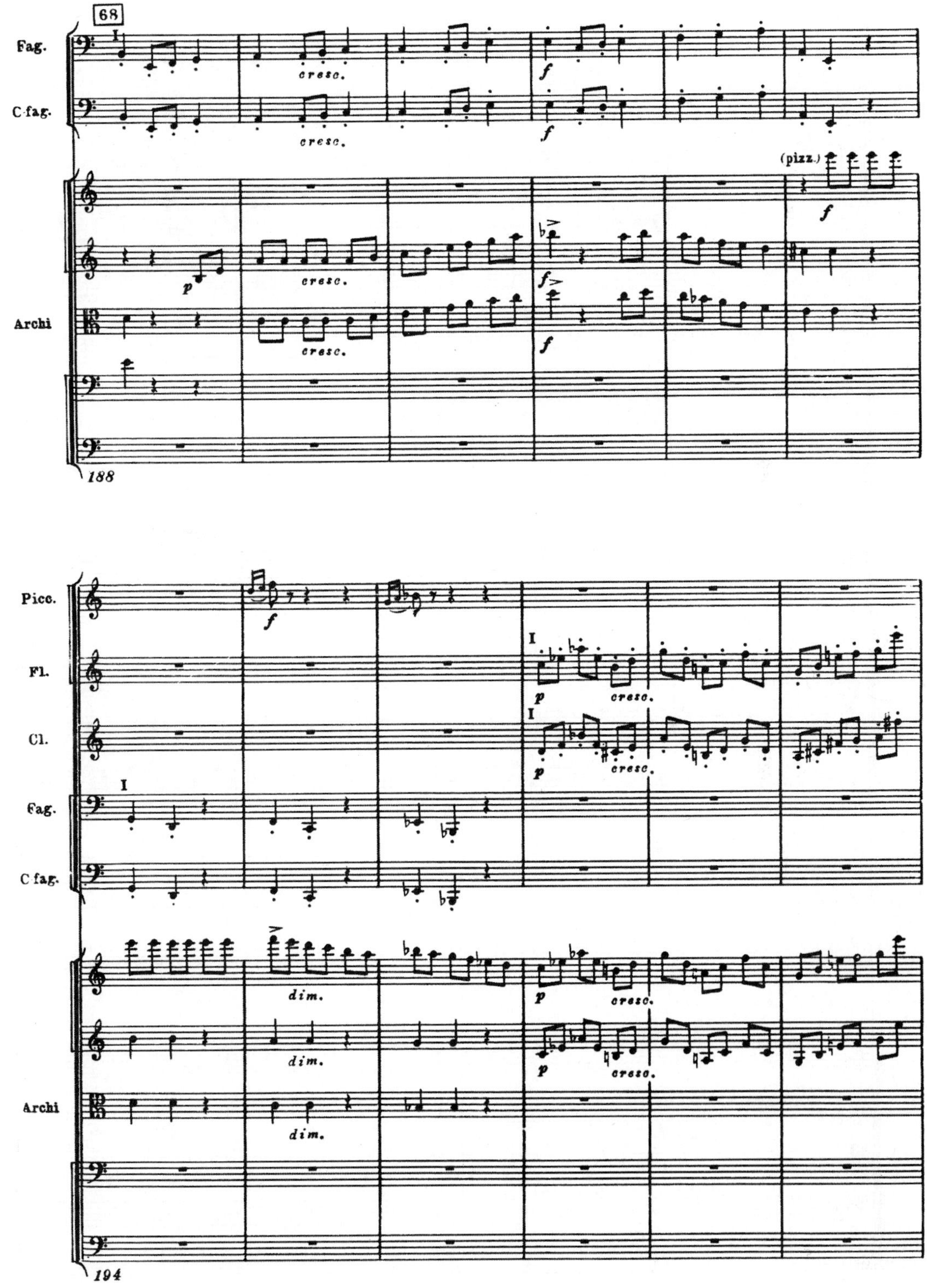

Picc.
Fl.
Cl.
Fag.
C fag.
Archi
I
f
p
cresc.
dim.
194

23
69
Picc.
a 2
Fl.
Ob.
Cl. picc.
Cl.
Fag.
C-fag.
Cor.
Tr-be
Tr-ni e Tuba
Timp.
P-tti
Sil.
Archi
(pizz.)
pizz.
200

Picc.
a2
Fl.
a2
Ob.
Cl. picc.
a2
Cl.
Fag.
f marc.
C-fag.
Cor.
Tr-be
Tr-ni e Tuba
Timp.
P-tti
Sil.
Archi
arco
f marc.
arco
f marc.
204

70
Picc.
Fl.
Ob.
Cl. picc.
Cl.
Fag.
C-fag.
Cor.
Tr-be
soie
Tr-ni e Tuba
Timp.
T-ro
Sil.
70
Archi
208

Picc.
Fl.
a2
ff
Ob.
a2
ff
Cl. picc.
ff
Cl.
a2
ff
Fag.
C-fag.
Cor.
Tr-be
Tr-ni e Tuba
ff
Timp.
T-ro
f
Sil.
arco
ff marc.
arco
ff marc.
Archi
212

24
71
Picc.
Fl.
a2
Ob.
II
p
Cl. picc.
Cl.
Fag.
p sub.
C-fag.
Cor.
Tr-be
sf
Tr-ni e Tuba
Timp.
T-ro
Sil.
Archi
arco
pizz.
218

Picc.
Fl.
II
Ob.
Cl. picc.
II
Cl.
Fag.
C-fag.
p
Cor.
Tr-be
Tr-ni e Tuba
Timp.
Sil.
f
p
Archi
222

72
Picc.
f marc.
Fl.
ff
Ob.
a2
ff
Cl. picc
ff
Cl.
Fag.
cresc.
ff
C fag.
Cor.
a2 soli
ff
soli
ff
Tr-be
mf cresc.
mf cresc.
Tr-ni e Tuba
mf
cresc.
mf
Timp.
72
Archi
cresc.
cresc.
cresc.
cresc.
cresc.
ff
226

Picc.
Fl.
a 2
ff
Ob.
Cl. picc.
Cl.
Fag.
C-fag.
Cor.
Tr-be
Tr-ni e Tuba
Timp.
T-ro
f
ff marc.
gliss.
Archi
arco
231

73
Picc.
Fl.
Ob.
Cl. picc.
Cl.
Fag.
C-fag.
Cor.
Tr-be
Tr-ni e Tuba
Timp.
T-ro
Archi
a2
ff
f
[ff]
gliss.
236

Picc.
a2
Fl.
a2
I solo
Ob.
Cl. picc.
a2
Cl.
pp
Fag.
pp
C-fag.
a2
Cor.
a2
a2
Tr-be
a2
Tr-ni e Tuba
soli
Timp.
ff
dim.
pp
pizz.
p
Archi
240

74
Picc.
Fl.
Ob.
Cl. picc.
Cl.
Fag.
C-fag.
Cor.
Tr-be
Tr-ni e Tuba
Timp.
Sil.
Archi
ff
a2
I
(pp)
muta in A
arco div.
arco
246

Dmitri Shostakovich earned international recognition at the age of nineteen with performances of his First Symphony (1926) and enjoyed celebrity status in the Soviet Union throughout the next decade. Thus he was stunned when in 1936 the Communist Party newspaper *Pravda*, at the instigation of Soviet dictator Joseph Stalin, suddenly denounced the modernist compositional style of his opera *Lady Macbeth of the Mtsensk District*. Unsure of his future in a time of political purges, Shostakovich shelved his already completed but thoroughly modernist Fourth Symphony and composed his Fifth Symphony in a more moderate idiom. His desire to regain state approval was encapsulated in a critic's description of the piece as "a Soviet artist's reply to just criticism." The work was premiered on November 21, 1937, in Leningrad (now St. Petersburg) by the Leningrad Philharmonic, conducted by Evgeny Mravinsky. The reception by the audience was overwhelming, and Shostakovich was once again viewed favorably by the communist regime.

Compared to many of his earlier works, the Fifth Symphony represents a retrenchment of style, with simpler formal procedures and more direct expression. While this change in approach may be linked to political pressures, it also represents a new idea that Shostakovich had been developing, inspired by studies of Mahler. The symphony, set in a classical four-movement structure, evokes the heroic spirit of the orchestral works of Beethoven and Tchaikovsky.

The second movement, marked Allegretto, is a scherzo in the style of an Austrian Ländler (as are several of Mahler's scherzos). For the most part, Shostakovich follows the form of the dance movement in a classical symphony, as can be observed in the diagram below. The overall form is ternary (Scherzo-Trio-Scherzo), with a trio in written-out binary form (i.e., with the repetitions written out and slightly varied rather than marked with repeat signs) and a scherzo in modified binary form.

Section:	Scherzo							Trio				Scherzo							Coda
Music:	A			B		B'		C	C'	D	D'	A'			B''		B'		
	a	b	a'	c	d	c'	d	e	e'	f	f'	a''	b'	a'''	c''	d'	c'	d	e''
Key:	a			c	F	c	F	C				a			c♯	F♯	c	F	a
Measure:	1	11	29	45	56	64	75	87	103	119	138	157	167	185	201	212	220	231	241

(Note that the measure numbers in this score are below the bottom staff rather than above the top staff as usual.)

Mahler's influence can be heard in the orchestration, the jarring contrasts of mood, the occasionally satirical tone, and the use of counterpoint. The vigorous, rather awkward, and tonally ambiguous melody in the low strings at the beginning of the movement introduces a number of motives that will be incorporated in later thematic ideas, such as the rising scale and the repeated notes. The horns (measure 11) usher in a new, playful or even sarcastic tune played primarily in the E-flat clarinet. The upper woodwinds present another idea with repeated notes (measure 20), and the bassoon follows with an extended solo. In Mahleresque fashion, the bassoon melody obscures the return of the opening low string theme at measure 29, and suggestions of the woodwind figures appear in the violins at measure 37. Thus the first part of the scherzo continually presents and develops ideas, yet it still hints at the structure one would expect at the beginning of a scherzo: a musical period that is stated (measures 1–28) and repeated (measures 29–44), constituting the first half of a binary form.

An abrupt shift to C minor marks the beginning of the second part of the scherzo (measure 45). Two divergent ideas are presented and then repeated: a crude waltz and a boisterous march (at measure 56). The first of these incorporates two $\frac{4}{4}$ measures that comically offset the established triple meter, and the second, with blaring horns, suggests a military fanfare. In the repetition of the waltz, the winds and strings reverse roles. Although the two halves of the scherzo differ in mood and melodic content, several recurring motives link them together. One notable example is the trilled figure in measures 14–15, which returns prominently in measures 52–54.

For those who know of and sympathize with Shostakovich's political situation at the time he wrote this symphony, the comic touches here—such as the rowdy fanfare—may suggest that he was mocking the government that threatened to censor him. Yet the circumstances were far too dangerous for anyone to mock Stalin, and we should be cautious about reading into the music meanings the composer may not have intended. More likely, Shostakovich was emulating the jesting, ironic tone of Mahler's scherzos, and leaving it to the listener to decide what the music might mean.

The trio begins with an elegant waltz tune played by a solo violin and accompanied by a harp and pizzicato cello. In the repetition of this sixteen-measure tune by the flute, the delicate mood is enhanced by glissandos in the harp and low strings. Unison strings rudely interrupt with the second half of the trio (at measure 119), which shifts briefly to B major for a phrase from the waltz theme (measures 129–33). On the repetition, the unison figure is given to the woodwinds.

Shostakovich continues to reverse the roles of winds and strings at the reprise of the scherzo. The opening bass melody is now in bassoon and contrabassoon, and pizzicato strings play the themes first introduced by horns and woodwinds. In a nod from one Fifth Symphony to another, Shostakovich's distinctive timbre of bassoon with pizzicato strings recalls the corresponding section in the scherzo of Beethoven's Symphony No. 5. The second part of the scherzo begins a half-step higher than it was originally presented, in C♯ minor, and the march tune, now in F♯ major, is given to the trumpets. Order is restored with the repetition, as the original key areas return and the horns play the march theme one last time. The coda opens with a brief recollection of the trio melody, which is abruptly and forcibly brought to a final cadence.

Although the overall harmonic scheme of the movement is traditional (A minor, with the relative major C in the trio), Shostakovich's harmony is full of modern elements. Alongside the occasional dominant-tonic cadence, there are many moments when the harmony takes an unexpected turn, lurching onto a new chord or into a new key with little or no preparation. Examples include the abrupt shifts of key mentioned above and, on a more local level, the succession in the C-major trio theme of A major, G major, F minor, and G minor chords leading right back to C major (measures 97–102). Ultimately, the tonal centers seem more often asserted than established, as if this were neotonal music pretending to be tonal—an apt metaphor for a modernist composer trying to conform to the restrictions imposed by a totalitarian state.

In writing for orchestra, Shostakovich had an array of outstanding musicians available to him in the Soviet Union, which is reflected in his virtuoso treatment of all sections, including the percussion. With its technical demands and wide range of emotions, this symphony remains popular with audiences and continues to test the limits of modern professional orchestras.

177

Silvestre Revueltas (1899–1940)

Sensemayá

Symphonic poem
1937–38

CD 13|25 CD 6|45

 The analysis mentioned in the commentary is in Ricardo Zohn-Muldoon, "The Song of the Snake: Silvestre Revueltas' *Sensemayá*," *Latin American Music Review* 19 (Fall/Winter 1998): 133–59.

16
Eng. Hn.
Cl. E♭
Cls. B♭
Bass Cl.
Bsns. I II
Hn. I
Tpt. I
Tuba
Con Sordina I
mf
f
Claves
Tom-Toms
B. Dr.
Bass

20
Eng. Hn.
Cl. E♭
Cl. B♭ I
Bass Cl.
Bsns. I II
Hn. I
Tpt. I
Tuba
mf espr. e misterioso
pp
mf
ppp
Con Sord. I
mf espr. e misterioso
pp
ppp
Claves
Tom-Toms
B. Dr.
Bass

24
Eng. Hn.
Cl. E♭
Cls. B♭ I II
Bass Cl.
Bsns. I II
Hns.
Tpt. I
Tuba
Claves
Tom-Toms
B. Dr.
Bass

28
Eng. Hn.
Cl. E♭
Cls. B♭ I II
Bass Cl.
Bsns. I II
Hns. I III
con sord. I-III
Tpt. I
Tuba
Claves
Tom-Toms
B. Dr.
Bass

32
Picc. I
Fl. I
Ob. I
Eng. Hn.
Cl. Eb
Cls. Bb I II
Bass Cl.
Bsns.
Hns.
Tpts.
Trbs.
Tuba
Timp.
Claves
Tom-Toms
Raspador
B. Dr.
Vls.
Vla.
Vcl.
Bass
Con Sord.
Con Sord.
a2
pp
mf
ppp
sfff
p
mf
f
più f

36
Picc. I
Fls. I II
Ob. I
Eng. Hn.
Cl. E♭
Cls. B♭ I II
Bass Cl.
Bsns. I II
III
Hns. I II
III IV
Tpts. I II
III IV
Trbs. I II
III
Tuba
Timp.
Claves
Tom-Toms
Raspador
Vls. I
II
Vla.
Vcl.
Bass

40
Picc. I
Fls. I II
Ob. I
Eng.Hn.
Cl. E♭
Cl. B♭ I II
Bass Cl.
Bsns. I II III
Hns. I II III IV
Tpts. I II III IV
Trbs. I II III
Tuba
Timp.
Claves
Tom-Toms
Raspador
Vls. I II
Vla.
Vcl.
Bass
f
fff
ppp
a2
ff

26
46
44
Picc. I
Fl. I
Ob. I
Eng. Hn.
Cl. E♭
Cls. B♭ I II
Bass Cl.
Bsns. I II III
Hns. I II III IV
Tpts. I II III IV
Trbs. I II III
Tuba
Timp.
Claves
Tom-Toms
S. Indian Dr.
Raspador
Vls. I II
Vla.
Vcl.
Bass
ppp
ff
f staccatissimo
with hard sticks
mf
più f

48
Picc.
Fls.
Obs.
Eng. Hn.
Cl. Eb
Cls. Bb I II
Bass Cl.
Bsns.
Hns.
a2
ff
Tpts.
Trbs.
Tuba
Timp.
Claves
S. Indian Dr.
Raspador
Vls.
Vla.
Vcl.
Bass

52
Picc.
I
Fls.
II
Ob.
Eng. Hn.
Cl. E♭
Cls. B♭ I II
Bass Cl.
I II
Bsns.
III
I II
Hns.
III IV
I II
Tpts.
III IV
Trbs. I II
Tuba-III
Timp.
Claves
S. Indian Dr.
Raspador
I
Vls.
II
Vla.
Vcl.
Bass
pp
pp
a2
ff
a2
ff
f
ff
f
ff
I-II
a2
f e marcato
III
sf
sf
sf
sf

56
Picc.
I
Fls.
II
Ob.
Eng. Hn.
Cl. E♭
Cls. B♭ I II
Bass Cl.
I II
Bsns.
III
I II
Hns.
III IV
I II
Tpts.
III IV
Trbs. I II
Tuba-III
Timp.
Claves
S. Indian Dr.
I
Vls.
II
Vla.
Vcl.
Bass
ff
f
sf
sempre f e marcato

60
Picc.
Fls I II
Obs. I II
Eng. Hn.
Cl. Eb
Cls. Bb I II
Bass Cl.
Bsns. I II III
Hns. I II III IV
Tpts. I II III IV
Trbs. I II
Tuba-III
Timp.
Claves
S. Indian Dr.
Vls. I II
Vla.
Vcl.
Bass
fff
sf
ff

63
Picc. I II
a2
Fls. I II
Obs. I II
Eng.Hn.
Cl. E♭
Cls.B♭ I II
Bass Cl.
Bsns. I II III
Hns. I II III IV
Tpts. I II III IV
Trbs. I II
Tuba-III
Timp.
Cym.
Claves
S.Indian Dr.
B.Dr.
Vls. I II
Vla.
Vcl.
Bass

66
Picc. I II
Fls. I II
Obs. I II
Eng.Hn.
Cl.E♭
Cl.B♭ I II
Bass Cl.
Bsns. I II III
Hns. I II III IV
Tpts. I II III IV
Trbs. I II
Tuba III
Timp.
Cym.
Claves
B.Dr.
Vls. I II
Vla.
Vcl.
Bass
sostenuto ff
sostenuto ff
sostenuto ff
sostenuto ff
sostenuto ff
sostenuto ff
ff
ff
ff
ff

69
27
47
Picc.
Fls.
Obs.
Eng. Hn.
Cl. E♭
Cl. B♭
Bass Cl.
Bsns.
Hns.
Tpts.
Trbs.
Tuba-III
Trb. III
Timp.
Tom-Toms
B. Dr.
Vls.
Vla.
Vcl.
Bass

72
Picc.
Fls.
Obs.
Eng.Hn.
Cl.E♭
Cl.B♭
Bass Cl.
Bsns.
Hns.
Tpts.
mf molto espr.
p
Trbs.
sf
mf
Timp.
Tom-Toms
B.Dr.
Vls.
Vla.
Vcl.
Bass

75
28
48
Picc.
Fls.
p molto espr.
Obs.
pp
Eng. Hn.
Cl. E♭
Cl. B♭ I
Bass Cl.
Bsns.
pp
ppp
senza sord
Hns.
p espr.
Tpts.
mf molto espr.
pp
Trbs.
f
Timp.
Tom-Toms
B. Dr.
Vls.
pizz
mf
Vla.
Vcl.
Bass

78
Picc.
Fls.
Obs.
pp
mf
Eng. Hn
Cl. E♭
Cls. B♭
Bass Cl.
Bsn.
Hns.
molto legato sempre
p
Tpts.
Trbs.
Timp.
Tom-Toms
B. Dr.
Vls.
Vla.
Vcl.
Bass

81
Picc.
Fls.
I
II
Obs. I II
Eng. Hn.
Cl. E♭
Cl. B♭ II
Bass Cl.
Bsns.
II
III
Hns.
I
III IV
Tpts.
I II
III IV
a2
Trbs.
I II
III
Timp.
Tom-Toms
B.Dr.
Vls.
I
II
Vla.
Vcl.
Bass
ff
f

84
Picc.
Fls.
Obs.
Eng. Hn.
Cl. E♭
Cl. B♭ I
Bass Cl.
Bsns.
Hns.
Tpts.
Trbs.
Timp.
Tom-Toms
Bass Dr.
Vls.
Vla.
Vcl.
Bass
ff
ppp
molto dim.

29
49
87
Picc. I II
Fls. I II
Obs. I II
Eng. Hn.
Cl. Eb
Cls. Bb I II
Bass Cl.
Bsns. I II III
Hns. I II III IV
Tpts. I II III IV
Trbs.
Tuba
Xyl.
Cym.
Gong
Tom-Toms
B. Dr.
Piano
Vls. I II
Vla.
Vcl.
Bass
fff
ff
a3
a2
sff
f
pizz.
arco
ppp

90
Picc. I II
Fls. I II
Obs. I II
Eng. Hn.
Cl. E♭
Cls. B♭ I II
Bass Cl.
Bsns. I II III
Hns. I II III IV
Tpts. I II III IV
Trbs. I II III
Tuba
Xyl.
Cym.
Gong
Tom-Toms
Piano
Vls. I II
Vla.
Vcl.
Bass
a2
pizz.
arco

93
Picc. I II
Fls. I II
Obs. I II
Eng.Hn.
Cl.E♭
Cls.B♭ I II
Bass Cl.
Bsns. I II III
Hns. I II
III IV
Tpts. I II
III IV
Trbs. I II
III
Tuba
Xyl.
Cym.
Gong
Tom-Toms
B.Dr.
Piano
Vls. I
II
pizz.
Vla.
Vcl.
Bass

96
Picc.
Fls.
Obs.
Eng. Hn.
Cl. E♭
Cls. B♭
Bass Cl.
Bsns.
Hns.
Tpts.
Trbs.
Tuba
Xyl.
Cym.
Gong
Tom-Toms
B. Dr.
Piano
Vls.
Vla.
Vcl.
Bass

99
30
50
Picc. I II
Fls. I II
Obs. I II
Eng. Hn.
Cl. E♭
Cls. B♭ I II
Bass Cl.
Bsns. I II
Hns. I II III IV
Tpts. I II III IV
Trbs. I II III
Tuba
Xyl.
Tom-Toms
S. Indian Drum
Piano
Vls I II
Vla
Vcl.
Bass
pp sempre

102
Bass Cl.
Bsns.
Trbs.
Tuba
Claves
Tom-Toms
S.Indian Drum
106
Obs.
a2
Eng.Hn.
Bass Cl.
Bsns.
Tpts.
Con Sord.
Con Sord.
Trbs.
Tuba
Claves
Tom-Toms
S.Indian Drum
Vl. I
Bass

109
Picc.
Fls.
Obs I II
p
pp
ff
sff
Eng. Hn.
Cl. E♭
Cls. B♭ I II
Bass Cl.
Bsns. I II III
Hns.
Tpts. I II III IV
mf
Trbs. I III
Tuba
Xyl.
Claves
Tom-Toms
S. Indian Drum
7/16
7/8
Vlns. I II
Vla.
Vcl.
Bass
pizz.

112
Picc.
Fls.
Obs. I II
Eng. Hn.
Cl. Eb
Cls. Bb
Bass Cl.
Bsns.
Hns.
Tpts.
Trbs.
Tuba
Xyl.
Cym.
Claves
Tom-Tom
S. Indian Drum
Vls.
Vla.
Vcl.
Bass
a2
7
16
7
8

115

Picc. I II
Fls. I II
Obs. I II
Eng. Hn.
Cl. E♭
Cls. B♭ I II
Bass Cl.
Bsns. I II III
Hns. I II III IV
Tpts. I II III IV
Trbs. I III
Tuba
Xyl.
Cym.
Claves
Tom-Toms
S. Indian Drum
Vls. I II
Vla.
Vcl.
Bass

a2 ff fff pp mf f sff ppp

118
Picc.
Fl. I
Obs. I II
Eng.Hn.
Cl. E♭
Cls.B♭ I II
Bass Cl.
Bsns I II III
Hns.
Tpts. I III
Trbs. I III
Tuba
Xyl.
Cym.
Claves
Tom-Toms
S.Indian Drum
Vls. I II
Vla.
Vcl.
Bass
a2
p espr. molto
ppp sub.
pizz sempre

121
Fl. I
Cl.E♭
Bass Cl.
Bsn. III
Hn. I
Tpts. I III
Xyl.
Cym.
S.Indian Drum
Vl. I
Bass
ppp
pp
p
sf

124
Fl. I
Cl.E♭
Bass Cl.
Bsn. III
Hn. I
Tpts. I III
Xyl.
Cym.
S.Indian Drum
Vl. I
Bass
mf
sf
f

127
Picc.
Fl. I
Obs. I II
Eng.Hn.
Cl.E♭
Cls.B♭
Bass Cl.
Bsns. I III
Hns. I
Tpts. I III
Trbs.
Tuba
Xyl.
gliss.
Cym.
S.Indian Drum
Vls. I II
Vla.
Vcl.
Bass

130
Picc.
Fl. I
Obs. I II
Eng. Hn.
Cl. E♭
Cls. B♭
Bass Cl.
I
Bsns.
III
I
Hns.
I II
Tpts.
III IV
più f
sff
Trbs.
Tuba
Xyl.
Cym.
f
S. Indian Drum
7 16
7 8
7 16
7 8
I
Vls.
II
Vla.
Vcl.
Bass

31
51
133
Picc.
Fls.
Obs.
Eng. Hn.
Cl. E♭
Cls. B♭
Bass Cl.
Bsns.
Hns.
Tpts.
Trbs.
Timp.
Claves
Tom-Toms
Piano
Vls.
Vla.
Vcl.
Bass
a2
ff marcatiss.
f marcatiss.
pp
ppp
f
mf
sff

136
Picc.
Fls.
Obs.
Eng.Hn.
Cl.E♭
Cls.B♭
Bass Cl.
Bsns.
Hns.
Tpts.
Trbs.
Timp.
Claves
Tom-Toms
Piano
Vls.
Vla.
Vcl.
Bass
ff
pp
ppp
f
sff
mf
7
16
7
8

139
Picc. I II
Fls. I II
Obs. I II
Eng. Hn.
Cl. E♭
Cls. B♭ I II
Bass Cl.
Bsns. I II III
a3
Hns. I II
III IV
Tpts. I II
III IV
Trbs. I II
III
Tuba
Timp.
Claves
Tom-Toms
Piano
Vls. I
II
Vla.
Vcl.
Bass
pp sul ponticello
pp sul ponticello

32 52

142

Picc. I II

Fls. I II

Obs. I II

Eng. Hn.

Cl. E♭

Cls. B♭ I II

Bass Cl.

B'sns. I II III

Hns. I II

III IV

Tpts. I II

III IV

Trbs. I II

III

Tuba

Timp.

Gong

Claves

Tom-Toms

Piano

145
Picc. I II
Fls. I II
Obs. I II
Eng. Hn.
Cl. E♭
Cls. B♭ I II
Bass Cl.
Bsns. I II III
Hns. I II
III IV
Tpts. I II
III IV
Trbs. I II
III
Tuba
Gong
Cym.
Piano
Vls. I
II
Vla.
Vcl.
Bass
div.
gliss.

33 53
148
Picc.
Fls.
Obs.
Eng. Hn.
Cl. E♭
Cls. B♭
Bass Cl.
Bsns.
Hns.
Tpts.
Trbs.
Tuba
Timp.
Gong
Gourd
Cym.
Tom-Toms
Piano
Vls.
Vla
Vcl.
Bass
a2
Gourd
Claves
with hard sticks
pizz

151
molto cresc.
Picc. I II
Fls. I II
Obs. I II
Eng. Hn.
Cl. E♭
Cls. B♭ I II
Bass Cl.
Bsns. I II III
Hns. I II III IV
Tpts. I II III IV
più f
Trbs. I II III
Timp.
Gourd
Claves
Tom-Toms
molto cresc.
Piano
Vls. I II
Vla.
Vcl.
Bass
sff

*Violins divided in 4. Half play tremolo; half, sostenuto cantabile.

**Half of the cellos tremolo sul ponticello; half, natural and cantabile.

157
Picc. I II
Fls. I II
Obs. I II
Eng. Hn.
Cl. E♭
Cls. B♭ I II
Bass Cl.
a2
Bsns. I II III IV
a2
Hns. I II III IV
Tpts. I II III IV
fff
fff
Trbs. I II
III-Tuba
Timp.
Xyl.
Glocken.
Gourd
Tom-Tom
Piano
Vls. I II
Vla.
Vcl.
Bass
3
3

160
Picc. I II
Fls. I II
Obs. I II
Eng. Hn.
Cl. E♭
Cls. B♭ I II
Bass Cl.
Bsns. I II III IV
Hns. I II III IV
Tpts. I II III IV
Trbs. I II
III-Tuba
Timp.
Xyl.
Celesta
Gourd
Tom-Tom
Piano
Vls. I II
Vla.
Vcl.
Bass
fff
ff

162
Picc. I II
Fls. I II
Obs. I II
Eng.Hn.
Cl.E♭
Cls.B♭ I II
Bass Cl.
Bsns. I II III IV
Hns. I II III IV
Tpts. I II III IV
fff
Trbs I II
III-Tuba
Timp.
Xyl.
Celesta
Gourd
Tom-Tom
Piano
fff
Vls. I II
Vla.
Vcl.
Bass

164
Picc. I II
Fls. I II
Obs. I II
Eng. Hn.
Cl. E♭
Cls. B♭ I II
Bass Cl.
Bsns. I II III IV
Hns. I II III IV
Tpts. I II III IV
fff
fff
Trbs. I III
Tuba
Timp.
Xyl.
Celesta
Gourd
Tom-Tom
Piano
Vls. I II
Vla.
Vcl.
Bass

166
Picc. I II
Fls. I II
Obs. I II
Eng. Hn.
Cl. E♭
Cls. B♭ I II
Bass Cl.
Bsns. I II III IV
Hns. I II III IV
Tpts. I II III IV
Trbs. I II III
Tuba
Timp.
Xyl.
Celesta
Gourd
Tom-Tom
Piano
Vls. I II
Vla.
Vcl.
Bass

168
Picc.
Fls.
Obs.
Eng. Hn.
Cl. E♭
Cls. B♭
Bass Cl.
Bsns.
Hns.
Tpts
Trbs.
Tuba
Timp.
Xyl.
Gourd
Tom-Tom
Piano
Vls.
Vla.
Vcl.
Bass
G.P.
unis
arco
ff
fff
score autographed by J.P. Bruno
Mexico City, March 6, 1938

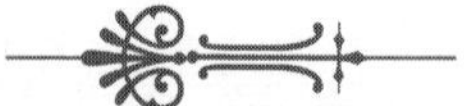

Silvestre Revueltas composed *Sensemayá* for chamber ensemble in 1937, then reworked it for large orchestra the next year. The work is based on a poem by Cuban poet Nicolás Guillén that reenacts a magical rite of the African-Cuban Mayombe sect. The ritual centers around a large figure, carried by a skilled dancer, that represents a snake—a symbol of threat—and during the ritual the snake is symbolically killed. The word *sensemayá*, which repeats throughout the poem, may stand for the snake or for the ritual; it apparently is a combination of *sensa*, a Bantu word for "Providence," and *Yemenyá*, an Afro-Cuban goddess whose name comes from the Yoruba language of west Africa. As composer Ricardo Zohn-Muldoon has demonstrated, Revueltas apparently set the text of the poem to music and then used the resulting melody throughout the piece, accompanied by other ideas and interspersed with interludes. The result is literally a song without words for orchestra.

According to Zohn-Muldoon's analysis, the piece falls into four large sections, following the course of the poem:

Measure	Section	Poem	Text/Thematic Material
1	1	(Introduction)	"Sen-se-ma-yá" rhythm (throughout section 1)
9			Snake theme
45		Stanza 1	Incantation: "¡Mayombe-bombe-mayombe!"
55		Stanza 2	Description of snake
65		Stanza 3	Incantation: "¡Mayombe-bombe-mayombe!"
68		Stanza 4	How to kill the snake
76		(Interlude)	Theme of man
88	2	(Interlude)	Altered "sen-se-ma-yá" rhythm
93		Stanza 5	Confrontation with the snake
100	3	(Interlude)	Material from section 1 introduction, with interjections
119			Continues, with theme of man
133		Stanza 6	Describes dead snake
142		(Interlude)	Striking the snake
145			Snake's dying convulsions
150	4	(Interlude)	Material from section 1
154		Stanza 7	Incantation "¡Mayombe-bombe-mayombe!" and narration of death *plus* snake theme *plus* theme of man

At the beginning of the work, a repeating pattern in the percussion of alternating eighth notes and eighth rests in $\frac{7}{8}$ meter suggests the word "sen-se-ma-yá" (measure 1), which continues throughout the first section. Revueltas overlays this pattern with ostinatos in the bass clarinet and bassoon, later joined or replaced by other instruments. A theme representing the snake enters in the tuba (measures 9–20), is completed by the horn, and is repeated twice in other instruments.

After this introduction, the ostinatos continue underneath the first four stanzas of the poem. The strings state the melody for the first stanza, a repeated incantation "¡Mayombe-bombe-mayombé!" (measures 46–49), interleaved with elements from the snake theme and other ideas. The melody for the second stanza, describing the snake, appears in trombones I and II (measures 55–65). The strings return with the third stanza, a repetition of the first, and then the trombones state the fourth, describing how to kill the snake, using material from the second stanza. The first large section concludes with an interlude that presents a new theme representing man (i.e., humanity; trumpet, E♭ clarinet, and flute, measures 76–84), as the string incantation joins the other ostinatos. The music fades, perhaps to represent the act of sneaking up quietly on the snake.

The loud, exciting, and relatively brief second section (measures 89–99) depicts the confrontation with the snake suggested by the fifth stanza of the poem, altering the "sen-se-ma-yá" rhythm and setting the rhythm and accents of the text in the trombones (with a new meter of $\frac{9}{8}$).

The third section begins as if it were a return to the first, but the musical flow is frequently interrupted by single measures of $\frac{7}{16}$, with rapid sixteenth-note figures (as at measures 106 and 110) suggesting the struggle between human and snake. The theme of man reappears in this context (measure 119). Then the trombones state the melody for the poem's sixth stanza (measures 133–42), which describes what the dead snake will no longer be able to do: eat, whistle, walk, run, watch, drink, breathe, or bite. The following interlude pictures the violent blows to the snake (measure 142) and the writhing snake's death-agony (measure 145).

The final section is a celebratory postlude, setting the final stanza of the poem. That stanza joins the incantation of the first stanza (violin II and viola, measures 154–56) to a narration of the snake's death (violin I and winds, measures 160–67). The themes of the snake and of man are heard again as well, along with numerous ostinati, in a climactic conclusion of overwhelming power.

As in most program music, knowing the relationship of the music to the poem that inspired it helps us follow the succession of events and understand why the piece takes the shape it does. Yet the work also makes sense in more abstract musical terms, presenting, layering, and juxtaposing a variety of ideas in a logical manner. Each of the ostinatos and melodies appears at only one pitch level, creating a sense of tonal location and lending coherence to the work even though a tonal center is not firmly established.

The emphasis on winds, brass, and percussion in this piece, along with the driving rhythm and alternating blocks of sound, shows the influence of Stravinsky, especially *The Rite of Spring*. The percussion features several Cuban or Mexican instruments, including *claves* (resonant short wooden sticks), *raspador* (a rasp or scraper), Indian drum, tom-toms (small tuned drums), and gourd.

178

EDGARD VARÈSE (1883–1965)

Hyperprism

Work for winds, brass, and percussion

1922–23

From Edgard Varèse, *Hyperprism* (New York: G. Ricordi, 1961). Used by permission of Universal Music MGB Publications.

6
(♩.=♩ préc.)
Fl.
Cl. mi♭
1. Cors en fa
2. Cors en fa
3.
ppp
f
(heavy)
sff
mf sf sf sff
mf
sf p
1. Trptts 2.
gliss.
T. Trbns B.
fff
mf
fff
molto
ppp
(con sord.)
sans sourd.
pp
mp
ff
p
pp
(1) sur le rebord
(2) membrane
S. D.
I. D.
B. D.
Tamb.
L.V.
mp
Cr. Cymb.
2 Cymb.
T. t.
à 2
Trgl.
Anvil
Sl. St.
2 Ch. Bl.
L. R.
Rttl
Big Rttl
Sl. Blls
Siren
sf

Très calme
(harmonique)
12
a tempo
accel. molto
très agité
animant
Fl.
Cl. mi♭
Cors en fa
Trptts
Trbns
ouvert
(non troppo)
bouché
con sord.
senza sord.
haletantes (en dehors)
(sans sord.)
sempre p
S. D.
I. D.
B. D.
Tamb.
Cr. Cymb.
2 Cymb.
T. t.
Trgl
Anvil
Sl. St.
2 Ch. Bl.
L. R.
Rttl
Big Rttl
Sl. Blls
Siren
L.V.
L.V. et séteindre
morendo

Calmato a tempo
18
Fl.
dans un sentiment sourd. et tumultueux
f
cédez légèrement
Cl. mi♭
1. Cors en fa
2. Cors en fa
3.
1. Trptts
2.
pppp
T. Trbns
B.
dans un sentiment sourd. et tumultueux
(voilé)
Calmato a tempo
(1) rebord
(2) membrane
S.D.
I.D.
B.D.
Tamb.
voilé
Cr. Cymb.
2 Cymb.
T. t.
étouffées
L.V.
étouffées
Trgl.
Anvil
Sl. St.
sec.
2 Ch. Bl.
L.R.
Rttl.
Big Rttl.
Sl. Blls
Siren

Tempo initial
23
Prenez petite Flûte
Petite Flûte
sec
Fl.
Cl. mib
1. Cors en fa 2. Cors en fa 3.
sans Sourd
con sord.
1. Trptts 2.
T. Trbns. B.
Tempo initial
(1) sur rebord
(2) membrane
Voilé
S. D.
I. D.
B. D.
L.V.
Tamb.
Cr. Cymb.
(1) frottées l'une contre l'autre
2 Cymb.
(1) agitez l'une contre l'autre
T. t.
Trgl.
Anvil
Sl. St.
2 Ch. Bl.
L. R.
Rttl
Big Rttl
Sl. Bls
Siren
sourd.

35
30
Pesante
Prenez grande Flûte
pte Fl.
Cl. mi♭
ouvert très en dehors
1.
Cors en fa
2.
Cors en fa
3.
ouvert
ouvert
1.
Trptts
2.
T.
Trbns
B.
Pesante
S. D.
I. D.
B. D.
Tamb.
(bois)
sec.
(bois)sec.(mailloche)
Cr. Cymb.
etouffées
2 Cymb.
T. t.
Trgl.
Anvil
Sl. St.
2 Ch. Bl.
L. R.
Rttl
Big Rttl
Sl. Blls
Siren

36
Lent
Flûte
Fl.
Cl. mi ♭
rall. pesantissimo
lunga
1.
Cors en fa
2.
Cors en fa
3.
sf molto
sff
fff
très chaud
très chaud
sans sourd.
avec sourd.
1.
Trptts
2.
avec sourd.
avec sourd.
T.
Trbns
B.
Lent
S.D.
I.D.
B.D.
Tamb.
Cr. Cymb.
2 Cymb.
T. t.
Trgl.
Anvil
Sl. St.
2 Ch. Bl.
L. R.
Rttl
Big Rttl
Sl. Blls
Siren

*) dans le < comme le > la 1ère Trompette legèrement dominante

47
Vif
a tempo
Mosso
Vif
Cl. mi♭
1. Cors en fa
2. Cors en fa
3.
1. Trptts
2.
T. Trbns
B.
S.D.
I.D.
B.D.
Tamb.
Cr. Cymb.
2 Cymb.
T.t.
etouffées
Trgl
Anvil
Sl.St.
2 Ch. Bi.
L.R.
Rttl
Big Rttl
Sl. Blls
Siren

55
a tempo
Mosso
pte Fl.
Cl. mi♭
1.
Cors en fa
2.
Cors en fa
3.
1.
Trptts
2.
T.
Trbns
B.
a tempo
Mosso
S.D.
I.D.
B.D.
Tamb.
Cr. Cymb.
2 Cymb.
T.t.
Trgl
Anvil
Sl. St.
2 Ch.Bl.
L.R.
Rttl
Big Rttl
Sl. Blls
Siren

36
59
Moderato
pte Fl.
Cl. mi♭
1. Cors en fa
2. Cors en fa
3.
ouvert
gliss.
1. Trptts 2.
T. Trbns B.
(1). rebord
(2) membrane
S. D.
I. D.
B. D.
Tamb.
Cr. Cymb.
2 Cymb.
T. t.
L.V.
Trgl
Anvil
Sl. St.
2 Ch. Bl.
L. R.
Rttl
Big Rttl
Sl. Blls
Siren

63
pte Fl.
Cl mi♭
1. Cors en fa
2. Cors en fa
3.
1. Trptts
2.
T. Trbns
B.
(laughing)
(1) rebord
(2) membrane
S.D.
I.D.
B.D.
Tamb.
Cr. Cymb.
2 Cymb.
T. t.
etouffées
(frottées)
L.V.
Trgl
Anvil
Sl. St.
2 Ch. Bl.
L.R.
Rttl
Big Rttl
Sl. Blls
Siren
morendo

68
pte Fl.
Cl. mi♭
1. Cors en fa 2. Cors en fa 3.
1. Trptts 2.
T. Trbns B.
S. D.
I. D.
B. D.
Tamb.
Cr. Cymb.
2 Cymb.
T. t.
Trgl.
Anvil
Sl. St.
2 Ch. Bl.
L. R.
Rttl
Big Rttl
Sl. Blls
Siren
subito

72
hurlant
Vif très souple, mystérieux (quasi à 1)
pte Fl.
Cl. mi♭
1. Cors en fa 2. Cors en fa 3.
1. Trptts 2.
T. Trbns B.
Vif très souple, mystérieux (quasi à 1)
S.D.
I.D.
B.D.
Tamb.
Cr. Cymb.
2 Cymb.
T.t.
Trgl
Anvil
Sl. St.
2 Ch. Bl.
L.R.
Rttl
Big Rttl
Sl. Blls
Siren

37
82
Allegro molto
très long
pte Fl.
Cl. mi ♭
ouvert
1.
Cors en fa
2.
Cors en fa
3.
Sans sourd.
1.
Trptts
2.
T.
Trbns
B.
S.D.
I.D.
B.D.
Tamb.
avec baguettes tambour
(Très serrè)
Cr. Cymb.
2 Cymb.
T. t.
Trgl
Anvil
Sl.St.
2 Ch. Bl.
L.R.
Rttl
Big Rttl
Sl. Blls
Siren

Edgard Varèse wrote *Hyperprism* in 1922–23 and conducted its premiere in New York on March 4, 1923, in a concert of the International Composers' Guild, a group he had cofounded that specialized in presenting new music. The performance sparked catcalls by some in the audience but also drew an offer from London music publisher J. Curwen & Sons to publish the piece, and it appeared the following year.

No doubt *Hyperprism* startled some of its first listeners because it does not do what most music does. Varèse conceived of his music spatially. It is not rhetorical, shaped like a speech or intending to communicate a feeling or experience, as so much music since the Renaissance has been; nor is it organic, each part relating to the others like cells of a living organism, as in a piece by Brahms or Webern. Rather, it is like a dance in sound, in which "sound masses" move through an imagined musical space. Many of the sounds Varèse uses suggest motion, in one or more diminsions: a pitch that rises and falls implies movement up and down, an increase or decrease in volume simulates moving closer or farther away, and a pitch or other sound that changes timbre or moves from one instrument to another seems to move horizontally—and may do so literally in a live concert.

Percussion instruments are well suited to this type of music. Some of the special instruments Varèse uses suggest motion in the very sounds they make, including the siren and the lion's roar (played by pulling on a string attached to a drum head, which makes the drum vibrate with changing pitch and volume, heard near the beginning of the piece in its first complete measure). Moreover, Varèse uses different combinations of percussion instruments to suggest sound masses that move, change, alternate, or interpenetrate. At the beginning, a composite, rapidly changing sound mass is initiated by a cymbal clash and tam-tam (flat gong) and continued by bass drum, moving from metallic to drum sounds. When this sound mass next appears in measure 5, the bass drum initiates it, and other drum and metallic sounds join in: crash cymbal, snare drum, and tambourine. This sound mass repeats in various forms in measures 7, 16–17, and 23, alternating with other ideas in the percussion. One such idea is a beat pattern in the Indian drum that is linked with a constantly changing array of other instruments, including siren, rattles, triangle, sleigh bells, anvil, and Chinese blocks (see measures 3, 6, 8, 11, 18, 20, and 24–25). When this idea repeats and varies, it sometimes merges with the sounds of the first sound mass (as in measures 16–22).

Meanwhile, the nine wind and brass instruments do not play themes and rarely play melodies. Instead, like the percussion, they produce sounds that suggest static or moving sound masses. The tenor trombone introduces the pitch *c♯'* and embellishes it with accents and glissandos, in alternation with the horns playing crescendos, *sforzandos*, and flutter-tonguing on the same note (measures 2–12; the horns are in F and sound a fifth lower than notated). This constitutes a sound mass with a static central pitch, but with a constantly changing timbre—using effects that most listeners in 1923 would have called noise rather than music.

Since the purpose of the pitches in this music is to create sound masses, Varèse avoids combinations that suggest familiar chords or scales. Instead, both melodically and harmonically, he tends to use notes that are next to each other in the chromatic scale but separated by one or more octaves. Such dissonances are prominent throughout the first section (measures 1–29). Thus the *c♯'* in tenor trombone and horns is joined by *D* two octaves below it in the bass trombone. (Interestingly, that low D offers Varèse an opportunity to link the brass and percussion sounds directly; it alternates with the lion's roar and siren, and all three are constantly changing dynamic level, giving them somewhat similar sound contours.) At measure 12, when the C♯ shifts up an octave to the trumpets and E♭ clarinet (which sounds a minor third higher than written), it is joined by C in flute and trombone over gentle metallic sounds in the percussion. As the clarinet and flute sustain their dissonance, the other instruments enter to form a chord containing the nine chromatic notes from B♭ to F♯ spread over a range of four and a half octaves (measures 15–16). The instruments do not all begin or end the chord together but enter and exit in groups, staggered in a manner that is typical of Varèse. Having explored chromatic harmonies of from two to nine notes, Varése now turns to melodic chromaticism: the flute melody that follows (measures 19–24) includes all twelve chromatic notes, ending with a minor ninth against the trumpet, which sustains the flute's next-to-last note. The section closes with another major seventh in the high winds (the piccolo A sounds an octave higher than written).

Varèse believed that the form of a work grew out of its material, and typically this results in an episodic structure. What we have examined so far is the first section, unified by the recurring sound masses in the percussion but subdivided into three units by the changing sound masses in the winds and brass: the sustained C♯ (measures 1–11), the chromatic chord (measures 12–18), and the flute melody (measures 19–29).

Everything changes at once at measure 30, launching the second section. Here the texture suddenly becomes homorhythmic, with brass and percussion moving together in the first subsection (measures 30–39). The percussion drop out entirely while the winds and brass engage in counterpoint (measures 40–43), and then all three instrumental families participate in a counterpoint of blocks, layering and juxtaposing figures that each repeat in only one instrument or group of instruments (measures 44–58).

The third section somewhat resembles the first. In the first subsection (59–68), horn 1 and tenor trombone decorate F♯, then the trombone plays a chromatic descending melody with octave displacements, ending over a quarter tone in the bass trombone notated as D half-flat (♭½). Piccolo and clarinet then play angular chromatic figures in rhythmic unison (measures 68–75), sounding together all but two notes of the chromatic scale: D and C♯, the immediate neighbors of that D half-flat. The brief coda (measures 84–89) sounds all twelve notes of the chromatic scale to end the piece.

Varèse's music is very distinctive and original in conception, but he draws on his immediate predecessors. The use of layers, block construction, and juxtaposition are indebted to Stravinsky. The nondevelopmental approach, focus on timbre as an essential musical element, and identification of each musical idea with a particular timbre or with changing timbres are characteristics of both Stravinsky and Debussy. Yet the pitch organization, with its focus on chromaticism and use of chromatic saturation to demarcate sections, relates to Schoenberg's atonal music, which Varèse came to know during his days in Berlin before emigrating to the United States.

In the original score shown here, Varèse laid out the percussion by type, making it easy to track the sounds he was using but leaving it to the players to figure out who played what when. A revised edition by Richard Sacks distributes the percussion parts to nine players but is essentially the same in sound.

Henry Cowell (1897–1965)

The Banshee

Piano piece

1925

The Banshee

Explanation of Symbols

"The Banshee" is played on the open strings of the piano, the player standing at the crook. Another person must sit at the keyboard and hold down the damper pedal throughout the composition. The whole work should be played an octave lower than written.

R. H. stands for "right hand." L. H. stands for "left hand." Different ways of playing the strings are indicated by a letter over each tone, as follows:

(A) indicates a sweep with the flesh of the finger from the lowest string up to the note given.

(B) sweep lengthwise along the string of the note given with flesh of finger.

(C) sweep up and back from lowest A to highest B-flat given in this composition.

(D) pluck string with flesh of finger, where written, instead of octave lower.

(E) sweep along three notes together, in the same manner as (B).

(F) sweep in the manner of (B) but with the back of finger-nail instead of flesh.

(G) when the finger is half way along the string in the manner of (F), start a sweep along the same string with the flesh of the other finger, thus partly damping the sound.

(H) sweep back and forth in the manner of (C), but start at the same time from both above and below, crossing the sweep in the middle.

(I) sweep along five notes, in the manner of (B).

(J) same as (I) but with back of finger-nails instead of flesh of finger.

(K) sweep along in manner of (J) with nails of both hands together, taking in all notes between the two outer limits given.

(L) sweep in manner of (C) with flat of hand instead of single finger.

CD 13|38

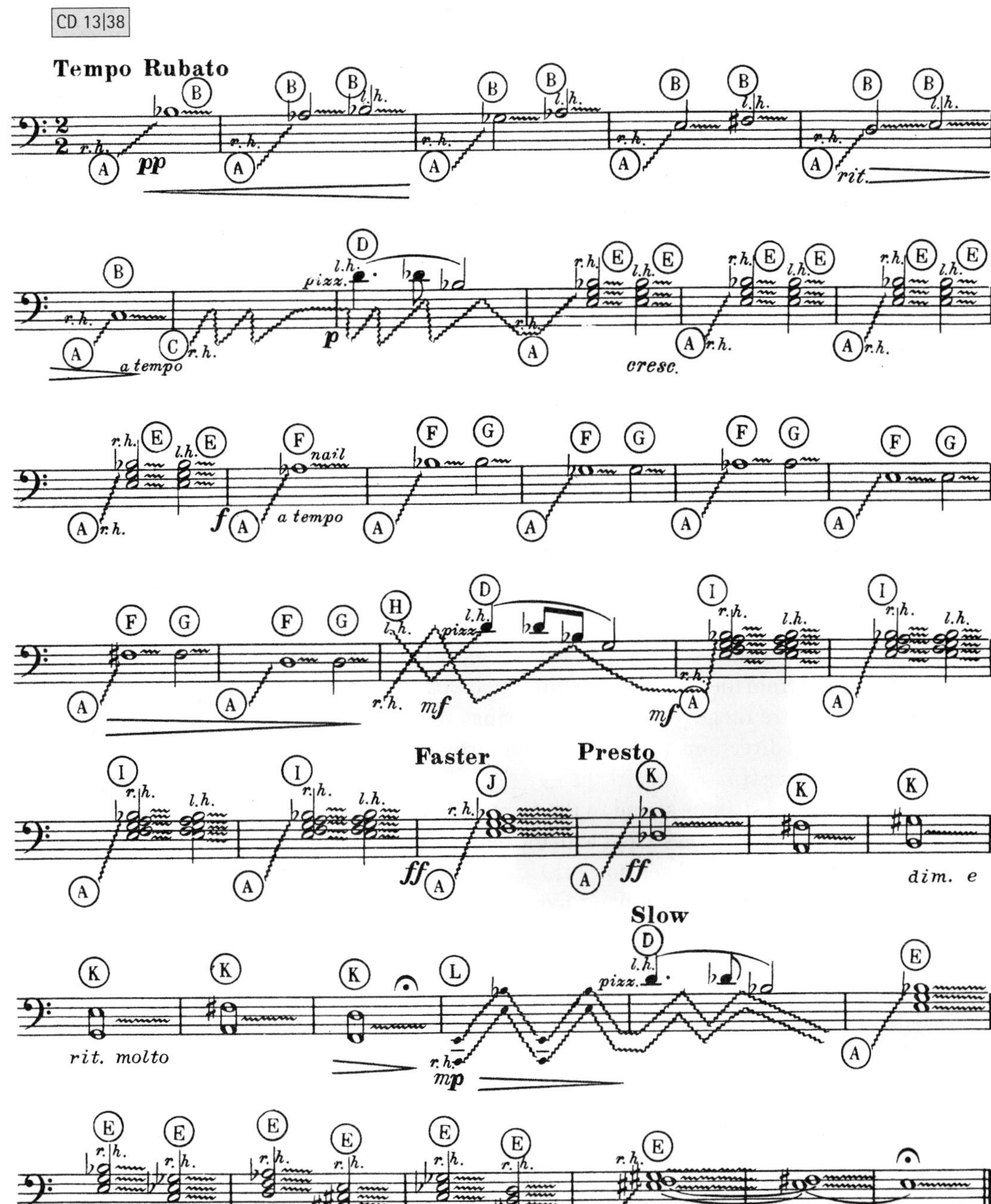
Tempo Rubato
r.h.
l.h.
pp
rit.
a tempo
pizz.
p
cresc.
nail
f
mf
Faster
Presto
ff
dim. e
Slow
rit. molto
mp
ppp

Henry Cowell spent his career exploring new techniques and composing pieces to showcase them. *The Banshee*, which Cowell composed and premiered in early 1925, is typical, presenting sounds made by playing directly on the strings of a grand piano rather than by pressing the keys. With the lid up and the damper pedal held down by an assistant or a wedge so the strings resonate freely, the performer stands in the crook of the piano and plays the strings with fingers, fingernails, or the palm of the hand. To show the player how to produce these new sounds, Cowell had to invent a notation, which relies on letters keyed to brief instructions for each playing technique.

There are four types of sound in this piece. With one exception, Cowell uses only the lowest strings of the piano—from B♭ a ninth below middle C to A two octaves lower. These strings are tightly wound with wire, unlike the smooth wire strings in higher registers. (For ease of reading, he notates these strings an octave higher than they sound.) To understand this piece, it will be helpful to find a grand piano and try out these sounds:

1. The simplest sound to produce is a glissando made by sweeping the flesh of the finger across the wire-wound strings. There are several variants: a glissando from the lowest A to an indicated note (letter A); back and forth across the entire range of wire-wound strings (C); back and forth simultaneously in both directions (H); or back and forth with a flat hand rather than a single finger (L).
2. The most striking sound in the piece is created by rubbing along the length of the wire-wound strings with the flesh of the finger, whether on the strings for one note (B), three notes (E), or five notes (I). This is done with the palm facing downward, the hand moving away from the player, and the fingers extended and pressing down on the strings, so the friction of the fingers against the ridges in the wound wire causes the string to vibrate. If done correctly, this creates a howling or moaning sound with varying pitch, strangely similar to a human voice, that must have reminded Cowell of the banshee, a type of female spirit from Irish folklore who wails outside the house of someone who is about to die.
3. A more raspy or zingy sound is made by rubbing along the length of the string with the back of the fingernail, on the strings for one note (F), five notes (J), or nine notes, using both hands (K). This is performed using the same gesture as the finger rubs, only with the fingers curled under so the fingernails contact the strings. Cowell often modifies the one-string fingernail rub in mid-course by adding a flesh-of-the-finger rub in the other hand on the same string (G).
4. The most familiar sound in the piece is made by plucking strings with the flesh of the finger (D), in a descending melodic motive, *d′–d♭′–b♭* (with added *g* the second time through). This is the one element that is played on the smooth wire strings, in the piano's middle range, and sounds as notated rather than an octave lower.

Of these sounds, the first and last can be imagined from the notation; the plucked pitches are obvious, and the glissandos are notated graphically with a wavy line adapted from the sign for arpeggiating a chord. But nothing in the notation can prepare the ear for the weird sound of rubbing along a wire-wound string with a finger or fingernail. The pitches one hears may be entirely different from those that are notated. At these spots, the notation serves as a kind of tablature, telling the player what to do rather than symbolizing the resulting sound (compare the lute tablatures in NAWM 61 and 73). For this reason, and because of differences among pianos and performers, the actual sounds of this piece can vary a great deal between performances.

With this repertoire of sounds, Cowell organized the piece in four short sections articulated by the plucked motive, which appears at the end of each of the first three sections accompanied by a new variant of the glissando (letters C, H, and L, each of which appears only once in the piece). The first section (measures 1–8), predominantly quiet, introduces the glissandos and finger rubs. The second (measures 9–20) grows louder, adding three-finger rubs and fingernail rubs. Louder still is the third section (measures 21–33), with multi-finger and multi-fingernail rubs. After the plucked motive is heard for the third time, the last section (measures 34–40) is quiet, with only glissandos and three-finger rubs. The overall shape suggests the visit of a banshee, who approaches and begins wailing softly, intensifies her cries, and subsides.

What is the role of the title and implied program in this piece? In the nineteenth century, composers often introduced extraordinary sounds or events to convey a program or scene, such as the flutter-tonguing in brass and wind instruments to imitate the bleating of sheep in Strauss's *Don Quixote* (NAWM 149). One could imagine that Cowell encountered the legend of the banshee and sought musical means to represent it. But given his lifelong interest in new resources, it is far more likely that he was experimenting with sounds that could be made on the piano strings, discovered the banshee-like wailing that resulted from rubbing the wire-bound strings lengthwise, and conceived the piece to demonstrate the techniques he had discovered. In this sense, the piece is a prime example of experimental music, which explores and presents new musical resources for their own sake. The title suggests a possible meaning for the new sounds and makes them easier to accept—and more interesting.

The performance on the accompanying recording is by Cowell himself, and we can assume that it reveals the sounds he intended to create. Comparing his performance with the score, he takes some liberties, adding some gestures and omitting or hurrying through others, suggesting that the overall shape and effect were most important to him.

Ruth Crawford Seeger (1901–1953)

String Quartet 1931: Fourth movement, Allegro possibile

String Quartet

1931

CD 13|39 CD 6|54

Allegro possibile

5

ff

pp sempre con sordino

pp sempre con sordino

pp sempre con sordino

sempre ff

10

From Ruth Crawford, *String Quartet, 1931* (Bryn Mawr, Pa.: Merion Music, 1941), 16–22. © 1941 by Merion Music, Inc./Theodore Presser, Inc. Reprinted by permission of Theodore Presser. Accidentals apply only to the notes directly following. For example, the fourth note in the fifth measure is D♮, not D♭, and the last note in the sixth measure is B♮, not B♭.

15
cresc. poco a poco to meas. 60
cresc. poco a poco to meas. 60
cresc. poco a poco to meas. 60
20
decresc. poco a poco to meas. 60
p
p
p
f
25
mp
mp
mp
mf
30
mp

40
55
35
40
45
mf
fz
f
p
3
5

50
pp
ff
fz
41
56
55
ffz
ffz p
60
pp
65
cresc. poco a poco to meas. 100
fz
decresc. poco a poco to meas. 101
decresc. poco a poco to meas. 101
decresc. poco a poco to meas. 101

70
75
80

85
mf
mp
mp
mp
90
f
p
p
p
95
più f

100
ff
pp
pp
pp
105
sempre ff
sempre pp
sempre pp
sempre pp
3
110
115
ffz
ffz
ffz

Ruth Crawford composed her String Quartet in 1931 during a year in Berlin and Paris on a Guggenheim Fellowship, the first awarded to a woman. Over the previous year, she had assisted her composition teacher Charles Seeger (whom she later married in 1932 after her return from Europe) in developing ideas of dissonant counterpoint for an unpublished book manuscript, and many of those ideas appear in her quartet. She saw his and her own work as representative of an American tradition in modern music, independent of the European modernists. Accordingly, while in Europe she studied with no one, avoided contact with Schoenberg (who was in Berlin), and met only briefly with Berg and Bartók. Her String Quartet was given the subtitle "1931" when it was published ten years later in *New Music*, a quarterly periodical of new scores by "ultramodern" composers, published by Henry Cowell.

The String Quartet is full of new ideas. Although it consists of four movements in a familiar order—fast, scherzo-like, slow, and fast—each movement is based on a different set of devices, most of which had never been tried in a quartet. The first movement is built on a counterpoint of almost wholly independent melodies. The second movement develops a three-note motive through constant shifts of accent and implied meter. In the third movement, all four instruments play almost constantly but swell to dynamic peaks at different times, and those peaks are heard as a kind of melody passed among the instruments.

The finale, included here, is the most systematic: a palindrome, whose second half is an exact retrograde of the first, transposed up a half step. (The pivot point is at measures 58–59, with the transposition beginning at the second eighth note of measure 60.) The texture consists of two contrapuntal lines. In the first half of the piece, the first violin plays one note, then two, then three, increasing the number of notes in succession to twenty-one, while getting gradually softer. The pitches and rhythms are freely chosen. Meanwhile the other three instruments, muted and playing in octaves, interject phrases of twenty notes, then nineteen, then eighteen, reducing the number of notes to one, while getting gradually louder. In contrast to the varied durations and freely chosen pitches of the first violin line, the lower instruments play only eighth notes (sometimes sustaining the last note in a phrase) and use pitches generated by permutations of a ten-note series. The result is a contrast of opposites: one line (in the violin) of free notes and rhythms, unmuted, that gradually decrescendoes through phrases that grow ever longer, and a second line (in the other instruments) of even notes and rhythms, that gradually crescendoes through phrases that grow ever shorter. After both lines arrive at their last note in measure 57, they sustain it at a soft dynamic level through the pivot point, and then everything reverses.

The series in the lower line is handled in an innovative manner. Rather than invert or retrograde the series, as in the twelve-tone music of Schoenberg, Berg, and Webern, Crawford permutes it through a process called *rotation*, taking the first note and moving it to the end, then doing this again with the second note, and so on:

D	E	F	E♭	F♯	A	A♭	G	D♭	C						
	E	F	E♭	F♯	A	A♭	G	D♭	C	D					
		F	E♭	F♯	A	A♭	G	D♭	C	D	E				
			E♭	F♯	A	A♭	G	D♭	C	D	E	F			
				F♯	A	A♭	G	D♭	C	D	E	F	E♭		etc.

The first phrase, with twenty notes, has the first two statements of this series (measures 3–5), the next phrase has all but the last note of the next two statements (adding up to nineteen notes, in measures 7–9), and so on, until the series has been stated ten times in all possible rotations, ending with the second eighth note of measure 21. At this point, the entire process unfolds again, with the series transposed up a whole step. (One note is missing in one of the rotations—can you find it?) After the second set of ten rotations is complete, the series returns in its original form and transposition (measures 47–54), and the process halts at the pivot point of the palindrome on what would be the first note of the next rotation.

This movement is unique in Crawford's output—no other piece works like this—and is therefore characteristic of Crawford, whose every piece is unique in its language and musical devices. The movement's intense conflicts between elements, such as the opposition in almost every parameter between the two contrapuntal lines, is also typical of her music. Such opposition introduces difficulties for the players in coordinating their parts, which is heightened here by an emphasis on duration and pulse, tending to obscure meter. The slurring in the lower line, which freely alternates groups of four, two, and three notes, also works against the meter, creating a free, rhapsodic interplay of opposing forces—the very embodiment of her and Seeger's notion of dissonant counterpoint.

Aaron Copland (1900–1990)

Appalachian Spring, Excerpt with Variations on *'Tis the Gift to Be Simple*

181

Ballet suite

1943–44, orchestrated 1945

CD 13|42 CD 6|57

5
Fl. I
Picc.
Ob. I. II
(in B♭) I.
Cl.
(in B♭) II
Fg. I. II
Tr. (B♭) I. II
Trb. I. II
Claves
Arpa
Pfte.
Vl. I
Vl. II
Vla.
Vc.
36
a 2
8va
mp
mf
sf

12

Cor. (F) I. II
Tr. (B♭) I. II
Trb. I. II
Vl. I
Vl. II
Vla.
Vc.
Cb.

mf *ff* *sfz* *p* *sf*

43 58

17

Accel. (37) Presto (𝅗𝅥 = 92) 8va

Fl. I. II.
Fg. I. II
Cor. (F) I. II

mp *p*

Accel. (37) Presto (𝅗𝅥 = 92)

non legato

Vl. I
Vl. II
Vla.

mp *mp* stacc. *p*

22
Fl. I
Cl. II (in B♭)
Fg. I. II
Vl. I
Vl. II
Vla.
non legato
mp
I.
II.
p
p stacc.
26
8va
38
Fl. I
Picc.
Ob. I. II
(in B♭) I.
Cl.
(in B♭) II.
Fg. I. II
Cor (F) I. II
Tr. (B♭) I. II
Vl. I
Vl. II
Vla.
Vc.
Soli
a 2
sf
sfz
mp
p
I. II. con sord.
I. II. con sord
pizz.
mf
non div.

31
a 2
Ob. I. II
(in B♭) I.
Cl.
(in B♭) II
Fg. I. II
mf
f
ff
p
39
senza sord.
Cor. (F) I. II
Tr. (B♭) I. II
arco
(pizz.)
Vl. I
Vl. II
Vla.
Vc.
Cb.
mp
pizz.
36
I.
con sord.
non legato
arco

41
40
Fl. I
Picc.
Ob. I. II
(in B♭) I.
Cl.
(in B♭) II
Fg. I. II
Cor. (F) I. II
Tr. (B♭) I. II
Trb. I. II
Vl. I
Vl. II
Vla.
Vc.
f marc.
non legato
con sord.
con sord.

46
Fl. I.
Picc.
Ob. I. II
(in B♭) I.
Cl.
(in B♭) II.
Cor. (F) I. II
Tr. (B♭) I. II
Trb. I. II
Timp.
Bass Dr.
Pfte.
Vl. I
Vl. II
Vla.
Vc.
Cb
41
8va
a 2
sf
f stacc.
marc.
div.
arco

51
8va
Fl. I
Picc.
Ob. I. II
(in B♭) I
Cl.
(in B♭) II
a 2
Cor. (F) I. II
Tr. (B♭) I. II
Trb. I. II
Timp.
B. Dr.
unis.
Vl. I
unis.
Vl. II
Vla.
Vc.
Cb.

54
42
8va
Fl. I
Picc.
Ob. I. II
(in B♭) I
Cl.
(in B♭) II
Cor. (F) I. II
a 2
Tr. (B♭) I. II
Trb. I. II
Timp.
B. Dr.
Vl. I
Vl. II
Vla.
Vc.
Cb.
cresc.
ff
mf
mp
At the frog
Mark the Bass

58
Fl. I
Picc.
Fg. I. II
Cor. (F) I. II
Vl. I
Vl. II
Vla.
Vc.
Cb.
8va
p
a 2
62

66
43
44
59
Fl. I
Picc.
Ob. I. II
a 2
(in B♭) I.
Cl.
(in B♭) II.
Fg. I. II
Cor. (F) I. II
senza sord.
Tr. (B♭) I. II
Trb. I. II
Claves
Arpa
Pfte.
Vl. I
Vl. II
Vla.
Vc.
Cb.
mf
f
sf
8va

74
44
Vl. I
Vl. II
Vla.
Vc.
Cb.
mf
79
a 2
Ob. I. II
f marc.
(in B♭) I.
Cl.
(in B♭) II.
Fg. I. II
Cor. (F) I. II
Tr. (B♭) I. II
mf
f
Pfte.
mf non legato
Vl. I
div.
Vl. II
Vla.
Vc.
Cb.

83
45
Solo
Fl. I
f
Picc.
Solo
a 2
Ob. I. II
(in B♭) I
Cl.
(in B♭) II
a 2
Fg. I. II
Cor. (F) I. II
a 2
Tr. (B♭) I. II
a 2
Trb. I. II
a 2
f
45
Pfte.
45
Vl. I
unis.
Vl. II
div. pizz.
div.
Vla.
p
div.
Vc.
div.
p
Cb.

88
46
Fl. I
8va
Picc.
Take Fl. II.
Près de la table
Arpa
p
46
div.
pizz.
arco
unis.
Vl. I
p
arco
Vl. II
Vla.
92
Fl. I
Fg.
I. II
I.
p
Tr. (Bb)
I. II
I.II con sord.
p
Arpa
Vl. I
Vl. II
unis.
Vla.
p

96

(47)

Fl. I.

Fl. II.

Ob. I. II

Cl. (in B♭) I

Cl. (in B♭) II

Fg. I. II

Tr. (B♭) I. II

Vl. I

Vl. II

Vla.

Vc.

Cb.

101
Fl.
I.
II.
Ob.
I. II
(in B♭) I
Cl.
(in B♭) II
Fg.
I. II
Cor. (F)
I. II
Tr. (B♭)
I. II
II. (senza sord.)
I. senza sord.
Vl. I
div.
pizz.
unis.
Vl. II
pizz.
Vla.
Vc.

106
48
I.
Fl.
II.
Ob. I. II
(in Bb) I
Cl.
(in Bb) II
Fg. I. II
Cor. (F) I. II
Tr. (Bb) I. II
Trb. I. II
Xylo.
Pfte.
Vl. I
Vl. II
Vla.
Vc.
secco
a 2
arco
marc.
cresc.
8va

111
8va
8va
a 2
I.
Fl.
II.
Ob. I. II
(in B♭) I
Cl.
(in B♭) II
Fg. I. II
a 2
Cor. (F) I. II
Tr. (B♭) I. II
Trb. I. II
Xylo.
8
Pfte.
Vl. I
Vl. II
Vla.
Vc.

116

(49)

I.
Fl.
II.
Ob. I. II
(in B♭) I
Cl.
(in B♭) II
Fg. I. II
Cor. (F) I. II
Tr. (B♭) I. II
Trb. I. II
Timp.
Xylo.
Pfte.
Vl. I
Vl. II
Vla.
Vc.
Cb.

sf
a 2
ff
II.
8va
marc.
div.
unis.

121
I.
Fl.
II.
sf
Ob. I. II
(in B♭) I
Cl.
(in B♭) II
a 2
Fg. I. II
Cor. (F) I. II
Tr. (B♭) I. II
Trb. I. II
Timp.
Xylo.
Claves
ff
Arpa
8va
Pfte
unis.
div.
Vl. I
Vl. II
Vla.
Vc.
Cb.

127

50

More deliberate tempo (♩ = 120)

I. Fl. II.

Ob. I. II

(in B♭) I. Cl. (in B♭) II.

Fg. I. II

Cor. (F) I. II

Tr. (B♭) I. II

Trb. I. II

Xylo. Timp.

Claves

Arpa

Pfte.

Vl. I

Vl. II

Vla.

Vc.

Cb.

a 2 ten. Xyl. Timp. *f* 8va unis. *sf* pizz.

45
60
134
ten.
rit.
Meno mosso (𝅗𝅥 = 96)
51
I.
Fl.
II.
Ob.
I. II
a 2
I. Solo
sub. mf cant. espress.
(in B♭) I.
Cl.
(in B♭) II
Fg.
I. II
Cor. (F)
I. II
Tr. (B♭)
I. II
Trb.
I. II
Timp.
sf
Arpa
mf (brittle)
8va
Vl. Solo
cant.
sub. mf
dolce
Vl. I
Vl. II
Vla.
Vc.
Cb.
p dolce
arco
pizz.
(pizz.)
p

141
52
Fl. I
ppp
I.
Ob. I. II
Solo
Cl. I (in B♭)
p cant.
p
ppp
I.
Fg. I. II
p
pp
Solo
p
8va
Arpa
8va
Vl. Solo
52
div.
Vl. I
p
ppp
div.
Vl. II
p
ppp
Vla.
p
ppp
arco
pizz.
Vc.
p
ppp
arco
Cb.
p
ppp

46
61
As at first (slowly)
53
Fl. I.
Cl. (in B♭) I.
Cl. (in B♭) II
Fg. I. II
Tr. (B♭) I. II
Arpa
Vl. II
Vla.
Vc.
Solo
I. Solo
I. Solo con sord.
div.
54
Fl. I.
Cl. I.
Fg. I. II
Tr (B♭) I. II
Arpa
Vl. I
Vl. II
Vla.
Vc. Cb.
unis.
Vc.,Cb.

★ Shaker melody "The gift to be simple"

48
63
57
A trifle faster (♩ = 80)
186
Fl. I
Picc.
Take Fl. II
Ob. I. II
II.
I. Solo
(in B♭) I.
Cl.
(in B♭) II
Solo
Solo
Fg. I. II
I. Solo
II. Solo
Tr. (B♭) I. II
con sord.
Arpa
193
58
I.
Fl.
II.
Ob. I. II
I.
a 2
(in B♭) I
Cl.
(in B♭) II
Fg. I. II
a 2
Cor. (F) I. II
(Open)
Tr. (B♭) I. II
Tri.

49
64
200
I.
Fl.
II.
mf
(a 2)
I. Solo
Ob.
I. II
(in B♭) I
Cl.
(in B♭) II
Solo
Fg.
I. II
II.
Cor. (F)
I. II
Glock.
sounds 8va
p
8va
Arpa
Pfte.
senza Ped.
Vl. I
div.
pizz.
Vl. II

208
59
I.
Fl.
II.
p leggiero
p leggiero
Ob. I. II
p leggiero
(in B♭) I
Cl.
(in B♭) II
p leggiero
p leggiero
Fg. I. II
p leggiero
Cor. (F) I. II
con sord.
p
Trb. I. II
I. Solo cant.
mf dolce
Glock. sounds 8va
8va
Arpa
59
8va
Pfte.
59
Vl. I
Vl. II
Vla.
mf cant. dolce

214
60
I.
Fl.
II.
Ob. I. II
(in Bb) I
Cl.
(in Bb) II
Fg. I. II
Cor. (F) I. II
senza sord. a 2
f cant.
Tr. (Bb) I. II
Trb. I. II
I.
a 2
Glock. sounds 8va
8va
Arpa
8va
Pfte.
cant. sonore
div.
f
Vl. I
Vl. II
Vla.
Vc. Cb.
f sonore

220
I.
Fl.
II.
Ob.
I. II
(in B♭) I
Cl.
(in B♭) II
Fg.
I. II
a 2
Cor. (F)
I. II
Tr. (B♭)
I. II
a 2
Trb.
I. II
Glock.
sounds 8va
8va
Arpa
8va
Pfte.
Vl. I
Vl. II
Vla.
Vc.
Cb.

226
I.
Fl.
II.
Ob.
I. II
(in Bb) I
Cl.
(in Bb) II
Fg.
I. II
a 2
Cor. (F)
I. II
Tr. (Bb)
I. II
a 2
Trb.
I. II
Glock.
sounds 8va
8va
Arpa
8va
Pfte.
Vl. I
Vl. II
Vla.
Vc.
Cb.

232
61
Solo
I.
Fl.
II.
Ob.
I. II
I. Solo
(in B♭) I
Cl.
(in B♭) II
Solo
Fg.
I. II
p
Cor. (F)
I. II
a 2
Tr. (B♭)
I. II
Trb.
I. II
Glock.
sounds 8va
8va
Arpa
Pfte.
Vl. I
Vl. II
arco
p sostenuto
Vla.
Vc.
Cb.
pizz.

50
65
238
(♪=♩)
62 Doppio movimento.
Fl. I
Ob. I. II
(in B♭) I
Cl.
(in B♭) II
Fg. I. II
mf
cresc.
non legato
Cor. (F) I. II
mf
cresc.
Vigoroso e marc.
a 2
Tr. (B♭) I. II
mf
cresc.
f
II.
Vigoroso e marc.
a 2
Trb. I. II
mf
cresc.
f
(♪=♩)
62 Doppio movimento
div.
Vl. I
mf
cresc.
Vl. II
f cresc.
Vla.
mf
cresc.
Vc.
mf
cresc.
248
a 2
Tr. (B♭) I. II
a 2
Trb. I. II
unis.
Vl. I
f
Vla.
f

256
63
Ob. I. II
a 2
f sf Vigoroso e marc.
(in B♭) I
Cl.
(in B♭) II
f sf Vigoroso e marc.
f sf Vigoroso e marc.
Cor. (F) I. II
a 2 sf
Tr. (B♭) I. II
a 2
sf
Trb. I. II
a 2 sf
264
Ob. I. II.
a 2
(in B♭) I
Cl.
(in B♭) II
Cor. (F) I. II
a 2
Tr. (B♭) I. II
a 2
Trb. I. II
a 2
Vl. I
Vla.

270
64 A trifle slower (♩ = 66)
Ob I. II
I. Solo
mf
Solo
(in B♭) I
Cl.
(in B♭) II
I. Solo
Fg. I. II
Tr. (B♭) I. II
a 2
p
Trb. I. II
Vl. I
Vla.
arco
Vc. Cb.
278
I.
Fl.
II.
Ob. I. II
Fg. I. II

51
66
288
(𝅗𝅥=𝅗𝅥) Broadly (in 2)
65
I.
Fl.
II.
Ob. I. II
(in B♭) I.
Cl.
(in B♭) II
Fg. I. II
Cor. (F) I. II
Tr. (B♭) I. II
Trb. I. II
Timp.
Arpa
Pfte.
Vl. I
Vl. II
Vla.
Vc.
Cb.
fff legato e marc.
a 2
fff
marc.
unis.
8va

297
66
I.
Fl.
II.
Ob.
I. II
a 2
(in Bb) I
Cl.
(in Bb) II
Fg.
I. II
a 2
Cor. (F)
I. II
Tr. (Bb)
I. II
Trb.
I. II
a 2
Timp.
Arpa
Pfte.
8va
Vl. I
Vl. II
Vla.
Vc.
Cb.
sf
p

Modern dancer and choreographer Martha Graham used Aaron Copland's dissonant and rhythmically complex *Piano Variations* (1930) as the music for a solo dance in 1931, and the result was so successful that the composer and choreographer looked for an opportunity to collaborate. Their chance came in 1942, when Elizabeth Sprague Coolidge, a prominent patron of modern music, commissioned three ballet scores for Graham, including one from Copland. Graham devised the scenario, which went through many changes even after Copland had begun composing the music. The final version of the ballet centers around a couple about to be married in rural nineteenth-century Pennsylvania, who are feted by a minister and neighbors on the completion of their farmhouse.

In accordance with the commission, Copland scored the original ballet for a chamber ensemble of thirteen instruments. He called the piece simply "Ballet for Martha" while working on it, and only when he arrived in Washington, D.C., for the October 30, 1944, premiere did he learn the title she had given the work, *Appalachian Spring.* He was later amused how often people said to him, "When I listen to that ballet of yours, I can just *feel* spring and *see* the Appalachians," since neither was in his mind as he composed. The ballet was a great success, and the music won Copland the Pulitzer Prize and the New York Music Critics' Circle Award. He later arranged the piece as a suite for full orchestra, premiered on October 4, 1945, in New York, and in that form it has become his most widely known work.

During the 1930s, Copland turned from the astringent modernism typified by the *Piano Variations* to a deliberately simpler, more accessible style, seeking to appeal to a broader public. Without leaving behind the dissonance, counterpoint, motivic unity, and juxtaposed blocks of sound that had marked his modernist works, he incorporated diatonic melodies and harmonies, transparent textures, and recognizable allusions to familiar types and styles of music, including some direct quotations of folk or popular songs. His new style is exemplified in *Appalachian Spring*, which evokes country fiddling, dancing, and singing and captures the spirit of rural America.

In the Allegro and Presto sections that begin the excerpt included here, the shifting meters, offbeat accents, and sudden changes of texture show Stravinsky's influence (see NAWM 164 and 165). But the predominantly diatonic melodies and harmonies, syncopation, and guitarlike chords give this passage a flavor of American folk music. Many passages vertically combine consonant and dissonant notes of the diatonic scale in a technique that has been called *pandiatonicism.* The rapid melodic figuration of the Presto (measure 18 of the excerpt) suggests country fiddling, while counterpoint (as at measures 35–38, 61–65, and 74–87) and motivic links between the Allegro and Presto (the figure from measures 5–6 recurs throughout the Presto) show the heritage of the European classical tradition.

At the Meno mosso (measure 138 of the excerpt), leaps of fourths and fifths in the violin and oboe solos and wide spacing of the chords suggest a sparsely populated landscape. This texture, together with diatonic melodies and lightly dissonant diatonic chords, established a distinctive sound that has been used ever since to depict the open spaces and rugged people of frontier America. A recollection of the opening passage of the ballet ("As at first," measure 151) includes the ballet's characteristic sound, superimposed tonic and dominant or tonic and subdominant triads (measures 152–55 and 158–61, respectively).

At the Doppio movimento (Double time, measure 171), Copland begins a set of variations on the Shaker hymn *Simple Gifts*, by Elder Joseph Brackett (1797–1882):

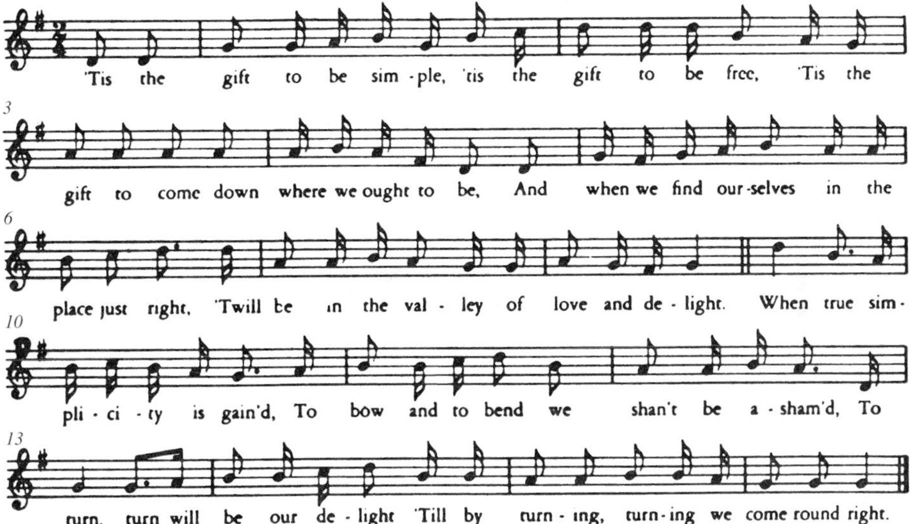

The Shakers were a religious sect who practiced celibacy and lived communally, raising their own food and making virtually everything they used themselves. Their hymns were used in religious services, sung in unaccompanied unison while most of the congregation danced. Copland discovered the tune in a published collection of Shaker hymns and thought it ideally suited Graham's scenario because of its links to dance and to rural America, although the people in her ballet were not Shaker (and there never were Shaker settlements in rural Pennsylvania).

Copland's approach to varying this monophonic hymn tune is to change the melody relatively little but to place it in a series of contrasting settings. The one alteration he consistently makes is in the phrasing, treating the first two notes of the hymn's final phrase as if they were the last two notes of the third phrase and thereby emphasizing the long note on "turn" in measure 13 of the tune. The first variation, in A♭ major, is for clarinet, accompanied quite simply by irregularly alternating dominant and tonic sustained tones in flutes and harp. The second variation (measure 191) has a similar texture, a step lower, with the melody in the oboe, paralleled by bassoon a tenth lower, and accompanied by brass and other winds. The third variation gives the melody, half as fast, to trombones and violas, who are later joined in canon by the horns and first violins, but omits the second half of the tune (measures 207–33). The melody passes to the trumpet and to C major in the fourth variation (measure 240), accompanied by trombone, doubled by winds in the third phrase, and joined for the second and fourth phrases by violins and violas fiddling in rapid scales. The final variation presents the two halves of the tune in reverse order: the opening motive in bassoon (measure 272) turns out to be a counterpoint to the second half of the melody in the clarinet, and then the entire orchestra proclaims the first half of the theme over a slowly descending bass (measure 288).

Like many other composers from Berlioz to Stravinsky (see commentary for NAWM 165), Copland often conducted his own works. The performance on the accompanying recording is of the version for full orchestra, conducted by Copland in 1970.

William Grant Still (1895–1978)

Afro-American Symphony (Symphony No. 1): First movement, Moderato assai

182

Symphony

1930

CD 13|52

Moderato assai ♩ = 88

2
a tempo
3 Fl's.
Oboi
E. H.
Cl's. in B♭
Bass Cl.
B'ssns.
Horns in F
1st Tpt. in B♭
Solo
Harmon mute
Harmon mutes
Trb. ni.
Timp.
Sm. Cymb.
damped
Sn. Dr.
B. D.
soft stick
sempre p
Harp
1st Vl.
2nd Vl.
Vla.
Vc.
Bass
arco
pizz.
(4)

11
Fl's.
Oboi
E. H.
Cl's. in Bb
Bass Cl.
B'ssn's
Horns in F
1st Tpt in Bb
Trb-ni.
Timp. (Db-Eb-Ab)
Sm. Cymb.
Sn. Dr. B. D.
Harp
1st Vl.
2nd Vl.
Vla.
Vc.
Bass
damped
pizz.

53
3
16
Fl's.
Piccolo
Oboi
E.H.
Solo
Clar's. in B♭
Bass Cl.
B'ss'ns.
Horns in F
Trpt in B♭
Trb-ni.
Timp. (D♭-E♭-A♭)
damped
Sm. Cymb.
B.D.
(12)
Harp
col legno
1st Vl.
2nd Vl.
Vla.
(arco)
Vc.
pizz.
Bass
arco
mp col legno
3

21
Fl's.
Picc.
Oboi
E. H.
Clar-s. in Bb
Bass Cl.
B'ss'n's.
Horns in F
Trpt in Bb
Trb.-ni
Timp.
Harp
Vl. I.
Vl. II.
Vla.
Vc.
Bass
mf
mp

27
Fl's.
Picc.
Oboi
E. H.
Clar's. in Bb
Bass Cl.
B'ss'n's.
Solo
Horns in F
Tpt. in Bb
Trb.-ni.
Timp.
Harp
Vl. I.
Vl. II.
Vla.
Vc.
Bass
pizz.
rit. poco a poco

54

32 accel.

[+] Più mosso ♩ = 112

Fl's. 1 2 mp mf

Picc. mp mf

Oboi 1 2 mp mf

E.H.

Clar's. in Bb 1 2 3 mf

Bass Cl. accel.

B'ss'n's. 1 2 rit. accel.

Horns in F 1 2 3 4 mp mf

Trpt. in Bb

Tro.-ni.

Timp. Più mosso ♩ = 112 p mp

Harp accel. mp mf

Vl. I. arco accel. p mp mf

Vl. II. arco p accel. mp mf

V'la. arco mp mf

Vc. arco mp mf

Bass arco mp mf

accel. [+]

37
Fl's.
Picc.
Change to Fl.
Oboi
unis.
E. H.
Cl's. in B♭
Bass Cl.
B'ss'ns.
Horns in F
Tpt's. in B♭
senza sord.
Trb.-ni
senza sord.
Tuba
Timp.
D♭–E♭–A♮
Tria.
Sn. Dr. B. D.
Cymb.
Harp
Vl. I.
Vl. II.
Vla.
Vc.
Bass
pizz.
arco
rit.

55
Andante cantabile ♩=72
5
poco a poco
42
Fl. 1.
Oboi
E. H.
Clar. 1. in B♭
Bass Clar.
Horn 1.
F♯-B♮-E♭
Timp.
Vibr.
Harp
Vl. I. div.
Vl. II.
Vle. div.
Vc. div.
Bass
Solo
mf teneramente
mp
mf
pp
p
(div.) mp
div.
5

48
rit.
Un poco più lento
accel.
G
Poco più mosso
Fl. 1.
Oboi
E. H.
Clar. 1. in Bb
Bass Clar.
legatissimo
Horns in F
mf tenuto
Timp.
Vibr.
Celesta
Harp
Vl. I. div.
2 Solo Violins
All of the Violins
Soli
passionato
Vl. II.
legatissimo
Vle. div.
f legatissimo
Vc. div.
Bass
div.

come prima
rall.
Solo
54
Fl's.
Fl.
E. H.
rall.
Cl's. in Bb
Bass Cl.
Bassoons
rall.
come prima
Horns in F
Tpts.
Trb.-ni
rall.
come prima
Timp.
Cymb.
rall.
come prima
mp tenuto
Celesta
Harp
rall.
Come prima
Vl. I.
Vl. II.
Vle. div.
unis.
Vc.
Bass
rall.
come prima

7
60
Fl's.
Change to Piccolo
Clar's. in Bb
Bass Clar.
B'ss'ns.
Horns in F
Tpts. in Bb
Trb.-ni.
Tuba
Cymb.
Celesta
mp tenuto
Vibraphone
Vibra.
Harp
mf normal position
Vl. I.
Vl. II.
Vle div.
Vc.
Soli
ardente
Bass
*) with nails, and close to the sounding board.
7

56
8 Più mosso (non tanto)
poco riten.
accel. poco a poco sin al Allegro
Fl's.
Picc.
Clar's. in Bb
Bass Cl.
B'ss'ns.
Horns in F
Tpt's. in Bb
Trb-ni
Tuba
G-B♮-E♭
Timp.
Damped
Damp quickly
Suspended Cymbal
Più mosso (non tanto)
Harp
sul G
f sonore
Vl. I.
Vl. II.
Viola
Vc.
Bass
8

9 Allegro ♩ = 160
72
Fl's. 1 2
Picc.
Oboi 1 2
Clar's. in B♭ 1 2 3
Bass Clar.
Bassoons 1 2
Horns in F 1 2 3 4
Tpts. in B♭ 1 2 3
mf (Harmon mutes)
Trb.-ni 1 2 3
f stacc.
Tuba
Timp.
A♭-B♮-E♭
Sn. Dr.
Cymb.s
Allegro ♩ = 160
Harp
Vl. I.
Vl. II.
Viola
Vc.
Bass
pizz.
staccatiss.
a 2
9

77

Fl's. 1 2

Picc.

Oboi 1 2

Clar's. in Bb 1 2 3

Bass Clar.

staccatiss.

B'ss'ns. 1 2

Horns in F

a4

Tpts. in Bb 1 2 3

mf

Trb.-ni. 1 2 3

f stacc.

Tuba

f stacc.

Timp.

sf

Sn. Dr.

sf

Cymb.s

sf

Harp

ff

Vl. I.

arco

pizz.

Vl. II.

arco

pizz.

Vla.

arco

pizz.

Vc.

arco

pizz.

Bass.

(pizz.)

82

Fl's. 1 2 — *mf*

Picc. — *mf*, *f*

Oboi 1 2 — a2, *f*

Clar's. in Bb 1 2 3 — *mf*, *mf stacc.*, *f*

Bass Clar. — *f stacc.*

B'ss'ns. 1 2 — *mf stacc.*, *f*

Horns in F 1 2 3 4 — *mf*

Tpt's. in Bb 1 2 3 — Harmon mute, *f*

Trb.-ni 1 2 3 — *mf*

Tuba — *mf*

Timp. — *mf*

Sn. Dr. B. D. — *mf*

Damped Cymb.

Cymb.

Harp — *mf*, *f*

Vl. I. — arco, *f*

Vl. II. — arco, *mf*, *f*

Vla. — arco, *f*

Vc. — arco, *f*

Bass — arco, *f stacc.*

87
10
Fl's.
Picc.
Oboi
Clar's. in Bb
Bass Clar.
B'ss'ns.
Horns in F.
Tpt's. in Bb
Senza sord.
Trb-ni
Tuba
Timp.
Sn. Dr. B. D.
Damped Cymb.
Cymb.s.
Harp.
Vl. I.
Vl. II.
Vla.
Vc.
Bass
unis.
cresc.
stacc.
10

92

unis.
Fl's.
Picc.
Change to Fl.
Oboi
unis.
Solo
E. H.
Clar's. in B♭
Bass Clar.
B'ssns.
stacc.
Tpt's.
Trb.-ni
Tuba
Timp.
Sn. Dr. B. D.
Cymb.-s.
Harp
Vl. I.
Vl. II.
Vla.
Vc.
Bass

57

98
Fl's.
Oboi
E. H.
Solo
Clar's.
Solo
Bass Clar.
Bassoons
Horns in F
Tpt's. in B♭
Trb-ni.
Timp.
Cel.
Harp
Vl. I.
Vl. II.
Vle.
3 Solo Vle.
Vc.
Bass
pizz.
ritard.
tenute

11
Andante cantabile ♩ = 72
104
Fl's.
Oboi
Clar's. in B♭
Bass Clar.
B'ss'ns.
Horns in F
Tpt's.
Trb.-ni.
Vibr.
Sm. Cymb.
W. Br.
Harp
Vl. I.
Vl. II.
Vla.
Vc.
Bass.
tenute
mf tenute
Fl.
mf
mp
Solo
p
mf sempre
espressivo
all
mf espressivo
arco
11

58
110
12
Tempo I, ♩ = 88
poco rit.
Fl's.
Oboi
E. H.
Clar's. in Bb
Bass Cl.
B'ss'ns.
Horns
Tpt's. in Bb
Harmon mutes
Trb--ni
Timp.
Vibr.
(damped)
Sm. Cymb.
mp sempre
W. Br.
Harp
With rhythmic precision
Vl. I.
div.
Vl. II.
pizz.
Vla.
Vc.
Bass

*) The dotted 8ths and 16ths should be played as though written as follows:

121
Fl's.
Oboi
E. H.
Clar's. in Bb
Bass Cl.
B'ss'ns.
I.
Horns in F
Tpt's. in Bb
Trb.-ni.
Timp.
Sm.-Cymb.
W. Br.
Harp
Vl. I.
Vl. II.
Vla.
Vc.
Bass
mf

126
rit.
13 Meno
Fl's.
Oboi
E.H.
Clar's. in Bb
Bass Clar.
Solo
mf tenuto
B'ss'ns.
Horns.
Tpt's. in Bb
stacc.
Tr-b.-ni.
mf Harmon mutes
Timp.
Sn. Cymb.
W. Br.
Solo
Meno
Harp
Vl. I.
unis.
gliss.
div.
Vl. II.
arco
Vla.
Vc.
Bass
pizz.
rit.
13

William Grant Still composed his *Afro-American Symphony* in 1930. When it was premiered in 1931 by the Rochester Philharmonic Orchestra conducted by Howard Hanson, it became the first symphony by an African-American composer to be performed by a major orchestra. Other black composers followed in Still's wake, including Florence Price, whose Symphony in E Minor was played by the Chicago Symphony Orchestra in 1933, and William Dawson, whose *Negro Folk Symphony* was premiered by the Philadelphia Orchestra in 1934. As a pathbreaker—

and one of the most prolific American composers of his era—Still became known as the dean of African-American composers. His symphony was published in 1935, and he later revised it in 1969, having written four more symphonies in the interim.

The *Afro-American Symphony* has the traditional four movements, with a sonata-form first movement, a slow movement, a scherzo, and a fast finale. The movements are not explicitly programmatic, but each is a character sketch that is also linked to verses from a poem by Paul Laurence Dunbar (1872–1906), who wrote about African-American life in the South, using folk materials and dialects. Originally Still also gave each movement a subtitle appropriate to its content: *Longings*; *Sorrows*; *Humor*; and *Aspirations*.

The first movement blends sonata form with an archlike ABCBA form, since the two main themes appear in reverse order in the recapitulation. The movement opens with a brief introductory melody in the English horn, followed by a first theme in the trumpet in the form of a twelve-bar blues in A♭ (measures 7–18; see the blues in NAWM 170 and 171). In addition to the blues melody (in classic AAB form) and harmonic progression, many other elements reflect characteristic features of African-American music. Syncopations appear in both melody and accompaniment, and phrases often end just before rather than on a strong beat. The call-and-response structure of African-American song is echoed in the frequent interjections by other instruments between the short phrases of melody. Lowered fifth, third, and seventh scale degrees in the melody (as in measures 2–4 and 15–16) imitate blue notes, as do chords that include both major and minor thirds (measures 4–5 and 7). Instrumental timbres are varied and often unusual, including groupings and sounds typical of jazz bands: trumpets and trombones with Harmon mutes, which give a distant, pinched, metallic sound (measures 6–8); steady taps on the bass drum and dampened strikes on the cymbal; winds and brass used in groups of similar sound, like sections in a jazz band, and voiced in chords of four notes (as in measures 7–10); and, later in the movement, a vibraphone (see especially measures 133–35).

The first theme repeats in the clarinet with interjections from other winds, accompanied by strings playing *col legno* (with the wood of the bow) to create a percussive effect. Then the transition begins (measure 33), developing motives from the first theme, as is typical of European symphonies. The second theme (measures 45–67), in the surprising key of G major (a half step below the tonic A♭, rather than the expected dominant, E♭), has the pentatonic contours and melancholy air of a spiritual, which along with blues and jazz was the type of music most widely identified with African Americans. The theme is in ABA' form, beginning in the oboe and moving in turn to violins, flutes, cello, and harp. Once again, interjections by other instruments between phrases of the oboe theme suggest the call-and-response of African-American song.

As the second theme concludes, the tempo picks up and the development section begins (measure 68). As in the earlier transition, here the procedures are those of a European sonata-form movement, fragmenting and developing elements from both themes and from the opening English horn melody. After calm is restored, the recapitulation brings back the two main themes in reverse order (measures 104 and 114 respectively), the second in the tonic A♭ minor and the first in A♭ major, with almost no transition between them. This time, the first theme appears in swinging rhythms (alternating long and short notes) rather than even ones; because Still knew that some orchestral musicians might not know what was intended, he marked in a note (at measure 116) that the dotted-eighth-sixteenth rhythms should be played like triplets, the usual ratio of swing. A brief coda (measures 128–36) brings the movement to a close with a reminiscence of the introduction, emphasizing the archlike structure of the entire movement.

The combination of blues and spiritual is appropriate to the sense of longing Still sought to capture in the movement, and to the verses of Dunbar he linked to it:

> 'All my life long twell de night has pas'
> Let de wo'k come ez it will,
> So dat I fin' you, my honey, at last,
> Somewhaih des ovah de hill.'

To a listener today, the way Still uses the orchestra in the *Afro-American Symphony* can sound like movie music. This is neither coincidence nor a sign of unoriginality; in 1934, Still moved to Los Angeles, where he composed for films while continuing to write concert music in classical forms. The manner in which he integrated the string sounds of the symphonic orchestra with the distinctive wind and brass sounds of the jazz orchestra helped to define a style that many other composers and arrangers used for films and popular music.

Charlie Parker (1920–1955) and Dizzy Gillespie (1917–1993)

Anthropology

Bebop tune and solo

1945

(a) Lead sheet

(b) Transcription of Charlie Parker's solo

CD 13|59 CD 6|67

Transcription of Charlie Parker's solo from *Charlie Parker Omnibook for All Bass Clef Instruments: Transcribed from His Recorded Solos* (New York: Atlantic Music, 1978).

33 Bb7 Eb7 Ab7 Bb G7 CM7 F7
37 Bb CM7 F7 DM7 G7 CM7 F7
41 Bb7 Eb7 Ab7 Bb
45 D7 G7
49 C7 F7
53 Bb CM7 F7 Bb G7
56 CM F7 Bb7 Eb7 Ab7 Bb G7 CM7 F7
61 69
61 Bb CM7 F7 DM7 G7 CM7 F7
65 Bb7 Eb7 Ab7 Bb CM7 F7

69
Bb
CM7
F7
DM7
G7
CM7
F7
73
Bb7
Eb
Ab7
Bb
77
D7
G7
81
C7
F7
85
Bb
CM7
F7
DM7
G7
CM7
F7
62
70
89
Bb7
Eb7
Ab7
Bb
CM7
F7
93
Bb
CM7
F7
DM7
GM7
CM7
F7
97
FM7
Bb7
Eb7
Ab7
Bb7
CM7
F7
101
Bb
CM7
F7
Bb
G7
CM7
F7

Anthropology is one of dozens of mid-1940s collaborations between Charlie "Bird" Parker and John Birks "Dizzy" Gillespie. The two met in Kansas City, Parker's home town, when Gillespie was on tour with Cab Calloway's big band. In the early 1940s, Parker, Gillespie, and other young jazz virtuosos convened in New York City clubs such as Minton's Playhouse and Monroe's Uptown House to play and improvise together in lengthy after-hours sessions. Out of these jam sessions grew a new musical language known as *bebop,* featuring breakneck speeds, complex chord changes, and angular melodies.

Like many bebop compositions, *Anthropology* is a contrafact—a new tune composed over a harmonic progression borrowed from another song. Specifically, like Duke Ellington's *Cotton Tail* (NAWM 172), it is a contrafact on "rhythm changes," jazz musicians' term for the chord progression from the chorus of

George Gershwin's *I Got Rhythm* (NAWM 169). Contrafacts were a major source for new bebop compositions because they constituted a common language for jazz musicians, could easily be molded into a new tune for a last-minute recording session, and did not require payment of royalties to the composer of the original tune. Contrafacts were especially important for Parker: new tunes built over the blues, rhythm changes, and the standard *Honeysuckle Rose* account for much of Parker's output.

The version of *Anthropology* that is included on the accompanying recording is from a live broadcast made on March 31, 1951, at Birdland, the New York jazz club named after Parker's nickname, where Parker was the headliner. The broadcast was recorded and released on LP as *Summit Meeting at Birdland.* The players were all stars, with Parker on alto saxophone and Gillespie on trumpet supported by a rhythm section made up of Bud Powell on piano, Tommy Potter on bass, and Roy Haynes on drums. Through most of the performance, the bass and cymbal keep steady time, and the piano and drums provide irregular punctuations.

The tune begins with the *head*, a lead melody in AABA form played in unison or octaves by the melody instruments at the beginning and end of the song. The musicians play from a lead sheet, shown here as NAWM 183a, that includes only the head and the chord changes. Everything else is improvised or worked out by ear in rehearsal. In this performance, after the head, Parker plays a solo that fills up three choruses (statements of the AABA harmonic progression), shown here in transcription as NAWM 183b. (The transcription includes the head; the solo begins at measure 29.) Gillespie then solos for three choruses, followed by Powell on piano for two. For the next two choruses, Parker and Gillespie "trade fours" with Haynes, alternating four measures of melody instrument with four measures of drum solo for each eight-measure phrase. The song ends as it began, with Parker and Gillespie leading the way in another statement of the head.

The musicians play at a blistering pace that is characteristic of bebop. The many syncopations (as in measures 8–10) and sudden stops, starts, and silences throughout the tune and Parker's solo keep the rhythm fresh and surprising. The convoluted, highly decorated melody is also typical of bebop: both the head and Parker's solo are full of chromatic notes, and the melody is dissonant with the underlying harmony almost as often as it is consonant. Because the solo is so chromatic, the transcriber has transcribed it without a key signature.

The solos do not offer variations on the tune, but spin out a constant variety of new ideas that fit within the harmonic progression. In each chorus, Parker uses different material, introduces rests and phrasing at different places, and reconceives his approach to each section, especially the B section (called the bridge). The virtuosity is astonishing, as the performers meant it to be. Occasionally, Parker repeats ideas (for example, measures 113–15 repeat measures 81–83), suggesting that at least in some places he is using formulas or routines worked out in advance that he can use at will, allowing him to keep up his breakneck speed. At measures 117–21, near the end of his solo, Parker quotes the song *Temptation* by Nacio Herb Brown to lyrics by Arthur Freed, sung by Bing Crosby in the 1933 movie *Going Hollywood*. Such quotations are frequent in Parker's solos, showing his sly wit and his intention to dazzle the listener. With bebop, jazz came to be recognized as an art music worthy of the same intent listening as classical music.

Olivier Messiaen (1908–1992)

Quartet for the End of Time: First movement, *Liturgie de cristal*

Quartet for violin, clarinet, violoncello, and piano

1940–41

CD 13|67 CD 6|75

Bien modéré, en poudroiement harmonieux

(comme un oiseau)

VIOLON

ppp

(son flûté, vers la pointe)

CLARINETTE en SI ♭

(comme un oiseau)

p expressif

VIOLONCELLE

ppp (vibrato)

A **Bien modéré**, en poudroiement harmonieux (♩=54 environ)

PIANO

pp legato (très enveloppé de pédale)

Von

Clar.

Velle

glissando

(*)

gliss.

B

From Olivier Messiaen, *Quatuor pour la fin du temps* (Paris: Durand, 1942), 1–6. © 1941 by Editions DURAND. Used by permission.

10
von
Clar.
vcelle
gliss.
3
13
C
8
3
16
glissando
gliss.

18
Von
Clar.
Vcelle
D
21
3
gliss.
23

25
Von
Clar.
Velle
pp
pp p
gliss.
E
28
gliss.
gliss.
3
30
8
cresc.
F

32
Von
Clar.
velle
f
dim.
glissando
34
pp
p
gliss.
36
3
cresc.
G

Olivier Messiaen wrote his *Quartet for the End of Time* during World War II in the winter of 1940–41 while interned at a prisoner-of-war camp in Silesia. He had been captured by the Germans the previous May as he was serving in the French army. He wrote the piece for performance by himself as pianist, together with a violinist, clarinetist, and cellist who were also imprisoned there. They gave the work its first performance in the camp, in the middle of winter, for their fellow prisoners.

The title refers to the biblical prophecy of the Apocalypse, which will bring the end of time as a progression of finite moments and the beginning of eternity. The score, published in 1942 after Messiaen had been released from captivity, carries the inscription, "In homage to the Angel of the Apocalypse, who raises his hand to the heavens and says, 'There will be no more Time.'" Four of the eight movements are for all four players, but the third is for clarinet alone, the fourth omits piano, the fifth is for cello and piano, and the eighth is for violin and piano.

The quartet is a study of time—measured, finite time, and timelessness, or eternity. Although the quartet lacks a text, it is a piece of sacred music, as is a great deal of Messiaen's output. Religion is not so much on the surface of his compositions as it is the motivation and goal for his creative effort.

The first movement, *Liturgie de cristal* (Crystal Liturgy), included here, conveys a sense of ecstatic contemplation of the passage of time. The clarinet and violin each play stylized birdcalls (of the blackbird and nightingale respectively), a type of melody that Messiaen often used to suggest nature as a divine gift. The figures do not develop, but change in unpredictable ways. Like the birds they imitate, each instrument sticks to its own repertoire of sounds. The rhythm of the birdcalls is also that of nature, having a pulse but no clear meter.

The cello and piano lay out complex patterns of duration and pitch that repeat in cycles. The cello constantly repeats a five-note sequence (C–E–D–F♯–B♭) in high harmonics (see below), using a pattern of fifteen durations. New statements of the pattern begin on the second quarter note of measure 8, the last eighth of measure 13, and so on, every five-and-a-half measures. These melodic and rhythmic cycles are like the *color* (repeating melody) and *talea* (repeating rhythm) of fourteenth-century isorhythm (see NAWM 24 and 25). The durational pattern Messiaen has chosen here combines two *non-retrogradable rhythms*, his term for rhythms that are palindromes, the same forward and backward: the first three notes (respectively 4, 3, and 4 eighth notes in duration) and the remaining twelve (which form the pattern 4–1–1–3–1–1–1–1–3–1–1–4, again counting eighth notes). Such rhythms remain the same whichever direction time runs, and thus suggest the unchangeable, the divine, and the eternal.

The cycles in the piano are more complex, with a series of twenty-nine chords overlapping a rhythmic pattern of seventeen durations. The rhythmic cycle begins again on the downbeat of measure 6 and every thirteen beats thereafter. The second statement of the chord cycle begins on the last eighth note of measure 8, with different rhythms because of the new alignment with the durational pattern. It would take twenty-nine repetitions of the rhythmic pattern and seventeen repetitions of the chord cycle, or a total of 377 beats, to return to the original alignment, and a total of 12,441 beats (4147 measures, or approximately three hours and fifty minutes) if the cello pattern is taken into account. Perhaps Messiaen meant this to imply a very long cycle, of which we hear only a part, as a metaphor for time everlasting, during which we each exist for only a moment.

The combination of the repeating cycles with variable alignment and freer repetition and variation in the violin and clarinet creates music that combines constancy and change. This presentation of ideas is typical of Messiaen, whose works embody a kind of meditation on a few materials that parallels meditative prayer.

The cello harmonics are played on the instrument's highest string, tuned to the A just below middle C. While the index finger of the left hand presses the string against the fingerboard to select the pitch, the smallest finger lightly touches the string at a spot a fourth higher (indicated by a diamond-shaped note), which produces a harmonic two octaves higher than the notated pitch. The ethereal sound, in the same range as the high birdcalls in the violin, lends height and depth to the scene suggested in the music.

Benjamin Britten (1913–1976)

Peter Grimes: Act III, Scene 2, *To hell with all your mercy!*

Opera

1944–45

10
largamente
51
Peter roars back at the shouters.
Fog-horn
P.
agitato
home! come home! come home!
Peter Grimes! Peter Grimes! Peter Grimes! Peter Grimes!
S.
Peter Grimes! Peter Grimes! Pe-ter Grimes!
A.
CHORUS (off)
T.
dim
Peter Grimes! Peter Grimes! Pe-ter Grimes!
B.
dim.
13
poco a poco dim.
Peter Grimes! Peter Grimes! Grimes! Grimes! Grimes! Peter Grimes! Peter Grimes! Peter Grimes!
dim.
Grimes!
14
Ellen and Balstrode come in, and stand waiting till Peter has calmed.
lento
rall.
Grimes! Pe-ter Grimes!
Grimes!
69
17 ELLEN
Ellen goes up to Peter.
dolce
espress.
parlando
Pe - ter We've come to take you home. O come home out of this dreadful night! See, here's Balstrode.

Peter does not notice her. The voices are now very distant.
52 Andante comodo e molto tranquillo (♩=54)
18
E.
Pe-ter don't you hear me?
S.
A.
T.
B.
CHORUS (off)
pp
Grimes, Grimes, Grimes! Grimes!
Pe-ter Grimes! Pe-ter! Pe-ter! Pe-ter! Pe-ter!
22
Fog-horn
colla parte
ppp
PETER
dolcissimo
What har - - - - bour shel - ters peace,
senza voce
a-way from ti-dal waves, a-way from storms!
Grimes! Grimes!
Pe-ter! Pe-ter! Pe-ter! Pe-ter! Grimes!
26
P.
cantando
What har - - bour can em - brace terrors and tragedies.
Grimes! Grimes! Grimes!
Pe-ter! Pe-ter! Pe-ter! Pe-ter! Pe-ter! Grimes!

BALSTRODE: *(Crossing to lift Peter up)* Come on, I'll help you with the boat.
ELLEN: No!
BALSTRODE: Sail out till you lose sight of the Moot Hall. Then sink the boat. D'you hear? Sink her. Good-bye Peter.

There is a crunch of shingle as Balstrode leads Peter down to his boat, and helps him push it out. After a short pause, he returns, takes Ellen by the arm, and leads her away.

70

Down slowly begins and the Borough slowly comes to life. Some stragglers of the manhunt go

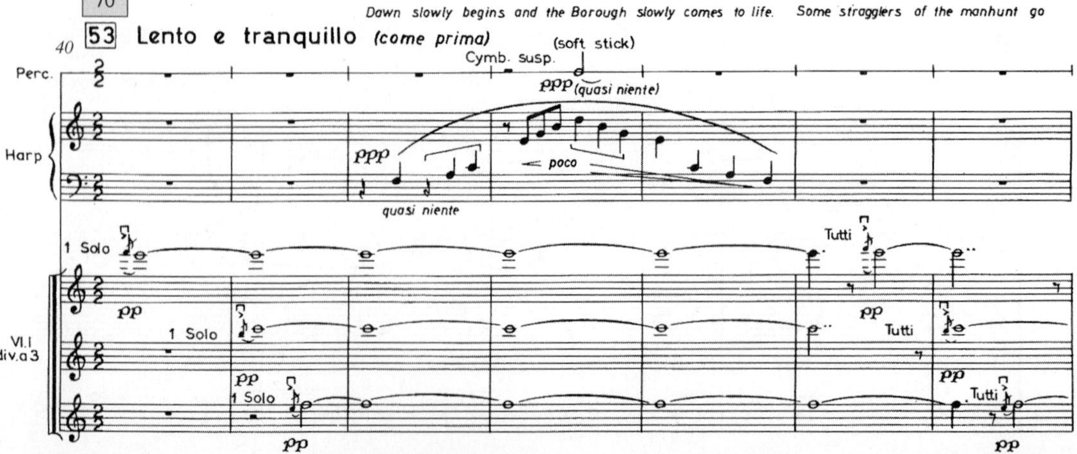

47
across the street to their houses. Shutters are drawn back.
Fl.
1. Solo
ppp poco a
Cl. in B♭
1. Solo
ppp
3
pp
Perc.
Cymb.
ppp
Harp
ppp
3
più
pp
Vl. Solo
f
pp
pp cresc.
ppp
pp cresc.
Vl. I div. a 3
ppp
ppp
pp cresc.
Vl. II div. a 3
53
1.
Fl.
poco e più espress.
f
tr
pp
Tutti
mf
dim.
Vl. I div. a 3
pp cresc.
mf
dim.
pp cresc.
mf
dim.
mf
dim.
Vl. II div. a 3
pp cresc.
mf
dim.
pp cresc.
mf
dim.

71
59
1.
a2
Fl.
pp sempre
Cl. in B♭
pp
mf
3
Bsn.
ppp sempre
D. Bsn.
ppp sempre
1.2
Hn. in F
3.4
ppp sempre
ppp sempre
1.2
Tbn.
3
Tuba
ppp sempre
(in the Orchestra)
ppp sempre
tr
Timp.
ppp sempre
Perc.
Cymb.
pp
veloce
Harp
mf
ppp
Vl. I. II
div. a 3
pp sempre
pp sempre
pp sempre
Sola
Vla.
div.
Vc.
pp sempre
Db.
pp sempre

54
Some women carry nets down to the shore.
Fl.
Cl. in B♭
Bsn.
D. Bsn.
Hn. in F
Tbn.
Tuba
Timp.
Perc.
Cymb.
Harp
SOPRANO
1st Solo (off)
distinto
Cho.
To those who pass, the Borough sounds be- tray
54
Vl. I. II div. a 3
Vla. div.
Vc.
Db.
sost.

More and more of the Borough people come casually to their daily jobs.
70
a2
Fl.
Bsn.
D.Bsn.
1.2
Hn.in F
3.4
Tr. 2 in C
ppp sost.
Tbn.
3 Tuba
dim.
pp
Timp.
Perc.
B.D.
ALL SOPRANOS
semplice
Cho.
The cold be - gin-ning of an - o - ther
sim.
Vl.I.II div.a 3
Vla.
Vc.
Db.

55
Swallow comes in and speaks to some fishermen.
76
Fl.
Cl. in B♭
Bsn.
D. Bsn.
Hn. in F
Tbn.
Tuba
Timp.
Perc.
Cymb.
Harp
CHORUS
S.
A.
day.
And houses sleep-ing by the wa-ter side Wake.
Vl. I. II div. a 3
Vla. div.
Sola
Vc.
Db.
poco cresc.
pp sost.
mf dim.

82
Fl.
Cl. in B♭
Bsn.
D.Bsn.
Hn. in F
Tbn.
Tuba
Timp.
Perc.
Harp
1. Solo
72
Cymb.
SWALLOW
There's a boat sinking out at sea, Coastguard reports.
A FISHERMAN (BASS)
Within reach?
CHORUS
S.
A.
— to the measured rip-ple of the tide.
Vl. I. II div. a 3
Vla. div.
Sola
Vc.
Db.

56
88
a2
ppp poco cresc.
p
Fl.
Cl. in B♭
1.
a2
p f
Bsn.
D. Bsn.
ppp
p
1.2
Hn. in F
3.4
1.2
Tbn.
3
Tuba
tr
Timp.
Cymb.
Perc.
mf
Harp
Sw.
No!
f marc.
Fisher-man
Let's have a look thro' the glasses.
TENOR
mf semplice
Or measured cadence of the lads who tow
BASS
mf semplice
CHORUS
Vl. I. II div. a 3
poco cresc.
Sola
pp
Vla. div.
Tutte div.
Vc.
Db.

94
Fl.
Cl. in B♭
Bsn.
D. Bsn.
1.2
Hn. in F
3.4
1.2
Tbn.
3
Tuba
Timp.
Perc.
Cymb.
Harp
CHORUS
T.
B.
Some en- tered hoy to fix her in her row.
Vl. I. II
div. a 3
Vla.
div.
Vc.
Db.
a2
p cresc.
(p) cresc.

Auntie comes out of the pub door.
57
73
100
Fl.
Ob.
Cl. in B♭
Bsn.
D.Bsn.
1.2
Hn. in F
3.4
1.2
Tbn.
3
Tuba
Timp.
Perc.
Cymb.
Harp
AUNTIE
What is it?
CHORUS
T.
B.
Or hol-low sound that from the passing bell To some de-part-ed spi-rits bids fare-well.
Vl. I. II
div. a 3
Vla.
div.
Vc.
Db.

106
Fl.
Cl. in B♭
D. Bsn.
Hn. in F
Tr. 1.2 in C
Tbn.
Tuba
Timp.
Cymb. (tr)
Perc.
cresc.
B.D.
Harp
TWO NIECES
In ceaseless motion
AUNTIE and Mrs. SEDLEY
A.
BOLES
One of these ru - - mours!
In cease-less motion
Nothing I can see.
BOLES and RECTOR
In ceaseless motion
KEENE
In ceaseless motion
SWALLOW and HOBSON
In ceaseless motion
S.
A.
CHORUS
T.
B.
In ceaseless motion
In ceaseless motion
In ceaseless motion
Vl. I. II div. a 3
cresc. molto
Vla. div.
Vc.
Db.

The stage is now filled with people singing at their daily work.
111
Fl.
Ob.
Cl. in B♭
Bsn.
D. Bsn.
Hn. in F
Tr. 1.2 in C
Tbn.
Tuba
Timp.
Perc.
Cymb.
B.D.
Harp
2 N.
A. & Mrs. S.
Bol. & Rec.
K.
Sw. & H.
CHORUS
S.
A.
T.
B.
comes and goes the tide.
Flow - ing it fills the channel broad and wide,
div.
unis.
Vl. I. II div. a 3
Vla.
Vc.
Db.

117
58
Fl.
Ob.
Cl. in B♭
Bsn.
D. Bsn.
Hn. in F
Tr. in C
Tbn.
Tuba
Timp.
Perc.
Cymb.
B.D.
Harp
2 N.
A. & Mrs. S.
Bol. & Rec.
K.
Sw. & H.
CHORUS
S.
A.
T.
B.
Vl. I. II div. a 3
Vla.
Vc.
Db.
poco a poco dim.
sost.
meno f
Then back to sea with strong ma - jestic sweep It
(cambiare l'arco ad lib.)

SLOW CURTAIN
122
Fl.
Cl. in B♭
Bsn.
D. Bsn.
Hn. in F
Tr. in C
Tbn.
Tuba
Timp.
Perc.
B.D.
Cymb.
Harp
2 N.
A. & Mrs. S.
Bol. & Rec.
K.
Sw. & H.
CHORUS
S.
A.
T.
B.
Vl. I. II div. a 3
Vla. div.
Vc.
Db.
meno f
ancora meno f
rolls in ebb yet ter-ri-ble and deep.
rolls in ebb yet ter-ri-ble, yet ter-ri-ble and deep.

128
molto rall.
Fl.
a2
Cl. in B♭
Bsn.
D. Bsn.
Hn. 4 in F
1.2 Tbn.
3 Tuba
Tuba
Timp.
Perc.
Cymb.
B.D.
Harp
Bol. & Rec.
K.
Sw. & H.
CHORUS
T.
B.
molto rall.
Vl. I, II div. a 3
Vla. div.
Sola
Vc.
pizz.
Db.
pizz.
End of Opera

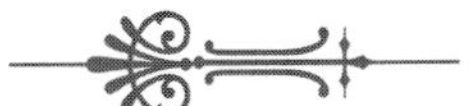

Benjamin Britten took his character Peter Grimes from *The Borough* (1810), a narrative poem by English poet George Crabbe about the people of Aldeburgh, a coastal town in Suffolk near Britten's childhood home. The story of Grimes, a fisherman who beat his apprentices, lost them in accidents, and went mad, might seem an unpromising plot for an opera. But for Britten and his life partner, tenor Peter Pears, Grimes's life as an outcast paralleled their own lives as pacifists, as conscientious objectors to all wars (including World War II, then raging), and as homosexuals, hated beyond reason by a society that could not accept them as they were. Grimes himself was neither a pacifist nor a homosexual, nor even a very sympathetic character. Instead, the focus of the libretto, written by Montagu Slater from the scenario Britten and Pears had conceived, was on the crowd's persecution of Grimes simply for being different, and on the way his internalization of their hatred leads to his destruction.

Britten composed the music between January 1944 and February 1945, assisted by a commission from the Koussevitzky Musical Foundation. *Peter Grimes* was premiered at Sadler's Wells Theatre in London on June 7, 1945, just a month after the war ended in Europe, with Pears in the title role. The opera's powerful message about the relationship between the individual and the state resonated deeply in the postwar world, and its emotional, accessible music established Britten's and Pears's reputations as the leading English composer and tenor of their time, respectively. The opera was soon staged throughout Europe and North America and has become one of the most popular postwar operas.

The opera begins with a prologue, an inquest into the death of Peter's apprentice on a fishing trip when they ran out of drinking water. Although Peter is exonerated, the townspeople blame him for the boy's death, and he is advised not to take on another apprentice unless he can get a woman to look after the boy. One solution would be to marry Mrs. Ellen Orford, a widowed schoolmistress and one of the few people friendly to Peter. But Grimes is not ready to marry Ellen, even though he is in love with her, because he feels he must prove himself to the town first by making lots of money. Knowing that Peter cannot handle his boat by himself, Ned Keene, the apothecary, finds him a new boy from the workhouse. Ellen is sympathetic to the boy, but when she discovers a bruise on him, she reproaches Peter for his temper. Peter strikes her and forces the boy to leave with him. This moment, when Peter accepts the town's brutalized image of him, is the crux of the drama, and it begins the downward spiral. Propelled by rumors that he is mistreating the boy, the townspeople come looking for Peter and his apprentice, only to find Peter's home, an old upturned boat beside a cliff, neatly kept but unoccupied. They do not know that their coming spurred Peter to hurry down to his boat and set out to sea, and on the way the boy slipped and fell into a chasm. After a few days with no sign of the boy, rumors fly and the townspeople again come after Peter, unaware that they themselves caused the boy's death. Ellen and the retired merchant skipper Balstrode, who has supported Peter in the past, encounter him wandering in the fog, overcome by grief and stress. Ellen wants to comfort him, but Balstrode advises him to take his boat out to sea and sink with it, which Peter proceeds to do.

The excerpt included here, from the very end of the opera, begins as the offstage chorus of townspeople repeatedly calls Peter's name, and he answers them in a florid and meandering recitative. This tragic scene eloquently displays the remarkable dramatic effects that Britten creates from simple means. Here, the only accompaniment to the chorus's calls and Peter's raving is the foghorn, on the pitch center of E♭. The rest of the scene recalls earlier music, as is appropriate to the final moments of a tragedy. When Peter cries out, "To hell with all your mercy! To hell with your revenge, And God have mercy upon you!," he echoes the motive introduced at the crucial scene when he hit Ellen, to the words "And God have mercy upon me!," which has pervaded the opera ever since. When Ellen comes to take him home, Peter does not respond to her directly, but recalls his song from Act I when he imagined finding a safe harbor in her love (measures 26–41 of this excerpt). When Balstrode helps Peter cast off, there is no music at all; here, Britten recognized that silence is more meaningful.

At the end, what remains are the sea and the townspeople, equally indifferent to Peter's fate. Britten captures that indifference through bitonality, returning to earlier music associated with sea and town, in two simultaneous keys, like two mutually indifferent planes of sound. The calm sea is depicted by sustained tones (*e''', c''', and f''*) in the upper strings decorated with grace notes, like flecks on the surface, with occasional waves suggested by arpeggiated thirds in harp and clarinet that encompass all the notes of the C-major scale, and a haunting melody in the flute (measures 56–63). Against this backdrop and supported by chords in the brass, the townspeople sing in A major (starting at measure 68) a song in hymn style about their daily routines, first heard at the opening of Act I. Between verses, someone mentions a report of a sinking boat (measures 88–93), but it is dismissed as a rumor (measures 109–13)—ironically, the only rumor in the entire opera that is true. The townspeople sing the final verse of their hymn, about the ceaseless, unpitying motions of the tide, this time inverting the second half of the melody into a majestic descent, and the curtain slowly falls.

The performance on the accompanying recording is conducted by Britten himself, with Peter Pears as Peter Grimes. Since Britten wrote this and most of his tenor parts for Pears, the music is ideally suited for Pears's reedy, flexible voice.

Samuel Barber (1910–1981)

Hermit Songs, Op. 29: No. 8, *The Monk and His Cat*

Song cycle

1952–53

186

**Notes marked(–) in these two measures should be slightly longer, pochissimo rubato; also on the fourth page.

10
mf
p
For you it is hunt-ing, for me stud-y.
mf
mf
p
Ped. Ped.
14
mf
Your shin - ing eye
mf
Ped. Ped. Ped. Ped. Ped. simile
17
p
watch - es the wall; my fee - ble eye is fixed on a
p
75 77
20
f declamato
book. You re-joice when your
8
pp
f subito

23
cantabile
p
claws En-trap a mouse; I re-joice when my mind Fath-oms a prob-lem.
27
rall.
a tempo, tranquillo mp
espr.
Pleased with his own art, Neith-er
mp
31
mf
p
hin-ders the oth-er; Thus we live e - ver With-out te-dium and en -
mf
p
36
76 78
- - vy.
poco rall.
Tempo I
cantando la melodia
p

40
p
Pan-gur, white Pan-gur, How hap-py we are A-lone to-geth-er,
43
p
Scho-lar and cat.
mf
46
sempre in tempo
pp
Pan-gur, white Pan-gur,
p espr.
How hap-py we are.
pp
49
ten. senza rall.
(in tempo)
pp
senza Ped.

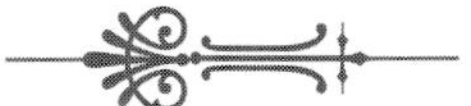

Samuel Barber wrote his *Hermit Songs* between November 1952 and January 1953, on a commission from the Elizabeth Sprague Coolidge Foundation. Inspired by a trip to Ireland the previous summer, he chose ten short anonymous texts, written between the eighth and thirteenth centuries by Irish monks and scholars and translated into modern English by a number of poets. Varying from religious visions to sly observations about monastic life, these short poems or fragments, most written in the margins of manuscripts the monks were preparing, are windows into their world. The song cycle was premiered on October 30, 1953, by soprano Leontyne Price with Barber at the piano, at the Library of Congress in Washington, D.C. Barber dedicated the song included here to Isabelle Vengerova, his piano teacher at the Curtis Institute in Philadelphia.

The Monk and His Cat, with a text translated by W. H. Auden, celebrates the happy life of scholar and cat, contentedly living together while each focuses on his own work, theology and mouse control respectively. Several musical devices depict the medieval monk: melodic open fifths in the piano left hand (for instance, between the last five notes in measure 1), suggesting the open harmonies of medieval music; parallel fifths as in medieval organum (the left hand in measures 8–9); a slowly moving chantlike melody in the piano (measures 1–5, returning at measures 16 and 39); and a later, more rapid line in the voice that alternates groups of twos and threes (as in chant) while hovering around a reciting tone (measures 29–37). The cat, meanwhile, is evoked by half steps and whole steps that resolve outward chromatically to thirds (as in measures 6–9), as though the cat himself is walking on the keys; and by sudden, loud, brief chords surrounded by rests (measures 12 and 22–23), to suggest the cat pouncing on a mouse.

The form is simple yet subtle, interweaving looks at the monk and the cat. The poem is in five sentences, each punctuated in the middle, like a psalm verse (compare NAWM 4a), with the first sentence (or verse) repeated at the end of the song. Some verses vary the opening phrase (A), and most are separated from the next by the catlike dissonances (B). But others introduce contrasting material, often changing midway to mark the two halves of the sentence (designated as a and b below). The result is a sort of rondo form:

Verse:	1		2a	2b		3		4a	4b	5	1		1a	
Music:	A	B	C1(~B)	C2	B	A'	B	D1	D2	E	A	B	A''	B
Key:	F							A		F♯	F			
Measure:	1	6	8	12	14	16	20	22	24	28	39	44	46	50

Barber used traditional techniques in his music (rather than inventing a new musical language as Schoenberg and other modernists did), but he gives each element a novel twist to create an individual sound. Although the song is clearly in F major, the harmony is suffused with gentle dissonances, consonant chords are rare, and the excursions to A major and F♯ major are unusual. The meter and rhythm are especially notable. In this as in all the songs of the set, Barber omits the time signature and freely changes the number of beats per measure to follow the accents of the text. The piano shifts from $\frac{9}{8}$ to $\frac{6}{8}$, $\frac{3}{4}$, $\frac{5}{8}$, and even $\frac{11}{8}$ over the course of the song. The vocal melody often contradicts the implied meter in the piano; for instance, in measures 2–4, each measure in the voice seems to suggest a $\frac{4}{4}$ measure beginning on the second eighth. These syncopations against the piano, augmented by the marked rubato in measures 3 and 4, create an agile, flexible line well suited both to the rhythm of the words and to the image of the cat. An appreciation of the vocal line's subtle beauty is heightened by the realization that it is a decorated paraphrase of the piano's chantlike melody, paralleling the latter a fourth higher:

Barber's ability to create fresh-sounding music from traditional elements has endeared him to audiences and performers alike. *Hermit Songs* has become a staple of the vocal repertoire, often performed in student recitals. The songs are tuneful yet present many performing problems, especially in rhythm and coordination between voice and piano.

John Cage (1912–1992)

Sonatas and Interludes: Sonata V

Suite for prepared piano

1946–48

TABLE OF PREPARATIONS

[MUTES OF VARIOUS MATERIALS ARE PLACED BETWEEN THE STRINGS OF THE KEYS USED, THUS EFFECTING TRANSFORMATIONS OF THE PIANO SOUNDS WITH RESPECT TO ALL OF THEIR CHARACTERISTICS.]

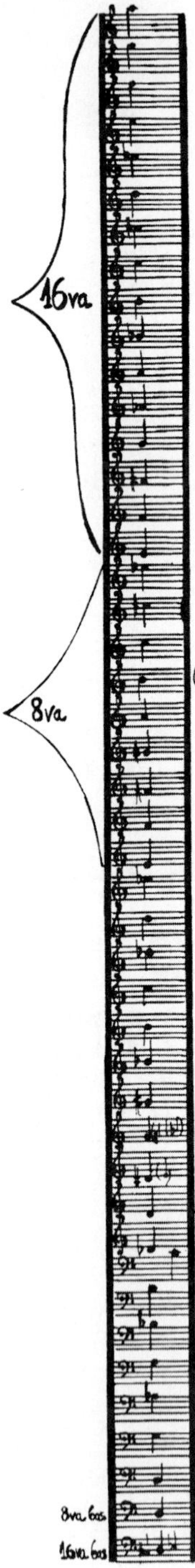

TONE	MATERIAL	STRINGS LEFT TO RIGHT	DISTANCE FROM DAMPER (INCHES)	MATERIAL	STRINGS LEFT TO RIGHT	DISTANCE FROM DAMPER (INCHES)	MATERIAL	STRINGS LEFT TO RIGHT	DISTANCE FROM DAMPER (INCHES)	TONE
16va				SCREW	2-3	1 1/4*				A
				MED. BOLT	2-3	1 3/8*				G
				SCREW	2-3	1 5/8*				F
				SCREW	2-3	1 13/16*				E
				SCREW	2-3	1 3/4*				E♭
				SM. BOLT	2-3	2*				D
				SCREW	2-3	1 11/16*				C♯
				FURNITURE BOLT	2-3	2 3/16*				C
				SCREW	2-3	2 1/2*				B
				SCREW	2-3	1 7/8*				B♭
				MED. BOLT	2-3	2 7/8*				A
				SCREW	2-3	2 1/4*				A♭
				SCREW	2-3	3 3/4*				G
				SCREW	2-3	2 15/16*				F♯
	SCREW	1-2	3/4*	FURN. BOLT + 2 NUTS	2-3	2 1/8*	SCREW + 2 NUTS	2-3	3 1/4*	F
				SCREW	2-3	1 13/16*				E
8va				FURNITURE BOLT	2-3	1 7/8				E♭
				SCREW	2-3	1 15/16				C♯
				SCREW	2-3	1 1/16				C
	(DAMPER TO BRIDGE = 4 7/16; ADJUST ACCORDINGLY)			MED. BOLT	2-3	3 3/4				B
				SCREW	2-3	4 7/16				A
	RUBBER	1-2-3	4 1/2	FURNITURE BOLT	2-3	1 1/4				G♯
				SCREW	2-3	1 3/4				F♯
				SCREW	2-3	2 5/16				F
	RUBBER	1-2-3	5 3/4							E
	RUBBER	1-2-3	6 1/2	FURN. BOLT + NUT	2-3	6 7/8				E♭
				FURNITURE BOLT	2-3	2 9/16				D
	RUBBER	1-2-3	3 5/8							D♭
				BOLT	2-3	7 1/8				C
				BOLT	2-3	2				B
	SCREW	1-2	10	SCREW	2-3	1	RUBBER	1-2-3	8 1/4	B♭
	(PLASTIC (see G))	1-2-3	2 5/16				RUBBER	1-2-3	4 1/2	G♯
	PLASTIC (OVER 1 UNDER 2-3)	1-2-3	2 7/8				RUBBER	1-2-3	10 1/8	G
	(PLASTIC (see D))	1-2-3	4 1/4				RUBBER	1-2-3	5 7/16	D♯
	PLASTIC (OVER 1 - UNDER 2-3)	1-2-3	4 1/8				RUBBER	1-2-3	9 3/4	D
	BOLT	1-2	15 1/2	BOLT	2-3	11/16	RUBBER	1-2-3	14 1/8	D♭
	BOLT	1-2	14 1/2	BOLT	2-3	7/8	RUBBER	1-2-3	6 1/2	C
	BOLT	1-2	14 3/4	BOLT	2-3	9/16	RUBBER	1-2-3	14	B
	RUBBER	1-2-3	9 1/2	MED. BOLT	2-3	10 1/8				B♭
	SCREW	1-2	5 7/8	LG. BOLT	2-3	5 7/8	SCREW + NUTS	1-2	1	A
	BOLT	1-2	7 1/8	MED. BOLT	2-3	2 1/4	RUBBER	1-2-3	4 1/8	A♭
	LONG BOLT	1-2	8 3/4	LG BOLT	2-3	3 1/4				G
				BOLT	2-3	11/16				D
8va bas.	SCREW + RUBBER	1-2	4 7/16							D
16va bas.	ERASER (OVER D UNDER C♯ + E♭) AM. PENCIL CO. #346	1	6 3/4							D

*MEASURE FROM BRIDGE.

CD 13|77 CD 6|79

𝅗𝅥 = 92

6

11

16

78 80

21

28

mf

34

John Cage was primarily a composer of music for percussion when he invented the prepared piano around 1940. Commissioned to write music to accompany a modern dance work (*Bacchanale*) that was to be staged in a hall too small to fit a percussion ensemble, he discovered that he could create percussion-like sounds on the piano by inserting small objects between the strings. He was inspired by the work of his former teacher, Henry Cowell, who also experimented with producing new sounds on the piano. In Cowell's *The Banshee* (NAWM 179), the performer plays on the strings directly, but all the sounds in a prepared piano piece are produced by playing on the keyboard. Placing material between the strings makes the piano into a one-person percussion orchestra. After writing several prepared piano scores for dances, Cage began to compose concert works for the instrument as well. His masterpiece for the prepared piano is *Sonatas and Interludes*, composed in 1946–48 and published in 1949 by Cowell's New Music Edition. The score is in Cage's own distinctive handwriting. He dedicated the work to pianist Maro Ajemian, who premiered it at Carnegie Hall in New York in January 1949.

In composing each piece for prepared piano, Cage first settled on what he called a gamut of sounds, the repertoire of sounds he would use in the piece, and on the particular insertions that would produce those sounds, which he had learned by experiment over several years. The Table of Preparations in the score for *Sonatas and Interludes* shows the forty-five preparations required for the piece, indicating what material to use and exactly where to place it, since the exact position affects the sound. Each piece in the set of sixteen sonatas and four interludes uses only some of the prepared sounds, giving it a distinctive palette. Some use unaltered piano sounds as well. The notation is in most respects like standard piano notation, but the sound that comes out when a key is pressed may be on a different pitch and may not sound like a piano at all. Thus the notation becomes like tablature (see the lute tablature in NAWM 61 and 73), telling the player where to place the fingers and how long to play each note, but not what sound will result.

Sonata V is an ideal example to demonstrate how the material inserted between the strings affects their sound, because each hand plays repeatedly on a small group of keys in a limited range, making it easy to compare the effect of each insertion. At the outset, the "melody" in the right hand goes down and up a segment of the chromatic scale from *b*′ to *e*♭″. As shown in the Table of Preparations, the strings for these notes have had different materials inserted in them:

- a metal bolt between the second and third strings for *b*′ and *c*″
- a piece of rubber in *d*♭″
- a metal furniture bolt between the second and third strings for *d*″
- rubber *and* a metal furniture bolt and nut in the strings for *e*♭″

Listen to the "melody" as the right hand goes back and forth through this gamut of sound. What sounds do you hear, and how do those sounds relate to the material inserted between the strings?

Adding a metal bolt between the strings creates a gonglike sound: the string vibrates freely but in a different way because of the additional mass, and there may be more than one pitch because the tension on the strings holding the bolt may differ. Adding weight to the strings also lowers the pitch. Indeed, in the performance on the accompanying recording, the pitch obtained by playing *d*″ sounds lower than the pitch made by playing *c*′, because the furniture bolt in the strings of the former is heavier than the normal bolt in the latter.

In all three cases in which only a bolt is inserted, it is placed between the second and third strings for each note. This leaves the first string unaltered, so that it resonates at the usual notated pitch. When the *una corda* ("one string") pedal on the piano is pressed, indicated by a dashed line under the music, the hammers that strike the strings are all moved slightly to the right, so that they do not strike the first string. In the first half of the piece, when the *una corda* pedal is held down, we hear only the gonglike sound of the strings with the bolts inserted between them. But in measures 21–27 and 37–40, when the *una corda* pedal is not pressed, the hammers hit the unaltered strings as well, and we hear two different sounds, the gong and the piano tone.

Adding a piece of rubber has a very different result: it deadens the sound, so we hear a sharp attack and little sustain. This makes the *e*♭″ and *d*♭″ sound like small drums or woodblocks rather than a piano. The combination of rubber with a bolt on the *e*♭″ sounds particularly woodlike in the accompanying recording. As the "melody" goes up and down in the right hand, we hear an alternation between woodlike and metallic sounds.

Meanwhile, the notes in the left hand move quickly up and down between *b* and *e*♭′, an octave below the right hand as notated, although the sounds are far from exact octaves apart. Here the preparations are different:

- two metal bolts plus a piece of rubber for *b*, *c*, and *d*♭′
- a piece of plastic plus a piece of rubber for *d*′ and *e*♭′

Because of their similar preparations, these five notes are fairly consistent in sound, suggesting a series of tuned log drums.

Most of the piece focuses on these ten sounds, but later on Cage introduces four more. The *a*♭ in the right hand in measures 28–29 is prepared with a piece of rubber and two bolts, one somewhat larger ("medium bolt"), and produces a sound like a tin can with a spoon in it that is immediately damped. The *g*′ and *a*♭′ in the left hand in measures 32–33 are prepared with plastic and rubber, so sound like the *d*′ and *e*♭′ below them. And the high *g*″ grace note in measure 37 is entirely unaltered, so it sounds like a piano note. In each case, the new notes are grouped with other notes that have similar sounds. Even the pure piano tone of the *g*″ is combined with the *b*′, *c*″, and *d*″, which include unaltered piano strings, and Cage allows the sounds to mingle by keeping the damper pedal down for two measures (indicated by the solid bracket under the music).

Given this gamut of sounds, how does Cage shape the piece?

Thirteen of the sixteen sonatas in *Sonatas and Interludes*, including this sonata, are in simple binary form, in two sections with a marked repeat of each section. This invokes a comparison to the keyboard sonatas of Domenico Scarlatti (see

NAWM 106), a deliberate reference to a historical model that is unusual for Cage, although as we have seen such references are quite common for other twentieth-century composers such as Schoenberg (NAWM 160a and 161), Webern (NAWM 163), Stravinsky (NAWM 165), and Bartók (NAWM 166). Sonatas IX, X, and XI add a third, unrepeated section, respectively at the beginning, at the end, or between the two repeated sections. There are also four interludes, the first two through-composed, the last two in four repeated sections. The first interlude falls after Sonata IV, the second and third after Sonata VIII, and the fourth after Sonata XII, breaking the sonatas into groups of four in a symmetrical arrangement.

In addition to these outward forms based on repetition, each movement also uses a type of structure based on duration that Cage first devised for his percussion pieces, in which the proportions within the whole piece are reflected within each unit. The units are marked off by double barlines and grouped into larger sections. In Sonata V, the first section has two nine-measure units, and the second section has two and a half (the last measure, in 3/2, counts as one-and-a-half measures of 2/2). When each section is repeated, the overall structure is 2+2+2½+2½. The same proportions can be seen within each unit, demarcated by the musical material. Cage sometimes referred to this structure as *square root form*, because it features the same number of units as there are measures in each unit—in this case, nine complete units of nine measures each—so that the total number of measures in each piece is the square of the number of measures in each unit (here, 9 x 9 = 81), and thus the number in each unit is the square root of the total.

Having examined the sounds and the durational structure Cage uses in this piece, we are ready to see how they interact to create the piece's overall shape:

- The first unit (measures 1–9) is characterized by an ostinato in the left hand and varied "melody" in the right. The longest notes—the dotted quarter notes in measures 1, 3, 5, and 7—demarcate the sub-units of 2+2+2½+2½ measures. These are also particularly distinctive sounds: the striking wood-like sound notated *e*♭″ and the more drumlike sound on *d*♭″, both quite different from the metallic sounds on the other notes.
- The second unit begins like the first but quickly changes to emphasize long gonglike sounds. The 2+2+2½+2½ proportion is less clearly articulated; there is no change at measure 12, the gong changes at measure 14 together with the accompanimental ostinato (now five quarter notes long), and only the ostinato changes in the middle of measure 16 (back to its original form). Then the first two units repeat as a section.
- The third unit (measures 19–27) begins the second section. It continues the long gongs of the second unit, now softer, and the ostinato figure is varied and stated only once within each sub-unit. Because the *una corda* pedal is released, the gong sounds are joined for the first time by pure piano tones. The 2+2+2½+2½ measure groupings are very clear, articulated by gong sounds and the re-initiation of the ostinato figure.
- The fourth unit (measures 28–36) is the loudest and most active, returning to the opening material and varying it while also introducing three new sounds on *a*♭, *g*′, and *a*♭′. The 2+2+2½+2½ measure groupings are marked by changes of material.

- The last unit—really half a unit (measures 37–40)—drops the ostinato entirely and features only the gongs and piano tones. Thus overall the piece moves from a mixture of wood and gong sounds to gong and piano tones, even creating the sense of a cadence at the end. As a half unit, these measures have just a 2+2½ grouping of measures (half the usual length), delineated by releasing the damper pedal and all notes but *c″* on the downbeat of measure 39.

As Cage discovered in playing his prepared piano pieces on various pianos and hearing them played by a number of pianists, the variability beween pianos and pianists means that the exact sounds created by the preparations will differ as well. This can be heard by comparing several recordings. His inability to precisely determine the sounds of the prepared piano was one factor that led Cage to take up indeterminacy in his later music. Yet the general move from woody to metallic timbres described here will be true of any performance, and so will the rhythm, so the shape of the piece will remain the same.

188

John Cage (1912–1992)

Music of Changes: Book I

Chance composition for piano

1951

CD 13|79

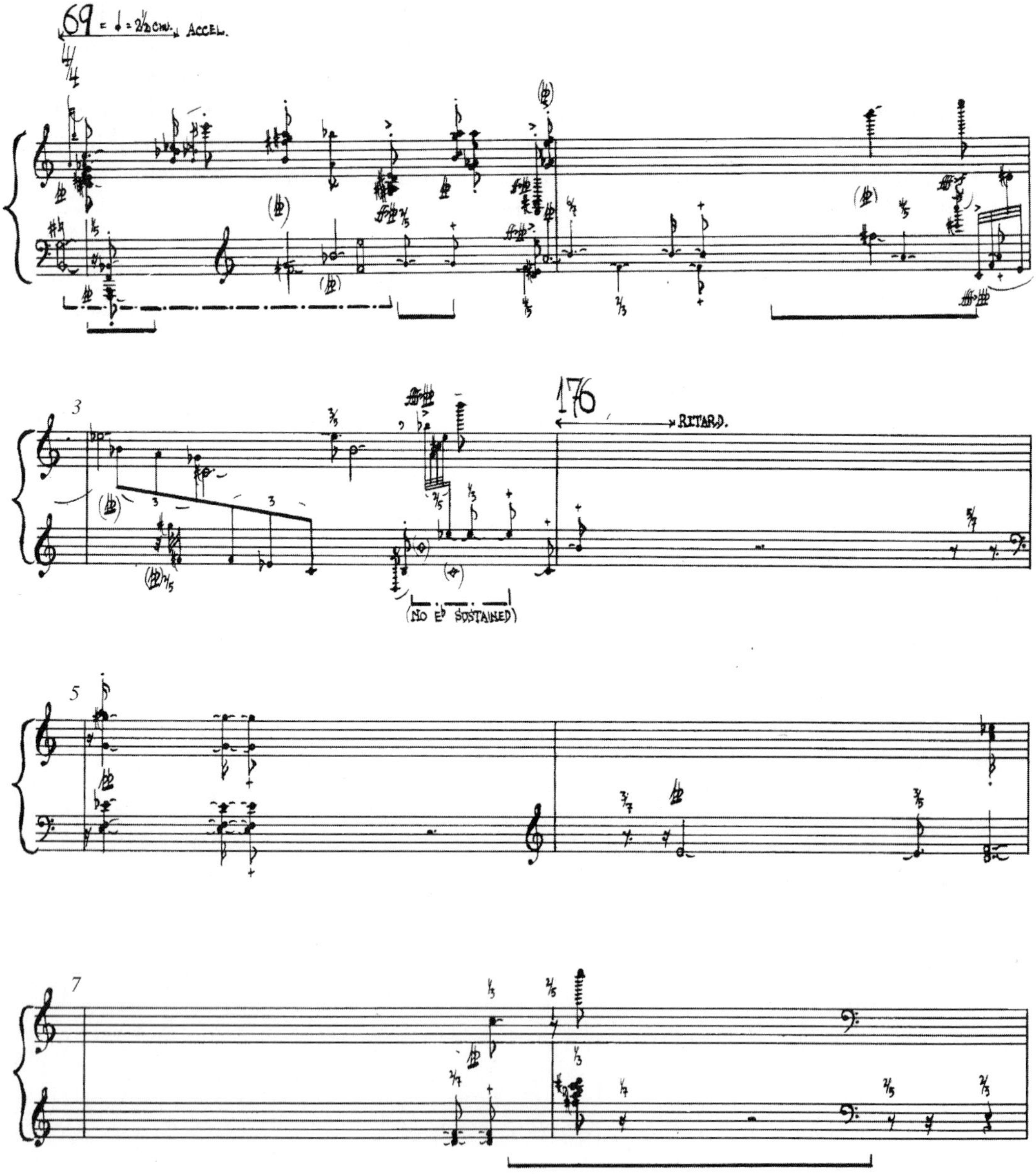

100
9
11
13
15
(100)
17

19
21
100
RITARD.
23
25
27
58
29

80
58
31
33
58
ACCEL.
35
37
39
76

41
43
45
ACCEL.
47
L.H.
R.H.
49

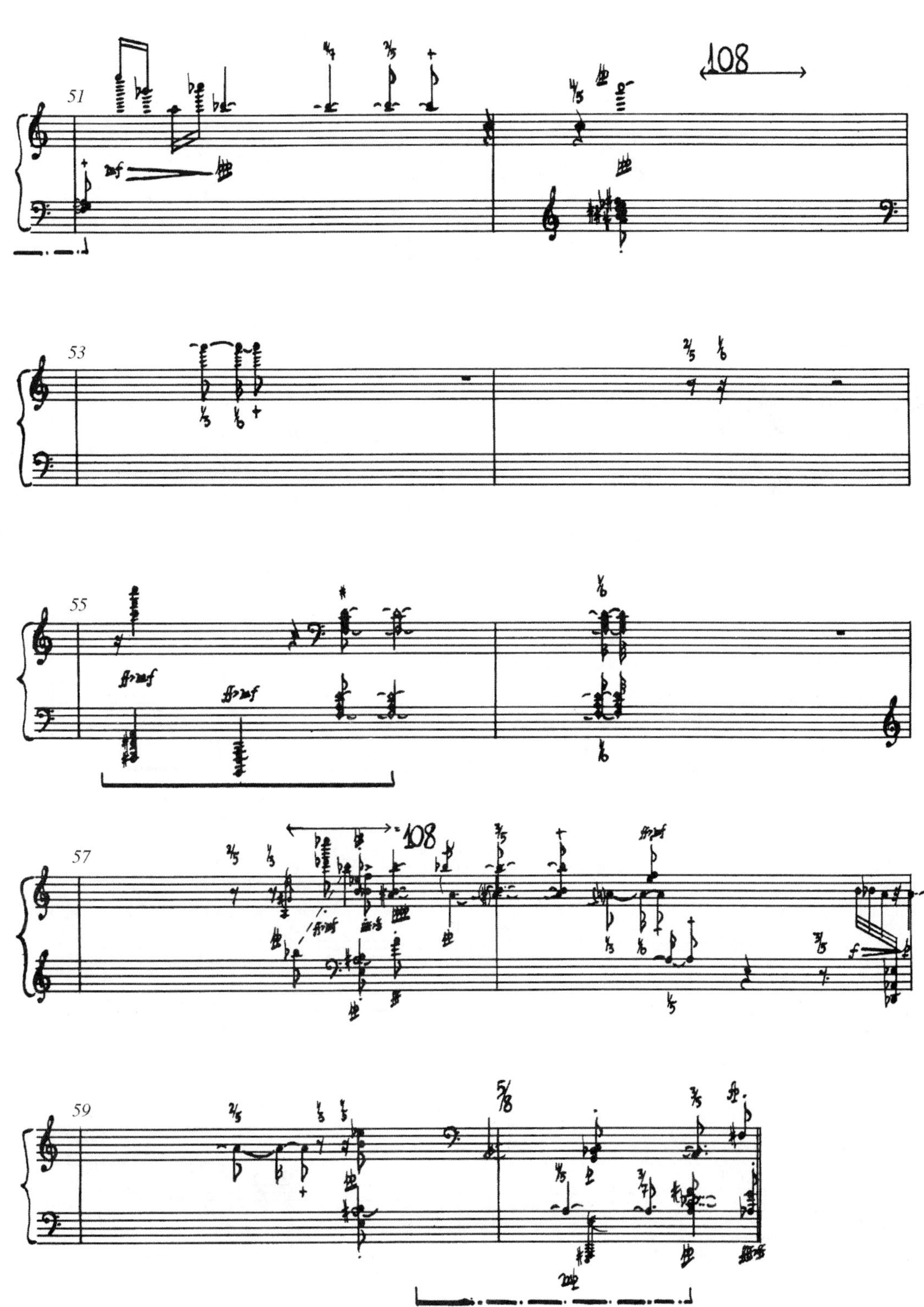
51
108
53
55
57
108
59
5/8

81

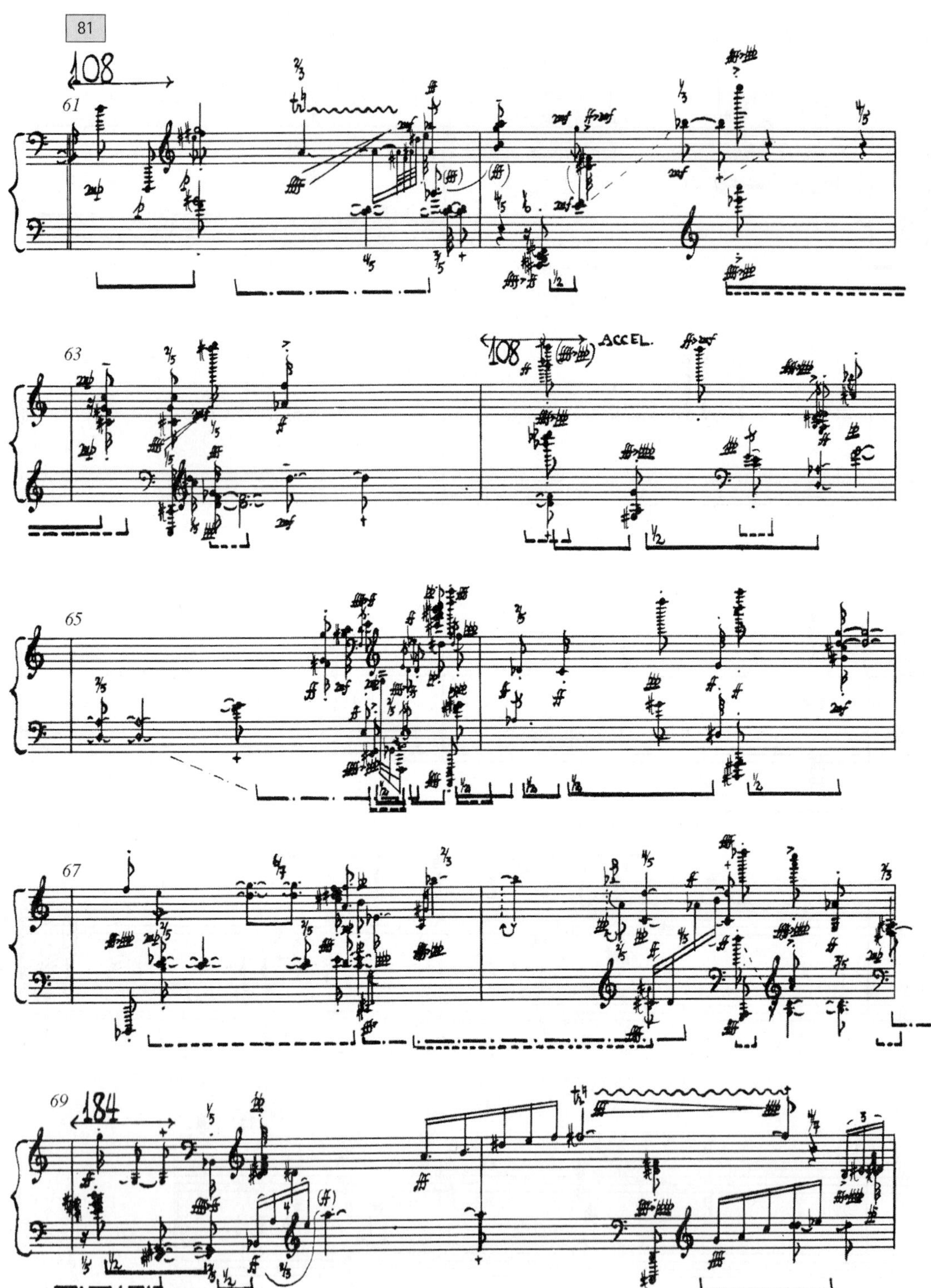

71
73
75
184
77
79

184
RITARD.
63
5-16-51
J.C.

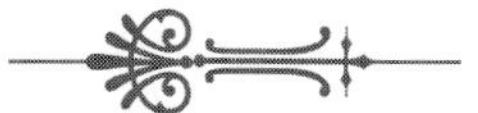

Music of Changes was one of the first pieces in which John Cage explored the possibility of determining aspects of the music by chance operations. He composed the work in four sections he called "books." Book I, included here, was composed in May 1951 and premiered that August by pianist David Tudor at the University of Colorado in Boulder; the other three books were completed later that year, and Tudor premiered the entire work in New York in January 1952.

The form of the piece was designed in advance. Cage used forms based on duration, particularly square-root form, in which the large-scale divisions of the work as a whole are reflected within each unit (see explanation in NAWM 187). A simple version might have seven units of seven measures each, but *Music of Changes* is far more complex, with a structure of durations based on a total of 29⅝ durational units, each 29⅝ measures long. Both the piece as a whole and each unit are divided into segments defined by the ratios 3–5–6¾–6¾–5–3⅛. Book I contains the first three units (measures 1–30, 31–60, and 61–90); in each, the last measure is only ⅝ as long as the others, for a total of 29⅝ measures. The divisions within each unit—of 3, 5, 6¾, 6¾, 5, and 3⅛ measures respectively—can be seen in the score, delineated by indications of tempo (see the tempo markings in the first unit, at measures 4, 9, 15, 22, and 27) and by changes of musical material and density.

Once Cage designed the durational structure, he filled it using chance operations. The title of the work refers to the ancient Chinese book *I-Ching* (Book of Changes), which contains a method for consulting an oracle by tossing coins six times to determine an answer from a list of sixty-four possible outcomes. For *Music of Changes*, Cage set up a series of charts, each with sixty-four elements that he chose using the same system. One chart determined how many events would occur during a particular segment; another determined the tempo (there were thirty-two tempos and thirty-two blanks, which if chosen maintained the previous tempo). Then there were eight charts each for sounds, dynamics (including accents), and durations. In the charts for sounds, half the possibilities were silences; the rest ranged from single notes to chords to "constellations" (several quick notes in a row) to noises (such as striking or slamming the lid of the keyboard). All these sounds were also designed in advance, so that only their selection for a particular position was determined by chance.

The result, as Cage noted, is a piece whose sequence of sounds is determined neither by the taste or psychology of the composer, nor by the traditions of past music. Neither the composer, the performer, nor the listener needs to make any value judgments, and no message is being communicated. The sounds are simply themselves, to be appreciated for their own sake.

The notation (in Cage's own distinctive handwriting) is unusual, but what the performer plays is completely determined. The "beat" set by the tempo is the quarter note, or one-fourth of a measure, shown by a line (2.5 centimeters long in the original score, here reduced). The notation is proportional: a note's place in time is shown precisely by its position in the measure, reading the length of the measure as an exact timeline. Diamond-shaped notes indicate keys (sometimes a single key, sometimes a range of keys, as at the beginning) that are depressed silently to raise the dampers, which are then kept off the strings by the sostenuto (sustain) pedal (marked with a dash-and-dot line under the notes), so that the strings resonate with harmonics generated by other notes. Other indications include using the damper pedal (marked with a solid line under the notes) and *una corda* pedal (which shifts the hammers to strike one instead of three strings for each note, marked with a dashed line, as in measures 33–34) and releasing a key to stop the tone (a plus above the note). Full of unusual techniques and rhythms, the piece is quite difficult to play, but the performer can take comfort from Cage's comment about this and other pieces generated by chance: "A 'mistake' is beside the point, for once anything happens it authentically is."

Morton Feldman (1926–1987)

Projection I

Cello piece

1950

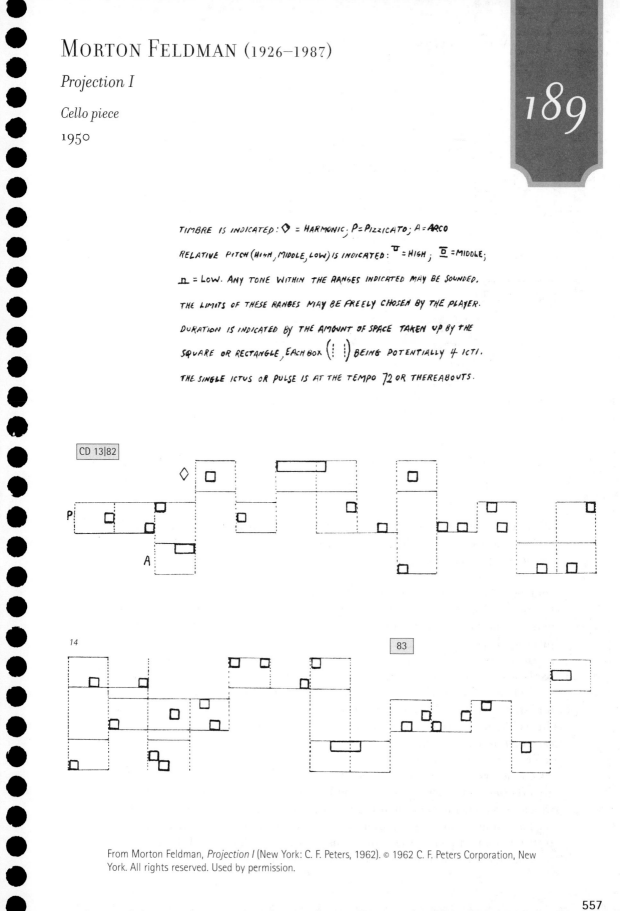

TIMBRE IS INDICATED: ◇ = HARMONIC; P = PIZZICATO; A = ARCO

RELATIVE PITCH (HIGH, MIDDLE, LOW) IS INDICATED: ⊓ = HIGH; ⊓ = MIDDLE;

⊓ = LOW. ANY TONE WITHIN THE RANGES INDICATED MAY BE SOUNDED.

THE LIMITS OF THESE RANGES MAY BE FREELY CHOSEN BY THE PLAYER.

DURATION IS INDICATED BY THE AMOUNT OF SPACE TAKEN UP BY THE

SQUARE OR RECTANGLE, EACH BOX (¦ ¦) BEING POTENTIALLY 4 ICTI.

THE SINGLE ICTUS OR PULSE IS AT THE TEMPO 72 OR THEREABOUTS.

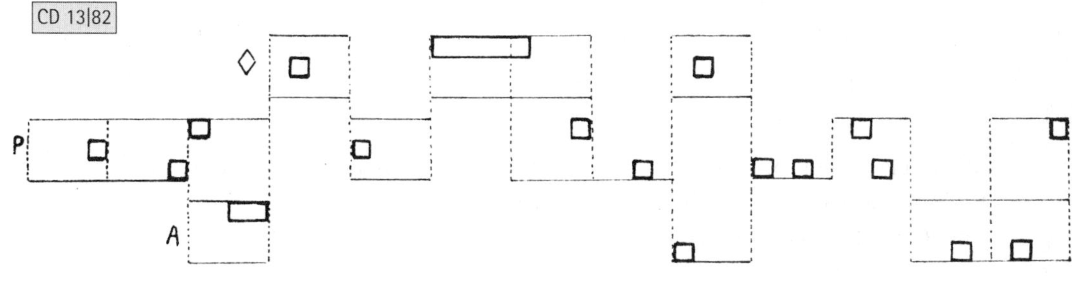

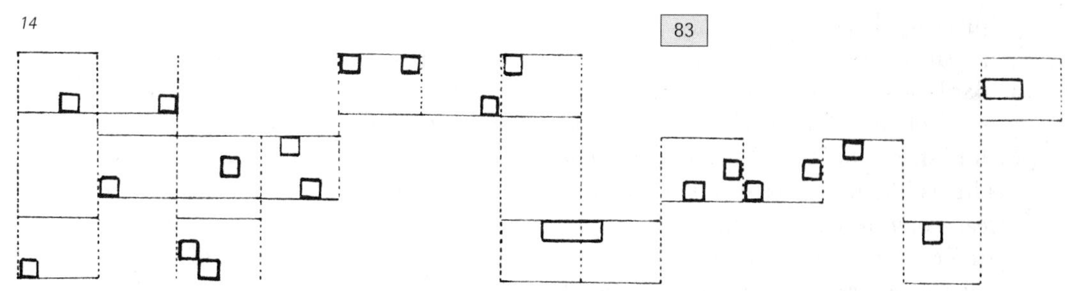

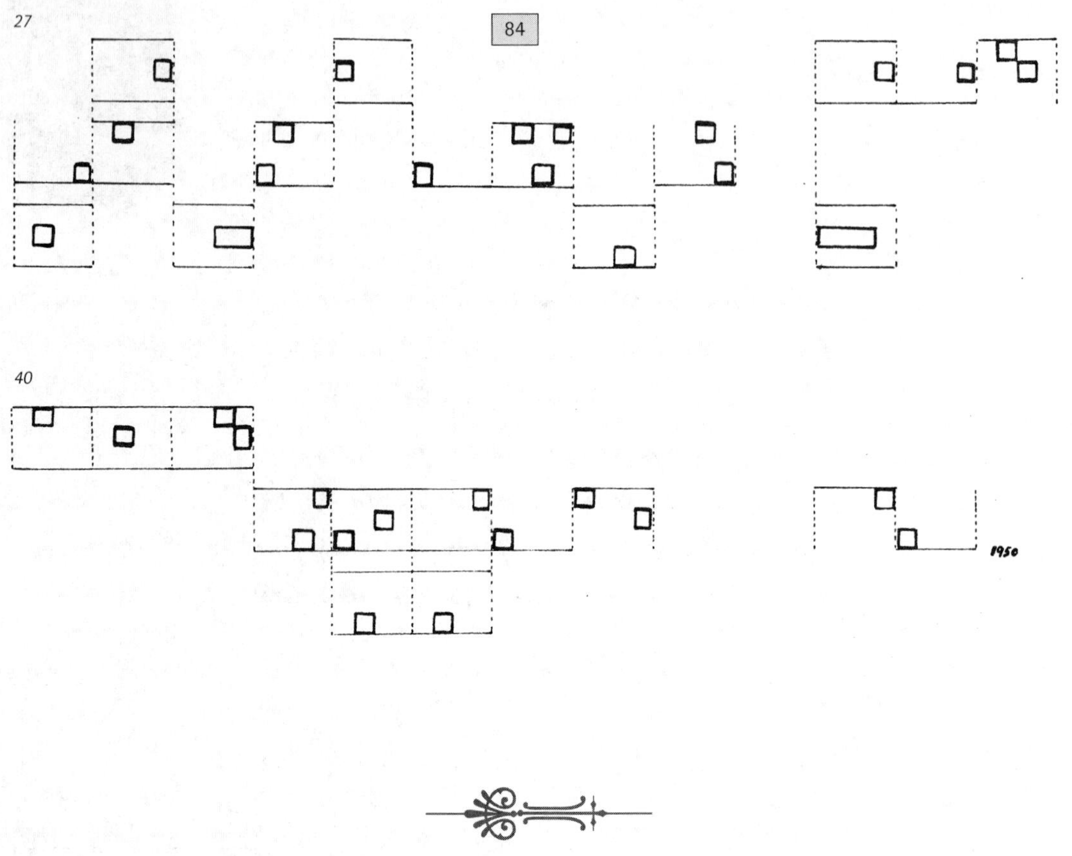

Morton Feldman composed *Projection I* for the cellist Seymour Barab. It was one of the first pieces to use graphic notation, which allowed Feldman to leave the exact pitches unspecified. Dynamics and articulation are also left to the player's discretion. These musical elements are *indeterminate*, rather than being chosen by the composer. Yet the piece is not random. By leaving these aspects of the music indeterminate, Feldman brings other parameters to the forefront: timbre, register, density, and the contrast between sound and silence. He uses these to give the piece its shape.

The notation Feldman devised for this piece shares several features with standard musical notation. It is read from left to right. Vertical dotted lines mark off units of duration, each with four sub-units Feldman calls *icti* (plural of *ictus*, Latin for "stress" or "beat") that come at about the tempo of 72 per minute; essentially, this is like measures of 4/4 meter at a tempo of 72 quarter notes per minute. (For ease of reference, in the following discussion these units of four icti will be referred to as measures, with the understanding that there is no sense of emphasis on the first ictus of the measure.) There are three styles of playing the cello—arco (bowed), pizzicato (plucked), and harmonics (bowed high notes produced with a finger touching but not pressing down the string)—which are laid out from the bottom to the top of the score, as if these three timbres were three different instruments in a piece of chamber music. Within each of these three "parts," musical notes are indicated by square or rectangular boxes. Although the exact pitch is not indicated, the placement of the box at the top, in the middle, or at the bottom of the space indicates whether the player is to choose a note that is in the high, middle, or low range. In all of these ways, Feldman's graphic notation uses conventions familiar from standard notation, reading duration from left to right with regularly recurring barlines, aligning different instruments vertically, and using relative height on the page to indicate relative height of pitches. Besides the refusal to specify exact pitch, the greatest departure from standard notation is the indication of duration for each note using the width of the box, which varies from one to five icti, and the use of empty space rather than rests to indicate silence.

Most music, from Renaissance modal counterpoint to twelve-tone music, uses pitch to provide structure. Without that as a resource, Feldman focuses on elements that are in some ways more basic than pitch.

One is the contrast between sound and silence. Throughout the piece, one note may immediately follow another, or there may be a silence of one to three icti between them. Only five times is there a silence of four or more icti: at measures 21–22, 32–33, 36, 41–42, and 48–50. Music has long been articulated by silence, from breaths between phrases of ancient songs to the rests between phrases of Mozart sonatas and Schoenberg's atonal works. On the same principle, these relatively longer silences in *Projection I* can be understood to delineate sections.

If we accept this view, an overall shape to the piece emerges—no matter what pitches the player selects. One shaping factor is the length of the sections. The first is the longest (21 measures), the second (11 measures) and third (4 measures) rapidly decrease in length, the fourth (5 measures) and fifth (8 measures) increase moderately, and the last (2 measures) is the shortest of all. The density of attacks in each section is fairly steady, usually one or two in each measure, but the progression toward shorter sections means a somewhat higher ratio of silence to sound as the piece progresses.

The sections are also characterized by different sound profiles created by timbre and register:

1. The first section (measures 1–21) uses all three ranges within all three timbres. It is dominated by pizzicatos, half of them in a low register. At the beginning and end, high bowed notes and harmonics are also featured, balanced in the middle of the section by low bowed notes and harmonics.
2. The second section (measures 22–32) omits the high and low range of harmonics and the low arco range. Again, it is dominated by pizzicatos, half in a low register, with some middle-range harmonics and arco notes.
3. The brief third section (measures 33–36) uses only high and low pizzicatos, with one low arco note; the other ranges are not used, and no harmonics appear.
4. The fourth section (measures 37–41) is virtually the opposite of the third: no pizzicatos appear, there is only one middle-range arco note, and the rest is harmonics in the high and middle range.
5. Pizzicatos in all three ranges return to dominate the fifth section (measures 42–49), joined only by one high and one mid-range harmonic and two low arco notes.
6. Section six (measures 50–51) has only two notes, a high and low pizzicato.

Overall, the piece moves from a long, inclusive section to shorter, more specialized ones, beginning and ending with a predominance of pizzicatos and moving to the opposite extreme in section four.

Such a piece is a model of indeterminacy, leaving important choices to the player. Every performance will sound different, especially in pitch. By leaving undetermined an element that is central to almost all other music, the piece challenges our basic definitions of music. Yet the piece still has an individual profile created by timbre, register, density, and silences that will be recognizable in any performance. By highlighting these parameters, Feldman makes us aware how much they contribute to our experience of music, even in traditional styles.

KARLHEINZ STOCKHAUSEN (1928–2007)

Kreuzspiel: Part 1

Chamber work for piano, oboe, bass clarinet, and percussion

1951

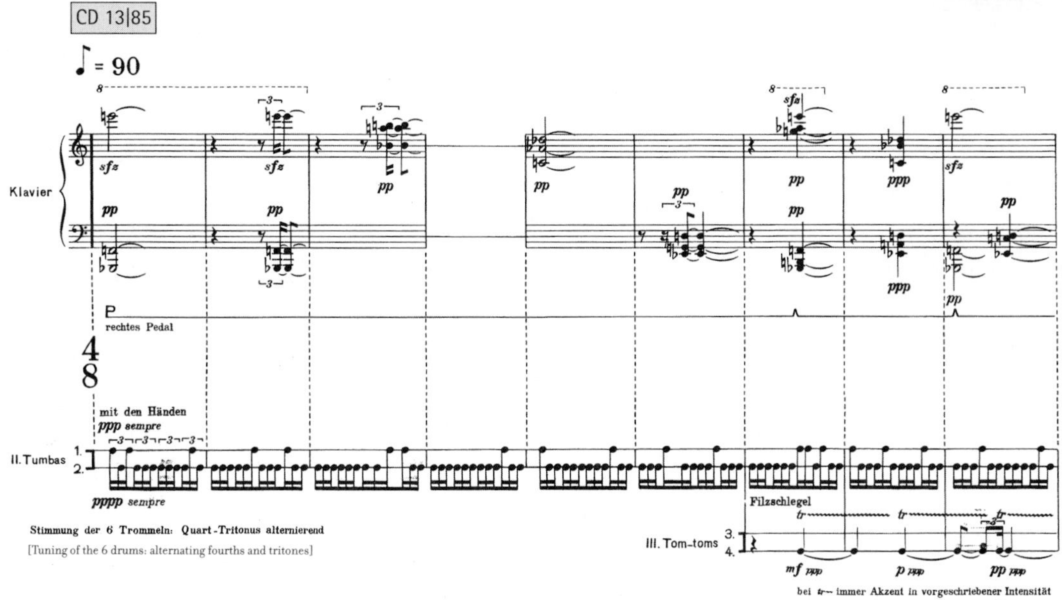

 The figures and parts of the analysis are based on Jonathan Harvey, *The Music of Stockhausen* (Berkeley: University of California Press, 1975), 14–20.

① *sfz*, *sffz* = Fell und Holzrand mit Filzkopf und Stiel gleichzeitig anschlagen [Strike drumskin and rim simultaneously with felt mallet-head and stick]

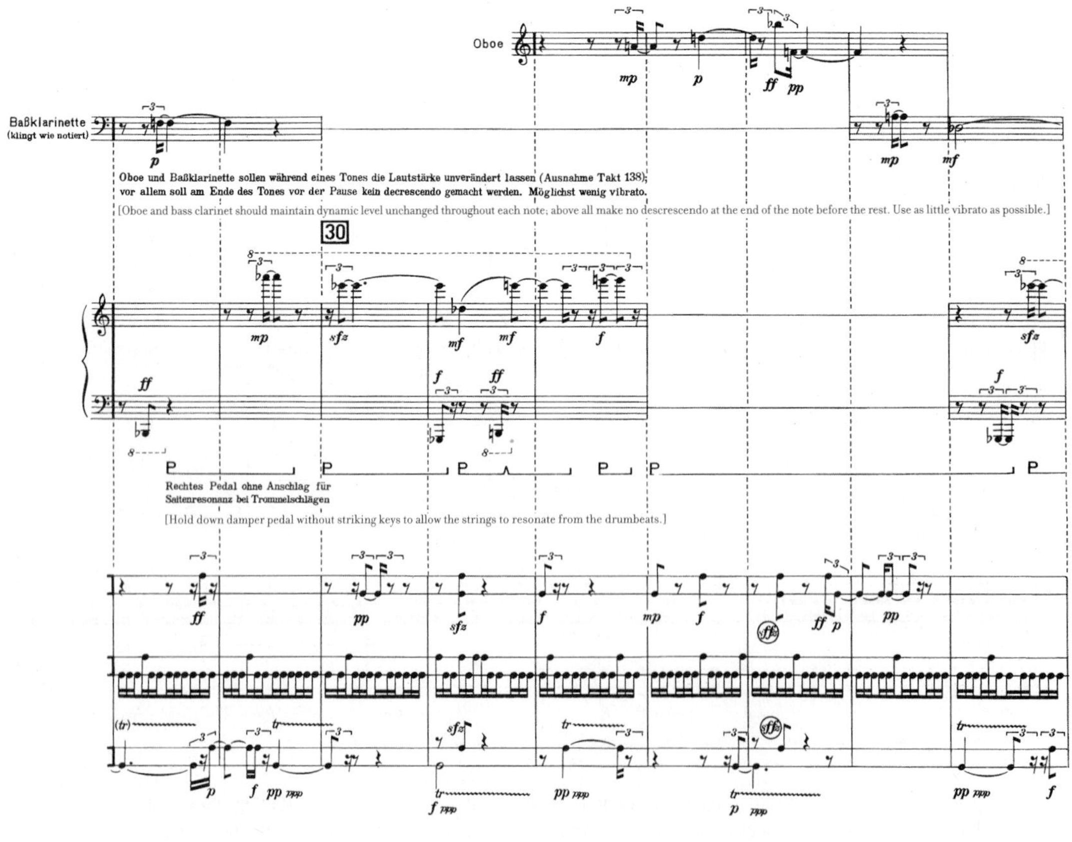

Oboe

Baßklarinette (klingt wie notiert)

mp p ff pp

p mp mf

Oboe und Baßklarinette sollen während eines Tones die Lautstärke unverändert lassen (Ausnahme Takt 138); vor allem soll am Ende des Tones vor der Pause kein decrescendo gemacht werden. Möglichst wenig vibrato.

[Oboe and bass clarinet should maintain dynamic level unchanged throughout each note; above all make no descrescendo at the end of the note before the rest. Use as little vibrato as possible.]

30

mp sfz mf mf f sfz

ff f ff f

Rechtes Pedal ohne Anschlag für Seitenresonanz bei Trommelschlägen

[Hold down damper pedal without striking keys to allow the strings to resonate from the drumbeats.]

ff pp sfz f mp f sffz ff p pp

(tr) p f pp ppp f ppp pp ppp sffz p ppp pp ppp f

40
87
50
Woodblock
rechte Hand schlägt Woodblock [Strike woodblock with right hand]

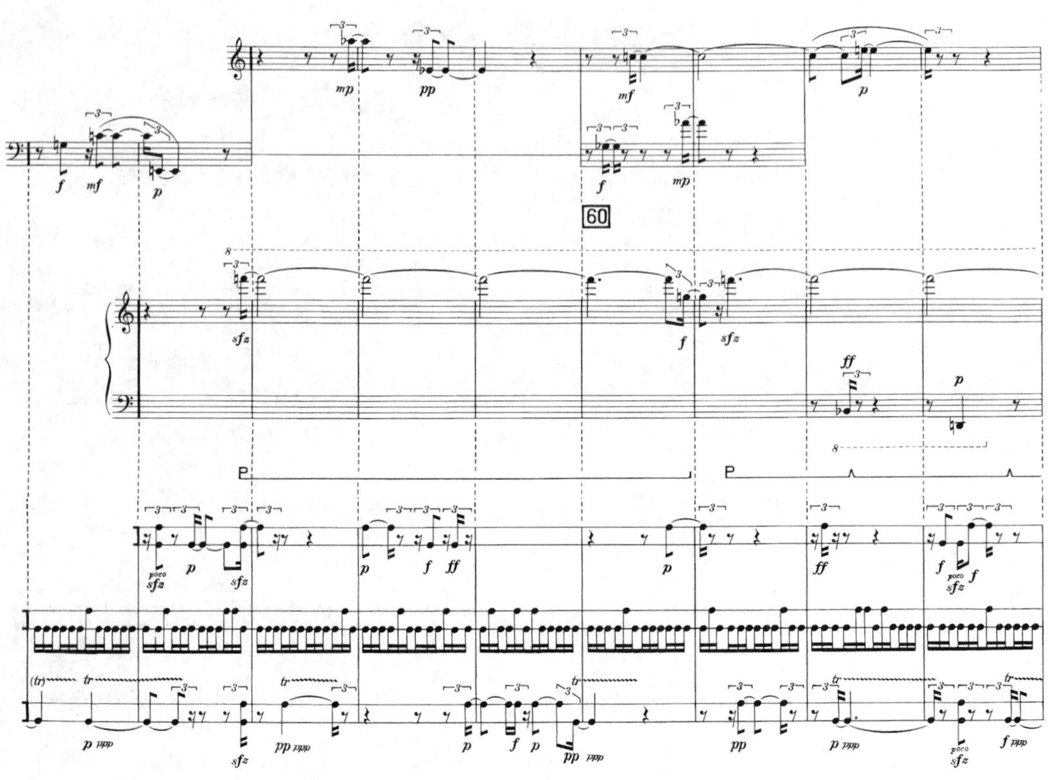
60

70

80

90

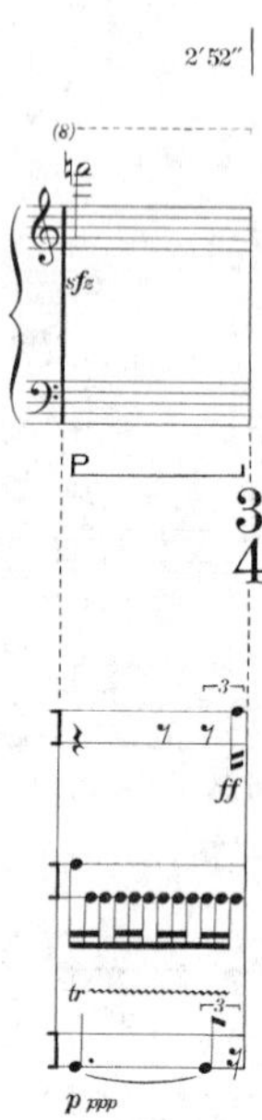

In the summer of 1951, Karlheinz Stockhausen attended the Darmstadt Summer Course for New Music for the first time. There he performed in Karel Goeyvarts's *Sonata for Two Pianos* and heard a recording of Olivier Messiaen's *Mode de valeurs et d'intensités* (Mode of Durations and Intensities) for piano solo, and he was struck by the novel ideas these pieces introduced. Messiaen based his piano piece on a "mode" of thirty-six pitches in which each pitch is assigned a duration, dynamic level, and articulation that are used with that pitch every time it appears. Goeyvarts, a student of Messiaen's, used a different system to link the four parameters of each note in his sonata, and in its middle movements material introduced in the highest register gradually moves down to the lowest, and vice versa. Stockhausen combined these ideas with new serial procedures in composing *Kreuzspiel* in the fall of 1951, making this one of the first pieces to explore serializing parameters other than pitch. It was premiered the next summer at Darmstadt, provoking an uproar and helping to make Stockhausen's reputation. Stockhausen revised it in 1959 before its publication in 1960, and dedicated it to his wife Doris Andreae.

Kreuzspiel is thoroughly systematic, applying serial principles to register, dynamics, and duration as well as pitch. The piece is in three parts or movements played without a break, of which the first part is included here. The title means "cross-play," and the piece is full of crossings.

Some crossings are audible, especially the crossing of register. After a thirteen-measure introduction (marked ♪ = 90), the main portion of Part 1 (marked

♪ = 136) begins with notes in the extreme registers of the piano, six notes of the chromatic scale near the bottom and the other six near the top (measure 14 to the first half of measure 20). Over the course of Part 1, the low notes gradually rise, passing through the low middle range played by bass clarinet and the high middle range played by the oboe, and end up in the highest range of the piano (second half of measure 85 through measure 91). Meanwhile, the notes that begin in the highest register of the piano trace the opposite path, so that the whole part is defined by this crossing of register. Part 2 begins in the middle range, moves out to the extremes, and returns to the middle. Part 3 combines the motions of the first two parts, creating a complex fabric of crossing registers.

A preview of this registral crossing can be heard in the introduction (measures 1–13). The piano presents three groups of chords, each of which includes all twelve chromatic pitch-classes. The first (measure 1 through the first half of measure 7) and last (measures 9–13) use chords of three notes, the middle group chords of six notes. The damper pedal is held down through each group of chords, allowing all twelve notes to resonate simultaneously, then is briefly released to articulate the beginning of the next group. As shown in the example below, most of the notes remain in the same register through all three groups, but several notes cross register: B descends four octaves and A♭ rises two octaves, then both return to their original positions, crossing each other twice; A descends three octaves and G rises four octaves, then both move an octave in the opposite direction; and C stays the same at first, then descends an octave. The result is a complex of registral crossings, heard against the static background of the other pitches.

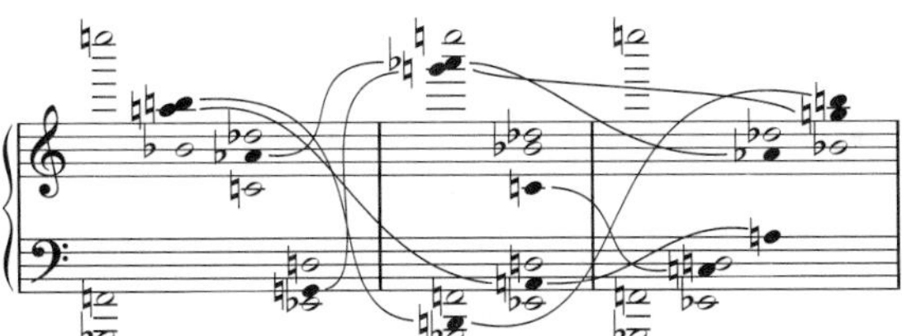

Other crossings are present in the compositional design, but may not be audible to a listener. One aspect full of such crossings is the sequence of pitches. After the introduction, through the rest of Part 1 only one pitch is attacked at a time, although pitches in different registers are often sustained long enough to overlap. The sequence of 144 pitches consists of twelve successive twelve-tone rows, and each new row is derived from the previous one by moving notes to new positions in the row in such a way that their paths cross in a symmetrical arrangement. The twelve rows and their derivations are shown in Figure 1, where the crossings are easier to see than they may be to hear in the music.

Stockhausen creates derived rows through a process of rotation akin to that in the finale of Crawford's String Quartet (NAWM 180) but much more elaborate. In this process, each note of the first hexachord is paired with its counterpart in the retrograde of the second hexachord (the first note of the row with the last, the second with the second to last, and so on). The two notes in each pair always move the same number of places, but in opposite directions. For example, the first and last notes of Row 1 are rotated into the middle of Row 2, each crossing over to join the

Figure 1: Pitch rows and their derivation

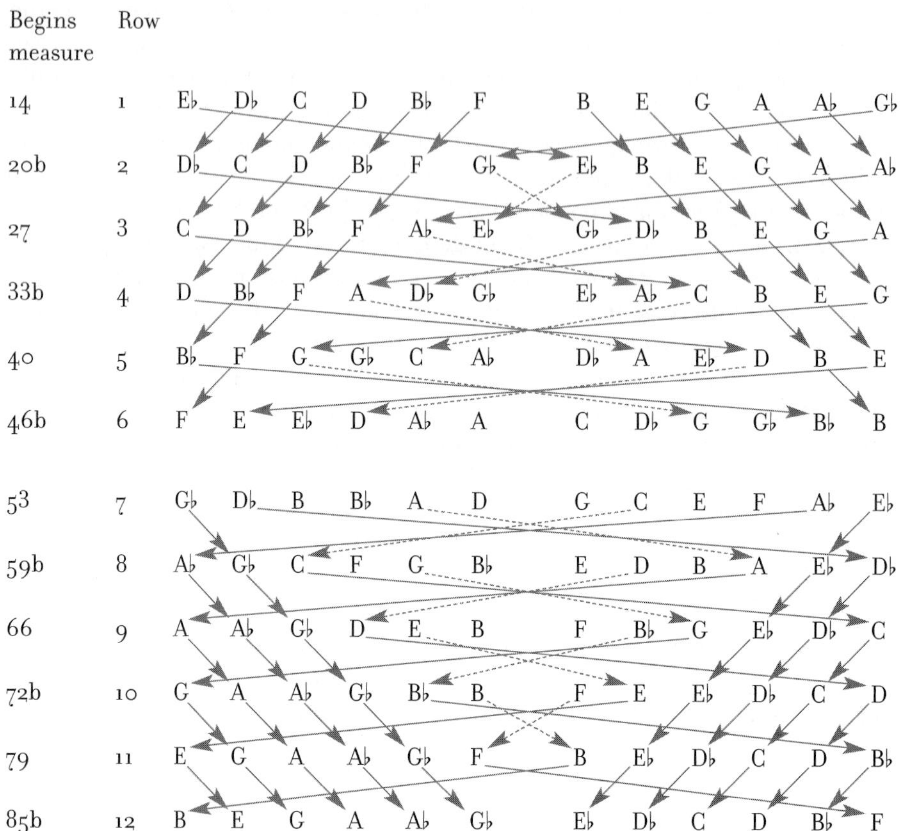

other hexachord, while the rest of each hexachord moves outward. The changes are shown by arrows. Similar transformations generate the next four rows, except that the notes in the middle of the row continue to cross back and forth between hexachords in a free rather than systematic way; the first subsequent crossing of each pair is shown by dotted arrows. Rows 7–12 follow a similar process in reverse, ending with a variant of the original row with the two hexachords reversed.

Thus the pitches in Part 1 are entirely systematic, derived through complex manipulation of the original twelve-tone row. The measure each row begins is shown in Figure 1, using "b" with the measure number to indicate that it begins on the second half of the measure. Occasionally, Stockhausen changes the order slightly in the piece itself: the E and E♭ in Row 6 are reversed (see measures 47–48), and the order at the beginning of Row 8 is reshuffled (see measures 59–61).

The registral placement of the pitches is determined by another serial procedure. A typical modern piano has a range of seven octaves (plus four extra notes at the top, which are not used in this piece). Each octave is assigned a number, with 7 for the lowest octave (from the A that is the piano's lowest note to the G♯ above it) and 1 for the highest octave. The pitch-classes that are introduced in the lowest octave during the statement of Row 1 in measures 14–20 move upwards through the registers in the order 7–2–5–4–3–6–1; those first presented in the highest octave move downward in the opposite order, 1–6–3–4–5–2–7. In the statement of Row 12, the notes that began in octave 7 are in octave 1 and vice versa. Pitches in the extreme ranges are played on the piano, pitches in the middle ranges on bass clarinet or oboe. Thus at the beginning and end of the process, the piano plays all the pitches. The number of pitches played by the wind instruments gradually increases until they play ten of the twelve in Row 6, then decreases again as the pitches move out of the instruments' ranges.

The pitch-classes start and end their motions through the registers at different times: F is the first to change register in measure 22, then A in measure 25, D in measure 27, and so on. Once a pitch-class starts to move, it keeps changing register with each new row until it arrives at its ultimate destination, then it stays there. The first time and the last time each pitch-class changes register, it is highlighted by a short, *sforzando* attack played by two or more tom-toms.

Duration is also serialized, in three different ways.

First, each pitch-class is assigned a duration, and each time that pitch-class is sounded, in any octave or instrument, there is the same length of time before the next pitch is played in the same or any other instrument. Thus the durations are serially ordered, in exactly the way the pitches are. A pitch may be sustained for a longer or shorter time, but its duration for the purpose of this structure is the length of time to the next attack. The duration for each pitch-class is given in Figure 2 in numbers of triplet sixteenth notes, from 1 to 12. The pitch-classes are listed in the order of the original row. The origin of these durations will be explained below.

Figure 2: Pitch-classes and their associated durations and dynamic levels

Pitch-class	E♭	D♭	C	D	B♭	F	B	E	G	A	A♭	G♭
Duration	11	5	6	9	2	12	1	10	4	7	8	3
Dynamics	***sfz*** (***pp***)	***mf***	***mf***	***p***	***ff***	***pp*** (***sfz***)	***ff***	***p***	***f***	***mp***	***mp***	***f***

There are twelve triplet sixteenth notes in each measure of 2/4 meter. The sum of the numbers from 1 to 12 is 78, or 6.5 times 12, so each complete statement of a row takes six and a half measures. This divides Part 1 into a series of units, each six and a half measures long.

In addition to duration, each pitch-class is associated with a particular dynamic level, also shown in Figure 2. In general, the shorter the duration, the louder the dynamic. There are rare spots in the music where Stockhausen changes the dynamic level associated with a particular pitch, and mid-way Stockhausen exchanges the dynamic levels for E♭ and F—another kind of crossing.

A second treatment of serialized duration is in the four tom-toms, in a process entirely independent of the *sforzando* attacks mentioned above. During the second half of the introduction (measures 7–13), the tom-toms play a series of diminishing durations, from 12 to 1 triplet sixteenth notes. Once again, the duration is the interval of time between one attack and the next. For the rest of Part 1, the tom-toms move through a sequence of twelve durational rows, shown in

Figure 3: Duration rows in the tom-toms and their derivation

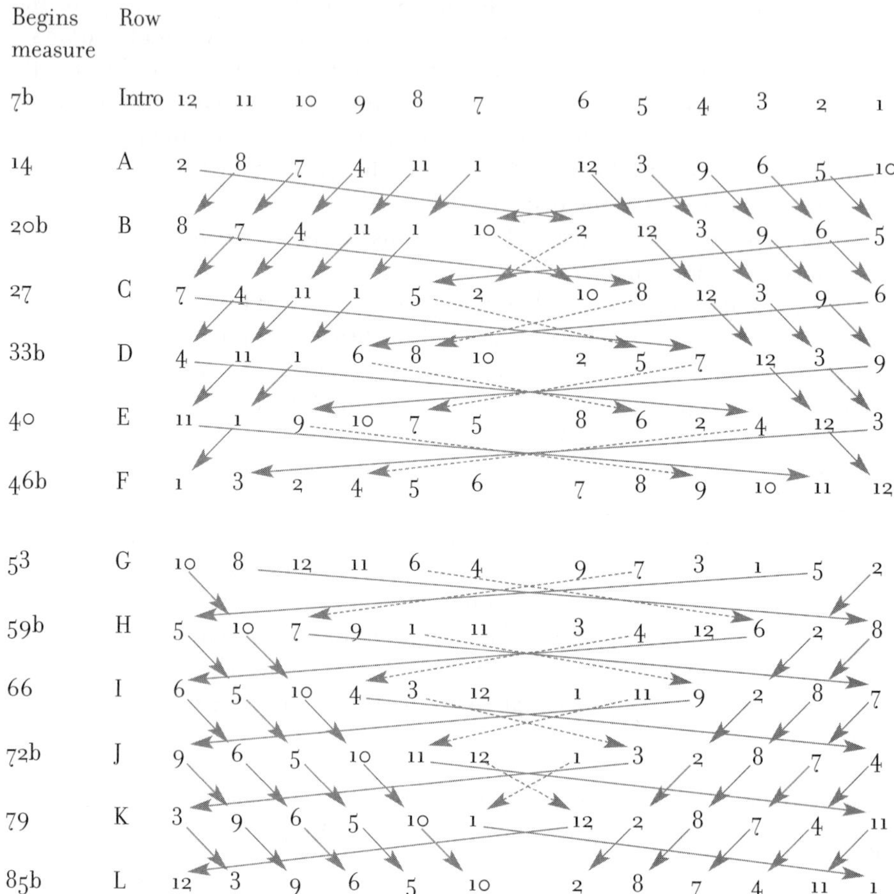

Figure 3 as Rows A through L. Each row includes all twelve numbers between 1 and 12. These rows also take six and a half measures each, and they are precisely coordinated with the pitch rows (Row A with Row 1, Row B with Row 2, and so on). The first row is the inverse of the durational series associated with the pitches in Row 1, shown in Figure 2. That is, subtracting each number in Figure 2 from 13 produces the numbers in Row A. Successive rows are derived using the same procedures as in Figure 1. Stockhausen makes only one alteration to this sequence of durations in the music itself; in measure 46, the durations of 3 and 2 are reversed, so that Row F becomes a statement of the twelve durations in increasing order from 1 to 12.

Like the pitches, the durations in the tom-toms are also assigned dynamic levels that stay constant throughout the piece. In addition, each duration is given to a specific drum. Durations 1, 4, and 7 are played on the first (highest) tom-tom, 3, 6, and 8 on the second, 2, 5, and 9 on the third, and 10, 11, and 12 on the fourth (lowest).

The tumbas or conga drums (paired drums, one higher pitched than the other, that are played with the hands) present yet a third sequence of rows, shown in

Figure 4: Duration rows in the tumbas and their derivation

Begins measure	Row											
1	Intro	2	8	7	4	11	1	12	3	9	6	5	10
7b		1	2	3	4	5	6	7	8	9	10	11	12
14		2	3	4	5	6	12	1	7	8	9	10	11
20b		3	4	5	6	12	11	2	1	7	8	9	10
27		4	5	6	12	11	10	3	2	1	7	8	9
33b		5	6	12	11	10	9	4	3	2	1	7	8
40		6	12	11	10	9	8	5	4	3	2	1	7
46b		12	11	10	9	8	7	6	5	4	3	2	1
53		11	10	9	8	7	1	12	6	5	4	3	2
59b		10	9	8	7	1	2	11	12	6	5	4	3
66		9	8	7	1	2	3	10	11	12	6	5	4
72b		8	7	1	2	3	4	9	10	11	12	6	5
79		7	1	2	3	4	5	8	9	10	11	12	6
85b		1	2	3	4	5	6	7	8	9	10	11	12

Figure 4. The tumbas keep time throughout Part 1, articulating every triplet sixteenth note at a soft level, like a pulsation in the background. The durational groupings are initiated by the higher-pitched tumba, which is also played slightly louder than the other. In the introduction, the tumbas play the pattern from the tom-toms' Row A, then their own series, the durations from 1 to 12 in increasing order. During the rest of Part 1, this series is rotated as shown in Figure 4. The tumbas' durational series is much simpler than those of the pitched instruments or the tom-toms, and they follow a rotation which is much simpler than those in Figures 1 and 3, making their process of permutation the easiest to hear in the music.

The metaphor of crossing is particularly apt for the top half of Figure 4, in which every duration crosses over to the other side of the series, resulting in a complete reversal from an ascending sequence of durations in measures 7b–13 to a descending one in measures 46b–52. The latter is pointed out in the music by playing the beginning of each grouping on a woodblock (played by the pianist) rather than on the higher tumba.

This moment (measures 46b–52) is in fact the crux—the main crossing—of the whole movement. This is where Row F in the tom-toms is a series of increasing durations from 1 to 12, exactly countering the decreasing durations in the woodblock and tumba. This is where the process of changing registers is crossing in the middle register, with ten of the twelve pitches of Row 6 sounded in the wind instruments. Moreover, with Row 6 (altering the position of the second and third note, as Stockhausen does in the music), the durations and dynamics are now in progressive order, with decreasing duration and increasing intensity:

Figure 5: Pitches in measures 46b–52 and their durations and dynamic levels

Pitch-class	F	E♭	E	D	A♭	A	C	D♭	G	G♭	B♭	B
Duration	12	11	10	9	8	7	6	5	4	3	2	1
Dynamics	*pp*	*pp*	*p*	*p*	*mp*	*mp*	*mf*	*mf*	*f*	*f*	*ff*	*ff*

This explains the derivation of the durations and dynamics for the pitch series. Compare Figure 5 to Figure 2 above, which showed the durations and dynamics at their first appearance with Row 1. The ascending dynamics are matched in the woodblock, emphasizing them. The first three and last two notes sound simultaneously with the woodblock, as they all should; but whimsically, Stockhausen delays notes 4 through 10 of his pitch row by one triplet sixteenth note, so that they sound just after rather than together with the woodblock.

How much of this elaborate structure is audible to the listener? The overall process of registral crossing, the move from piano notes to wind instruments and back, the coordination of elements at measures 46b–52, and the patterns of rising and falling duration in the tumbas should all be possible to hear. But without careful study of the score, listeners may be completely at sea, or may simply focus on the interesting sounds of varying dynamic levels, timbres, and pitches, all heard over a constant, yet constantly changing, quiet pulsation in the tumbas.

In a note to the score, Stockhausen indicates how the players should be arranged onstage. The grand piano's lid should be removed and the piano positioned with its keyboard facing front, so that the pianist's back is to the audience. The oboist is to the left (from both the pianist's and the audience's perspective), the bass clarinet to the right, and the three percussionists are arranged around the piano, with Percussion I (playing tom-toms 1 and 2) on the right behind the bass clarinetist, Percussion II (playing tumbas) behind the piano, and Percussion III (playing tom-toms 3 and 4) behind the oboist. Although just six players are involved, precise coordination is both so necessary and so difficult to achieve that the piece usually requires a conductor, standing just to the left of the piano keyboard. Stockhausen himself conducts the performance on the accompanying recording.

Pierre Boulez (b. 1925)

Le marteau sans maître: Movement 6, *Bourreaux de solitude*

Chamber song cycle

1953–55

191

CD 14|1

 For a comprehensive analysis, including the series given below and its derivations, see Lev Koblyakov, *Pierre Boulez: A World of Harmony* (London: Harwood Academic Publishers, 1990), 35–76 and 139–94.

Fl. en sol
Xyl.
Vibr.
Mrc. (sonn.)
Guit.
Alto avec sourd.
2
cédez
Voix
Le pas s'est é - loi -

Tempo
poco rall.
court
Fl. en sol
Xyl.
Vibr.
Mrc. (sonn.)
Guit.
Voix
-gné
Alto avec sourd.

Tempo poco più lento (♩ = 104) (♩ = 52)
plus long
Ancora più lento (♩ = 96) (♩ = 48)
long
Fl. en sol
Xyl.
Vibr.
Mrc. (sonn.)
Guit.
Voix
Le
mar
cheur
s'est
tu
Alto avec sourd.
pizz.
(pizz.)
arco

Tempo I
Fl. en sol
Xyl.
Vibr.
Mrc. (sonn.)
Guit.
Alto avec sourd.

Fl. en sol
Vibr.
Mrc. (sonn.)
Guit.
Alto avec sourd.

33
Fl. en sol
Xyl.
Vibr.
Guit.
sul A
Alto avec sourd.

36
Fl. en sol
Xyl.
Vibr.
Mrc. (sonn.)
Guit.
Alto avec sourd.

Fl. en sol
Xyl.
Vibr.
Mrc. (sonn.)
Guit.
Alto avec sourd.
Voix
Flzg.
Etouffer ces sonorités en jouant ceci avec le plat de la main
[Dampen these notes one by one by touching the bars with the flat of the hand in the following rhythm]
Sur le ca -

46
Fl. en sol
Xyl.
Vibr.
Mrc. (sonn.)
Guit.
harmonique hauteur réelle
jouer ceci
Voix
dran de l'I mi ta
Alto avec sourd.
50
Fl. en sol
Xyl.
Vibr.
Mrc. (sonn.)
Guit.
Voix
tion
Le
Alto avec sourd.
pizz.

54
Fl. en sol
poco cresc.
Xyl.
Vibr.
Mrc. (sonn.)
Guit.
Voix
molto
Ba - lan - - - - - - - cier
Alto avec sourd.
arco
59
Fl. en sol
Xyl.
Vibr.
Mrc. (sonn.)
Guit.
Voix
lan - - - - - -
Alto avec sourd.
pizz.
arco

63
Fl.
en sol
Xyl.
Vibr.
Mrc.
(sonn.)
Guit.
sul E
Voix
-ce
sa
char
ge
de
Alto
avec sourd.

serrer
Tempo
66
Fl.
en sol
Vibr.
Mrc.
(sonn.)
Guit.
sul E
Voix
gra - nit
ré - flexe
Alto
avec sourd.
pizz.
arco
pizz.
arco

poco accel.
70
Fl. en sol
Xyl.
Vibr.
Mrc. (sonn.)
Guit.
Alto avec sourd.
long

Meno lento (♪ = 120) (♩ = 60)
poco più accel.
75
Fl. en sol
Xyl.
Vibr.
Mrc. (sonn.)
Guit.
Alto avec sourd.
moins long

3
Ancora méno lento (♪ = 132) (♩ = 66)
79
Fl. en sol
Xyl.
Vibr.
Mrc. (sonn.)
Guit.
sul E
Alto avec sourd.

82
Fl. en sol
Xyl.
Vibr.
Mrc. (sonn.)
Guit.
sul C
Alto avec sourd.

BOURREAUX DE SOLITUDE

Le pas s'est éloigné le marcheur s'est tu

Sur le cadran de l'Imitation
Le Balancier lance sa charge de granit
reflexe.

—RENÉ CHAR

EXECUTIONERS OF SOLITUDE

The footstep has moved away the walker
is silent

On the dial of the Imitation
The Pendulum launches its load of
reflex granite.

Pierre Boulez began *Le marteau sans maître* (The Hammer without a Master) in 1953, intending it for the Donaueschingen Festival in 1954. When the performance had to be postponed, he revised the piece and added the ninth movement. It was finally premiered in June 1955 in Baden-Baden, and it soon became his most famous work. He dedicated the published score to Hans Rosbaud, who conducted the premiere.

Boulez based this piece on texts drawn from René Char's collection of surrealist poetry, *Le marteau sans maître* (1934). He arranged the work in three cycles, each centered on one poem. In two cases, instrumental movements precede and follow the song setting, treating the same basic material in different ways; in the third, there are two settings of the song. But instead of placing these three cycles one after the other, Boulez interleaved them:

Mvt	First cycle	Second cycle	Third cycle
1	Before *L'artisanat furieux*		
2		Commentary I on *Bourreaux de solitude*	
3	*L'artisanat furieux*		
4		Commentary II on *Bourreaux de solitude*	
5			*Bel édifice et les pressentiments*, first version
6		*Bourreaux de solitude*	
7	After *L'artisanat furieux*		
8		Commentary III on *Bourreaux de solitude*	
9			*Bel édifice et les pressentiments*, second version

The second cycle occupies the even-numbered movements. Its focus is the song setting in the sixth movement, included here.

The work is scored for alto voice, alto flute (in G, sounding a fourth lower than written), xylorimba (a large xylophone, sounding an octave higher than written), vibraphone, percussion, guitar (sounding an octave lower than written), and viola (called by its French name *Alto* in the score). The use of low female voice, alto flute, and viola gives the music a darker quality than the more predictable soprano, flute, and violin, while the plucked sounds of the guitar and the percussive sounds of the vibraphone and xylophone offer a lighter texture than a piano. The xylophone and vibraphone are both percussion instruments played with mallets, with bars for different pitches laid out like a keyboard over open tubes that serve as resonators; they differ in that the xylophone's bars are wood while the vibraphone's are metal, and the latter has electrically powered turning wheels in its resonating tubes that create a vibrato or pulsation. As in Schoenberg's *Pierrot lunaire* (NAWM 160), a different group of instruments plays in each movement. All seven performers participate in *Bourreaux de solitude*, although the percussionist plays only maracas.

At this point in his career, Boulez was committed to serial procedures for organizing pitch, duration, and dynamics, but he used them in a very complex manner. The row manipulations in Stockhausen's *Kreuzspiel* (NAWM 190) are child's play compared to those in Boulez's *Le marteau sans maître*. In Boulez's view, the rigid patterning in *Kreuzspiel* (and in his own early pieces that applied serial principles to duration and other parameters) was not the same as composition, which requires the exercise of taste and expressivity. By deploying rows in novel ways, deriving subsidiary series in each parameter from a basic row, and varying his material in many ways simultaneously, he made his music much more diverse, fluid, and expressive, but he also made his path in constructing the music extraordinarily difficult to follow.

Even knowing the basic row for the second cycle is little help:

The row is used in this form only once in this song, in its final measures. The chord on the second sixteenth note of measure 92 contains the first seven notes (with their proper durations and dynamics), and the final chord contains the last five (with the right dynamics, but slightly shortened durations). Elsewhere, Boulez deploys a number of derived series, created using a variety of methods.

Some aspects lie relatively close to the surface. For example, in the first measure, all twelve pitch-classes are sounded once. Each has a different duration, increasing progressively up the chromatic scale from D (one sixteenth note) to C♯ (twelve sixteenths, equal to a dotted quarter note). Each also has a unique dynamic level, increasing as the pitch-classes descend the chromatic scale from A (***pp***) to B♭ (accented ***ff sfz***). The composite rhythm includes an attack on every sixteenth note. The inclusion of all pitch-classes, durations, attack points, dynamic levels, and instruments makes clear that these parameters are systematically organized, while providing a great diversity of sounds for the listener. The rest of the instrumental introduction (measures 1–13) follows similar procedures, although the precise procedures and the underlying pulsation change with each statement of all twelve notes.

When the voice enters at the pickup to measure 14, the sound of the music changes greatly. The singer begins her first phrase on the same note as the alto flute, moves to a note the guitar has just played, and ends on a note shared with viola. When other instruments join in measures 17–18, they play notes she has already sung, or that other instruments have just played, although we have not yet heard all twelve in this section. This duplication of notes between instruments and within phrases gives a very different sound to the main part of the song, in which the voice alternates with short instrumental interludes. The closing section (measures 79–94) is again entirely instrumental, and like the introduction it is marked by twelve-tone saturation and relatively regular rhythm.

While these large-scale factors give shape to the piece, the difficulty of analyzing the particulars of the pitch content, durations, and dynamics in this piece suggests that analysis is really beside the point. Like Schoenberg or Wagner, Boulez does not want us to take apart his music to expose his secrets. Instead, he creates an ever-changing, diverting surface with a highly individual mixture of sounds that can be attractive and engaging. Our very inability to explain his music may allow us to experience it directly, rather than as an example of a complex system.

The difficulty of performing such music is obvious: the rhythms are unusual, the dynamics are constantly changing, the melodies awkward. Clearly, the singer must have perfect pitch. It may seem helpful to the singer to have her pitches matched by other instruments, but that may simply make any errors more obvious. A sign of how difficult the piece is to coordinate is that it needs a conductor, even for an ensemble of only seven—and that Boulez dedicated it to the conductor, not the singer, of the premiere performance.

The performance on the accompanying recording is conducted by the composer himself, who in the decades since this piece's premiere has become more widely known as a conductor than as a composer.

Luciano Berio (1925–2003)

Sequenza III

Solo for female voice

1965–66

The performer (a singer, an actor or both) appears on stage already muttering as though pursuing an off-stage thought. She stops muttering when the applause of the public is subsiding; she resumes after a short silence (at about the 11'' of the score). The vocal actions must be timed with reference to the 10'' divisions of each page.

● = sung tones } to be held to next sound or to ˥, ˩
○ = whispered, unvoiced sounds }

ɸ, Φ = sung and whispered sounds as short as possible

= different speeds of periodically articulated sounds

= can be performed as fast as possible

= as fused and continuous as possible

etc. = all grace notes as fast as possible

Although the borderline between s p e a k i n g and s i n g i n g voice will often be burred in actual performance, the vocal actions written on one line (a) are "spoken" while those written on three or five lines are "sung". On three lines, only relative register positions are given (b); dotted lines connect notes of exactly the same pitch (c). On five lines (d) precise intervals are given, but their pitch is not absolute: each sequence of intervals (between "spoken" sections) can be transposed to fit the vocal range of the performer; dotted lines indicate that the change of vocal colors on the same pitch must occur smoothly and without accents (e).

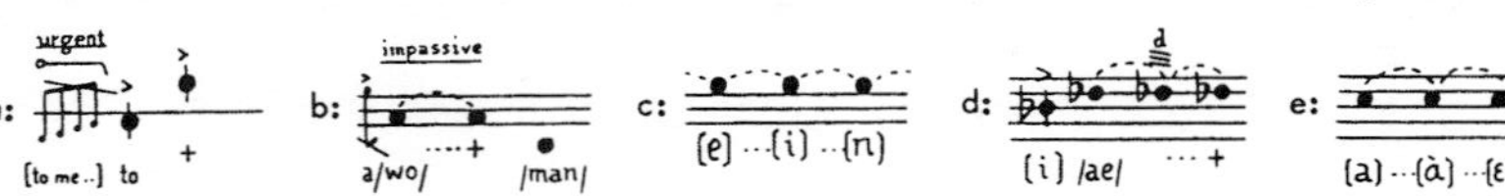

= intonation contour

The text is written in different ways:

1) Sounds or groups of sounds phonetically notated: [a], [ka], [u], [i], [0], [ø], [ait], [be], [e], [ɛ] etc.
2) Sounds or groups of sounds as pronounced in context: /gi/ as in give, / wo / as in woman, / tho / as in without, / co / as in comes etc.
3) Words conventionally written and uttered: "give me a few words" etc.

Sounds and words lined up in parenthesis as (/a tru to me/) must be repeated quickly in a random and slightly discontinuous way.

Groups of sounds and words in parenthesis as (to me...), (be/lo/...), (/co//ta/...) etc. must be repeated quickly in a regular way. At 15'' of the score, for instance, (to me...) to is equivalent to to me to me to; at 30'', ([e] [a]...)[a] is equivalent to [e][a] [e][a] [e] [a]; at 1' the group (/ta/[ka] be...)must be repeated as many times as possible for about 2''.

L. Laughter must always be clearly articulated on a wide register.

[?] = bursts of laughter to be used with any vowel freely chosen

= mouth clicks

= cough

= snapping fingers gently

\+ = with mouth closed

o, o— = breathy tone, almost whispered

= breathing in, gasping

= tremolo

= dental tremolo (or jaw quivering)

= trilling the tongue against the upper lip (action concealed by one hand)

= tapping very rapidly with one hand (or fingers) against the mouth (action concealed by other hand)

(hm) = hand (or hands) over mouth

(hm) = moving hand cupped over mouth to affect sound (like a mute)

(hd) = hands down

Hand, facial and bodily gestures besides those specified in the score are to be employed at the discretion of the performer according to the indicated patterns of emotions and vocal behavior (t e n s e, u r g e n t, d i s t a n t, d r e a m y etc.). The performer, however, must not try to represent or pantomime tension, urgency, distance or dreaminess but must let these cues act as a spontaneous conditioning factor to her vocal action (mainly the color, stress and intonation aspects) and body attitudes. The processes involved in this conditioning are not assumed to be conventionalized; they must be experimented with by the performer herself according to her own emotional code, her vocal flexibility and her "dramaturgy".

CD 14|4

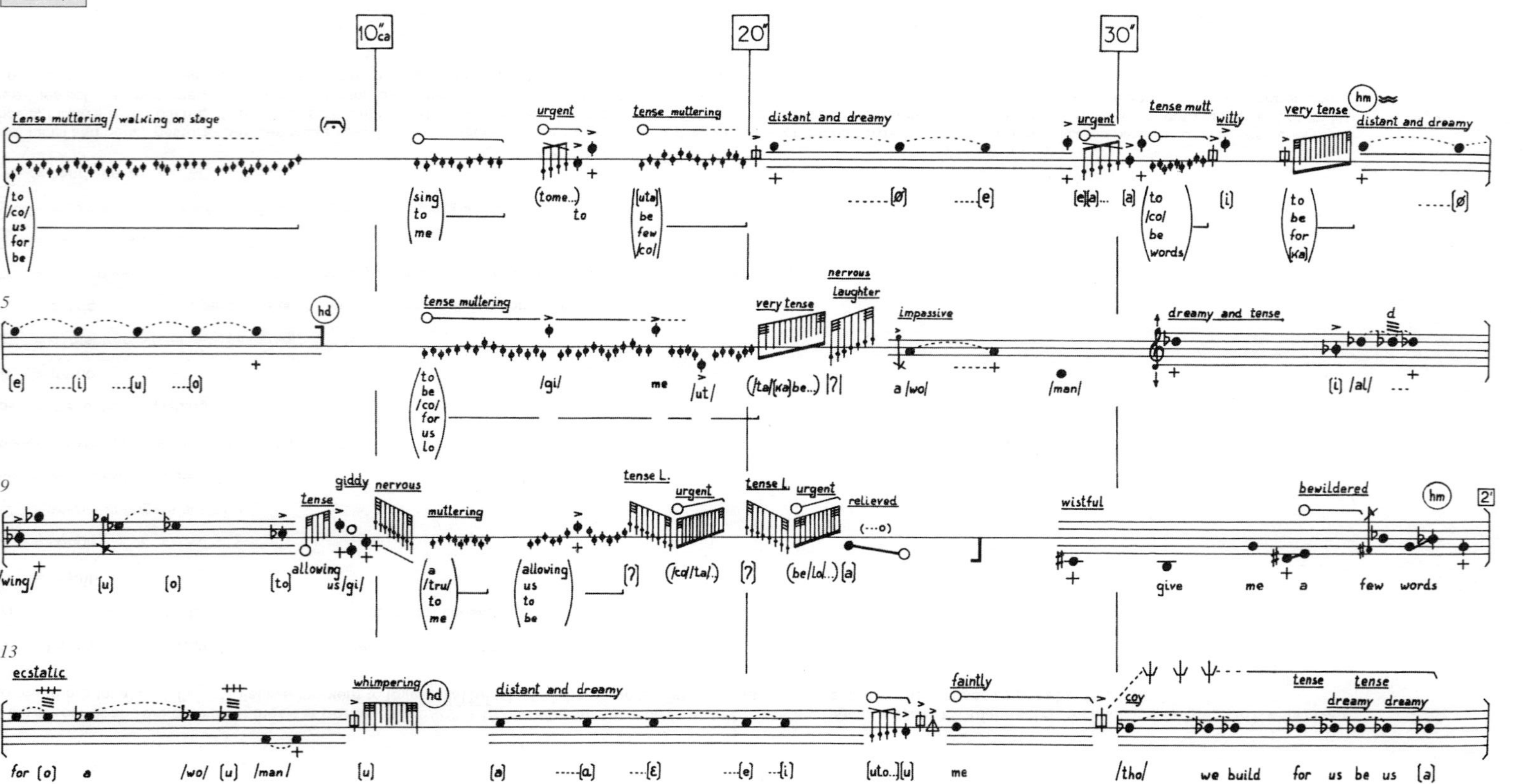

10"ca
20"
30"
tense muttering / walking on stage
urgent
tense muttering
distant and dreamy
urgent
tense mutt.
witty
very tense
hm
distant and dreamy
to /co/ us for be
sing to me
(tome...) to
[uta] be few /co/
[ø]
[e]
[e][a]... [a]
to /co/ be words
[i]
to be for [ka]
tense muttering
very tense
nervous laughter
impassive
dreamy and tense
hd
[e] [i] [u] [o]
to be /co/ for us lo
/gi/
me
/ut/
(ta)(ka)be...) [?]
a /wo/
/man/
[i] /al/
giddy
nervous
tense
muttering
tense L.
urgent
tense L.
urgent
relieved
wistful
bewildered
hm
2"
/wing/ [u] [o] [to] allowing us /gi/
a /tru/ to me
allowing us to be
[?] (ka/ta/.) [?] (be/lo/..) [a]
give me a few words
ecstatic
whimpering
hd
distant and dreamy
faintly
coy
tense
tense
dreamy
dreamy
for [o] a /wo/ [u] /man/
[u]
[a] [a] [ɛ] [e] [i]
[uto..][u]
me
/tho/ we build for us be us [a]

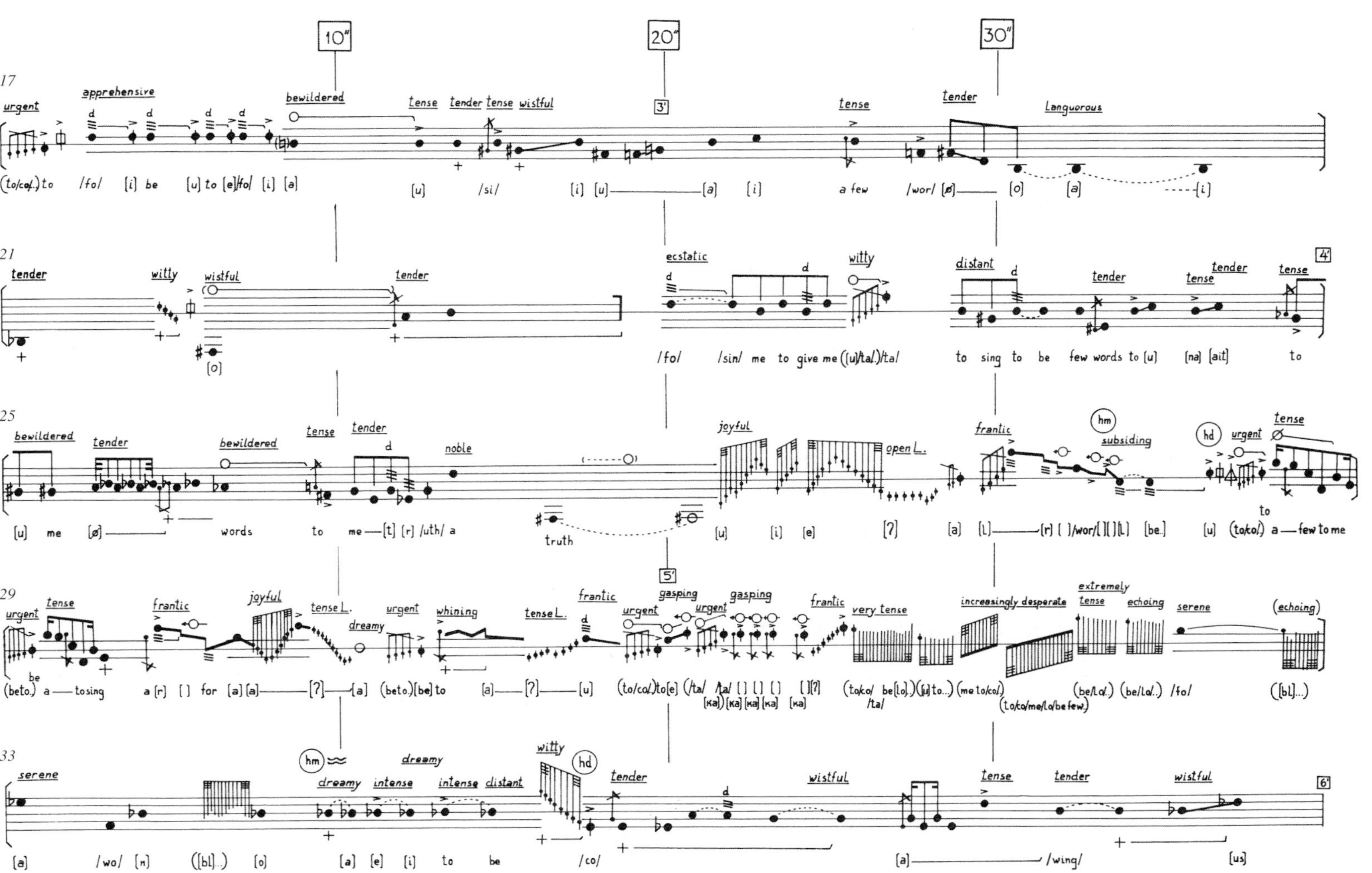
10"
20"
30"
17
urgent
apprehensive
bewildered
tense
tender tense wistful
3'
tense
tender
Languorous
(to/co/.) to /fo/ [i] be [u] to [e]/fo/ [i] [a]
[u] /si/ [i] [u] [a] [i] a few /wor/ [ø] [o] [a] [i]
21
tender
witty
wistful
tender
[o]
ecstatic
witty
distant
tender
tense
tender
tense
4'
/fo/ /sin/ me to give me ([u]/ta/.)/ta/
to sing to be few words to [u] [na] [ait] to
25
bewildered
tender
bewildered
tense
tender
noble
joyful
open L.
frantic
hm
subsiding
hd
urgent
tense
[u] me [ø] words to me [t] [r] /uth/ a
truth
[u] [i] [e] [?] [a] [L] [r] [ ] /wor/ [ ] [ ] [L] [be.]
[u] (to/co/.) a few to me
to
29
urgent
tense
frantic
joyful
tense L.
dreamy
urgent
whining
tense L.
frantic
5'
urgent
gasping
urgent
gasping
frantic
very tense
increasingly desperate
extremely
tense
echoing
serene
(echoing)
(beto.) a tosing
be
a [r] [ ] for [a] [a] [?] [a] (beto.)[be] to [a] [?] [u]
(to/co/.)to[e] (/ta/ /ta/ [ ] [ ] [ ] [ ][?]
[ka] [ka] [ka] [ka] [ka]
(to/co/ be[lo].)([u] to...) (me to/co/.)
/ta/
(to/co/me/lo/be few)
(be/lo/.) (be/lo/.) /fo/ ([bl]...)
33
serene
hm
dreamy
dreamy
intense
intense
distant
witty
hd
tender
wistful
tense
tender
wistful
6'
[a] /wo/ [n] ([bl]...) [o] [a] [e] [i] to be /co/
[a] /wing/ [us]

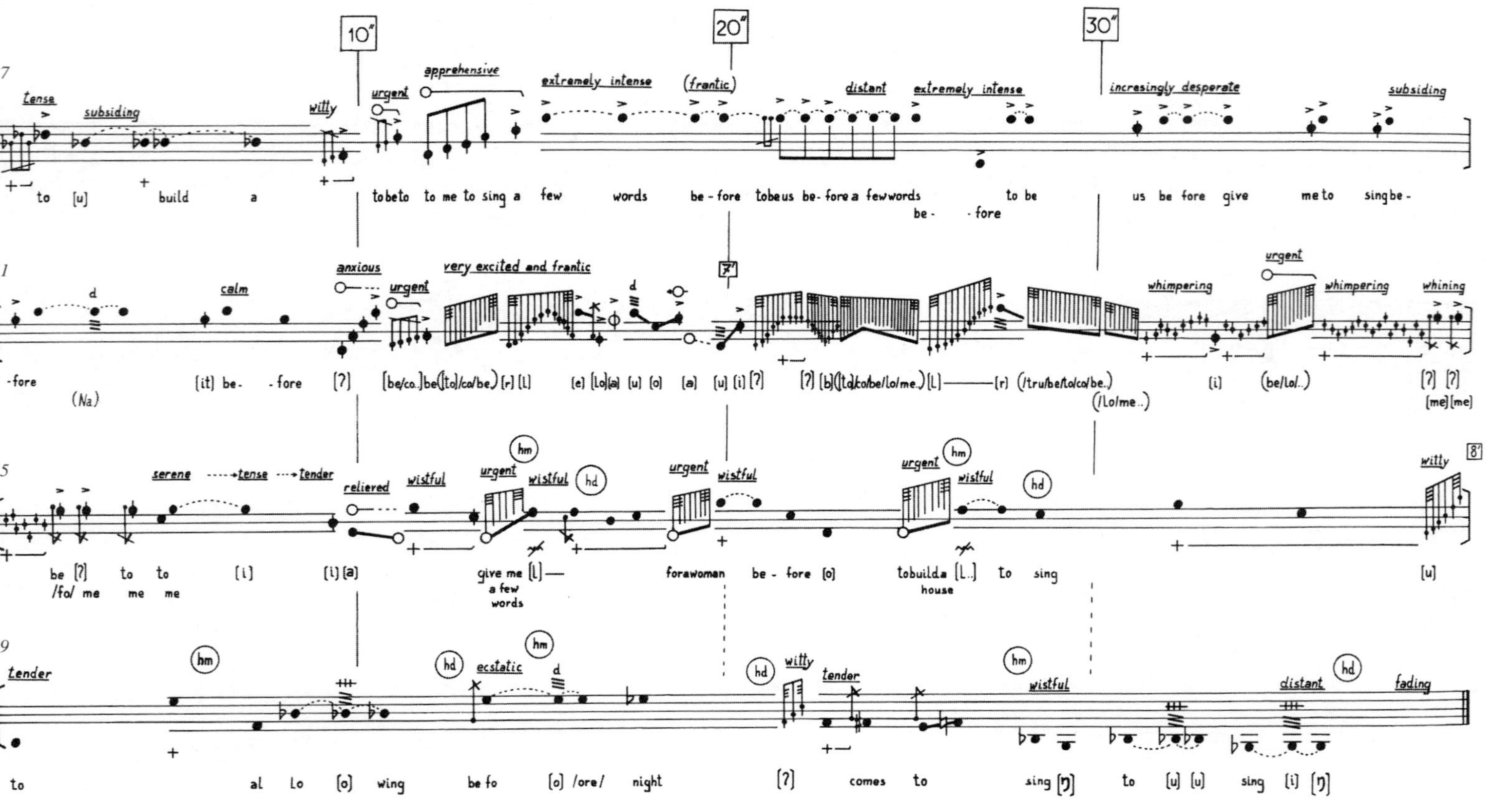
37
10"
20"
30"
tense
subsiding
witty
urgent
apprehensive
extremely intense
(frantic)
distant
extremely intense
increasingly desperate
subsiding
to [u] build a tobeto to me to sing a few words be - fore tobeus be- fore a fewwords to be be- - fore us be fore give me to singbe -
41
calm
anxious
urgent
very excited and frantic
whimpering
urgent
whimpering
whining
-fore (Na) [it] be- -fore [?] [be/co.]be([to]/co/be.) [r] [L] [e] [Lo][a] [u] [o] [a] [u] [i] [?] [?] [b]([ta]/co/be/lo/me.) [L] [r] (/tru/be/to/co/be..) (/lo/me..) [i] (be/lo/..) [?] [?] [me] [me]
45
serene ----→tense ---→tender
relieved
wistful
urgent
wistful
urgent
wistful
urgent
wistful
witty
be [?] to to /fo/ me me me [i] [i] [a] give me a few words [L] forawoman be - fore [o] tobuilda house [L..] to sing [u]
49
tender
ecstatic
witty
tender
wistful
distant
fading
to al Lo [o] wing be fo [o] /ore/ night [?] comes to sing [ŋ] to [u] [u] sing [i] [ŋ]

give me	a few words	for a woman
to sing	a truth	allowing us
to build a house	without worrying	before night comes

— MARKUS KUTTER

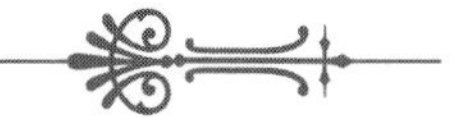

Luciano Berio worked with many outstanding performers who specialized in new music. Intrigued by the possibilities their virtuosity allowed, he composed a series of fourteen solo works called *Sequenza*, each for a different instrument and written for a particular performer with whom he had worked. After the first two, for flute (1958) and harp (1963), he turned to explore the voice as an instrument in *Sequenza III.* He composed it in 1965–66 for American soprano Cathy Berberian (1925–1983), his longtime collaborator and former wife, and dedicated the piece to her.

Berberian was distinguished not only by her attributes as a virtuoso singer—clear tone, wide range, perfect pitch, flexibility, and varied tone color—but also by her diverse background. She had training in dance and mime as well as in voice and opera, and she had worked with non-Western music and dance (including Indian and Armenian). Berberian's versatility encouraged Berio to create a solo piece that was theatrical as well as musical, and that included a wide variety of sounds beyond traditional singing. This score is not a work that must be reproduced exactly the same each time; rather, much like Baroque vocal music, a Broadway song, or a jazz standard, this is a platform for performance, intended to allow the performer a great deal of leeway for dramatization.

Berio was interested in exploring the relationship between sound and sense. He asked Swiss writer Markus Kutter for a brief text that he could use as a basis. The result, given above, is not a poem per se but a set of modules or phrases, although the modules can be read in sequence to form a brief poem whose opening words sound like Berio's request ("give me a few words for a woman to sing"). This text is not set as in a traditional song, nor does it ever appear whole. Rather, it is treated as source material for interesting vocal sounds, from individual vowels and consonants to syllables, whole words, and occasional phrases. Berio uses the International Phonetic Alphabet in brackets to write individual sounds or groups of sounds. At the other extreme are words written normally, all taken from Kutter's text. In between are syllables written between slashes (such as /co/ at the beginning), which are pronounced as they are in the words of Kutter's text (in this case, like "co" in "comes"). Text or syllables between parentheses are rattled off as quickly as possible, and so will also likely be heard as sounds.

The notation is indeterminate in some respects, yet quite specific in others. The piece is laid out on thirteen lines, each marked off in four segments of approximately ten seconds each. For ease of identification, these segments are numbered and will be referred to as measures, although there is no meter. (The performance on the accompanying recording is about a minute shorter than the eight minutes and forty seconds suggested by the notation.) Two pages of directions explain the novel notation, which the singer must memorize in order to perform the piece. Filled-in noteheads are sung or voiced and are held to the next sound or bracket; open noteheads are whispered, and a vertical slash makes either kind of sound as short as possible. A full five-line staff, read with treble clef, indicates singing with precise intervals (although not necessarily absolute pitch; these sections can be transposed to fit the singer's range). A three-line staff indicates relative registers, and notation with only one line indicates speaking voice. Other signs indicate laughter, mouth clicks, coughs, gasps, and other sounds.

The title *Sequenza* (Sequence) refers to a sequence of entities that are introduced and explored in turn. In most of the *Sequenzas*, these entities are predominantly pitch fields, mined for their harmonic and melodic possibilities. But in *Sequenza III*, fixed pitch is only one of many types of sound that Berio includes. The organization is based on a sequence in which new sounds are introduced and old ones dropped over the course of the piece. For example, the piece begins with tense muttering, which then alternates with other material and gradually grows less prominent until it is heard for the last time in measure 10. Meanwhile, other sounds are introduced in measures 2–3 that trace their own paths: quickly rising voiced sounds, which recur intermittently through most of the piece; a mouth click, heard nine times until measure 28, about mid-way through the piece; and a high "distant and dreamy" sustained tone, heard just three times through measure 15. Dozens of other sounds and gestures are introduced and explored over the course of the piece, which builds in intensity and relaxes several times before descending at the end to a calm close. The directions to the singer include many suggestions of mood, from tense to calm and bewildered to ecstatic, but these seem intended to increase the variety of sounds rather than to trace an emotional arc that might suggest a story or sequence of events.

Berio was aware of research into how vocal sounds are produced, and his knowledge is reflected in some of the sequences of sounds that he uses. For example, phoneticians define eight principal vowel sounds, known as *cardinal vowels*, based on the position of the tongue in the mouth:

	Front	Back
Closed (tongue high)	i	u
	e	o
	ɛ	ɔ
Open (tongue low)	a	ɑ

The vowel [i] (as in "see") is produced with the tongue arched high and close to the front of the mouth, with the lips spread; [e] (as in "say") is similar, with the tongue not quite as high and the lips less spread; [u] (as in "goo") is made with the tongue as high and far back as possible, with the lips pursed; and [o] (as in "go") is similar, with the tongue not as high and the lips less pursed. All are relatively closed vowels. In measure 5, on a sustained pitch, the singer moves through all of them, going clockwise around the circle from [e] through [i] and [u] to [o], then closes her mouth (as marked by a plus sign). In measures 14–15, the singer starts with the relatively open vowels [a] ("aahh"), [ɑ] (as in "sat"), and [ɛ] (as in "set"), then moves up the chart to [e], [i], [u], and [o]. In these and many other passages, Berio orders the raw vocal sounds in ways that exploit their basic characteristics and create coherent sequences of tone color.

Such gradations of vowel sound have parallels in other aspects of the piece, such as the way sound gestures alternate and gradually replace one another; the gradations between approximate and exact pitches and between speech and song; and the gradiant from individual vowels or consonants to syllables, words, and phrases. While the shape of the piece cannot be described exactly, Berio's careful control of these gradations, and his exploration of the contrasts and commonalities in his material, help the very diverse sounds in *Sequenza III* flow together in a logical sequence.

193

George Crumb (b. 1929)

Black Angels: Thirteen Images from the Dark Land: Images 4 and 5

Electric string quartet

1970

(a) Image 4: *Devil-Music*

CD 14|5 CD 6|81

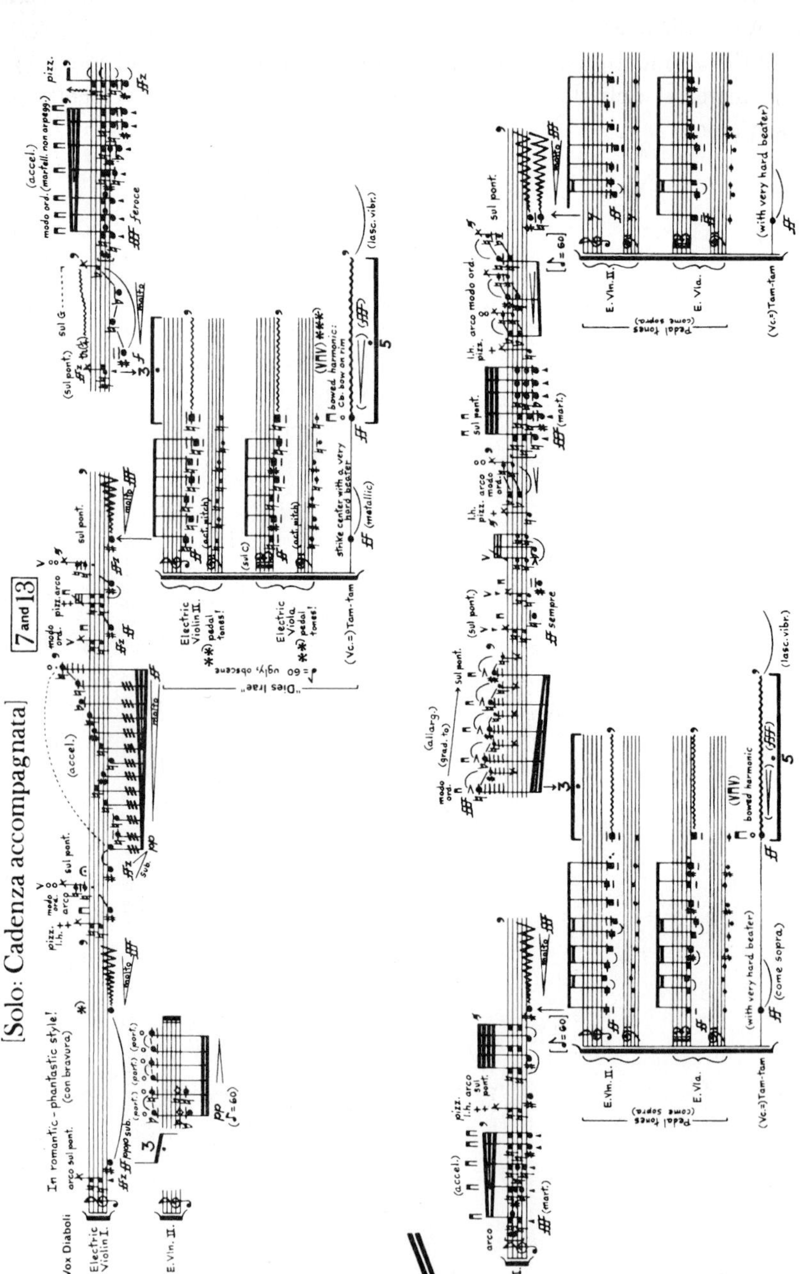

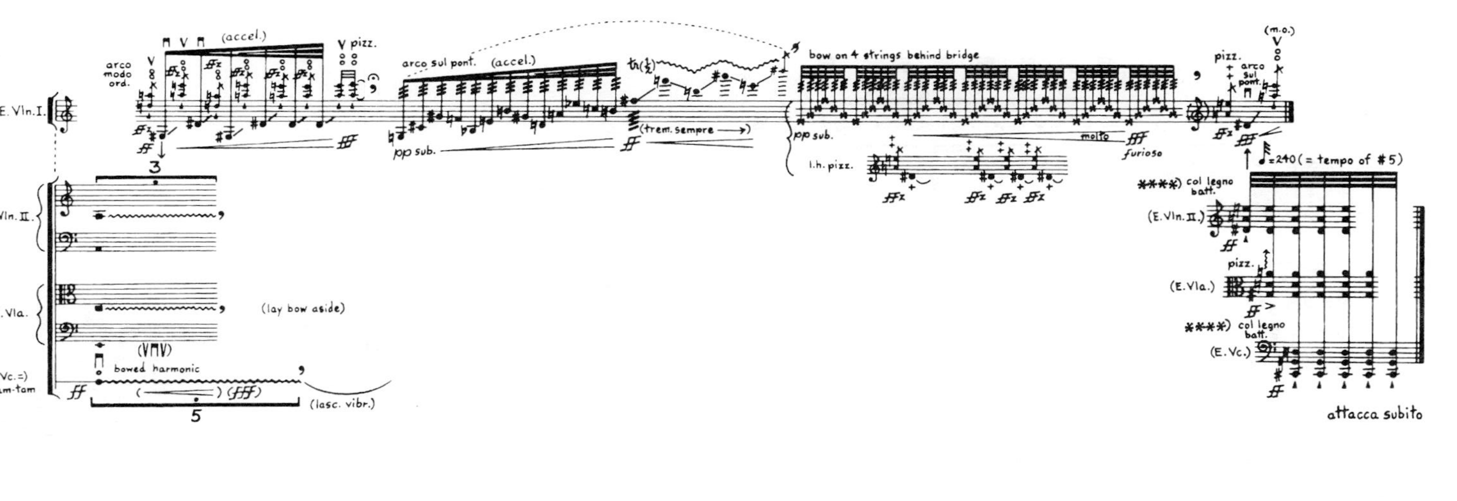

(b) Image 5: *Danse macabre*

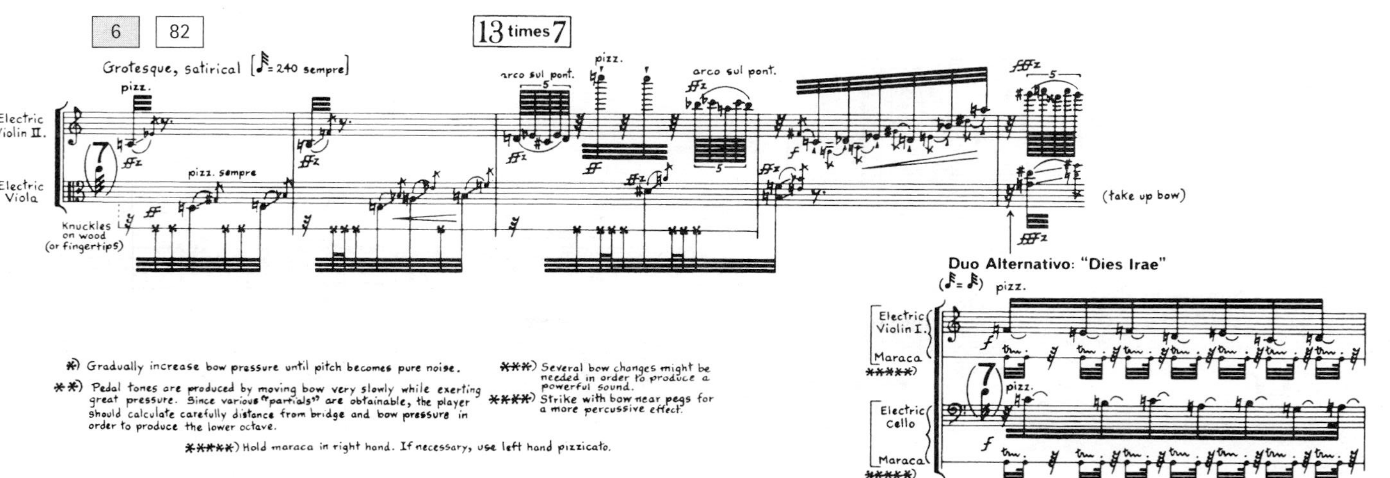

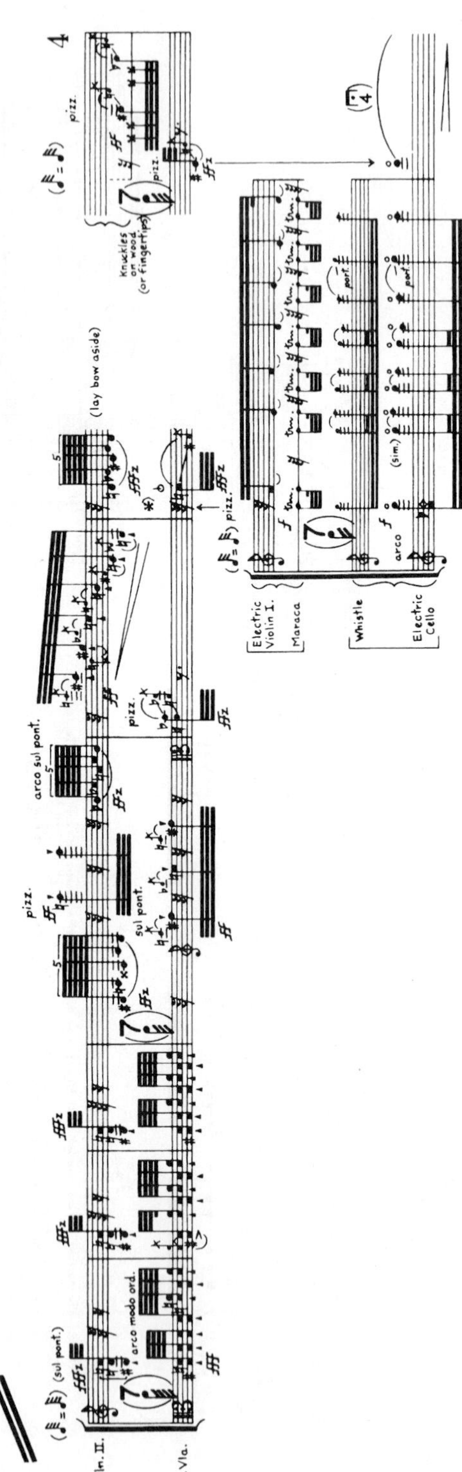
E. Vln. II.
E. Vla.
(sul pont.)
arco modo ord.
pizz.
sul pont.
arco sul pont.
(lay bow aside)
Knuckles on wood (or fingertips)
Electric Violin I.
Maraca
Whistle
Electric Cello
arco
port.
(sim.)
4

E. Vln. II.
E. Vla.
(pizz. sempre)
(pizz.)
arco sul pont.
(take up bow)
Whistle
Electric Violin I.
Electric Cello
Maraca
arco sul D sempre
arco modo ord.
(sul pont.)
port.
mp
4

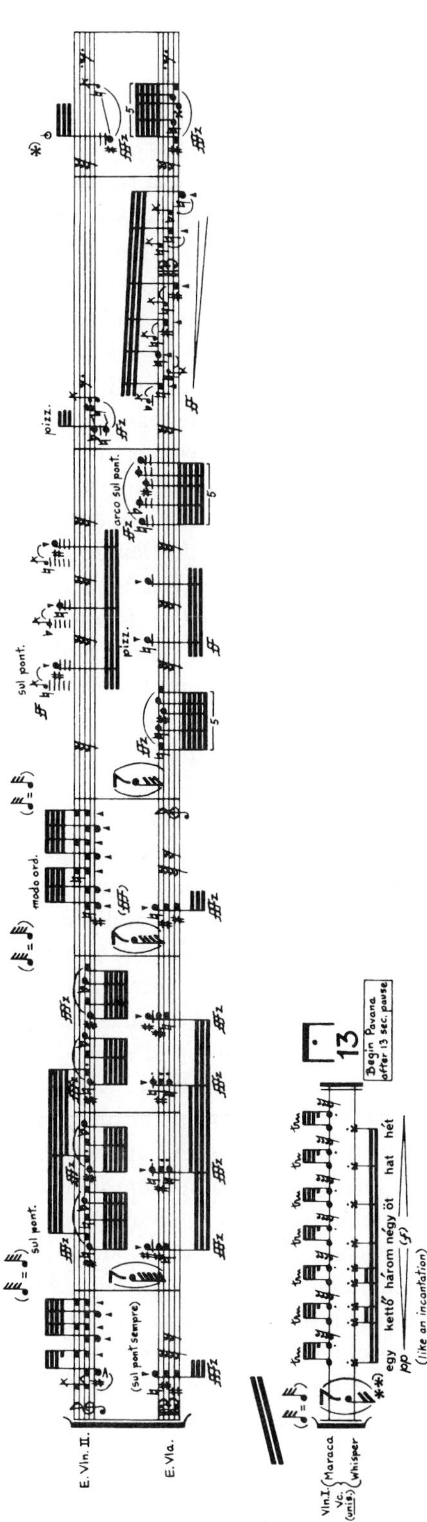

*) ɸ = a percussive pizzicato (string rebounds from fingerboard)

**) The Hungarian numerals one through seven. Pronounce: ehdy, keh-tuh, hah-rohm (trilled r), naydy, oeht (ö like German), haht, hate.

The late 1960s and early 1970s were turbulent years in the history of the United States. The Vietnam War and other issues were vehemently debated, especially on college campuses. George Crumb, a professor at the University of Pennsylvania, was deeply affected by this strife, as were many of his artist colleagues across the country. For a commission from the University of Michigan, Crumb composed *Black Angels* in 1970, inscribing at the end of the score "in tempore belli" (in time of war). The work is both a protest against the Vietnam War and a reaction to the troubled world of the late 1960s. The premiere by the Stanley Quartet in Ann Arbor, Michigan, on October 23, 1970, received a standing ovation.

A black angel is a conventional image used by painters to represent a fallen angel. According to the composer, the work represents three stages in the journey of the soul: fall from grace (the section marked "Departure," including Images 1–5), spiritual annihilation ("Absence," Images 6–9), and redemption ("Return," Images 10–13). The subtitle *Thirteen Images from the Dark Land* suggests the pervasive numerology underlying this work. The score contains numerous references to the numbers 7 and 13, which Crumb characterized as "fateful numbers"—numbers that are considered to be lucky or unlucky. These numbers affect duration, pitch, harmony, and melody. Several of the movements, for example, are based on a prominent chord with *d*♯'–*a*'–*e*''; counting downward in semitones from the *e*'', these pitches represent the numbers 0–7–13. At the conclusion of the work, Crumb duly noted: "finished on Friday the Thirteenth, March 1970."

Crumb creates a surrealistic, dreamlike character through his imaginative use of color. An electronically amplified string quartet can produce a variety of unique sounds, and Crumb explores unusual means of bowing, such as striking the strings near the pegs with the bow, holding the bow underhand in the manner of viol players, and bowing between the left-hand fingers and the pegs, along with glissandos, *sul ponticello* (on the bridge, creating a thin, metallic sound), and percussive pizzicato. In addition, the performers are asked to play a variety of percussion instruments, including maracas, tam-tams, and water-tuned crystal glasses, and to make vocal sounds, such as clicking, whistling, whispering, and chanting. The spoken words involve ritualistic counting focusing on the numbers seven and thirteen in German, French, Russian, Hungarian, Japanese, and Swahili. These effects are not mere striving for novelty; the composer employed them to create a nightmarish atmosphere as a substrate for his poetic message.

Image 4, *Devil-Music*, and Image 5, *Danse macabre*, should be considered as a pair. There is no break between them, they share a common theme, and they have similar structures. Indeed, one can hear *Devil-Music* as an improvisatory introduction to *Danse macabre*. The titles of both movements refer to medieval artworks in which the devil is shown playing the violin and leading various dancing figures to their deaths. These images were also treated in two celebrated compositions from the nineteenth century, Franz Liszt's *Totentanz* for piano and orchestra, and Camille Saint-Saëns's *Danse macabre* for violin and orchestra. The titles of both can be translated as "dance of death." Images 4 and 5 share several characteristics with these orchestral works. As in *Totentanz*, Death is associated with the Gregorian chant melody from the Requiem Mass, *Dies irae*, first used with such association in the finale of Berlioz's *Symphonie fantastique* (NAWM 130). As in Saint-Saëns's *Danse macabre*, Death plays the violin, and the tritone involving an open string is emphasized. For Saint-Saëns, the sound of open strings and a tritone represented the devil tuning his violin. In the medieval era, the tritone was called *diabolus in musica* (devil in music).

In both Images 4 and 5, the first three phrases of *Dies irae* alternate with contrasting material. In *Devil-Music* the principal line, labeled *Vox Diaboli* (devil's voice), features an intense solo cadenza for the first violinist. Virtuosic effects include triple-stopped chords, pizzicato notes plucked by the left hand (normally used only for fingering), and harmonics. In several instances, the soloist is instructed to press on the bow until "pitch becomes pure noise." Throughout the cadenza, perfect fifths and diminished fifths can be heard, often incorporating open strings; the *d♯'–a'–e''* sonority, which uses two open strings (*a'* and *e''*), predominates. Interspersed in the brief breaks of the cadenza are the phrases of the *Dies irae* played by the second violin and viola in pedal tones—pitches an octave lower than notated (and lower than the instruments can normally play), produced by moving the bow slowly while exerting great pressure. The cellist accompanies with the tam-tam. For the final cadence, all of the instruments present a version of the principal three-note chord. The bottom three string parts employ the percussive effects of pizzicato or *col legno* (hitting the strings with the wood side of the bow).

Danse macabre alternates material played by the second violin and viola with the phases of the *Dies irae* in the first violin and cello. The second violin and viola lines rely heavily on pizzicato and other unusual effects, such as tapping on the viola with knuckles. Embedded in the second and fourth statements of these two instruments are brief quotations from Saint-Saëns's *Danse macabre*. The *Dies irae* is also presented with unusual timbres, involving pizzicato, harmonics, maracas, and whistling. At the conclusion of this Image, the first violinist and cellist whisper the numbers one through seven in Hungarian.

A performance of *Black Angels* demands considerable technical skills, creativity, and theatricality. Because a string quartet plays without a conductor, Crumb requires each performer to play from the score (rather than from a single part, as customary) so that the coordination of the parts is every player's responsibility. As an aid to the musicians, Crumb simplified the notation by omitting unnecessary rests, and he created oversized scores that can be read easily from a distance (but which had to be reduced to fit into a book this size). The score is in his own neat, very distinctive handwriting. In addition to numerous explanations and suggestions, Crumb includes a chart showing a preferred arrangement of percussion instruments. This work has become a staple in the repertory of several young professional quartets, including the Concord String Quartet heard in the recording.

Milton Babbitt (b. 1916)

Philomel: Section I

Monodrama for soprano, recorded soprano, and synthesized sound

1964

CD 14|7 CD 6|83

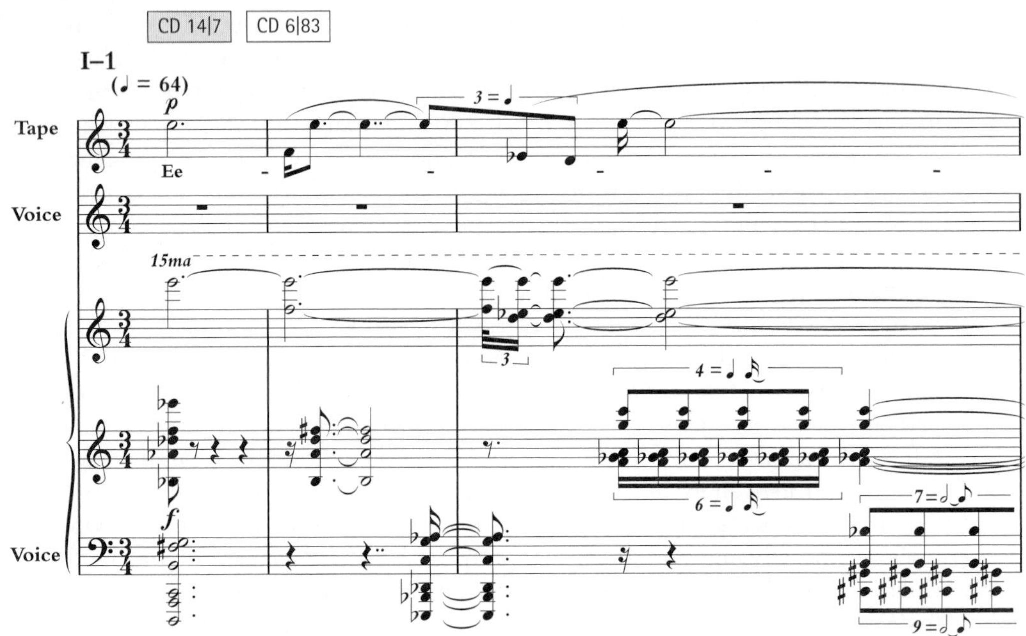

Accidentals affect only those notes they immediately precede, with the exception of tied notes.

(gliss.)
pp
5 =
T.Vc.
Ee
Ee
Vc.
Ee
ee
15ma
8 =
f
p
11 =
pp
p
f
ff
11 =
ff

3 =
2 =
T.Vc.
ee
ee
Vc.
ee
ee
ee
ee
ee
ee
15ma
pp
f
f
p
7 =
f
10 =

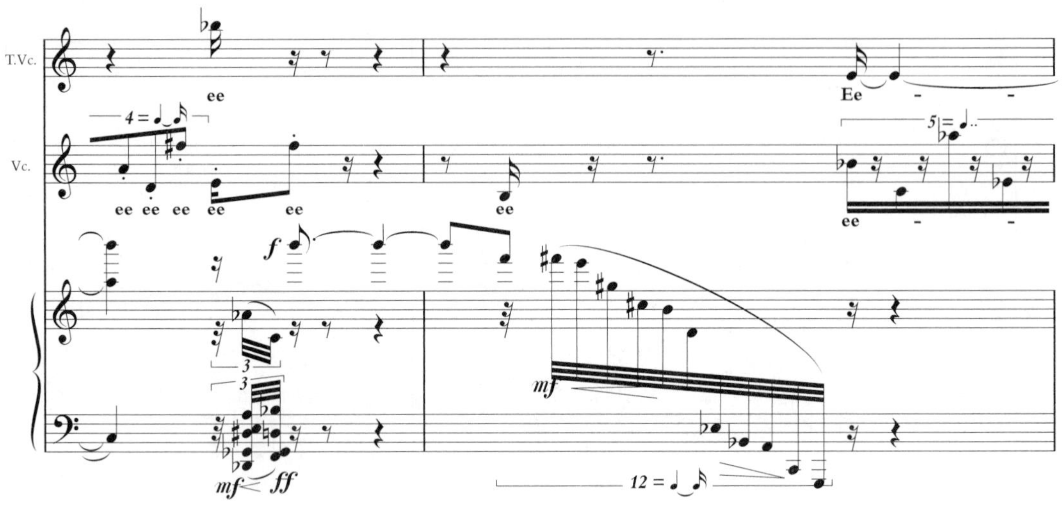
T.Vc.
ee
Ee
Vc.
4 =
ee ee ee ee ee
ee
5 =
ee
f
mf
mf
ff
12 =

7 =
T.Vc.
ee
ee
ee
Vc.
4 =
ee
ee
ee
3 =
6 =
p
f
f
f
3
3
p
6 =
3 =
6 =

6 =
T.Vc.
(gliss.)
Ee
Vc.
ee
9 =
7 =
11 =
p
ff
pp
f

5 =
T.Vc.
ee
ee
Ee
3 =
Vc.
Ee Ee
4 =
6 =
f
pp
p

T.Vc.
Vc.
2 =
5 =
Fee - ee - ee - -
8va
f
p
f
f
12 =

Vc.
4 =
3 =
3
I fee - l.
Feel a mil - lion trees
And the
pp

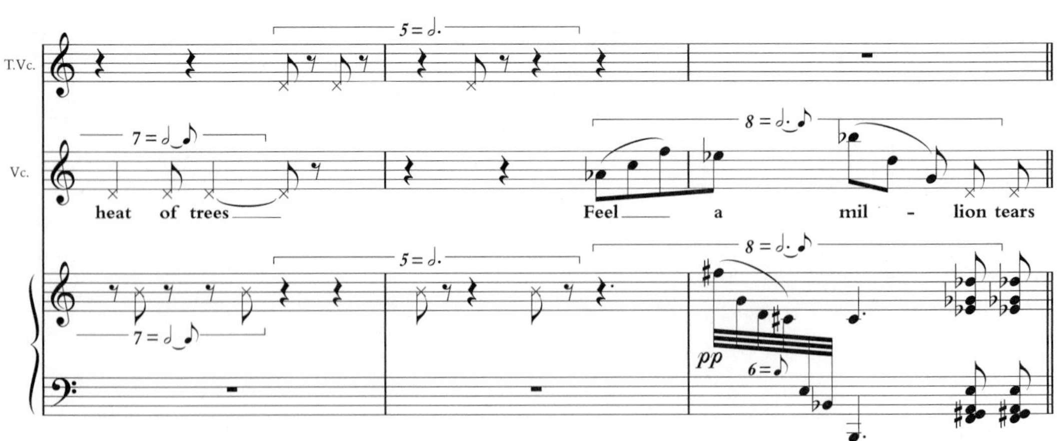
T.Vc.
Vc.
5 =
7 =
8 =
heat of trees
Feel a mil - lion tears
pp
6 =

INTERLUDE (Tape)

Not true tears — Not true trees —

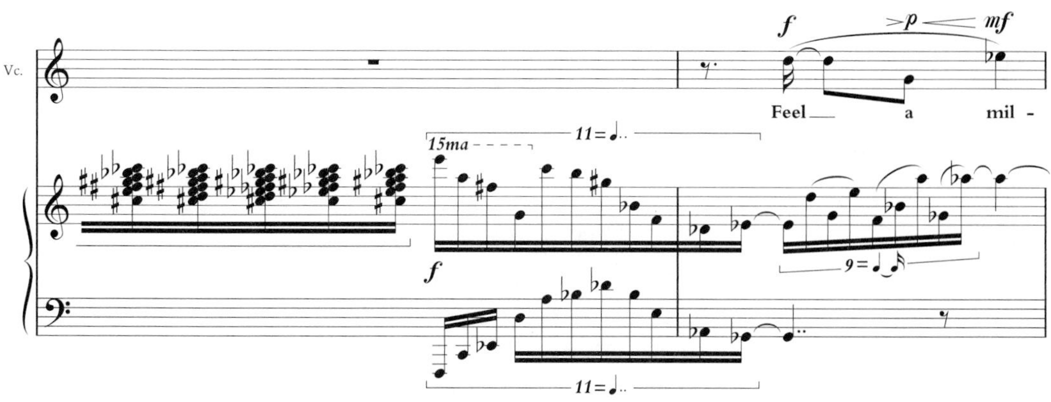

Vc.
lion fil - a ments; Fear the tear-ing, the
feel - ing Trees of e - phem - er - al leaves
Trees tear, And I bear Fam - i - lies of tears
cresc.

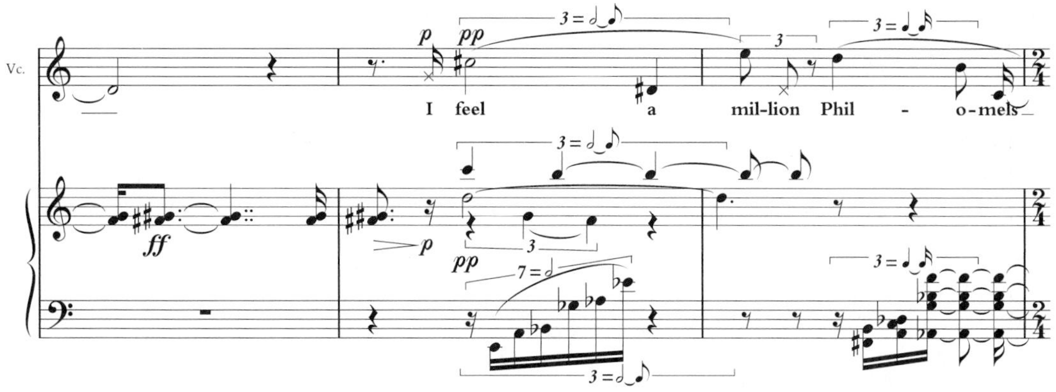
Vc.
I feel a mil-lion Phil - o-mels

T.Vc.
Trees filled with mel - low -
Vc.

T.Vc.
ing
Fe - lo-nious fame—

INTERLUDE

I–3
9
85
(♩ = 80)
Vc.
I feel trees in my hair and on the ground,
Hon - ey - mel - ons foul - ing My knees and feet
Sound-less - ly in my Flight through the for - est;

Vc.
I found-er in qui - et.

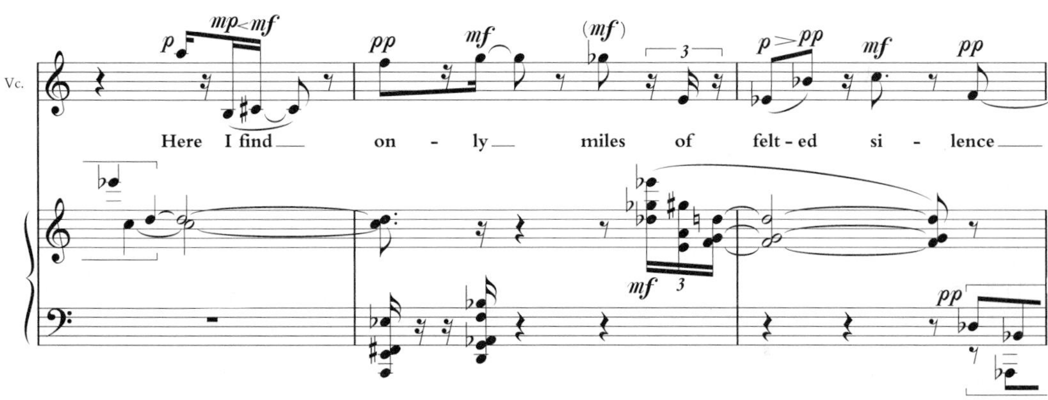
Vc.
Here I find on - ly miles of felt - ed si - lence

Vc.
Un-wind - ing be - hind me, Lost,

INTERLUDE

TAPE VOICE: Pillowing melody, honey unheard —

I–4 10 86

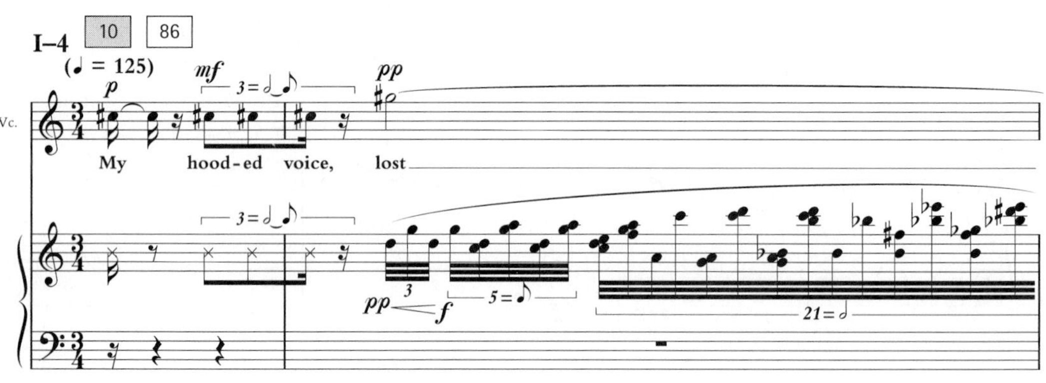

Vc.
Forced as my last Un - feath - ered de - fense

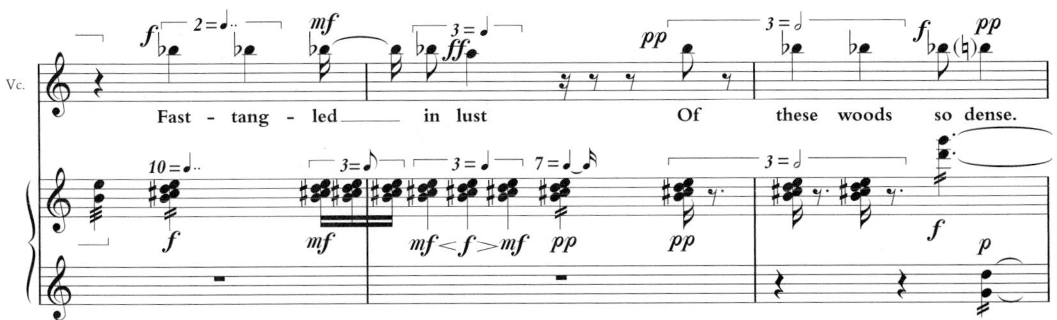
Vc.
Fast - tang - led in lust Of these woods so dense.

Vc.
Emp - tied, un - feel - ing

Vc.
and un - filled By trees here where no birds

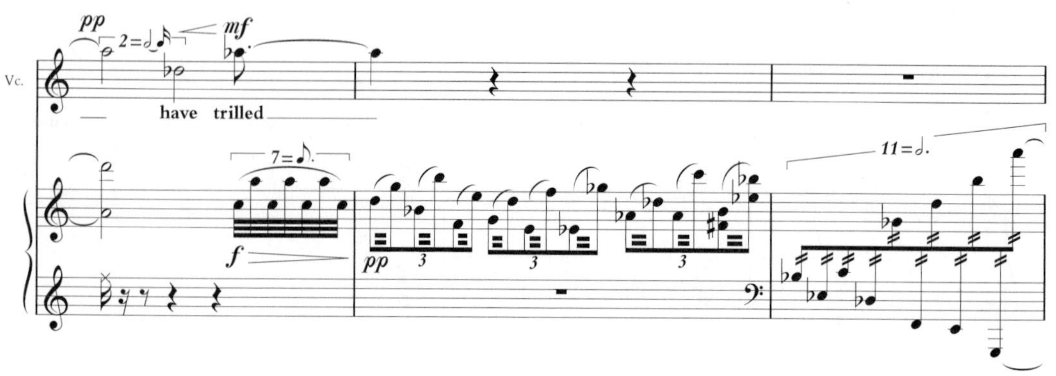
pp
2 = 𝅗𝅥 𝅘𝅥𝅮
mf
Vc.
have trilled
7 = 𝅘𝅥𝅮.
f
pp
3
3
3
11 = 𝅗𝅥.

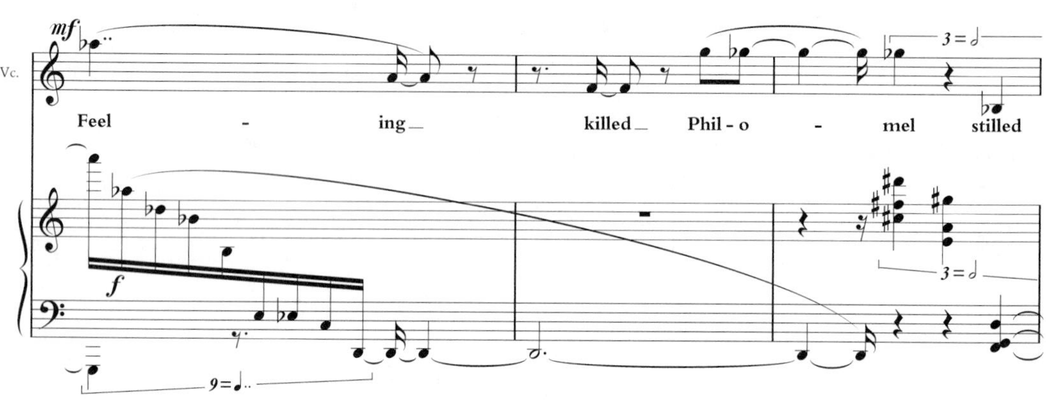
mf
Vc.
Feel - ing killed Phil - o - mel stilled
3 = 𝅗𝅥
f
9 = 𝅘𝅥..
3 = 𝅗𝅥

Vc.
Her hon - ey un - ful - filled.
3
3
5 = 𝅘𝅥𝅮

INTERLUDE

TAPE VOICE: Feeling killed, Philomel stilled, Her honey unfulfilled.

11
87
I–5
(♩ = 80)
Vc.
What is that sound? A voice found?
8va

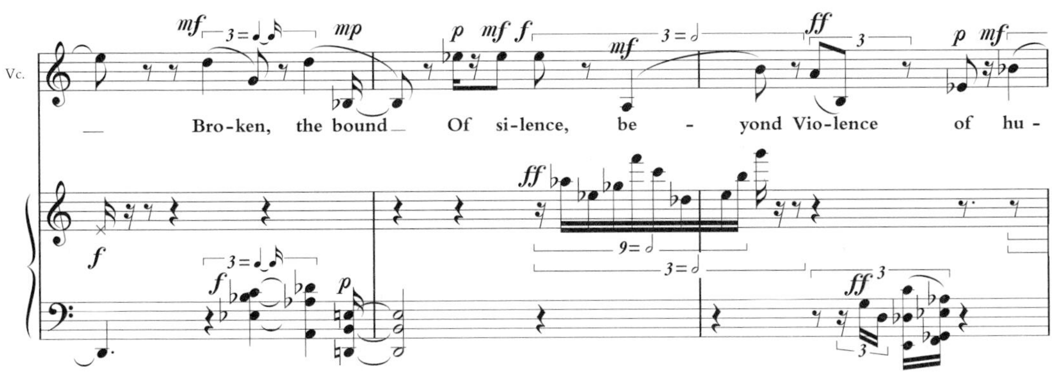
Vc.
Bro-ken, the bound Of si-lence, be - yond Vio-lence of hu -

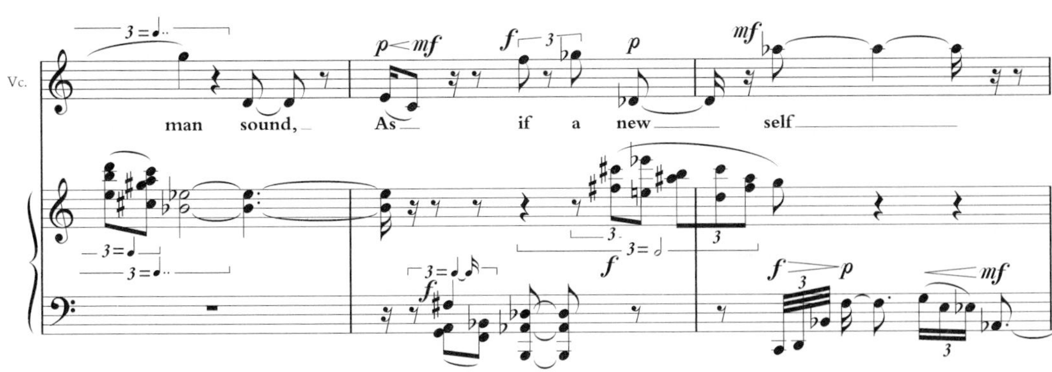
Vc.
man sound, As if a new self

Vc.
mf
Could
be
found - ed
pp
13 =
6 =
4 =
mf
pp
3

Vc.
on
sound.
The trees
are as -
5 =
3
4 =
6 =
2
4

T.Vc.
pp
3
mf
What
is
Vc.
- tound
ed!
What
is
3 =
11 =
9 =
12 =
p
f

T.Vc.
Vc.
this hum - ming?
I am be -
com - ing
My–
ow - n
song!
11 = ♩♪
3 = 𝅗𝅥
6 = 𝅝
9 = 𝅗𝅥
11 = 𝅗𝅥
8va
pp
p
f
mf
ff

TAPE

(Recorded Soprano)
(Eeeeeeeeeeeeeeeeee)

PHILOMEL

Eeeeeeeeeeeeeeeeeee!
Eeeeeeeeeeeeeeeeee!
Feeeeeeeeeeeeeeeeeee!
I feel
Feel a million trees
And the heat of trees

TAPE

Not true trees—

PHILOMEL

Feel a million tears

TAPE

Not true tears—
Not true trees—

PHILOMEL

Is it Tereus I feel?

TAPE

Not Tereus: not a true Tereus—

PHILOMEL

Feel a million filaments;
Fear the tearing, the feeling
Trees, of ephemeral leaves
Trees tear,
And I bear
Families of tears
I feel a million Philomels

TAPE

Trees filled with mellowing
Felonous fame—

PHILOMEL

I feel trees in my hair
And on the ground,
Honeymelons fouling
My knees and feet
Soundlessly in my
Flight through the forest;
I founder in quiet.
Here I find only
Miles of felted silence
Unwinding behind me,
Lost, lost in the wooded night.

TAPE

Pillowing melody,
Honey unheard—

PHILOMEL

My hooded voice, lost
Lost, as my first
Unhoneyed tongue;
Forced, as my last
Unfeathered defense
Fast-tangled in lust
Of these woods so dense.
Emptied, unfeeling and unfilled
By trees here where no birds have
   trilled—
Feeling killed
Philomel stilled
Her honey unfulfilled.

TAPE

Feeling killed
Philomel stilled
Her honey unfulfilled

PHILOMEL

What is that sound?
A voice found?
Broken, the bound
Of silence, beyond
Violence of human sound,
As if a new self
Could be founded on sound.
The trees are astounded!

PHILOMEL AND TAPE
(simultaneously)

What is this humming?
I am becoming
My own song . . .

—JOHN HOLLANDER

Milton Babbitt's *Philomel* was commissioned by the Ford Foundation for the soprano Bethany Beardslee and premiered by her in 1964. Probably Babbitt's most popular work, it combines live performance with prerecorded tape and synthesized sounds. The soprano soloist is heard against a tape that incorporates an altered recording of her own voice, a kind of distorted echo, together with electronic sounds. The "score" shown here includes the complete part for voice and—with exceptions—a total representation of the rhythmic and pitch content of the synthesized and recorded accompaniment in all those sections of the work in which the singer participates. The exceptions occur when, to avoid notational complexity, the rhythmic representation is only closely approximate, and registral relations are simplified. Such a score is unusual for electronic music, in which "composition" typically happens on tape rather than on paper, but is useful for the singer. The tape interludes, in which the singer does not participate, are not notated.

The poem, written expressly for this setting by John Hollander, is based on a fable by Ovid (*Metamorphoses* 6:412–674). Procne, wife of Tereus, king of Thrace, is eager to see her sister, Philomela, after an absence of many years, and sends Tereus to fetch her. On the return trip Tereus rapes Philomela in a Thracian wood and cuts out her tongue to prevent disclosure, but his guilt is exposed nevertheless by a tapestry in which Philomela weaves her story. Procne, horrified, avenges herself against her husband by killing their son and feeding Tereus from the butchered corpse. In a rage, Tereus pursues the two sisters, but before he can catch them the gods transform him into a hoopoe bird, Procne into a swallow, and Philomela into a nightingale. In the metamorphosis Philomela regains her voice. The sung text begins at this point.

Babbitt's composition, like John Hollander's poem, is in three sections. In the first, excerpted here, Philomel screams as she recalls the pain of violation; dazed, she expresses her feelings in vivid but incoherent images. She runs through the forest in fear and confusion. In Section 2, Philomel seeks answers about her predicament from a thrush, a hawk, an owl, and a gull. In the third section, she sings a strophic lament, joined in refrains by her taped voice.

The taped voice often answers the soloist by distorting her line or, speaking, comments like a Greek chorus. Every detail in the vocal sections was worked out in serial terms. The vocal sections alternate with unnotated synthesized and tape interludes that are more freely composed.

The vocal melody is extremely disjunct, with leaps of major sevenths, ninths, and even elevenths. Some of the notes are sung in Sprechstimme, marked by an X instead of a notehead, and expressive glissandos punctuate some phrases. The pitch-class E, the first note sung by the taped voice, is central to the construction of the opening passage. The twelve-tone row is stated, then transposed, in such a way that E becomes successively the first, second, third, fourth, and fifth pitch-class in the row. With each unfolding of the row, the taped voice claims more of the row's pitch-classes up to E—in the second measure two, in the third three, and so on. The accompaniment each time claims the remainder of the row or aggregate (the twelve pitch-classes of the chromatic scale). The first sonority, as the taped soprano screams "Eeeeeee" on E, contains all twelve pitch-classes and covers a seven-octave span. Subsequent simultaneities are less populated, with increasingly arpeggiated and pointillistic unfoldings of the row. The high E is heard as a steady pedal note through the first eight measures. When Philomel's natural voice enters, it begins on F, and E is now the last member of the row, appearing as the highest note in the accompaniment in measure 9.

Like Schoenberg in *Pierrot lunaire* (NAWM 160), Babbitt tore some leaves from the book of the sixteenth-century madrigalists. The pitch E for the scream is a madrigalian conceit, as are the synthesized trills on the word "trilled." But he went beyond the madrigalists in the second section of the poem, where, instead of bird imitations, he introduced recorded birdsong.

This work is extraordinarily difficult to perform. The score and tape can be rented from the publisher; since the tape uses Bethany Beardslee's voice, most sopranos try to match her sound, though some have made their own tape. The piece requires a singer with perfect pitch, outstanding command of rhythm, and total control of dynamic contrasts. It exemplifies the trend among some composers in the 1960s to write music only for the very best performers and to challenge their abilities to the utmost. The performance on the accompanying recording features Beardslee herself.

Krzysztof Penderecki (b. 1933)

Threnody: To the Victims of Hiroshima

Tone poem for string orchestra

1960

195

CD 14|12

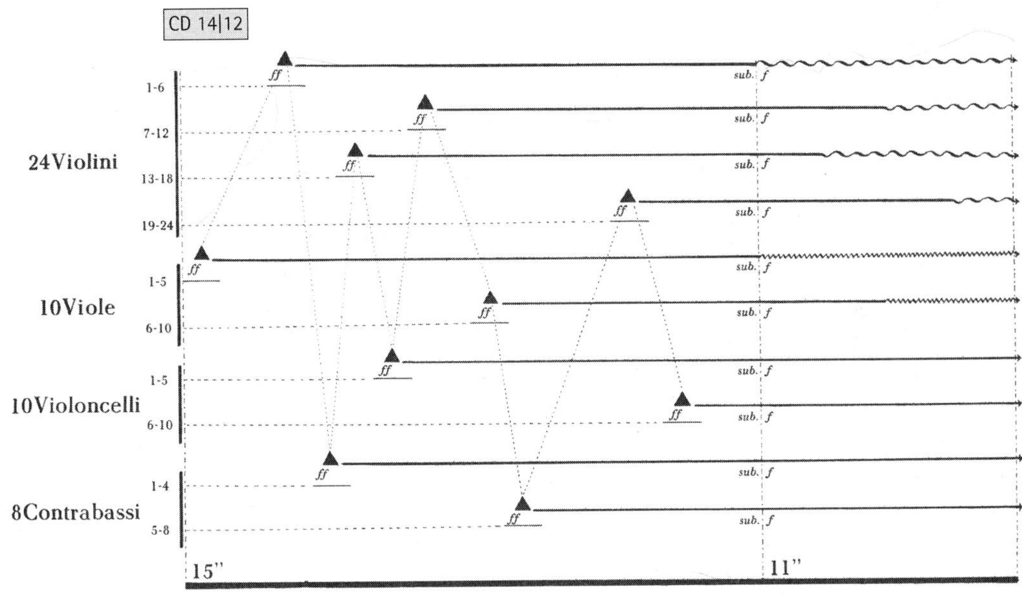

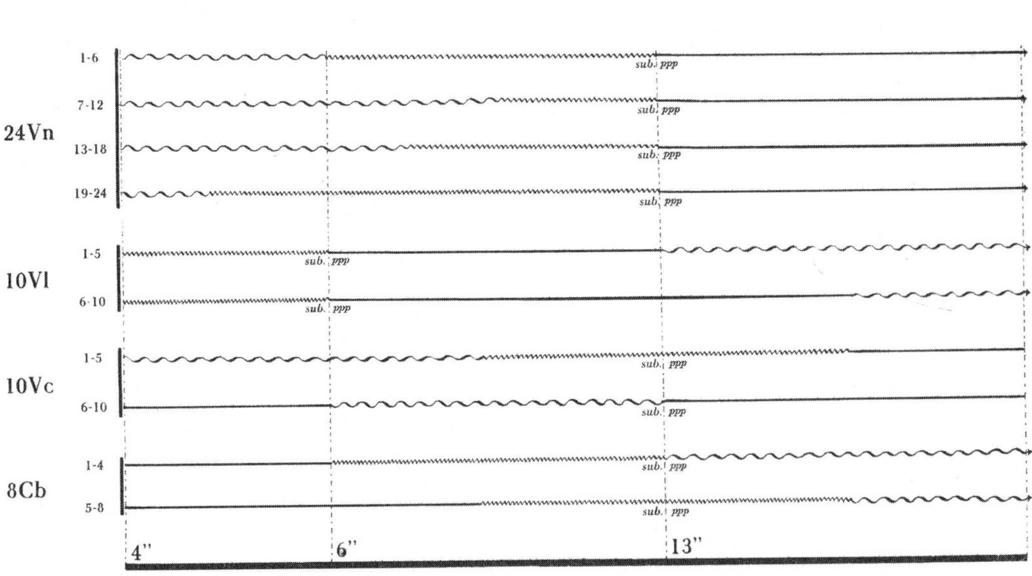

 For a guide to the notation, see page 1298.

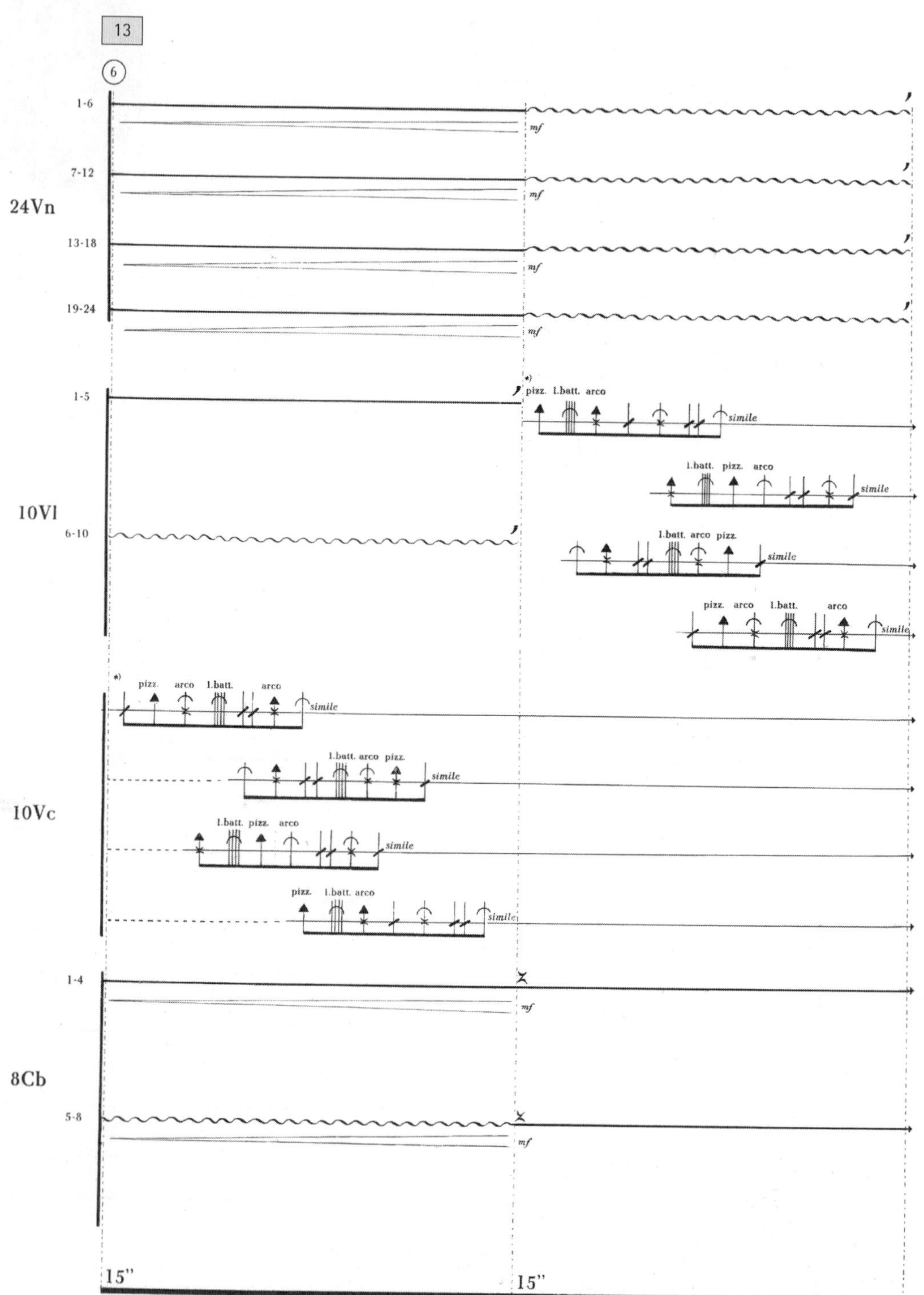

*) Each instrumentalist chooses one of the four given groups and executes it (within a fixed space of time) as rapidly as possible.

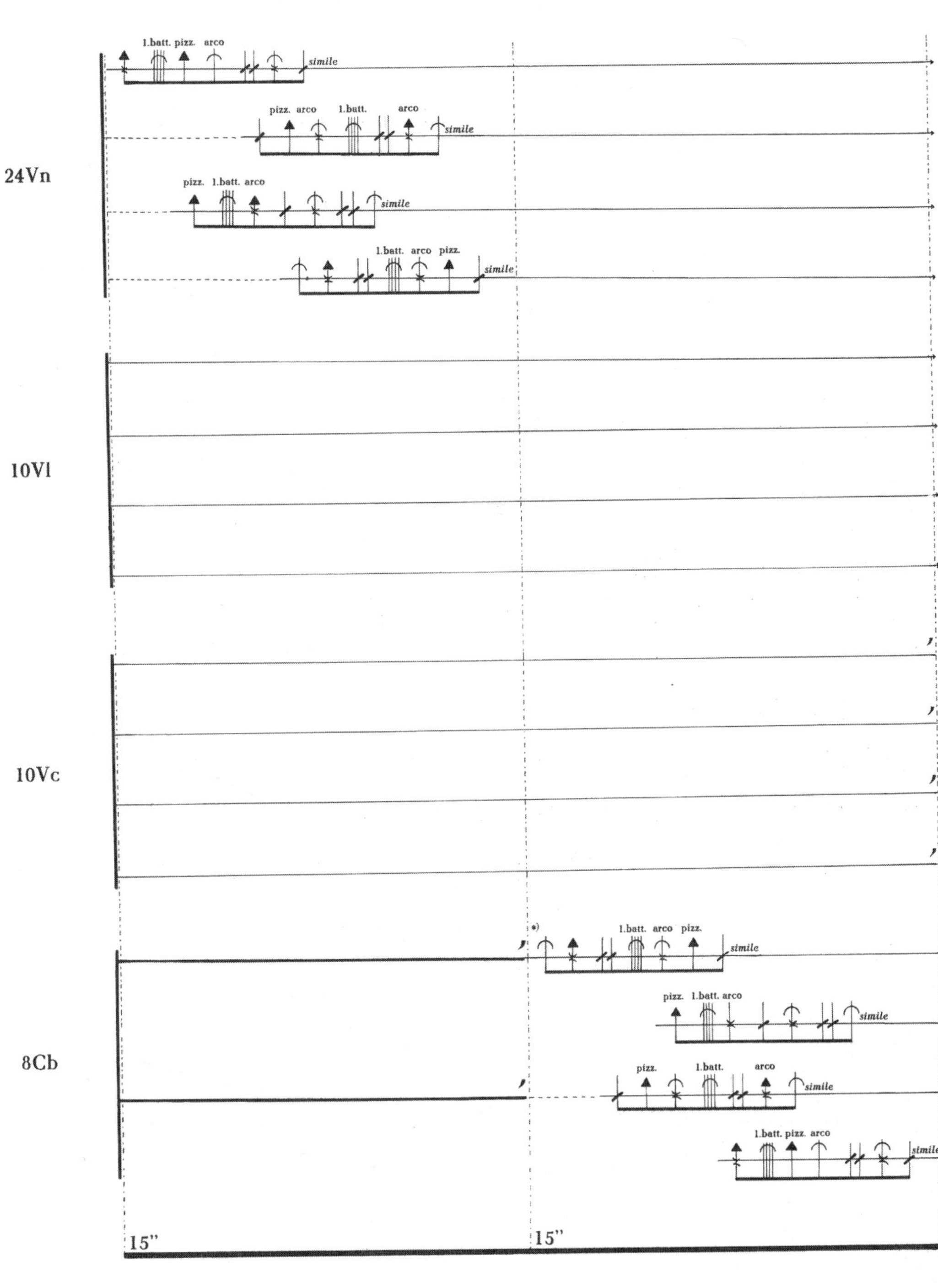
1.batt. pizz. arco
simile
pizz. arco 1.batt. arco
simile
24Vn
pizz. 1.batt. arco
simile
1.batt. arco pizz.
simile
10Vl
10Vc
*)
1.batt. arco pizz.
simile
pizz. 1.batt. arco
simile
8Cb
pizz. 1.batt. arco
simile
1.batt. pizz. arco
simile
15"
15"

14

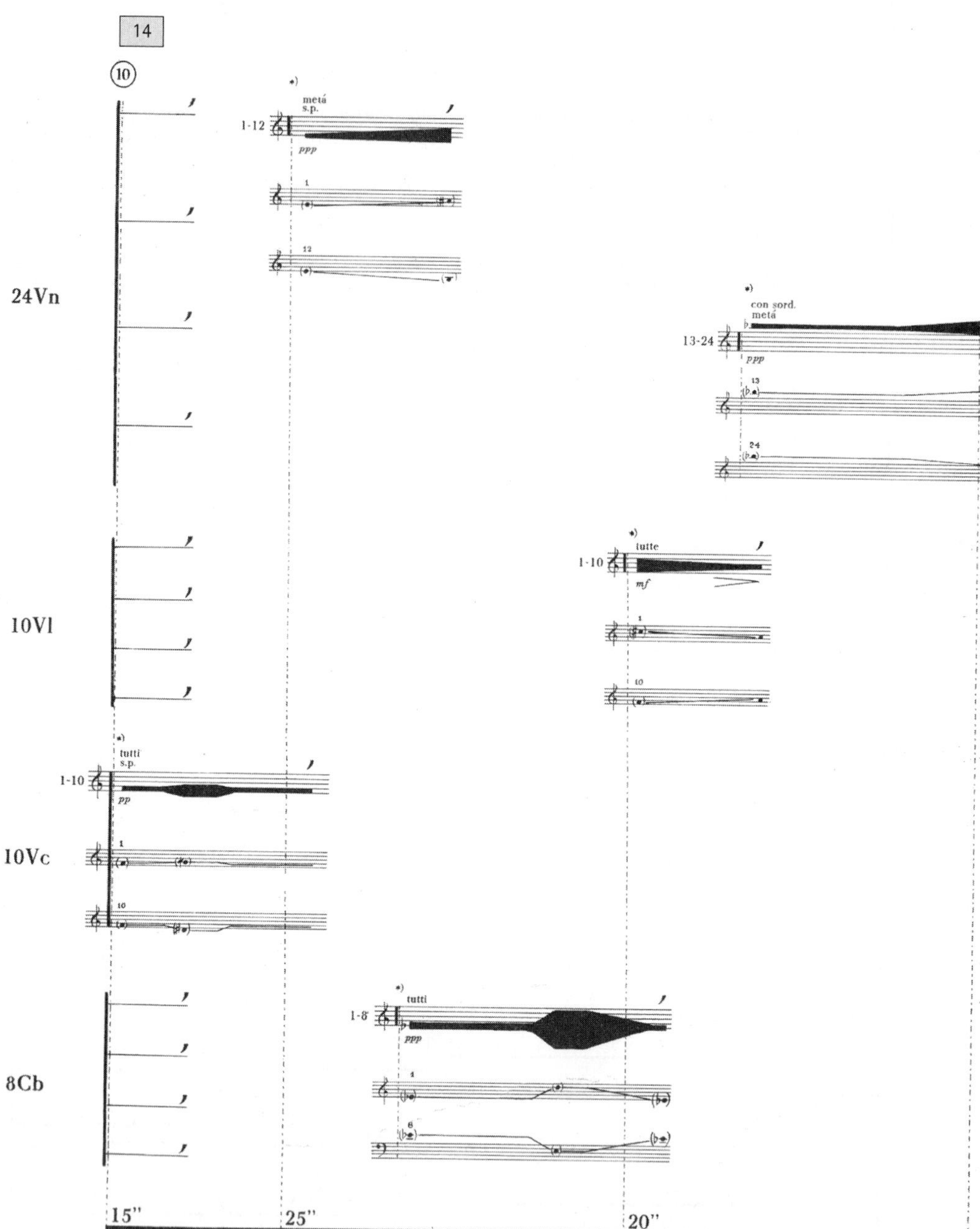

*) Exact notation is given in the parts.

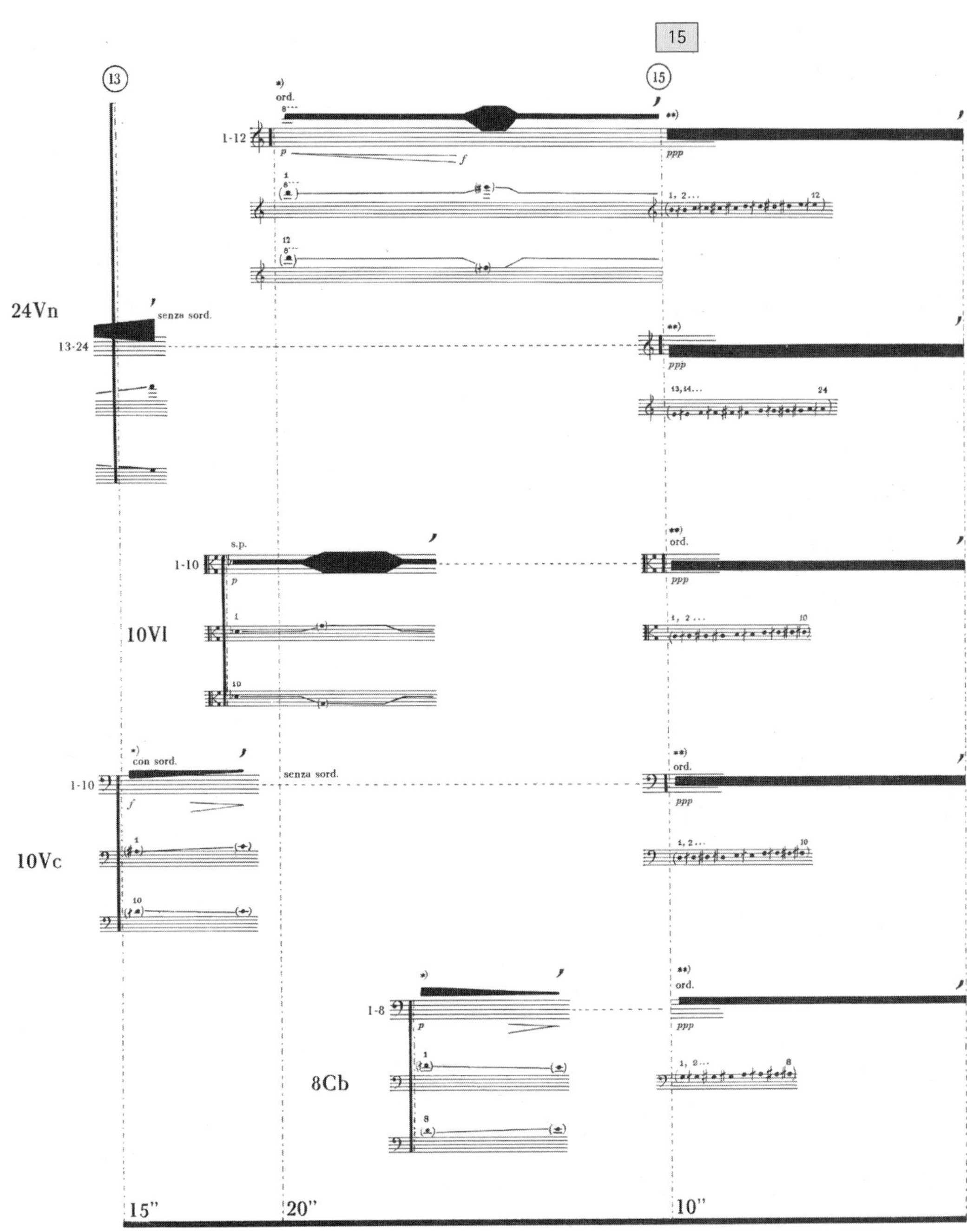

*) See previous note.

**) Each instrumentalist plays the tone allocated to his instrument, so that the whole quarter-tone scale between the indicated lowest and highest tones sounds simultaneously.

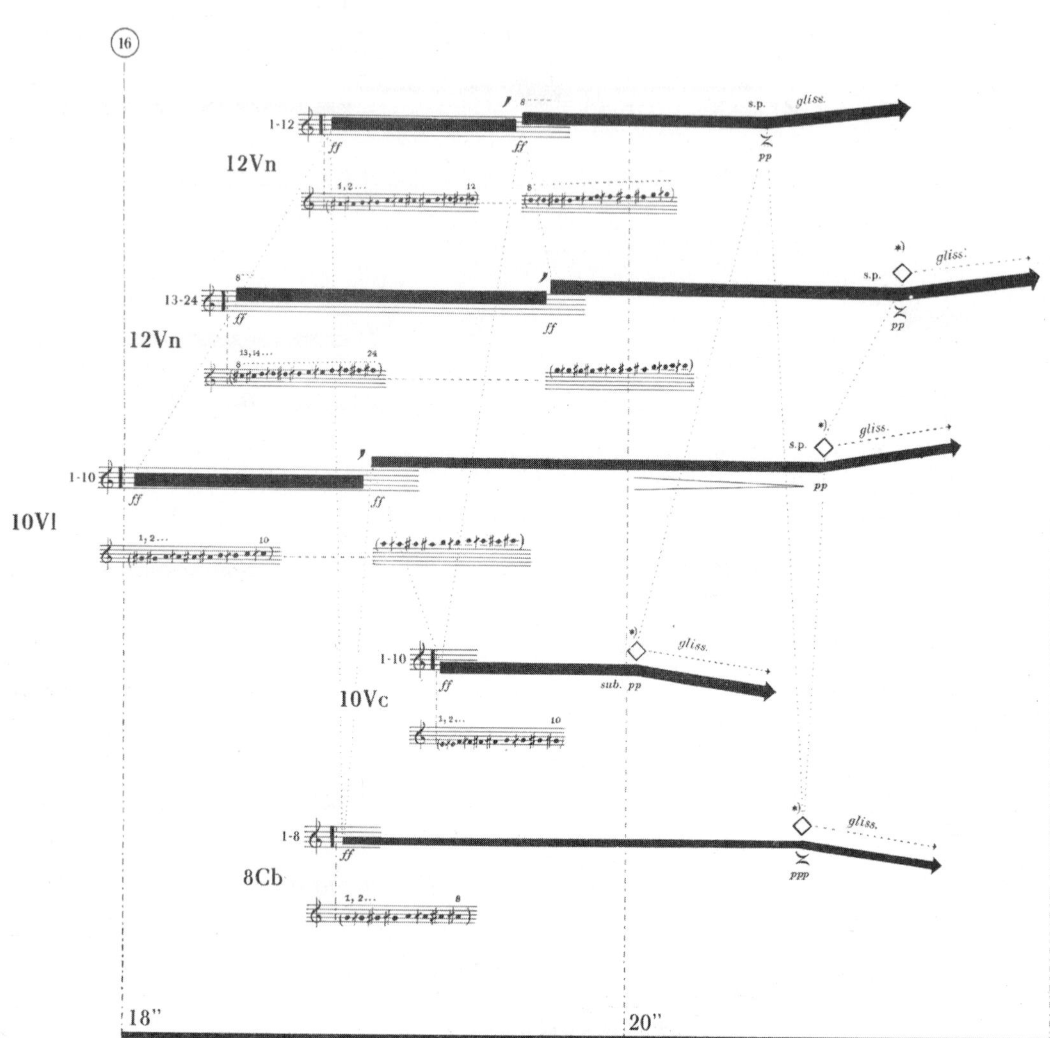
16
1-12
12Vn
ff
ff
s.p.
gliss.
pp
13-24
12Vn
ff
ff
s.p.
gliss.
pp
1-10
10Vl
ff
ff
s.p.
gliss.
pp
1-10
10Vc
ff
sub. pp
gliss.
1-8
8Cb
ff
gliss.
ppp
18"
20"

*) Harmonics

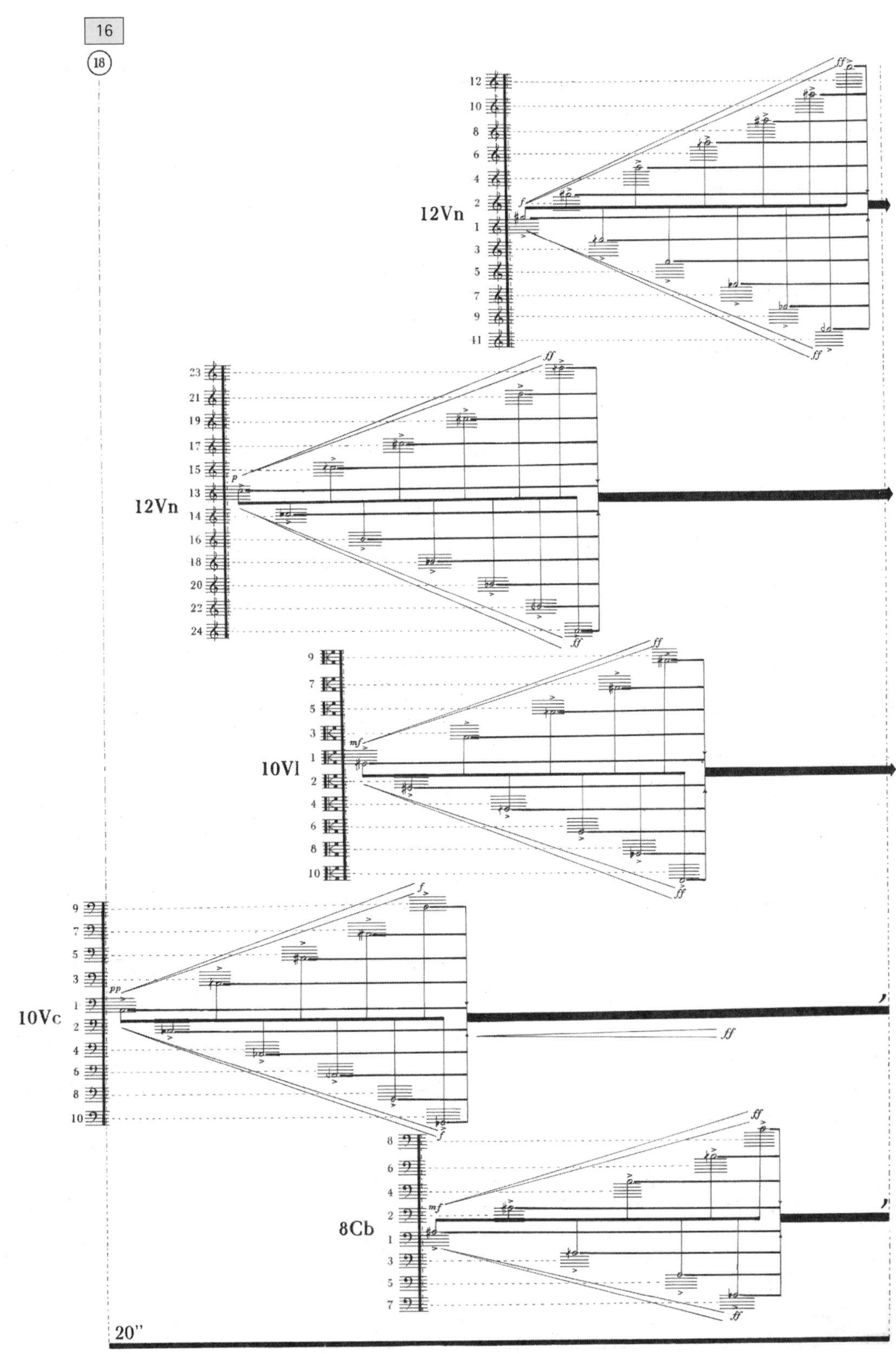
16
18
12Vn
12Vn
10Vl
10Vc
8Cb
20"

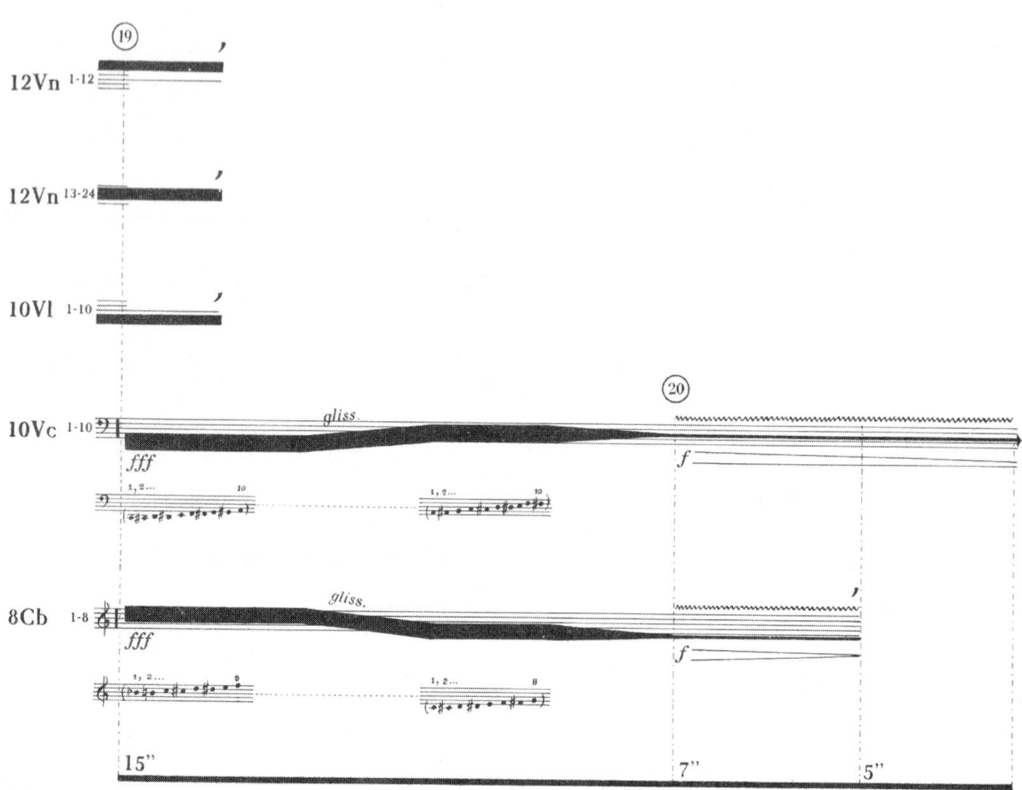
19
12Vn 1-12
12Vn 13-24
10Vl 1-10
20
10Vc 1-10
gliss.
fff
f
1, 2...
10
8Cb 1-8
gliss.
fff
f
1, 2...
8
15"
7"
5"

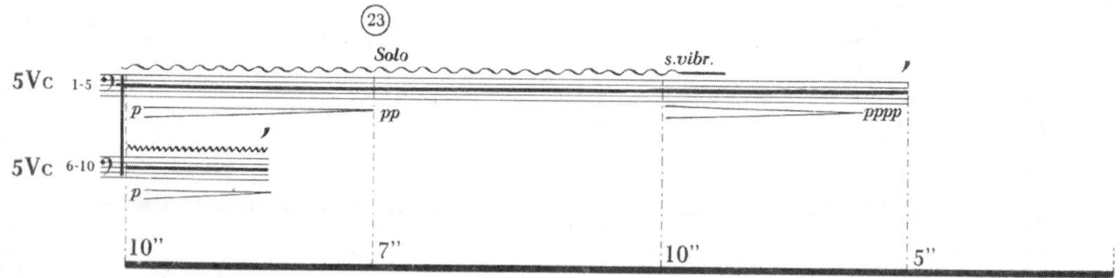
23
Solo
s.vibr.
5Vc 1-5
p
pp
pppp
5Vc 6-10
p
10"
7"
10"
5"

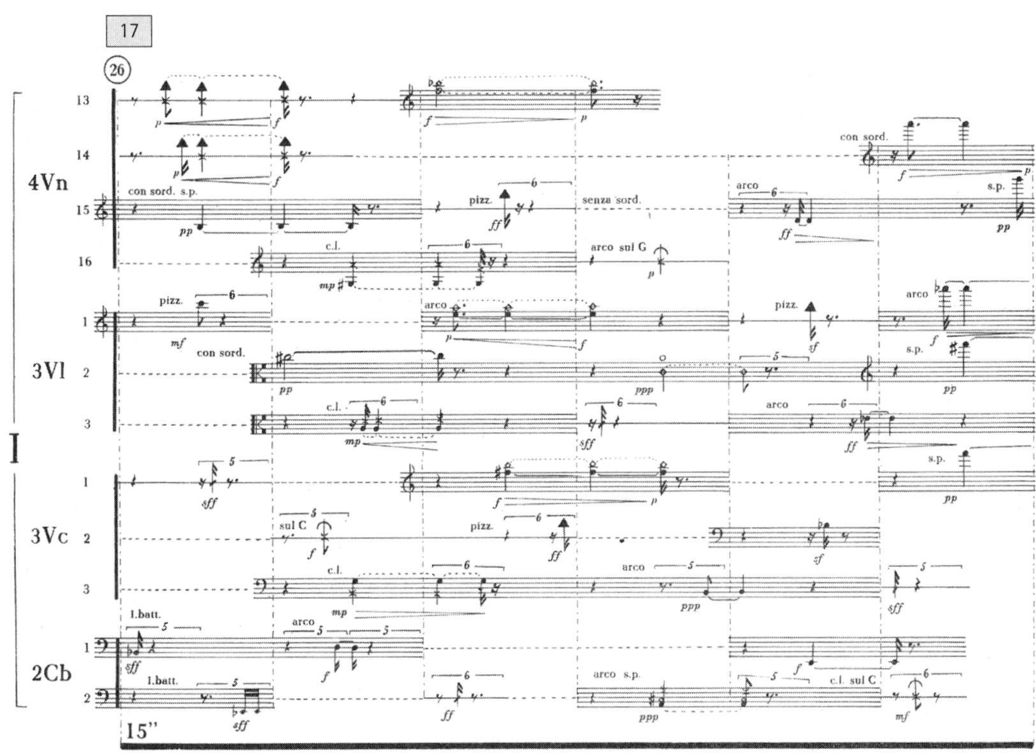
17
26
4Vn
3Vl
3Vc
2Cb
I
con sord. s.p.
pizz.
senza sord.
arco
arco sul G
con sord.
c.l.
sul C
l.batt.
arco s.p.
c.l. sul C
15"

32
4Vn
3Vl
3Vc
2Cb
I
s.p.
senza sord.
arco ord.
c.l. ord.
pizz.
sul D
ord. c.l.
c.l.
15"

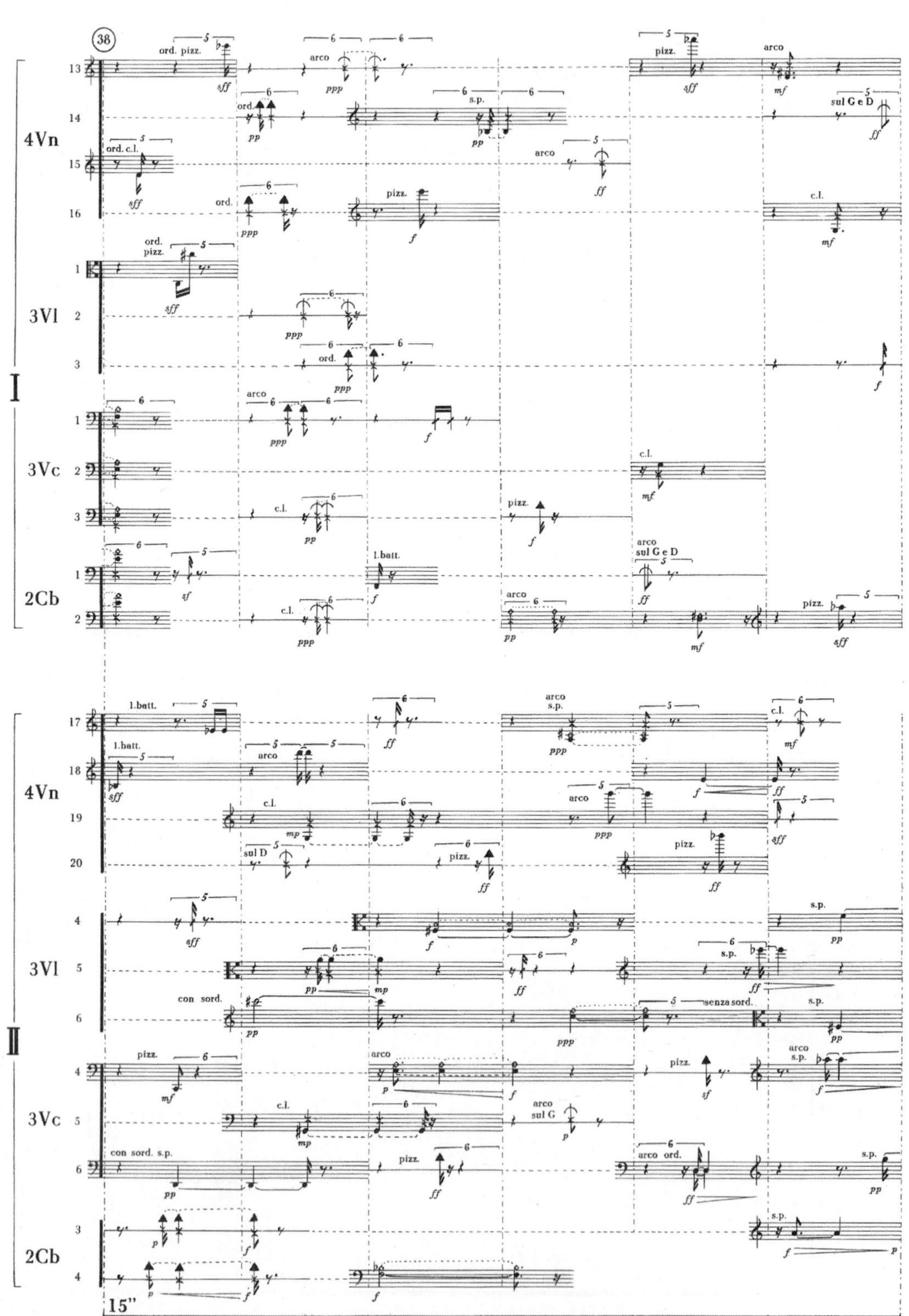
38
4Vn
3Vl
3Vc
2Cb
I
II
ord. pizz.
arco
pizz.
ord.
s.p.
sul G e D
ord. c.l.
c.l.
l.batt.
sul D
con sord.
senza sord.
con sord. s.p.
arco ord.
arco sul G
15"

14
50
4Vn
3Vl
3Vc
2Cb
I
II
III
c.l.
arco sul D
arco
s.p.
ord.
pizz.
l.batt.
sul G e D
sul C e E
sul D
15''

18
56 arco
15
1.batt.
arco
pizz.
4Vn
3Vl
3Vc
2Cb
I
ff sempre
s.p.
pp
ppp
pizz.
f
p
II
l.batt.
ff sempre
sff
mf
c.l.
III
10"

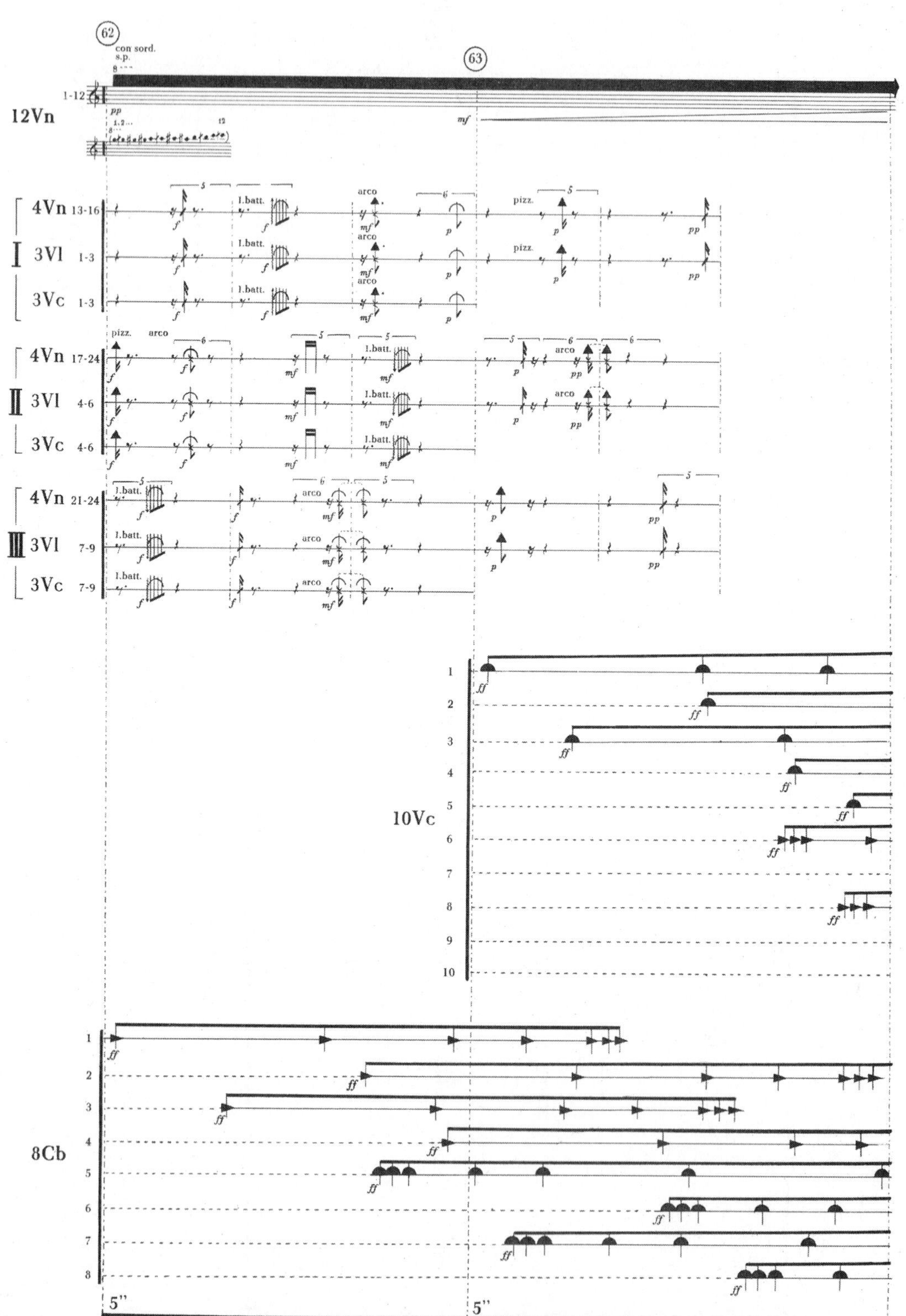
62
con sord.
s.p.
63
1-12
12Vn
pp
mf
4Vn 13-16
I 3Vl 1-3
3Vc 1-3
l.batt.
arco
pizz.
4Vn 17-24
II 3Vl 4-6
3Vc 4-6
4Vn 21-24
III 3Vl 7-9
3Vc 7-9
10Vc
8Cb
5''
5''

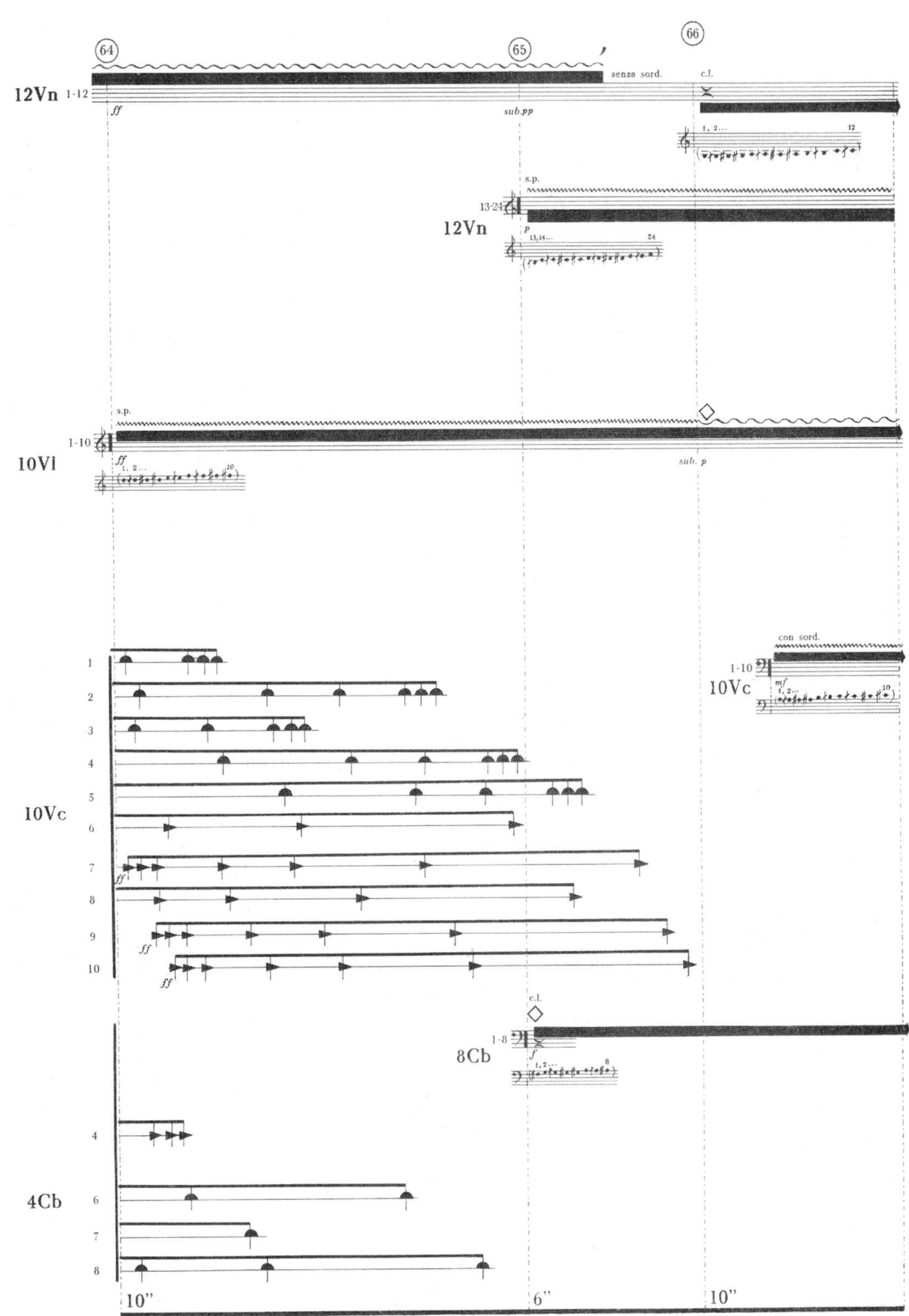

64
65
66
12Vn 1-12
ff
senza sord.
sub.pp
c.l.
1, 2...
12
s.p.
13-24
12Vn
p
13,14...
24
s.p.
1-10
10Vl
ff
1, 2...
10
sub. p
con sord.
1-10
10Vc
mf
1, 2...
10
10Vc
1
2
3
4
5
6
7
8
9
10
ff
c.l.
1-8
8Cb
f
1, 2...
8
4Cb
4
6
7
8
10"
6"
10"

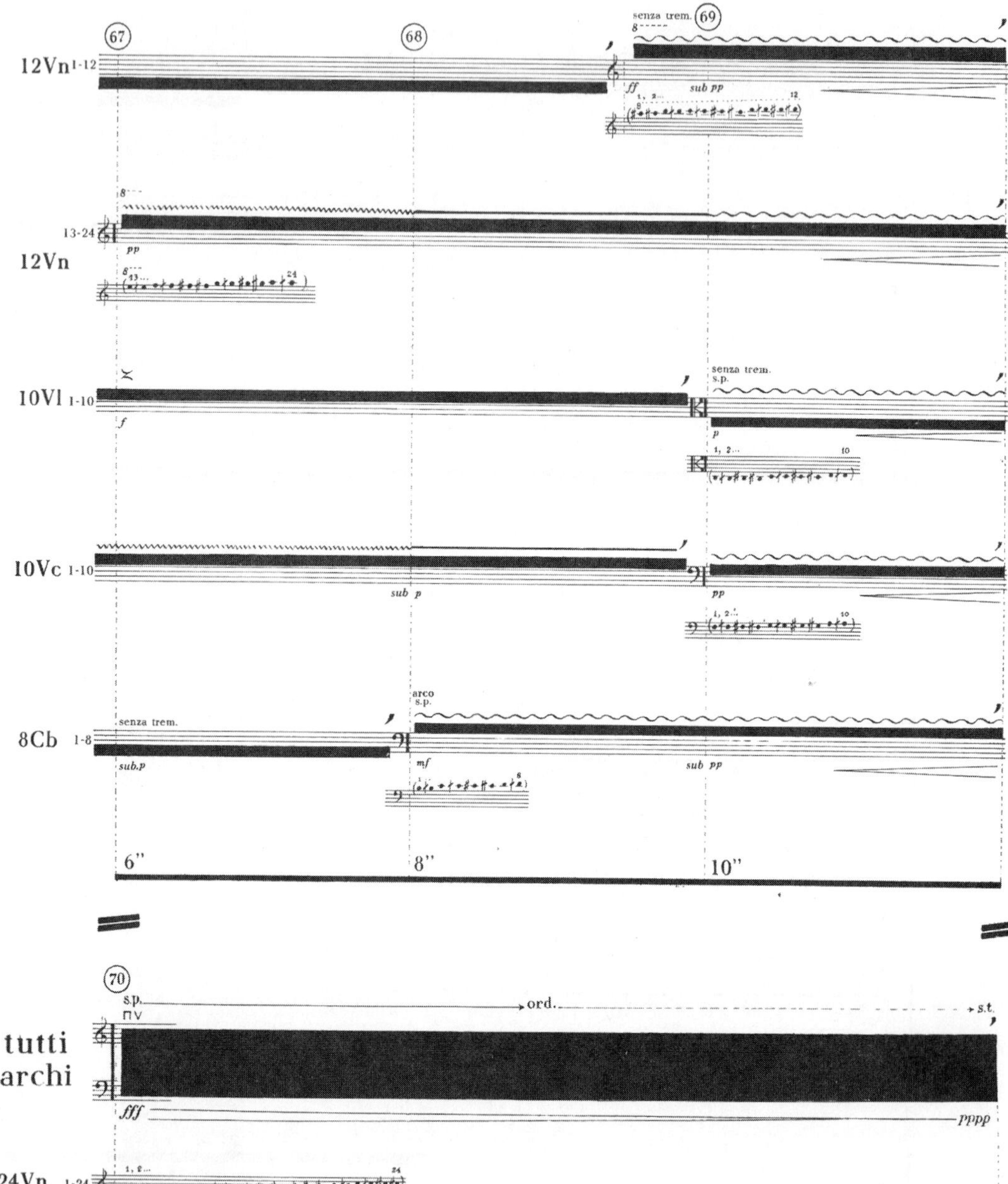

70
s.p. → ord. → s.t.
tutti archi
fff
pppp
24Vn 1-24
10Vl 1-10
10Vc 1-10
8Cb 1-8
30"

GUIDE TO NOTATION

s. p. = sul ponticello [bow on the bridge]
s. t. = sul tasto [bow above the fingerboard]
c. l. = col legno [bow with the wood of the bow]

l. batt. = col legno battuto [strike the string with the wood of the bow]
ord. = ordinario [in an ordinary manner, canceling any of the above indications]

= raised by $\frac{1}{4}$ tone

= raised by $\frac{3}{4}$ tone

= lowered by $\frac{1}{4}$ tone

= lowered by $\frac{3}{4}$ tone

= highest note of the instrument (indefinite pitch)

= play between bridge and tailpiece

= arpeggio on 4 strings behind the bridge

= play on tailpiece (arco) [bowed]

= play on bridge

= percussion effect: strike the upper sounding board of the violin with the nut [of the bow] or the finger-tips

= several irregular changes of bow direction in succession

= molto vibrato

= very slow vibrato with a $\frac{1}{4}$ tone frequency difference produced by sliding the finger

= very rapid non-rhythmical tremolo

Polish composer Krzysztof Penderecki (pronounced KZHISH-toff pen-de-RETS-ki) is one of the most recognized and influential figures of the post–World War II generation. With the liberalization of communism after the end of Stalinism in 1956, the Polish government began to promote new music, and Penderecki began to explore new compositional techniques and styles. International attention quickly focused on him when he composed a series of sensational works, including *Threnody.* After winning the UNESCO Prize of the International Composers Jury in 1961, this work, for string orchestra, premiered to great acclaim later that year at the Warsaw Autumn Festival, and it remains his most famous piece.

Penderecki initially conceived of the composition as an abstract work, calling it *8'37''*, a name derived from its performance length. The change of title to *Threnody* (a song of lamentation) with the subtitle *To the Victims of Hiroshima* gave the piece a powerful image and message. For contemporary audiences, it not only depicted a horrific event of the recent past—the destruction of a Japanese city by the first atomic bomb used in war—but also suggested the imminent future in the aftermath of a possible World War III.

Traditional concepts of melody, harmony, and meter are absent in this work. Instead, Penderecki creates a sense of form by moving through several sections of diverse sounds. *Threnody* is written for 52 strings: 24 violins, 10 violas, 10 cellos, and 8 double basses. Each performer is given a unique part, often requiring the use of unusual performance techniques and notation (explained in the chart on the previous page). These distinctive timbres help to delineate five large sections, some of which overlap:

Section	Measure	Sounds
1	1	high pitched dissonant clusters
2	6	varied texture of multiple sound effects in rapid succession
3	10	sustained tones and quarter-tone clusters linked with glissandos
4	26	isolated pitches and various sound effects, in canon
5	56	unison sound effects and clusters that lead to the final climactic chord

The sound effects and sustained tone clusters in section 5 recall the sounds of sections 2 and 3, a relationship that is reinforced by parallel climaxes in measures 19 and 70. Based on this sense of return, it is possible to view the entire work as a modified ABA' structure, with the first three sections as the initial A.

Section 1 immediately establishes the mood of the work. Ten groups of four to six instruments enter in quick succession, alternating relatively high and low instruments. Each performer is instructed to play the highest note possible on the instrument; since the highest note differs from player to player, the result is intense high-pitch clusters that suggest screaming. Beginning in measure 2, the sound is varied through dynamic changes and the addition of two kinds of vibrato (variations in pitch)—one rapid, the other wide and slow.

Several unusual effects are featured in section 2. Penderecki requires seven different sounds, including striking the soundboard of the instrument with the hand or bow and bowing on the strings between the bridge and tailpiece (which produces very high but indeterminate notes on these short lengths of string). These sounds are arranged in four patterns, and the performers are instructed to choose one pattern and play it repeatedly as fast as possible, entering in imitative fashion by section (first cellos, then violas, violins, and contrabasses). The resultant effect has been likened to the sound of static from a shortwave radio.

In section 3, Penderecki divides the strings into the five groups of a traditional string orchestra. For the first time, sustained pitches are heard in the middle-to-lower registers, as the various groups swell with glissando effects between unisons and quarter-tone clusters. The score is written in a graphic notation that conveys the effect of a thickening and narrowing band of sound; the individual parts are shown in standard notation (with glissandos and the signs for quarter-tones). Two further variants of the clusters occur in this section. At measure 15, clusters in each group crescendo before dissolving with upward or downward glissandos. At measure 18, the clusters are formed as each successive instrument in a group enters on a note a quarter-tone higher or lower than is already sounding, and the sound crescendos into a climax at measure 19, before resolving to a solo cello in measure 23.

Section 4 presents the most complex passage of the composition. Penderecki divides the ensemble into three orchestras and initiates what can be analyzed as a three-part canon. Each orchestra has twelve independent parts playing a variety of sounds, pitches, and even rhythmic gestures with traditional notation. The entrance of Orchestra II at measure 38 is at the same pitch level as Orchestra I, but the registers are inverted. Orchestra I begins with a B♭ followed by two E♭s in the double-basses; at the entrance of Orchestra II, these pitches appear in the violins, with the other material similarly reversed. Orchestra III, which enters at measure 44, omits the first four measures of the material and transposes the remaining pitches either up a fourth or down a fifth. The material of all three orchestras begins to appear in retrograde with reverse registers after their seventeenth measure.

The final section begins at measure 56, as each of the three orchestras in succession turns to playing the sound effects from section 2, but now all at the same time. At measure 62, the first 12 violins, absent for section 4, return with a sustained quarter-tone cluster, supported by the lower strings bowing over their tailpieces and bridges. Gradually returning to the five-part division of the strings, Penderecki soon has all groups playing sustained quarter-tone clusters with vibrato. At measure 70, the instruments converge, and each performer sounds a different pitch in a stunning pitch cluster of 52 quarter tones, played *fortissississimo*. This remarkable chord is sustained for thirty seconds, gradually diminishing in volume as the players move from playing *sul ponticello* (over the bridge, producing a metallic sound) to *ordinario* (normal playing) to *sul tasto* (over the fingerboard for a rich, somewhat hollow sound). The chord then fades to nothing, bringing the piece to a silent and somber close.

For this work, Penderecki employed an effective notation (shown on page 637) that communicates complex effects in relatively simple terms. He incorporated features of traditional notation to denote specific pitches and rhythms when needed. The standard symbol for glissandos, a diagonal line, is the basis for notating shifting tone clusters, which is readily understood by string players. To indicate specific quarter-tone pitches, Penderecki used variants of the symbols for sharps and flats, and for vibrato he simply added a wavy line. For some of the unusual performance techniques, such as playing behind the bridge, Penderecki developed images that can easily be linked to those effects. For example, a small arch suggests the bridge, and four lines represent the four strings. Professional performers would have little difficulty memorizing these symbols.

Since measure lengths in this work are defined in seconds rather than beats (except in section 4), the primary roles of the conductor are to keep time and give cues. Some conductors use a stopwatch in order to be as precise as possible, but others treat time more freely. The recording accompanying this anthology maintains a fairly strict time, but many performances are longer than the indicated eight minutes and twenty-six seconds. Indeed, one of the recordings with Penderecki himself conducting extends to nine minutes and forty-five seconds.

196

Karel Husa (b. 1921)

Music for Prague 1968: First movement, Introduction and Fanfare, Adagio—Allegro

Concert band suite

1968

CD 14|19

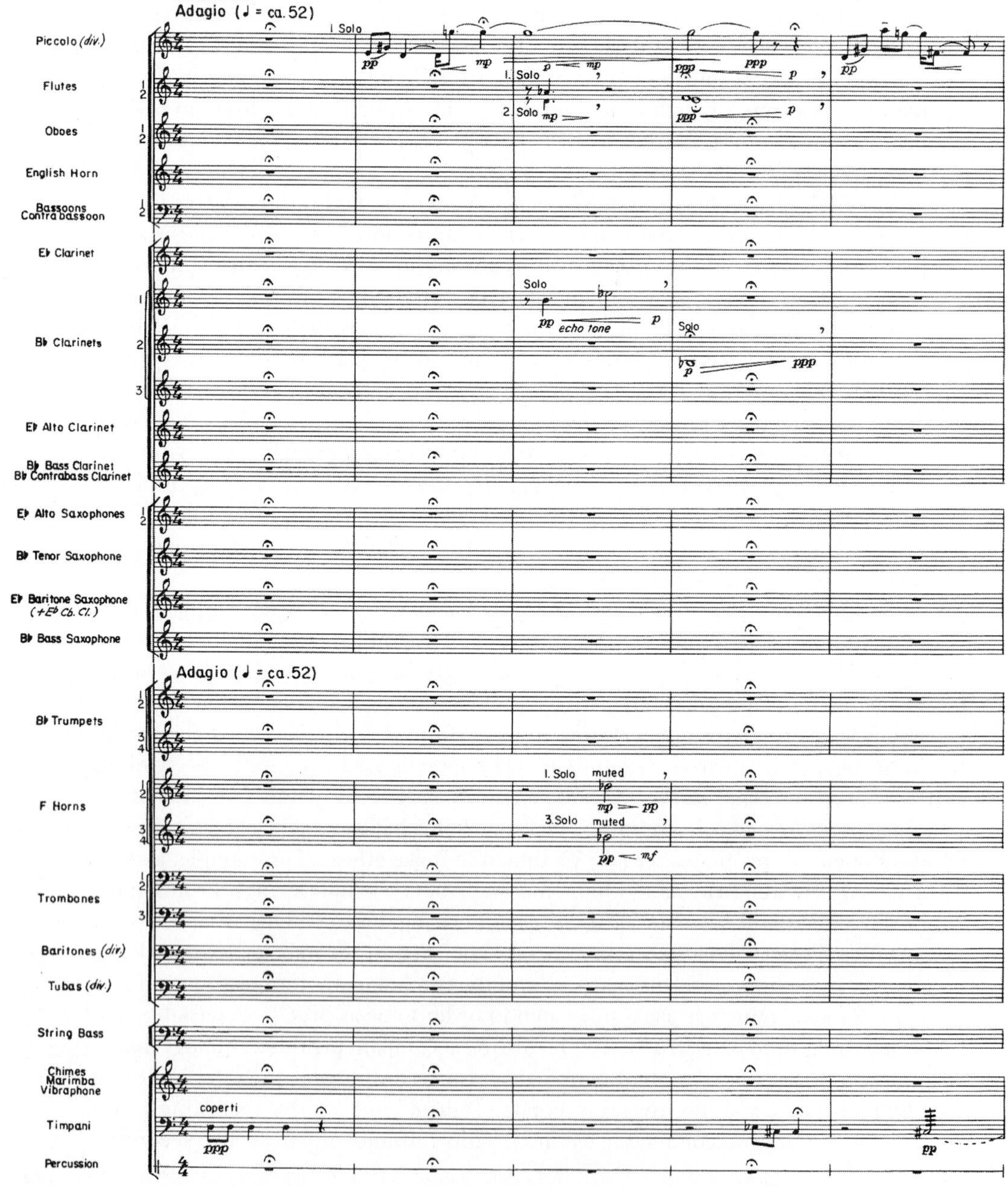
Adagio (♩ = ca. 52)
Piccolo (div.)
Flutes
Oboes
English Horn
Bassoons
Contrabassoon
E♭ Clarinet
B♭ Clarinets
E♭ Alto Clarinet
B♭ Bass Clarinet
B♭ Contrabass Clarinet
E♭ Alto Saxophones
B♭ Tenor Saxophone
E♭ Baritone Saxophone (+E♭ Cb. Cl.)
B♭ Bass Saxophone
B♭ Trumpets
F Horns
Trombones
Baritones (div.)
Tubas (div.)
String Bass
Chimes
Marimba
Vibraphone
Timpani
Percussion
I Solo
1. Solo
2. Solo
Solo
echo tone
I. Solo
muted
3. Solo
coperti

From Karel Husa, *Music for Prague 1968* (New York: Associated Music Publishers, 1969), 4–30.

6
Picc.
Fls.
Obs.
E.H.
Bns.
Cbn.
E♭ Cl.
B♭ Cls.
A.Cl.
B.Cl.
Cb.Cl.
A. Saxs.
T. Sax.
Bar. Sax.
B. Sax.
Tpts.
Hns.
Tbns.
Bars.
Tuba
St. B.
Vib.
Timp.
Perc.
cantando
Solo Harmon mute, stem out
Solo Harmon mute, stem out
perdendosi

20
11
Picc.
Fls.
fl.t.
Obs.
E.H.
Bns.
Cbn.
E♭ Cl.
B♭ Cls.
A.Cl.
B. Cl.
Cb.Cl.
A.Saxs.
T.Sax.
Bar.Sax.
B.Sax.
Tpts.
Hns.
Tbns.
Bar.
Tuba
St. B.
Mar.
Vib.
soft sticks, motor on
let vibrate
Timp.
Perc.

15
A
Picc.
Fls.
Solo
mf espr.
p
mf
pp
Obs.
E. H.
Bns.
Cbn.
E♭ Cl.
I Solo
senza vibrato
pp
B♭ Cls.
dim.
2 Soli
pp senza vibrato
A. Cl.
B. Cl.
Cb. Cl.
A. Saxs.
T. Sax.
Bar. Sax.
B. Sax.
Tpts.
Hns.
Harmon mute, stem in
fl. t.
gradually decrease speed of tremolo
mp
Tbns.
Bar.
Tuba
pizz.
f
St. B.
medium sticks
Mar.
Vib.
Timp.
Perc.

19
Picc.
Fls.
Obs.
E.H.
Bns.
Cbn.
Eb Cl.
Bb Cls.
A. Cl.
B. Cl.
Cb.Cl.
A. Saxs.
T. Sax.
Bar. Sax.
B. Sax.
Tpts.
Hns.
Tbns.
Bar.
Tuba
St. B.
Mar.
Timp.
Perc.
ppp (no cresc.)
cresc. poco a poco
dim.
div. a 3
mf dim
1. Harmon mute, stem in
Solo
4. St. mute
I. mute
Large Tam-tam
scrape w. Trgl. stick
let vibrate

23
Tutti
Picc.
Fls.
Obs.
E. H.
Bns. Cbn.
E♭ Cl.
B♭ Cls.
A. Cl.
B. Cl. Cb. Cl.
A. Saxs.
T. Sax.
Bar. Sax.
B. Sax.
Tpts.
Hns.
2. mute
Tbns.
Bar. Tuba
St. B.
Mar.
Timp.
Perc.
mf cresc. poco a poco
mp cresc.
cresc. poco a poco

27
B
Picc.
Fls. 1 2
a 2
Obs. 1 2
E.H.
Bns. 1 2
Cbn.
E♭ Cl.
B♭ Cls. 1 2 3
div. a 3
A. Cl.
B. Cl. Cb.Cl.
B.Cl.
ossia
pp sonore
A.Saxs. 1 2
T.Sax.
Bar.Sax.
B. Sax.
p cresc. poco a poco
Tpts. 1 2 3 4
Hns. 1 2 3 4
a 2 (mute)
a 2 mute
poco
Tbns. 1 2 3
St. mute
Bar.
Tuba
mute
St. B.
Mar.
Vib.
Timp.
Perc.
cresc. poco a poco
dim.

* ↑ = quartertone higher (valid for the following note only).

21
35
C Allegro (♩ = 108 - 112)
Picc.
Fls. 1 2
Obs. 1 2
E.H.
Bns. 1 2 Cbn.
E♭ Cl.
B♭ Cls. 1 2 3
all
A. Cl.
B. Cl.
Cb.Cl.
A. Saxs. 1 2
T. Sax.
Bar. Sax.
B. Sax.
C Allegro (♩ = 108 - 112)
open
ff brassy
(open)
Tpts. 1 2 3 4
Hns. 1 2 3 4
Tbns. 1 2 3
Bar. 1 2
Tuba
St. B.
Mar.
Vib.
Timp.
nat., hard stick
Susp. Cym. 2 wooden sticks, at the edge
sm.
m.
l.
Perc.
fff

39
Picc.
Fls. 1 2
Obs. 1 2
E. H.
Bns. 1 2
Cbn.
E♭ Cl.
B♭ Cls. 1 2 3
A. Cl.
B. Cl.
Cb. Cl.
A. Saxs. 1 2
T. Sax.
Bar. Sax.
B. Sax.
Tpts.
ff
Hns.
open
ff brassy
f
Tbns.
Bar.
Tuba
St. B.
Mar.
Vib.
Timp.
Perc.
Tam-t.
sm.
m.
l.
let vibrate

44
D
Picc.
Fls. 1 2
Obs. 1 2
E.H.
Bns. 1 2
Cbn.
E♭ Cl.
B♭ Cls. 1 2 3
A. Cl.
B. Cl.
Cb. Cl.
Cb. Cl.
A. Saxs. 1 2
T. Sax.
Bar. Sax.
B. Sax.
Tpts.
fl.t.
fp cresc. molto
Hns. 1 2 3 4
Tbns. 1 2 3
Bar. 1 2
Tuba
St. B.
Mar.
hardest plastic stick
sempre ff
Vib.
hardest plastic sticks
Ped.
sempre ff
Timp.
Perc.

48
Picc.
Fls. 1 2
Obs. 1 2
E.H.
Bns. 1 2 Cbn.
Cbn.
ff
E♭ Cl.
B♭ Cls. 1 2 3
A. Cl.
B. Cl. Cb. Cl.
Cb. Cl.
f
cresc. poco a poco
A. Saxs. 1 2
a2
T. Sax.
Bar. Sax.
B. Sax.
Tpts. 1 2 3 4
Hns. 1 2 3 4
a 2
Tbns. 1 2 3
Bar. 1 2
ff sfp
cresc.
Tuba
open
St. B.
arco
Mar.
Vib.
Timp.
Perc.

52
Picc.
Fls. 1 2
Obs. 1 2
E.H.
Bns. 1 2 Cbn.
Cbn.
Bns.
E♭Cl.
B♭ Cls. 1 2 3
a 2
A.Cl.
B.Cl.
Cb.Cl.
A.Saxs. 1 2
T.Sax.
Bar.Sax.
B.Sax.
Tpts. 1 2 3 4
Hns. 1 2 3 4
dim. poco a poco
dim. poco a poco
Tbns. 1 2 3
gliss.
gliss.
Bar. 1 2
Tuba
St. B.
Mar.
Vib.
Timp.
Perc.
2 Cym.

56
Picc.
Fls. 1 2
Obs. 1 2
E.H.
Bns. 1 2
Cbn.
E♭ Cl.
B♭ Cls. 1 2 3
A. Cl.
B. Cl.
CbCl.
A. Saxs 1 2
T. Sax.
Bar. Sax.
B. Sax.
Tpts. 1 2 3 4
Hns. 1 2 3 4
Tbns. 1 2 3
Bar. 1 2
Tuba
St. B.
Mar.
Timp.
Perc.
a 2
8va ad lib.
ff sub.
a 3

22
60
E
Picc.
Fls. 1 2
ff ma cantando
Obs. 1 2
ff ma cantando
E.H.
ff ma cantando
Bns. 1 2
ff
Cbn.
ff ma cantando
E♭ Cl.
a 3
B♭ Cls. 1 2 3
ff ma cantando
A. Cl.
ff
B. Cl.
ff
Cb.Cl.
mf cresc. poco a poco
A. Saxs. 1 2
mf cresc. poco a poco
T. Sax.
mf cresc. poco a poco
Bar. Sax.
mf cresc. poco a poco
B. Sax.
mf cresc. poco a poco
E
Tpts.
nat.
ff ma cantando
Hns.
nat.
ff
Tbns.
nat.
ff
Bar.
nat.
ff ma cantando
Tuba
ff ma cantando
St. B.
ff ma cantando
Mar.
Timp.
Perc.

63
Picc.
Fls. 1 2
fl.t.
ff
Obs. 1 2
E.H.
f
Bns. 1 2
Cbn.
(Bns.)
E♭ Cl.
p cresc. poco a poco
B♭ Cls. 1 2 3
a 3
p cresc. poco a poco
A. Cl.
p cresc. poco a poco
B. Cl.
Cb. Cl.
A. Saxs. 1 2
T. Sax.
Bar. Sax.
B. Sax.
Tpts. 1 2 3 4
campana in aria
Harmon mute, stem in
ff
campana in aria
Cup mute
ff
campana in aria
St. mute
ff
campana in aria
Hns. 1 2 3 4
Tbns. 1 2 3
Bar. 1 2
unis.
Tuba
St. B.
Mar.
Vib.
f
Timp.
Perc.

66
Picc.
Fls 1 2
Obs. 1 2
E. H.
Bns. 1 2
Cbn.
E♭ Cl.
B♭ Cls. 1 2 3
a2
A. Cl.
B. Cl. Cb. Cl.
B. Cl.
mp cresc.
cresc.
A. Saxs. 1 2
T. Sax.
Bar. Sax.
B. Sax.
Tpts. 1 2 3 4
(open)
Hns. 1 2 3 4
Tbns. 1 2 3
Bar. 1 2
Tuba
St. B.
Mar.
Vib.
Perc.

69
F
Picc.
Fls. 1 2
Obs. 1 2
E.H.
Bns. 1 2 Cbn.
a 2
E♭ Cl.
B♭ Cls. 1 2 3
A. Cl.
B. Cl.
Cb. Cl.
A. Saxs. 1 2
T. Sax.
Bar. Sax.
B. Sax.
Tpts. 1 2 3 4
fp molto cresc.
Hns. 1 2 3 4
brassy
Tbns. 1 2 3
Bar. 1 2
Tuba
St. B.
Mar.
Vib.
Perc.
Susp. Cym.
at edge

72
23
Picc.
Fls. 1 2
Obs. 1 2
E.H.
Bns. 1 2
Cbn.
E♭Cl.
B♭ Cls. 1 2 3
A. Cl.
B. Cl
Cb. Cl.
A.Saxs. 1 2
T. Sax.
Bar.Sax.
B.Sax.
Tpts. 1 2 3 4
ossia
Hns. 1 2 3 4
a2 nat.
a 2 nat.
Tbns. 1 2 3
gliss.
Bar. 1 2
a2
Tuba
div.
unis.
St.B.
Mar.
Vib.
Perc.
Tom-t. i.
Tom-t. m.
Tom-t. l.
hard felt Timp.sticks

Picc.
Fls. 1 2
Obs. 1 2
E.H.
Bns. 1 2
Cbn.
E♭ Cl.
B♭ Cls. 1 2 3
A. Cl.
B. Cl.
Cb. Cl.
A. Saxs. 1 2
T. Sax.
Bar. Sax.
B. Sax.
Tpts. 1 3 2 4
Hns. 1 2 3 4
Tbns. 1 2 3
Bar. 1 2
Tuba
St.B.
Mar.
Vib.
Perc.
3 Tom-t
sm.
m.
l.
G
fl.t.
cresc.
ff
open
ff staccatiss.
a 2
mp cresc. poco a poco
cresc. poco a poco
fff
mf
f

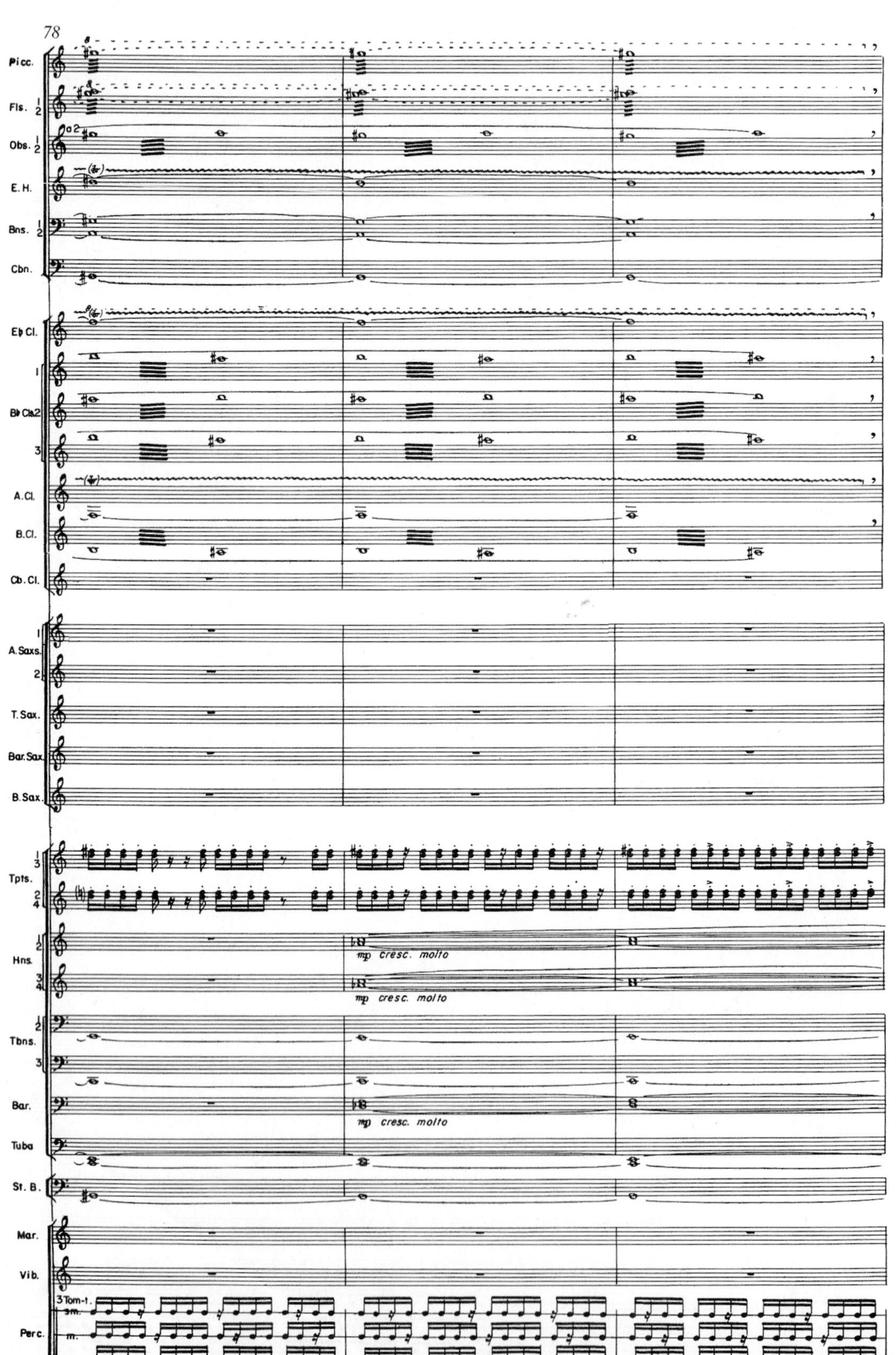
78
Picc.
Fls. 1 2
Obs. 1 2
a2
E. H.
Bns. 1 2
Cbn.
E♭ Cl.
B♭ Cls. 1 2 3
A. Cl.
B. Cl.
Cb. Cl.
A. Saxs. 1 2
T. Sax.
Bar. Sax.
B. Sax.
Tpts. 1 3 2 4
Hns. 1 2 3 4
mp cresc. molto
mp cresc. molto
Tbns. 1 2 3
Bar.
mp cresc. molto
Tuba
St. B.
Mar.
Vib.
Perc.
3 Tom-t.
sm.
m.
l.

24
81
The notes are to be played at random, preferably different all the time; they must be fast, fff and staccatissimo.
The notation indicates approximate direction up and down.
Broken triads ought to be avoided.
Picc.
Fls. 1 2
Obs. 1 2
E.H.
Bns. 1 2
Cbn.
E♭ Cl.
B♭ Cls. 1 2 3
a2
A. Cl.
B. Cl.
Cb. Cl.
mf cresc. poco a poco
A. Saxs. 1 2
T. Sax.
Bar. Sax.
B. Sax.
Tpts. 1 2 3 4
repeat freely and irregularly
accelerate to H
Hns. 1 2 3 4
gliss.
Tbns. 1 2 3
Bar.
Tuba
St. B.
Mar.
Vib.
Perc.
3 Tom-t.
sm.
m.
l.
fff
ff

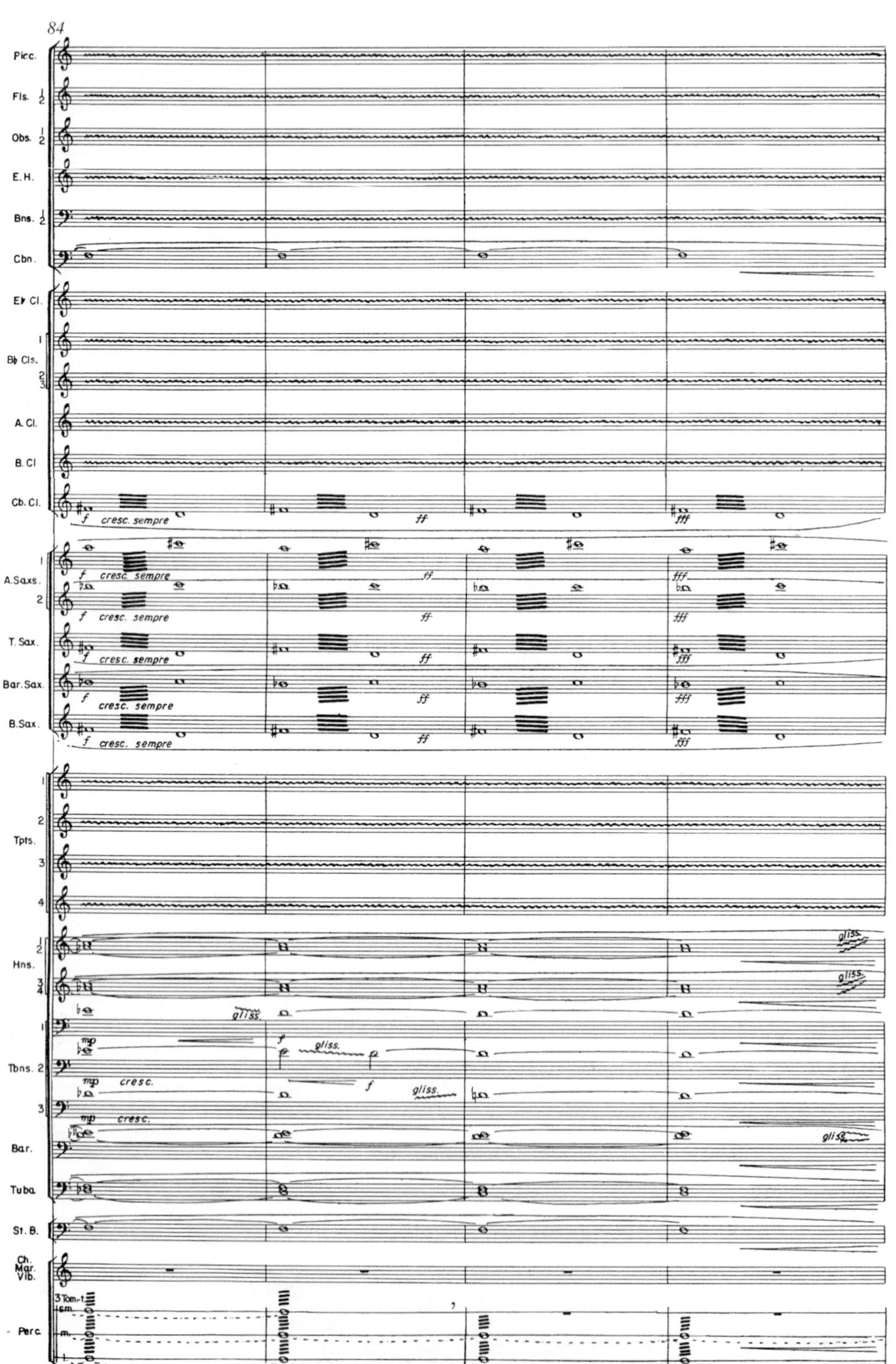
84
Picc.
Fls. 1 2
Obs. 1 2
E. H.
Bns. 1 2
Cbn.
E♭ Cl.
B♭ Cls. 1 2 3
A. Cl.
B. Cl
Cb. Cl.
f cresc. sempre
ff
fff
A. Saxs. 1 2
T. Sax.
Bar. Sax.
B. Sax.
Tpts. 1 2 3 4
Hns. 1 2 3 4
gliss.
Tbns. 1 2 3
mp cresc.
f
Bar.
Tuba
St. B.
Ch. Mar. Vib.
3 Tom-t.
Perc.

25
88
H
rit. poco a poco
Picc.
Fls.
dim. poco a poco
staccatiss. as fast as possible, unmeasured
Obs.
E. H.
Bns.
Cbn.
E♭ Cl.
B♭ Cls.
ossia staccatiss. as fast as possible
A. Cl.
B. Cl.
Cb. Cl.
A. Saxs.
T. Sax.
Bar. Sax.
B. Sax.
Tpts.
Hns.
Tbns.
Bar.
Tuba
St. B.
Ch.
let vibrate
Mar.
slow down progressively
Vib.
Timp.
dim.
2 Tom-t.
Perc.

91
sempre rit. poco a poco
Picc.
Fls.
slow down progressively
dim. sempre
Obs.
E.H.
Bns.
Cbn.
slow down progressively
E♭ Cl.
B♭ Cls.
div. in 2
A. Cl.
B. Cl.
Cb.Cl.
A.Saxs.
T. Sax.
Bar.Sax.
B.Sax.
sempre rit. poco a poco
Tpts.
Hns.
Tbns.
Bar.
Tuba
St. B.
Mar.
Vib.
Timp.
Perc.

95
sempre rit.
Picc.
Fls.
fl.t. slow down progressively
mp dim.
perdendosi
ppp
Obs.
mp dim.
dim.
E.H.
ppp
Bns.
Cbn.
E♭ Cl.
one half dim.
Bb Cls.
dim.
1. Solo mp
ppp
2. Solo
A. Cl.
dim.
ppp
B. Cl.
pp
Cb.Cl.
A.Saxs.
T. Sax.
Bar. Sax.
B.Sax.
sempre rit.
Solo Harmon mute, stem in
p
Tpts.
mp
Hns.
Tbns.
Bar.
Tuba
St.B.
Ch.
pp let ring
Mar.
dim.
Vib.
dim.
Timp.
mp
Perc.

100
Adagio(♩ = ca. 52)
Solo
p
dim.
dim.
pp
Picc.
Fls.
Solo
pp
perdendosi
Obs.
E.H.
Bns.
Cbn.
E♭ Cl.
B♭ Cls.
2.
perdendosi
A. Cl.
B. Cl.
Cb.Cl.
A.Saxs.
T. Sax.
Bar.Sax.
B.Sax.
Adagio(♩ = ca. 52)
Tpts.
Hns.
Tbns.
Bar.
Tuba
St. B.
Ch.
Mar. Vib.
Timp.
pp
ppp
pppp
Perc.

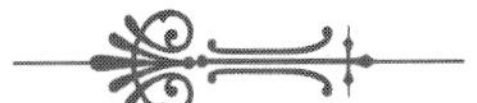

In the twentieth century, band conductors sought to develop a repertoire of music for band and for wind ensemble that attained the same seriousness and level of artistry as the masterpieces of orchestral music, going beyond the marches, medleys, arrangements, and solo display pieces traditionally played by bands. Over the century, a repertoire of classics for band developed, and one of its central pieces is Karel Husa's *Music for Prague 1968*. Commissioned by the Ithaca College Concert Band and composed during the summer and fall of 1968, the work was premiered on January 31, 1969, at the Music Educators National Conference in Washington, D.C., and has been performed over eight thousand times since then. In 1970, Husa rescored the piece for orchestra, and it has been played many times in that form as well.

Husa was born in Prague, Czechoslovakia (now in the Czech Republic), and educated there and in Paris. Stranded in France when the communists assumed power in his native country in 1948, he came to the United States to teach at Cornell University in 1954 and became a naturalized American citizen in 1959. He was inspired to write *Music for Prague 1968* by the events of August 1968, when Soviet tanks rolled into Prague to overthrow the liberal communist government of Alexander Dubček and reassert Soviet control. The piece is in four movements: Introduction and Fanfare; Aria; Interlude (for percussion alone); and Toccata and Chorale.

The central thematic idea of the piece is the first phrase from a fifteenth-century Czech chorale tune, previously used by Czech composer Bedřich Smetana in his tone poems *Tábor* and *Blaník*, the last two movements of *Má vlast* (My Country, ca. 1872–79), and by Antonín Dvořák in *Husitská* (1883). The chorale "You Who Are God's Warriors" was a song of the Hussites, followers of religious reformer Jan Hus (ca. 1369–1415), whose fortress at Tábor became a symbol of Czech resistance to outside oppression. Legend held that in times of need, the Hussite warriors would ride out of their hiding places to save the Czech nation. By using the chorale, Husa invoked the legend, surely appropriate during the crisis in 1968. But he also alluded to the two great Czech nationalist composers and to music almost every Czech would know.

In an apt metaphor for the gathering of the warriors, Smetana's *Tábor* develops the theme in fragments before stating it whole at the end, making it an early example of cumulative form (see Ives's *General William Booth*, NAWM 168). *Music for Prague 1968* is also in cumulative form, both as a four-movement work and in the first movement. The whole chorale phrase, shown in the example on the next page, appears only at the end of the last movement, having been developed over the course of the entire piece. In the first movement, the first two measures of the tune soar triumphantly in the brass near the end of the movement (measures 74–76), and reappear soon afterward in the timpani, now with the first three notes of the third measure as well (measures 90–94). The last few notes continue, unable to complete the phrase, as the music dwindles away, waiting for the finale to gather the complete band of warriors in full force.

At the beginning of the movement, the timpani softly presents fragments of the chorale: the first measure in the right rhythm (measure 1), but the second distorted intervallically, so that the rising whole step and falling major third (D–E–C) of the original tune become a rising half step and falling whole tone (D–E♭–C♯), as shown in the example below. The timpani persists with these ideas throughout the slow introduction. Then at the start of the fanfare (measure 35), the trumpets take up the notes from the timpani to create a four-note idea (D–E♭–D♭–C), ultimately derived from the chorale. This motive becomes the main material for the fanfare, presented in retrograde, inverted, and permuted forms as well as in its original form. Development of this motive builds to the climactic presentation of the first two measures of the chorale. In the second movement, the fanfare motive (transposed) and its retrograde become segments of the twelve-tone row that underlies the entire movement. Meanwhile, the piccolo and flute solos that dominate the introduction of the first movement are suffused with ideas drawn from the chorale or the fanfare figure, and a three-chord motive (measures 3–4) that becomes important in this and later movements is also related to the fanfare figure. All these relationships are also shown in the example. Thus, most of the motivic material in the piece ultimately derives from the chorale theme, symbolizing the reliance of the Czech people on their historical traditions of resistance.

In addition to using developing variation and twelve-tone procedures, Husa draws on other modern methods in some passages. Instruments often have contradictory dynamics, so that chords change as they sound (as at measures 3–4), and at times dynamics themselves become a virtual melody (see clarinet 1, measures 10–14). The brass use a variety of mutes to create different colors, and the alto saxophone plays quarter tones (measures 33–34). In order to achieve maximum density at the climax (measures 81–87), Husa uses indeterminate notation, instructing the winds to play notes "at random," fast, loud, and staccato, and the trumpets to repeat a note "freely and irregularly." The effect is overwhelming, and the passage is easier to perform than it would be if each note were written out.

Such a piece is as intricately worked out as an orchestral composition by Webern or Bartók (compare NAWM 163 and 167) and is a far cry from the light entertainment music that dominated the band repertoire before World War II. It also resembles orchestral music in offering a profound emotional experience that is appropriate to its program. From quiet stillness, the Adagio introduction slowly gathers force through dissonant chords and a slow development of ideas, then the Allegro fanfare builds layers and density to a visceral climax of rage and defiance before it gradually calms. Over the course of all four movements, Husa touches a wide range of emotions ranging from grief to exhilaration. The work ends with the chorale as a commitment that, however long it takes, the Czech people will be free.

197

Steve Reich (b. 1936)

Tehillim: Part IV

For four solo voices and ensemble or chamber orchestra

1981

8
A11
Ob.
E.H., Bsn.
1
Tamb.
2
2
Voices
3
nim va - u - gav, Ha - le - lu - hu ba - tzil - tzi - lay sha - ma,
nim va - u - gav, Ha - le - lu - hu ba - tzil - tzi - lay sha - ma,
Vln. I
Vln. II
Vla.
Vc.
Cb.

15
AIII
Ob.
E.H., Bsn.
1
Tamb.
2
2
Voices
3
Ha - le - lu - hu ba - tzil - tzi-lay ta - ru - ah, Kol han - sha - mah ta -
Ha - le - lu - hu ba - tzil - tzi-lay ta - ru - ah, Kol han - sha - mah ta -
unis.
div.
Vln. I
Vln. II
Vla.
Vc.
Cb.

21
AIIIa
Ob.
E.H., Bsn.
1
Tamb.
2
2
Voices
3
ha - lail - yah Ha - le - lu - yah. Kol han - sha - ma ta -
ha - lail - yah Ha - le - lu - yah. Kol han - sha - ma ta -
Vln. I
Vln. II
Vla.
Vc.
Cb.

27
B I
27
Ob.
E.H., Bsn.
Clar. 1, 2
mf
Clar. 3, 4
1
Tamb.
2
2
Voices
3
Voice 1 (Lyric S.)
ha - lail - yah Ha - le - lu - yah. Ha - le - lu - hu ba -
ha - lail - yah Ha - le - lu - yah.
Vln. I
Vln. II
Vla.
Vc.
Cb.

33
Clar. 1
Clar. 2
mf
Tamb.
1
2
Voices
1 (Lyric S.)
tof u - ma-chol, Ha - le - lu - hu ba - mi - nim va - u - gav,
2 (Lyric S.)
Ha - le - lu - hu ba - tof u - ma - chol, Ha - le - lu - hu ba - mi - nim va -
Vln. I
Vln. II
Vla.
Vc.
Cb.

40
BII
Clar. 1
Clar. 2
1
Tamb.
2
1
Voices
Ha - le - lu - hu ba - tzil - tzi - lay sha - ma, Ha - le - lu - hu ba-tzil - tzi - lay ta -
2
u - gav, Ha - le - lu - hu ba-tzil-tzi-lay sha - ma, Ha - le - lu - hu
unis.
div.
Vln. I
Vln. II
Vla.
Vc.
Cb.

49
BIII
Clar. 1
Clar. 2
Tamb.
1
2
Voices
1
ru - ah, Kol han - sha - ma ta - ha - lail - yah Ha - le - lu -
2
ba-tzil - tzi - lay ta - ru - ah, Kol han - sha-ma ta - ha - lail - yah
Vln. I
Vln. II
Vla.
Vc.
Cb.

55
BIIIa
Clar. 1
Clar. 2
Tamb.
1
2
Voices
1
yah. Kol han - sha - ma ta - ha - lail - yah Ha - le - lu - yah.
2
Ha - le - lu - yah. Kol han - sha - ma ta - ha - lail - yah Ha - le - lu -
Vln. I
Vln. II
Vla.
Vc.
Cb.

28
62
C
Maracas
Tamb.
1
2
fade
pp
Organ 1
Organ 2
Voices
1
2
3
4
Ha - le - lu - hu ba - tof u - ma - chol, Ha - le -
Ha - le - lu - hu ba - tof u - ma -
Ha - le - lu - hu ba - tof
Ha - le - lu - hu
div.
Vln. I
Vln. II
Vla.
Vc.
Cb.

67
D
Maracas
Organ 1
Organ 2
Voices
1
lu - hu ba - mi - nim va - u - gav, Ha - le - lu - hu ba -
2
chol, Ha - le - lu - hu ba - mi - nim va - u - gav,
3
u - ma-chol, Ha - le - lu - hu ba - mi - nim va - u - gav,
4
ba - tof u - ma - chol, Ha - le - lu - hu ba - mi - nim va -
Vln. I
Vln. II
Vla.
Vc.
Cb.

72
Maracas
Organ 1
Organ 2
Voices
1
tof u - ma - chol, Ha - le - lu - hu ba - mi - nim va - u - gav,
2
Ha - le - lu - hu ba-tof u - ma - chol, Ha - le-lu - hu ba - mi-nim va -
3
Ha - le - lu - hu ba-tof u - ma-chol, Ha - le-lu - hu ba -
4
u - gav, Ha - le - lu - hu ba - tof u - ma - chol, Ha - le-lu - hu -
Vln. I
Vln. II
Vla.
Vc.
Cb.

78
Maracas
Organ 1
Organ 2
1
Ha - le - lu - hu ba - tof u - ma - chol, Ha - le - lu - hu ba - mi -
2
u - gav, Ha - le - lu - hu ba - tof u - ma - chol, Ha -
Voices
3
mi-nim va - u - gav, Ha - le - lu - hu ba - tof u - ma-chol,
4
ba - mi - nim va - u - gav, Ha - le - lu - hu ba - tof u - ma -
Vln. I
Vln. II
Vla.
Vc.
Cb.

84
E
Maracas
Organ 1
Organ 2
Voices
1
nim va - u - gav, Ha - le - lu - hu ba - tof u - ma - chol,
2
le - lu - hu ba - mi-nim va - u - gav, Ha - le - lu - hu u - ma -
3
Ha - le - lu - hu ba - mi - nim va - u - gav, Ha - le-lu - hu -
4
chol, Ha - le - lu - hu ba - mi-nim va - u - gav, Ha - le -
Vln. I
Vln. II
Vla.
Vc.
Cb.

90
F
Maracas
Organ 1
Organ 2
Voices
1
Ha - le - lu - hu ba - mi - nim va - u - gav, Ha - le - lu - hu ba-
2
u - ma - chol, Ha - le-lu - hu ba - mi-nim va - u - gav,
3
ba - tof u - ma - chol, Ha - le - lu - hu ba - mi-nim va - u - gav,
4
lu - hu ba - tof u - ma - chol, Ha - le - lu - hu ba - mi - nim va -
Vln. I
Vln. II
Vla.
Vc.
Cb.

96
Maracas
Organ 1
Organ 2
Voices
1
tof u - ma - chol, Ha - le - lu - hu ba - mi - nim va - u - gav,
2
Ha - le - lu - hu ba-tof u - ma - chol, Ha - le - lu - hu ba-mi - nim va -
3
Ha - le-lu - hu ba-tof u - ma-chol, Ha - le - lu - hu ba -
4
u - gav, Ha - le - lu - hu ba-tof u - ma - chol, Ha - le-lu - hu
Vln. I
Vln. II
Vla.
Vc.
Cb.

29
G
102
Maracas
Organ 1
Organ 2
Voices
1
Ha - le - lu-hu ba - tzil - tzi - lay sha - ma, Ha - le - lu - hu ba - tzil -
2
u - gav, Ha - le - lu - hu ba-tzil - tzi-lay sha - ma, Ha - le -
3
mi-nim Ha - le - lu - hu ba - tzil - tzi - lay sha - ma,
4
ba Ha - le - lu - hu ba - tzil - tzi - lay sha -
unis.
Vln. I
Vln. II
Vla.
Vc.
Cb.

109
H
Maracas
Organ 1
Organ 2
Voices
1
tzi-lay ta - ru - ah, Ha - le - lu - hu ba - tzil - tzi - lay sha - ma,
2
lu - hu ba-tzil - tzi-lay ta - ru - ah, Ha - le - lu - hu ba - tzil - tzi-lay
3
Ha - le - lu - hu ba - tzil - tzi - lay ta - ru - ah, Ha - le - lu - hu ba -
4
ma, Ha - le-lu - hu ba - tzil - tzi-lay ta - ru - ah, Ha - le - lu -
div.
Vln. I
Vln. II
Vla.
Vc.
Cb.

116
I
Maracas
Organ 1
Organ 2
Voices
Ha - le - lu - hu ba-tzil - tzi-lay ta - ru - ah, Ha - le - lu - hu ba-
— sha - ma, Ha - le - lu - hu ba-tzil - tzi-lay ta - ru - ah,
tzil - tzi - lay sha - ma, Ha - le - lu - hu ba - tzil - tzi-lay ta - ru - ah.
hu ba - tzil - tzi-lay sha - ma, Ha - le - lu - hu ba-tzil - tzi-lay ta - ru -
Vln. I
Vln. II
Vla.
Vc.
Cb.

122
Maracas
Organ 1
Organ 2
Voices
1
tzil - tzi - lay sha - ma, Ha - le - lu - hu ba - tzil - tzi - lay ta - ru - ah,
2
Ha - le - lu - hu ba-tzil - tzi-lay sha - ma, Ha - le - lu - hu ba-tzil - tzi - lay
3
Ha - le - lu - hu ba - tzil - tzi - lay sha - ma, Ha - le - lu - hu ba-tzil
4
ah, Ha - le - lu - hu ba - tzil-tzi-lay sha - ma, Ha - le - lu - hu
Vln. I
Vln. II
Vla.
Vc.
Cb.

30
J
129
Maracas
Organ 1
Organ 2
Voices
Kol han-sha - ma ta-ha - lail - yah Ha - le - lu - yah. Kol
Kol han-sha-ma ta - ha - lail - yah Ha - le - lu - yah.
Kol han - sha - ma ta-ha - lail - yah
Kol han - sha-ma ta - ha -
unis.
Vln. I
Vln. II
Vla.
Vc.
Cb.

138
K
Maracas
Organ 1
Organ 2
Voices
1
han - sha - ma ta - ha - lail - yah Ha - le - lu - yah. Kol
2
Kol han - sha-ma ta-ha - lail - yah Ha - le - lu - yah.
3
Ha - le - lu - yah. Kol han - sha - ma ta - ha - lail - yah
4
lail - yah Ha - le - lu - yah. Kol han - sha-ma ta - ha -
Vln. I
Vln. II
Vla.
Vc.
Cb.

146
L
Maracas
Organ 1
Organ 2
Voices
1
han-sha - ma ta-ha - lail - yah Ha - le - lu - yah. Kol
2
Kol han - sha-ma ta - ha - lail - yah Ha - le - lu - yah.
3
Ha - le - lu - yah. Kol han - sha - ma ta-ha - lail - yah
4
lail - yah Ha - le - lu - yah. Kol han - sha-ma ta - ha -
div.
Vln. I
Vln. II
Vla.
Vc.
Cb.

M
154
Maracas
Organ 1
Organ 2
Voices
1
han - sha - ma ta - ha - lail - yah Ha - le - lu - yah. Kol
2
Kol han - sha-ma ta - ha - lail - yah Ha - le - lu - yah.
3
Ha - le - lu - yah. Kol han - sha - ma ta - ha - lail - yah
4
lail - yah Ha - le - lu - yah. Kol han - sha - ma ta - ha -
Vln. I
Vln. II
Vla.
Vc.
Cb.

162
N
Maracas
Organ 1
Organ 2
Voices
1
han - sha - ma ta - ha - lail - yah Ha - le - lu - yah.
2
Kol han - sha - ma ta - ha - lail - yah Ha - le - lu
3
Ha - le - lu - yah. Kol han - sha - ma ta - ha - lail - yah
4
lail - yah Ha - le - lu - yah. Kol han - sha-ma
unis.
Vln. I
Vln. II
Vla.
Vc.
Cb.

31
170
O I Poco accel.
Clar. 1
Ob.
E.H., Bsn.
Maracas
Tamb. 1
2
Voices
4 (High S.)
2 (Lyric S.)
Ha - le - lu - hu ba - tof u - ma - chol,
3 (Alto)
Ha - le - lu - hu ba - tof u - ma - chol,
Vln. I
Vln. II
Vla.
Vc.
Cb.

174
♩= 152
Ola
Clar. 1
Ob.
E.H., Bsn.
Maracas
Tamb. 1
2
4
Voices 2
Ha - le - lu - hu ba - mi - nim va - u - gav,
3
Ha - le - lu - hu ba - mi - nim va - u - gav,
Vln. I
Vln. II
Vla.
Vc.
Cb.

179
OII
Clar. 1
Ob.
E.H., Bsn.
Maracas
1
Tamb.
2
4
Ha - le - lu - - hu ba - tzil - tzi -
Voices 2
Ha - le - lu - - hu ba - tzil - tzi -
3
Ha - le - lu - - hu ba - tzil - tzi -
div.
Vln. I
div.
Vln. II
Vla.
Vc.
Cb.

184
OIIa
Clar. 1
Ob.
E.H., Bsn.
Maracas
1
Tamb.
2
4
lay sha - ma sha - ma,
Voices 2
lay sha - ma sha - ma, Ha - le -
3
lay sha - ma sha - ma, Ha - le -
Vln. I
Vln. II
Vla.
Vc.
Cb.

189
Clar. 1
Ob.
E.H., Bsn.
Maracas
1
Tamb.
2
4
Voices 2
lu - hu ba - tzil - tzi - lay ta - ru - ah,
3
lu - hu ba - tzil - tzi - lay ta - ru - ah,
Vln. I
non div.
Vln. II
Vla.
Vc.
pizz.
Cb.

193
Clar. 1
Ob.
E.H., Bsn.
Maracas
1
Tamb.
2
4
Kol han - sha - ma
Voices 2
Kol han - sha - ma ta - ha - lail - yah Ha -
3
Kol han - sha - ma ta - ha - lail - yah Ha -
Vln. I
unis.
Vln. II
div.
unis.
Vla.
Vc.
Cb.
arco

197
OIIIa
Clar. 1
Ob.
E.H., Bsn.
Maracas
1
Tamb.
2
4
Voices 2
le - lu - yah. Kol han - sha - ma ta - ha - lail -
3
le - lu - yah. Kol han - sha - ma ta - ha - lail -
div.
Vln. I
Vln. II
Vla.
Vc.
Cb.

202
Clar. 1
Ob.
E.H., Bsn.
Maracas
1
Tamb.
2
4
Ha - le - lu - yah.
Voices 2
yah Ha - le - lu - yah.
3
yah Ha - le - lu - yah.
Vln. I
Vln. II
Vla.
Vc.
Cb.

32
207
P I
Clar. 1
Ob.
E.H., Bsn.
Maracas
1
Tamb.
2
4
Voices 2
3
non div.
Vln. I
non div.
Vln. II
Vla.
Vc.
Cb.

210
Pla
Clar. 1
Ob.
E.H., Bsn.
Maracas
Tamb.
1
2
Voices
4
2
3
Vln. I
Vln. II
Vla.
Vc.
Cb.

213
Clar. 1
Ob.
E.H., Bsn.
Maracas
Tamb.
1
2
4
Voices
2
3
Vln. I
Vln. II
Vla.
Vc.
Cb.

216
PII
Clar. 1
Ob.
E.H., Bsn.
Maracas
Tamb.
1
2
4
Voices
2
3
Vln. I
Vln. II
Vla.
Vc.
Cb.

219
PIIa
Clar. 1
Ob.
E.H., Bsn.
Maracas
Tamb. 1
2
Voices 4
2
3
Vln. I
Vln. II
Vla.
Vc.
Cb.

223
Clar. 1
Ob.
E.H., Bsn.
Maracas
Tamb. 1
Tamb. 2
Voices 4
Voices 2
Voices 3
Vln. I
Vln. II
Vla.
Vc.
Cb.

*This movement contains no letter Q.

228
RIa
Clar. 1
Ob.
E.H., Bsn.
Maracas
1
Tamb.
2
4
chol,
Ha - le -
Voices 2
chol,
Ha - le -
3
chol,
Ha - le -
Vln. I
Vln. II
Vla.
Vc.
Cv.

231
Clar. 1
Ob.
E.H., Bsn.
Maracas
Tamb.
1
2
Voices
4
lu - hu ba - mi - nim va - u - gav,
2
lu - hu ba - mi - nim va - u - gav,
3
lu - hu ba - mi - nim va - u - gav,
Vln. I
Vln. II
Vla.
Vc.
Cb.

234
RII
Clar. 1
Ob.
E.H., Bsn.
Maracas
Tamb. 1
2
Voices 4
Ha - le - lu - hu ba - tzil - tzi - lay
2
Ha - le - lu - hu ba - tzil - tzi - lay
3
Ha - le - lu - hu ba - tzil - tzi - lay
Vln. I
Vln. II
Vla.
Vc.
Cb.

237
RIIa
Clar. 1
Ob.
E.H., Bsn.
Maracas
Tamb.
Voices
sha - ma, Ha - le - lu - hu ba -
Vln. I
Vln. II
Vla.
Vc.
Cb.

241
Clar. 1
Ob.
E.H., Bsn.
Maracas
Tamb. 1
Tamb. 2
Voices 4
tzil - tzi - lay ta - ru - ah,
Voices 2
tzil - tzi - lay ta - ru - ah,
3
tzil - tzi - lay ta - ru - ah,
Vln. I
Vln. II
Vla.
Vc.
Cb.

243
RIII
Clar. 1
Ob.
E.H., Bsn.
Maracas
Tamb.
Voices
Kol han - - sha - ma ta - ha - lail - yah, Ha -
Vln. I
Vln. II
Vla.
Vc.
Cb.

246
RIIIa
Clar. 1
Ob.
E.H., Bsn.
Maracas
Tamb. 1
Tamb. 2
Voices 4
le - lu - yah, Kol han - sha - ma ta - ha - lail -
Voices 2
le - lu - yah, Kol han - sha - ma ta - ha - lail -
Voices 3
le - lu - yah, Kol han - sha - ma ta - ha - lail -
Vln. I
Vln. II
Vla.
Vc.
Cb.

250
Clar. 1
Ob.
E.H., Bsn.
Maracas
Tamb.
1
2
Voices
4
2
3
yah
Ha - le - lu - yah,
Vln. I
Vln. II
Vla.
Vc.
Cb.

*sounds an octave higher
**damp vibraphone note on every rest with hand not holding mallet.

256
Picc.
Fl.
Clar. 1
Clar. 2
Ob.
E.H.
Bsn.
Maracas
Crotales
hard rubber mallets
f
Vibes 1
Vibes 2
Tamb. 1 2
Org. 1
Org. 2
Voices 4 1
Voices 2 3
Ha - le - lu - yah,
Ha - le - lu - yah,
Vln. I
Vln. II
Vla.
Vc.
Cb.
f
f

260
T
Picc.
Fl.
Clar. 1 2
Ob.
E.H.
Bsn.
Maracas
Crotales
Vibes 1 2
Tamb. 1 2
Org. 1
Org. 2
Voices 4 1 2 3
Ha - le - lu - yah, Ha - le - lu - yah, Ha -
Voice 3
Vln. I
Vln. II
Vla.
Vc.
Cb.
pizz.
f

265
Picc.
Fl.
Clar. 1 2
Ob.
E.H.
Bsn.
Maracas
Crotales
Vibes 1 2
Tamb. 1 2
Org. 1
Org. 2
Voices 4 1
le - lu - yah, Ha - le - lu - yah, Ha -
3
le - lu - yah, Ha - le - lu - yah, Ha -
Vln. I
Vln. II
Vla.
Vc.
Cb.

270
U
Picc.
Fl.
Clar.
Ob.
E.H.
Bsn.
Maracas
Crotales
Vibes
Tamb.
Org. 1
Org. 2
Voices
le - lu - - yah,
Ha - le - lu -
le - lu - yah,
Vln. I
Vln. II
Vla.
Vc.
Cb.

275
Breathe here if necessary.
Picc.
Fl.
Breathe here if necessary.
Clar. 1 2
Breathe here if necessary.
Ob.
E.H.
Bsn.
Maracas
Crotales
Vibes 1 2
Tamb. 1 2
Org. 1
Org. 2
Breathe here if necessary.
Voices 4 1
yah, Ha - le - lu - yah,
2 3
Ha - le - lu - yah, Ha - le - lu - yah,
Vln. I
Vln. II
Vla.
Vc.
arco
Cb.

281
Picc.
Fl.
Clar. 1 2
Ob.
E.H.
Bsn.
Maracas
Crotales
Vibes 1 2
Tamb. 1 2
Org. 1
Org. 2
Voices 4 1
Ha - le - lu - yah,
Voices 2 3
Ha - le - lu - yah,
Vln. I
Vln. II
Vla.
Vc.
Cb.

287
V
Picc.
Fl.
Clar. 1 2
Ob.
E.H.
Bsn.
Maracas
Crotales
Vibes 1 2
Tamb. 1 2
Org. 1
Org. 2
Voices 4 1 2 3
Ha - le - lu - yah, Ha -
Ha - le - lu - yah, Ha -
Vln. I
Vln. II
Vla.
Vc.
Cb.

292
Picc.
Fl.
Clar. 1 2
Ob.
E.H.
Bsn.
Maracas
Crotales
Vibes 1 2
Tamb. 1 2
Org. 1
Org. 2
Voices 4 1 2 3
le - - - lu - yah, Ha - le - lu -
le - - - lu - yah, Ha - le - lu -
Vln. I
Vln. II
Vla.
Vc.
Cb.

296
Picc.
Fl.
Clar.
Ob.
E.H.
Bsn.
Maracas
Crotales
Vibes
Tamb.
Org. 1
Org. 2
Voices
yah, Ha - le - lu - yah, Ha - le - lu -
yah, Ha - le - lu - yah, Ha - le - lu -
Vln. I
Vln. II
Vla.
Vc.
Cb.

300
Picc.
Fl.
Clar. 1 2
Ob.
E.H.
Bsn.
Maracas
Crotales
Vibes 1 2
Tamb. 1 2
Org. 1
Org. 2
Voices 4 1
yah,
Ha - le - lu -
2 3
yah,
Ha - le - lu -
Vln. I
Vln. II
Vla.
Vc.
Cb.

304
Picc.
Fl.
Clar. 1 2
Ob.
E.H.
Bsn.
Maracas
Crotales
damp
Vibes 1 2
Tamb. 1 2
Org. 1
Org. 2
Voices 4 1
yah,
Ha - le - lu - yah.
Voices 2 3
yah,
Ha - le - lu - yah.
Vln. I
Vln. II
Vla.
Vc.
Cb.
ff
fine

Hal-le-lú-hu ba-tóf u-ma-chól,	Praise him with drum and dance,
Hal-le-lú-hu ba-mi-ním va-u-gáv.	praise him with strings and winds.
Hal-le-lú-hu ba-tzil-tz-láy sha-máh,	Praise him with sounding cymbals,
Hal-le-lú-hu ba-tzil-tz-láy ta-ru-áh.	praise him with clanging cymbals.
Kol han-sha-má ta-ha-láil Yah,	Let all that breathes praise the Eternal,
Ha-le-lu-yáh.	Hallelujah.

—Psalm 150:4–6

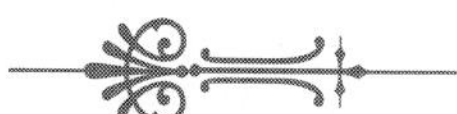

Steve Reich made his reputation in the 1960s and 1970s composing pieces in minimalist style, based on obsessive repetition of melodic or rhythmic figures over a steady pulse, with a focus on slow processes of musical change and on the material itself rather than on communicating a feeling or meaning. *Tehillim* marked a departure, continuing many elements of his earlier style while broadening it to embrace longer melodies, chordal harmonies, canons, constantly changing irregular meters, and expressive setting of words. This is Reich's first work to engage his own Jewish heritage and the first in many years to use a text, which accounts for the change in style. The title means "psalms" in Hebrew, and the text, excerpts from four Psalms in Hebrew, is at the center of the piece, both conceptually and musically. As Reich commented in notes to the original recording, he felt a need to set the psalm verses to melodies that reflected the rhythm and meaning of the words, and the other elements of the piece flowed from that decision. The tuned tambourines without jingles and the small pitched cymbals were meant to evoke ancient instruments mentioned in the psalms, and the four vocal soloists are asked to sing without vibrato in the manner of early music (music before 1750). The work was commissioned by West German Radio in Cologne, South German Radio in Stuttgart, and The Rothko Chapel in Houston, and was premiered in September 1981 by Reich's ensemble, Steve Reich and Musicians, on West German Radio. Reich later scored an alternate version with chamber orchestra, which is used on the accompanying recording.

Tehillim is in four parts, each using a different psalm excerpt and setting it in a different way in the four solo voices. Part I begins with a complete melodic setting of the text, then treats phrases of the melody in a series of canons. Part II sets the text syllabically in two-voice and then in three-voice homophony, then sets it again with longer melismas. Part III presents the text in short phrases in a dialogue between voices or pairs of voices, with the final syllable sustained at greater length as the text repeats several times. Part IV, shown here, combines aspects of all three procedures. The main melody appears at the outset with the complete text (including a repetition of the last of the three psalm verses), followed by four variations and a final section on "Haleluyah":

Measure	Section	Musical Description
1	1	Main melody in two-voice homophony
31	2	Main melody in two-voice canon
62	3	First phrase in four-voice canon, stated five times
102		Second phrase in four-voice canon, stated three times
129		Third phrase in four-voice canon, stated five times
170	4	Main melody varied, in lengthened durations with some altered pitches and brief melismas, alternating two-voice and three-voice homophony
207	5	Instrumental interlude (string chords for following vocal passage)
225		Main melody varied in top voice, transposed up a perfect fifth and elaborated with melismas and altered notes, in three-voice homophony
253	6	"Haleluyah" in short phrases in dialogue between paired voices, and later in four-voice homophony

The procedures from the preceding movements appear in order: sections 1 through 3 use procedures from Part I; sections 1, 4, and 5 use procedures from Part II; and section 6 uses those from Part III. In the canons, the following voices often decorate the opening of a phrase by adding a passing tone or other melodic variants, as at measures 33, 42, and 62–65. Reich uses rehearsal letters combined with roman numerals and lower-case letters to delineate sections and subsections; for example, the first section is marked with rehearsal letter A, the three psalm verses are designated AI, AII, and AIII, and the repetition of the third verse is marked AIIIa (see measures 1, 10, 19, and 25).

The main melody has more skips and leaps than steps, giving it an active, joyous character appropriate to the text. Both the melody and its counterpoints are diatonic, mostly in the D minor (or F major) scale, then moving back and forth between the F, G, and D major scales from measure 243 to the end. The contrasts of scale collection increase the intensity and sense of elation near the end of the piece, and they exploit a particular quality of the melody: its second half (measures 19–30) uses only the notes D, E, G, and A, which are shared as common tones among all three scales. The main melody appears to be modal, with each phrase ending on either A or E, but the accompanying lines and the chords in the orchestra do not clearly reinforce either as a modal center. The final sonority, combining notes of the A-major and G-major triads with A as the highest and lowest notes, emphasizes A, although Reich's own note on the piece says it ends in D major.

The singers are doubled by wind instruments and organs, and the strings play sustained diatonic but dissonant chords of five to seven notes. Up through measure 128, the strings play a repertoire of only five chords. The strings shift to the G-major scale collection for the third canon in section 3 (measure 129), then return to the original D minor with a much more varied palette of chords. At measure 207, the strings are featured in an interlude, then at measure 225 those same chords accompany the voices. From measure 243 to the end, the strings change diatonic collections frequently, along with the singers. Nowhere is there a clear sense of harmonic progression, or resolution to a pitch center; rather, the chords project the scale collection within which the voices move.

The meter is constantly changing in response to the natural speech rhythms of the text. The barlines follow the rhythm of the voices at the beginning, and usually of the top voice when the rhythmic patterns conflict, as they do during the canons in sections 2 and 3. Because of the fast pace, the eighth notes go by too quickly for the performers to count or for the conductor to beat. The rhythm is best conceived in terms of long beats (three eighth notes long) and short beats (two eighth notes long), as in Bulgarian dance meters (see discussion in NAWM 167). These groups of three and two are indicated in the score to aid the conductor, the threes by triangles and the twos by vertical lines.

The percussion rhythms derive from those of the voices, articulating every vocal note but also reflecting the groups of three and two. In section 1, for example, the first tambourine plays on the first and last eighth note of each group of three, and on the first eighth note of each group of two, resting on the second eighth notes. The second tambourine reinforces the downbeat of almost every measure and otherwise plays when the first tambourine rests, except that both rest together to mark the end of each line of text (as in measure 4) or the words "Halleluhu" ("praise him," as in measure 6), "Kol hanshamah" (measures 19–20, perhaps illustrating the text, "let all that breathes"), and "Haleluyah." When the first canon begins in section 2, the procedure is similar, but tambourine 1 is paired with voice 1 and tambourine 2 with voice 2.

At the beginning of section 3, the tambourines fade out and the maracas enter, continuing to play without a break until the end. The maracas player moves at twice the pace of the others, moving up and down in unbroken sixteenth notes. In order to avoid tiring out, the player alternates hands, playing for awhile with one hand, then starting to move the empty hand together with the first, then holding the instrument with both hands, and gradually passing it off to the second hand so the first can rest. In the final section, the vibraphones reinforce the tambourines, and the crotales (tuned cymbals) add echoes of the vocal Haleluyahs (measure 256).

John Adams (b. 1947)

Short Ride in a Fast Machine

Orchestral fanfare

1986

CD 14|35

Delirando (𝅗𝅥 = 152)

Clarinets in A*

Horns in F

Tpts.: always *extremely* short quarters

Trumpets in C

Trombones

High Wood Block

sim.

Percussion 1

Synthesizer 1**

N. B.: Volume balance between the two synthesizers must be *exactly* equal.

Synthesizer 2**

Cls. in A

Hns. in F

Tpts. in C

Tbns.

(High Wd. Blk.)

Perc. 1

Synth. 1

Synth. 2

* Clarinets 3 & 4 are optional.

** Synthesizer: the sound should be similar to an "analog brass" voice with a moderately fast attack, for example the "Anna Brass" preset on the Yamaha SY77. The speakers should be placed directly behind the players. The sound should never be mixed into the auditorium PA system. The level should be adjusted to mix with the rest of the orchestra and not predominate. The synthesizer parts are optional.

From John Adams, *Two Fanfares for Orchestra* (New York: Hendon Music, Boosey & Hawkes, 1992), 23–66.

Cls. in A
Hns. in F
Staccato quarters should be played as short as staccato eighths.
Tpts. in C
1. & 2.
Tbns.
(High Wd. Blk.)
sempre sim.
Perc. 1
Synth. 1
Synth. 2
Fl. 1 Picc. 1
a2
Fl. 2 Picc. 2
più f

Fl. 1
Picc. 1
ff
sim.
Fl. 2
Picc. 2
Obs.
Cls. in A
Hns. in F
Tpts. in C
Tbns.
(High Wd. Blk.)
Perc. 1
Synth. 1
Synth. 2

24
25
26
27
Fl. 1
Picc. 1
Fl. 2
Picc. 2
Obs.
Cls. in A
Hns. in F
Tpts. in C
Tbns.
(High Wd. Blk.)
Perc. 1
Sn. Dr. (rim shots)
Perc. 2
Synth. 1
Synth. 2
ff
sffz

28
29
30
31
Fl. 1
Picc. 1
Fl. 2
Picc. 2
Obs.
Cls. in A
ff
Hns. in F
sffz
Tpts. in C
mf
Tbns.
(High Wd. Blk.)
Perc. 1
(Sn. Dr. [rim shots])
Perc. 2
To Glock.
Synth. 1
Synth. 2

32
33
34
35
Fl. 1 Picc. 1
Fl. 2 Picc. 2
Obs.
Cls. in A
Hns. in F
Tpts. in C
Tbns.
Perc. 1
Perc. 2
Perc. 3
Synth. 1
Synth. 2
(High Wd. Blk.)
Glock. (metal mallets)
Crotales (metal mallets)
L.V.
sim.
ff
f

36
37
38
Fl. 1
Picc. 1
Fl. 2
Picc. 2
Obs.
Cls. in A
Hns. in F
Tpts. in C
Tbns.
Perc. 1
Perc. 2
Perc. 3
Synth. 1
Synth. 2
(High Wd. Blk.)
(Glock.)
(Crot.)
L.V.
sim.
ff

Fl. 1 Picc. 1
Fl. 2 Picc. 2
ff
Obs.
Cls. in A
Hns. in F
Tpts in C
Tbns.
(High Wd. Blk.)
Perc. 1
To Susp. Cym.
(sponge mallets)
Perc. 3
p
Synth. 1
Synth. 2

Fl. 1 Picc. 1
Fl. 2 Picc. 2
Obs.
Cls. in A
Hns. in F
fff
mf subito
Tpts. in C
Tbns.
(High Wd. Blk.)
Perc. 1
(Susp. Cym.)
(Let ring)
Perc. 3
ff
Synth. 1
Synth. 2

46
47
48
Fl. 1
Picc. 1
Fl. 2
Picc. 2
Obs.
Cls. in A
Hns. in F
Tpts. in C
Tbns
(High Wd. Blk.)
Perc. 1
(Sn. Dr. [rim shots])
To Crotales
Perc. 2
Synth. 1
Synth. 2
ff
p
sffz

49
50
51
Fl. 1
Picc. 1
Fl. 2
Picc. 2
Obs.
Cls. in A
Hns. in F
Tpts. in C
Tbns.
f
sffz
(High Wd. Blk.)
Perc. 1
(Crotales)
Perc. 2
mf
ff
L.V.
(Susp. Cym.)
Perc. 3
(cut off immediately)
Synth. 1
Synth. 2

* A regular bass drum with hand-held beater played by another percussionist may be substituted here for greater intensity.

56
57
58
59
Fls. 1 2
Obs. 1 2
Eng. Hn.
Cls. in A 1 3
2 4
Bsns. 1 2
3
Hns. in F 1 2
3 4
(High Wd. Blk.)
Perc. 1
sfz
(Ped. Bs. Dr.)
Synth. 1
Synth. 2
Vln. I
(non div.)
Vln. II
Vla.
Vcl.

Fls.
Obs.
Eng. Hn.
Cls. in A
Bsns.
Hns. in F
Tpts. in C
Tbns.
(High Wd. Blk.)
Perc. 1
(Ped. Bs. Dr.)
sfz
Synth. 1
Synth. 2
(non div.)
Vln. I
Vln. II
Vla.
Vcl.

64
65
66
67
Fls. 1 2
Obs. 1 2
Eng. Hn.
Cls. in A 1 3 2 4
Bsns. 1 2 3
Hns. in F 1 2 3 4
Tpts. in C 1 2 3 4
Tbns. 1 2 3
(High Wd. Blk.)
Perc. 1
(Ped. Bs. Dr.)
sfz
Synth. 1
Synth. 2
Vln. I
Vln. II
Vla.
Vcl.

Fls. 1 2
Obs. 1 2
Eng. Hn.
Cls. in A 1 3 2 4
Bsns. 1 2 3
Hns. in F 1 2 3 4
Tpts. in C 1 2 3 4
Tbns. 1 2 3
Timp.
Perc. 1
Perc. 2
Synth. 1
Synth. 2
Vln. I
Vln. II
Vla.
Vcl.
68
69
70
71
sffz
a2
gliss.
ff
Wood sticks
(High Wd. Blk.)
(Ped. Bs. Dr.)
sfz
Large Bs. Dr.
On the string - (non div.)
On the string
div.
unis.

72
73
74
Fls. 1 2
Obs. 1 2
Eng. Hn.
Cls. in A 1 3 2 4
Bsns. 1 2 3
Hns. in F 1 2 3 4
Tpts. in C 1 2 3 4
Tbns. 1 2 3
Timp.
Perc. 1
(High Wd. Blk.)
Perc. 2
(Large Bs. Dr.)
Perc. 3
Sizzle Cym.
L. V.
Synth. 1
Synth. 2
Vln. I
Vln. II
Vla.
Vcl.
sffz
ff
sff

75
76
77
Fls. 1 2
Obs. 1 2
Eng. Hn.
Cls. in A 1 3 2 4
Bsns. 1 2 3
Hns. in F 1 2 3 4
ff
Tpts. in C 1 2 3 4
Tbns. 1 2 3
Timp.
sffz
fff
(High Wd. Blk.)
Perc. 1
(Large Bs. Dr.)
Perc. 2
Sn. Dr. (rim shots)
(Sizzle Cym.)
Sizzle Cym.
Perc. 3
Synth. 1
Synth. 2
Vln. I
Vln. II
Vla.
Vcl.

37
Fls. 1 2
Obs. 1 2
a2
f staccato!
Eng. Hn.
f staccato!
Cls. in A 1 3 2 4
to Cls. in B♭
to Cls. in B♭
Bsns. 1 2 3
Hns. in F 1 2 3 4
Tpts. in C 1 2 3 4
Tbns. 1 2 3
Timp.
(High Wd. Blk.)
Low Wd. Blk.
Perc. 1
(Large Bs. Dr.)
Perc. 2
To Tamb.
(Sizzle Cym.)
Perc. 3
Dampen immediately
Synth. 1
Synth. 2
Vln. I
Vln. II
f Off the string
Vla
f Off the string
Vcl.

82
83
84
85
86
Obs. 1 2
Eng. Hn.
Cls. 1 in B♭ 2
Bsns. 1 2 3
Contra-Bsn.
f secco
Hns. 1 in F 2
Trb. 3 Tuba
a2
(Low Wd. Blk.)
Perc. 1
Ped. Bs. Dr.
Tamb.
Perc. 2
mf
Synth. 1
Synth. 2
(non div.)
Vln. I (div.)
sfz
Vln. II
div.
Vla.
Vcl. Cbs.
ff

Obs. 1 2
Eng. Hn.
Cls. 1 in B♭ 2
Bsns. 1 2 3
Contra-Bsn.
Trb. 3 Tuba
(Low Wd. Blk.)
Perc. 1
(Ped. Bs. Dr.)
(Tamb.)
Perc. 2
Synth. 1
Synth. 2
Vln. I
sim.
Vln. II
Vla. (div.)
(non div.)
Vcl. Cbs.

92
93
94
95
96
Obs. 1 2
Eng. Hn.
Cls. 1 in B♭ 2
Bsns. 1 2 3
Contra-Bsn.
Tbn. 3 Tuba
(Low Wd. Blk.)
Perc. 1
(Ped. Bs. Dr.)
(Tamb.)
Perc. 2
Synth. 1
Synth. 2
Vln. I
(non div.)
Vln. II
Vla.
Vcl. Cbs.

97
98
99
100
101
Piccs. 1 2
Fls. 1 2
Obs. 1 2
Eng. Hn.
Cls. 1 in B♭ 2
Bsns. 1 2 3
Contra-Bsn.
Hns. in F 1 2 3 4
Tpts. in C 1 2 3 4
Tbn. 3 Tuba
* Tbn. 3: omit low G's if necessary
Timp.
Felt sticks
Perc. 1
(Low Wd. Blk.)
Perc. 2
(Ped. Bs. Dr.)
(Tamb.)
Perc. 3
Sn. Dr. (ord.)
Synth. 1
Synth. 2
Vln. I
Vln. II
Vla.
Vcl. Cbs.
subito f

102
103
104
105
106
Piccs. 1 2
always extremely short quarters
sff
sim.
Fls. 1 2
Obs. 1 2
ff
f
Eng. Hn.
Cls. 1 in B♭ 2
Bsns. 1 2 3
Contra-Bsn.
Hns. in F 1 2 3 4
Tpts. in C 1 2 3 4
sffz
Tbns. 1 2
Tbn. 3 Tuba
Timp.
sempre f
(Low Wd. Blk.)
Perc. 1
(Ped. Bs. Dr.)
(Tamb.)
Perc. 2
(Sn. Dr.)
Perc. 3
Synth. 1
Synth. 2
(div.)
Vln. I
Vln. II
Vla.
Vcl. Cbs.

107
108
109
110
Piccs. 1 2
Fls. 1 2
Obs. 1 2
Eng. Hn.
Cls. 1 in B♭ 2
Bsns. 1 2 3
Contra-Bsn.
Hns. in F 1 2 3 4
Tpts. in C 1 2 3 4
Tbns. 1 2
Tbn. 3 Tuba
Timp.
(Low Wd. Blk.)
Perc. 1
(Ped. Bs. Dr.)
(Tamb.)
Perc. 2
(Sn. Dr.)
Perc. 3
Synth. 1
Synth. 2
Vln. I
Vln. II
Vla.
Vcl. Cbs.
ff
f

111
112
113
114
Piccs. 1 2
Fls. 1 2
Obs. 1 2
Eng. Hn.
Cls. in B♭ 1 2
Bsns. 1 2 3
Contra-Bsn.
Hns. in F 1 2 3 4
Tpts. in C 1 2 3 4
Tbns. 1 2
Tbn. 3 Tuba
Timp.
Perc. 1
Perc. 2
Perc. 3
Synth. 1
Synth. 2
Vln. I
Vln. II
Vla.
Vcl. Cbs.
sempre ff
(Low Wd. Blk.)
(Ped. Bs. Dr.)
(Tamb.)
(Sn. Dr.)
(divisi if necessary)

115
116
117
118
Piccs. 1 2
Fls. 1 2
Obs. 1 2
Eng. Hn.
Cls. 1 in B♭ 2
Bsns. 1 2 3
Contra-Bsn.
Hns. in F 1 2 3 4
Tpts. in C 1 2 3 4
Tbns. 1 2
Tbn. 3 Tuba
Timp.
(Low Wd. Blk.)
Perc. 1
(Ped. Bs. Dr.)
(Tamb.)
Perc. 2
(Sn. Dr.)
Perc. 3
To Sizzle Cym.
Synth. 1
Synth. 2
Vln. I
Vln. II
Vla.
Vcl. Cbs.

38
119
120
121
122
Piccs. 1 2
Fls. 1 2
Obs. 1 2
Eng. Hn.
Cls. 1 in B♭ 2
Bsns. 1 2 3
Contra-Bsn.
Hns. in F 1 2 3 4
Tpts. in C 1 2 3 4
Tbns. 1 2
Tbn. 3 Tuba
Timp.
Perc. 1
Perc. 2
Perc. 3
Synth. 1
Synth. 2
Vln. I
Vln. II
Vla.
Vcl. Cbs.
very short quarters
to Cls. in A
a2
(Low Wd. Blk.)
(Ped. Bs. Dr.)
(Tamb.)
Sizzle Cym.
(High Wd. Blk.)
L. V.

Piccs.
Fls.
Obs.
Eng. Hn.
Bsns.
Bsn. 3 C. Bsn.
Hns. in F
Tpts. in C
Tbns.
Tuba
Timp.
Perc. 1
Synth. 1
Synth. 2
Vln. I (div.)
Vln. II (div.)
Vla.
Vcl. Cbs.
sempre fff
(High Wd. Blk.)
(non div.)
(div.)
sim.

Piccs. 1 2
Fls. 1 2
Obs. 1 2
Eng. Hn.
Bsns. 1 2
Bsn. 3 C. Bsn.
Hns. in F
Tpts. in C
Tbns.
Tuba
Timp.
(High Wd. Blk.)
Perc. 1
Ped. Bs. Dr.
Perc. 2
Bs. Dr.
Large Tam Tam
Perc. 3
Synth. 1
Synth. 2
Vln. I
Vln. II
Vla.
Vcl. Cbs.

Piccs.
Fls.
Obs.
Eng. Hn.
Cls. in A
Bsns.
Bsn. 3 C. Bsn.
Hns. in F
Tpts. in C
Tbns.
Tbn. 3 Tuba
Timp.
Perc. 1
Perc. 2
Perc. 3
Synth. 1
Synth. 2
Vln. I
Vln. II
Vla. (div.)
Vcl.
Cbs.
sim.
(High Wd. Blk.)
Med. Wd. Blk.
mf (subito)
(Ped. Bs. Dr.)
sfff sempre
(Bs. Dr.)
(Large Tam Tam)
dampen immediately
Bsn. 3
div.
unis.
(half)

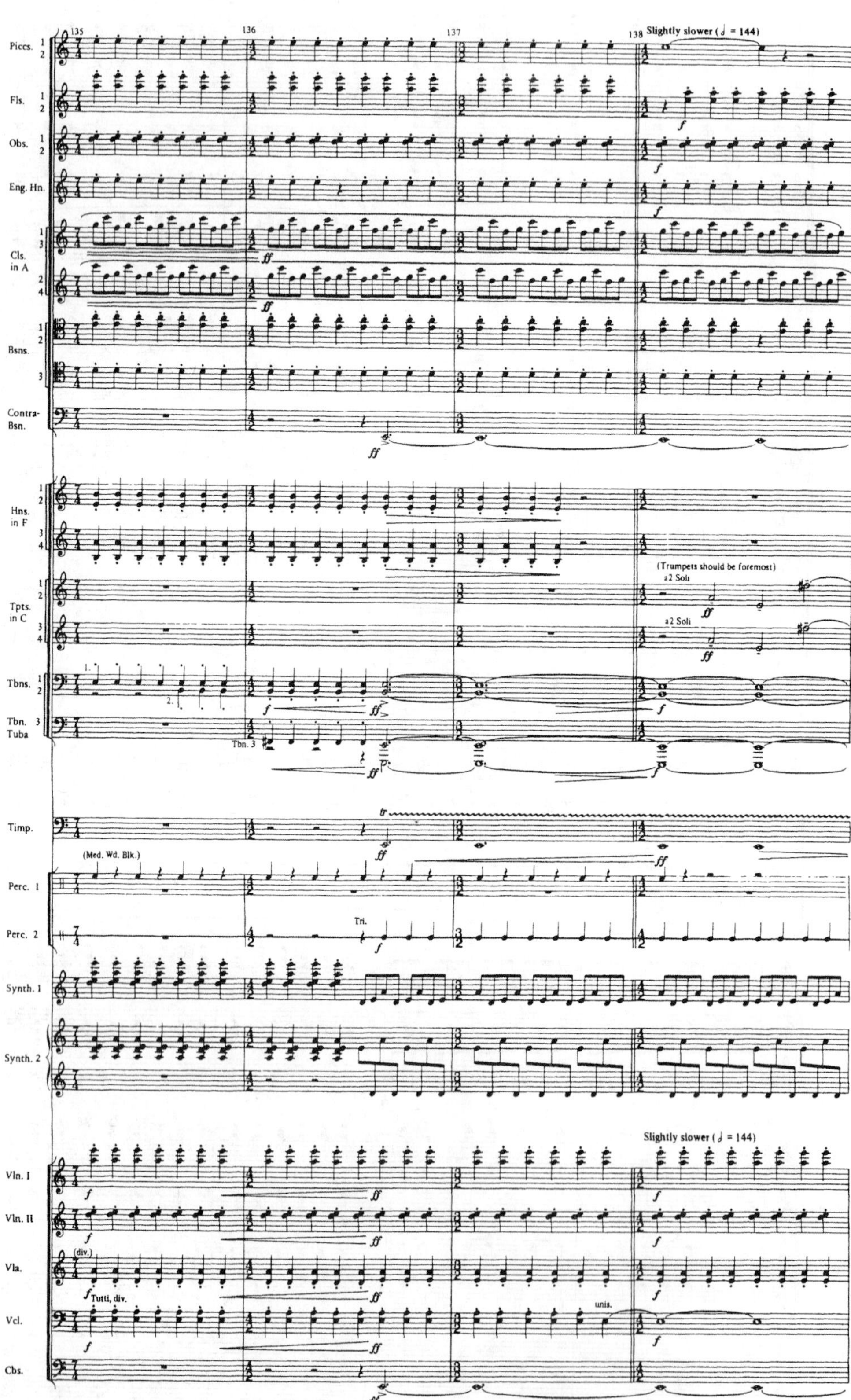
135
136
137
138 Slightly slower (♩ = 144)
Piccs. 1 2
Fls. 1 2
Obs. 1 2
Eng. Hn.
Cls. in A 1 3 2 4
Bsns. 1 2 3
Contra-Bsn.
Hns. in F 1 2 3 4
(Trumpets should be foremost)
a2 Soli
Tpts. in C 1 2 3 4
Tbns. 1 2
Tbn. 3 Tuba
Tbn. 3
Timp.
(Med. Wd. Blk.)
Perc. 1
Perc. 2
Tri.
Synth. 1
Synth. 2
Slightly slower (♩ = 144)
Vln. I
Vln. II
(div.)
Vla.
Tutti, div.
unis.
Vcl.
Cbs.

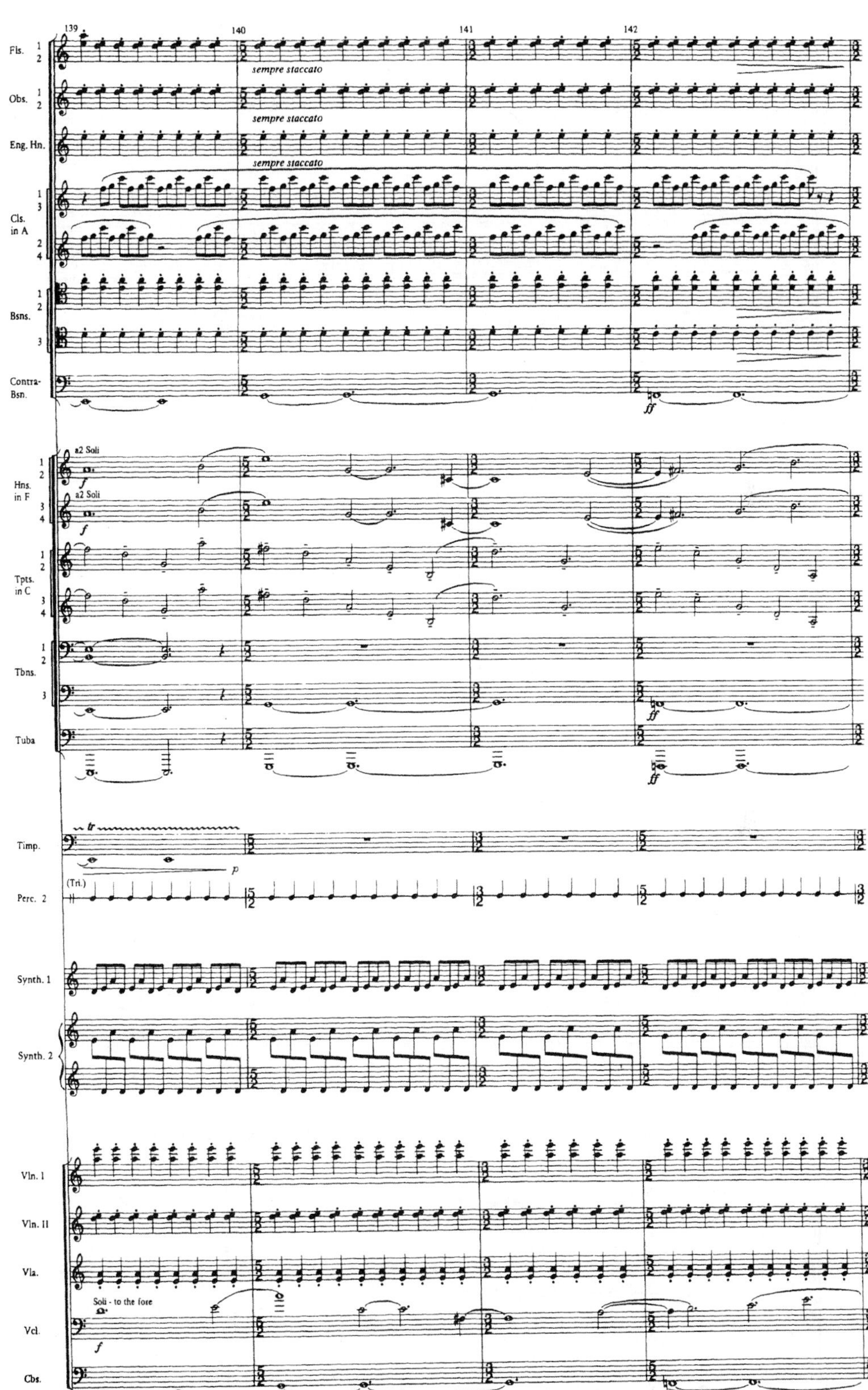
139
140
141
142
Fls. 1 2
sempre staccato
Obs. 1 2
sempre staccato
Eng. Hn.
sempre staccato
Cls. in A 1 3 2 4
Bsns. 1 2 3
Contra-Bsn.
ff
Hns. in F 1 2 3 4
a2 Soli
f
Tpts. in C 1 2 3 4
Tbns. 1 2 3
Tuba
Timp.
tr
p
Perc. 2
(Tri.)
Synth. 1
Synth. 2
Vln. I
Vln. II
Vla.
Vcl.
Soli - to the fore
Cbs.

143
144
145
146
Piccs. 1 2
Obs. 1 2
Eng. Hn.
Cls. in A 1 3
2 4
Bsns. 1 2
a2
Bsn. 3 C. Bsn.
Hns in F 1 2
3 4
Tpts. in C 1 2
3 4
Tbn. 3 Tuba
Perc. 1
Xylo. (hard mallets)
Perc. 2
(Tri.)
Perc. 3
Crot. (metal beaters)
L. V.
ff
p
Synth. 1
Synth. 2
Vln. I
Vln. II
Vla.
Vcl.
Cbs.

(Dynamic envelopes apply only to Piccolos)
147
148
149
150
Piccs. 1 2
sempre staccato
ff
Fl. 1
Ob. 1
sempre staccato
Fl. 2
Ob. 2
sempre staccato
Eng. Hn.
sempre staccato
Cls. in A
Bsns. 1 2
Bsn. 3
C. Bsn.
Hns. in F
Tpts. in C
Tbn. 3
Tuba
Timp.
tr
(Xylo.)
Perc 1
p
(Tri.)
Perc. 2
sempre f
(Crot.)
Perc. 3
L. V.
Synth. 1
Synth. 2
sempre staccato
Vln. I
Vln. II
(unis.)
Vla.
Vcl.
Cbs.

151
152
153
154
Piccs. 1 2
ff
ff
f
ff
Fl. 1
Ob. 1
Fl. 2
Ob. 2
Bsn. 1 2
Bsn. 3
C. Bsn.
Hns. in F 1 2 3 4
f
f
Tpts. in C 1 2 3 4
Tbn. 3
Tuba
f
Timp.
tr
pp
(Xylo.)
Perc. 1
ff
ff
f
ff
(Tri.)
Perc. 2
(Crot.)
Perc. 3
L. V.
ff
Synth. 1
Synth. 2
Vln. I
sempre ff
Vln. II
sempre ff
Vla.
sempre ff
Vcl.
Cbs.
f

155
156
157
158
Piccs. 1 2
Fl. 1 Ob. 1
Fl. 2 Ob. 2
Cls. in A
Bsns. 1 2
Bsn. 3 C. Bsn.
Hns. in F
Tpt. in C
Tbn. 3 Tuba
Timp.
(Xylo.)
Perc. 1
(Tri.)
Perc. 2
sempre ff
Sizzle Cym.
Perc. 3
L. V
Synth. 1
Synth. 2
Vln. I
Vln. II
Vla.
Vcl.
Cbs.

Picc. 1 2
Fls. 1 2
Obs. 1 2
Eng. Hn.
Cls. in A 1 3 2 4
Bsns. 1 2
Bsn. 3 C. Bsn.
Hns in F 1 2 3 4
Tpts. in C 1 2 3 4
Tbn. 3 Tuba
Timp.
(Xylo.)
Perc. 1
(Tri.)
Perc. 2
Synth. 1
Synth. 2
Vln. I
Vln. II
Vla.
Vcl.
Cbs.
159
160
161
162

163
164
165
166
Piccs.
Fls.
Obs.
Eng. Hn.
Cls. in A
Bsns.
Bsn. C. Bsn.
Hns. in F
Tpts. in C
Tbns.
Tbn. Tuba
(Xylo.)
Perc. 1
(Tri.)
Perc. 2
(Sizzle Cym.)
Perc. 3
L. V.
Synth. 1
Synth. 2
8va
Vln. I
(unis.)
Vln. II
Vla.
Vcl.
Cbs.

167
168
169
170
Piccs. 1 2
Fls. 1 2
Obs. 1 2
Cls. in A 1 3 2 4
Bsns. 1 2
Bsn. 3 C. Bsn.
Hns. in F 1 2 3 4
Bells in the air
Bells in the air
Tpts. in C 1 2 3 4
Tbns. 1 2
Tbn. 3 Tuba
Timp.
(Xylo.)
Perc. 1
(Tri.)
Perc. 2
(Sizzle Cym.)
Perc. 3
Synth. 1
Synth. 2
(8va)
Vln. I
Vln. II
Vla.
Vcl.
Cbs.

Poco allargando
171
172
173
174
Piccs. 1 2
Fls. 1 2
Obs. 1 2
Eng. Hn.
Cls. in A 1 3 2 4
Bsns. 1 2
Bsn. 3 C. Bsn.
Hns. in F 1 2 3 4
Tpts. in C 1 2 3 4
Tbns. 1 2
Tbn. 3 Tuba
Timp.
(Xylo.)
Perc. 1
(Tri.)
Perc. 2
To Tam Tam
(Sizzle Cym.)
Perc. 3
Synth. 1
Synth. 2
Poco allargando
(8va)
Vln. I
sim.
Vln. II
sim.
Vla.
sim.
Vcl.
Cbs.

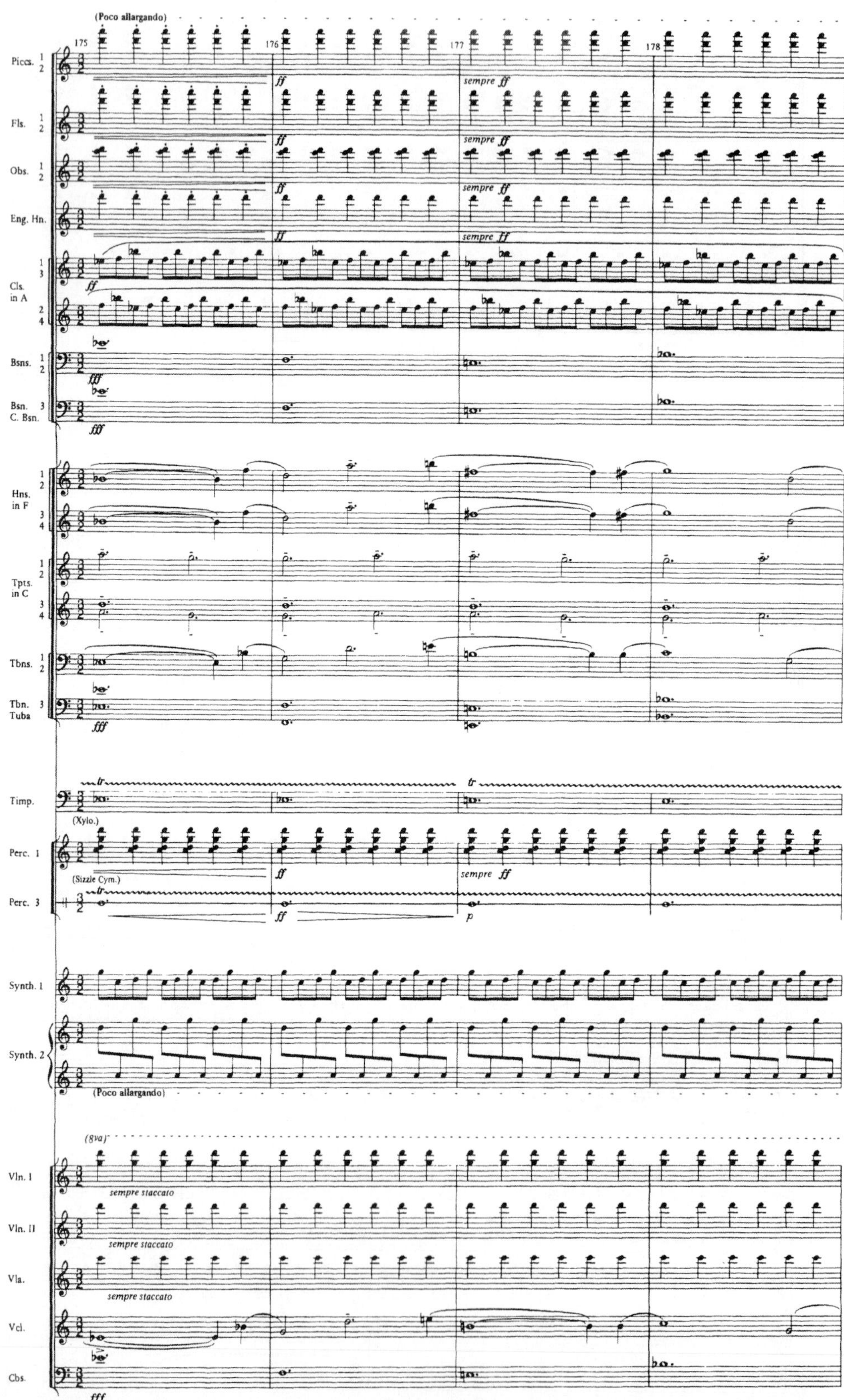
(Poco allargando)
175
176
177
178
Piccs. 1 2
ff
sempre ff
Fls. 1 2
Obs. 1 2
Eng. Hn.
Cls. in A 1 3 2 4
Bsns. 1 2
fff
Bsn. 3 C. Bsn.
Hns. in F 1 2 3 4
Tpts. in C 1 2 3 4
Tbns. 1 2
Tbn. 3 Tuba
Timp.
tr
(Xylo.)
Perc. 1
(Sizzle Cym.)
Perc. 3
p
Synth. 1
Synth. 2
(8va)
Vln. I
sempre staccato
Vln. II
Vla.
Vcl.
Cbs.

(Poco allargando)
Tempo I (𝅗𝅥 = 152)
179
180
181
182
Piccs. 1 2
Fls. 1 2
Obs. 1 2
Eng. Hn.
Cls. in A 1 3 2 4
Bsns. 1 2
Bsn. 3 C. Bsn.
Hns. in F 1 2 3 4
Tpts. in C 1 2 3 4
Tbns. 1 2
Tbn. 3 Tuba
Timp.
(Xylo.)
Perc. 1
To Tamb.
Tam Tam
Perc. 2
L. V.
To Sn. Dr.
(Sizzle Cym.)
Perc. 3
To Crot.
Synth. 1
Synth. 2
(Poco allargando)
Tempo I (𝅗𝅥 = 152)
(loco)
(div.)
Vln. I
div.
Vln. II
Vla.
Vcl.
Cbs.

183
184
185
186
187
188
Picc. 1
Fl. 1
Picc. 2
Fl. 2
Obs.
Cls. in A
Bsns.
Bsn. 3
C. Bsn.
Hns. in F
Tpts. in C
Tbns.
Tbn. 3
Tuba
Timp.
Perc. 1
Perc. 2
Perc. 3
Vln. I
Vln. II
Vla.
Vcl.
Cbs.
Fl. 1
Picc. 1
Fl. 2
Picc. 2
fff
sfff
Tamb.
Sn. Dr. (rim shots)
Bass Dr.
Crot.
sim.
non div.

John Adams's *Short Ride in a Fast Machine* was commissioned by the Great Woods Festival in Massachusetts and premiered in 1986 by the Pittsburgh Symphony Orchestra, conducted by Michael Tilson Thomas. Adams called it a "fanfare for orchestra," and it has some of the spirit of a fanfare, featuring the brass and building to a rousing climax. The title refers to the rapid, motoric rhythm of the piece, whose exhilarating effect and audience appeal have made it one of Adams's most frequently programmed compositions.

Like several of his other works of the 1980s, such as the symphonic suite *Harmonielehre* and the opera *Nixon in China*, this piece uses minimalist techniques to create a complex musical fabric that hardly deserves the word "minimalist." Building on a minimalist foundation of constant pulsation and repetition of simple rhythmic and melodic material, Adams enriched his music with more rapid changes, greater harmonic variety, and emotional surges. Most of the ideas are simple, but by varying and layering them in unpredictable ways, he creates ever-changing textures. A woodblock establishes a steady pulse, and the other instruments play off it, some moving in lockstep with it while others feature contrasting meters, syncopations, or irregular accents. Very common throughout are groupings of three at different metric levels; for instance, in measures 7–13, the woodblock and synthesizer 2 articulate half-notes in the $\frac{3}{2}$ meter, the brass chords repeat in groupings of three quarter notes, and the clarinet and synthesizer 1 ostinatos move in groups of three eighth notes, so that $\frac{3}{8}$, $\frac{3}{4}$, and $\frac{3}{2}$ meters all sound at once.

The piece begins and ends on a pitch center of D, but the harmony is not tonal. Rather, a sense of harmonic motion is suggested by changing the pitch collection, the set of notes in circulation at any moment. Sometimes several notes in the collection will change at once. Adams calls these points of change "gates," a term borrowed from electronic music, referring to the switches that regulate the flow of electrical current. At other times, single notes will be added, dropped, or altered chromatically, creating a sense of gradual movement Adams calls "landscape," as if one is moving through a landscape that gradually changes character. As in music by Debussy and Stravinsky, changes of pitch collection are often coordinated with changes of figuration and timbre, especially at section breaks.

In the first section, the woodblock sets the pace, joined by rapid ostinatos in clarinets and optional synthesizers that create a twittery background and establish the initial pitch collection of D, E, and A (the clarinets are in A, sounding a minor third lower than written). Over this the trumpets enter, playing repeated chords with the same notes, at first with the woodblock pulse and then in a hemiola against it. Other brass join in on the chords, adding new notes to the collection in the manner of Adams's landscape (F♯ in measure 10, C in measure 13, G in measure 14) as the rhythms grow more complex. Flutes and oboes add quick filigree figures in the upper register, and other percussion instruments join in as well. At measure 39, the pitch collection changes (D, E, F♯ and A continue to sound, but G and C move to G♯ and B), marked by a change in figuration in the upper winds, but the other parts keep rolling along.

A new section begins at measure 52 with the entrance of the strings and bassoons. Brass, winds, and strings now all move in rhythmic unison, playing repeated chords against the background of woodblock, clarinets, synthesizers, and percussion. The new section is set off by a gate: while the D–E–A ostinato continues, the rest of the pitch collection changes from an E-major triad in the preceding measures to a B♭-major triad at measure 52. Now the ostinatos and the repeated chords both change the harmony every few measures; a C-major triad is added at measure 57, and then other combinations appear, adding E-minor, F♯-minor, and E♭-major triads to the mix, which grows more dissonant as the section builds to a climax.

The machine changes gears in the middle of measure 79, introducing the contrasting middle section. The steady pulse continues, but on a lower woodblock; after 254 hits on the high woodblock, the new sound is a very audible change. The pitch content is stripped down to E♭ and B♭—the last two notes to be added in the previous section. Then, through the rest of the middle section, the collection of pitches in the pulsing chords and ostinatos changes every two to four measures. Over this a new idea appears: a staccato line in the bass instruments, marching in a meter of four beats per measure against the prevailing $\frac{3}{2}$ meter. The staccato bass line starts with alternating thirds but gradually expands its range and repertoire of intervals, eventually including all but the major seventh. As it becomes increasingly unpredictable, it moves through all twelve notes of the chromatic scale by measure 101 (the D♭ on the downbeat is the twelfth). At this point new layers are added to the texture, more prominently *sforzando* brass and wind chords, snare drum, and timpani. The chord progression of measures 80–100 repeats with variations and omissions, and the staccato bass line continues to expand its range, going through a second round of all twelve notes. The end of the section (measures 117–21) is marked by a crescendo, rolls in drums and cymbal, a descending bass line, and a gradual return to ostinatos and harmonies on D, E, and A, preparing the varied return of the opening section.

The return at measure 122 is marked by the high woodblock, the synthesizer ostinatos, and the rhythms in the brass and wind chords (compare the brass rhythms in measures 37–45 of the first section). A new element is the bass line, which leaps an octave and a sixth back and forth between C and A. After a brief halt at measure 133, the opening D–E–A chord and the clarinet ostinatos return as well.

The final section begins at measure 138 as the ostinatos and pulsating chords continue, the woodblock drops out, and three-part counterpoint begins between three wide-ranging lines: a quickly moving melody in trumpets, a slower mid-range line in horns and cellos, and a still slower bass line in trombones, tuba, contrabassoon, and contrabass. The pulsing chords and ostinatos change pitch collection more slowly now and remain exclusively diatonic, setting off the chromatic melodies in all three contrapuntal lines. From being the main event at the beginning of the piece, the ostinatos and repeating chords have now become the background accompaniment, the typical role such textures play in traditional tonal music. Once more the music swells to a climax, and after a brief fanfare-like coda, the piece concludes on a D major triad.

Music like this can be very hard to play, demanding pinpoint rhythm, rapid playing in the winds, and attention to small changes. It can be difficult to keep track of one's place when repeating a figure as the measures are flying by, but each performer has to be prepared for the next change in an ostinato or rhythm, such as the few spots where the woodblock varies its otherwise incessant beat (measures 59, 63, 121, and 132–35). After the continuously repeating chords, the emergence of a moving bass line in the middle section and then of intertwining, arching melodies in the brass, low strings, and bassoons seems like an emotional release, as satisfying to the players as it is for the listeners.

György Ligeti (1923–2006)

Étude No. 9, *Vertige*

Étude

1990

CD 14|39

Prestissimo *)**sempre molto legato,** 𝅝 **= 48** (very even / *sehr gleichmäßig*) **)

ppp

una corda
senza ped.

(4) ***)

(7)

(10)

(13)

*) So fast that the individual notes—even without pedal—almost melt into continuous lines.

**) The piece has no rhythmic metre—it consists of a continuous flow—therefore the bar lines only serve as a guideline.

***) The first four "bars" serve as a model indicating the compositional structure of the whole piece. After this point consistent notation has been dispensed with in order not to complicate the appearance of the music unnecessarily. The whole piece, however, should be interpreted as shown in the first four "bars": the chromatic runs break over each other like waves from different directions, and the interference pattern is irregular i.e. the time intervals between the entry points of the runs vary constantly. In addition, legato slurs have been omitted with one exception: everything should be played legato according to the example of "bars" one to four.

(16)

(19)

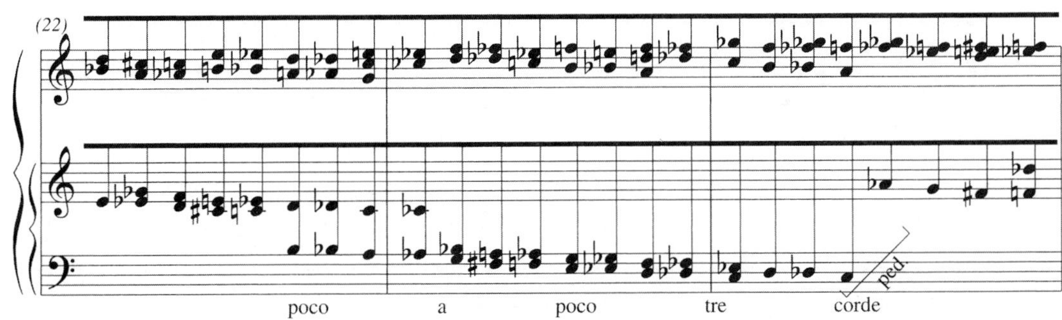
(22)
ped.
poco a poco tre corde

(25)
(ppp)
cresc. poco a poco
mp
cresc. poco a poco
poco ped.
emphasize the melody / die Melodie hervorheben

(28)
(cresc.)
mf
pp sub.
pp
una corda
(cresc.)
f
quasi senza ped.
(31)
emphasize the melody / die Melodie hervorheben
(34)
(pp sempre)
poco ped.
tre corde mp
mp ped.
(37)
ppp
mp
mp
p una corda
(40)

(43)
cresc. poco a poco
mf tre corde
emphasize the melody
die Melodie hervorheben
(46)
(cresc.)
mp
più ped.
(mf)
(49)
cresc.
mf
(mp) cresc.
mf
cresc. poco a poco
f
f
f
(52)
8
cresc. poco a poco
f
(cresc.) f
ff
f
f
non arp.
f
ff
ff
fff

(55)
8
ff
cresc.
f
ff
ff
ff
f
non arp.
fff
(58)
(cresc.)
ff
ff
ff
ff
fff
fff
fff
fff (A - F♯ simultaneously)
(A - Fis simultan)
dim. poco a poco
p dim.
pp
(61)
ff
p
p
pp
(>)
fff emphasize the melody
die Melodie hervorheben
ff dim.
f
poco a poco
mf
mp
mp
poco a poco meno ped.
(64)
pp sempre
poco ped.

(67)
(70)
(73)
(76)
dim. poco a poco al -
poco a poco una corda
(79)
ppp

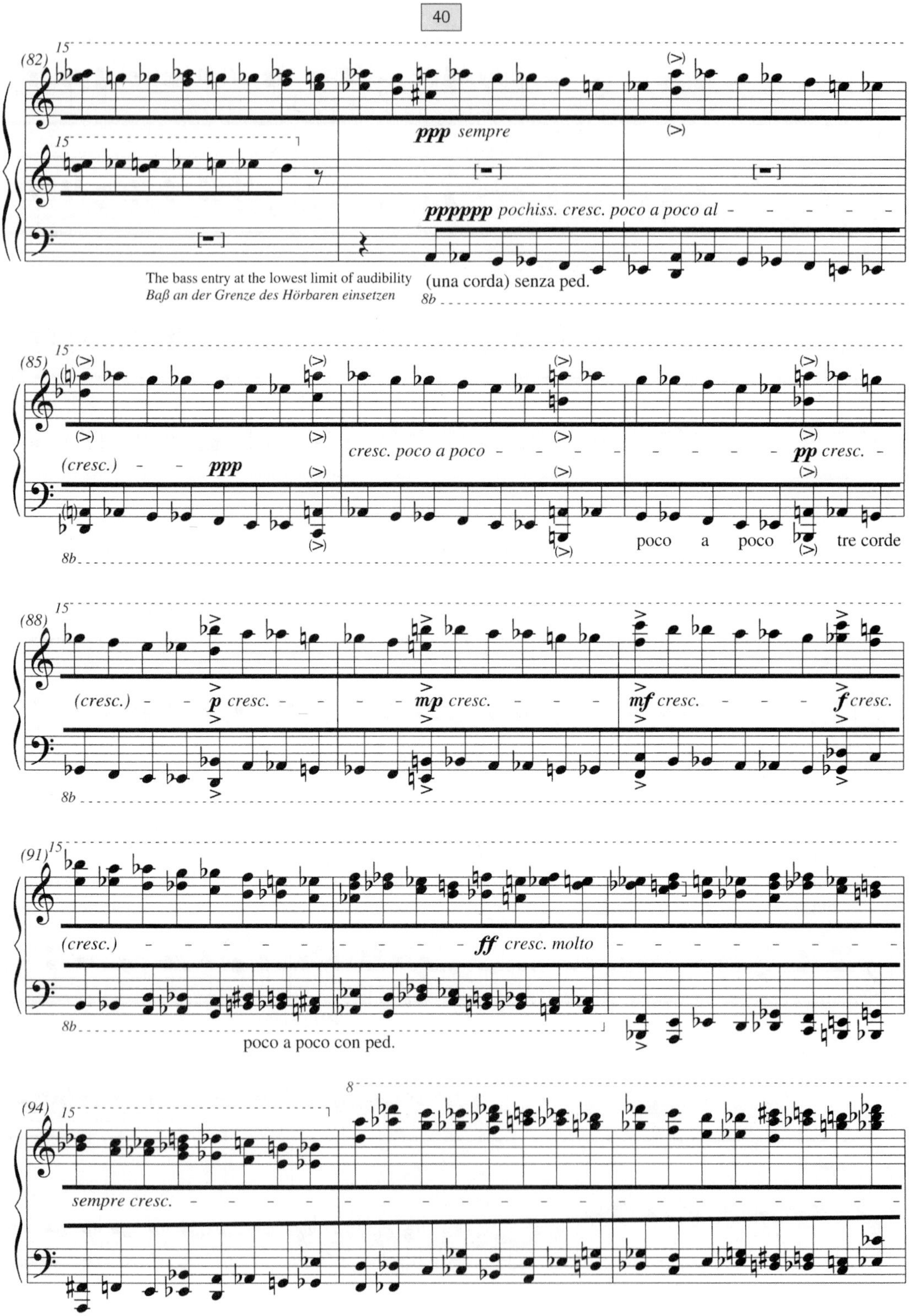

40

(82) 15

ppp sempre

pppppp pochiss. cresc. poco a poco al – – – – –

The bass entry at the lowest limit of audibility
Baß an der Grenze des Hörbaren einsetzen

(una corda) senza ped.

8b

(85) 15

(cresc.) – – *ppp*

cresc. poco a poco – – – – – – – – – – *pp cresc.* –

poco a poco tre corde

8b

(97)
8
(cresc.)
fff cresc.
ffff cresc.

(100)
8
(cresc.)
sempre cresc., tutta la forza

(103)
8
(sempre cresc., tutta la forza)

(105)
8
(sempre cresc., tutta la forza)

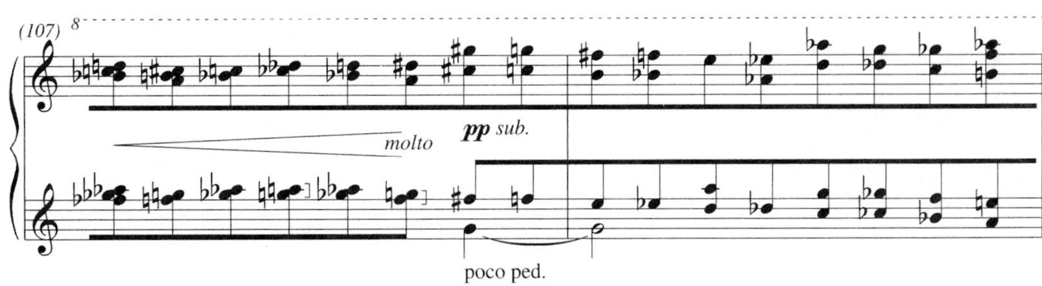
(107)
8
molto
pp sub.
poco ped.

cresc. poco al - - - - - p cresc. al - -
(109)
cresc. molto al - - - - - - - - - -
emphasize the melody
die Melodie hervorheben
poco a poco più ped.

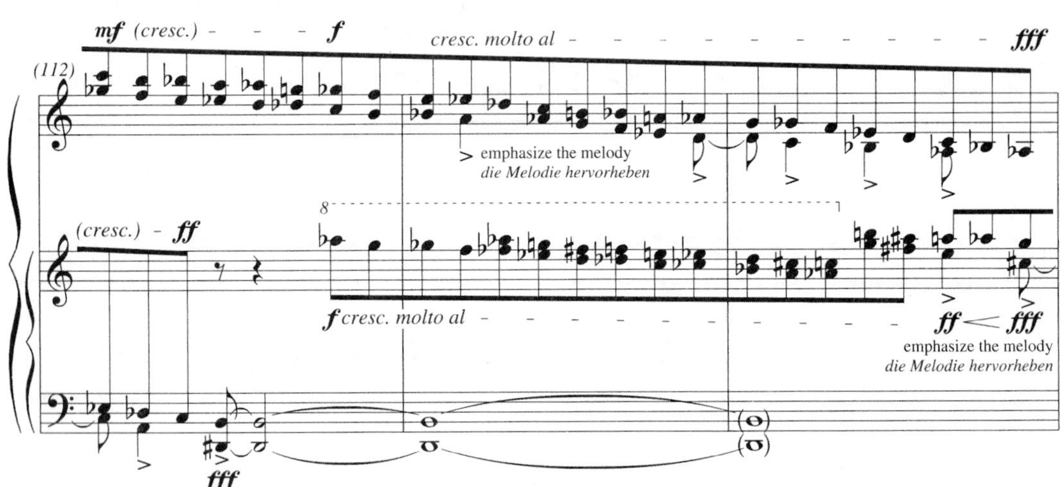
mf (cresc.) - - - - f
cresc. molto al - - - - - - - - - - - - - - fff
(112)
emphasize the melody
die Melodie hervorheben
(cresc.) - ff
f cresc. molto al - - - - - - - - - - - - ff fff
emphasize the melody
die Melodie hervorheben
fff

(115)
sub.
pp (mp) cresc. al - - - - - - - fff
fff sempre
fff sempre
ffff

(118)
8

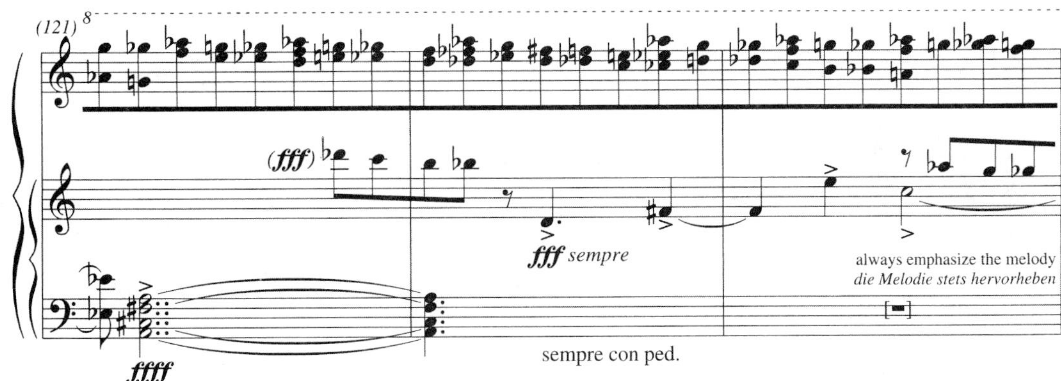
(121)
8
(fff)
fff sempre
ffff
sempre con ped.
always emphasize the melody
die Melodie stets hervorheben

dim. - - - - - - - p - mf - mp - - p dim. - - -
(124)
8
ff dim. - f - - mf p dim. - - - - - - - - - - - -

8
ppp
(127)
poco ped.
meno ped.
cresc. -
ppp
meno ped.
una corda
cresc. -

cresc.
(130)
(cresc.) - - f mf
mf
mf cresc. al
(cresc.) - - f più ped.
tre corde
ff
f f
emphasize the melody
die Melodie hervorheben
cresc. al - - f
(133)
cantabile
pp sub.
ppp
pppp dim. al
(cresc.) - - f
ff cresc.
pp sub.
una corda
pochiss. ped.
dim.
ppp dim.
(136)
15
(dim.)
8b
(dim.) - pppp dim. poco a poco
15
(139)
(dim.)
quasi niente
pppppp quasi niente
8b
dim. al „niente"
pppppp
veramente niente pppppppp
release pedal very gradually
Pedal sehr allmählich heben
Durata ca. 3′03″

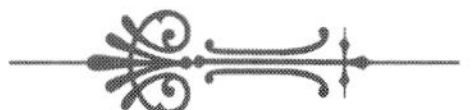

György Ligeti made his international reputation in the 1950s and 1960s with pieces for orchestra, voices, or other ensembles that focused on texture and processes of change rather than themes, melody, or harmony. One of his basic tools was what he called *micropolyphony*, in which a large number of instruments or voices had independent contrapuntal lines (sometimes canonic or nearly so) that could not be heard separately but that combined to create a gradual process of movement, such as a gradually rising cluster of sound. In his eighteen études for solo piano, composed between 1985 and 2001, Ligeti blended many of his earlier concerns with the nineteenth-century tradition of the étude for a virtuoso pianist, in the spirit of his fellow Hungarian Franz Liszt (see NAWM 128). *Vertige* (Vertigo), his ninth étude, was commissioned by the city of Gütersloh in northwest Germany for a concert in May 1990 in honor of composer Mauricio Kagel, to whom the piece is dedicated. It was published as part of Ligeti's second book of études.

The whole piece is based on overlapping, rapidly descending chromatic scales of various lengths, which create the sense of vertigo (suggested by the title) through a novel application of micropolyphony. As Ligeti explains in performance notes, there is no meter (the barlines are there for ease of reading), and the notes should move so fast and be played so legato that they blur into continuous lines. This is the étude part of the piece, and it takes enormous skill to play. The emotional effect comes from what those lines do.

At the outset, each descending line begins on *b*′ (sometimes notated *c*♭″) and ends on *a*♭, beginning in the right hand and moving seamlessly into the left. (The motion of each line from one hand to the other is made clear by the beams in the opening measures, but it would be cumbersome to continue this notation throughout the piece.) The descending lines enter at irregular intervals between eight and two eighth-notes apart, so that the number of simultaneous lines varies from two to four. These overlapping lines are like waves, all moving within the same range and thereby creating a sense of constant falling without actually getting any lower. This is a paradoxical auditory illusion known as the Shepard effect, invented by computer scientist Roger Shepard and developed further by computer music composer Jean-Claude Risset. Here Ligeti transfers the effect to an acoustic instrument.

From this very regular start, the music moves toward increasing variety over the course of the piece. No definable form emerges, only a series of events marked by constant variation (see chart on page 792).

In measure 14, the range begins to expand outward in both directions. The beginning note rises chromatically, and the lowest note gradually drops from *g* to *c*. But now not all lines descend through the entire range (the first not to do so begins in measure 16), so the texture grows more variable.

A melody in longer notes and at a higher dynamic level emerges in the left hand in measure 25, comprising a half step, a series of thirds, and a descending fifth, followed by a chord. This melody begins on B (like the opening scales) and ends on a B-minor triad, hinting at a tonal center amid all the chromatics. The

Measure	Events
1	Multiple descending chromatic lines, overlapping (continues throughout, except in measures 83–90)
14	Range expands outward
25	Falling melody in bass
30	Range rises
34	Falling melody in treble, range expands downward
45	Falling melody in bass, followed by rising figures and chords
64	Range rises into highest octave
83	Contrasting texture: parallel descending chromatic lines six octaves apart
90	Return to original texture of overlapping descending chromatic lines, in extreme ranges, gradually converging in high range
110	Falling melody varied twice, followed by rising figures varied
126	Range expands downward
130	Chords, falling melody, and rising figures varied, disappear in extreme ranges

descending lines continue, crescendoing along with the melody, and for the first time near the end of the melody there are brief rising chromatic segments (measures 28–29, both hands).

The descending lines rise into the upper register—another paradox, achieved by making the lines enter more quickly one after another, and making each one shorter so that the bottom of the range gradually drops away. The melody appears again at measure 34, now at the top of the texture, loud against the soft background of the scales. Meanwhile, the scales slowly expand lower again, with each new low note emphasized by being accented and sustained (measures 31–45). The melody emerges a third time at measure 45 and expands into a much longer series of notes and chords, now marked more by rising gestures than falling ones, as if resisting the constantly falling motion of the scales.

Both the scales and the other ideas gradually crescendo. After a climax in measures 54–61, the rising gestures fade, and the falling scales continue softly, moving into the upper reaches of the piano and gradually thinning in texture as each scale grows shorter. Suddenly at measure 83 a new texture begins, with the two hands playing in parallel, six octaves apart, accenting the beginning of each descending scale. The scales begin every seven eighth-notes, then every six, increasing the pace as the music gradually crescendos. Just as suddenly, the texture returns to that of multiple descending lines in measure 90. As the intensity continues to build, the right hand slowly descends from its stratosphere and the left hand works its way upward until the two meet and the left hand returns to playing the continuation of scales that originated in the right hand (measure 100).

After a sudden *pianissimo* (measure 107), the melodic idea returns in new variations. Triads on F♯ minor, F major, and B major (measures 121 and 130–31) again suggest tonal sounds within the chromaticism, but nothing is confirmed. After a final climax on the B-major triad, the music fades to nothingness.

Besides maintaining the constant flow of descending scales, the pianist must also distinguish between a wide range of dynamic levels, including simultaneous contrasting ones. There are many changes of pedaling as well, often changing gradually, such as the shift from *una corda* (one string) at the beginning to *tre corde* (three strings, the normal piano sound) on the second page.

200

Ellen Taaffe Zwilich (b. 1939)

Symphony No. 1: First movement

Symphony

1982

From Ellen Taaffe Zwilich, *Symphony No. 1 (Three Movements for Orchestra)* (Newton, Mass.: Margun Music, 1983), 3–51.

accel. d=52
Pic.
Fl.
Ob.
E.H.
Cl.
Bs.Cl.
Bsn.
Cbsn.
Hn.
Tbn.
Sus. Cym.
Pf.
Hp.
7
8
9
10
11
Vln. I
Vln. II
Vla.
Vlc.
Cb.

42
riten.
a tempo (♩=52)
accel.
ten.
a2
cresc. poco a poco
sub mf
L.V.
8basso
A-Ab
Bb-B♮
loco
12
13
14
15
16
17
riten.
a tempo (♩=52)
accel.
unis.
cresc. poco a poco

(accel.) d=60
Pic.
Fl.
Cl.
Bs.Cl.
Bsn.
Cbsn.
cresc. poco a poco
Hn.
Tpt.
Tbn.
Timp.
Sus. Cym.
l.v.
tubular bell
Pf.
8va
18
19
20
21
22
Vln. I
Vln. II
Vla.
Vlc.
Cb.

accel.
23
24
25
26
27
accel.
pizz

(accel.) d=68
Pic.
Fl.
Ob.
E.H.
Cl.
Bs.Cl.
Bsn.
Cbsn.
Hn.
Tpt.
Tbn.
Tu.
Timp.
Tub. Bells
Pf.
Vln. I
Vln. II
Vla.
Vlc.
Cb.
sord.
pizz
28
29
30
31
32

Sizz.
Cym.
33
34
35
36

accel. d=76
Pic.
Fl.
Cl.
cresc. poco a poco
ff
Bs.Cl.
Bsn.
Bs.Cl.
Hn.
Tpt.
Sizz. Cym.
Pf.
loco
sub f
37
38
39
40
41
sul G
Vln. I
Vln. II
Vla.
Vlc.
Cb.

f
sub f
div.
sffz
mf
L.V.
ff
8va
42
43
44
45

accel.
♩=84
Pic.
Fl.
Ob.
Cl.
Bs.Cl.
Hn.
Tpt.
Pf.
Hp.
46
47
48
49
50
Vln. I
Vln. II
Vla.
Vlc.
Cb.

accel.
51
52
53
54
55
accel.

𝅗𝅥=92
accel.
𝅗𝅥=100
Pic.
Fl.
Ob.
Cl.
Hn.
Tpt.
Tbn.
senza
cresc.
Hp.
56
57
58
59
60
61
Vln. I
Vln. II
Vla.
Vlc.

accel.
a2
loco
(senza)
62
63
64
65
66
accel.

(accel.) ♩= 108
G.P.
accel.
Pic.
Fl.
Ob.
E.H.
Cl.
Bs.Cl.
Bsn.
Hn.
Tpt.
Tbn.
Timp.
Pf.
67
68
69
70
Vln. I
Vln. II
Vla.
Vlc.
div.

(decel)
♩= 116
8va
loco
fp
sfzp
71
72
73
74
75
8va

43
riten.
Allegro ♩= ca. 124
(Pesante)
Pic.
Fl.
Ob.
E.H.
Cl.
Bs.Cl.
Bsn.
Hn.
Tpt.
Tbn.
Tu.
Timp.
Sus. Cym.
Pf.
Hp.
Vln. I
Vln. II
Vla.
Vlc.
Cb.
a2
molto f
fp
pizz
loco
76
77
78
79
80

Sn.Dr.
secco
SNARE DRUM
crisp
ARCO
non-div.
81
82
83
84
85

Pic.
Fl.
Ob.
Cl.
TAKE CONTRA
Hn.
Tpt.
Tbn.
Timp.
(ultra-stacc)
Sus. Cym.
Pf.
Hp.
86
87
88
89
90
Vln. I
Vla.
Vlc.
PIZZ

fp
f
fp
fp
f
f
mf
mf
mf
fp
fp
f
f
f
f
f
I
fp
SMALL SUSP. CYMB.
mf
ff
8va
91
92
93
94
ARCO
mf
ff

Pic.
Fl.
Cl.
Tpt. 1 2
1 2 Tbn. 3
Sus. Cym.
Hp.
Vln. I
Vln. II
Vla.
Vlc.
95
96
97
98
99
100
PIZZ
ARCO
L.V.

l.v.
mf
f
mf
ff
101
102
103
104
105
106
107

Fl.
Cl.
Bsn.
Cbsn.
Tpt. 1 2
Tbn. 1 2 3
Tu.
S.D.
Sn. Dr.
Pf.
(fingernail)
Hp.
108
109
110
111
112
Vln. I
Vln. II
Vla.
Vlc.
Cb.
ARCO

113
114
115
116
mf
sul G
f
sul G
f (4)

Pic.
Fl.
Ob.
E.H.
Cl.
Bs.Cl.
Bsn.
Cbsn.
Hn.
Tu.
Tamb.
Sus. Cym.
Pf.
Hp.
117
118
119
120
Vln. I
Vln. II
Vla.
Vlc.
Cb.
* arpeggio always before the beat, highest note on the beat

TAMBOURINE
L.V.
(thumb roll)
L.V.
121
122
123
124
125
SUL G
SUL G
non div.
ARCO

Pic.
Fl.
Cl.
Bs.Cl.
Bsn.
Cbsn.
Hn.
Tpt.
Tu.
Tamb.
Sn.Dr.
Pf.
Hp.
Vln. I
Vln. II
Vla.
Vlc.
Cb.
126
127
128
S.D.
L.V.

a2 I open
II st. mute
II via sord.
Sizz. Cym.
sizzle cymb
L.V.
(tight)
2 Large cymbals
8va
loco
129
130
131

44
G.P.
Cl.
Bs.Cl.
Bsn.
Cbsn.
Hn.
Timp.
Sn.Dr.
(hard)
small B.D.
damp cymbals
Pf.
Hp.
132
133
134
135
136
137
Vln. I
Vln. II
Vla.
Vlc.
Cb.
pizz

Sm.
Bs. Dr.
138
139
140
141
142

Pic.
Fl.
Ob.
E.H.
Cl.
Bs.Cl.
Bsn.
Tpt. 1 2
Tbn. 1 2 3
Sus. Cym.
Bs. Dr.
Vln. I
Vln. II
Vla.
Vlc.
143
144
145
146
147
148

Sus. Cym.
Bs. Dr.
149
150
151
152
153
B.D.
L.V.
ARCO

Fl.
Ob.
E.H.
Cl.
Bs.Cl.
Bsn.
Cbsn.
Hn.
Tpt.
Tbn.
Timp.
Bs.Dr.
Pf.
Hp.
154
155
156
157
Vln. I
Vln. II
Vla.
Vlc.
Cb.

158
159
160
161
162

Bs.Cl.
Bsn.
Cbsn.
Tbn.
Bs. Dr.
Sus. Cym.
Pf.
Hp.
163
164
165
166
167
Vla.
Vlc.
Cb.

mf
mf
f
mf
f
mf
8ba
f
168
169
170
171
172
sul C

Fl.
Cl.
Bs.Cl.
Bsn.
Cbsn.
a2
Hn.
Tpt. 1 2
Tbn.
Tu.
L.V.
B.D.
Crisp
Sus. Cym.
Hp.
173
174
175
176
177
178
Vln. I
Vln. II
Pizz
ARCO
Vla.
Vlc.
Cb.

Bs. Dr.
179
180
181
182
non-div.

Pic.
Fl.
Ob.
Cl.
Bsn.
Cbsn.
Hn.
Tpt.
Tbn.
Sus. Cym.
Pf.
Hp.
183
184
185
186
Vln. I
Vln. II
Vla.
Vlc.
Cb.

187
188
189
190
191
8va
loco
pizz
pizz

cresc. poco a poco
Pic.
Fl.
Ob.
E.H.
Cl.
Bs.Cl.
Bsn.
Cbsn.
Hn.
Tpt.
Tbn.
Tu.
Sus. Cym.
Pf.
Vln. I
Vln. II
Vla.
Vlc.
Cb.
192
193
194
195
196
197
(senza)
molto f
Arco
pizz

45
Tub.
Bells
Sus.
Cym.
tubular bell
L.V.
div.
198
199
200
201
202
203
non div.
ARCO
(VПV, staggered)

Pic.
Fl.
Ob.
E.H.
Cl.
Bs.Cl.
Bsn.
Cbsn.
Tub. Bells
Pf.
204
205
206
207
208
Vln. I
Vln. II
Vla.
Vlc.
Cb.

mf
p
partial damp
mp
209
210
211
212
213

Tbn.
Tu.
214
215
216
217
Vln. I
Vln. II
Vla.
Vlc.
Cb.
con sordino
mp
dim.
pp
morendo

warm
mp
warm
mp
warm
mp
218
219
220

Fl.
Ob.
Bsn.
Cbsn.
Hn.
Tbn.
Vln. I
Vln. II
Vla.
Vlc.
Cb.
221
222
223
224
rall.
mp
pp
2 players
div.

46
d = 62
rall.
a tempo
morendo
225
226
227
228
229
230
231
warm
p
pp

ritard
cédez
Pic.
Fl.
Pf.
Ped.
8ba
Hp.
232
233
234
235
236
Vln. I
Vln. II
Vla.
Vlc.
Cb.
div.
tutti

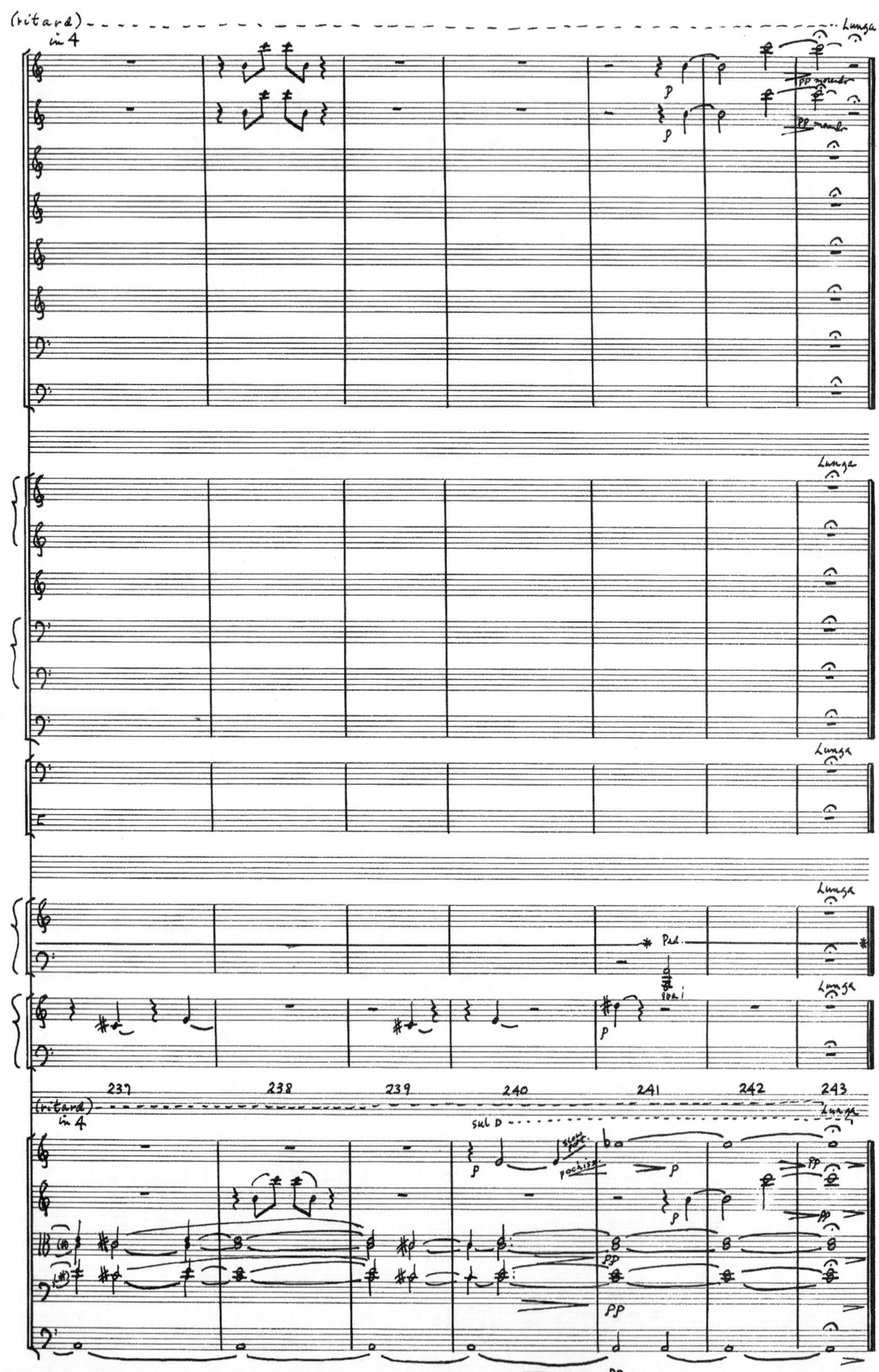
(ritard)
in 4
Lunga
pp morendo
Lunga
Lunga
Lunga
Ped.
Lunga
237
238
239
240
241
242
243
(ritard)
in 4
Lunga
sul D
pp
pp

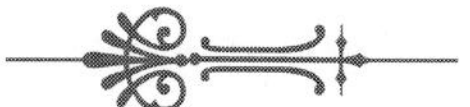

Ellen Taaffe Zwilich's Symphony No. 1 (originally titled *Three Movements for Orchestra*) was commissioned by the American Composers Orchestra and the National Endowment for the Arts and also supported by the Guggenheim Foundation. It was premiered at Lincoln Center in New York on May 5, 1982, by the American Composers Orchestra, conducted by Gunther Schuller. The work was well received by the audience and praised by reviewers, and the following year it earned Zwilich the Pulitzer Prize in Music, the first ever awarded to a woman.

Almost all the material in the first movement evolves from the opening fifteen measures, in a process of *developing variation.* The term was coined by Arnold Schoenberg more than fifty years earlier to describe procedures of constant development he found in Bach and Brahms and adopted in his own music (see commentaries for NAWM 147, 148, and 160). Zwilich's work descends from the same tradition. Yet where Schoenberg used complex ideas and developed them rapidly, Zwilich uses relatively simple elements, develops them gradually, and repeats material more often than Schoenberg does, making her music easier to follow. Although the piece is not tonal in a traditional sense, it uses familiar harmonic materials, including tonal centers, prominent thirds and fifths, and occasional triads. Zwilich frequently uses gestures reminiscent of the expressive sweep of Romantic symphonies. Certain moments, such as the E-major triad and passionate melody at measure 13, sound almost like Mahler.

The piece opens with a threefold rising minor third, *a′–c′*, played *accelerando* (with gradually increasing tempo). This motive establishes A as the tonal center for the movement. The third is answered by a rising fifth, *c♯′–g♯′*, introducing notes that both form 014 sets with the initial third (G♯–A–C, and A–C–C♯). This set, containing both a minor and a major third as well as a half step, becomes the central material for the movement, appearing in a variety of guises. One such guise, combining two overlapping 014 sets, is the motive C–E♭–B–D, which appears at measures 8–11 in the winds. (The C–E♭ is in English horn and clarinet, both of which are transposing instruments, whose parts are notated respectively a fifth higher and a whole step higher than they sound.) Other melodies derived from 014 sets appear in the violins at measures 9–10 (*g–(a)–b♭–b♮′–g♯*) and at measures 13–14 (*b‴–c‴–b″–e♭‴–c‴–d‴–c♯″*). Thus, each of the principal ideas in the movement can trace its ancestry back to the opening gestures, giving the music coherence at the same time it embraces constant change. All these ideas recur throughout the movement, in new variations; the last melody, for instance, impassioned when first heard, reappears in a calm and contemplative mood near the end, transposed and slower in the cellos (measures 227–33).

The opening motto is heard several times in the first section, each time associated with an accelerando, as the tempo gradually increases. This process leads to the central part of the movement, an Allegro (measure 78). Its theme begins *a–c′–c♯″*, another instance of the 014 set, and secondary ideas introduced at measures 100 and 114 also draw on the set. The Allegro builds to a climax at measures 128–31, then subsides to a pause, and material returns in a new order (compare measures 143–93 to measures 99–123, 78–85, 110–15, and 92–98). The final section (measures 199–243) returns to a slow tempo and to ideas from the first section, now in a much sparser texture, and gradually calms to a close.

Arvo Pärt (b. 1935)

Seven Magnificat Antiphons: Excerpts

Choral antiphons

1988, revised 1991

(a) No. 1: *O Weisheit*

21
1
3
1
3
in und ord - nest al - les
1
in Kraft und Mil - de ord - nest du al - les:
1
in Kraft und Mil - de ord - nest du al - les:
1
in und ord - nest al - les

29
1
5
1
komm of - fen - ba - re den der
O komm und of - fen - ba - re uns den Weg der
O komm und of - fen - ba - re uns den Weg der
komm of - fen - ba - re den der

37
3
1
3
1
3
und Ein - sicht
1
Weis - heit
1
Weis - heit und der Ein - sicht.
1
O Weis - heit
1
Weis - heit und der Ein - sicht.
1
O Weis - heit
1
und Ein - sicht Weis - heit

O Weisheit, hervorgegangen aus dem Munde des Höchsten,
die Welt umspannst du von einem Ende zum andern,
in Kraft und Milde ordnest du alles:

o komm und offenbare uns den Weg der Weisheit und der Einsicht.

O Wisdom, sprung forth from the mouth of the most high,
you embrace the world from one end to the other,
in strength and mildness you put everything in order;
O come and reveal to us the way of wisdom and understanding.

(b) No. 6: *O König aller Völker*

mp
Sehn - sucht, Schluß - stein,
mf
zusammen-hält: o komm und er- ret - te den Menschen, den du aus Er - de ge - bil -
mp
o komm und er- ret - te den Men - schen, den
mp
o komm und er- ret - te den Men - schen, den

mf
der den Bau zu - sam - men - hält:
f
det! O Kö - nig al - ler Völ - ker, ih - re Er - wartung und Sehnsucht,
mf
du aus Er - de ge - bil - det! O Kö - nig al - ler
mf
du aus Er - de ge - bil - det! O Kö - nig al - ler

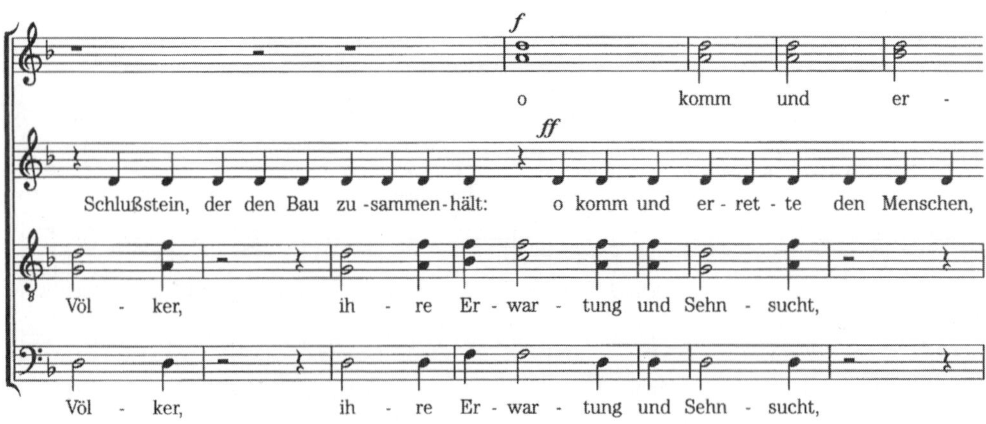
f
o komm und er -
ff
Schlußstein, der den Bau zu -sammen-hält: o komm und er - ret - te den Menschen,
Völ - ker, ih - re Er - war - tung und Sehn - sucht,
Völ - ker, ih - re Er - war - tung und Sehn - sucht,

O König aller Völker,
ihre Erwartung end Sehnsucht,
Schlußstein, der den Bau zusammenhält:
o komm und errette den Menschen, den
du aus Erde gebildet!

O king of all peoples,
their expectation and longing;
keystone, which holds the building together:
O come and redeem mankind, whom you
have fashioned out of clay!

Arvo Pärt left his native Estonia (then a constituent republic of the Soviet Union) in 1980 and settled in Berlin, seeking greater international opportunities. In 1988, he wrote *Seven Magnificat Antiphons*, his first major choral work in German, the language of his adoptive country. The texts are translations of the Latin antiphons that are sung just before and after the Magnificat in Vespers services on the seven evenings immediately preceding Christmas Eve. These seven antiphons, one for each evening's service, are known as the "O Antiphons" because they all begin with the exclamation "O" and conclude with a line beginning "O come," appropriate for the season of Advent. The work is dedicated to the RIAS-Kammerchor, the chamber choir of RIAS (Radio in the American Sector).

The *Magnificat Antiphons* exemplify Pärt's distinctive *tintinnabuli* style (named after the Latin word for ringing bells), which he devised in the mid-1970s after studying Gregorian chant and early polyphony. In this technique, one voice presents a diatonic melody that generally moves by step around a central pitch, and the other voices sound notes of the tonic triad that are determined by a preset system. The two movements included here demonstrate different ways of applying this simple method.

The text of *O Weisheit* is set syllabically and homophonically. Measure lines are used to indicate lengths of individual words but do not suggest a meter. One-syllable words are set with half notes, but longer words are set with a whole note on the syllable that receives the greatest stress. Throughout, the soprano and bass sing every other word, regardless of syllable lengths or declamation, and a three-beat measure of rests follows every comma.

The principal melody appears in the tenor, where it is doubled in parallel thirds. The tenors reiterate a C♯ and E for each half note, and alternate moving up and down a step for whole notes. The entire melodic range remains within the span of a third. The other voices of the ensemble derive their pitches from the A-major triad. The bass and soprano lines are limited to E and A, arranged as a perfect fourth or fifth. The repetition of these open harmonies at irregular intervals suggests the ringing of a bell. The upper and lower alto lines sing the two pitches from the A-major triad that are higher than and closest to the notes of the comparable tenor lines. For the most part, the altos remain on *e'* and *a'*, but when the tenors descend to *b* and *d'*, the altos move down to a *c♯'* and *e'*.

As a result of this simple construction, the movement has only six different harmonies; the tenors and altos sound a first-inversion A-major triad on each half note and alternate two four-note dissonant diatonic sonorities on the whole notes, and each of these three chords may either sound alone or be accompanied by the notes in the bass and soprano. This simplicity, coupled with the sustained quiet dynamics, effectively supports the antiphon's plea for wisdom and understanding. The movement recalls the recitation of prayers in Gregorian chant and the sonorities of early polyphony. In the process, Pärt also foreshadows the principal tonal centers of the work as a whole. The first two chords contain all the pitches that will serve as tonal centers for the seven movements: A–F♯–C♯–A–E–D–A.

O König aller Völker employs tintinnabuli techniques in a different manner. The texture is divided into three distinct parts. The sopranos sing with half notes and whole notes, following a pattern similar to that observed in *O Weisheit*, although some single-syllable words at the beginning of phrases receive whole notes. The tenors and basses sing the same rhythmic values as the sopranos, but in diminution. The third line is provided by the altos, who chant independently on D in quarter notes.

The principal melody is sung by the second tenor and the second soprano in a canon in augmentation. As in *O Weisheit*, the melody moves primarily by step within a limited range. The other voices draw their pitches from the D-minor triad in a predetermined manner. The first soprano always sings the pitch from the D-minor triad that is above and closest to the note of the second soprano. The bass and first tenor are given pitches that are second closest to those of the second tenor, respectively below and above it. In the first measure, for example, the second tenor and second soprano are on A. The closest higher pitch to A in the D-minor triad is D, which is sung by the first soprano. The second closest higher pitch is an F, heard in the first tenor. The second closest pitch below A in the D-minor triad is D, which is given to the bass.

In *O König aller Völker*, because of the shifting relationship between the voices, harmonies are more varied than in *O Weisheit*, dissonances are more prevalent, and there are no rests in all voices at once—a note is always sounding in at least one voice. The recited D in the alto line also builds in intensity. Initially, it echoes the text as presented in the lower voices, but as the dynamics climb, the alto line pushes forward so that it must repeat the line "o komm und errette den Menschen" (O come and redeem mankind) twice before the work comes to a dramatic fortissimo close.

The utmost simplicity of Pärt's music makes it rewarding and approachable for choirs and audiences alike, yet the frequent small changes maintain interest. The rhythmic complexities of *O König aller Völker* present some challenges to performers. Traditional beating patterns from the conductor cannot be applied, since there are three different rhythmic notations in the score. The unifying factor in these lines is the beat, indicated as a quarter note.

Sofia Gubaidulina (b. 1931)

Rejoice! Sonata for Violin and Violoncello: Fifth movement, *Listen to the still small voice within*

Sonata

1981

CD 14|49

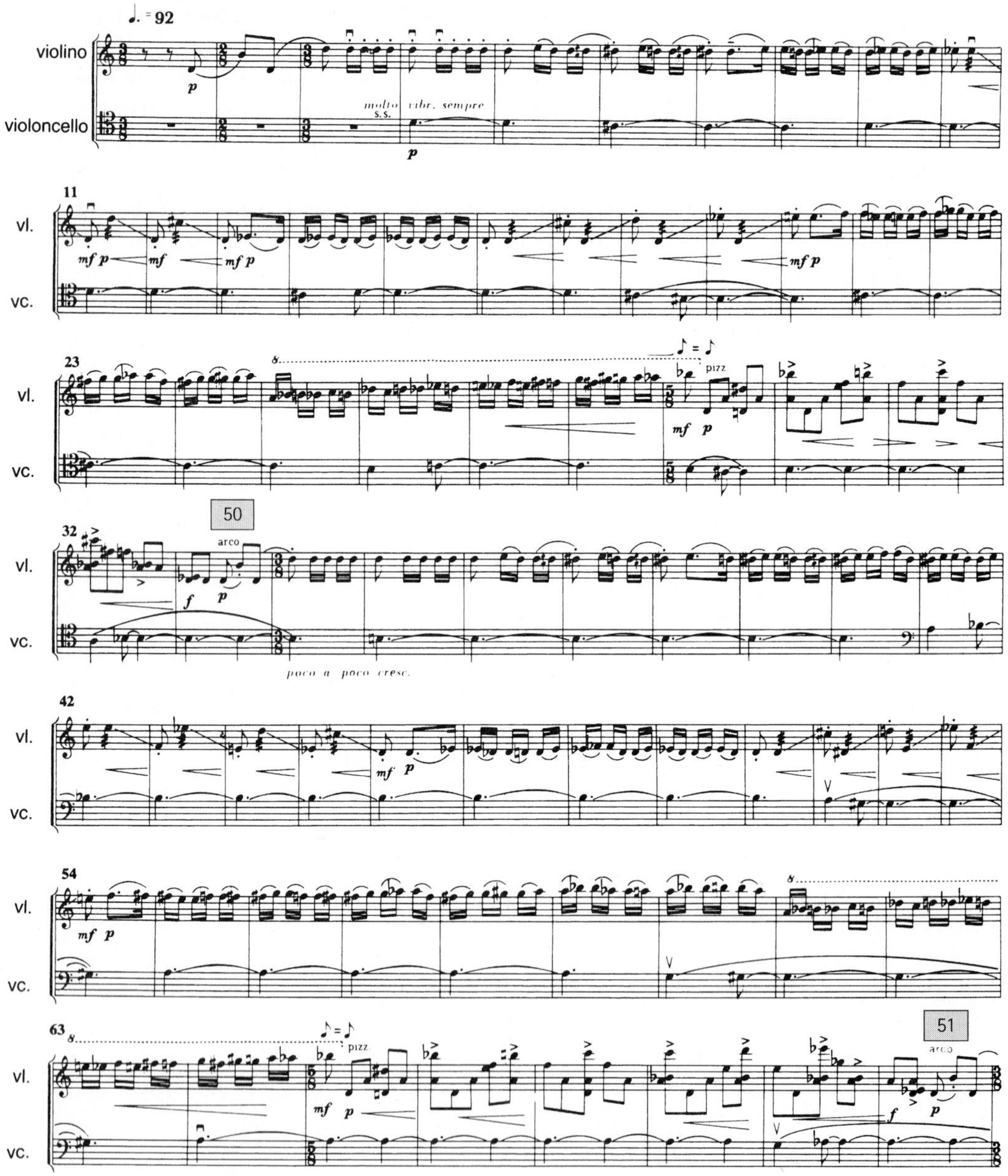

52
71
vl.
vc.
mf
p
81
87
53
mf
94
f
103
mf
110
pizz
f
mf
54
118
arco
f
p
127
mf
p

135
vl.
vc.
143
151
160
169
poco a poco cresc.
180
190
55
199
gliss.

Sofia Gubaidulina was born in the Tatar Republic, an autonomous region in central Russia, four hundred miles east of Moscow. Her childhood there, together with her combined Tatar, Russian, Polish, and Jewish heritage, led to a profound interest in blending sounds and influences. As she once said, "I am the place where East and West meet." Her sensitivity to sound is reflected in *Rejoice!*, a duo sonata for violin and cello that is a study in chromaticism, glissandos, tremolos, and harmonics. The piece also reflects her interest in spirituality, which put her at odds with the Soviet authorities. Like many of her works, this sonata was first performed outside the Soviet Union; it was premiered in Kuhmo, Finland, in 1988, seven years after she composed it. The quotations heading the movements are from the spiritual lessons of the Ukrainian philosopher Grigory Skovoroda (1722–1794).

In the fifth movement, *Listen to the still small voice within*, Gubaidulina introduces a sequence of gestures, then offers three variations on the same series of ideas. There are four principal motives in the violin: a leaping and pulsing figure, A (measures 1–5); a neighbor-note figure, B (measures 5–10); a tremolo glissando, C (measures 10–13); and a pizzicato jumping figure, D (measures 29–33). All of them suggest a tonal center on the note D, which is often the lowest or most frequently repeated note in the phrase. The cello, playing with intense vibrato throughout, traces a slowly moving, mostly chromatic line that gradually winds down two octaves from *d'* to *D* over the course of the piece, confirming D as the pitch center.

Figure A remains essentially the same at each appearance, serving to introduce each main section (at measures 1, 33, 70, and 122). Figure D undergoes extension but is also otherwise unchanged, closing off each section but the last. But figures B and C are constantly changing. In the first section, B appears in three variants—in the upper octave (measures 5–10), in the lower octave (measures 13–16), and climbing into the stratosphere (measures 20–28)—and C in two, either falling (measures 10–13) or rising (measures 16–20). Neither ever returns in exactly the same form. In the second section, B is lengthened at each occurrence, and in later sections it ranges widely, adding large leaps alongside its original stepwise motion (see at measures 93–104 and 151–74). C is transformed even more radically, as the glissandos morph into diatonic scales (measures 80–93), arpeggios (measures 104–7, 134–38, and 142–46), and rising and falling waves of glissandos (175–81).

Near the end, soon after the cello descends to *D*♯, its lowest note so far, the violin soars up to *c*♯'''', where it becomes transfixed (measure 194). The cello finally finds its voice, moving around chromatically and then rising repeatedly in a glissando from low *E*♭ to a natural harmonic on the C string. Gubaidulina commented about this sonata that the transition from normal sound to harmonics was a metaphor for transfiguration, a "transition to another plane of existence," representing both the "voice within" of the movement's title and the emerging joy suggested by the title of the entire sonata. After the cello touches its low D *col legno* (with the wood of the bow), the piece ends with high natural harmonics in both instruments, sounding an inverted F♯-major triad.

Most of the notation is traditional, but at the end several new signs are used. The notation for the violin in measure 198—featuring stems without noteheads and beams that are not parallel, but gradually merge together—is used to indicate that the player repeats the same note while gradually slowing down from sixteenth notes to eighths (and even slower, as signaled by the widening distance between the stems). The wavy beams in measures 206 and 219 indicate wide vibrato, a fast rocking of the finger against the fingerboard that changes the pitch slightly. Measure 219 calls for each player to repeat a pattern, without coordinating it with the other player, for about ten seconds, until both performers stop at the same time.

Alfred Schnittke (1934–1998)

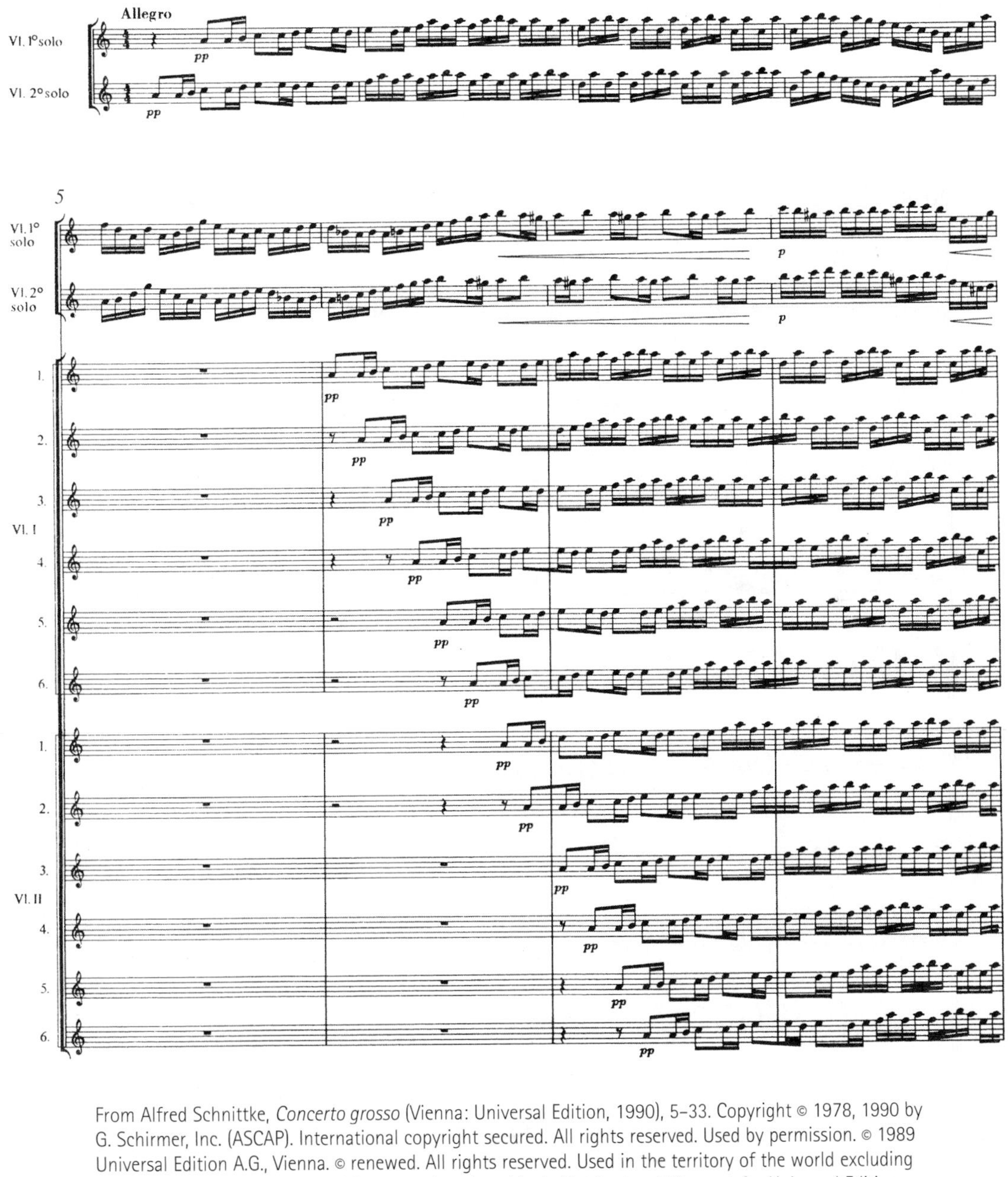

Concerto Grosso No. 1: Second movement, Toccata

Concerto

1976

5
Vl. 1° solo
Vl. 2° solo
p
Vl. I 1. 2. 3. 4. 5. 6.
Vl. II 1. 2. 3. 4. 5. 6.
pp

9
Vl. 1° solo
mp
mf
Vl. 2° solo
mp
mf
1.
2.
3.
Vl. I
4.
5.
6.
1.
2.
3.
Vl. II
4.
5.
6.

13
Vl. 1° solo
Vl. 2° solo
Vl. I
Vl. II
Vle.
Vc.
f
pp

17
Vl. 1° solo
f
Vl. 2° solo
f
Cemb.
(f)
1.
2.
3.
Vl. I
4.
5.
6.
pp
1.
2.
3.
Vl. II
4.
5.
6.
pp
2.
Vle. 3.
4.
1.
Vc.
2.

21
Vl. 1° solo
f
Vl. 2° solo
f
Cemb.
(f)
1.
2.
3.
Vl. I
4.
5.
6.
pp
1.
2.
3
Vl. II
4.
5.
6.
pp
1.
2.
Vle.
3.
4.
pp
1.
2.
Vc.
3.
4.
pp

25
Vl.1° solo
Vl.2° solo
Cemb.
(f)
Vl. I
Vl. II
Vle.
Vc.
f

29
58
Vl.1° solo
Vl.2° solo
Cemb.
(pp)
p
Vl. I
Vl. II
Vle.
Vc.
Cb.
ff

34
Vl. 1° solo
Vl. 2° solo
Cemb.
1.
2.
Vl. I
3.
4.
1.
2.
Vl. II
3.
4.
pp
pizz.
gliss.
1.
2.
Vle.
3.
4.

40
Vl.1°
solo
f
Vl.2°
solo
f
Cemb.
1.
mp
2.
mp
Vl.I 3.
mp
4.
mp
5.
6.
a2
mp
1.
mp
2.
mp
Vl.II 3.
mp
4.
mp
5.
6.
a2
mp
Vle.
(unite) arco
mp
Vc.
(uniti)
mp
Cb.
mp

45
Vl. 1° solo
Vl. 2° solo
(uniti)
Vl. I
(uniti)
Vl. II
Vle.
Vc.
Cb.
49
Vl. 1° solo
Vl. 2° solo
Vl. I
pp 2:6.
Vl. II
pp
Vle.
Vc.
Cb.
pizz.
(pp)

53
(pp)
Vl.I
1.
2.
3.
4.
5.
6.
pp
Vl.II
Vle.
Vc.
Cb.

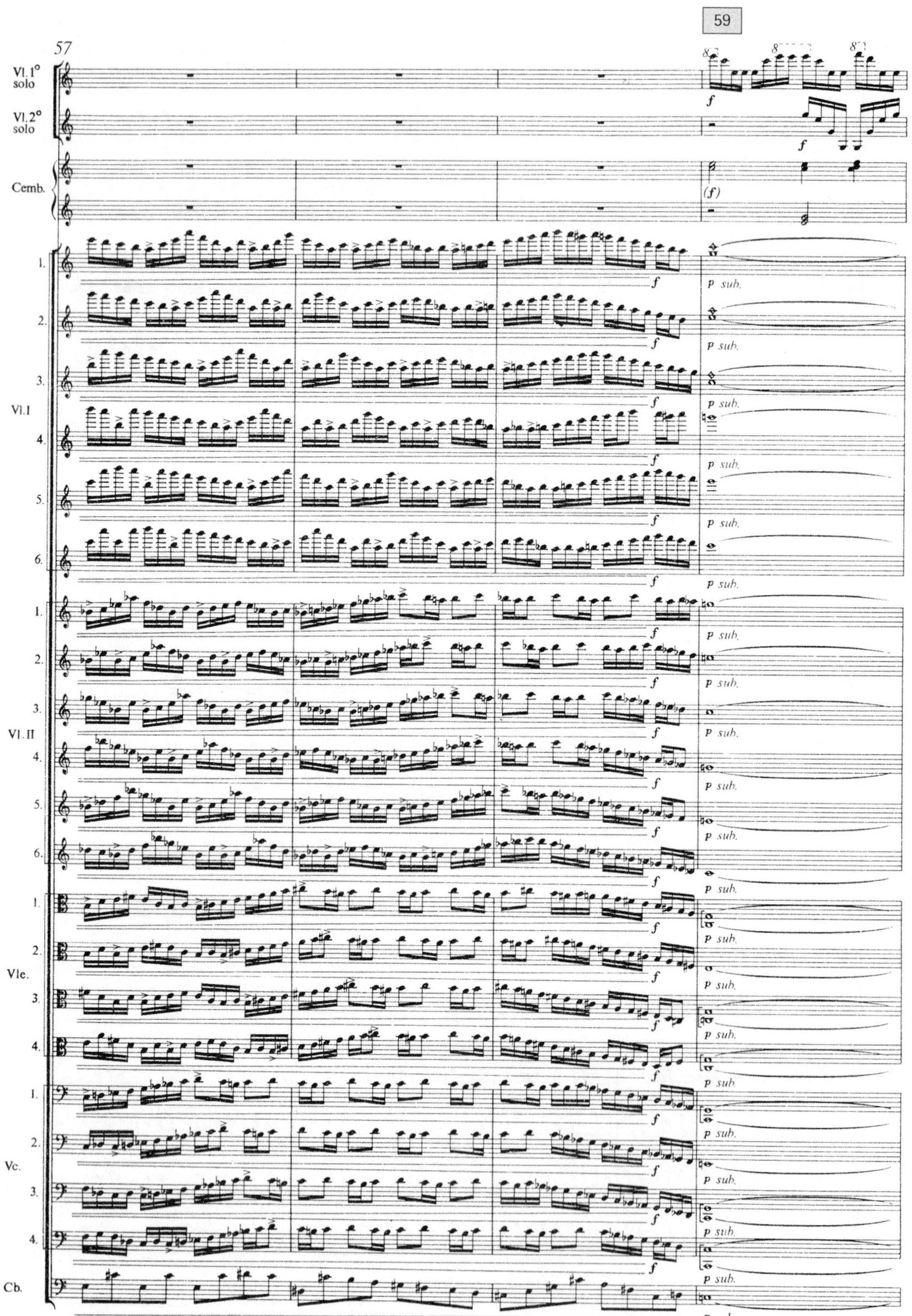
59
57
Vl.1° solo
Vl.2° solo
Cemb.
Vl.I
Vl.II
Vle.
Vc.
Cb.
f
(f)
p sub.

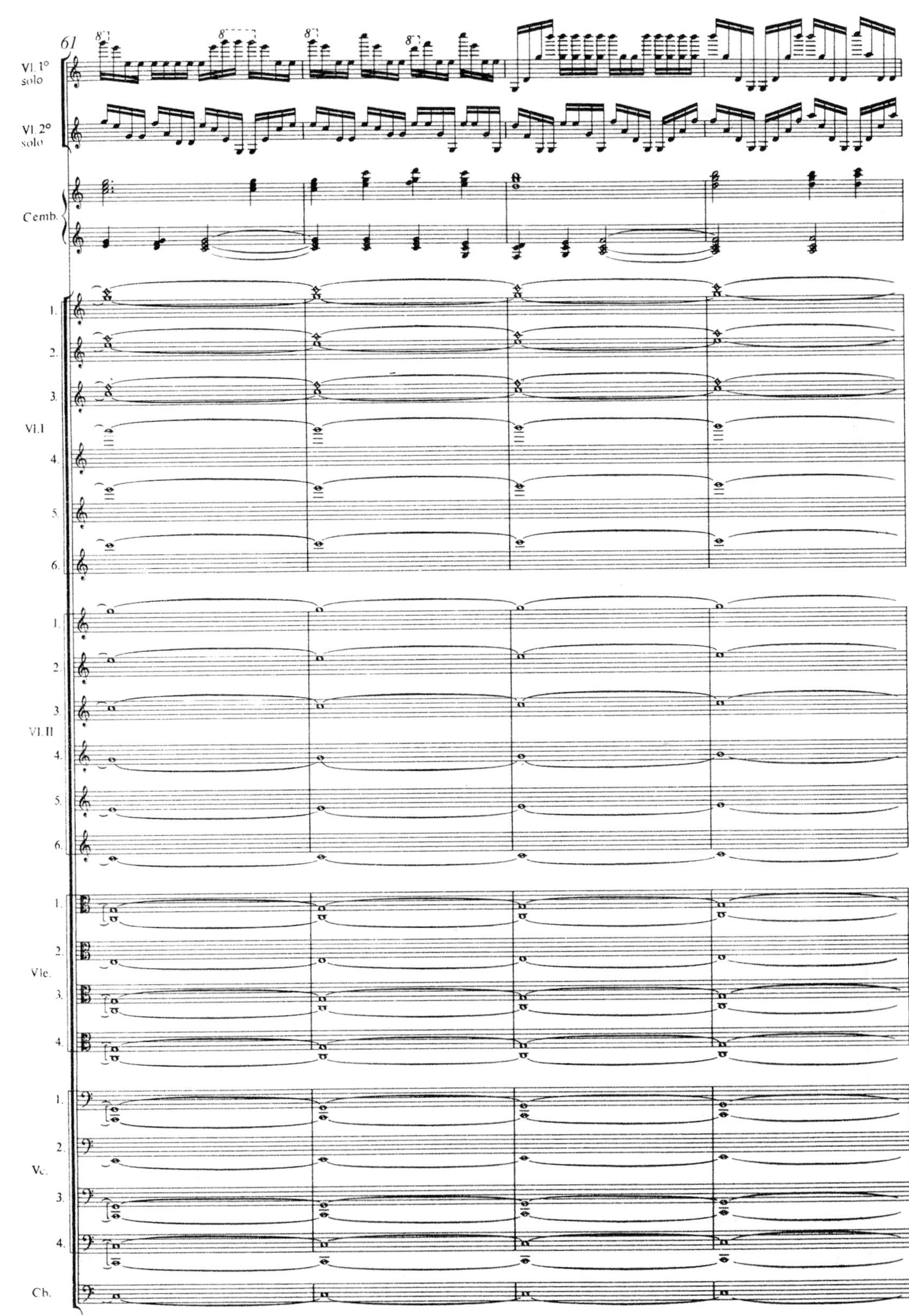
61
Vl. 1° solo
Vl. 2° solo
Cemb.
1.
2.
3.
Vl. I
4.
5.
6.
1.
2.
3.
Vl. II
4.
5.
6.
1.
2.
Vle.
3.
4.
1.
2.
Vc.
3.
4.
Cb.

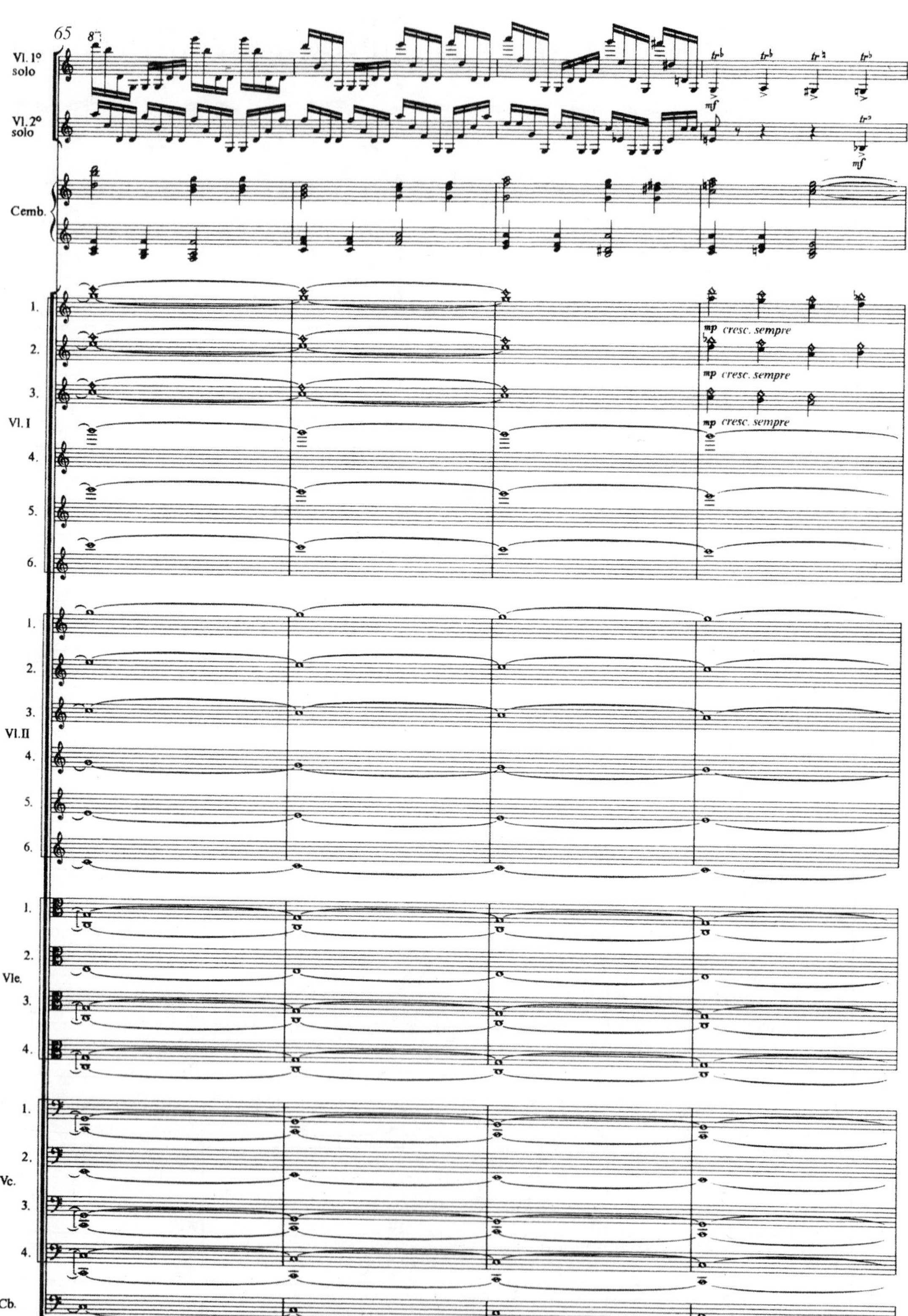
65
Vl. 1º solo
Vl. 2º solo
Cemb.
Vl. I
Vl. II
Vle.
Vc.
Cb.
mf
mp cresc. sempre
mp cresc. sempre
mp cresc. sempre

69
Vl.1° solo
Vl.2° solo
f
f
Cemb.
Vl. I
mp cresc. sempre
mp cresc. sempre
mp cresc. sempre
Vl. II
mf cresc. sempre
mf cresc. sempre
mf cresc. sempre
mf cresc. sempre
mf cresc. sempre
mf cresc. sempre
Vle.
Vc.
Cb.

73
Vl. 1° solo
Vl. 2° solo
ff
ff
Cemb.
Vl. I
1.
2.
3.
4.
5.
6.
Vl. II
1.
2.
3.
4.
5.
6.
Vle.
1.
2.
3.
f cresc. sempre
f cresc. sempre
f cresc. sempre
Vc.
1.
2.
3.
4.
f cresc. sempre
f cresc. sempre
f cresc. sempre
Cb.

77
60
Vl.1° solo
Vl.2° solo
Cemb.
Vl. I
Vl. II
Vle.
Vc.
fff
mp
(mp)
ff

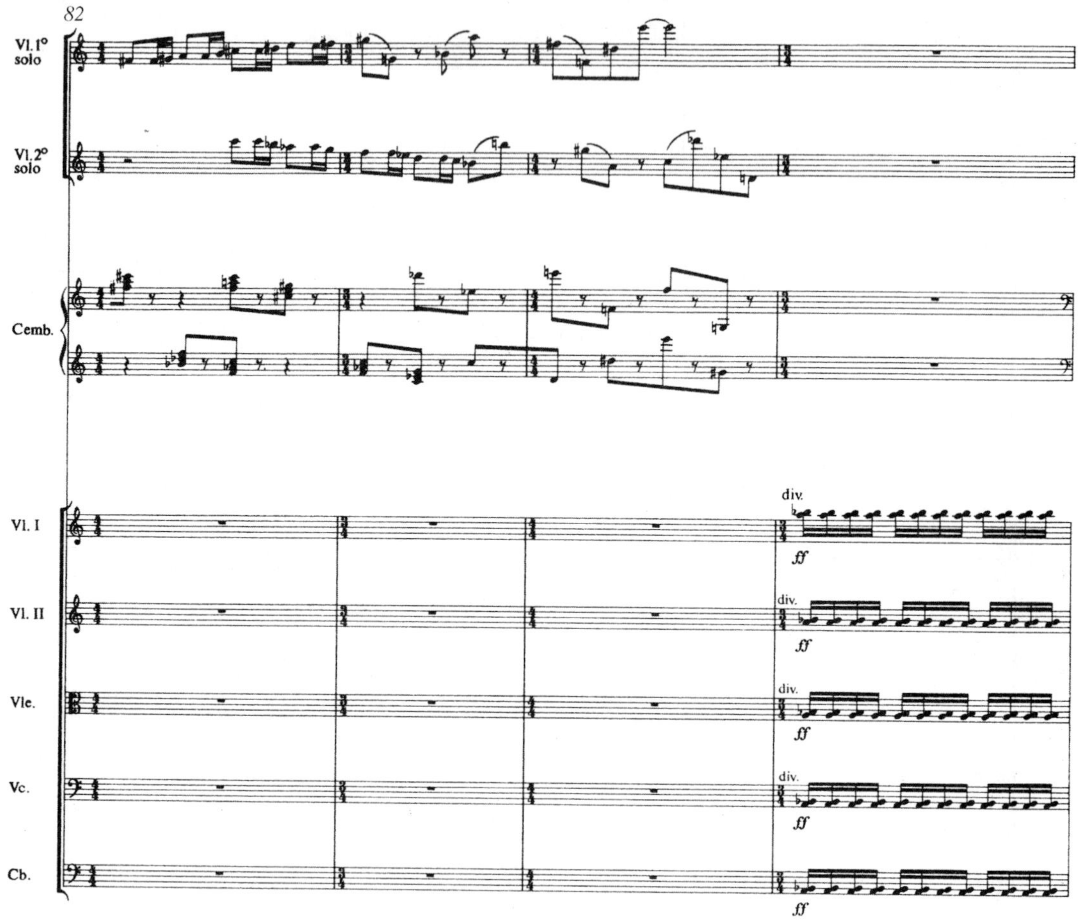

82
Vl. 1° solo
Vl. 2° solo
Cemb.
Vl. I
div.
ff
Vl. II
div.
ff
Vle.
div.
ff
Vc.
div.
ff
Cb.
ff

86
Vl. 1° solo
mp
Vl. 2° solo
mp
Cemb.
(mp)

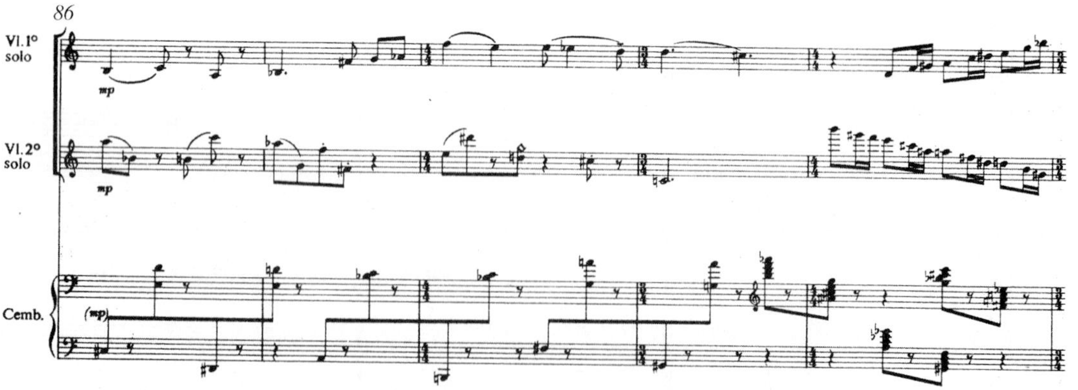

91

Vl.1° solo

mp

Vl.2° solo

mp

Cemb.

(mp)

a3

Vl.I

ff

a3

ff

a3

Vl.II

ff

a3

ff

a2

Vle.

ff

a2

ff

a2

Vc.

ff

a2

ff

Cb.

ff

100
Vl. 1° solo
Vl. 2° solo
Cemb.
Vl. I
Vl. II
Vle.
Vc.
Cb.
ff
sul pont.
pp
pizz.

104
Vl. I
Vl. II
Vle.
Vc.
Cb.

108
61
Vl. solo
Vl. solo
Cemb.
(f)
f
Vl. I
Vl. II
Vle.
Vc.
Cb.

111
Vl.1° solo
Vl.2° solo
Cemb.

114
Vl.1° solo
Vl.2° solo
Cemb.

118
Vl.1° solo
Vl.2° solo
Cemb.

121
Vl. 1° solo
Vl. 2° solo
Cemb.
uniti ord.
Vl. I
pp
uniti ord.
Vl. II
pp
unite
Vle.
pp
arco
Cb.
pp
125
Vl. I
ff
Vl. II
ff
Vle.
ff
Vc.
ff
Cb.
ff

133

Vl.1° solo

Vl.2° solo

Vl.I 1. 2. 3. 4. 5. 6.

mf

Vl.II 1. 2.

mf

Vle. 1. 2. 3. 4.

pizz.

mf

137
Vl.1° solo
Vl.2° solo
Vl.I
Vl.II
Vle.
Vc.
Cb.
mf
pizz.
f

140
Vl.1° solo
Vl.2° solo
1.
2.
3.
Vl.I
4.
5.
6.
1.
2.
3.
Vl.II
4.
5.
6.
1.
2.
Vle.
3.
4.
1.
2.
Vc.
3.
4.
Cb.

144
Vl. 1° solo
Vl. 2° solo
Vl. I
Vl. II
Vle.
Vc.
Cb.
ff

148
Vl.1° solo
fff
Vl.2° solo
fff
Cemb.
(fff)
Vl.I
1.
2.
3.
4.
5.
6.
Vl.II
1.
2.
3.
4
5.
6.
fff
Vle.
1.
2.
3.
4.
arco
Vc.
1.
2.
3.
4.
Cb.
arco
fff
attacca

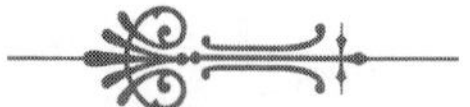

Alfred Schnittke's Concerto Grosso for two violins, harpsichord (doubling on piano), and string orchestra was commissioned by violinists Gidon Kremer and Tatiana Grindenko and premiered with them as soloists in March 1977 in Leningrad. Kremer, one of the leading young Soviet violinists, and his wife Grindenko played the concerto in several Soviet cities that year and took it on tour through West Germany and Austria, helping to establish Schnittke's reputation in the West.

The concerto is in six movements: Preludio, Toccata, Recitativo, Cadenza, Rondo, and Postludio. The titles of the work and its movements invoke Baroque models. The alternation of soloists and orchestra resembles that of a Vivaldi concerto (see NAWM 93), although the fast movements do not use Vivaldi's ritornello form. Some of the musical material, such as the figure that opens the Toccata, is close to Vivaldi's style. And the harpsichord is identified with Baroque music.

But not all is Baroque. Schnittke was interested in contrasting elements of diverse styles with each other, an approach he called *polystylism*. In this concerto, he plays off three stylistic categories: eighteenth-century styles, modern atonality, and what he called "banal popular music," represented here by a hymnlike tune presented at the beginning of the Preludio. This juxtaposition of very different styles gives new meaning to the word and genre *concerto*, which originally meant a work that combined diverse performing forces to work in concert. Schnittke took some of the material from film scores he had composed, and this adds another level of juxtaposition, between the popular medium of film music and the classical genre of the concerto.

The Toccata alternates sections with contrasting thematic material and stylistic allusions (see chart on page 887). Part of the point of combining styles from the past and present, and from the classical and popular traditions, is that all these types of music coexist in the modern world. The same is true in the piece. Each style is evoked through melodic material and procedures associated with that style, but no style appears in its pure form. Rather, the traits of each style are mixed with modernist procedures, bringing that style into the modern era, and in the final section all the thematic material appears simultaneously, representing a coming together of all these contrasting types of music.

In the A section (measures 1–30), Schnittke uses Baroque ideas and material to generate modern textures. The main theme (measures 1–8) is a motoric melody in A minor marked by sequences, scales, arpeggiations, and other Vivaldi-like figuration. It is introduced by solo violin 2, joined in canon a beat later by solo violin 1. The initial entrance of the soloists sounds neoclassical, almost Baroque. What could be more Baroque than a canon? But when the orchestra comes in, Schnittke uses canon to create a very un-Baroque texture. A twelve-part canon in the violins on the main theme, imitated at the unison and at the time interval of one eighth note, has an effect similar to Ligeti's micropolyphony (see NAWM 199), creating a mostly diatonic wash of sound. Over this the soloists modulate around the circle of fifths from A minor to F minor (measures 8–11). This adds polytonality to the

Measure	Section/ Theme	Style invoked	Traditional devices	Modern procedures
1	A	Baroque/Vivaldi	Canon at unison, circle-of-fifth progressions	Micropolyphony, diatonic dissonance, canon at semitone, chromatic saturation, polytonality
31	B	Galant/Haydn	Melody-accompaniment texture, tonal harmony, canon at octave	Micropolyphony, canon at semitone, polytonality, chromatic saturation, clusters
52	A'	Baroque/Vivaldi	Canon at unison, canon in augmentation	Micropolyphony, canon at semitone, polytonality, chromatic saturation
60	C	Popular/hymnlike	Tonal harmony, homophonic harmonization, canon in inversion	Diatonic dissonance, polytonality, canon at semitone, chromatic saturation
78	D	Twelve-tone plus Stravinskian blocks	Twelve-tone techniques, canon in inversion, juxtaposing blocks	Micropolyphony, polytonality
109	B' + C'		Canon	Clusters, polytonality
129	All		Twelve-tone techniques, canon in inversion, augmentation	Canon at semitone, polytonality, micropolyphony

mix, plus chromatic saturation—because, through the modulations, the soloists touch upon all the chromatic notes that were missing from the theme. Although the basic ideas—the Vivaldi-like theme, canon, sequence, and motion down the circle of fifths—are all typical of Baroque concertos, Schnittke uses them to create a very modern effect.

At measure 14, the violins stop and the violas and cellos begin their own canon, based on the middle segment of the A theme. The first viola plays this segment in F♯ minor, and each of the other five instruments descends from one to five semitones and then begins to play the same segment in canon with the others, until the six minor keys from F♯ down to C♯ are all sounding at once. This texture recurs in the violins at measure 19 with all twelve minor keys in order from B minor on down, and again at measures 23 and 27 in the entire orchestra, starting on E minor and A minor respectively. The beginning keys in these four canons create another circle-of-fifths motion, F♯–B–E–A. These passages expand on the micropolyphony, polytonality, and chromatic saturation already evident in the opening section.

In between these canonic passages in the orchestra, the soloists play their own canons over descending-third patterns in the harpsichord. Each successive canon is at a closer interval in time, shrinking from three sixteenth notes to one. Each canon rapidly moves through a circle of fifths. Throughout measures 14–27, the alternation of soloists and orchestra, the motoric theme, the canons and sequences, and the circle-of-fifth motions are all right out of Vivaldi's playbook, but the sound is nothing Vivaldi would have ever imagined.

The canons end on a total chromatic cluster in measure 29, and the B section begins (measures 30–51). Here the style changes to something like the galant style of the mid-to-late eighteenth century. If we extract from the texture just the harpsichord and solo violin 2, the two sound like a passage from a Classic-era sonata: the keyboard plays a simple accompaniment, the violin a Classically phrased melody, and both follow a tonal harmonic progression in C♯ minor. But again Schnittke uses canon to create a more complex texture. Solo violin 1 echoes the melody, first a measure later, then half a measure (measure 35), and finally just a beat later (measure 39). Meanwhile, the orchestral strings treat the melody in canon at the semitone, creating chromatic clusters. In measures 44–51, the soloists play dissonant double stops that fill in notes necessary for chromatic saturation.

At measure 52 the A theme returns, now in an incredibly complex 21-part canon in the five chromatic keys from C♯ minor (in the contrabass, in augmentation) down to A minor (in the first violins)—the keys of the B and A sections, respectively.

Section C begins at measure 60 with a more dramatic contrast of style. The orchestral lines converge on an expansive C-major triad. The harpsichord plays the hymnlike tune introduced at the beginning of the concerto's first movement, harmonized homophonically, and echoed in inverted canon in the harpsichord's left hand. Over this the soloists play widely spaced arpeggiations and double stops, drawing notes from the chords in the harpsichord. At measure 68 the soloists begin a new, chromatic figuration of trills and arpeggios. Simultaneously, the orchestra instruments begin another canon, based on an undulating ostinato in the upper three instruments that repeats in six-beat cycles; it is imitated by successively lower trios of instruments, each entering a major seventh lower and five beats later.

So far, Schnittke has used techniques of tonal styles to generate unusual modernist textures. In the D section (measures 78–108), he evokes two modern styles: twelve-tone music (see NAWM 161 and 163) and the pulsating style of Stravinsky's *Rite of Spring* (NAWM 164). The twelve-tone melody starts with B–A–C–H (B♭–A–C–B♮) in measure 78, an allusion both to Bach and to Schoenberg, whose row for his Piano Suite also includes BACH (see NAWM 161). The pulsating dissonances also build from B♭ and A (measure 85) to B♭, A, and C (measure 93) and finally to all four notes of BACH (measure 101). After being juxtaposed as alternating blocks several times—a Stravinskian technique—the twelve-tone and pulsating styles combine at measure 102. Meanwhile, hints of the A theme have appeared periodically in inverted canon (measures 82, 90, and 98) and canon at the semitone (measures 106–7, hidden in the pulsating texture).

The rest of the piece mixes the elements already presented. In the next section (measures 109–128), material from section B returns (in reverse order) in the solo violins, joined by the C theme at measure 113 in the harpsichord (with the melody in F♯ minor and accompaniment in C minor). The orchestra enters at measure 121 with the first part of the B theme in canon at the semitone. The final section (measures 129–51) combines all the themes at once: the soloists play twelve-tone canons derived from the D theme; the orchestral violins play the B theme in canon in all minor keys from G down to G♯; the violas and cellos play the A theme in augmentation in all minor keys from G down to C; and the contrabass plays the C theme in augmentation in C♯ minor. The movement ends with repeating dissonant figures in the solo instruments and a closing twelve-note chord in the orchestra. In this final section, the stylistic contrasts in the movement are resolved paradoxically, with all the themes coexisting, but in a modernist world of maximal density and complexity.

Michael Daugherty (b. 1954)

Dead Elvis

For solo bassoon and chamber ensemble

1993

CD 14|63

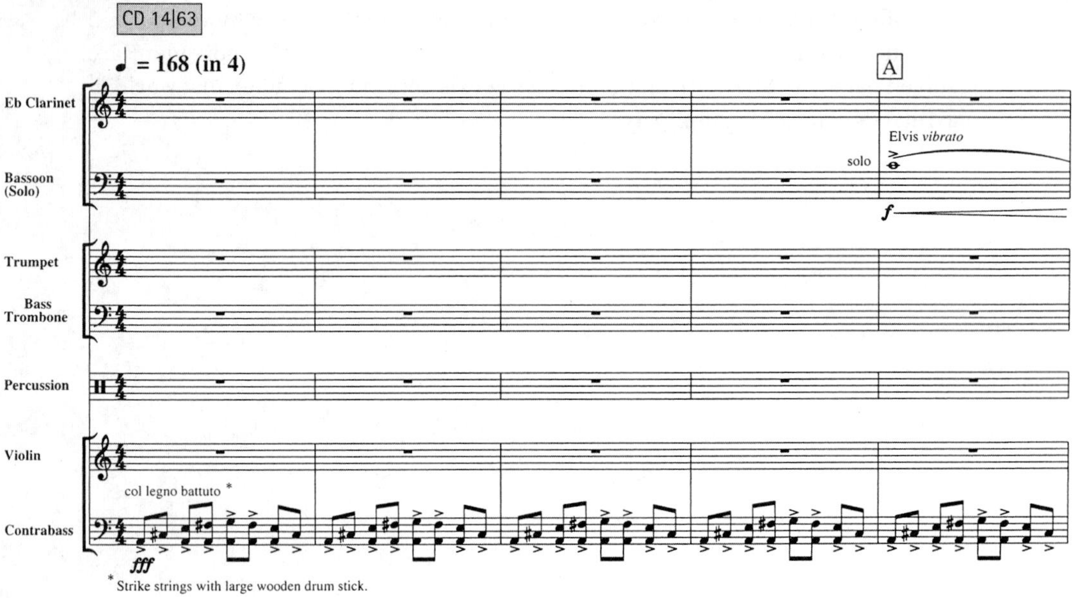

 All instruments sound at notated pitch except for contrabass, which sounds an octave lower.

12
B
Cl.
Bn.
f
ff
sfffz
Tpt.
Tbn.
Perc.
Vn.
Cb.
18
C
damp Crotale
accented, full bow
ff
Straight metal mute
staccato
gl.
f
sffz
l.v.
simile
(col legno battuto)
fff

24
D
Cl.
Bn.
Tpt.
Tbn.
Perc.
Vn.
Cb.
simile
gl.
senza sord.
damp Crotale
l.v.
ff
f
sfffz
30
E
staccato
open
p
(col legno battuto)

36
F
Cl.
Bn.
ff
sfffz
f
Tpt.
Tbn.
simile
gl.
p < sffz
Perc.
Vn.
Cb.
42
G
(l.v.)

64
H
48
Cl.
Bn.
f
ff
sffz
ff
Tpt.
Tbn.
f
gl.
p
sffz
Perc.
Large Cowbell
(drum sticks)
p
Vn.
ff
l.v. open strings
(col legno battuto)
pizz., secco
Cb.
ff
53
Cl.
Bn.
Tpt.
Tbn.
Perc.
Vn.
Cb.

57
I
Elvis vibrato
fff espr.
Cl.
Bn.
Tpt.
Tbn.
Cymbal
bell
pp
Perc.
Vn.
Bartók pizz.
Cb.
61
Cl.
Bn.
Tpt.
Tbn.
Perc.
Vn.
Cb.

65
Cl.
Bn.
Tpt.
Straight metal mute
Tbn.
p
cresc. poco a poco
mp
Perc.
cresc. poco a poco
mp
Vn.
Cb.
69
J
Cl.
f cresc.
fff
f
fff
Bn.
ff
Tpt.
ffpp
ff
Tbn.
(cresc.)
f
ff
mf
ff
secco
Perc.
(cresc.)
mf
f
mp
f
secco
Vn.
mf
ff
rest stick
Cb.
mf
ff

K
L
74
Cl.
Bn.
Tpt.
Tbn.
Perc.
Vn.
Cb.
secco
cresc.
80
65
M
♩ = 66
Elvis vibrato
(solo)
ff espr. à la Las Vegas
(cresc.)
(Cym.)
bell
Bongos
low
high
Cowbell
full bow
(pizz.) *
* strike strings with palm of hand to create backbeat

molto rit.
84
Cl.
Bn.
Tpt.
Tbn.
Perc.
Vn.
Cb.
f operatically
plunger
edge
88
N ♩ = 168
dim.
(cym.)
bell
Brake dr.
(drum stick)
arco (with bow)

O
Elvis vib.
p espr.
fp
ff
p
plunger
ffp
pp
sfffz
edge
f
Cl.
Bn.
Tpt.
Tbn.
Perc.
Vn.
Cb.

103
Cl.
Bn.
Tpt.
Tbn.
(Cym.)
Perc.
(Bongo)
Vn.
Cb.
107
P
cresc.
cresc. poco a poco
(cowbell)
(l.v.)

111
Cl.
(cresc.)
ff
Bn.
Tpt.
ffp
pp
Tbn.
p
sfffz
(Cym.)
Perc.
(Bongo)
Vn.
(cresc.)
ff
Cb.
115
Cl.
(cresc.)
fff
Bn.
Tpt.
pp
ffp
pp
ffp
pp
open
p
Tbn.
p
sfffz
Perc.
Vn.
(cresc.)
fff
Cb.

119
Cl.
Bn.
Tpt.
Tbn.
Perc.
Vn.
Cb.
cresc. poco a poco
(open)
sffz
123
66
Q
(cresc.)
ffff
fff
ff
gliss.
p
edge
fpp
cresc.
f
bell
pp
arco
with energy

127
Cl.
Bn.
Elvis vib.
ff
Tpt.
Tbn.
edge l.v.
Perc.
cresc.
sfz
Vn.
f
Cb.
130
Cl.
Bn.
fff
ff
fff
ff
(open)
Tpt.
pp
p
pp
p
Tbn.
Crotale
laissez vibrer
Brake Dr., Metal beater
simile
Perc.
f
Vn.
Cb.

133
Cl.
Bn.
fff
ff
Tpt.
pp
p
Tbn.
Perc.
Vn.
Cb.
136
R
Cl.
Bn.
fff
ff
Tpt.
pp
p
mf cresc.
sffz
Tbn.
Perc.
(l.v.)
Vn.
Cb.

139
Cl.
Bn.
Tpt.
Tbn.
Cowbell
Crotale
(l.v.)
Cowbell
simile
Perc.
Vn.
Cb.
142

145
S
Cl.
Bn.
Tpt.
Tbn.
Perc.
Vn.
Cb.
f
fp
fff
pp
p
f cresc.
148
sffz
ff
(cresc.)
(plunger)
long gliss.
sfffz
Cym., Drum sticks
Bongo low
f driving energetic groove

151
Cl.
fp
sffz
f
Bn.
ff
fff
Tpt.
p
sfz
long gliss.
Tbn.
fp
sfffz
Perc.
Vn.
Cb.
153
Cl.
fp
sffz
f
Bn.
ff
fff
Tpt.
p
long gliss.
Tbn.
fp
sfffz
Perc.
Vn.
Cb.

155
Cl.
Bn.
Tpt.
Tbn.
Perc.
Vn.
Cb.
fp
sffz
f
ff
fff
sfz
p
long gliss.
sfffz
67
T
157
secco
sul G
fff

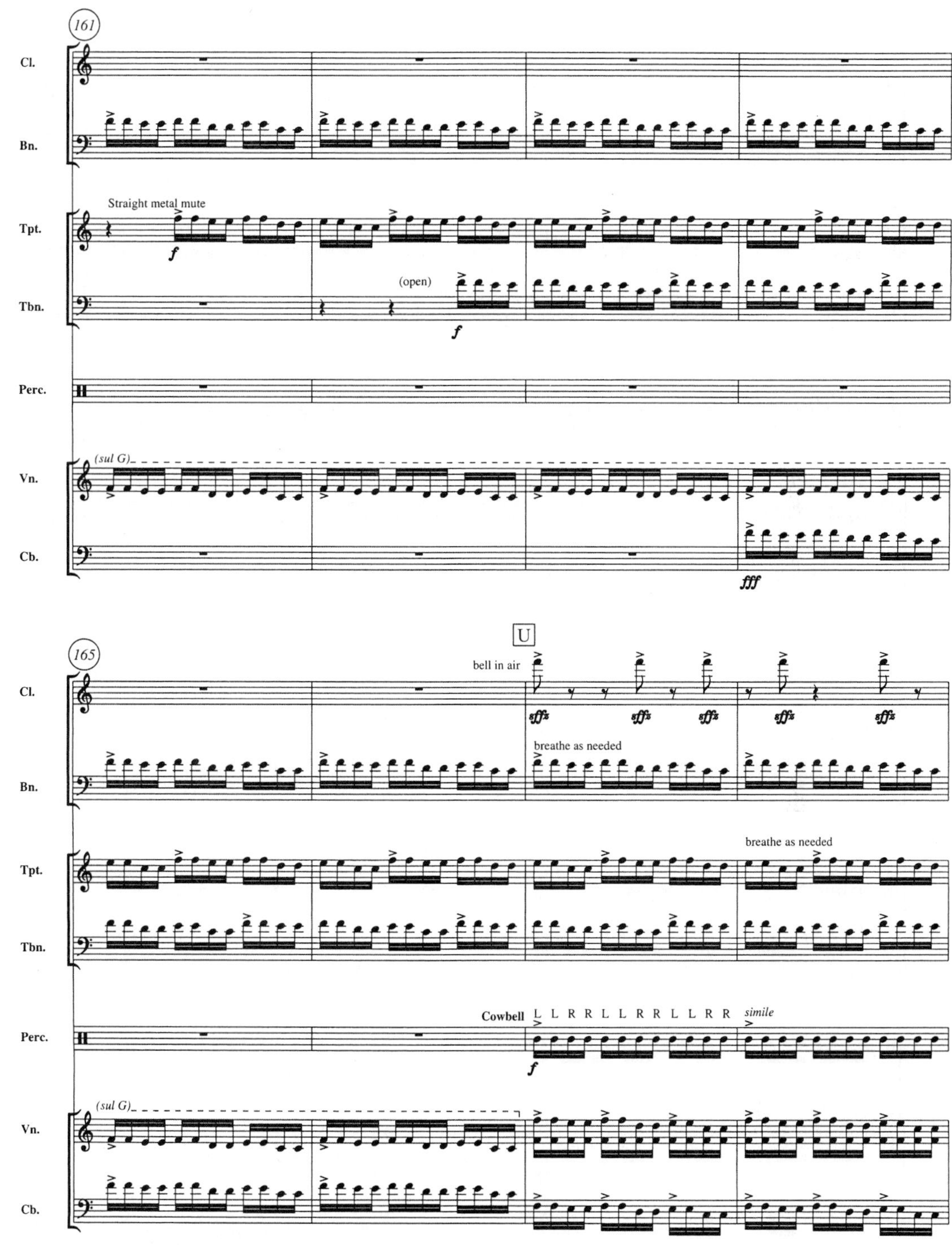
161
Cl.
Bn.
Straight metal mute
Tpt.
f
(open)
Tbn.
f
Perc.
(sul G)
Vn.
Cb.
fff
U
165
bell in air
Cl.
sffz
sffz
sffz
sffz
sffz
breathe as needed
Bn.
breathe as needed
Tpt.
Tbn.
Cowbell
L L R R L L R R L L R R
simile
Perc.
f
(sul G)
Vn.
Cb.

169
Cl.
Bn.
Tpt.
breathe as needed
Tbn.
cresc. poco a poco
Perc.
Vn.
Cb.
173
G.P.
V
G.P.

68
178
G.P.
W ♩. = 56 (in 2)
Cl.
Bn.
Tpt.
Tbn.
(Cowbell)
Perc.
pizz.
sul A
sul E
sul A
sim.
Vn.
Cb.
183
8va
solo
molto vib.
gliss
gl.
espr.

191
X
Cl.
Bn.
solo
f
7
ff
p
Tpt.
Tbn.
Perc.
Vn.
Cb.
(8va)
vibrato gliss.
ff
pp
196
8va
gliss.

* emphasize backbeat, do not cover bassoon

210
Cl.
Bn.
Tpt.
Tbn.
slow gliss.
slow gliss.
Perc.
Vn.
slow gliss.
slow gliss.
Cb.
215
AA
Cl.
pp
p
Bn.
ff
fff
Tpt.
pp
p
Tbn.
slow gliss.
pp
p
Perc.
pp
p
Vn.
slow gliss.
pp
p
Cb.
pp
p

219
Cl.
Bn.
Tpt.
Tbn.
Perc.
Vn.
Cb.
slow gliss
gl.
224
BB
pp
p dim.
ff
fff
slow gliss

228
Cl.
(dim.)
Bn.
dim.
Tpt.
(dim.)
slow gliss
Tbn.
(dim.)
Perc.
(dim.)
slow gliss
Vn.
(dim.)
Cb.
(dim.)
CC
233
Cl.
pp
p
secco
Bn.
mf
fff
Tpt.
gliss
Tbn.
Perc.
gl.
Vn.
Cb.

* *gliss.* immediately, exaggerated, and very slowly

69
EE
249
♩ = subito 176 (in 4)
Cl.
Bn.
sffz
f
14
senza sord.
Tpt.
Tbn.
Perc.
Vn.
rest bow
Cb.
255
ff with energy

* Measures 261–292: Trumpet and Trombone should project over the ensemble.

264
Cl.
Bn.
Tpt.
Tbn.
Perc.
p
f
Vn.
Cb.
267
GG
fp
gl.

270
Cl.
Bn.
Tpt.
Tbn.
Perc.
Vn.
Cb.
p
273
Cl.
Bn.
Tpt.
Tbn.
Perc.
f
Vn.
Cb.

276
HH
Cl.
Bn.
Tpt.
Tbn.
Perc.
fp
f
Vn.
gl.
cb.
accel. poco a poco
280
cresc.
f (cresc.)
Cb.

11
rubato, freely
quasi cadenza
283
Cl.
Bn.
ff
Tpt.
(cresc.)
fff
senza sord.
Tbn.
(cresc.)
fff
senza sord.
Perc.
secco
(cresc.)
ff
Vn.
gl.
gl.
Cb.
287
rit.
♩ = 168
Cl.
Bn.
Elvis vibrato
(cresc.)
fff
Tpt.
Tbn.
Perc.
Vn.
Cb.

* Strike strings with wooden drum stick

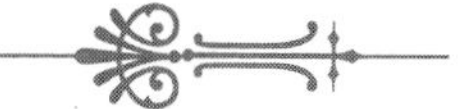

Michael Daugherty composed *Dead Elvis* in 1993 on a commission from bassoonist Chuck Ullery together with the Grand Tetons Festival and Boston Musica Viva. According to his own account, he began the piece by asking a group of musicians to improvise on the basic ideas, recorded the session, and used those materials in planning the work. It was premiered in July of that year at the Grand Tetons Festival in Jackson Hole, Wyoming, with Ullery as soloist and the composer conducting. Ullery also appears as the soloist on the recording that accompanies this anthology.

The piece is part of Daugherty's series of works on icons of American popular culture. It memorializes Elvis Presley, who made his reputation in the mid-1950s as a gyrating star of rock and roll, appeared in several Hollywood films, ended his career in the 1970s singing shows in Las Vegas wearing a white polyester jumpsuit studded with rhinestones, and died at age 42, reclusive and overweight, at his Graceland estate. But the piece also takes on the phenomenon of Elvis impersonators, who dress as he did in Las Vegas and lip-synch or sing his music—or, in this case, play the bassoon. Daugherty explains in a note in the score:

> No rock and roll personality seems to have inspired as much speculation, adulation, and impersonation as Elvis Presley (1935–77). In *Dead Elvis* (1993), the bassoon soloist is an Elvis impersonator accompanied by a chamber ensemble. It is more than a coincidence that *Dead Elvis* is scored for the same instrumentation as Stravinsky's *Histoire du Soldat* (1918), in which a soldier sells his violin, and his soul, to the devil for a magic book. I offer a new spin on this Faustian scenario: a rock star sells out to Hollywood, Colonel Parker [Presley's manager], and Las Vegas for wealth and fame. I use *Dies irae*—a medieval Latin chant for the Day of Judgment—as the principal musical theme in my composition to pose the question, is Elvis dead or alive beyond the grave of Graceland? In *Dead Elvis* we hear fast and slow fifties rock and roll ostinati in the double bass, violin, and bongos, while the bassoonist gyrates, double-tongues, and croons his way through variations of *Dies irae*.
>
> Elvis is part of American culture, history, and mythology, for better or for worse. If you want to understand America and all its riddles, sooner or later you will have to deal with (Dead) Elvis.

In using *Dies irae* as a symbol of death and the diabolical, Daugherty continues a long musical tradition established by Berlioz in *Symphonie fantastique* (NAWM 130), while taking his subject much less seriously.

The piece unfolds in a series of sections, each invoking certain musical styles and creating an appropriate atmosphere.

At the opening, the contrabass plays a boogie-woogie bass, popular in early rock and roll. But instead of bowing or plucking the strings, the player is directed to hit them with a stick, recalling the *col legno* sound (hitting the strings with the wood of the bow) Berlioz used in the finale of *Symphonie fantastique*. The bassoon plays a comic repeating figure that alternates between an "Elvis vibrato" and an explosive *sforzando* on the lowest note in its range. The percussion has a similar figure alternating a high crotale (tuned cymbal) with low sound on a brake drum. Over this texture, the violin and trombone introduce *Dies irae.*

In the next section (measure 51), the bassoon takes over *Dies irae,* repeating its first phrase obsessively, echoed by violin. The clarinet adds a meandering, mostly chromatic descant. (The clarinet and trumpet are notated in the score at sounding pitch.)

At measure 82, the bassoon croons Presley's chart-topping 1960 hit *It's Now or Never,* to the tune of the old Italian song *O sole mio.* Marked "*espr[essivo] à la Las Vegas,*" the melody appears in the bassoon's highest range. The violin keeps up the chant in a contrasting meter over a twelve-tone pizzicato bass line, and the bongos and cowbell introduce a Cuban sound.

As the tune comes to a close in measure 89, the violin and bass begin the chant in parallel dominant seventh chords, in a Latin syncopated rhythm. The Latin feel is reinforced by cymbal and bongos. The bassoon joins the bass at measure 95, while the violin and clarinet drift upwards chromatically and the trombone and trumpet play their own statement of *Dies irae* with plunger mutes, evoking a jazz sound. When the trombone and trumpet begin a repetition at measure 109, the bassoon starts on its lowest note and slowly treks upward chromatically to the top of its range, keeping in rhythm with the bass, as everyone crescendos to a peak.

At measure 125, the opening material returns, varied and with additions, including the Latin-rhythm violin figure from measure 89 (which enters at measure 129, playing the chant in parallel tritones); rapid rising scales in bassoon and clarinet; and a new version of the chant in the trumpet (measure 137). Here Latin meets boogie-woogie. Like the previous section, this all gradually moves higher in the range and grows ever louder.

A new variation of the chant follows at measure 157, a repeating figure in sixteenth notes launched by the bassoon and picked up by the other instruments.

The mood changes suddenly at measure 181. The pizzicato violin slowly arpeggiates an E-minor triad, evoking the background accompaniment used for slow songs from Bellini operas (see NAWM 138) to pop ballads. Over this, the contrabass plays a distorted G-major *Dies irae* in two-note segments, scooping up an octave to the first note of each pair and swelling on it before moving on to the second. The bassoon does the same in E minor, then the two play together in parallel thirds. At measure 209, the bassoon soars to a high sustained E, the bass takes over the E-minor arpeggiation, and the other instruments play the chant softly in parallel seventh chords, often moving in glissandos. Beginning in measure 225, as the other instruments continue, the bassoon slowly sinks chromatically from the top of its range to the bottom, at first in long notes, then in syncopated sixteenth-note octave sputters, diminuendoing as it sinks, like a dying beast. If Elvis dies during the piece, this is the moment.

The final section (measure 249) turns active again. The bassoon initiates the chant in short *sforzandos,* joined by the quickly pulsing violin playing it in parallel tritones as before. At measure 261, the trumpet and trombone join the chant, and bassoon, clarinet, contrabass, and percussion play repeating figures, establishing a jazzy groove in the Latin-influenced style of Lalo Schifrin. The texture breaks for a cadenza, a rising chromatic scale in the bassoon from the bottom to the top of its range (measure 285). After a few loud chords and a reminder of the opening section, the piece ends on a *sforzando* chord with the bassoon holding its lowest note as loud and long as possible.

Dead Elvis is a virtuoso workout for the soloist, who has to play at the extremes of the range, act like Elvis, and negotiate the white jumpsuit, hairpiece, and pasted-on lambchop sideburns. The percussion instruments—ride cymbal, crotale, cowbell, high and low bongos, and brake drum, arrayed from high to low on the percussion staff—are all associated with styles of popular music, and so lend the proper atmosphere. So do the mutes on the brass instruments, especially the plunger (literally, the rubber part of a bathroom plunger) and the Harmon mute (or wah-wah mute), which are common in jazz; when these are used, a plus sign (+) over the note means the mute is closed over the instrument's bell, producing a stopped sound, and a circle over the note means the mute is open, allowing air to pass through.

205

Bright Sheng (b. 1955)

Seven Tunes Heard in China: No. 1, *Seasons*

For solo cello

1995

CD 14|70 CD 6|88

Bright Sheng was born in Shanghai, China, and worked in the Qinghai province near Tibet for seven years during the Cultural Revolution (1966–76), China's repressive mass mobilization, when young intellectuals were exiled to rural areas to work beside and be "reeducated" by the peasants. When the universities finally reopened in 1978, Sheng was one of the first music students accepted at the Shanghai Conservatory, and four years later he came to the United States. Conversant in both Chinese traditional music and Western classical music, he has synthesized the two traditions in many works. His *Seven Tunes Heard in China* for solo cello was commissioned by the Pacific Symphony on behalf of a patron, George Cheng, and was dedicated to his wife, Arlene Cheng. Sheng wrote the piece for cellist Yo-Yo Ma, who premiered it at Cheng Hall at the University of California, Irvine, in 1995.

In this suite, Sheng combines features of the Bach cello suites, including dancelike rhythms, double stops, motivic repetition, sequences, and simulated polyphony, with the character and style of Chinese music. Each of the seven movements presents a melody Sheng heard in a different province in China, and the ornamentation, glissandos, and free treatment of meter suggest a Chinese performance style. During the course of the suite, the cello imitates the sounds of several Chinese string, wind, and percussion instruments, including the two-stringed bowed *erhu* and the plucked *qin*.

The first movement, *Seasons*, freely treats a melody from the Qinghai province. The tune contains several short melodic ideas that are highly rhythmic, suggesting the playful nature of the song text:

Spring is coming,
Narcissi are blooming,
The maiden is out from her boudoir seeking,
My love boy, lend me a hand, please.

The opening three measures establish A as the initial pitch center and present two of the recurring motives—the rising fourths followed by descending motion in measure 1 and the repeated pentatonic idea in measures 2–3. The next three measures complete the principal theme, rising to a high vibrato note followed by two mostly pentatonic phrases, and closing with a scalar descent. The remainder of the movement develops these motives.

Numerous characteristics of Chinese music appear in the melody, including quick ornamental turns, slides between pitches, and long held notes that crescendo with an intense vibrato (measures 4 and 16). Yet Sheng also develops motivic ideas in a traditional Western manner. In measures 7–11, the repeated motive with its alternating registers and double stops suggests two-part imitative counterpoint in the manner of J. S. Bach, culminating in a cadence on A in measure 12. The pitch center starts to wander with a move to E♭ in measure 13, and simulated imitation in measures 14–15 suggests polytonality, as motivic statements alternate centers on B♭ and E (measures 14–15). A varied statement of the second phrase of the theme, transposed up a fifth (beginning in the last beat of measure 15), leads to more quasi-polytonal alternations that highlight tritone transpositions between E and B♭ (measures 17–20 and 23–26) and A and E♭ (measures 21–22). The movement comes to a quiet close on an E♭, a tritone away from the pitch center at the beginning.

A performance of this work requires experience with both Western and Asian music. Yo-Yo Ma, heard on the accompanying recording, is ideally suited to these needs, combining mastery of the Bach cello suites with understanding of Chinese instruments and performance manners. He also edited the published score of the work. Indications of fingerings are not abundant, but his suggestion that the first measure should be played primarily with one finger establishes a technique that can be applied to the entire movement.

INSTRUMENT NAMES AND ABBREVIATIONS

The following tables set forth the English, Italian, German, and French names used for the various musical instruments in these scores, and their respective abbreviations.

WOODWINDS

English	*Italian*	*German*	*French*
Piccolo (Picc.)	Flauto piccolo (Fl. Picc.); Ottavino (Ott.)	Kleine Flöte (kl. Fl.)	Petite flûte
Flute (Fl.)	Flauto (Fl.), pl. Flauti; Flauto grande (Fl. gr.)	Flöte (Fl.), pl. Flöten; Große Flöte (gr. Fl.)	Flûte (Fl.)
Alto flute	Flauto alto (Fl. alto); Flauto contralto (fl.c-alto)	Altflöte	Flûte en sol
Oboe (Ob.)	Oboe (Ob.), pl. Oboi	Hoboe (Hb., Hob.), pl. Hoboen; Oboe (Ob.), pl. Oboen	Hautbois (Hb., Hautb.)
English horn (E.H.)	Corno inglese (C. ing., C. ingl., Cor. ingl., C.i.)	Englisches Horn, Englisch Horn (engl. Horn, Egl. H.)	Cor anglais (C.A., Cor ang.)
Sopranino clarinet	Clarinetto piccolo (clar. picc.)		
Clarinet (C., Cl., Clt., Clar.)	Clarinetto (Cl., Clar.), pl. Clarinetti (Cltti.)	Klarinette (Kl., Klar.), pl. Klarinetten; Clarinette (Cl.)	Clarinette (Cl.)
Alto clarinet (A. Cl.)			
Bass clarinet (B. Cl.)	Clarinetto basso (Cl. b., Cl. bas., Cl. basso, Clar. basso); Clarone (Clne.)	Bass Klarinette, Bassklarinette (Bkl., B.-Kl., Basskl.), Bassclarinette (Basscl., B.-Cl.)	Clarinette basse (Cl. bs.)
Contrabass clarinet (Cb. Cl.)			
Saxophone (Sax.) [alto, tenor, baritone, bass]	Sassofone	Saxophon	Saxophone
Bassoon (Bn., Bsn., Bssn.)	Fagotto (Fag., Fg.), pl. Fagotti	Fagott (Fag., Fg.), pl. Fagotte	Basson (Bssn., Bon.)
Contrabassoon (C. Bn., C. Bsn.); Double bassoon (D. Bsn.)	Contrafagotto (Cfg., C. Fag., Cont. F.)	Kontrafagott (K.-Fag., Kfg.)	Contrebasson (C. bssn.)
Cornett	Cornetto	Zink	Cornet-à-bouquin

BRASS

English	Italian	German	French
Horn, French horn (Hr., Hn.)	Corno (Cor., C., Cr.), pl. Corni	Horn (Hr.), pl. Hörner (Hörn., Hrn.)	Cor; Cor à pistons
Trumpet (Tpt., Trpt., Trp., Tr.)	Tromba (Tr., Trb.), pl. Trombe (Trbe., Tbe.); Clarino, pl. Clarini	Trompete (Tr., Trp., Trpt., Tromp.), pl. Trompeten	Trompette (Tr., Trp.)
Piccolo trumpet	Tromba piccola (Tr. picc.)		
Bass trumpet	Tromba bassa (Tr. bas.)		
Cornet	Cornetta, pl. Cornetti	Kornett	Cornet à pistons (C. à p., Pist.)
Trombone (Tr., Tbe., Tbn., Trb., Trm., Trbe.) [alto, tenor]	Trombone (Trbn., Tromb.), pl. Tromboni (Tbni., Trbni., Trni.) [alto, tenore]	Posaune (Ps., Pos.), pl. Posaunen [alt, tenor]	Trombone (Tr., Trb.)
Bass trombone (B. Tbn.)	Trombone basso (Trne. B.)	Bass Posaune	
Contrabass trombone	Cimbasso (Cimb.)		
Baritone horn (Baritone, Bar.)			
Tenor tuba		Tenortuba	
Tuba (Tb.)	Tuba (Tb., Tba.), pl. Tube	Tuba (Tb.); Basstuba (Btb.)	Tuba (Tb.)
Ophicleide	Oficleide	Ophikleide	Ophicléide

STRINGS

English	Italian	German	French
Violin (V., Vl., Vn., Vln., Vi.)	Violino (V., Vl., Vn., Vln., Viol.), pl. Violini (Vni.); Viola da braccio	Violine (V., Vl., Vln., Viol.), pl. Violinen; Geige (Gg.), pl. Geigen	Violon (V., Vl., Vln., Von.)
Viola (Va., Vl., pl. Vas.)	Viola (Va., Vla., Vl.), pl. Viole (Vle.)	Bratsche (Br.), pl. Bratschen	Alto (A., Alt.)
Violoncello, Cello (Vcl., Vc.)	Violoncello (Vc., Vcl., Vcll., Vcllo., Vlc.), pl. Violoncelli	Violoncell (Vc., Vcl., Violinc.), pl. Violoncelli (Vcll.)	Violoncelle (Vc., Velle., Vlle., Vcelle.)
Double bass (D. B., D. Bs.); String bass; Bass viol	Contrabasso (Cb., C. B.), Basso, pl. Contrabassi or Bassi (C. Bassi, Bi.); Violon, violone [may also designate or include cello or bass viola da gamba]	Kontrabass (Kb., K.-B.), pl. Kontrabässe; Contrabass (Contrab., C.-B.); Bass, pl. Bässe	Contrebasse (C. B.)
Viola da gamba; Viol; Gamba	Viola da gamba	Gambe	Viole

PERCUSSION

English	Italian	German	French
Percussion (Perc.)	Percussione	Schlagzeug (Schlag.)	Batterie (Batt.)
Timpani (Timp.); Kettledrums (K. D.)	Timpani (Timp., Tp.)	Pauken (Pk.)	Timbales (Timb.)
Snare drum (S. D., Sn. Dr.); Side drum	Tamburo piccolo (Tamb. picc.); Tamburo militare (Tamb. milit.); Tamburo (Tro.)	Kleine Trommel (Kl. Tr.)	Caisse claire (C. cl.); Tambour militaire (Tamb. milit.)
Tenor drum	Cassa rullante	Rührtrommel	Caisse roulante
Indian drum			
Tom-tom			
Tumba; Conga drum		Tumba	
Bongos			
Bass drum (B. drum, Bass dr., Bs. Dr.)	Gran cassa (Gr. Cassa, Gr. C., G. C.); Cassa (C.); Gran tamburo (Gr. Tamb.)	Große Trommel (Gr. Tr.)	Grosse caisse (Gr. c., G. C.)
Tambourine (Tamb.)	Tamburino (Tamb.)	Schellentrommel, Tamburin	Tambour de Basque (T. de Basq., T. de B., Tamb. de Basque), Tambourin (Tambin., Tin.)
Lion's roar			
Cymbals (Cym., Cymb.)	Piatti (P., Ptti., Piat.); Cinelli	Becken (Beck.)	Cymbales (Cym., Cymb.)
Suspended cymbal (Sus. cym., Susp. cymb.)			
Sizzle cymbal (Sizz. cym.)			
Hi-Hat			
Tam-Tam (Tam-T.); Gong	Tam-Tam (Tam-T., T-tam)	Tam-Tam	Tam-Tam
Triangle (Trgl., Tri.)	Triangolo (Trgl.)	Triangel (Trgl.)	Triangle (Triang.)
Anvil			
Glockenspiel (Glocken.)	Campanelli (Cmp., Campli.)	Glockenspiel (Glsp.)	Carillon
Bells; Tubular bells (Tub. bells); Chimes	Campane (Cam., Camp., Cmp.); sing. Campana (Cna.)	Glocken	Cloches
Japanese bells	Campanelli giapponesi (Camp. giapp.)		
Cowbells	Cencerro	Kuhglocken	Sonnailles
Sleighbells	Sonagli	Schellen	Grelots
Crotales (Crot.); Antique Cymbals	Crotali; Piatti antichi	Antiken Zimbeln	Cymbales antiques (Cym. ant.)
Xylophone (Xyl., Xylo.)	Xilofono, Silofono	Xylophon (Xyl.)	Xylophone (Xyl.)
Xylorimba			Xylorimba
Vibraphone (Vibr.)			Vibraphone (Vibr.)
Marimba			
Woodblock (Wd. Blk.)	Cassa di legno	Holzblock	Bloc de bois

(Percussion continued on page 934)

PERCUSSION (continued)

English	*Italian*	*German*	*French*
Chinese blocks			
Slap stick			
Rattle			
Claves			
Raspador			
Gourd			
Maracas; Maraca			Maracas (Mrc.)
Siren			

OTHER INSTRUMENTS

English	*Italian*	*German*	*French*
Harp (Hp., Hrp.)	Arpa (A., Arp.); Harpa	Harfe (Hfe., Hrf.)	Harpe (Hp.)
Piano (Pno.)	Pianoforte (P.-f., Pft., Pfte.); Piano	Klavier	Piano
Celesta (Cel.)	Celesta (Cel.)		Céleste
Harpsichord	Cembalo (Cemb.); Clavicembalo	Cembalo	Clavecin
Organ (Org.)	Organo (Org.) [Organo di legno is an organ with wooden pipes]	Orgel	Orgue
Synthesizer			
Guitar (Gtr.)	Chitarra	Gitarre (Git.)	Guitare (Guit.)
Lute	Lauto, leuto, liuto	Laute	Luth
Theorbo	Teorba; Chitarrone	Theorb; Chitarron	Téorbe
Archlute	Arcileuto	Erzlaute	Archiluth
Banjo			

Transposing instruments and timpani tunings are indicated using the following pitch names:

English	C	D♭	D	E♭	E	F	G	A♭	A	B♭	B
Italian	Do	Re♭	Re	Mi♭	Mi	Fa	Sol	La♭	La	Si♭	Si
French	Ut	Ré♭	Ré	Mi♭	Mi	Fa	Sol	La♭	La	Si♭	Si
German	C	Des	D	Es	E	F	G	As	A	B	H

For transposing instruments, if the music is written in C major, it will sound in the designated key; thus "in A" means that a notated C will sound as A, and every notated pitch will sound a minor third lower than written. Horns, clarinets in B♭ and A, and trumpets in B♭ sound lower than written; clarinets in D and E♭ and trumpets in D and F sound higher than written. English horns are in F, sounding a fifth lower than written; alto flutes are in G, sounding a fourth lower.

GLOSSARY OF SCORE AND PERFORMANCE INDICATIONS

For a glossary of general music terms, see *A History of Western Music*, 8th ed.

a, à The phrases *a 2* (*à 2*), *a 3* (*à 3*, etc.) indicate that the part is to be played in unison by 2, 3 (etc.) players, or that the group is to divide into 2, 3 (etc.) different parts (which meaning holds is usually obvious from the context); when a simple number (1., 2., etc.) is placed over a part, it indicates that only the first (second, etc.) player in that group should play.
A Alto.
a tempo At the (basic) tempo.
ab Off; *Dämpfer ab*, remove mute.
abdämpfen Damp; stop from vibrating.
aber But.
accelerando (accel.) Growing faster.
accompagnato, accompagnata Accompanied.
ad libitum (ad lib.) An indication giving the performer liberty; for example, to vary from strict tempo, to include or omit the part of some voice or instrument, or to include a cadenza of one's own invention.
adagio Slow, leisurely.
agitato, agité Agitated, excited.
al Until.
alla marcia Like a march; in march tempo.
allargando (allarg.) Growing broader or slower.
alle All; tutti.
allegretto A moderately fast tempo, between allegro and andante.
allegro A rapid tempo, between allegretto and presto.
allegro moderato At a moderately fast tempo.
allegro molto Very rapid tempo.
allegro possibile As fast as possible.
alto, Alt (A); pl. alti The deeper of the two main divisions of women's (or boys') voices; in vocal music in four or more parts, a part above the tenor and below the highest voice.
altri The others; used to designate the other players in an orchestral section when one or more players in the section are given separate parts.
am Griffbrett On a string instrument, bow near, or over, the fingerboard; *sul tasto.*
am Steg On a string instrument, bow over or very near the bridge, producing a thin, metallic sound; *sul ponticello.*
ancora Still, even.
andante A moderately slow tempo, between adagio and allegretto, about walking speed.
animant Growing more animated.
animato, animé Animated.
archi Strings, the string section of the orchestra.
arco Played with the bow; used to mark a return to bowing after a pizzicato passage.
ardente Ardent, passionate.
arpège Arpeggio, arpeggiation.
arpeggiando, arpeggiato (arpeg., arpegg., arp.) Arpeggiated; played in harp style, sounding the notes of the chord in quick succession rather than simultaneously.
assai Very.
assez lent Quite slow.
at the frog Play with the part of the bow nearest the player's hand (the *frog* of the bow).
attacca, attacca subito Begin the next movement or section without pause.
attacca *pp* Very soft attack.
auf On; *Dämpfer auf*, put mute in place.
auf der Bühne (a.d. Bühne) On stage.
avec With
avec une émotion naissante With new feeling.
avec une joie de plus en plus tumultueuse With a joy growing more and more tumultuous.
avec une joie voilée With veiled joy.

B Bass.
bacchetta (bacch.) Drumstick.

bacchetta di legno (bacch. di legno) Wooden drumstick.
bacchetta di triangolo (bacch. di Triang.) Metal stick used to play the triangle.
baguettes, baguettes tambour Drumsticks.
bass, basso, Baß (B); pl. bassi, Bässe A low male voice, or the lowest part in a vocal or instrumental work.
bedeutet Means, indicates.
begleitend Accompanying; indicates that another part has the leading voice in the texture.
Bartók pizzicato (Bartók pizz.) On a bowed string instrument, a sharp pizzicato plucked by two fingers with such force that the string snaps against the fingerboard.
bell in the air Sign for horn players to lift the bell of the instrument (where the sound comes out) to direct the sound forward.
ben Very, well.
bewegt, bewegte Agitated.
bien Very, well.
bois Wood; play with wooden drumstick.
bouché Stopped; play horn with hand in bell to mute the sound.
bravura Skill, virtuosity.
brushes Play with wire brushes rather than drumsticks.
Bühne Stage.

ca Circa.
cadenza A short or extended passage for solo instrument or voice in free, improvisatory style, usually at or just before or after a cadence.
calando Diminishing in volume and speed.
calmato a tempo Calming to return to the previous tempo.
calme Calm.
cambiare l'arco ad lib. Change bow direction as necessary; used to indicate that on a sustained tone the entire section should not bow simultaneously.
campana in aria On a brass instrument, play with the bell raised to achieve an especially prominent tone.
cantabile (cant., cantab.) In a singing style.
cantando Singing; in a singing manner.
cantando la melodia Emphasize the melody as if singing it.
cédez Hold back.
chaud Warm.
Chorauszug Transcription of the chorus parts, used for rehearsal or for cues during performance.
chorus (1) Group of singers, normally several on each part. (2) In a popular song, the refrain.
circa (ca.) About.
col, colla, coll' With the.
colla parte With the part; indicates that the player is to follow or coordinate with another part in tempo and expression.
col legno (c.l.) With the wood of the bow.
col legno battuto (col legno batt., c. l. batt., l.batt.) Striking the strings with the wood of the bow.
come sopra As above, as previously.
comme Like, as.
comme une fanfare Like a fanfare.
comme un oiseau Like a birdcall.
comodo Comfortable, easy.
con With.
con sordino (con sord.) (1) With mute. (2) In piano music, press the *una corda* pedal.
coperto, coperti Of a drum, covered with a cloth to muffle the sound.
coro Chorus.
court Short, brief.
crescendo (cresc.) Increasing in volume.
cuivré, cuivrez On a horn, play with a loud, brassy tone.
cup mute Mute for trumpet or trombone, like a straight mute but with a cup on the wide end that covers the bell of the instrument.

da capo (D.C.) Repeat from the beginning, through the first section of the movement.
daher Therefore, hence.
damp, dampen Muffle, silence; stop from vibrating.
damped Of a cymbal, muffled as soon as it is struck.
damper pedal On a piano, the pedal farthest to the right, which lifts the dampers off the strings and lets notes continue to sound after the fingers have left the keys.
Dämpfer (Dpf., Dpfr.) Mute.
dann Then.
dans In; during.
dans en sentiment sourd. et tumultueux With a muffled and tumultuous feeling.
de plus en plus More and more, gradually.
declamato Sung in declamatory fashion.
decrescendo (decresc., decres.) Decreasing in volume.
delirando Raving, delirious.
descendez le "la" un demi-ton plus bas Tune the A string a semitone lower.

détaché Detached; with a broad, vigorous bow stroke, each note bowed singly.
deutlich Distinctly.
di Of.
die The.
diese, dieser This, these.
diminuendo (dim., dimin.) Decreasing in volume.
distinto Distinctly.
divisi, divise (div.) Divided; indicates that the group should be divided into two or more parts to perform the passage in question.
dolce Gentle, soft.
dolcissimo (dolciss.) Very gentle.
dominante Dominant, dominating.
Doppelgriff Double stop; on string instruments, playing two strings at once
doppio movimento Twice as fast.
Dpf., Dpfr. *Dämpfer*; mute.

e And.
echo tone, Echoton Like an echo.
éclatant Sparkling, brilliant.
ein, eine One; a.
en In.
en dehors Emphasized, prominent.
en poudroiement harmonieux In a harmonious ray of sunlight (literally, airborne dust made visible by the sun's rays).
enchaînez Play the next movement without a break.
encore Still, yet (as in *encore plus lent,* still more slowly).
enveloppé de pedale Veiled or enveloped by the damper pedal, which allows notes on the piano to continue sounding and thus blur the harmony.
environ About.
espressivo (espress., espr.) Expressive, expressively.
et And.
étouffée Damped, muted.
etwa *Circa*; about.
etwas Somewhat, rather.
eventuell nur eine (event. nur eine) If necessary, only one player.
expressif (express.) Expressive.

f Forte.
feroce Ferocious.
ff Fortissimo.
fff Fortississimo.
fine End, close.
Filzschlegel Felt-covered drumstick.
Flageolet (Flag.) Harmonic.
Flatterzunge Flutter-tongue.
flautando (flaut.) On a string instrument, producing a flute-like tone by bowing lightly and swiftly above the fingerboard.
flüchtig Fleeting, transient.
flutter-tongue, Flatterzunge (fl. t., Flttzg., Flzg.) Very fast tonguing technique for wind and brass intruments, producing a rapid trill-like sound.
folgt There follows.
forte (*f*) Loud.
forte-piano (*fp*) Loud, then immediately soft on the same note.
forte-pianissimo (*fpp*) Loud, then immediately very soft on the same note.
fortissimo (*ff*) Very loud.
fortississimo (*fff*) Extremely loud; ***ffff*** indicates a still louder dynamic.
fortsetzend Continuing.
forza Force.
forzando, forzato (*fz*) Play with a strong accent.
fp Forte-piano; loud, then immediately soft.
fpp Forte-pianissimo.
frog The part of the bow nearest the player's hand, used to tighten the bowhairs.
frottées l'une contre l'autre Rubbing against each other.
fz Forzando, forzato.

gebrochen Broken, arpeggiated.
gedämpft Muted; for a horn, stopped by inserting the right hand in the bell.
gehende Moderate tempo, walking speed; andante.
Generalpause (G.P.) Rest for the complete ensemble.
geschlagen (geschl.) Struck.
gesprochen Spoken.
gestopft Stopped; for the notes of a horn obtained by placing the hand in the bell.
gestoßen Detached, not legato.
gestrichen (gestr.) Bowed.
gesungen Sung.
geteilt (get.) Divided, divisi; indicates that the group should be divided into two or more parts to perform the passage in question.
gewöhnlich (gew., gewöhnl.) Usual, customary; used to cancel an indication to play in an unusual manner, such as *am Steg* or *col legno.*
giusto Moderate.
gleichmässig Equal; even; at a steady pace.

gleichsam versuchend, eine Begleitung für das Lied Wozzecks zu finden As if seeking to devise an accompaniment for Wozzeck's song.
gli altri The others; used to designate the other players in an orchestral section when one or more players in the section are given separate parts.
glissando (gliss., gl.) Rapidly gliding over strings or keys, producing a fast scale on a harp or piano or a fast continuous slide on string instruments, timpani, or trombone.
G.P. *Generalpause*; rest in all parts.
grazioso Graceful.
Griffbrett Fingerboard of a string instrument.
gross, groß, große Large, big.

H *Hauptstimme* or *Hauptrhythmus*.
haletantes Breathless, panting.
Halt Stop, hold, pause.
Harmon mute Mute for trumpet or trombone that can be adjusted or covered with the hand to allow different amounts of air through, producing a more or less distant sound.
harmonic, harmonique (harm.) A flute-like sound produced on a string instrument by bowing while lightly touching the string with the finger instead of pressing down on the string (natural harmonic), or by stopping the string with one finger and lightly touching the string at another point, usually a perfect fourth higher (artificial harmonic). On a harp, a harmonic is produced by plucking the string while touching it precisely in the middle of the string, and sounds an octave higher. On a wind instrument, a harmonic is produced by fingering the note indicated and blowing lightly to produce a note an octave higher.
Hauptrhythmus Principal rhythm; the main rhythmic pattern.
Hauptstimme Principal voice; the most important part in the texture.
hauteur réelle Actual pitch.
hervor Given prominence.
hervortretend Prominent; coming to the fore.
hörbar Audible.
hurlant Blaring out.

im Tempo, im Takt In tempo.
immer Always, still.
impetuoso Impetuous, violent.
in Used for indicating transposing instruments or changes of pitch. An instrument *in C* sounds as written, but one designated as in another key sounds in that key when its notated part is in C major; thus a clarinet *in A* will sound an A when it plays a C. See the chart of pitch names, p. 934.
in tempo Resume the previous tempo; used after a ritardando or other variation in tempo.
innig Sincere, tender, fervent.

jouer ceci Play this.

klingen lassen Let ring; allow to sound.
klingt wie notiert Sounds as written, meaning that the score shows the sounding pitches for transposing instruments (like horn in F or clarinet in A) as a convenience to the score-reader; the normal transpositions appear in the parts from which the instruments play.
kurz Short.
kurzer Halt Brief pause.

la, le, l' The.
laissez vibrer, laissez vibrer et s'éteindre, lascia vibrare (lasc. vibr., l.v.) Let vibrate; an indication to the player of a harp, cymbal, etc., that the sound must not be damped but should be allowed to die away.
langsam Slow, slowly.
langsamer Slower.
largamente Broadly.
largo A very slow tempo.
l.batt. Col legno battuto.
Le trille indique le pouce, l'accent le coup frappé avec le poing In notation for tambourine, the trill indicates rubbing the side of the drumhead with the thumb (to produce jingles), and the accent indicates striking the instrument with the fist.
legatissimo Very legato.
legato Performed without any perceptible interruption between notes; the opposite of staccato.
legèrement Lightly, gently, slightly.
leggiero Light and graceful.
leggio (legg.) Music stand; in an orchestral score, *legg. 5.6.* indicates the players at the fifth and sixth stands in the section (normally there are two players at each stand in the string sections).
legno The wood of the bow.
lent Slow, slowly.
lento A slow tempo, between andante and largo.
l.h. Left hand; play with the left hand.
loco To be played where written; cancels an *octava* sign.

lumineux Luminous, brilliant.
lunga Long; hold for a long time.
l.v. Let vibrate; *laisser vibrer, lascia vibrare.*

m. *Mit*; with.
ma But.
ma non troppo But not too much.
maestoso Majestic; stately.
mailloche Mallet, beater.
mais But.
mano destra (m.d.) Play with the right hand.
mano sinistra (m.s.) Play with the left hand.
marcatissimo (marcatiss.) With very marked emphasis.
marcato (marc.) Marked, with emphasis.
marcia March.
marqué Marked, with emphasis.
martellato (mart., martell.) Hammered.
m.d. *Main droite, mano destra*; play with the right hand.
m.D., m.Dpf. *Mit Dämpfer*; with mute.
m.d. Pianino *Mit dem Pianino*; with the upright piano.
membrane On the drumskin.
meno Less.
meno mosso Less fast.
Menuett Minuet.
metà Half of the indicated group of players.
metronome marking Indicates metronome setting for the correct tempo, in beats per minute.
mezzo forte (*mf*) Moderately loud.
mezzo piano (*mp*) Moderately soft.
mf Mezzo forte.
misterioso Mysteriously.
mit (m.) With; *mit dem, mit den,* with the.
mit den Händen Play with the hands.
moderato, modéré At a moderate tempo.
modo ordinario (modo ord.) In an ordinary fashion; cancels a previous indication to play in an unusual manner, such as *sul ponticello.*
moins Less.
molto Very, much.
morendo Dying away; becoming very soft.
mosso Rapid; with movement.
mp Mezzo piano.
muta in Change the tuning of the instrument as specified; or change to another instrument as specified.
m.s. *Mano sinistra*; play with the left hand.
mysterieux Mysteriously.

N⌐ *Nebenstimme.*
Nachschlag Auxiliary note at the end of a trill.
naturale (nat.) Natural; used to cancel a previous indication for an unusual technique (such as *coperto* for a drummer), or to indicate a natural harmonic on an open string.
Nebenstimme The second most important voice in the texture; compare *Hauptstimme.*
nehmen, nimmt Take; used to indicate a change of instrument, as from flute to piccolo, or adding a mute.
nerveux Nervous.
neue New.
nicht Not.
niente Nothing; inaudible.
nimmt Takes; used to indicate a change of instrument, as from bass clarinet to clarinet.
noch Still, yet.
non Not.
non troppo, non tanto Not too much.
Noten Notes.

o. *Ohne*; without.
octava (okt., 8va, 8.) Octave; *8va alto* means an octave higher, *8va basso* an octave lower. If not otherwise qualified, the notes marked should be played an octave higher than written if *8va* is written above the affected notes, or an octave lower if written below them. *15ma* indicates two octaves higher.
offen Open; cancels *gedämpft.*
ohne (o.) Without.
open (1) In brass instruments, the opposite of muted or stopped. (2) In string instruments, refers to the unstopped string (i.e., sounding at its full length).
ordinario, ordinairement, ordinèrement (ord.) In the usual way; cancels an instruction to play in some special manner, such as *sul ponticello.*
ossia Or rather; used to indicate an optional alternate reading of a passage.
ouvert Open.

p Piano (the dynamic level); soft.
passionato Passionate, impassioned.
pause Rest; pause.
pavillon en l'air (pav. en l'air) Bell in the air; sign for horn players to lift their bells to direct the sound forward.
pedal, pedale (ped., P.) In piano music, indicates that the damper pedal should be depressed; an asterisk indicates the point of release (brackets below the music are also used to indicate pedalling).
perdendosi Gradually dying away.

pesante (pes.) Heavy.
pesantissimo Very heavy.
peu Little, a little.
Pianino Upright piano.
pianissimo (*pp*) Very soft.
pianississimo (*ppp*) Extremely soft; ***pppp*** indicates a still softer dynamic.
piano (*p*) Soft.
più More.
più mosso Faster.
pizzicato (pizz.) On a string instrument, plucked with the finger instead of played with the bow; compare *arco*.
plötzlich Sudden, suddenly, immediately.
plunger A kind of mute for brass instruments used in jazz to create a wah-wah effect.
plus More.
pochissimo (pochiss.) Very little.
poco, un poco Little, a little.
poco a poco Little by little.
ponticello (pont.) The bridge of a string instrument.
portamento (port.) Fast slide between notes.
pp Pianissimo.
ppp Pianississimo.
précise (préc.) Precisely.
prenez Take; used to indicate a change of instrument, as from flute to piccolo.
près de la table On the harp, pluck the strings near the soundboard, producing a metallic sound.
prestissimo Very fast; faster than presto.
presto A very quick tempo (faster than allegro).
prima, primo (Imo) First, as in first bassoon part.

quasi Almost, as if.
quasi Echo Like an echo.
quasi in den Tanz einfallend As if joining in the dance.
quasi niente Almost nothing, i.e., as softly as possible.

rallentando (rall., rallent.), ralentir Growing slower.
rapido, rapide Fast.
rasch Fast.
rascher Faster.
rebord The rim of a drum.
rechtes Pedal Damper pedal.
Rezitation Reciting voice.
r.h., R.H. Right hand; play with the right hand.
rim shot On a snare drum, striking both the drum skin and the rim simultaneously with the same drumstick; or laying one drumstick on the drum, with its tip on the skin and its shaft on the rim, and striking it with the other drumstick.
risoluto Resolute.
ritardando (rit., ritard.) Gradually slackening in speed.
ritardierte Slowed-down.
ritenuto (riten.) Holding back.
ritmico Rhythmic.
rubato A certain elasticity and flexibility of tempo, speeding up and slowing down the performance of written music.
ruhig Calm.
ruhig schreitend Calm pace, moderate Andante tempo.
ruhiger Calmer; more calmly.

S Soprano.
Saite String; e.g., *C-Saite* means C string.
sans Without.
sans nuances Without nuances; do not vary dymanic level.
Schnellpolka Fast polka tempo.
schon bei geschlossenem Vorhang verhaltend Stop when the curtain closes.
Schwammschlägel Sponge-headed drumstick.
schwerer Heavier.
secco, sec Dry.
segno Sign; especially one indicating the beginning of a section to be repeated.
sehr Very.
semplice Simple, in a simple manner.
sempre Always, continually.
senza Without.
senza vibrato (s.vibr.) Without vibrato.
serré Hard, strong.
serrer Push ahead.
sforzando, sforzato (*sfz*, *sf*) With sudden emphasis.
sforzando-piano (*sfp*) Sforzando, then suddenly soft.
simile (sim.) Likewise; continue in a similar manner.
sin al, sino al Until, up to (usually followed by a new tempo or dynamic marking, or by a dotted line indicating a terminal point).
Singstimme Singing voice; vocal line.
soft stick Use padded or sponge drumstick.
solo, sola (pl. soli) (1) To be played by one performer. (2) Indicates the most prominent part in an ensemble texture.

sombre Dark, somber.
son flûté, vers la pointe On a string instrument, played near the tip of the bow, producing a flute-like sound.
sonore Sonorous, with full tone.
soprano, Sopran (Sop., S, Sopr.), pl. Soprani, Soprane The voice with the highest range.
sordino (sord., pl. sordini) Mute.
sostenuto (sost.) (1) Sustained. (2) In piano music, press the *sostenuto* (middle) pedal, which sustains the notes that are being held when the pedal is first pressed.
souple Flowing, smooth.
sourdement (sourd.) Muffled, muted.
sourdine (sourd.) Mute.
soutenu Sustained.
s.p. Sul ponticello.
staccato (stacc.) Detached, separated; held for less than the full notated duration.
staccatissimo (staccatiss.) Very staccato.
Steg Bridge on a string instrument; see *am Steg*.
stem in, stem out On a Harmon mute, indicates whether the stem of the plunger is pushed in, cutting off most of the air flow, or pulled out, allowing more air through.
straight mute (st. mute, str. mute) Conical mute for brass instruments, placed in the bell and held there by cork strips that allow some air through.
stringendo (string.) Quickening.
subito (sub.) Suddenly, immediately.
suivant les dynamiques, employer baguettes douces ou dures Following the dynamics, employ soft or hard drumsticks.
suivre Follow; *suivre le Ier*, follow the first player.
sul On the (as in *sul G*. on the G string).
sul ponticello (sul pont., s.p.) On a string instrument, bow over or very near the bridge; this emphasizes the higher harmonics to produce a thin, metallic sound.
sul tasto (s.t.) On a string instrument, bow near, or over, the fingerboard; this minimizes the harmonics to produce a flute-like, ethereal sound.
sur On.
sur la touche On a string instrument, bow near, or over, the fingerboard; *sul tasto*.
sur rebord On the rim.
s.vibr. Senza vibrato.

T Tenor.
Takt Bar, beat.
tanto So much.
tasto Fingerboard of a string instrument; sul tasto.
tempo (1) The speed or relative pace of the music. (2) A tempo; used after *rit.* or *calando*.
tempo blues In the tempo of a blues.
tempo di marcia March tempo.
tempo giusto Moderate or appropriate tempo.
tempo primo (tempo I, I. Tempo, 1° tempo), tempo initial At the original tempo.
tempo rigoreux Keep rigorously to the tempo.
tempo rubato Play with rubato.
teneramente Tenderly.
tenor, tenore, Tenor (T., ten.), pl. tenori, Tenöre High male voice or part; in choral music, the second voice from the bottom of the texture.
tenuto, tenute (ten.) Held, sustained.
tiefer Lower.
touche Fingerboard or fret (of a string instrument).
tr Trill.
tranquillo Quiet, calm.
tre corde, tre corda Three strings; cancels *una corda* marking.
tremolo (trem.) (1) On string instruments, a quick reiteration of the same tone, produced by a rapid up-and-down movement of the bow. (2) A similar effect on another instrument or voice.
très Very.
trill (*tr*) The rapid alternation of a given note with the note above it. In a drum part it indicates rapid alternating strokes with two drumsticks.
Triller ohne Nachschlag Trills without final auxiliary or grace note.
Trio Second or middle section of a minuet and trio, a scherzo, a march, or a rag.
Triole Triplets.
troppo Too much.
tumultueuse Tumultuous.
tutta forza, tutta la forza Full force.
tutti, tutte Literally, "all"; usually means all the instruments in a given category as distinct from a solo part; cancels the designation *solo*.

übergreifen Reach over; in piano music, indicates that one hand should reach over the other.
übertönend Drowning out.

übrigen (d. Übrig.) The others, the remaining; used to designate the other players in an orchestral section when one or more players in the section are given separate parts.
un, una, une One; a.
un poco, un peu A little.
una corda One string; tells the player of a grand piano to depress the left pedal, which shifts the hammer mechanism over so that only one string is struck for each note (rather than three or two).
und (u.) And.
unison (unis.) The same notes or melody played by several instruments at the same pitch. Often used to emphasize that a phrase is not to be divided among several players; cancels *divisi*.
unite, uniti Unison.
unmittelbar anschließend Immediately following.
Unterbrechung Interruption, breaking off.

vamp Brief introduction which may be repeated ad libitum until the singer begins.
veramente Truly.
verklingen lassen Let the sound die away; do not damp.
verstimmt Out of tune; *ein verstimmtes Pianino*, an out-of-tune upright piano.
Verwandlung Change of scene.
vibrato, vibrez (vib., vibr.) Slight fluctuation of pitch around a sustained tone.
via Away; *via sord.*, remove mute.
Viertel Quarter note; *die neuen Viertel . . . sind gleich den Vierteln der vorigen Triole*, the new quarter note is equivalent to the quarter notes in the preceding triplets.
vif Quick, lively.
vigoroso Vigorous, strong.
voce Voice.
voilé Veiled.
voix Voice.
Vorhang auf Curtain up.
Vorhang fällt, Vorhang zu Curtain down.
voriges, vorigen Preceding.

wieder Again; still more.
womöglich If possible.

ziemlich Rather, fairly.
zusammen (zus.) Together; unison.

INDEX OF COMPOSERS

INDEX OF TITLES

INDEX OF FORMS AND GENRES

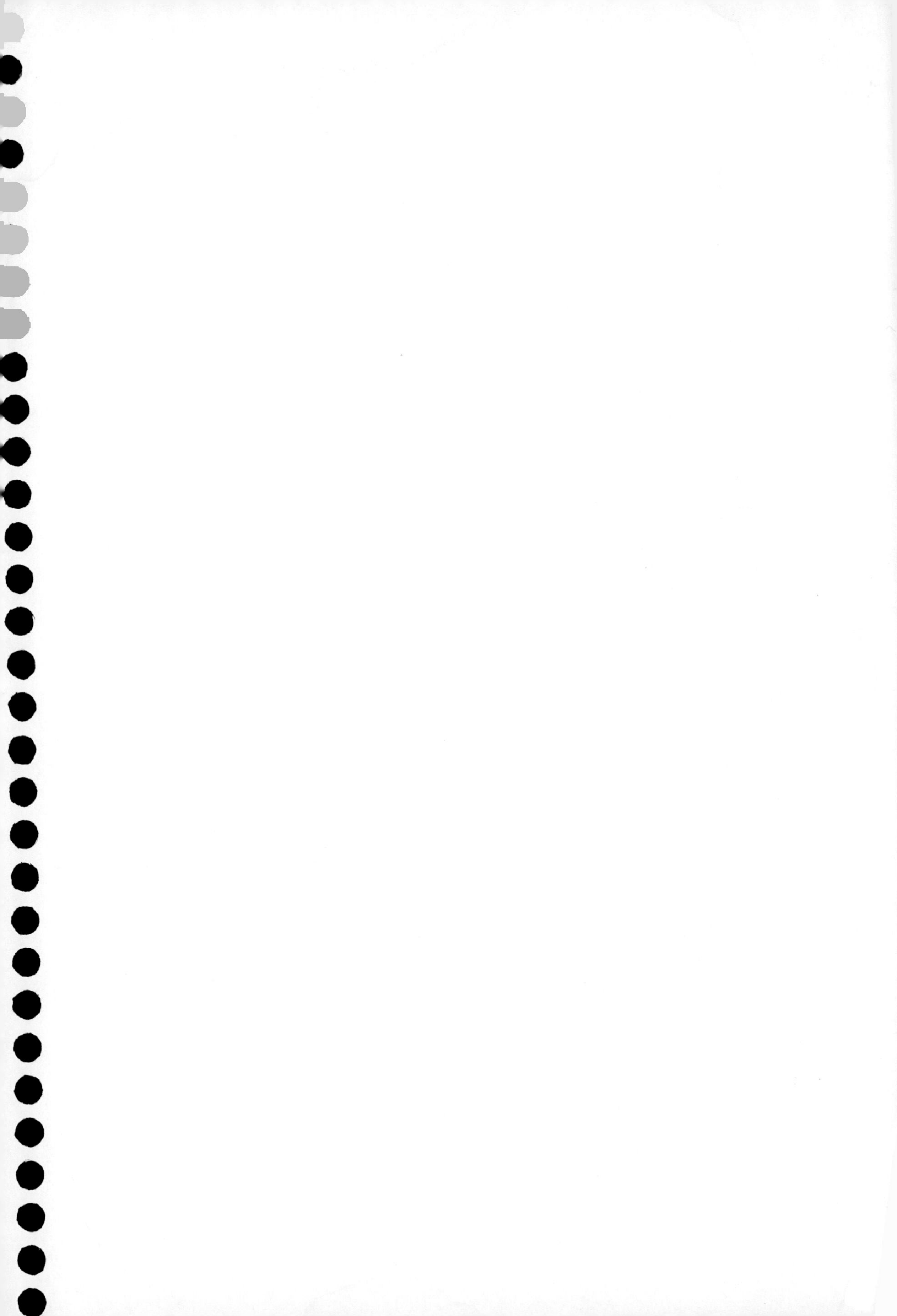